COMPANION TO THE POLITICAL ECONOMY OF RENT SEEKING

Gordon Tullock 1922–2014

A dedicated scholar
An unsurpassed original thinker of twentieth-century political economy
A principal founder of the public choice school
The initiator of the study of rent seeking
And, for many of the contributors to this book, a missed friend

Companion to the Political Economy of Rent Seeking

Edited by

Roger D. Congleton

BB&T Professor of Economics, West Virginia University, USA

Arye L. Hillman

William Gittes Chair and Professor of Economics, Bar-Ilan University, Israel

Edward Elgar
PUBLISHING

Cheltenham, UK • Northampton, MA, USA

Published by
Edward Elgar Publishing Limited
The Lypiatts
15 Lansdown Road
Cheltenham
Glos GL50 2JA
UK

Edward Elgar Publishing, Inc.
William Pratt House
9 Dewey Court
Northampton
Massachusetts 01060
USA

A catalogue record for this book
is available from the British Library

Library of Congress Control Number: 2014957082

This book is available electronically in the Elgaronline
Economics subject collection
DOI 10.4337/9781782544944

MIX
Paper from
responsible sources
FSC® C013056

ISBN 978 1 78254 493 7 (cased)
ISBN 978 1 78254 494 4 (eBook)

Typeset by Servis Filmsetting Ltd, Stockport, Cheshire
Printed and bound in Great Britain by T.J. International Ltd, Padstow

Contents

Contributors

J. Atsu Amegashie received his PhD in Economics from Simon Fraser University, Canada. He is Associate Professor of Economics at the University of Guelph, Canada and a Research Fellow at CESifo in Munich, Germany and the Tshepo Institute, Wilfrid Laurier University, Canada. He has held visiting positions at Oxford University, UK and the University of Munich, Germany. He is a member of the editorial boards of the *European Journal of Political Economy*, *Defense and Peace Economics* and *Journal of Behavioral and Experimental Economics* (formerly the *Journal of Socio-Economics*). His fields of specialization are public choice, public economics, development economics and applied microeconomics.

Michael Brooks is Associate Professor in the Tasmanian School of Business and Economics at the University of Tasmania in Hobart, Australia. He trained initially to be a high school teacher, completing a Diploma of Education, but was drawn back to economics, completing a Masters of Economics at Monash University and in 1983 a PhD at Virginia Polytechnic Institute and State University, USA. His recent research topics include the political economy of taxation, expressive voting, political leadership and the economics of esteem.

Roger D. Congleton is the BB&T Professor of Economics at West Virginia University, USA. He joined the Department of Economics at West Virginia University in 2011, after a long association with the Department of Economics and the Center for Study of Public Choice at George Mason University, USA. He has lectured and published widely on the political economy of rent seeking, public policy, institutions and constitutional theory. His books include *Perfecting Parliament: Liberalism, Constitutional Reform, and the Emergence of Western Democracy* (2011), *Politics by Principle, Not Interest: Towards Nondiscriminatory Democracy* (co-authored with James M. Buchanan, 1998) and two collections of rent-seeking publications, *The Economic Analysis of Rent Seeking* (with R.D. Tollison, 1995) and *40 Years of Rent Seeking Research* (with A.L. Hillman and K.A. Konrad, 2008). He has been a visiting Fellow at the Amsterdam Center for Law and Economics, at Oxford University (Nuffield, Politics), a Fulbright Distinguished Professor of American Studies at the University of Southern Denmark and was the Adam Smith Professor of Economics and Philosophy at the University of Bayreuth, Germany. He is co-editor of the journal *Constitutional Political Economy*. His PhD in Economics is from Virginia Polytechnic Institute and State University, USA, where he wrote under James Buchanan.

Giuseppe Dari-Mattiacci is Professor of Law and Economics and holds appointments at both the Faculty of Law and the Faculty of Economics (by courtesy) at the University of Amsterdam, the Netherlands. He is Director of the Amsterdam Center for Law and Economics and Fellow of the Tinbergen Institute. He is editor of the *International Review of Law and Economics* and a former editor of *Review of Law and Economics*. He has been a BFI Fellow at the University of Chicago Law School, USA and a recipient of the VIDI grant from the Netherlands Organization for Scientific Research (NWO). He studied law at the University of Rome, Italy (D.Jur. 1997), law and economics at Utrecht University (LLM 2000 and PhD 2002) and mathematics at the University of Amsterdam (BA 2011). He has published numerous articles on the law and economics of torts, property, litigation and lawmaking in various journals including the *University of Chicago Law Review*, *Journal of Legal Studies*, *Journal of Law, Economics and Organization*, *Journal of Law and Economics* and *Journal of Economic History*. His recent scholarship focuses on law, economics and history and examines the evolution of legal institutions from ancient Rome to modern times. His current research projects include the economic analysis of ancient law, comparative variation of legal rules and the economics of endogenous institutional change.

Robert T. Deacon is Professor of Economics Emeritus at the University of California, Santa Barbara, USA. His research specialties are natural resource and environmental economics, with special emphasis on the role of political institutions. His research has been published in leading general interest and specialty professional journals for economics, including the *American Economic Review*, *Journal of Political Economy*, *Journal of Law and Economics*, *Journal of Environmental Economics and Management*, *Public Choice* and *Land Economics*. He has served on editorial positions for several journals and was managing editor of the *Journal of Environmental Economics and Management*. He has held fellowships and visiting faculty positions at universities in the USA and abroad and is University Fellow at Resources for the Future.

Gil S. Epstein is Professor of Economics and Dean School of Graduate Studies at Bar-Ilan University in Israel. He is a Research Fellow at IZA (Bonn, Germany) as well as at CreAM (London, UK) and a Fellow at Centro Studi Luca d'Agliano (Milan, Italy). He has been awarded several prestigious grants and is frequently invited to present his research at international conferences and institutes around the world. He has published widely, with over 90 publications on political economy, public choice, labor economics, migration and public policy in leading academic journals. He is associate editor of the *Journal of Population Economics* and associate editor of *e-economics*.

Sabine Flamand is a Post-doctoral Researcher at the Nova School of Business and Economics in Lisbon, Portugal. Her primary research interests are political economy, microeconomics and public economics. She has applied contest theory to the study of separatist conflict and intra-party competition. Her research has been published in *Public Choice*. She holds a PhD in Economics from the Universitat Autonoma de Barcelona in Spain.

Rune Jansen Hagen is Professor at the Department of Economics at the University of Bergen, Norway and affiliated Researcher at the Choice Lab (Norwegian School of Economics). His PhD is from the Norwegian School of Economics. His main field of expertise is development economics, particularly issues related to flows of external finance to poor countries. With regard to foreign aid, he has done applied theoretical research on fungibility, the Samaritan's Dilemma and the role of the International Monetary Fund. His research papers have been published in the *Journal of International Economics*, *Journal of Development Economics* and *Review of Income and Wealth*, as well as other journals.

Arye L. Hillman is the William Gittes Professor of Economics at Bar-Ilan University in Israel. His research interest is political economy, in particular with regard to international trade policy and more generally in the context of public policy. His research papers have appeared in various journals including the *American Economic Review*, *Quarterly Journal of Economics*, *Economic Journal*, *European Journal of Political Economy*, *Public Choice*, *Journal of International Economics* and *Journal of Public Economics*. He is the author of *The Political Economy of Protection* (1989, reprinted in 2001). His book *Public Finance and Public Policy: Responsibilities and Limitations of Government* (2nd edition 2009) has been translated into several languages. Edited volumes include *Markets and Politicians: Politicized Economic Choice* (1991). He has been a visiting Professor at UCLA, Princeton in the USA and Paris 1-Panthéon-Sorbonne in France. He has a BA (first class honors and the University Medal) from the University of Newcastle, Australia and a PhD in Economics from the University of Pennsylvania, USA. Between 1994 and 2014 he was editor and editor-in-chief of the *European Journal of Political Economy*. He is a past President of the European Public Choice Society. Together with Heinrich W. Ursprung, he is a recipient of the Max-Planck Prize for Humanities Sciences.

Randall G. Holcombe is DeVoe Moore Professor of Economics at Florida State University, USA. He taught at Texas A&M University and Auburn University prior to coming to Florida State in 1988. He was a member of Florida Governor Jeb Bush's Council of Economic Advisors from 2000 to 2006. He is a past President of the Public Choice Society and the Society for the Development of Austrian Economics. He is the author of 15 books and more than 150 articles published in academic and professional journals. His books include *From Liberty to Democracy: The Transformation of American Government* (2002) and *Producing Prosperity* (2013). He received his PhD in Economics from Virginia Tech.

Chen Kang is Professor of Economics at the National University of Singapore. He has published widely on issues relating to macroeconomic modeling, China's economic reform and development and the economic role of government in professional journals, including the *Journal of Comparative Economics*, *European Journal of Political Economy*, *China Economic Review* and *Economic Modelling*. He is the author of *The Chinese Economy in Transition: Micro Changes and Macro Implications* (1995). He currently serves on the editorial board of the *European Journal of Political Economy* and on the advisory boards of *China Economic Quarterly* and *World Economic Papers*. He was the Wang Yanan Chair Professor of Economics at Xiamen University, China. He has a PhD in Economics from the University of Maryland, USA.

Mwangi S. Kimenyi is Senior Fellow and Director of the Africa Growth Initiative in the Global Economy and Development Program of The Brookings Institution in Washington DC, USA. He has been a faculty member of the Department of Economics at the University of Mississippi and the University of Connecticut, a visiting Professor at the University of Wisconsin-Madison, a visiting Fellow at the Hoover Institution at Stanford University and Research Associate with the Centre for the Study of African Economies at Oxford University, UK. He is the Founding Executive Director of the Kenya Institute for Public Policy Research and Analysis. He received his undergraduate degree at the University of Nairobi-Kenya and completed graduate studies at Ohio

University and George Mason University, USA where he obtained a Doctorate in Economics in 1986. He has also studied for certificate programs at the University of Michigan and Harvard. His research focuses on institutions and economic development, Africa's political economy and policies for economic growth and poverty reduction. He has authored or co-edited eight books and six policy monographs and published widely in professional journals and books. He is the recipient of many honors and awards including the Georgescu-Roegen Prize in Economics (1991) and jointly the Outstanding Research Award (2001) by Global Development Network (GDN).

Eric Langlais is Professor of Economics and of Law and Economics at the University of Paris Ouest Nanterre La Défense in France and leader of the research program for 'Law, Institutions and Regulations' at EconomiX (UMR CNRS and University of Paris Ouest). His research interests cover the fields of economics of risk and uncertainty, public economics, tort law and liability, criminality, and economics of litigations and justice. He is co-editor of the *Journal of Advanced Research in Law and Economics* and associate editor of the *Review of Finance and Banking* and the *International Review of Law and Economics*. His publications have appeared in *Annals of Economics and Statistics*, *Economics Letters*, *Theory and Decision*, *Review of Economics of the Household*, *Journal of Institutional and Theoretical Economics*, *Public Choice*, *Louvain Economic Review*, *Journal of Public Economic Theory*, *International Review of Law and Economics*, *European Journal of Law and Economics* and in other journals. He is joint author of *The Economics of Class Actions* (*Economie des Actions Collectives*) (with Bruno Deffains and Myriam Doriat-Duban, 2008), and co-editor of *Economics of Law* (*Analyse Economique du Droit*) (with Bruno Deffains, 2009). He qualified for the Habilitation to Supervise Theses at the University of Orléans (1993) and has a PhD in Economics from the University of Paris 1-Panthéon-Sorbonne (1992).

Mark I. Levin is Professor at the National Research University in the Higher School of Economics, Moscow, Russia. He also lectures at Moscow State University and the Russian Presidential Academy of National Economy and Public Administration. He has a PhD in Systems Analysis and a DSc in Mathematical Economics from the Central Institute of Mathematical Economics of the Russian Academy of Science, Moscow, where he is Chief Researcher. His fields of interest are mathematical economics, analysis of disequilibrium economies and data analysis. In recent years his research has focused on corruption and xenophobia in Russia. He is author and co-author of more than 70 papers and four books.

Ngo Van Long is James McGill Professor of Economics at McGill University, Canada. He has contributed to the rent-seeking and lobbying literature, including in the context of international trade. His other research interests are the economics of natural resources and the environment, international trade theory, dynamic games and applied microeconomic theory (industrial organization theory, taxation theory). He has published in a variety of journals, including *Econometrica*, *Quarterly Journal of Economics*, *Journal of Economic Theory*, *International Economic Review*, *Economic Journal*, *European Journal of Political Economy*, *Journal of Public Economics*, *Journal of International Economics*, *Games and Economic Behavior* and *Journal of Public Economic Theory*. He is associate editor of the *Journal of Public Economic Theory* and the *Review of International*

Economics. He is on the editorial board of the *European Journal of Political Economy*. He is author or editor of nine books, including *A Survey of Dynamic Games in Economics* (2010). He has a BA (first class honors) from Latrobe University, Australia and a PhD in Economics from Australian National University.

Bruno Lovat is Associate Professor in Economics and Finance at the University of Lorraine, France. He is a member of the Bureau for Economic Theory and Applications, a research laboratory of the French National Centre for Scientific Research. He teaches mathematics and risk theory. His research interests concern the evolution of law and legal institutions, strategic delegation, incentive schemes and pension systems. His publications have appeared in *Revue française d'économie*, *Nonlinear Analysis, Positivity*, *Dynamics of Continuous, Discrete and Impulsive Systems*, *Public Choice*, *Journal of Economic Behavior and Organization* and in other journals. He has a PhD in Mathematics from the University of Metz, France (1995).

Barbara Luppi is a faculty member of the Department of Economics at the University of Modena and Reggio Emilia in Modena, Italy. Her research interests are in the field of law and economics and focus primarily on contract and tort law. She has had visiting positions at Tel Aviv University, Israel and at the Center of Law and Rationality, University of Minnesota and at the University of St Thomas, USA. Her publications have appeared in the *Journal of Legal Studies*, *Public Choice*, *International Journal of Law and Economics*, *European Journal of Law and Economics*, *Review of Law and Economics*, *Harvard Law Review Forum*, and other journals. She has a MSc in Economics with distinction from the London School of Economics and Political Science, UK (2001), a PhD in Political Economics from the University of Bologna, Italy (2005) where her thesis was 'Essays on economic applications of human cognitive limitations', and a PhD in Economics from the London School of Economics and Political Science (2010) where her thesis was on 'The consequences of behavioral bias: bandit problems and product liability law'.

Sugata Marjit is the Reserve Bank of India Professor of Industrial Economics and the Project Director of the Centre for Training and Research in Public Finance and Policy at the Centre for Studies in Social Sciences, Calcutta (CSSSC) in India. He has been the Director of CSSSC and the Chairman of the State Higher Education Council, which is the most senior academic position in the higher education system of the state of West Bengal. He is among very few to have received two prestigious national awards for economists in India, the VKRV Rao National Prize for Social Science and the Mahalanobis Medal of the Indian Econometric Society. A visiting Professor in more than 25 universities spanning continents, his PhD in Economics is from the University of Rochester (1985), USA. He has published more than 100 research papers in major journals and his books have been published by major academic publishers.

John Mukum Mbaku is Brady Presidential Distinguished Professor of Economics, Willard L. Eccles Professor of Economics and John S. Hinckley Fellow at Weber State University, USA and former (1986–2007) associate editor (Africa) of the *Journal of Third World Studies*. He is also a Nonresident Senior Fellow at The Brookings Institution and an Attorney and Counselor at Law (licensed in the State of Utah). He received his PhD in Economics and the J.Dure (law) from the University of Georgia and the Graduate

Certificate in Natural Resources and Environmental Law from the S.J. Quinney College of Law at the University of Utah. He is the author of many books, book chapters and peer-reviewed journal articles.

Yosef Mealem is Lecturer in the School of Banking and Finance at the Netanya Academic College, Israel. His research interests include applications of game theory, political economy and public economics. His past positions include Chief Economist and Macroeconomic Manager at large finance companies, Chairman of the Board at a number of finance companies, member of advisory committees to the Supervisor of Insurance and the Supervisor of the Capital Market in the Ministry of Finance of Israel and member of the Research Department of the Bank of Israel. He received the PhD in Economics from Princeton University, USA.

Thomas Moutos is Professor of Economics in the Department of International and European Economic Studies, at the Athens University of Economics and Business, Greece, and a Research Fellow at CESifo. His research interests have covered topics in macroeconomics, international economics and labor economics, often focusing on the political economy aspects of public policies. His publications have appeared in various professional journals. He is the co-author of *Human Capital, Employment, and Bargaining* (with Robert A. Hart, 1995). Edited volumes include *Managing European Union Enlargement* (with Helge Berger, 2004) and *Designing the New European Union* (with Helge Berger, 2006). He has a PhD in Economics from McMaster University, Canada.

Dennis C. Mueller is Professor Emeritus at the University of Vienna, Austria. Prior positions were at the Science Center Berlin, Germany, University of Maryland, Cornell University, Brookings Institution, USA and Simon Fraser University, Canada. He is a past President of the Public Choice Society, European Public Choice Society, Southern Economic Association, European Association for Research in Industrial Economics, Industrial Organization Society and the International Joseph A. Schumpeter Society. He is author or editor of 22 books and author of over 150 research papers. His book *Public Choice* (3rd edition 2003) was the first comprehensive compilation of the public-choice literature.

Vivekananda Mukherjee is Associate Professor in the Department of Economics, Jadavpur University, Kolkata, India. His research interest is in the area of institutional economics. He has published in the *European Journal of Political Economy*, *Journal of Institutional and Theoretical Economics*, *Environment and Development Economics*, *Ecological Economics*, *Review of Law and Economics*, *Theory and Decision*, *Journal of International Trade and Economic Development*, *Annals of Public and Cooperative Economics*, *Journal of Economic Development* and *Economics Bulletin*. He received his PhD from Jadavpur University on the topic of 'Theoretical models of corruption'.

Shmuel Nitzan is the Sir Issac Wolfson Professor of Economics at Bar-Ilan University in Israel. His primary research interests are political economy, social choice, voting theory and collective decision making under uncertainty. His publications have appeared in various professional journals including *Econometrica*, *American Political Science Review*, *Quarterly Journal of Economics*, *Journal of Public Economics*, *Journal of*

Economic Theory, *International Economic Review*, *European Economic Review*, *Public Choice*, *Social Choice and Welfare* and *European Journal of Political Economy*. He is the author of *Collective Preference and Choice* (2010), *Endogenous Public Policy and Contests* (2007, with Gil Epstein) and *Collective Decision Making: An Economic Outlook* (1985, with Jacob Paroush). He has a PhD in Economics from the Hebrew University of Jerusalem. He is a former editor of the *European Journal of Political Economy*. He is President of the Israeli Economic Association (2014–16).

Martin Paldam is Professor Emeritus at the Department of Economics, University of Aarhus, Denmark. His degrees are Candidate of Economics from the University of Copenhagen and Doctorate in Economics from the University of Aarhus. He is the author of some 260 scientific articles and book chapters and eight books. He has been a consultant for the Danish Council of Economic Advisors, United Nations Development Programme, World Bank and Organisation for Economic Co-operation and Development. He is a past President of the European Public Choice Society.

Francesco Parisi is the Oppenheimer Wolff and Donnelly Professor of Law at the University of Minnesota Law School, USA and Professor of Economics at the Department of Economics, University of Bologna, Italy. He received his D.Jur. degree from the University of Rome 'La Sapienza', LLM, JSD and MA degree in Economics from the University of California at Berkeley and a PhD in Economics from George Mason University, USA. He is the author of ten books and over 200 articles in the field of law and economics. His articles have appeared in journals that include the *American Law and Economics Review*, *Journal of Legal Studies*, *International Review of Law and Economics*, *Public Choice*, *Journal of Institutional Economics*, *Journal of Institutional and Theoretical Economics*, *Harvard Law Review Forum*, *American Journal of Jurisprudence* and *American Journal of Comparative Law*. His books include *The Economics of Lawmaking* (with Vincy Fon, 2011) and *The Language of Law and Economics* (2013). He is editor of the *Oxford Handbook of Law and Economics* (2015) and editor-in-chief of the *Review of Law and Economics*. From 2002 to 2008 he was editor of the *Supreme Court Economic Review*. He is on the board of editors of the *International Review of Law and Economics*, *Public Choice* and *American Journal of Comparative Law*.

Lambros Pechlivanos is Assistant Professor of Economics in the Department of International and European Economic Studies at the Athens University of Economics and Business, Greece. He has been visiting Professor at the University of Passau, Germany and Researcher at IDEI, University of Toulouse, France and at the Foundation of Economic and Industrial Research in Athens, Greece. His research interests include economics of information and organization, contract theory, auctions and market design. His research papers have appeared in various professional journals that include the *Journal of Labor Economics*, *Games and Economic Behavior* and *European Journal of Operation Research*. He has edited and contributed to various collective volumes. He has a PhD in Economics from Boston University, USA.

Liu Qijun is Associate Professor of Economics at the School of Public Administration, Huazhong University of Science and Technology, in Wuhan, China. He has been a visiting Professor at Bar-Ilan University, Israel. His research interests are the political economy of public policy and rent seeking. In recent years, his research has focused on corruption in China. To unfold the mystery of endemic or ongoing corruption and to study the causes and consequences of corruption, he has compiled a databank of corrupt activities based on convictions for corruption-related crimes. He is the author of *An Economic Analysis of Rent Seeking Behavior* (2008) and his publications have appeared in the *European Journal of Political Economy*, *CASS Journal of Political Science*, *China Public Administration* and other professional journals. He has a PhD in Economics from Huazhong University of Science and Technology.

Ashwin Rode is a Post-doctoral Scholar in the Department of Economics, University of Chicago, USA. His research interests include environmental and natural resource economics and political economy. His recent research has applied the rent-seeking framework to topics in environmental and natural-resource economics. He received a PhD in Economics from the University of California, Santa Barbara, USA (2014). His dissertation research was supported in part by the Joseph L. Fisher Fellowship from Resources for the Future.

Georgy A. Satarov is Professor in the Russian Presidential Academy of National Economy and Public Administration, Moscow, Russia. He has a PhD in Applied Mathematics from the Institute of Systems Research of the Russian Academy of Science, Moscow. His fields of research interest have been mathematical methods and data analysis in social and humanitarian sciences. He is the author of more than 100 papers and publications. In recent years his research has focused on corruption in Russia. In 1990 he founded the first Russian independent applied political research center INDEM, subsequently renamed Fond INDEM. Between 1994 and1997 he was political assistant of the President of the Russian Federation.

Roman M. Sheremeta is Assistant Professor of Economics at the Weatherhead School of Management at Case Western Reserve University, USA and a Research Associate at the Economic Science Institute at Chapman University, USA. He is associate editor at the *Journal of Economic Behavior and Organization*. He received a PhD in Economics from Purdue University, USA (2009). He is a recipient of many research and teaching awards, as well as multiple grants. His main research interests are experimental and behavioral economics, conflict and conflict resolution and game theory. He has published 35 research papers in a variety of academic journals.

William F. Shughart II is J. Fish Smith Professor in Public Choice at Utah State University's Jon M. Huntsman School of Business, USA, Research Director and Senior Fellow of the Independent Institute, editor-in-chief of *Public Choice* and past President of the Southern Economic Association. A co-editor of two editions of *The Elgar Companion to Public Choice* and the author or editor of ten other books, 59 book chapters, 130 peer-reviewed journal articles, 37 book reviews and nearly 200 signed editorials, published, inter alia, in the *Wall Street Journal*, *Investor's Business Daily*, *Los Angeles Times* and *Chicago Tribune*. He earned a PhD in Economics from Texas A&M University, USA.

Diana W. Thomas is Associate Professor of Economics and Associate Director of the Creighton Economic Institute at the Heider College of Business, Creighton University, USA. She received her PhD in Economics from George Mason University, USA in 2009. In her research, she explores the unintended consequences of regulation and the role that political entrepreneurs play in changing the rules that govern society. Her research papers have appeared in a number of professional journals including *Public Choice*, *Kyklos*, *Southern Economic Journal* and *Journal of Banking and Finance*.

George Tridimas is Professor of Political Economy in the Business School of the University of Ulster, Ireland. He obtained a BA from the University of Athens, Greece and an MPhil and DPhil in Economics from the University of Oxford, UK. He has held positions at the University of the Witwatersrand in South Africa and the University of Reading in the UK. He is on the editorial board of the *European Journal of Political Economy*. His research and publications are principally on the political economy of direct democracy, with special focus on ancient Athens, mechanisms of collective decision making, the size of government, publicly provided goods and economic behavior and the economic analysis of the judiciary.

Orestis Troumpounis is Lecturer at Lancaster University, UK. He obtained a PhD in Economics from Universidad Autonoma de Barcelona, Spain (2011). His published and ongoing research uses game-theoretic concepts and aims at understanding how institutions shape individuals' and parties' strategies in different political contexts. His research has focused on the analysis of attributes of electoral systems such as proportional representation and participation quorums and on sharing rules in collective rent seeking.

Roland Vaubel is Professor of Economics at the University of Mannheim, Germany. He has been Professor of Economics at Erasmus University Rotterdam, the Netherlands and visiting Professor of International Economics at the Graduate School of Business, University of Chicago, USA. He is a member of the Advisory Council to the German Federal Ministry of Economics and Energy. He is associate editor of the *Review of International Organizations* and a member of the editorial board of the *European Journal of Political Economy*. His research publications have appeared in various professional journals. He has co-edited several books on interjurisdictional competition and international organizations. His monographs and books include *The European Institutions as an Interest Group* (2009) and *The Centralisation of Western Europe: The Common Market, Political Integration, and Democracy* (1995). Edited volumes include *The Political Economy of International Organizations: A Public Choice Approach* (with Thomas D. Willett, 1991). He received a BA in Philosophy, Politics and Economics from the University of Oxford, UK, an MA from Columbia University, USA and a doctorate from the University of Kiel, Germany.

Karl Wärneryd is Associate Professor in the Department of Economics at the Stockholm School of Economics, Sweden. He has made contributions to the theory of rent seeking and his research interests more generally involve the applications of game theory to economic and political-economy issues. His research has appeared in *Economic Theory*, *Games and Economic Behavior*, *International Journal of Game Theory*, *Journal of Economic Theory*, *RAND Journal of Economics*, *Scandinavian Journal of Economics*, *European Economic Review*, *Journal of Public Economics*, and other professional journals. He is on the editorial board of the *European Journal of Political Economy*. He has had visiting positions at Tilburg University, the Netherlands and George Mason University, USA. His PhD is from the Stockholm School of Economics.

Preface

Resources can be used unproductively to claim output or wealth that already exists or to seek policies that create privileged benefits. Such unproductive behavior is known as rent seeking. Much of rent seeking involves government or political decisions and is therefore in the domain of political economy but rent seeking also takes place in personal relations and within firms and bureaucracies.

The contributions in this volume are intended to be accessible to students, researchers, and policy practitioners, although the chapters in Part II require familiarity with techniques used in economic modeling. Because each chapter is preceded by a summary, we can be quite brief in describing the contents of the chapters.

Part I consists of two introductory chapters by the editors. Chapter 1 is an introduction to the concept of rent seeking and its roots in human behavior. Chapter 2 places rent seeking, in conjunction with rent creation and rent extraction, in the context of the political economy.

Part II is concerned with contest models. Chapter 3 by Ngo Van Long is an overview of rent-seeking contests. Chapter 4 by Gil Epstein and Shmuel Nitzan reviews models in which policies are contested and contests provide personal benefit for policymakers. Chapter 5 by Giuseppe Dari-Mattiacci, Eric Langlais, Bruno Lovat and Francesco Parisi describes consequences of asymmetries among rent seekers. In Chapter 6 by Sabine Flamand and Orestis Troumpounis, rent seeking is by interest groups or coalitions. Chapter 7 by Karl Wärneryd describes how organizational structure affects rent seeking. Chapter 8 by Yosef Mealem and Shmuel Nitzan describes the design of contests for rent extraction when the contest designer can choose between all-pay auctions and lottery contest-success functions. In Chapter 9 by J. Atsu Amegashie, there is sabotage in contests. Chapter 10 by Roman Sheremeta extends the theory of contests to behavioral dimensions. Together the chapters in Part II provide a comprehensive overview of theoretical models of contests involving rents.

Part III describes applications of the theory. Chapter 11 by William Shughart and Diana Thomas uses rent seeking to explain why government regulation of industry can result in 'capture' of the regulatory process. Chapter 12 by Arye Hillman considers why there have been dual expositions of the conduct of international trade policy with exclusion and inclusion of rents. Chapter 13 by Michael Brooks shows how rent seeking fundamentally changes the welfare conclusions of the theory of public finance. Chapter 14 by Robert Deacon and Ashwin Rode relates the resource curse to rent seeking. Chapter 15 by Rune Jansen Hagen describes the relation between rent seeking and development aid. Chapter 16 by Roland Vaubel explains why rent seeking is basic to understanding incentives, behavior and consequences of international organizations. Chapter 17 by Francesco Parisi and Barbara Luppi places rent seeking in the context of judicial institutions.

Part IV provides case studies of different societies. Chapter 18 by Dennis Mueller compares rents in the United States and Europe. Chapter 19 by Martin Paldam describes rents in a modern welfare state, Denmark. Chapter 20 by Mark Levin and Georgy Satarov describes rent seeking in Russia. Chapter 21 by John Mukum Mbaku and Mwangi S. Kimenyi describes Africa. Chapter 22 by Chen Kang and Liu Qijun describes China. Chapter 23 by Sugata Marjit and Vivekananda Mukherjee describes India. Chapter 24 by Thomas Moutos and Lambros Pechlivanos places modern Greece in a rent-seeking perspective. Chapter 25 by George Tridimas takes us back in time to ancient Greece and Athens. The chapters in Part IV show that principles associated with rents and rent seeking explain behavior and outcomes across locations and through time.

Part V describes the relation between rent seeking and institutions. Chapter 26 by Randall Holcombe places the theory of rent seeking in a context of constitutional political economy and contrasts the 'politics-as-exchange' and rent-seeking approaches to political decisions. Chapter 27 by Roger Congleton describes how potential rent-seeking losses have informed the institutional designs of all durable organizations; were this not the case, rent dissipation would have eliminated the net benefits of organizations and society would have returned to various Hobbesian jungles in which all potential net gains are dissipated through conflict.

The contributions in this volume provide a 'companion' for research on rent seeking and related rent creation and extraction. Together the chapters show that the scope of rent-related incentives and behavior is broad and central to the study of economics, politics, culture, public administration and history.

Roger D. Congleton and Arye L. Hillman
12 December 2014

PART I

INTRODUCTION

1. The nature of rent seeking

Roger D. Congleton

SUMMARY

This chapter provides a short introduction to the rent-seeking research program, including an analysis of the nature of rent seeking and its associated losses, evolutionary pressures for reducing those losses and the extent to which modest rent-seeking losses are natural and unavoidable.

1.1 THE ORIGIN OF THE LITERATURE ON RENT SEEKING

The term rent seeking was coined by Anne Krueger (1974) in her study of the resources drawn into the import and export businesses of Turkey and India because of their monopoly structure. She argued that competition for the 'rents' associated with those monopolies caused a good deal of competition for positions in those industries that consumed scarce resources – talent, time, training and other resources, without increasing the magnitude of industry rents. Competition to participate in import-export monopolies could thus to be a wasteful use of resources, and Krueger estimated that 7 percent of gross domestic product (GDP) in India and 10 percent of GDP in Turkey were wasted in that process. She called the activity of pursuing the higher wages available in the monopolized sectors, 'rent seeking'.

Unbeknownst to her, Gordon Tullock had undertaken a similar analysis of crime, tariffs and monopoly privileges nearly a decade earlier (1967 [2008]). This was pointed out, the literatures joined, and a new field of public policy analysis was launched. Rent seeking, from the perspective of that early literature, was the wasting of resources in the pursuit of 'unearned' profits or wages, which often were obtained through public policies that were widely acknowledged by economists to be counterproductive.

This core idea produced a substantial literature that attempted to analyze the extent of losses from monopoly and a variety of public policies that tend to increase market power. The new methodology included losses associated with the pursuit of rents – broadly construed – in addition to the conventional deadweight loss triangles of mainstream welfare economics. New estimates implied that losses from monopoly and 'protective' policies were far larger than formerly believed. For example, estimates of losses from monopoly in the United States suggested that rent-seeking losses were approximately 2 percent of gross national product (Posner 1975 [2008]), whereas the older estimates of welfare losses were only 0.1 percent of GNP. Rent-seeking losses were 20 times larger than the original deadweight loss estimates of Harberger (1954).

1.2 QUESTIONS EXPLORED BY THE LITERATURE ON RENT SEEKING

The core ideas were generalized to include the nonproductive use of resources in a wide variety of contests. In rent-seeking contests, resource investments are made by all the participants without significantly increasing the prize competed for or producing significant benefits for persons outside the contests of interest. Other contests may be productive, in that competition increases net value, rather than diminishes it, as might be said of competitive markets, contests for political office or sporting games. Rent-seeking contests are not value increasing for the rivals in the contests or for those affected by them, because the opportunity cost of the resources consumed exceed any benefits produced by the contest. Theft has this character. Warfare has this character. Many lobbying contests over public policy have this character. Many status games also have this character.

To analyze how contests may elicit unproductive conflict, the theoretical literature on rent seeking investigates how different rules affect investments in contests in which no-net benefits are produced, as in contests in which rivalry over a fixed pie occurs. In such contests it is clear that the rules of the game affect losses by encouraging or discouraging competitive efforts. Another strand of the theoretical literature explores incentives of governments to create or eliminate contests in which such losses accrue. Some rent-seeking contests are arguably accidental features of policy making, but others seem to be the result of intent. In either case, different rules could have reduced rent-seeking losses.

To what extent are such loss-affecting rules adopted? An answer requires integrated models of rent-seeking behavior and officeholders with the authority or power to establish the rules of rent-seeking contests.

One major strand of the rent-seeking literature analyzes what might be regarded to be accidental losses from rent-seeking activities. In some political settings, contests emerge which elicit efforts to persuade government to adopt policies that reduce competition in markets, without producing much of value. This process requires information campaigns, the wining and dining of pivotal decision makers and perhaps the giving of gifts (or bribes). As long as the overall net benefits generated by the policies are not significantly increased by those efforts, it is clear that all the efforts to secure favors for oneself or one's industry can be regarded as a deadweight loss, because the resources invested in the contest could have been used elsewhere to produce new net benefits for consumers or others.

Losses from such counterproductive contests would be reduced if each competitor simply reduced its efforts by half (or more). In this sense, rent-seeking losses are conceptually avoidable, although reducing them is not always politically feasible under existing institutions, nor is it always obvious that particular reforms will reduce or increase losses.[1] Were policy makers to understand the nature of these losses, perhaps the mechanisms for selecting public policies would be modified to avoid such losses. The existence of rent-seeking activities and losses are thus relevant for the study of policy making and public economics, and many other areas of social science.

---

[1] The effects that institutions have on the extent of rent-seeking losses was first explicitly analyzed in Congleton (1980 [2008]).

Insofar as resources are unproductively consumed by rent-seeking contests, those expenditures are miscounted in GNP statistics, where expenditures are assumed to reflect marginal revenue products of inputs – that is to say, the extent to which an input increases national output. The salaries of lobbyists create benefits for the lobbyists themselves but without increasing national output. Insofar as GNP is intended to represent the value of final goods produced economy wide, GNP should be reduced by the amount of the resources consumed in unproductive contests. Laband and Sophocleus (1992) suggest that up to 25 percent of GNP is consumed in such contests in the United States.[2]

1.3 THE NORMATIVE CASE AGAINST RENT SEEKING

The usual method of measuring rent-seeking losses relies upon the Kaldor-Hicks measures that dominate applied work in public economics. However, the normative effects of rent seeking can also be analyzed from other perspectives, with similar conclusions. For example, from a contractarian perspective, those who anticipate being affected by rent-seeking contests would unanimously agree to ban all contests in which the expected net benefits are lower than alternative uses of resources. Risk-averse persons would go a bit further and agree to ban contests in which the expected net benefits are zero, insofar as uncertainty is present for persons caught up in such contests or affected by them. Similar bans would also be agreed to from a justice or fairness perspective, insofar as the result of rent-seeking contests tends to be 'unearned' or 'undeserved' income, or 'illegitimate' shifts of net benefits from their 'proper' owners to others or from the relatively poor to the relatively rich, as with trade protection and agricultural subsidies.

Tullock's (1967 [2008]) analysis of ordinary theft nicely illustrates the normative case against rent seeking and indirectly provides a clear utilitarian defense for private property. Suppose that 'Al' undertakes to grow some nice melons in her garden. Her neighbor 'Bob' likes melons but does not like gardening. He plans to simply harvest some of the melons grown by Al, when they are ripe. From a Kaldor-Hicks (K-H) perspective, this is mere redistribution and so no change in overall welfare occurs from Bob's action. However, Al realizes that Bob will attempt to take the melons and erects a fence around her melon patch at a cost of R^A. Bob may reciprocate by purchasing a ladder or fence cutters at a cost of R^B. The net benefits of the melon for each have clearly been reduced by this contest for control of the melons, and the K-H measure of social welfare is reduced by the amount spent on the fence and fence cutters, $R^A + R^B$, even if Al's gardening effort is unaffected by her efforts at fence building.

The K-H losses are even greater if the output of Al's garden falls as she redirects her time and energy to fence construction and maintenance. Such losses provide a reason to ban theft from a K-H perspective, but this conclusion is obvious only when the resource costs of the contest over the melons are accounted for.

---

[2] Several excellent compendiums of the rent-seeking literature have been assembled as the literature emerged. The first was by Buchanan et al. (1980). Others include Rowley et al. (1988), Tollison and Congleton (1995) and Congleton et al. (2008a, 2008b). The latter two volumes are the most extensive of the collections.

Theft would also be banned from a contractarian perspective for somewhat similar reasons. Essentially all persons can imagine themselves being in Al and Bob's situation – more than occasionally – and would realize that losses from such conflict can be reduced by establishing clear rights for gardeners over their produce. Similarly, a justice perspective might insist that Al is entitled to the fruits of her labor, rather than Bob. It is she that bore the cost of planting and tending to the melons and it is proper that she should realize the fruits of that effort, rather than her neighbor. Different meanings of fairness can affect one's conclusions, but it seems clear that if Bob could also raise his own melons at a reasonable cost, fairness would require that the melons produced by Al should be Al's, rather than Bob's.

All rent seeking involves costly investments to get more than one has 'earned', with results that run counter to mainstream normative theories. That rent seeking continues to occur provides evidence of the effectiveness of the efforts of rent seekers relative to all the rest of us (Olson 1965).

1.4 LIFE, EVOLUTION AND UNPRODUCTIVE CONFLICT

It bears noting that it is completely natural that individuals and organizations attempt to profit from their efforts, as rent seekers do. It is not a human or cultural defect, but a survival trait. To survive, every species needs to find more food than required in calories to obtain it and more water than spent in sweat and tears finding and transporting it. Although there are many ways to obtain a surplus, doing so is a nontrivial activity and a necessary one for all living things.

Biologists have catalogued a wide range of strategies through which organisms survive. Some species use sunlight and minerals to construct their fabric of life and flourish when both are available at particular ratios and densities. Others use the bodies of other organisms as their principal source of raw materials. The bodies of those organisms may in turn be used as sustenance for others, as grass grazers are food for meat eaters. In this manner, a chain of life is formed from simple more or less independent organisms to species that depend more on others further down the food chain. The latter are often, although not always, biologically more complex than those that produce life directly from minerals and sunlight.

There is conflict over sustenance throughout the chain: at and between levels of the biological system. An ecosystem is not one large harmonious circle of life. Conflict within and among species absorbs both calories and time that could be used in other ways. The rent-seeking literature implies that the nature of these contests can be such that as many or more calories are consumed in such contests as is produced by them (exact or super dissipation). However, conflict over scarce food sources can consume as many or more calories than at stake only for short periods of time. One or more species will fail to survive such intense conflict. Survival requires rules, strategies, or decision-making procedures that avoid both the exact and over-dissipation results of rent-seeking contests.

As a consequence, all species have evolved a variety of ways for reducing conflict and also for surviving the conflict that nonetheless occurs. Conflict is reduced in a number of ways. Specialization can reduce conflict by using resources for survival that other species cannot. Genetically transmitted rules of conduct can reduce conflict, as with territoriality and pecking orders. Indeed, that such rules become 'hard wired' in genetic codes demonstrates their importance. Hard shells, speed, stealth, self-repair, and fear responses further reduce losses from conflict. Statistical methods are also used; for example, reproduction rates tend to be much higher and average longevity somewhat shorter down the chain than up.

Evolution is sufficient to produce complex ecosystems in which conflict is reduced to less than all-consuming levels. This allows species and the overall pattern of life to be sustained for very long periods of time – until disrupted by major catastrophes, such as changes in climate, exhaustion of critical sources of sustenance or genetic innovation that increases competition or diminishes the effectiveness of older strategies to reduce it. Such strategies tend to be both efficient and robust in the sense that even after major disruptions, biological systems have been sufficiently flexible that a new balance has nearly always emerged, although occasionally with major disruptions in the composition of the biosphere, as with the disappearance of dinosaurs. The winners are not always the strongest or fastest, but the best at harvesting net calories from a given physical and biological environment.

Humans emerged rather late in this process and, like other species, were also predisposed to maximize net calories. Their success suggests that forward looking – rational – evaluation of alternative strategies and consequences may also help reduce such losses in dynamic or complex circumstances. As the particular talents of humanity were refined and knowledge and capital accumulated, they came to be so efficient at net-calorie maximization that essentially the entire food chain from brewer's yeast to whales could be used in the production of human sustenance – for food, shelter and comfort.

Humans subsequently began to create their own artificial ecosystems, choosing particular species to support and others to challenge. Husbandry replaced nature's Nash equilibrium of conflict over calories in many areas of the biosphere, which reduced losses from conflict for the desired species and often increased it for the undesired species. The result was fewer bears and wolves but more sheep, chickens and grapevines, as humans produced safe havens for domesticated animals and plants and organized efforts to exterminate their rivals.

Inter-human conflict has also occurred, and much of that had (and has) the structure of rent-seeking contests. It was clearly possible that more calories would be consumed (or destroyed) in warfare than realized as the fruit of battle. For those that survived, it was also possible that the quality of life would be reduced to levels below that which most humans sought, as argued by Hobbes in 1651. However, again, solutions emerged, although not only genetic ones.

Organizations were formed to realize the productivity gains of team production and to avoid the losses from conflict, as noted by Montesquieu (1748[1914]). Counterproductive conflict is often systematically punished through social norms or government coercion. For example ownership rights over particular resources may be established, and violations of those 'rights' punished by norms against theft and formal penalties imposed on thieves. That laws emerged to both encourage productive activities and discourage unproductive conflict is clear from the earliest recorded legal codes, such as the code of Hammurabi (1800 BCE). Whether the individual rules making up civil and criminal law resulted from intent or social evolution is less clear, but also less important.

Wasteful conflict among human organizations has proved to be more difficult to reduce than among individuals and families. Again, territoriality and norms for engaging in conflict have played important roles (international law). Bans on the most destructive forms of warfare and agreements to reduce stocks of military capital goods also tend to reduce losses, and so agreements to do so have also been negotiated, although they have often been violated or undermined through innovation. Warfare and piracy, with their associated losses, remain problems in spite of boundary and peace treaties negotiated between governments and civil laws enforced within the territories governed.

As stressed by the rent-seeking literature, one of the perennial problems of humankind is managing losses from conflict. Successful strategies for doing so, as Hobbes (1651 [1982]) pointed out, allow far richer societies to emerge, although those strategies have not been sufficient to eliminate all unproductive conflict.

1.5 THE UNPRODUCTIVE CONFLICT THAT REMAINS AND THE CONTRIBUTION OF THIS VOLUME

It is that residual of unproductive conflict that has attracted the attention of economists, political scientists and game theorists attempting to understand the nature of rent-seeking losses and to devise institutional solutions. Although societies in which the scholars live all have rules that reduce losses from rent-seeking activities, the results are imperfect. Losses continue to accumulate, and analyzing them explicitly has been a productive intellectual enterprise. It has produced a clearer understanding of the use of resources in contests and how changing the rules of the game can and have reduced associated losses.

This book contributes to our understanding of counterproductive conflict by providing a comprehensive overview of the rent-seeking literature that emerged after 1967 and its wide range of applications and implications. Although rent-seeking losses have been reduced by both biological and social evolution, and by conscious institutional designs, unproductive conflict continues to pose substantial risks for even relatively well-functioning contemporary societies. The game-theoretic strand of the literature on rent seeking has examined the extent to which competition and conflict tend to be increased or diminished by changes in rules. The applied literature, in turn, demonstrates that losses actually exist – that rent seeking remains a problem – and increases our understanding of the real-world institutions and strategies that produce those losses.

Distinguishing contests that increase social net benefits, as competition in markets tends to do, from those that diminish social net benefits, as warfare and other forms of political conflict often do, is an important field of research with important policy implications. Applied work addresses this distinction through a variety of case studies: one policy, one market, one region or one period at a time. Theoretical work attempts to find general ways to undertake this classification.

Overall the present volume demonstrates that rent-seeking behavior is important as both a theoretical possibility and as a real-world phenomenon. Rent seeking affects how institutions work and why they do not work as well as economists, political scientists and philosophers often imagine or wish they did. These conclusions are demonstrated with thorough literature reviews, game-theoretic analyses, conceptual extensions and case studies – all written in a manner that is accessible to those interested in understanding the counterproductive interactions that occur between and within political and economic systems.

REFERENCES

Buchanan, James M., Robert D. Tollison and Gordon Tullock (eds) (1980), *Toward a Theory of the Rent-seeking Society*, College Station, TX: Texas A&M Press.

Congleton, Roger D. (1980), 'Competitive process, competitive waste, and institutions', in James M. Buchanan, Robert D. Tollison and Gordon Tullock (eds), *Toward a Theory of the Rent-seeking Society*, College Station, TX: Texas A&M Press, pp. 153–79, reprinted in Roger D. Congleton, Arye L. Hillman and Kai A. Konrad (eds) (2008), *40 Years of Research on Rent Seeking 1 – The Theory of Rent Seeking*, Heidelberg: Springer, pp. 69–95.

Congleton, Roger D., Arye L. Hillman and Kai A. Konrad (eds) (2008a), *40 Years of Research on Rent Seeking 1 – The Theory of Rent Seeking*, Heidelberg: Springer.

Congleton, Roger D., Arye L. Hillman and Kai A. Konrad (eds) (2008b), *40 Years of Research on Rent Seeking 2 – Applications: Rent Seeking in Practice*, Heidelberg: Springer.

Harberger, Arnold C. (1954), 'Monopoly and resource allocation', *American Economic Review*, **44**(2), 77–87.

Hobbes, Thomas (1651), *Leviathan*, reprinted in 1982, Baltimore, MD: Penguin Books.

Krueger, Anne O. (1974), 'The political economy of the rent-seeking society', *American Economic Review*, **64**(3), 291–303, reprinted in Roger D. Congleton, Arye L. Hillman and Kai A. Konrad (eds) (2008), *40 Years of Research on Rent Seeking 2 – Applications: Rent Seeking in Practice*, Heidelberg: Springer, pp. 151–63.

Laband, David N. and John P. Sophocleus (1992), 'An estimate of resource expenditures on transfer activity in the United States', *Quarterly Journal of Economics*, **107**(3), 959–83.

Montesquieu, Charles Louis de Secondat (1748), *The Spirit of the Laws*, reprinted in 1914, London: G. Bell and Sons.

Olson, Mancur (1965), *The Logic of Collective Action*, Cambridge, MA: Harvard University Press.

Posner, Richard (1975), 'The social costs of monopoly and regulation', *Journal of Political Economy*, **83**(4), 807–27, reprinted in Roger D. Congleton, Arye L. Hillman and Kai A. Konrad (eds) (2008), *40 Years of Research on Rent Seeking 2 – Applications: Rent Seeking in Practice*, Heidelberg: Springer, pp. 45–65.

Rowley, Charles, Robert D. Tollison and Gordon Tullock (eds) (1988), *The Political Economy of Rent Seeking*, Boston, MA: Kluwer.

Tollison, Robert D. and Roger D. Congleton (1995), *The Economic Analysis of Rent Seeking*, Aldershot, UK and Brookfield, VT, USA: Edward Elgar Publishing.

Tullock, Gordon (1967), 'The welfare costs of tariffs, monopolies, and theft', *Western Economic Journal*, **5**(3), 224–32, reprinted in Roger D. Congleton, Arye L. Hillman and Kai A. Konrad (eds) (2008), *40 Years of Research on Rent Seeking 1 – The Theory of Rent Seeking*, Heidelberg: Springer, pp. 45–53.

Tullock, Gordon (1980), 'Efficient rent seeking', in James M. Buchanan, Robert D. Tollison and Gordon Tullock (eds), *Toward a Theory of the Rent-seeking Society*, College Station, TX: Texas A&M Press, pp. 97–112, reprinted in Roger. D. Congleton, Arye L. Hillman and Kai Konrad (eds) (2008), *40 Years of Research on Rent Seeking 1 – The Theory of Rent Seeking*, Heidelberg: Springer, pp. 105–20.

2. Rent seeking as political economy

Arye L. Hillman

SUMMARY

The theory of contests has added interesting refinements to understanding rent-seeking behavior. Rent seeking, in conjunction with rent creation and rent extraction, is also at the core of political economy.

2.1 RENT SEEKING

The insight of the theory of rent seeking is that resources can be used unproductively to seek unearned personal benefits. Gordon Tullock's observations (Tullock 1967 [2008]) and the papers in Buchanan, Tollison and Tullock (1980) were the foundations for the introduction of rent seeking into modern economic analysis. Anne Krueger (1974) helped with a name and then all but disappeared from the scene of study of rent seeking. The historical record shows that rent seeking has been part of human behavior from the onset of recorded time. Why work when it is possible to benefit from the productive effort of others? Rent seeking has often been violent. In the contemporary era, in high-income democracies, evidence of rent seeking is political exchange of privileged benefits for votes and campaign contributions and regulation that benefits the regulated industry. Illegal personal gain through corruption can also take place. In low-income countries that are often autocracies or 'weak' democracies, rent seeking can be overt and without pretension, and facilitated by but a few decision makers who need to be influenced in a quest for rents. Perhaps only the autocratic ruler needs to be persuaded.

The motivation for studying rent seeking has been the likelihood of significant social losses from government policies beyond Harberger deadweight losses (Harberger 1954). While market data can in principle be used to measure Harberger losses, data limitations make direct measurement of social losses from rent seeking basically impossible. There are no official statistics: governments cannot be expected to provide data on rent seeking even if in principle they could. Surveys could ask, 'Have you engaged in rent seeking and if so what is the value of the resources that you used?' but the question may be regarded as an affront and people may refuse to answer, whether they are rent seekers or not. Rent seekers may reply expressively (Hillman 2010) and deny involvement in rent seeking, even if answering anonymously.

With rent seeking not directly observable and survey evidence non-existent or unreliable, studies of rent seeking have inferred social loss from observed magnitudes of contested rents. A convenient assumption has been complete rent dissipation (that the value of resources used in contesting a rent equals the value of an observed rent). Observed monopoly profits can then, for example, be regarded as social loss. Complete rent dissipation was the assumption made by Anne Krueger (1974) in estimating social losses from rent seeking in India and Turkey; by Richard Posner (1975) in evaluating the social loss due to monopoly in the United States; by Keith Cowling and Dennis Mueller (1978 [2008]) in comparing the social cost of monopoly in the United States and the United Kingdom; and by Sharif Mohammad and John Whalley (1984) in measuring social losses from rent seeking in India. David Laband and John Sophocleus (1988, 1992) used values of government transfers to infer the social cost of rent seeking in the United States; Angelopoulos et al. (2009) calibrated a general-equilibrium model with interest groups to estimate the social cost of rent seeking in Europe given observed income transfers, subsidies, and preferential tax treatment; Eliakim Katz and Jacob Rosenberg (1989) suggested estimates based on the supposition that the social cost of rent seeking could be inferred from changes in the composition of a government budget.

To justify the assumption of complete rent dissipation, we look to the theory of contests (Konrad 2009). Justifications can be found (for example, Hillman and Samet 1987 [2008]) but the more general conclusion from the theory of contests is that complete rent dissipation cannot be assured. In the original contest proposed by Gordon Tullock (1980 [2008]), rent dissipation depends on the number of contenders and returns to scale in rent-seeking outlays. Rent dissipation also depends on risk aversion and on the value of a contested rent relative to initial wealth (Hillman and Katz 1984 [2008]), on whether rent seekers know against how many other rent seekers they are competing (Münster 2006; Myerson and Wärneryd 2006), and on various other aspects of contests including whether the rent is a public good (Ursprung 1990).

With rational Nash behavior and including countervailing outlays (for example, by consumers in the face of rent seekers who are seeking monopoly profits), the value of a contested rent is an upper bound to social loss (Ellingsen 1991). With mixed strategies, *ex post* over-dissipation is possible. Over-dissipation is observed in experiments and is described in behavioral rent-seeking models.

The possibility of under- or over-dissipation compromises the assumption that observed rents indicate social losses. Nonetheless, against the background of the murky processes of rent seeking, at best all we usually have to go on for evaluating losses from rent seeking are observed rents.

There can be a question as to whether rent seeking is taking place. In debating the magnitudes of social costs of monopoly in the United States and Great Britain, Keith Cowling and Dennis Mueller (1978 [2008]) assumed complete rent dissipation and took the position that all corporate profits could be regarded as social losses, because the profits were contestable rents. Advertising expenditures were viewed as rent-seeking outlays. Stephen Littlechild (1981 [2008]) took the position that monopoly profits are signals for competitive entry and that advertising expenditures can be informative. To judge who might be correct, we need to know whether monopoly profits result in competitive entry or in rent seeking to displace the incumbent monopolist (who can also use resources in defending a monopoly position). If competitive entry is blocked, rent seeking is the only possibility and social costs can then include violence, corrupt law enforcement, and the undermining of whatever trust there is in government (see, for example, Blanco 2013 on Mexico).

Other social costs of rent seeking are outcomes that are counter to meritocracy and competence. Low-valuation rent seekers can win contests (Hillman and Riley

1989 [2008]; Nti 1999 [2008]) and be assigned positions or income sources contrary to comparative advantage. Exchange after a contest has been won can be efficiency-improving but may confirm a rent-seeking contest that it is inconvenient to acknowledge. In contests of ingratiation, the advantage is with persons with the lowest value of time or whose comparative advantage is in rent seeking. A successful rent seeker can emerge controlling the activities or even lives of productive people.

2.2 RENT CREATION

Rent seeking is an important concept even if there are impediments to measurement. The parallel is with the hidden activities of shadow-economy transactions. Rent seeking requires the creation of rents, which can take place through public spending: Park et al. (2005) studied rent creation from 'state coffers'. Government regulation (Peltzman 1976) and protectionist international trade policies (Hillman 1982 [2008], 1989 [2001]) create rents. Opportunities for rent creation appear to underlie the incentive for creation of new political jurisdictions (Hillman 2005). Foreign aid can also create rents (Svensson 2000 [2008]; Easterly 2001).

2.3 RENT EXTRACTION

The political incentive for rent creation is rent extraction (Appelbaum and Katz 1987 [2008]). Fred McChesney (1987 [2008]) described politicians who propose policies that disadvantage groups with the aim of extracting payments for not proceeding with the policies. The examples of political extortion were from the United States. Political benefits from creating rents can take the form of political support in the form of campaign contributions or votes. Rents can also be extracted through corruption (Aidt 2003), at the highest levels of government or at low levels of a government bureaucracy (Tanzi 1998). Rent extraction can simply take the form of the strong in a society taking from the weak (Hillman 2004). In a government or bureaucratic hierarchy, rents extracted can be contested by contesting positions in the hierarchy. If placement in positions in a hierarchy is determined by higher-level officials, the higher-level positions will be contested – and so on as up the political or bureaucratic hierarchy, with rents that can be extracted providing the incentives for rent seeking (Hillman and Katz 1987 [2008]). Rent extraction introduces issues of contest design into rent seeking, through the incentives of rent extractors to maximize rents extracted (Gradstein and Konrad 1999 [2008]).

2.4 THE ACCEPTABILITY OF AN IDEA

Roger Congleton (1991 [2008]) described rent seekers as using ideology to further their objectives but also ideology can be involved in attitudes to existence of rent seeking. A declaration that 'rent seeking is exaggerated' can be an expressive statement of self-described identity as someone who believes that it is contrary to human nature to create and seek rents. Gordon Tullock, on the other hand, proposed that 'people are people' (Tullock 2000), implying that human nature does not change when utility-maximizing private citizens occupy political or bureaucratic positions. It is not incidental that rent seeking began as part of the repertoire of concepts of the public-choice school, which emphasized agency problems between governments and citizens.

Tullock (1981 [2004]) also proposed that income distribution in practice is not about governments choosing from among normative theories of social justice but reflects the outcomes that individuals and groups can achieve for themselves through political processes. The latter processes involve rent seeking. If ideology defines government income transfers as means of achieving social justice, the proposal that income distribution is the outcome of influence over public policy through rent seeking defies political correctness (Hillman 1998 [2008]). Stephen Morris (2001) suggested that political correctness inhibits appropriate policies; the appropriate policy may be to restrict income redistribution because the redistribution is the consequence of rent seeking but political correctness disallows limits on redistribution when redistribution is defined as in the pursuit of social justice. The view that associates government redistribution with social justice does not fit well with the proposal that income redistribution by government is the consequence of rent seeking.

Gordon Tullock recognized the social losses from rent seeking while living in the United States (although, during the course of government service, he had been in China). Had he sought to publish his 1967 paper on 'the welfare costs of monopoly, tariffs and theft' in a low-income country, the paper may not have been published – not for the reason that academic journals do not exist, but that raising the issue of rent seeking leads into questions about for whose benefit rents are created. The idea of rent seeking was not, at the onset, accepted as part of mainstream economic thinking in the United States (Congleton et al. 2008). Gordon Tullock's being the originator of the rent-seeking concept could have made him persona non grata in the welfare states of Europe.

2.5 THE POLITICAL ECONOMY OF RENT SEEKING

Rent seeking has been extensively studied in the theory of contests. The political economy of rent seeking goes beyond the theory of contests to relate incentives for rent creation and extraction to the literature on politicized policy decisions (for example, Peltzman 1976; Hillman 1982 [2008]; Hillman 1991; Grossman and Helpman 2001). Rent creation and extraction also underlie the motives for contesting political office and the seeking of positions as regulators and in government bureaucracies (Hillman 2009, chapter 2). In a context that includes incentives for creation and extraction of rents, the theory of rent seeking becomes a core part of political economy.

REFERENCES

Aidt, Toke S. (2003), 'Economic analysis of corruption: a survey', *Economic Journal*, **113**(491), F632–F52.

Angelopoulos, Konstantinos, Apostolis Philippopoulos and Vanghelis Vassilatos (2009), 'The social cost of rent seeking in Europe', *European Journal of Political Economy*, **25**(3), 280–99.

Appelbaum, Elie and Eliakim Katz (1987), 'Seeking rents by setting rents: the political economy of rent seeking', *The Economic Journal*, **97**(387), 685–99, reprinted in Roger D. Congleton, Arye L. Hillman and Kai A. Konrad (eds) (2008), *40 Years of Research on Rent Seeking 1 – Theory of Rent Seeking*, Heidelberg: Springer, pp. 555–69.

Blanco, Luisa R. (2013), 'The impact of crime on trust in institutions in Mexico', *European Journal of Political Economy*, **32**, 38–55.

Buchanan, James M., Robert D. Tollison and Gordon Tullock (eds) (1980), *Toward a Theory of the Rent-seeking Society*, College Station, TX: Texas A&M University Press.

Congleton, Roger D. (1991), 'Ideological conviction and persuasion in the rent-seeking society', *Journal of Public Economics*, **44**(1), 65–86, reprinted in Roger D. Congleton, Arye L. Hillman and Kai A. Konrad (eds) (2008), *40 Years of Research on Rent Seeking 2 – Applications: Rent Seeking in Practice*, Heidelberg: Springer, pp. 769–90.

Congleton, Roger D., Arye L. Hillman and Kai A. Konrad (2008), '40 years of research on rent seeking: an overview', in Roger D. Congleton, Arye L. Hillman and Kai A. Konrad (eds), *40 Years of Research on Rent Seeking – volume 1 Theory of Rent Seeking and volume 2 Applications: Rent Seeking in Practice*, Heidelberg: Springer, pp. 1–42.

Cowling, Keith and Dennis C. Mueller (1978), 'The social costs of monopoly power', *Economic Journal*, **88**(352), 727–48, reprinted in Roger D. Congleton, Arye L. Hillman and Kai A. Konrad (eds) (2008), *40 Years of Research on Rent Seeking 2 – Applications: Rent Seeking in Practice*, Heidelberg: Springer, pp. 67–88.

Easterly, William (2001), *The Elusive Quest for Growth. Economists' Adventures and Misadventures in the Tropics*, Cambridge, MA: MIT Press.

Ellingsen, Tore (1991), 'Strategic buyers and the social cost of monopoly', *American Economic Review*, **81**(3), 648–57.

Gradstein, Mark and Kai Konrad (1999), 'Orchestrating rent-seeking contests', *The Economic Journal*, **109**(458), 536–45, reprinted in Roger D. Congleton, Arye L. Hillman and Kai A. Konrad (eds) (2008), *40 Years of Research on Rent Seeking 1 – Theory of Rent Seeking*, Heidelberg: Springer, pp. 571–80.

Grossman, Gene M. and Elhanan Helpman (2001), *Special Interest Politics*, Cambridge, MA: MIT Press.

Harberger, Arnold C. (1954), 'Monopoly and resource allocation', *American Economic Review Papers and Proceedings*, **44**(2), 77–87.

Hillman, Arye L. (1982), 'Declining industries and political-support protectionist motives', *American Economic Review*, **72**(2), 1180–87, reprinted in Wilfred J. Ethier and Arye L. Hillman (eds) (2008), *The WTO and the Political Economy of Trade Policy*, Aldershot, UK and Brookfield, VT, USA: Edward Elgar Publishing, pp. 43–50.

Hillman, Arye L. (1989), *The Political Economy of Protection*, Chur: Harwood Academic Publishers; reprinted (2001), London: Routledge.

Hillman, Arye L. (ed.), (1991), *Markets and Politicians: Politicized Economic Choice*, Boston: Kluwer.

Hillman, Arye L. (1998), 'Political economy and political correctness', *Public Choice*, **96**(3–4), 219–39, reprinted in Roger D. Congleton, Arye L. Hillman and Kai Konrad (eds) (2008), *40 Years of Research on Rent Seeking 2 – Applications: Rent Seeking in Practice*, Heidelberg: Springer, pp. 791–811 (Presidential Address, European Public Choice Society, Prague, April 1997).

Hillman, Arye L. (2004), 'Nietzschean development failures', *Public Choice*, **119**(3–4), 263–80.

Hillman, Arye L. (2005), 'Political institutions, jurisdictional boundaries, and rent creation', *Keio Economic Studies*, **42**(1–2), 25–37, Special issue in honor of Michihiro Ohyama, ed. Wilfred J. Ethier and Makoto Yano.

Hillman, Arye L. (2009), *Public Finance and Public Policy: Responsibilities and Limitations of Government*, 2nd edn, New York: Cambridge University Press.

Hillman, Arye L. (2010), 'Expressive behavior in economics and politics', *European Journal of Political Economy*, **26**(4), 403–18.

Hillman, Arye L. and Eliakim Katz (1984), 'Risk-averse rent seekers and the social costs of monopoly power', *Economic Journal*, **94**(373), 104–10, reprinted in Roger D. Congleton, Arye L. Hillman and Kai A. Konrad (eds) (2008), *40 Years of Research on Rent Seeking 1 – The Theory of Rent Seeking*, Heidelberg: Springer, pp. 97–103.

Hillman, Arye L. and Eliakim Katz (1987), 'Hierarchical structure and the social costs of bribes and transfers', *Journal of Public Economics*, **34**(2), 129–42, reprinted in Roger D. Congleton, Arye L. Hillman, and Kai Konrad (eds) (2008), *40 Years of Research on Rent Seeking 1 – The Theory of Rent Seeking*, Heidelberg: Springer, pp. 523–36.

Hillman, Arye L. and John G. Riley (1989), 'Politically contestable rents and transfers', *Economics and Politics*, **1**(1), 17–39, reprinted in Roger D. Congleton, Arye L. Hillman and Kai Konrad (eds) (2008), *40 Years of Research on Rent Seeking 1 – The Theory of Rent Seeking*, Heidelberg: Springer, pp. 185–207.

Hillman, Arye L. and Dov Samet (1987), 'Dissipation of contestable rents by small numbers of contenders', *Public Choice*, **54**(1), 63–82, reprinted in Roger D. Congleton, Arye L. Hillman and Kai A. Konrad (eds) (2008), *40 Years of Research on Rent Seeking 1 – The Theory of Rent Seeking*, Heidelberg: Springer, pp. 165–84.

Katz, Eliakim and Jacob Rosenberg (1989), 'Rent seeking for budgetary allocation: preliminary results for 20 countries', *Public Choice*, **60**(2), 133–44.

Konrad, Kai A. (2009), *Strategy and Dynamics in Contests*, Oxford: Oxford University Press.

Krueger, Anne O. (1974), 'The political economy of the rent-seeking society', *American Economic Review*, **64**(3), 291–303, reprinted in Roger D. Congleton, Arye L. Hillman and Kai A. Konrad (eds) (2008), *40 Years of Research on Rent Seeking 2 – Applications: Rent Seeking in Practice*, Heidelberg: Springer, pp. 151–63.

Laband, David N. and John P. Sophocleus (1988), 'The social cost of rent seeking: first estimates', *Public Choice*, **58**(3), 269–75.

Laband, David N. and John P. Sophocleus (1992), 'An estimate of resource expenditure on transfer activity in the United States', *Quarterly Journal of Economics*, **107**(3), 959–83.

Littlechild, Stephen (1981), 'Misleading calculations of the social costs of monopoly power', *Economic Journal*, **91**(362), 348–63, reprinted in Roger D. Congleton, Arye L. Hillman and Kai A. Konrad (eds) (2008), *40 Years of Research on Rent Seeking 2 – Applications: Rent Seeking in Practice*, Heidelberg: Springer, pp. 89–104.

McChesney, Fred S. (1987), 'Rent extraction and rent creation in the economic theory of regulation', *Journal of Legal Studies*, **16**(1), 101–18, reprinted in Roger D. Congleton, Arye L. Hillman and Kai A. Konrad (eds) (2008), *40 Years of Research on Rent Seeking 2 – Applications: Rent Seeking in Practice*, Heidelberg: Springer, pp. 313–30.

Mohammad, Sharif and John Whalley (1984), 'Rent seeking in India: its costs and policy significance', *Kyklos*, **37**(3), 387–413.

Morris, Stephen (2001), 'Political correctness', *Journal of Political Economy*, **109**(2), 231–65.

Münster, Johannes (2006), 'Contests with an unknown number of contestants', *Public Choice*, **129**(3–4), 353–68.

Myerson, Robert B. and Karl Wärneryd (2006), 'Population uncertainty in contests', *Economic Theory*, **27**(2), 469–74.

Nti, Kofi O. (1999), 'Rent seeking with asymmetric valuations', *Public Choice*, **98**(3–4), 415–30, reprinted in Roger D. Congleton, Arye L. Hillman and Kai A. Konrad (eds) (2008), *40 Years of Research on Rent Seeking 1 – The Theory of Rent Seeking*, Heidelberg: Springer, pp. 149–64.

Park, Hyun, Apostolis Philippopoulos and Vanghelis Vassilatos (2005), 'Choosing the size of the public sector under rent seeking from state coffers', *European Journal of Political Economy*, **21**(4), 830–50.

Peltzman, Sam (1976), 'Toward a more general theory of regulation', *Journal of Law and Economics*, **19**(2), 211–40.

Posner, Richard A. (1975), 'The social costs of monopoly and regulation', *Journal of Political Economy*, **89**(4), 807–27, reprinted in Roger D. Congleton, Arye L. Hillman and Kai A. Konrad (eds) (2008), *40 Years of Research on Rent Seeking 2 – Applications: Rent Seeking in Practice*, Heidelberg: Springer, pp. 45–65.

Svensson, Jakob (2000), 'Foreign aid and rent seeking', *Journal of International Economics*, **51**(2), 437–61, reprinted in Roger D. Congleton, Arye L. Hillman and Kai A. Konrad (eds) (2008), *40 Years of Research on Rent Seeking 2 – Applications: Rent Seeking in Practice*, Heidelberg: Springer, pp. 165–89.

Tanzi, Vito (1998), 'Corruption around the world: causes, consequences, scope, and cures', *Staff Papers – International Monetary Fund*, **45**(4), 559–94, reprinted in George T. Abed and Sanjeev Gupta (eds) (2002), *Governance, Corruption, and Economic Performance*, Washington DC: International Monetary Fund, pp. 19–58.

Tullock, Gordon (1967), 'The welfare costs of tariffs, monopolies and theft', *Western Economic Journal*, **5**(3), 224–32, reprinted in Roger D. Congleton, Arye L. Hillman and Kai A. Konrad (eds) (2008), *40 Years of Research on Rent Seeking 1 – The Theory of Rent Seeking*, Heidelberg: Springer, pp. 45–53.

Tullock, Gordon (1980), 'Efficient rent seeking', in James M. Buchanan, Robert D. Tollison and Gordon Tullock (eds), *Toward a Theory of the Rent-seeking Society*, College Station, TX: Texas A&M Press, pp. 97–112, reprinted in Roger D. Congleton, Arye L. Hillman and Kai A. Konrad (eds) (2008), *40 Years of Research on Rent Seeking 1 – The Theory of Rent Seeking*, Heidelberg: Springer, pp. 105–20.

Tullock, Gordon (1981), 'The rhetoric and reality of redistribution', *Southern Economic Journal*, **47**(4), 895–907, reprinted in Charles K. Rowley (ed.) (2004), *The Selected Works of Gordon Tullock, volume 1, Virginia Political Economy*, Indianapolis: Liberty Fund, pp. 276–94 (Presidential Address, Southern Economic Association, Washington DC, November 1980).

Tullock, Gordon (2000), 'People are people', in Gordon Tullock, Arthur Seldon, and Gordon L. Brady (eds) (2004), *Government: Whose Obedient Servant?*, London: Institute of Economic Affairs, pp. 3–18, reprinted in

Charles K. Rowley (ed.) (2004), *The Selected Works of Gordon Tullock, volume 4, The Economics of Politics*, Indianapolis: Liberty Fund, pp. 32–45.

Ursprung, Heinrich W. (1990), 'Public goods, rent dissipation, and candidate competition', *Economics and Politics*, **2**(2), 115–32, reprinted in Roger D. Congleton, Arye L. Hillman and Kai A. Konrad (eds) (2008), *40 Years of Research on Rent Seeking 1 – Theory of Rent Seeking*, Heidelberg: Springer, pp. 329–46.

PART II

THEORY

3. The theory of contests: a unified model and review of the literature[1]

Ngo Van Long

3.1 INTRODUCTION

Contests are a pervasive fact of life, both in the human and the non-human spheres. Frank Knight (1935, p. 301) saw games of contest as an essential feature of economic life: 'The activity which we call economic, whether of production or of consumption or of the two together, is also, if we look below the surface, to be interpreted largely by the motives of the competitive contest or game, rather than those of mechanical utility functions to be maximized.'

In a similar fashion, Veblen (1924) emphasized the pervasiveness of emulation, which he defined as 'the stimulus of an invidious comparison which prompts us to outdo those with whom we are in the habit of classing ourselves'. He believed that 'with the exception of the instinct for self-preservation, the propensity for emulation is probably the strongest and most alert and persistent of economic motives proper'. Emulation can lead to direct contests, and to wasteful use of resources.

Contests may serve socially useful functions such as the selection of the best candidate for a position. Quite often, however, contests give rise to processes whereby individuals or groups try to influence political or bureaucratic decisions in their favor. As Congleton (1980 [2008], p. 154) put it, 'if one's opportunity set is not entirely determined externally by forces beyond the influence of an individual actor, situations are very likely to arise in which an economically rational individual will use the resources at his disposal to influence his range of options at the expense of others'. The theory of rent seeking views contests as an inevitable feature of political discretion.

This chapter reviews the theory of contests, with a primary focus on the relationship between the rent and the efforts to capture rent. In particular, we will identify situations where rent dissipation is, or is not, complete. One of the main reasons for investigating special features of rent-seeking contests is to establish guidelines for estimating the value of wasted resources in various rent-seeking situations. As Tullock (1967 [2008]), Krueger (1974 [2008]) and others have argued, estimates of national income should in principle be adjusted to deduct the wasteful use of real resources.[2]

---

[1] Reprinted from *European Journal of Political Economy* (2013), **32**, 161–81 with kind permission of Elsevier Ltd.

[2] Krueger (1974 [2008b]) calculated that in India in 1964, total rents amounted to 7.3 percent of gross domestic product (GDP). Two thirds of these rents were associated with import licenses. She found that in 1968, quota rents in Turkey was about 15 percent of GDP. By including other distortions, Mohammed and Whalley (1984) obtained a much higher estimate of contestable rents in India: around 30 percent to 45 percent of GDP. See also Angelopoulos et al. (2009) and Laband and Sophocleus (1992).

Since the publication of an excellent survey of the literature on contests (Nitzan, 1994), the economic profession has continued to add new insights to the analysis of rent seeking, some of which are reported in the present chapter. For a complementary and insightful survey with greater emphasis on conceptual issues, see Hillman (2013). A volume of readings on the theory of rent seeking edited by Congleton et al. (2008a) also contains a useful guide to the literature. Readers interested in greater technical details are referred to the beautifully crafted monograph by Konrad (2009).

In Section 3.2, a fairly general contest model is explained. We show that the Tullock contest model and the first-prize sealed-bid auction model are obtained as special cases, and their implications are explored. Section 3.3 deals with some important modifications of the basic model: hierarchical rent seeking, rent seeking under risk aversion, insecured rents and sabotage in rent-seeking contests. Section 3.4 discusses further extensions of the model: contest design, commitment and endogenous order of moves, and dynamic rent seeking. Section 3.5 offers concluding remarks.

3.2 THE BASIC MODEL

In this section we introduce the basic setting and show how two main contest models can be obtained from it: the first-prize sealed-bid all-pay auction and the standard Tullock contest.

3.2.1 The Basic Setting and Some General Results

Consider a simple setting. There are n contestants. A prize will be awarded to the winner of the contest.[3] Let V_i be contestant i's valuation of the prize. Without loss of generality, we can index the contestants such that $V_1 \geq V_2 \geq V_3 \geq \ldots \geq V_n > 0$. The contestants expend efforts (or outlays) in order to influence their probability of winning. Let y_i denote contestant i's effort. The cost of effort is $C(y_i) = y_i$.

Since contestants' efforts are not necessarily equally effective, to make them comparable, we assume a contestant's effort is turned into 'effective effort', denoted by z_i, under an 'effective effort production function' $f_i(y_i)$, which in general may differ across individuals:

$$z_i = f_i(y_i)$$

We assume that $f_i(y)$ is a monotone increasing function, with $f_i(0) = 0$ and $f'_i(y_i) > 0$.

The sum of the effective efforts is $Z = \sum_{j=1}^{n} z_j$. We call Z the aggregate effective effort.

---

[3] Here we assume that the prize is awarded to the winner of the contest. In a more general context, an interesting issue that may arise is: can contestants refuse to contest and, instead, opt to share the prize among themselves, through bargaining? If so, when would they prefer contesting to bargaining? For a model of contested water rights with the possibility of bargaining, see Ansink and Weikard (2009). They show that if there is the possibility of third party intervention in the event of contest, and contestants have different expectation of the success of third party intervention, they might prefer contesting to bargaining.

Assume that if $Z > 0$, then the probability that constestant i wins the contest, p_i, is equal to the ratio z_i/Z. We suppose that in the case where $Z = 0$, then all the contestants have an equal probability of winning, $1/n$.

Formally,

$$\pi_i = \begin{cases} \frac{z_i}{Z} = \frac{f_i(y_i)}{f_i(y_i) + \sum_{j \neq i}^{n} f_j(y_j)} & \text{if } Z > 0 \\ \frac{1}{n} & \text{if } Z = 0 \end{cases}$$

Let Z_{-i} denote the sum of the effective efforts of all contestants except that of i. Contestant i takes Z_{-i} as given, and chooses $y_i \geqslant 0$ to maximize her expected payoff:

$$\max_{y_i} \left(\frac{f_i(y_i)}{Z_{-i} + f_i(y_i)} V_i \right) - y_i$$

All contestants must choose their efforts simultaneously. The solution concept is Nash equilibrium. A pure strategy Nash equilibrium is an action profile $(y_1, y_2, \ldots, y_n)$ such that no contestant can improve her expected payoff by deviating from it. A mixed strategy Nash equilibrium is a profile of cumulative probability distributions $(F_1, F_2, \ldots, F_n)$ such that no contestant can improve her expected payoff by choosing a different cumulative probability distribution. We will discuss the conditions for existence and uniqueness of Nash equilibrium.

An interesting observation is that in the case of pure strategy Nash equilibrium, Z is always strictly positive. To prove this, suppose $Z = 0$. Then everyone has the probability of success $1/n$. Then player i, taking $Z_{-i} = 0$ as given, can deviate to improve her payoff, simply by increasing her effort level from zero to ε_i, where ε_i is an arbitrarily small positive number, and her winning probability becomes $\varepsilon_i/(\varepsilon_i + 0) = 1$. A consequence of this result is that in any pure strategy Nash equilibrium, at least two players will expend strictly positive effort levels. To show this, consider a candidate Nash equilibrium action profile $(y_1, y_2, \ldots, y_n)$ with $y_i > 0$ for some i and $y_j = 0$ for all $j \neq i$. Then player i can deviate to gain by reducing y_i marginally: her winning probability is still 1 while her effort cost is reduced.

While the functions $f_i(y_i)$ can be quite general, for tractability most authors restrict attention to a special case, which was proposed by Tullock (1980):

$$z_i = y_i^\beta \text{ where } \beta > 0$$

Under this specification, the probability that contestant i wins is

$$\pi_i = \begin{cases} \frac{z_i}{Z} = \frac{y_i^\beta}{y_i^\beta + \sum_{j \neq i}^{n} y_j^\beta} & \text{if } Z > 0 \\ \frac{1}{n} & \text{if } Z = 0 \end{cases} \tag{3.1}$$

This probability specification is known as the Tullock contest success function.[4] The transformation $z_i = y_i^\beta$ displays decreasing (respectively, increasing) returns to scale

4 This contest success of function was proposed by Tullock (1975 [2008], 1980). An earlier and somewhat more general functional form was introduced by Mills (1961), who used it to model promotional competition.

when $\beta < 1$ (respectively, $\beta > 1$). The case of constant returns to scale, $\beta = 1$, is simplest in terms of computation. This constant returns to scale case is called the Tullock lottery.[5]

A limiting case of the Tullock contest function is of particular interest: as *b* tends to infinity, contestant *i* will win with probability 1 if $y_i > y_j$ for all $j \neq i$. To see this, rewrite π_i as follows

$$\pi_i = \frac{1}{1 + \sum_{j \neq i} (\frac{y_j}{y_i})^\beta}$$

Clearly, with $y_i > y_j$ for all $j \neq i$, the term $(\frac{y_j}{y_i})^\beta$ approaches zero as β approaches ∞. It follows that, in this limiting case, the person whose effort exceeds that of each of her rivals will win. The Tullock contest with $\beta = \infty$ is equivalent to the 'first-price sealed-bid all-pay auction' game: all players must make their bids simultaneously, and pay their bids, and the highest bidder is the winner.

3.2.2 Analysis of the First-prize Sealed-bid All-pay Auction

Let us first consider the first-prize sealed-bid all-pay auction game where the contestants are not constrained by any upper bound on their effort level. The case where an upper limit is imposed will be considered later.

The first-prize sealed-bid all-pay auction has no Nash equilibrium in pure strategies, even in the simplest case of two players with identical valuations: $V_1 = V_2 = V$. To see this, consider any candidate action profile (y_1^*, y_2^*). Without loss, we can suppose that $y_i^* \leq V$, as no rational player will submit a bid exceeding V. Clearly, if $y_1^* = y_2^* < V$, the candidate (y_1^*, y_2^*) cannot be a Nash equilibrium, because a player, say contestant 1, can improve her payoff by deviating from it and choosing a slightly greater y_1, thus winning the prize with certainty.[6] If $y_1^* = y_2^* = V$, the payoff of each contestant is negative; again player 1, say, can deviate to improve her payoff by choosing $y_1 = 0$. If $y_2^* < y_1^* \leq V$, then player 1 can reduce y_1 marginally below y_1^* and still win; thus the candidate action profile (y_1^*, y_2^*) is not a Nash equilibrium.

We must therefore find a Nash equilibrium in mixed strategies. It is easy to see that, with two players, the equilibrium involves randomization using the uniform density function over the interval $[0, V]$. With the uniform density, the cumulative distribution for player 1 is

$$F_1(t) \equiv \Pr(y_1 < t) = \begin{cases} 0 & \text{if } t < 0 \\ \frac{t}{V} & \text{if } 0 \leq t \leq V \\ 1 & \text{if } t > V \end{cases}$$

Given this strategy of player 1, any choice of y_2 in the interval $[0, V]$ will yield player 2 an expected payoff of zero:[7]

---

[5] Tullock (1980, p. 99) explained this analogy.

[6] Whenever there are two contestants, I will use 'she' to denote player 1 and 'he' for player 2.

[7] And of course, any $y_2 > V$ will give him a negative payoff.

$$U_2 = \Pr(y_1 < y_2)V - y_2 = F_1(y_2)V - y_2 = \left(\frac{y_2}{V}\right)V - y_2 = 0$$

Therefore player 2 is indifferent among all pure strategies y_2 in $[0, V]$. He might as well randomize his choice using the same cumulative distribution as player 1. It follows that in the symmetric two-contestant case, randomization using the uniform density function constitutes a Nash equilibrium in mixed strategies. It can be shown that there is no other Nash equilibrium.

Generalizing to the case of n identical contestants, Hillman and Samet (1987 [2008]) show that for the first-prize sealed-bid all-pay auction game without upper bounds on the bids, in the symmetric equilibrium, all contestants will randomize their efforts, using the cumulative distribution function $F(y) = (y/V)^{1/(n-1)}$, for $0 \le y \le V$.[8] With identical valuations, it can be shown that for any n, the expected aggregate effort is equal to the prize, that is, rent is completely dissipated in the expectational sense (Hillman and Samet 1987 [2008]).[9]

Hillman and Riley (1989 [2008]) extend the analysis to the case of asymmetric valuations and show that rent is not completely dissipated. To see this, consider the simple case with two players. Suppose player 1, Heather, has a high valuation V_H, while player 2, Luke, has a lower valuation, V_L.

Assume $V_H > V_L > 0$. First, we show that there is no Nash equilibrium in pure strategies. The argument is similar to that we used in the case of two identical players. Let y_H denote Heather's effort level. For a given $y_H > 0$, it is optimal for Luke either to contribute just a little bit more than y_H and win (in which case $y_H > 0$ cannot be optimal for Heather), or to contribute zero, in which case y_H is also not optimal for Heather, for she can reduce y_H a bit and still win. The same argument applies for any given $y_L > 0$. And of course $(y_H, y_L) = (0, 0)$ cannot be an equilibrium. Therefore, a Nash equilibrium must involve mixed strategies by both players.

It is easy to verify that the Nash equilibrium strategy of the high valuation player is randomize her effort level using the uniform distribution over the real interval $[0, V_L]$, and that the low valuation player's equilibrium strategy is: set $y_L = 0$ with probability $(V_H - V_L)/V_H$, and with the complementary probability, randomize y_L using the uniform distribution over the interval $(0, V_L]$.

Given Luke's equilibrium strategy, Heather obtains an expected payoff of $V_H - V_L$ for any effort level y_H in the interval $(0, V_L]$, and a smaller payoff $(V_H - E_H)$ if $y_H > V_L$. Given Heather's equibrium strategy, Luke's expected payoff is zero for any non-negative $y_L \le V_L$ (and is negative if $y_L > V_L$). It can be shown that there is no other mixed strategy Nash equilibrium (Baye et al. 1996 [2008]).

Under the mixed strategy Nash equilibrium, Heather's expected effort cost is $V_L/2$

---

8 It follows that if $n = 2$, $F(y)$ is the cumulative probability of the uniform density function over [0. V], as noted by Hirshleifer and Riley (1978).

9 The complete dissipation result has been shown to apply also to some models with less extreme sensitivity of success to a marginal change in a player's effort. Alcalde and Dahm (2010) show that for a class of contest success functions, if the elasticity of a rent seeker's win probability with respect to her effort is sufficiently high, then there exists a mixed strategy equilibrium with complete rent dissipation.

and Luke's expected effort cost is $V_L^2/(2V_H)$. The sum of their expected effort is less than the low valuation V_L. The equilibrium displays an inefficiency: the contestant with the highest valuation does not always win the prize.

How does the result generalize to the case with n contestants? In the simple case where the top two valuations are strictly greater than the valuation of the remaining contestants, that is, $V_1 \geq V_2 > V_3 \geq V_4 \geq \ldots \geq V_n$, it is clear that the n – 2 lower valuation contestants will set their effort at zero. For other cases, there may exist multiple Nash equilibria (see Baye et al. 1996 [2008]). For example, if there are three players with the highest valuation, in one equilibrium, two players will use the strategies as described above while the third player chooses $y_3 = 0$; in another equilibrium, all three contestants randomize their effort levels.[10]

What happens if a minimum outlay $c > 0$ is required to enter the contest? Hillman and Samet (1987) demonstrated that with n identical contestants, the equilibrium distribution function of effort is

$$F(y) = \begin{cases} (y/V)^{1/(n-1)} & \text{for } c \leq y \leq V \\ (c/V)^{1/(n-1)} = F(0) & \text{for } 0 \leq y \leq c \end{cases}$$

In this case, for any finite n, the expected aggregate effort is less than the prize:

$$nE(y) = V - c^{n/(n-1)} < V$$

However, since the prize is not awarded if no contestant spends at least c, an event with probability $F(0)^n$, the expected prize is $[1 - F(0)^n]V$, which is equal to $nE(y)$. It follows that when the contestants have the same valuation, rent dissipation is complete, on average.

What happens if there is a prescribed upper bound $\bar{y}$ on individual effort? Congleton (1980 [2008], pp. 72–5) considered this case for two symmetric players, and Che and Gale (1997) analyzed the case with n asymmetric players. Suppose there are n contestants, indexed by i where $i = 1, 2, \ldots, n$. Without loss of generality, assume $V_1 \geq V_2 \geq V_3 \geq \ldots \ldots \geq V_n$. Let us first assume that $n\bar{y} < V_n$. Then the Nash equilibrium involves $y_i = \bar{y}$ for all i. To see this, suppose one contestant sets her y_i at the maximum $\bar{y}$. Any other contestant j then knows that setting $y_j < \bar{y}$ will give him a zero probability of winning, while setting $y_j = \bar{y}$ will give him a probability of at least $1/n$ of winning. Since $(1/n)V_i \geq (1/n)V_n > \bar{y}$, clearly it pays to choose the latter action, $y_j = \bar{y}$. (In the limiting case where $n\bar{y} = V_n$, the same equilibrium obtains, but the expected payoff is zero: the rent is completely dissipated.)

What happens if $\bar{y} > 1/n$? Let us define the following thresholds $\bar{y}_2 \equiv \frac{1}{2}V_2$,

---

[10] The model can be generalized to the case of all-pay auction with two objects that are ranked in the same way by all players. The player with the highest bid wins the most valuable object, and the second highest bidder wins the second best object. In the case with one dominant player and $n - 1$ identical players with weaker preferences, Cohen and Sela (2008) found that there is always an equilibrium with only three active players. They also found that the expected total effort may be higher in this two-prize contest than in an alternative contest where the two objects are combined to form a one-prize contest.

$\bar{y}_3 \equiv \frac{1}{3}V_3, \ldots, \bar{y}_j \equiv \frac{1}{j}V_j$. Then, as long as the prescribed upper bound $\bar{y}$ satisfies the inequality $\bar{y}_{k-1} < \bar{y} < \bar{y}_k$, only the top k players will actively contest, and will in equilibrium choose $\bar{y}$ as their effort level.

Finally, consider the case of convex effort cost, $C(y_i)$, with $C(0) = 0$, $C'(y_i) > 0$ and $C''(y_i) \geq 0$. Suppose there are two players with identical valuation V. Define y_{max} as the effort level that yields a player a net benefit of zero if he wins the prize:

$$C(y_{max}) = V$$

Clearly, no player will choose an effort level higher than y_{max}. Let $F_j(.)$ be the cumulative distribution of player j's effort level. Then if player i selects an arbitrary y, the probability that player j's bid is beow y is $F_j(y)$, and thus payer i's expected payoff under that choice is

$$F_j(y)\,V - C(y)$$

This payoff will be equal to zero for each y in the interval $[0, y_{max}]$ if and only if the function $F_j(y)$ is identical to the function $(1/V)C(y)$ for all y in this interval. Since the players have identical cost functions and identical valuation, it follows that in a symmetric equilibrium, players use the common cumulative distribution $F(y)$, which has the property that

$$F(y) = \frac{C(y)}{V}$$

(In the special case where $C(y)$ is linear, the cumulative $F(y)$ is the integral of the uniform density function.) Generalizing to the case of n identical players, we obtain $F(E) = [C(y)/V]^{1/n}$ for $y \in [0, y_{max}]$.

Let us consider some modifications of the model of first-prize sealed-bid all-pay auction.

So far, we have assumed that each contestant knows the valuations of other contestants. The case of incomplete information can be modeled as follows. Suppose there are two contestants. Contestant 1 does not know contestant 2's valuation V_2, but knows that V_2 has a cumulative distribution $F(.)$ over the interval $[0, \bar{V}]$, where $\bar{V}$ is known, and $F(\bar{V}) = 1$. Suppose that player 2 has the effort strategy $y_2 = \phi_2(V_2)$ such that the higher is V_2, the higher is the effort y_2, and $\phi_2(0) = 0$. Then the inverse function $V_2 = \phi_2^{-1}(y_2)$ exists. Given any number y, the probability that y_2 is lower than y is the probability that V_2 is smaller than $\phi_2^{-1}(y)$, that is, it is $F(\phi_2^{-1}(y))$.

Contestant 1's expected payoff from exerting effort y_1 is

$$U_1(y_1) = F(\phi_2^{-1}(y_1))\,V_1 - y_1$$

Her optimal y_1 therefore must satisfy the first order condition

$$V_1 F'(\phi_2^{-1}(y_1))\frac{d\phi_2^{-1}(y_1)}{dy_1} - 1 = 0$$

Given constestant 2's effort strategy, this equation determines y_1 as a function of V_1. Denote this function as $\phi_1(V_1)$. Then the first order condition for contestant 1 can be written as

$$V_1 F'(\phi_2^{-1}(\phi_1(V_1))d\phi_2^{-1}(\phi_1(V_1)) = d\phi_1(V_1)$$

Similarly, the first order condition for contestant 2 is

$$V_2 F'(\phi_1^{-1}(\phi_2(V_2))d\phi_1^{-1}(\phi_2(V_2)) = d\phi_2(V_2)$$

In a symmetric equilibrium, the effort strategies of the two contestants are identical: $\phi_1(.) = \phi_2(.) = \phi(.)$. The two first order conditions then give

$$VF'(V) = \frac{d\phi(V)}{dV}$$

This is a first order differential equation with the boundary condition $\phi(0) = 0$. Integration yields

$$\phi(V) = \int_0^V vF'(v)\,dv$$

For example, suppose $\overline{V} = 1/2$ and V is distributed in the interval [0, 1/2] with the cumulative distribution $F(V) = 4(V - V^2)$, then we can obtain the symmetric Nash equilibrium strategy,

$$\phi(V) = 4\left[\frac{V^2}{2} - \frac{2V^3}{3}\right], 0 \leq V \leq \frac{1}{2}$$

The contrast between the perfect information case and the imperfect information case is interesting. In the first case, each player knows the exact valuation of the opponent. A pure strategy equilibrium does not exist; both players must randomize their effort levels to support a Nash equilibrium. In the imperfect information case, each contestant i knows V_i, but does not know the valuation of the opponent. While any given opponent has a uniquely chosen effort level, since the opponent's type is not known, from an uninformed player's point of view, it is as if the opponent randomized his effort level.[11] Concerning efficiency, notice that in the former case inefficiency can occur in the sense that the prize is not necessarily awarded to the agent that values it most. In the latter case the winner is always the one with the highest valuation.

---

11 For further discussion of this point, and the duality relationship between the two strategic situations, see Amann and Leininger (1996).

3.2.3 Contest with Additive Noise

In the preceding subsection, the contestant that exerts the most effort will win. In the real world, efforts are not observed; only outcomes are. The relationship between efforts and outcomes is stochastic, because of the presence of noise. For example, identical levels of research efforts do not necessarily result in identical number of publications, because of noise in the reviewing process. The labor market tournaments provide primary examples of the importance of noise. (See Lazear (1995) for an excellent survey of the literature on labor market tournaments.)

Suppose there are two contestants. The winning contestant receives the prize V_W. The losing contestant is given a consolation prize $V_C < V_W$. Assume that contestant *i*'s effort y_i gives rise to an observed outcome $x_i = y_i + \varepsilon_i$ where ε_i is an unobservable random variable with zero mean. The prize is awarded to the contestant with the highest observed outcome x_i (in the case $x_1 = x_2$, each contestant will win with probability 1/2 by tossing a coin). Define the noise $\varepsilon = \varepsilon_2 - \varepsilon_1$. Then the probability that contestant 1 wins is

$$\pi_1(y_1, y_2, \varepsilon) = \begin{cases} 1 & \text{if} \quad y_1 - y_2 > \varepsilon \\ \frac{1}{2} & \text{if} \quad y_1 - y_2 = \varepsilon \\ 0 & \text{if} \quad y_1 - y_2 < \varepsilon \end{cases}$$

Assume that the noise *e* has a cumulative distribution $F(\varepsilon)$ over the support $[-\delta, \delta]$. For any given pair of effort levels (y_1, y_2) the probability that contestant 1 wins is the probability that the noise *e* is smaller than the difference $y_1 - y_2$, and this is measured by $F(y_1 - y_2)$. Notice that this probability is zero if $y_1 - y_2 < -\delta$ and is 1 if $y_1 - y_2 > \delta$. Each contestant has a strictly convex effort cost function $C(y_i)$ where $C'(y_i) > 0$ and $C''(y_i) > 0$. This assumption is made so that we can obtain a pure strategy Nash equilibrium, given a sufficiently strong degree of convexity.

Contestant 1 chooses effort level y_1 to maximize her expected payoff U_1, defined by

$$U_1 = -C(y_1) + V_C + (V_W - V_C)\Pr\{\varepsilon \leq y_1 - y_2\}$$

The first order condition is

$$-C'(y_1) + (V_W - V_C)\frac{\partial F(y_1 - y_2)}{\partial y_1} = 0$$

Note that the Nash equilibrium effort levels depend on the difference beween the prizes, and not on their absolute level. The consolation prize can be adjusted so that the expected payoff of each contestant is at least as high as the reservation utility level.

For illustration, consider the case where the noise *e* has the uniform density function. Then $F(\varepsilon) = (\varepsilon + \delta)/2\delta$ for $-\delta \leq \varepsilon \leq \delta$, and the derivative $\partial F(y_1 - y_2)/\partial y_1 = 1/(2\delta)$ as long as $-\delta < y_1 - y_2 < \delta$. Within this range, a small change in y_2 has no impact on the choice y_1. We then obtain the symmetric Nash equilibrium

$$y_1 = y_2 = y^* = (C')^{-1}\left(\frac{V_W - V_C}{2\delta}\right)$$

Since C' is an increasing function, so is its inverse function, $(C')^{-1}$. It follows that the wider is the range $[-\delta,\delta]$, the smaller is the Nash equilibrium effort level. This is an intuitively plausible result.

Notice that y^* depends on the difference $V_W - V_C$, and not on the absolute levels V_W and V_C. We may call $V_W - V_C$ the 'stake' of the game, and denote it by S. The greater is the stake, the higher is the equilibrium effort level. The consolation prize V_C must be chosen in such a way that the contestants are willing to participate: their expected utility at the Nash equilibrium, $(S)F(y^*(S)) + V_C - C(y^*(S))$, must be not less than the outside payoff U_0.

3.2.4 The Standard Tullock Contest

In the standard Tullock contest, the probability of winning is given by the Tullock contest success function (3.1).[12]

The most popular special case of the standard Tullock contest is the Tullock lottery contest success function, that is, $\beta = 1$, because it is analytically simple. Let us take a look at this case first. Assume for the moment that there are only two contestants, with $V_1 > 0$ and $V_2 > 0$. We have shown in Subsection 3.2.1 that in any Nash equilibrium involving n ³ 2 players, there are at least two players who exert strictly positive effort.

For any $y_2 > 0$, the first order condition of contestant 1 is

$$\frac{y_2}{[y_1 + y_2]^2} V_1 - 1 \leq 0$$

This yields the reaction function $y_1 = r_1(y_2)$:

$$y_1 = \max\{0, \sqrt{y_2 V_1} - y_2\} \text{ for } y_2 > 0 \tag{3.2}$$

Note that for all $y_2 \geq V_1$, contestant 1 will set $y_1 = 0$, and for all y_2 in the open interval $(0, V_1)$, player 1's best response is a unique positive number. It is important to point out that if $y_2 = 0$, the best reply of contestant 1 is not well defined. If she chooses $y_1 = 0$, her probability of winning will be only 1/2. If she chooses $y_1 = \varepsilon > 0$, her probability of winning will be 1. But then she would want to set ε as small as possible, as long as it is positive. There is no such ε! Thus $r_1(y_2)$ is not defined at $y_2 = 0$.

Similarly,

$$y_2 = \max\{0, \sqrt{y_1 V_2} - y_1\} \text{ for } y_1 > 0 \tag{3.3}$$

Let $Y = y_1 + y_2$. Since we have shown in Subsection 3.2.1 that at a Nash equilibrium efforts of the two players are strictly positive, we can solve for the Nash equibrium (y_1, y_2) by noting that at the equilibrium, the following conditions hold

---

[12] For an axiomatic approach leading to the Tullock contest success function, see Corchón (2007).

$$\frac{Y - y_1}{[Y]^2} V_1 = 1 \Leftrightarrow y_2 = Y - \frac{Y^2}{V_1} \tag{3.4}$$

$$\frac{Y - y_2}{[Y]^2} V_2 = 1 \Leftrightarrow y_1 = Y - \frac{Y^2}{V_2} \tag{3.5}$$

It follows that, by summation,

$$Y = 2Y - Y^2\left(\frac{1}{V_1} + \frac{1}{V_2}\right)$$

or

$$Y = Y^2\left(\frac{1}{V_1} + \frac{1}{V_2}\right)$$

Solving for Y

$$Y = \frac{1}{\frac{1}{V_1} + \frac{1}{V_2}} = \frac{V_1 V_2}{V_1 + V_2}$$

Substituting into equations (3.5) and (3.4), we obtain

$$y_i = \frac{1}{V_j}\left[\frac{V_1 V_2}{V_1 + V_2}\right]^2$$

We conclude that the Nash equilibrium is unique, and efforts are proportional to valuations:

$$\frac{y_1}{V_1} = \frac{y_2}{V_2}$$

The equibrium success probabilities are

$$\pi_i = \frac{V_i}{V_1 + V_2} \quad \text{for } i = 1, 2, \; j \neq i$$

The high valuation contestant has higher probability of success.

The results can be generalized to the case of n contestants with asymmetric valuations, except that we cannot conclude that all contestants will exert strictly positive efforts. Let us define the aggregate effort by $Y = \sum_{i=1}^{n} y_i$, and the combined effort of player i's opponents by $Y_{-i} = Y - y_i$. Since y_i cannot be negative, the first order condition for player i is

$$\frac{Y_{-i}}{[y_i + Y_{-i}]^2} V_i - 1 \leq 0$$

with inequality holding if $y_i = 0$. Since $Y = Y_{-i} + y_i$, this condition becomes

$$\frac{Y - y_i}{Y^2}V_i - 1 \leq 0$$

We can therefore express the relationship between player *i*'s optimal effort and the equilibrium aggregate effort as follows[13]

$$y_i = \max\left\{0, Y - \frac{Y^2}{V_i}\right\}$$

If equilibrium efforts are strictly positive for exactly *k* players, then summing over these players, we obtain

$$Y = \left(kY - Y^2\sum_{i=1}^{k}\tfrac{1}{V_i}\right)$$

or

$$Y = \left(\frac{k-1}{k}\right)\frac{k}{\sum_{i=1}^{k}\frac{1}{V_i}}$$

Thus, with *k* active participants, their total effort is a fraction $(k-1)/k$ of the harmonic mean of the individual valuations (Hillman and Riley 1989 [2008]). Using this approach, one can show that for any given number of contestants with possibly heterogeneous valuations, there exists a unique Nash equilibrium. Order the contestants so that $V_1 \geq V_2 \geq \ldots \geq V_j \geq V_{j+1}$ and so on. Let *k* be the number of contestants with strictly positive effort. Then *k* is the first positive integer such that V_{k+1} is smaller than $(k-1)/k$ times the harmonic mean of the top *k* valuations.

In the case of the Tullock lottery contest with *n* identical contestants, we can deduce from the preceding equation a simple result concerning the extent to which rent is dissipated:

$$Y = \left(\frac{n-1}{n}\right)V$$

That is, total effort is lower than the prize, for any finite *n*. This means that the expected rent for each player is positive, as long as *n* is finite. If there is free entry, we take the limit $n \to \infty$ and observe that the rent is completely dissipated.

The above existence and uniqueness result has been generalized to the case of concave y_i^β, where $0 < \beta \leq 1$, even for non-identical contestants (Szidarovszky and Okuguchi 1997 [2008]).[14]

For the increasing returns to scale case $\beta > 1$, the situation is more complicated. The first order condition is

---

13 This approach, linking equilibrium effort of a player to aggregate effort, has been used extensively in oligopoly theory (for example, Szidarovszky and Okuguchi 1997 [2008]; Long and Soubeyran 2000) and in a related class of games (Cornes and Hartley 2005).

14 Szidarovszky and Okuguchi (1997 [2008]) established sufficient conditions for existence and uniqueness under more general assumptions about the contest success function.

$$\frac{\beta y_i^{\beta-1} Z_{-i}}{[y_i^\beta + Z_{-i}]^2} V_i - 1 \leq 0$$

The second order condition is satisfied if

$$\frac{(\beta - 1) y_i^{\beta-2}[y_i^\beta + Z_{-i}] - 2\beta y_i^{2\beta-2}}{[y_i^\beta + Z_{-i}]^3} \leq 0$$

In the case of identical contestants, the existence of a Nash equilibrium and its uniqueness can be ensured, provided that $\beta \leq n/(n-1)$, for then the second order condition reduces to $y^{2(\beta-1)}((n-2)\beta - n) < 0$. If $\beta \leq n/(n-1)$ then $(n-2)\beta - n < 0$.

In this case, it can be shown that aggregate effort is

$$Y = \beta\left(\frac{n-1}{n}\right)V \tag{3.6}$$

Thus, if $\beta \leq n/(n-1)$, the ratio of aggregate effort to the prize, Y/V, will converge to β as n becomes arbitrarily large. Notice that Y is an increasing function of n: the larger the number of contestants, the greater will be the aggregate effort expended.

For the case $\beta > n/(n-1)$, typically there is no pure strategy equilibrium. A general result is that regardless of the value of β, a contestant's expected effort can never exceed the prize (Ellingsen 1991 [2008]).

What are the effects on an increase in heterogeneity among rent seekers? Assume $\beta \leq 1$. In the case of two constestants, the Nash equilibrium effort levels are

$$y_i = \frac{\beta V_i^{\beta+1} V_j^\beta}{[V_1^\beta + V_2^\beta]^2} \text{ for } i = 1, 2,\ j \neq i \tag{3.7}$$

The equilibrium success probabilities are

$$\pi_i = \frac{V_i^\beta}{V_1^\beta + V_2^\beta} \text{ for } i = 1, 2,\ j \neq i \tag{3.8}$$

and the equilibrium payoff is

$$U_i = \frac{[V_i^\beta + (1-\beta) V_j^\beta] V_i^{\beta+1}}{[V_1^\beta + V_2^\beta]^2} \text{ for } i = 1, 2,\ j \neq i \tag{3.9}$$

Observe that $E_i/E_j = V_i/V_j$, and $\pi_i/\pi_j = (V_i/V_j)^\beta$: the player with higher valuation expends proportionally greater effort, and has a higher probability of success. If we define the degree of heterogeneity between the players by the sum of the squared deviations from the mean valuation,

$$H = (V_1 - \overline{V})^2 + (V_2 - \overline{V})^2$$

where $\overline{V} = (V_1 + V_2)/2$, it can be shown that the greater the heterogeneity, the lower is the sum of efforts expended.

Cheikbossian (2008) studied two-dimensional heterogeneity in a rent-seeking game for public goods. Unlike the standard rent-seeking model, the prize is endogenous. There are two groups of rent seekers, and individuals are homegeneous within each group but heterogeneous (in terms of the strength of preference for public goods) across groups. The group sizes are different: this is the second dimension of heterogeneity. The government chooses the level of public good provision to maximize the weighted sum of group utilities, with weights given by the Tullock contest success function. He showed that in this endogenous-prize model, the total level of efforts expended is increasing in taste heterogeneity but decreasing in group size asymmetry.

Another source of heterogeneity is differences in valuations of members within each group of rent seekers. Lee (2012) assumes there are n groups, and group i consists of m_i members. The prize is fixed, and is awarded only to one group. The probability that group i wins is specified by the Tullock lottery $z_i/(z_i + Z_{-i})$ where z_i is group i's effective effort level. The valuation of the prize varies across members of the winning group. Unlike the standard model, Lee assumes that z_i is not equal to the sum of efforts x_{ij} of members of group i. Rather, it is equal to the lowest contribution among the group members:

$$z_i = \min\{x_{i1}, x_{i2}, \ldots, x_{im_i}\}$$

This formulation is known as the weakest-link technology, and was pioneered by Hirshleifer (1983, 1985). With this type of heterogeneity, it is found that within each group there is no free riding, and high valuation players would want to subsidize low valuation players. This is in sharp contrast to Baik (2008) who found that under the standard technology, where z_i is equal to the sum of efforts x_{ij} of members, only the highest valuation player in each group expends effort, and other members free ride.

Finally, the Tullock contest can be generalized to the case where valuations are private information. Hurley and Shogren (1998) and Sui (2009) considered two-sided incomplete information about valuations, in which a player may be of two or three types. Fey (2008) generalized to two rent seekers, each with possible valuations distributed according to the uniform density function. Under private information, with two players, expected equilibrium efforts tend to be lower than in symmetric contests with public information. However, Ryvkin (2010) shows that this result is not generalizable to the contests with more than two players and arbitrary density function.

3.3 EXTENSIONS OF THE BASIC MODEL

3.3.1 Hierarchical Rent Seeking

In the above model, given the prize, there is only one level of rent seeking: contestants expend resources (efforts) to improve the probability of winning. When we defined Y/V as the rate of rent dissipation, the implicit assumption was that Y are real resources that are used up. However, it seems plausible that contestants use parts of Y to pay bribes to the bureaucrats who potentially can influence the decision on the winner of the prize. At first, it might be thought that bribes are only transfer payments and therefore not a social waste. This would be so if the priviledged position of the bribe receiver were not contestable. In the real world, privileged positions are often contestable. It follows that in the case of contestability, the expectations of receiving bribes create incentives for a group of bureaucrats to contest for the privileged position. Then a given rent can create a hierarchy of rent-seeking contests. This line of arguments was advanced by Posner (1975 [2008]), and a formal model was proposed by Hillman and Katz (1987 [2008]).[15]

Suppose a primary rent V is created, and a winner is to be selected by bureaucratic discretion. There are $m - 1$ tiers in the bureaucracy. Then there are m contests, one for the primary rent, and $(m - 1)$ for the positions that entitle the occupant to a bribe.

Let Y be the aggregate equilibrium outlay by contestants for the primary rent. Assume $Y = q_1 V$. Assume a fraction $(1 - \alpha_1)$ of this outlay is paid as a bribe. The outlay for the second contest is $Y_2 = q_2 V_2$ where $V_2 = (1 - \alpha_1) Y = (1 - \alpha_1) q_1 V$.

Then $Y_2 = q_2(1 - \alpha_1) q_1 V$. The second-round bribe is $(1 - \alpha_2) Y_2 = (1 - \alpha_2) q_2 V_2 = (1 - \alpha_2) q_2(1 - \alpha_1) q_1 V$.

The total outlay made by contestants at level i is

$$Y_i = q_i \prod_{j=1}^{i-1} q_j(1 - \alpha_j) V$$

The value of real resource expended at level i is

$$w_i = \alpha_i q_i \prod_{j=1}^{i-1} q_j(1 - \alpha_j) V$$

Consider the simple case where $\alpha_i = \alpha$ and $q_i = q$ for all i. Then

$$w_i = \alpha q (q)^{i-1} (1 - \alpha_i)^{i-1}$$

If $\alpha > 0$ and $q = 1$, it is easy to show that as the number of levels in the hierarchy tends to infinity, the total value of real resources expended by all levels of contests is equal to V.

3.3.2 Rent Seeking Under Risk Aversion

So far, we have assumed that contestants are risk neutral. Does risk aversion reduce social waste in the rent-seeking process?

Hillman and Katz (1984 [2008]) and Long and Vousden (1987 [2008]) considered the case of risk averse rent seekers in the Tullock contest, while Hillman and Samet (1987 [2008]) studied the consequence of risk aversion in the first-prize sealed-bid all-pay auction. Konrad and Schlesinger (1997) examined the role of risk aversion in rent-augmenting games. Treich (2010) discussed the implication of prudence in rent-seeking games.

Let us consider the first-prize sealed-bid all-pay auction under risk aversion. Assume identical valuation of the prize. Let $\pi(y)$ denote the equilibrium probability

---

15 Clearly rent seeking can affect the desired size of government. See Park et al. (2005).

that a given contestant is the highest bidder given that she bids y. Let $u(V - y)$ be the utility if she wins, and $u(-y)$ be the utility if she loses, where u is a concave and increasing function. If she does not bid, her utility is $u(0) = 0$ by normalization. Equilibrium with randomization requires that the expected payoff is the same for all y in the interval $[0, V]$:

$$\pi(y)u(V-y)+[1-\pi(y)]\,u(-y) = u(0) = 0 \text{ for all } y \in [0, V]$$

If everyone uses the same randomization strategy, represented by the cumulative distribution $F(y)$, then $p(y) = F(y)^{n-1}$. It follows that the equilibrium distribution function is

$$F(y) = \left[\frac{-u(-y)}{u(V-y) - u(y)}\right]^{1/(n-1)} \text{ for } 0 \leq y \leq V$$

Hillman and Samet (1987 [2008]) used this property to show that if u is strictly concave (risk aversion), then for any n, the expected outlay is smaller than the prize. This is true even in the limit as $n \to \infty$.

Hillman and Katz (1984 [2008]) considered risk aversion in the Tullock contest. They focused on competitive rent seeking, that is, the situation where the equilibrium number of rent seekers is large enough to ensure that being a rent seeker gives the same expected utility as that of a non-rent seeker. Defining the extent of rent dissipation as the ratio of aggregate effort, ny, to the prize, V, they showed that under risk aversion, rent dissipation is strictly less than unity, even when the number of rent seekers approaches infinity. The dissipation approaches $1 - (k/2)R$ where R is the coefficient of risk aversion and k is the ratio of the prize V to the initial weath.[16]

Long and Vousden (1987 [2008]) considered a model where the prize is not awarded to a winner; rather the bureaucrat allocates a share s_i of the total rent V to each contestant i. Assume that the probability that contestant i's share is at least as great as a fraction t is dependent on both (i) his effort level and (ii) the sum of effort levels of other contestants. Denote these by y_i and Y_{-i}. Define

$$H^i(t, y_i, Y_{-i}) = \Pr(s_i \geq t | y_i, Y_{-i})$$

It is natural to assume that H^i is increasing in y_i and decreasing in Y_{-i}. Then

$$H_2^i \equiv \frac{\partial H^i}{\partial y_i} \geq 0, \; H_3 \equiv \frac{\partial H^i}{\partial Y_{-i}} \leq 0$$

Also, assume that an increase in Y_{-i} reduces the marginal effectiveness of y_i. Then

$$H_{23}^i \leq 0$$

[16] They assume that V is small enough so that higher order terms in the Taylor series expansion can be ignored.

Assume that H^i is homogeneous of degree zero in (y_i, Y_{-i}). This means that if all contestants increase their effort by the same percentage, there will be no change in the probability that $s_i \geqslant t$. Let $G^i = 1 - H^i$, and let g^i be the associated density function: $g^i(t, y_i, Y_{-i}) = -\partial H^i/\partial t$. Then $g^i(t, y_i, Y_{-i})$ is also homogeneous of degree zero in (y_i, Y_{-i}).

Each contestant i chooses y_i to maximize the expected net benefit, defined as the expected utility of his share of the prize $s_i V$ minus his effort cost $C^i(y_i)$.

$$\max_{y_i} \int_0^1 u(tV) g^i(t, y_i, Y_{-i})\, dt - C^i(y_i)$$

It is assumed that $C^i(.)$ is an increasing and convex function, and $u(.)$ is an increasing and concave function.

Long and Vousden showed that in a symmetric Nash equilibrium, the first order condition can be expressed as

$$V \int_0^1 u'(tV) H_2(t, y, (n-1)y)\, dt - C'(y) = 0$$

This condition says that the expected marginal return to effort is equated to the marginal effort cost.

Since $H_2(t, y,(n-1)y)$ is homogeneous of degree minus one in (y_i, Y_{-i}) it holds that

$$H_2(t, y, (n-1)y) = \frac{1}{y} H_2(t, 1, n-1)$$

Then, in equilibrium,

$$V \int_0^1 u'(tV) H_2(t,1,(n-1)1)\, dt = yC'(y)$$

Since the left-hand side is a positive constant and the right-hand side is a strictly increasing function of y, and is equal to zero at $y = 0$, there exists a unique symmetric equilibrium effort level $y^* > 0$.

Performing comparative statics, it is found that an increase in the prize V will lead to lower (respectively, higher) Nash equilibrium effort if the relative risk aversion is greater (respectively, smaller) than unity. This result can be explained as follows. If marginal utility were constant (the case of a linear u), an increase in V will increase the left-hand side. However, if marginal utility is diminishing, for any $t > 0$, the marginal utility $u'(tv)$ is smaller, the greater is V. This force tends to reduce the value of the left-hand side. Higher risk aversion will strengthen this effect.

Long and Vousden extended the model to allow for the possibility that the size of the total rent V is itself a random variable, with a known upper bound K. Assume that the probability that V is at least as large as a given number w where $w \in (0, K)$ can be increased by increasing the aggregate effort, Y. Under the assumption that individuals do not perceive that individual effort has an influence on this probability, it can be shown that an increase in the upper bound K will result in a greater symmetric Nash equilibrium individual effort if and only if the coefficient of relative risk aversion is smaller than unity. On the other hand, if rent seekers do to some extent perceive this influence, then an increase in this perception will lead to more effort, provided that the coefficient of relative risk aversion is smaller than unity.

Turning to the long run, one can find comparative static results when the number of rent seekers is endogenously determined by free entry. An increase in the size of the rent, V, will increase the equilibrium number of rent seekers, but each will expend less effort, if relative risk aversion exceeds unity. Finally, one can find out about the extent of rent dissipation, defined as as the ratio of aggregate effort cost (under free entry) to the value of the prize. It can be shown that under risk aversion and uncertain share of the total rent, rent dissipation is strictly below unity, even when the number of rent seekers approaches infinity. The dissipation is shown to approach $1 - (k/2)\delta R$ where R is the coefficient of risk aversion, k is the ratio of the prize V to the initial weath and δ is a positive term bounded above by 1, which is increasing in the variance of the distribution of individual share in the Nash equilibrium. Thus, the greater is the variance, the smaller is the dissipation.

The role of risk aversion has been further studied by Skaperdas and Gan (1995). For contests with risk aversion and heterogeneity, see Cornes and Hartley (2003).

3.3.3 Insecure Enduring Rents

So far, we have assumed that the winner of a rent-seeking contest is entitled to the rent sought. In many real world situations, the rent sought is not a fixed prize that a winner can appropriate instantaneously, or in one single period. Quite often, the rent is a stream of incomes that can only be appropriated gradually over time, and subject to risk of discontinuation. For example, a firm may have obtained the monopoly right to extract and sell an exhaustible resource from a mine, over a number of periods. However, that right may be insecure: a future government may nationalize the mine, or a future contest may arise between the incumbent firm and a new entrant.[17] Similarly, many forests are harvested under concession agreements. The concessionaires are quite often unsure about the security of their tenure.

How do contestants value the stream of future rents that are subject to discontinuation and/or new contests? If they are risk neutral, do they still expend resources, in spite of the uncertainty of tenure, to such an extent that rents are completely dissipated? These questions are considered by Aidt and Hillman (2008). They posit that durable rents are not everlasting. Deregulation, trade liberalization or reform of the bureaucracy can eliminate rents, either permanently or temporarily, with the possibility of being recreated for a new contest.[18]

Aidt and Hillman (2008) assume that n contestants compete to obtain the entitlement to an unsecured stream of rents. The rent per period is w. Think of w as the monopoly

---

[17] The problem of resource extraction under uncertainty about possible nationalization was analyzed in Long (1975).

[18] For another model of insecure enduring rent, see Bjorvatn and Naghavi (2011). They show that a government may try to pacify two opposition groups by handing out special favors. It is found that the chance of conflict is highest for intermediate levels of rents.

profit. Assume that the incumbent monopolist in period t faces the probability p that next period, $t + 1$, his monopoly rights will remain uncontested (that is, the incumbent continues to be in state M), and the probability $1 - p$ that the incumbent's monopoly rights will be terminated (T), in which case there are two possible scenarios. First, the scenario L (liberalization), under which there is no rent to be contested in period $t + 1$. Second, the scenario C, where the rent for period $t + 1$ remains at w, but must be contested, and the winner is assigned the rent, thus becoming the new incumbent. Conditional on T, liberalization occurs with probablity z, and a new contest occurs with probability $1 - z$. Once the economy is in state L, in the next period it will continue to be in that state with probability z, and it will change to state C with probability $1 - z$. (Thus for an economy with parameter value z equal to 1, once it is liberalized, it will remain liberalized for ever; for an economy with $z = 0$, liberalization never takes place, and the termination of an incumbent's monopoly right simply entails a new contest.)

Clearly, the case $p = 1$ implies perfectly secure property rights for the incumbent. Conversely, $p = 0$ implies that a winner is entitled to only one-period rent, w.

An incumbent in period t can thus expect that, in period $t + 1$, one of three things can happen to him: (i) his monopoly rights continue without contest, that is, he is in state M; (ii) his monopoly rights are terminated, but he is allowed to take part in the new contest, that is, he is in state C; and (iii) there is no rent for anyone (state L). These three mutually exclusive and exhaustive events occur with probability p, $(1 - p)(1 - z)$ and $(1 - p)z$, respectively.

When the economy is in state L, there are no contestants, and all the n agents have the same value $V(L)$. When the economy is in state C, all n agents are actively contesting, and they have the same value $V(C)$. When the economy is in state M, the incumbent has the value $V^I(M)$ while the non-incumbents have the value $V^N(M)$. The relationships among these four values are as follows. Let δ be the discount factor, where $0 < \delta < 1$. Then

$$V(L) = \delta z V(L) + \delta(1 - z) V(C)$$

$$V^I(M) = w + \delta[pV^I(M) + (1 - p)(1 - z)V(C) + (1 - p)zV(L)]$$

$$V^N(M) = \delta[pV^N(M) + (1 - p)(1 - z)V(C) + (1 - p)zV(L)]$$

$$V(C) = q[V^I(M) - w] + (1 - q)V^N(M) - y + qw$$

$$= -y + qV^I(N) + (1 - q)V^N(M)$$

where q is the probability that he wins the contest, and y is his effort.

From the second and the third equations, we obtain

$$V^I(M) - V^N(M) = \frac{w}{1 - \delta p}$$

Rewrite $V(C)$ as

$$V(C) = -y + q[V^I(M) - V^N(M)] + V^N(M)$$

$$= -y + q\left[\frac{w}{1 - \delta p}\right] + V^N(M)$$

The term $V^I(M) - V^N(M)$ may be called the 'stake' of the 'stage game.' It is equal to $w/(1 - \beta p)$. Thus, with $V^N(M)$ being taken as given, independent of effort y_i, when there is a contest, each contestant i will choose y_i to maximize

$$q_i(y_1, y_2 \ldots, y_n)\left[\frac{w}{1 - \delta p}\right] - y_i$$

Assume that a symmetric Nash equilibrium effort profile $(y_1^*, y_2^*, \ldots, y_n^*)$ exists and is unique. Assume further that the stake of the 'stage game' when the economy is in state C is completely dissipated.[19] Then it can be shown that the expected present value of resources expended if the economy is currently in the contest state, C, is

$$R(C, z, p) = \frac{w(1 - z\delta)}{(1 - \delta)(1 - \delta pz)}$$

On the other hand, given that the economy is in the contest state, the expected present value of the rent (discounted for the risk of liberalization, which is present if $p \neq 1$) can be solved as follows. Denote by U_L (repectively, U_{NL}) the expected present value of rent if the economy is currently in the liberalized state (respectively, non-liberalized state). They must satisfy the following equations

$$U_L = \delta(1 - z)U_{NL} + \delta z U_L$$

$$U_{NL} = w + \delta p U_{NL} + \delta(1 - p)[zU_L + (1 - z)U_{NL}]$$

Solving these two equations, we obtain

$$U_{NL} = \frac{w(1 - z\delta)}{(1 - \delta)(1 - \delta pz)}$$

It follows that the ratio $R(C, z, p)/U_{NL}$ is unity, independent of the values of the parameters p and z. This result is striking. Under the assumption that rent dissipation is complete in each stage game, neither the imperfect protection of rent ($p < 1$) nor the risks that rents disappear ($z > 0$) affect the rate of rent dissipation.

This result does not mean that the time path of waste is invariant to these parameters. In fact, if $p = 1$ (perfect protection), then all the waste occurs in the first contest, and there is no future waste. If $p = 0$ and $z = 0$, waste will occur every period. It is also worth noting that in democracies, because of frequent changes of governments, p is low, while authoritarian regimes may be able to commit to more lasting rents, which implies that under autocracy, rent-seeking resources are concentrated at the time rents are created. This results in low levels of deployment of productive resources in the early stage of

19 This would happen, for example, with the Tullock lottery contest success function.

development, which may provide an explanation of why economies ruled by autocracy failed to develop.

3.3.4 Sabotage in Rent-seeking Contests

Konrad (2000 [2008]) extended the rent-seeking activities to include sabotage. Suppose there are n contestants. Contestant 1 may try to harm contestant 2 by spreading rumors that damage his credibility. This may increase the winning probability of all contestants $j \neq 2$. Player 1's sabotage thus confers positive externalities on n players. One would expect that the larger is n, the weaker will be the incentive to sabotage.

Konrad supposed that contestant i directs s_{ij} units of effort at sabotaging contestant j, where $s_{ij} = 0$ by definition. Let $S_j \equiv \sum_{i=1}^{n} s_{ij}$ denote the sum of efforts directed against contestant j. Let e_i be contestant i's non-sabotage effort directed at the bureaucrat. Assume that the probability that contestant i is awarded the prize is

$$\pi_i = \frac{b_i^{\beta}}{\sum_{n=1}^{n} b_j^{\beta}}$$

where b_i is a function of both e_i and S_i, such that it is increasing and concave in e_i and decreasing and convex in S_i. Furthermore, assume $b_i(e_i, 0) = e_i$, and that an increase in S_i will decrease the marginal effectiveness of e_i.

Consider the case where contestants are homogeneous. If sabotage efforts are constrained to be zero, then using equation (3.6), the symmetric Nash equilibrium non-sabotage effort is e^0 where

$$e^0 = \frac{n-1}{n^2}\beta V$$

Konrad showed that if, for all contestants, the absolute value of derivative $\partial b_i/\partial S_i$, evaluated at $(e_i, S_i) = (e^0, 0)$, is not greater than $n - 1$, then the original symmetric equilibrium of the Tullock contest without sabotage is a symmetric equilibrium of the game where sabotage is permitted. This result shows that sabotage is observed only when the number of contestants is small.

Consider now the case where the above derivative condition is not met, and a symmetric equilibrium with positive sabotage exists. Denote this equibrium by (e^*, S^*). Does e* exceed e^0 (the equilibrium effort in the scenario where sabotage is constrained to be zero)? Konrad showed that this will occur if and only if an increase in S has a negative effect on $(1/b)b_e$.

What about rent dissipation? Define aggregate effort as $E = ne^* + nS^*$. As long as an equilibrium with positive sabotage exists, a small increase in n can decrease E. This is in sharp contrast to the case where sabotage is not possible, for then, according to equation (3.6), an increase in n always increases aggregate effort.[20]

Amegashie (2012) presents an alternative model of contests between two players who can sabotage each other. Unlike the model of Konrad (2000 [2008]) where a player's

[20] Note, however, that if n is large enough, there will be no sabotage in equilibrium.

sabotage effort directly affects his rival's probability of success, Amegashie assumes that the sabotage raises the per unit cost of the rival's productive effort. Furthermore, while Konrad assumes that each agent chooses his productive effort and his sabotage effort at the same time, the present model assumes a two-stage game: in stage 1, sabotage efforts are chosen by both players, and in stage 2, having observed the sabotage efforts, the players choose their productive efforts. The probability of success depends only on the productive efforts (as in Tullock's model).

Amegashie analyzes the two-stage game and found some interesting results. First, if the prize V is low, then the equilibrium sabotage efforts are zero. Second, if V is large, then sabotage is positive and increasing in V, and productive efforts do not increase with V. These results differ from Konrad's, because the two papers make different specifications of the contest success probability.

Amegashie also generalizes the model to the case of n players. In this case, it is not possible to prove the results analytically, so the author resorts to numerical analysis. He finds that if $n \geqslant 3$, there is no symmetric equilibrium with positive sabotage. This result is in line with Konrad, who found that if n is large, then sabotage disappears. The specific result of the present paper is of course dependent on the assumption that a player's per unit cost of productive effort is linear in the sum of sabotage efforts of other players.

Chen (2003) and Münster (2007) modeled sabotage in the context of promotion tournaments. They found that if contestants are heterogeneous, sabotage tends to narrow down the range of winning probabilities, because sabotage efforts tend to concentrate on the most productive agents.

3.4 STRUCTURAL ISSUES AND DYNAMICS

This section is devoted to two structural issues (contest design and endogenous order of moves), and extension of the contest model to a dynamic environment.

3.4.1 Contest Design

The politicians who allocate rent presumably value high rent-seeking efforts by contestants.[21] This suggests that they would want to design the contest to maximize aggregate rent-seeking effort. Politicians would value the effort in rent seeking if the effort were a benefit for them. However, the basic premise of rent seeking is that the effort is a social loss. In a bribery setting the total bribe would be valued but it was a major point of Tullock that bribes and rent seeking are different in that a bribe is a transfer of income and not in itself a source of efficiency loss – like a thief who steals (Tullock 1967 [2008]) engages in an activity that transfers income.

In Hillman and Katz (1987 [2008]), the bribes in the hierarchy are contestable, hence the social cost of rent seeking. The literature on evoking 'effort' through contest design suggests sports contests. However, if the transfers are contestable, the transfers are

---

[21] This view has been expressed by Downs (1957), Buchanan and Tullock (1962), Stigler (1971), Peltzman (1976), among others.

translated into rent-seeking prizes with associated social loss. A question: are the politicians who design the contests internalizing the contest that will arise from the attempt to become the beneficiary of the transfers?

Appelbaum and Katz (1987 [2008]) model how a self-seeking politician optimally sets the rent V so as to maximize his own payoff, taking into account possible adverse reaction from the public at large. Assume there are n contestants (say n firms that seek to win the total rent V). Under the Tullock lottery contest success function (that is, $\beta = 1$), rent seeking by n firms will result in aggregate rent-seeking effort $Y = V(n - 1)/n$. Assume a fraction α of Y will be paid to the politician as bribes. The politician's income is then α Y S where S is his salary (exogenously fixed). There is however some probability that he will be removed from his office, in which case his outside income is Z. This probability is assumed to be an increasing function of the dissatisfaction of the consumers (voters), which is in turn an increasing function of how much the firm extracts from them. Assume this extracted amount is V, which is determined by the politician. The politician then chooses V so as to maximize his expected income. An intuitive result from this model is that the rent set by the politician is decreasing in his salary S. Thus higher salary to politicians reduces social waste, since a proportion $(1 - \alpha)$ of Y is wasted. A more efficient rent-seeking technology (a lower α) may or may not benefit society.

In the long run, there is free entry of contestants. Assume the politician can set an entry fee, c, which he collects from firms and distributes to consumers. By definition of the long run, the expected net payoff of firms is zero. Thus in effect the politician is using firms as a means to extract transfers from the consumers to himself.

A related question is, instead of setting the rent, the contest designer may ask whether a simultaneous contest is better than a multi-stage contest if his objective is to maximize aggregate effort (which may of course result in maximizing his revenue from bribes). A problem of this type was analyzed by Gradstein and Konrad (1999 [2008]). They assume that in a single stage of a contest with n contestants, the success function is given by equation (3.1), which we reproduce below:

$$\pi_i = \frac{y_i^\beta}{\sum_{j=1}^{n} y_j^\beta}$$

where $\beta < n/(n - 1)$ to ensure that the second order condition is satisfied. The waste factor (the ratio of aggregate effort to the prize) is $\beta\,(n - 1)/n$, as shown by equation (3.6). Consider now a multi-stage contest among n participants with identical valuations. At each stage, they are divided into several groups, and compete within each group. The winner in each group goes up to the next round and so on. It can be shown that (i) at each stage, the number of contestants in each competing group is equal and (ii) for any given number of rounds, the optimal group size is the same across rounds.[22] Let g denote the group size and m the number of rounds. Given the number of contestants, n, one must choose the group size g and the number of rounds, m, subject to the constraint $n = g^m$. It can be shown that if $\beta < 1$, the optimal number of rounds is one. If $1 < \beta < (n - 1)/n$,

[22] In proving (i) and (ii), one ignores the difficulty that arises because the solution must be an integer.

the optimal m is the largest possible positive integer and g the smallest possible positive integer not less than 2, which must be consistent with $n = g^m$.

For related research on designing an optimal contest, see Dasgupta and Nti (1998) who proposed a modified contest success function, and Amegashie (2006) who found additional implications for such a function.

3.4.2 Commitment and Endogenous Order of Moves

In the standard Tullock contest it is assumed that the contestants simultaneously choose their effort levels. If there are two contestants with different valuations, at the Nash equilibrium, the one with higher valuation will have a higher probability of success, as implied by equation (3.8). Dixit (1987 [2008]) finds that in the case of two asymmetric contestants, the high valuation contestant, player 1, would gain (relative to her Nash equilibrium payoff) from being the first mover, and she would expend greater effort than at the Nash equilibrium. The low valuation contestant (player 2), if he were to move first, would want to commit to a lower effort level than his Nash equilibrium effort level. He concludes that 'the player favored to win is the one who has the strategic incentive to overexert, and the underdog, to ease up' (Dixit 1987 [2008], p. 893). In the context of rent seeking, if the high valuation contestant is given first access to the bureaucrat, her outlays will be greater than under the Nash equilibrium. This seems to suggest that strategic behavior leads to more social waste.

Dixit's conclusion is correct, but in a sense, not quite correct. It can be shown that for the high valuation contestant, even though her payoff from being a Stackelberg leader, say $U_1(S_1)$, is strictly greater than her payoff under the Nash equilibrium, say $U_1(N)$, her payoff if the low valuation contestant were to lead (resulting in a Stackelberg leadership point S_2) would be even greater still: $U_1(S_2) > U_1(S_1)$. This was pointed out by Baik and Shogren (1992 [2008]). For the higher valuation contestant, being a follower is better than being a leader.[23]

Baik and Shogren (1992 [2008]) establish definitively that if the order of moves is endogenized, the high valuation contestant would choose to be the second mover, and the low valuation contestant would choose to be the first mover.[24] They formalized the game as follows. Before choosing effort levels, the two contestants must play a non-cooperative commitment game where they simultaneously choose whether to commit to act late (L) or to commit to act early (E). Let the subscript denote the player. If their choices are (L_1, L_2) or (E_1, E_2), then the game proceeds to the next stage, where both must choose their efforts simultaneously (both acting late or both acting early, which amounts to the same thing, since there is no discounting). The outcome is then the Nash equilibrium in effort levels. If their choices are (L_1, E_2) then player 2 must choose his effort level y_2 before player 1 chooses y_1. If their choice are (E_1, L_2) then player 1 must choose her effort level before player 2.

Baik and Shogren (1992 [2008]) demonstrate that for the low valuation contestant, to

---

23 The reader can easily check this result in the case of the Tullock lottery, where reaction functions are given by equations (3.2) and (3.3).

24 Leininger (1993) independently discovered the same result.

choose E_2 is the dominant strategy. This is because his payoff when the higher valuation contestant is the Stackelberg leader in the Tullock contest is worse that his payoff at the Nash equilibrium, which is of course inferior to his payoff from being a Stackelberg leader. Knowing that E_2 is player 2's dominant strategy, player 1's choice between L_1 and E_1 amounts to whether she wants to be the second mover in the Tullock contest, or to be at the Nash equilibrium. Her payoff as follower is higher than at the Nash equilibrium. Therefore she chooses L_1. Therefore the equilibrium of the timing game is (L_1 E_1). The low valuation contestant is thus endogenously chosen to be the Stackelberg leader in the contest. It can be shown that at this equilibrium, both contestants expand less effort than at the Nash equilibrium of the standard contest. Baik and Shogren (1992 [2008], p. 362) concluded that 'strategic behavior in contests between two unevenly matched players should lead to underinvestment of effort and lower social costs' relative to Nash behavior.

The importance of commitment in the above formulation cannot be overemphasized. In fact, if after both players have made their contributions, there is another stage where they are given an opportunity to add to their effort, the Nash contribution levels of the standard contest game will be restored. This was formally proved by Romano and Yildirim (2005).

3.4.3 Dynamic Contests

Most models of contest use a static framework. There are a few models that take into account the temporal dimension. Dynamic models of rent seeking are potentially important, because we would want to know how this discount rate may affect the extent of real resources used in rent seeking, and how contestants interact over time.

Stephan and Ursprung (1998 [2008]) formulated a model of contest between two persons, A (the aggressor) and B (the defender) over an infinite horizon. The rate of discount is $r > 0$. In each period, they choose their effort levels L_A and L_B, repectively, which determine the success probability of B

$$\pi = \frac{L_B}{L_A + L_B}$$

and the success probability of A is $1 - \pi$. The effort cost is incurred by each contestant, whether one wins or loses. If the aggressor loses, he receives zero dollars for the current period, and next period, he starts the same contest again. If the aggressor wins, he receives 1 dollar for the period, and with probability z, there will be no more contest (and he will receive one dollar per period for ever), while with probability $1 - z$ he will have to face the same contest next period. Here z is the exogenous probability that the contest will come to a (permanent) end after the loss of the defending side.

It is assumed that the defender B's prize if he wins the current contest is b dollars for the current period, instead of 1. The amounts 1 and b are however not the stakes of the game, due to the dynamic considerations, which involve parameters such as z and r. For the aggressor A, his stake in the contest is the difference between his expected life-time payoff in the event of winning, W_A, and his expected life-time payoff in the event of losing, F_A. These are defined by the following recursive equations

$$F_A = -L_A + 0 + \frac{1}{1+r}[(1-\pi)W_A + \pi F_A]$$

$$W_A = -L_A + 1 + \frac{(1-z)}{1+r}[(1-\pi)W_A + \pi F_A] + \frac{z}{1+r}\sum_{i=0}^{\infty}\left(\frac{1}{1+r}\right)^i$$

The aggressor's stake is defined as

$$S_A \equiv W_A - F_A = \frac{z+r}{(1-\pi)z+r}\left(1 + \frac{zF_A}{z+r}\right)$$

The defender's stake S_B is defined in a similar way.

The parameter z is a measure of 'dynamic asymmetry'. If $z = 0$, we have an unconditionally repeated contest. At the other extreme, if $z = 1$, the game finishes after the loss of the defending side. Player B is disadvantaged if z is positive.

Since the structure of the game is Markovian (that is, the calendar time is of no consequence to any player), the authors focus on stationary effort choice.

The game is solved numerically. It is found that if $b < 1$ (that is, the defender values rent less than the aggressor), then an increase in dynamic asymmetry, z leads to a decrease in the expected total effort cost. If $b > 1$, then there exists an interval of dynamic asymmetry such that a small increase in dynamic asymmetry results in a higher dissipation of rent. This interval becomes wider as the rate of interest r increases.

Another source of dynamic consideration is that a contestant's influence may change over time, as he cultivates his relationship with the bureaucrats. Fujiwara and Long (2012) take up this issue in the context of the theory of government procurements, extending the work of Long and Stähler (2009). They constructed a model of a dynamic contest between a home firm and a foreign firm that compete for a new government procurement contract in each period, in an infinite horizon context. The crucial variable is the firm's relative stock of influence (or goodwill), which has an impact on the chance to win a procurement contract for the period. The firms invest in their stock of influence by cultivating their relationship with the bureaucrats that collectively make the decision about which firm should win a particular contract. Similarly to advertising models, where a firm's goodwill is a summary measure of the favorable attitude of its potential customers toward its product, in this contest model, a firm's relative goodwill is a measure of the favorable disposition of the bureaucrats who choose the winner. Denote by $w(t)$ the domestic firm's relative stock of influence, measured on a scale such that its smallest possible value is zero, and its greatest possible value is unity. Thus $w^*(t) \equiv 1 - w(t)$ is the foreign firm's relative stock of goodwill. The probability that the domestic firm wins the period t procurement contract is $p(w(t))$, where p is an increasing function of w, with $p(0) = 0$ and $p(1) = 1$. Then $1 - p(w(t))$ is the probability that the foreign firm wins. Assume $p(w) = w$ identically. At any point of time, the relative stock of goodwill is given. Over time, goodwill can be cultivated.

The authors model the evolution of $w(t)$ as follows. Assume $\dot{w}(t)$ depends on (i) the current stock level, $w(t)$, and (ii) the effective amount of money the domestic firm spends on lobbying, $s(t)$ in relation to its rival's effective spending, $\beta\, s^*(t)$. Here $\beta \in [0, 1]$ is a parameter that converts the foreign firm's nominal lobbying expenditure $s^*(t)$ into effective spending. For example, if $\beta = 0.75$, then only 75 cents out of each dollar that the foreign firm spends on lobbying are effective. Thus β is inversely related to the degree of bias against the foreign firm. If $\beta = 1$, there is no bias. The closer β is to zero, the greater the bias. Fujiwara and Long assume that the evolution of w is given by the following 'transition equation':

$$\frac{dw}{dt} = \alpha\left[\ln\left(\frac{s}{w}\right) - \ln\left(\frac{\beta s^*}{1 - w}\right)\right](1 - w)w \quad w(0) \in (0,1) \text{ given}$$

where $\alpha > 0$ is a parameter of the speed of adjustment of w. The term $(1 - w)w$ on the right-hand side ensures that w can never become negative, and it can never exceed 1. The term inside the square brackets indicates that the domestic firm's stock of goodwill increases if and only if the ratio of its lobbying expenditure to its relative goodwill, s/w, exceeds the foreign ratio $\beta\, s^*/(1 - w)$. By definition, the domestic government treats the foreign firm more equally as β increases toward 1. Trade liberalization in procurements is modeled as an exogenous increase in β.

Let V denote the domestic firm's gross profit if it wins the contest. The domestic government levies a profit tax rate τ on each firm. Taking τ as given, the domestic and foreign firms non-cooperatively choose their time paths of lobbying efforts to maximize their discounted streams of expected net profit. The underlying environment is formally described by the following dynamic game:

$$\max_{s} \int_0^{\infty} e^{-rt}[w(1 - \tau)V - s]dt$$

$$\max_{s^*} \int_0^{\infty} e^{-rt}[(1 - w)(1 - \tau)V^* - s^*]dt$$

subject to the transition equation, and where $w \in [0, 1]$ is the probability with which the domestic firm wins the contest. Here, $r > 0$ is a constant rate of discount. A dynamic Nash equilibrium is found, using the techniques of differential game.[25]

Now consider the welfare effects of an increase in β. Denote the domestic welfare by W. It is composed of the domestic firm's expected profit (net of lobbying cost) and tax revenue:

$$W \equiv (1 - \tau)wV - s + \tau wV + \tau(1 - w)V^* = wV + \tau(1 - w)V^* - s$$

The lobbying cost is assumed to be real resources that are used up in the lobbying process.

Similarly, world welfare is defined by

$$W^G \equiv w(1 - \tau)V - s + (1 - w)(1 - \tau)V^* - s^* + \tau wV + \tau(1 - w)V^*$$

$$= wV + (1 - w)V^* - s - s^*$$

---

[25] See Dockner et al. (2000) and Long (2010) for differential games in economics and management science.

Assume that under autarky without foreign competition, the domestic firm is always awarded the contract. Hence, the resulting domestic firm's profit is simply $V - s$ and it trivially chooses $s = 0$ since there is no reason to incur a positive effort when there is no rival. This in turn implies that welfare under autarky is V. The home country's welfare change from autarky to trade is

$$\Delta \equiv wV + \tau(1 - w)V^* - s - V = (w - 1)(V - \tau V^*) - s$$

A question of interest is how does an increase in β, interpreted as a trade liberalization in government procurement procedures, affect the home country's welfare. This is found by evaluating the following integral along the dynamic Nash equilibrium path of competition in lobbying, $s(t)$ and $s^*(t)$,

$$\int_0^\infty e^{-rt} \frac{d\Delta}{d\beta} dt$$

Fujiwara and Long find that trade liberalization, in the form of a reduction in bias against the foreign firm, improves both domestic and global welfare if (i) either the foreign firm's profit is sufficiently large or (ii) the initial degree of home bias is sufficiently small. If the initial home bias is large, a small reduction in the bias may reduce home welfare.

A reduction in bias (an increase in β) will raise steady-state lobbying efforts if and only if $1/\beta > V^*/V$ is positive. Recall that $1/\beta$ is the degree of bias toward the domestic firm. Liberalizing government procurements encourages more lobbying efforts of both firms if the initial bias toward the domestic firm is greater than the relative efficiency of the foreign firm. There is a parallel with the well-known procompetitive effect of trade liberalization in oligopolistic trade theory.

Another recent model of contest over time is Amegashie and Runkel (2008, 2012). Amegashie and Runkel (2008) offer a differential game model, which shows that 'revenge matters'. What they discover is 'the Paradox of Revenge': if both parties to a war derive pleasure from revenge, and both know this, they will exercise more restraint in their attacks. Therefore the steady state will show lower intensity of conflicts than in a model without a revenge motive.[26]

Their model is as follows. Let $D_i^j(t)$ be a summary measure of the past damages that country i inflicts on country j. Let $u_i(t)$ be the intensity of fighting of country i's army. Assume that

$$\frac{dD_i^j(t)}{dt} = u_i(t) - \delta D_i^j(t)$$

[26] This is in sharp contrast to the account of Mark Twain's character Buck (a friend of Huckleberry Finn): 'A feud is this way: A man has a quarrel with another man, and kills him; then that other man's brother kills *him*; then the other brothers, on both sides, goes [*sic*] for one another; then the *cousins* chip in – and by and by everybody's killed off, and there ain't no more feud. But it's kind of slow, and takes a long time.'

where $\delta > 0$ is the rate of decay of the memories. At any t, the probability that i wins the battle is

$$\pi^i(t) = \frac{1}{2} + \eta[u_i(t) - u_j(t)]$$

where it is assumed $\eta > 0$ and that the absolute value of $\eta\ [u_i(t) - u_j(t)]$ is bounded by $\frac{1}{2}$.

If i wins, its perceived prize is $\omega + R(D_j^i(t))$, where ω is a constant (for example, the monetary gains from resource grabbing), and $R(D_j^i(t))$ is a measure of pleasure derived from a revenge motive. Assuming that $R(D_j^i) = \alpha D_j^i$ where $\alpha > 0$. The effort cost of fighting at intensity u_i is $C^i(u_i)$. Assume

$$C^i(u_i) = \frac{1}{2}c_i u_i^2 \text{ where } c_i > 0$$

Country i seeks a time path of efforts $u_i(t)$ to maximize the integral of the discounted flow of period payoffs,

$$\int_0^{\infty} e^{-rt}[\pi^i[\omega + R(D_j^i(t))] - C^i(u_i(t))]\, dt$$

The game becomes a linear quadratic game. Amegashi and Runkel (2008) solve the model numerically, using linear strategies and quadratic value functions. They find that there are three Markov-perfect Nash equilibria leading to three different stationary states. Two of these equilibria involve steady-state fighting intensity that is lower than the intensity level that would prevail if there were no revenge motive. Amegashie and Runkel (2012) is a two-period version of the above continuous-time, infinite horizon model. A similar result is established: the revenge motive might temper the fighting intensity.

Finally, there is a literature of contests in the context of economic growth. Tornell (1997) presented a model of economic growth and decline with endogenous property rights. Two groups of infinitely-lived agents engage in a dynamic game over the choice of property rights regime. A dynamic equilibrium of the game may result in multiple switching of regimes. Each group's share of aggregate capital stock change after a switch takes place. The model generates a hump-shaped pattern of growth. Acemoglu and Robinson (2001, 2006) consider dynamic models where coups and revolutions can occur in response to exogenous economic shocks.[27] In Acemoglu and Robinson (2001), there are two groups of agents, the poor and the elite. Each group consists of infinitely-lived individuals. The elite has more capital than the poor. The majority of people are poor, and initially it is the elite that has the political power. The poor can attempt a revolution at any time, but revolution is costly (a fraction of national income is destroyed). If a revolution is succesful, a fraction of assets of the elite is expropriated. The elite can avoid a revolution by establishing a democracy. The productivity of capital is a random

[27] See also Acemoglu and Robinson (2012) for a less technical exposition. Besley and Persson (2011) provide a more formal approach. Jennings (2013) provides a comparative study.

variable, which is revealed at the beginning of each period: it can be low or high. The role of this random variable is to allow variations in opportunity costs of revolution in a non-democracy, and in the elite's opportunity costs of mounting a coup to overthrow a democracy.

Guriev and Sonin (2009) model a dynamic game between two oligarchs and a dictator. The oligarchs cooperate when choosing a new dictator at the start of a new period, but do not cooperate within the period. Dictators come in two types: a strong dictator can only be removed when the two oligarchs join forces, while a weak dictator can be removed by either oligarch. A strong dictator can expropriate one oligarch as long as he keeps the other oligarch happy. The dictator asks the oligarchs to contribute funds to him, and can choose 'strong protection' (thus banning rent seeking by the oligarchs) at a cost, or 'no protection' at zero cost. Guriev and Sonin (2009) characterize the equilibrium of the game, and find conditions under which a dictator will choose strong protection or no protection, as well as conditions under which a dictator will be removed.

Gonzalez (2005, 2007) and Gradstein (2004, 2007, 2008) assume that individuals allocate resources among consumption, investment, rent appropriating and rent-defending activities and study the effects of contests under imperfect property rights on growth and welfare.

Gonzalez (2005) studies how exogenous changes in property rights regime might affect welfare. Using a two-period model, Gonzalez (2005) shows that when property is sufficiently insecure, anticipation of conflict over economic distribution reduces incentives to adopt new technologies even if they are readily available at negligible costs.

In an endogenous growth model with infinitely-lived individuals Gonzalez (2007) demonstrates that piecemeal reform in property rights enforcements might not be in the interest of society, and a substantial reform might be necessary if it is to be welfare improving.

Gradstein (2004) models the determination of the property rights regime as a collective choice by identical individuals who allocate their unit of labor time between productive activity and unproductive activity. The citizens face a binary choice: either a given small fraction of income is protected or 100 percent of income is protected. In the latter case, they must pay a lump sum tax to finance property right enforcement. It is shown that when the economy is poor, people would prefer the first alternative.

Gradstein (2007) assumes that individuals allocate wealth between productive and unproductive rent-seeking activity. He shows that under perfect enforcement, inequality decreases over time, while it increases over time under the rent-seeking regime.

Gradstein (2008) introduces a publicly provided good financed from taxing investment. An individual's share of this good depends on the amount of resource he allocates to rent seeking and on institutional quality, which is chosen by voting, either under the one-man-one-vote regime or under the political bias regime, in which the political weight of an individual household is increasing with its income. The result is that institutional quality is higher under the one-man-one-vote regime. Gradstein (2008) shows that the preference of the politically decisive coalition to maintain the existing political bias regime increases with income inequality.

Leonard and Long (2012) model rent seeking and the evolution of the degree of enforcement of property rights in an overlapping generation framework. Parents have effective bequest motives. Adults allocate resources between production and rent seeking (appropriation of other people's wealth). The effectiveness of an individual's rent-seeking activity is a function of three variables: the amount of resources he or she devotes to rent seeking, the size of their investment and society's degree of enforcement of property rights, assumed to be a continuous variable. The cost of enforcement is a function of both the degree of enforcement, and the size of the economy (as measured by its capital stock). It is found that if individuals are homogeneous, as the economy grows, the endogenously determined degree of property rights enforcement increases. When there are heterogeneous groups, where the political power of a group depends both on its size and the wealth of its members, the model generates possible shifts in political power, and discrete changes in property rights regimes.

3.5 CONCLUSIONS

Economics is the study of resource allocation. At one extreme, one has the theory of allocation by the invisible hand: a price system that sends signals to price-taking agents about demand and supply conditions. Agents adjust their demand and supply in response to changes in prices. Under certain assumptions, such as the absence of externalities and non-increasing returns to scale, one can show that a competive equilibrium exists and is socially efficient. This theory is based on an additional set of assumptions that are not often explicitly stated: property rights are well defined and well protected, and public goods are either of no value and not provided or have positive values and are provided efficiently by benevolent governments.

In a world where those assumptions are not met, many important allocation decisions are no longer made in the most efficient manner. It becomes important to distinguish between allocative inefficiency and the source of inefficiency due to socially wasteful use of resources in rent seeking. One must model how decisions are made when rivalrous agents compete for positions or for shares of contestable resources, and determine to what extent real resources are wasted by the rent-seeking process. The theory of contests, and in particular, the rent-seeking literature, have shed much light on these issues. Research on rent seeking has shown that the analysis of institution is an essential key to the understanding of social waste, and is potentially useful for the design of better institutions.

ACKNOWLEDGMENTS

I wish to thank Arye L. Hillman for many helpful comments and suggestions.

REFERENCES

Acemoglu, D. and J. Robinson (2001), 'A theory of political transitions', *American Economic Review*, **91**(4), 938–63.
Acemoglu, D. and J.A. Robinson (2006), 'De facto Political power and institutional persistence', *American Economic Review*, **96**(2), 325–30.
Acemoglu, D. and J. Robinson (2012), *Why Nations Fail: The Origins of Power, Prosperity and Poverty*, London: Profile Books.

Aidt, T.S. and A.L. Hillman (2008), 'Enduring rents', *European Journal of Political Economy*, **24**(3), 545–53.

Alcalde, J. and M. Dahm (2010), 'Rent seeking and rent dissipation: a neutrality result', *Journal of Public Economics*, **94**(1–2), 1–7.

Amann, E. and W. Leininger (1996), 'Asymmetric all-pay auctions with incomplete information: the two-player case', *Games and Economic Behavior*, **14**(1), 1–18.

Amegashie, J.A. (2006), 'A contest success function with a tractable noise parameter', *Public Choice*, **126**(1), 135–44.

Amegashie, J.A. (2012), 'Productive versus destructive efforts in contests', *European Journal of Political Economy*, **28**(4), 461–8.

Amegashie, J.A. and M. Runkel (2008), 'The paradox of revenge in conflicts', Working Paper No. 2261, CESifo, Munich.

Amegashie, J.A. and M. Runkel (2012), 'The paradox of revenge in conflicts', *Journal of Conflict Resolution*, **56**(2), 313–30.

Angelopoulos, K., A. Philippopoulos and V. Vassilatos (2009), 'The social cost of rent seeking in Europe', *European Journal of Political Economy*, **25**(3), 280–99.

Ansink, E. and H.-P. Weikard (2009), 'Contested water rights', *European Journal of Political Economy*, **25**(2), 247–60.

Applebaum, E. and E. Katz (1987), 'Seeking rents by setting rents: the political economy of rent seeking', *Economic Journal*, **97**(387), 685–99, reprinted in R.D. Congleton, A.L. Hillman and K.A. Konrad (eds) (2008), *40 Years of Research on Rent Seeking 1 – The Theory of Rent Seeking*, Heidelberg: Springer, pp. 555–69.

Baik, K.H. (2008), 'Contests with group-specific public good prizes', *Social Choice and Welfare*, **30**(1), 103–17.

Baik, K.H. and J.F. Shogren (1992), 'Strategic behavior in contests – comment', *American Economic Review*, **82**(1), 359–62, reprinted in R.D. Congleton, A.L. Hillman and K.A. Konrad (eds) (2008), *40 Years of Research on Rent Seeking 1 – The Theory of Rent Seeking*, Heidelberg: Springer, pp. 439–42.

Baye, M.R., D. Kovenock and C.G. de Vries (1996), 'The all-pay auction with complete information', *Economic Theory*, **8**(2), 291–305, reprinted in R.D. Congleton, A.L. Hillman and K.A. Konrad (eds) (2008), *40 Years of Research on Rent Seeking 1 – The Theory of Rent Seeking*, Heidelberg: Springer, pp. 209–23.

Besley, T. and T. Persson (2011), *Pillars of Prosperity: The Political Economics of Development Clusters*, Princeton, NJ: Princeton University Press.

Bjorvatn, K. and A. Naghavi (2011), 'Rent seeking and regime stability in rentier states', *European Journal of Political Economy*, **27**, 740–48.

Buchanan, J.M. and G. Tullock (1962), *The Calculus of Consent*, Ann-Arbor, MI: University of Michigan Press.

Che, Y.K. and I. Gale (1997), 'Rent dissipation when rent seekers are budget-constrained', *Public Choice*, **92**(1–2), 109–26.

Cheikbossian, G. (2008), 'Heterogeneous groups and rent-seeking for public goods', *European Journal of Political Economy*, **24**, 133–50.

Chen, K.P. (2003), 'Sabotage in promotion tournaments', *Journal of Law, Economics, and Organization*, **19**(1), 119–40.

Cohen, C. and A. Sela (2008), 'Allocation of prizes in asymmetric all-pay auctions', *European Journal of Political Economy*, **24**, 123–32.

Congleton, R.D. (1980), 'Competitive process, competitive waste, and institutions', in J.M. Buchanan, R. Tollinson and G. Tullock (eds), *Toward a Theory of the Rent-seeking Society*, College Station, TX: Texas A&M University Press, pp. 153–79, reprinted in R.D. Congleton, A.L. Hillman and K.A. Konrad (eds) (2008), *40 Years of Research on Rent Seeking 1 – The Theory of Rent Seeking*, Heidelberg: Springer, pp. 69–95.

Congleton, R.D, A.L. Hillman and K.A. Konrad (eds) (2008a), *40 Years of Research on Rent Seeking 1 – The Theory of Rent Seeking*, Heidelberg: Springer.

Congleton, R.D, A.L. Hillman and K.A. Konrad (eds) (2008b), *40 Years of Research on Rent Seeking 2 – Applications: Rent Seeking in Practice*, Heidelberg: Springer.

Corchón, L.C. (2007), 'The theory of contests: a survey', *Review of Economic Design*, **11**(2), 69–100.

Cornes, R. and R. Hartley (2003), 'Risk aversion, heterogeneity and contests', *Public Choice*, **117**(1–2), 1–25.

Cornes, R. and R. Hartley (2005), 'Asymmetric contests with general technologies', *Economic Theory*, **26**(4), 923–46.

Dasgupta, A. and K.O. Nti (1998), 'Designing an optimal contest', *European Journal of Political Economy*, **14**, 587–603.

Dixit, A.K. (1987), 'Strategic behavior in contests', *American Economic Review*, **77**(5), 981–8, reprinted in R.D. Congleton, A.L. Hillman and K.A. Konrad (eds) (2008), *40 Years of Research on Rent Seeking 1 – The Theory of Rent Seeking*, Heidelberg: Springer, pp. 431–8.

Dockner, E., S. Jorgensen, N.V. Long and G. Sorger (2000), *Differential Games in Economics and Management Science*, Cambridge: Cambridge University Press.
Downs, A. (1957), *An Economic Theory of Democracy*, New York: Harper & Row.
Ellingsen, T. (1991), 'Strategic buyers and the social costs of monopoly', *American Economic Review*, **81**(3), 648–57, reprinted in R.D. Congleton, A.L. Hillman and K.A. Konrad (eds) (2008), *40 Years of Research on Rent Seeking 1 – The Theory of Rent Seeking*, Heidelberg: Springer, pp. 399–403.
Fey, M. (2008), 'Rent-seeking contests with incomplete information', *Public Choice*, **135**, 81–93.
Fujiwara, K. and N.V. Long (2012), 'Welfare effects of reducing home-bias in government procurements: a dynamic contest model', *Review of Development Economics*, **16**(1), 137–47.
Gonzalez, F. (2005), 'Insecure property and technological backwardness', *Economic Journal*, **115**(505), 703–21.
Gonzalez, F. (2007), 'Effective property rights, conflict and growth', *Journal of Economic Theory*, **137**(1), 127–39.
Gradstein, M. (2004), 'Governance and growth', *Journal of Development Economics*, **73**(2), 505–18.
Gradstein, M. (2007), 'Inequality, democracy and the protection of property rights', *Economic Journal*, **117**(516), 252–69.
Gradstein, M. (2008), 'Institutional traps and economic growth', *International Economic Review*, **49**(3), 1043–66.
Gradstein, M. and K.A. Konrad (1999), 'Orchestrating rent seeking contests', *Economic Journal*, **109**(458), 536–45, reprinted in R.D. Congleton, A.L. Hillman and K.A. Konrad (eds) (2008), *40 Years of Research on Rent Seeking 1 – The Theory of Rent Seeking*, Heidelberg: Springer, pp. 571–80.
Guriev, S. and K. Sonin (2009), 'Dictators and oligarchs: a dynamic theory of contested property rights', *Journal of Public Economics*, **93**(1–2), 1–19.
Hillman, A.L. (2013), 'Rent seeking', in M. Reksulak, L. Razzolini and W.F. Shughart II (eds), *The Elgar Companion to Public Choice*, 2 edn, Cheltenham, UK and Northampton, MA, USA: Edward Elgar Publishing, pp. 307–30.
Hillman, A.L. and E. Katz (1984), 'Risk-averse rent seekers and the social cost of monopoly power', *Economic Journal*, **94**(373), 104–10, reprinted in R.D. Congleton, A.L. Hillman and K.A. Konrad (eds) (2008), *40 Years of Research on Rent Seeking 1 – The Theory of Rent Seeking*, Heidelberg: Springer, pp. 97–103.
Hillman, A.L. and E. Katz (1987), 'Hierarchical structure and the social costs of bribes and transfers', *Journal of Public Economics*, **34**(2), 129–42, reprinted in R.D. Congleton, A.L. Hillman and K.A. Konrad (eds) (2008), *40 Years of Research on Rent Seeking 1 – The Theory of Rent Seeking*, Heidelberg: Springer, pp. 523–36.
Hillman, A.L. and J.G. Riley (1989), 'Politically contestable rents and transfers', *Economics and Politics*, 1(1), 17–39, reprinted in R.D. Congleton, A.L. Hillman and K.A. Konrad (eds) (2008), *40 Years of Research on Rent Seeking 1 – The Theory of Rent Seeking*, Heidelberg: Springer, pp. 185–207.
Hillman, A.L. and D. Samet (1987), 'Dissipation of contest rents by small numbers of contenders', *Public Choice*, **54**(1), 63–82, reprinted in R.D. Congleton, A.L. Hillman and K.A. Konrad (eds) (2008), *40 Years of Research on Rent Seeking 1 – The Theory of Rent Seeking*, Heidelberg: Springer, pp. 165–84.
Hirshleifer, J. (1983), 'From weakest-link to best-shot: the voluntary provision of public goods', *Public Choice*, **41**(3), 371–86.
Hirshleifer, J. (1985), 'From weakest-link to best-shot: correction', *Public Choice*, **46**(2), 221–3.
Hirshleifer, J. and J.G. Riley (1978), 'Auctions and contests', 'Working Paper No. 118B, University of California, Los Angeles.
Hurley, T. and J. Shogren (1998), 'Asymmetric information contests', *European Journal of Political Economy*, **14**, 645–65.
Jennings, C. (2013), 'Institutions and prosperity: a review of Timothy Besley and Torsten Persson, Pillars of Prosperity: The Political Economics of Development Clusters', *European Journal of Political Economy*, **29**, 252–8.
Knight, F.H. (1935), *The Ethics of Competition and Other Essays*, New York: Harper and Brothers.
Konrad, K.A. (2000), 'Sabotage in rent seeking contests', *Journal of Law, Economics, and Organization*, **16**(1), 155–65, reprinted in R.D. Congleton, A.L. Hillman and K.A. Konrad (eds) (2008), *40 Years of Research on Rent Seeking 1 – The Theory of Rent Seeking*, Heidelberg: Springer, pp. 409–19.
Konrad, K.A. (2009), *Strategy and Dynamics in Contests*, Oxford: Oxford University Press.
Konrad, K.A. and H. Schlesinger (1997), 'Risk aversion in rent-seeking and rent-augmenting games', *Economic Journal*, **107**(445), 1671–83.
Krueger, A.O. (1974), 'The political economy of the rent-seeking society', *American Economic Review*, **64**(3), 291–303, reprinted in R.D. Congleton, A.L. Hillman and K.A. Konrad (eds) (2008), *40 Years of Research on Rent Seeking 2 – Applications: Rent Seeking in Practice*, Heidelberg: Springer, pp. 151–63.
Laband, D.N. and J.P. Sophocleus (1992), 'An estimate of resource expenditure on transfer activity in the United States', *Quarterly Journal of Economics*, **107**(3), 959–83.
Lazear, E. (1995), *Personnel Economics*, Cambridge, MA: MIT Press.

Lee, D. (2012), 'Weakest-link contests with group-specific public good prizes', *European Journal of Political Economy*, **28**, 238–48.
Leininger, W. (1993), 'More efficient rent seeking – a Münchhausen solution', *Public Choice*, **75**(1), 43–62.
Leonard, D. and N.V. Long (2012), 'Endogenous changes in property rights regime', *Economic Record*, **88**(280), 79–88.
Long, N.V. (1975), 'Resource extraction under uncertainty about possible nationalization', *Journal of Economic Theory*, **10**(1), 42–53.
Long, N.V. (2010), *A Survey of Dynamic Games in Economics*, Singapore: World Scientific.
Long, N.V. and A. Soubeyran (2000), 'Existence and uniqueness of Cournot equilibrium: a contraction mapping approach', *Economics Letters*, **67**(3), 231–6.
Long, N.V. and F. Stähler (2009), 'A contest model of liberalizing government procurements', *European Journal of Political Economy*, **25**(4), 479–88.
Long, N.V. and N. Vousden (1987), 'Risk averse rent seeking with shared rents', *Economic Journal*, **97**(388), 971–85, reprinted in R.D. Congleton, A.L. Hillman and K.A. Konrad (eds) (2008), *40 Years of Research on Rent Seeking 1 – The Theory of Rent Seeking*, Heidelberg: Springer, pp. 293–307.
Mills, H.D. (1961), 'A study of promotional competition', in F.M. Bass (ed.), *Mathematical Models and Methods in Marketing*, Homewood, IL: R.D. Irwin, pp. 245–301.
Mohammed, S. and J. Whalley (1984), 'Rent seeking in India: its costs and policy significance', *Kyklos*, **37**, 398–413.
Münster, J. (2007), 'Selection tournaments, sabotage, and participation', *Journal of Economics and Management Strategy*, **16**(4), 943–70.
Nitzan, S. (1994), 'Modelling rent seeking contests', *European Journal of Political Economy*, **10**(1), 41–60.
Park, H., A. Philippopoulos and V. Vassilatos (2005), 'Choosing the size of the public sector under rent seeking from state coffers', *European Journal of Political Economy*, **21**, 830–50.
Peltzman, S. (1976), 'Towards a more general theory of regulation', *Journal of Law and Economics*, **19**(2), 211–40.
Posner, R.A. (1975), 'The social costs of monopoly and regulation', *Journal of Political Economy*, **83**(4), 505–29, reprinted in R.D. Congleton, A.L. Hillman and K.A. Konrad (eds) (2008), *40 Years of Research on Rent Seeking 1 – The Theory of Rent Seeking*, Heidelberg: Springer, pp. 45–56.
Romano, R. and H. Yildirim (2005), 'On the endogeneity of Cournot-Nash and Stackelberg equilibria: games of accumulation', *Journal of Economic Theory*, **120**(1), 73–107.
Ryvkin, D. (2010), 'Contests with private costs: beyond two players', *European Journal of Political Economy*, **26**(4), 558–67.
Skaperdas, S. and L. Gan (1995), 'Risk-aversion in contests', *Economic Journal*, **105**(431), 951–62.
Stephan, J. and H.W. Ursprung (1998), 'The social cost of rent seeking when victories are potentially transient and losses final', in K. Jäger and K.-J. Koch (eds), *Trade, Growth, and Economic Policies in Open Economies*, Berlin: Springer, pp. 101–10, reprinted in R.D. Congleton, A.L. Hillman and K.A. Konrad (eds) (2008), *Forty Years of Research on Rent Seeking*, Vols 1 and 2, Heidelberg: Springer, pp. 443–54.
Stigler, G.J. (1971), 'The theory of economic regulation', *Bell Journal of Economics*, **2**(1), 3–21.
Sui, Y. (2009), 'Rent-seeking contests with private values and resale', *Public Choice*, **138**, 409–22.
Szidarovszky, F. and K. Okuguchi (1997), 'On the existence and uniqueness of pure Nash equilibrium in rent-seeking', *Games and Economic Behavior*, **18**(1), 135–40, reprinted in R.D. Congleton, A.L. Hillman, and K.A. Konrad (eds) (2008), *40 Years of Research on Rent Seeking 1 – The Theory of Rent Seeking*, Heidelberg: Springer, pp. 271–8.
Tornell, A. (1997), 'Economic growth and decline with endogenous property rights', *Journal of Economic Growth*, **2**(3), 219–50.
Treich, N. (2010), 'Risk aversion and prudence in rent-seeking games', *Public Choice*, **145**(3), 339–49.
Tullock, G. (1967), 'The welfare costs of tariffs, monopolies and theft', *Western Economic Journal*, **5**, 224–32, reprinted in R.D. Congleton, A.L. Hillman and K.A. Konrad (eds) (2008), *40 Years of Research on Rent Seeking 1 – The Theory of Rent Seeking*, Heidelberg: Springer, pp. 45–53.
Tullock, G. (1975), 'On the efficient organization of trials', *Kyklos*, **28**, 745–62, reprinted in R.D. Congleton, A.L. Hillman and K.A. Konrad (eds) (2008), *40 Years of Research on Rent Seeking 2 – Applications: Rent Seeking in Practice*, Heidelberg: Springer, pp. 361–78.
Tullock, G. (1980), 'Efficient rent seeking', in J.M. Buchanan, R. Tollinson and G. Tullock (eds), *Toward a Theory of the Rent-seeking Society*, College Station, TX: Texas A&M University Press, pp. 97–112.
Veblen, T. (1924), *The Theory of the Leisure Class*, London: Allen and Unwin.

4. Contestable policies

Gil S. Epstein and Shmuel Nitzan

SUMMARY

Often contests involve the determination of the policies that are the source of rents, with prospective gainers and losers seeking to influence policy decisions and policy makers having an interest in the policy outcome. Policy-contest models describe the equilibrium outcomes that can arise.

4.1 INTRODUCTION

Rent-seeking models assume a contest for a fixed prize and focus on the social cost of rent seeking (Nitzan 1994; Hillman 2013; Long 2013). The decision maker who assigns the prize to the successful rent seeker is not explicitly present in the rent-seeking models. In another class of models, which can be called policy contests, the assigner of rents is explicitly present and the rent-seeking prize is endogenous. In the terminology of Appelbaum and Katz (1987 [2008]), policy makers may 'seek rents by setting rents'.[1]

The rents that are set have distributional consequences. Hillman and Riley (1989 [2008]) used the term 'transfer contests' to describe contests in which policies and rents are endogenous and losers in a contest make transfers to gainers. When there are competing groups seeking to gain rents or avoid payments, the social costs of rent seeking include resources used by both groups (Appelbaum and Katz 1986). An example is opposition to granting of monopoly (Ellingsen 1991 [2008]; Fabella 1995). Competing groups are also present in models of regulation and protectionist policies in which policy makers are constrained in providing special-interest benefits by voter discontent (Peltzman 1976; Hillman 1982 [2008]; Grossman and Helpman 1994 [2008]).

These latter models either set out the social cost of rent seeking when there is countervailing opposition or establish the politically chosen policy that balances political benefits and costs. This chapter goes beyond this literature by showing the complexity and varieties of outcomes in contests in which policy is contested and policy makers have interests in the policies.

The framework for policy contests, proposed in Epstein and Nitzan (2002) and presented in Sections 4.3 and 4.4, shows the dual importance of the government as an agenda setter and as a decision maker that approves or rejects policy proposals, while

[1] Congleton and Lee (2009), for example, analyze how a government's regulatory policies may be affected by revenues and other services generated by the efforts of rent seekers: a revenue-maximizing government oversees monopolization but sells monopoly privileges in a manner that promotes innovation and partially accounts for the deadweight losses associated with monopolized markets.

highlighting the significance of lobbying by organized interest groups engaged in rent-seeking activities. We do not consider the deadweight losses of policies – on which, see Becker (1983), Congleton (1988), Glazer and McMillan (1992) and Aidt (2003) – or the magnitudes of rent-seeking losses. We set out a micro-foundation for political-support and contest-success functions. Politicians or bureaucrats are viewed as choosing policies while taking into account both the lobbying outlays of interest groups and the welfare of the general public, as in the political-support models.[2] The lobbying outlays may benefit the politician or bureaucrat (see, for example, Congleton 1989, 2004; Congleton and Lee 2009). A simple, fundamental condition that rationalizes random behavior of political decision makers also ensures the existence of the contest-success function (CSF) that is assumed exogenous in the contest literature.[3]

The most commonly used CSFs are logit-form functions emanating from Tullock (1980 [2008]) and the function associated with all-pay auctions that awards the prize to the highest outlay (Hillman and Samet 1987 [2008]). In the standard contest literature, the government is assumed to be a passive player that only randomly approves or rejects policy proposals (see Epstein and Nitzan 2003, 2004 [2008]). In the extended public-policy contests described in this chapter, the government or political or bureaucratic decision maker is an active rational 'principal' who determines policy in two senses; by proposing the policy and randomly approving or rejecting the policy. That is, on the one hand, the political or bureaucratic decision maker acts rationally in selecting a proposed policy, anticipating the lobbying efforts of interest groups or in setting the agenda; on the other hand, the political or bureaucratic decision maker acts randomly (seemingly 'irrationally') in approving or rejecting the proposed policy. This chapter will show that under an appropriate mix of objectives encompassing public welfare and the objective of seeking lobbying outlays, random behavior is rational. The rationalization of the most widely studied contests will be illustrated.

Lobbying is part of the policy-making process in representative democracies.[4] Hillman and Ursprung (1988 [2008]) described lobbying with political competition among candidates for office and interest groups making campaign contributions to candidates. Grossman and Helpman (1996) model lobbying as a 'menu-auction'; the common-agency setting for lobbying leads candidates to select policies that are a compromise between the policy preferences of voters and the lobbies (as in the models of political-support models of Peltzman 1976, Hillman 1982 [2008] and Grossman and Helpman 1994 [2008]). Building on Besley and Coate (1997, 2001), Felli and Merlo (2001) study a citizen-candidate model of electoral competition with 'menu-auction' lobbying, assuming that the elected policy maker selects the lobbies that take part in the policy-making process. In their elaborate model, the equilibrium policy outcome is again a compromise, in this case between the policy preferences

2 The lobbying efforts on which we focus are interpreted as resources that buy influence (for example, campaign contributions) rather than resources involved in the dissemination of information by one means or another. For a detailed discussion on these alternative lobbying activities, see Grossman and Helpman (2001).

3 For an axiomatic characterization of CSFs, see Skaperdas (1996 [2008]).

4 For different perspectives on lobbying and influence, see, for example, Congleton (1986 [2008], 1991 [2008]), Grossman and Helpman (2001) and Persson and Tabellini (2000).

of the elected candidate and those of the (at most two) lobbies chosen by the policy maker.

In contrast to this literature, Glazer et al. (1998) demonstrate that extreme policies may appear, not in spite of but because of political opposition. More specifically, an incumbent may gain political support by adopting a policy the challenger is more likely to want to change. The awareness of voters of the high cost of the more likely policy change induces them to support the extreme policy proposed by the incumbent.[5]

In a 'menu-auction', an equilibrium comprises a set of contribution schedules that are optimal for the interest groups in light of the anticipated behavior of the politician who selects a policy that is his best response to the implicit offers of the interest groups. A complete political-economic equilibrium, however, includes the policy proposals that are optimal for the interest groups in light of the anticipated outcome of the lobbying contest that hinges on their lobbying efforts.[6] In Epstein and Nitzan (2004 [2008]), a reduced-form, two-stage lobbying game is described in which policies and rent-seeking activities are analyzed simultaneously. The policies proposed by the contenders tend to be restrained to reduce rent-seeking losses. In that model, as we show below, the implemented (winning) policy is always a compromise, that is, it belongs to the interior of the interval defined by the interest groups' (*ex post*) preferred policies. However, to use the terminology of Hillman and Riley (1989 [2008]), in an imperfectly discriminating contest, the proposals of the different groups will not coincide. Munster (2006) shows that in a perfectly discriminating contest (an all-pay auction), the proposed policies also tend to be restrained. In contrast to Epstein and Nitzan (2004 [2008]), Munster (2006) demonstrates that the policy proposals in the all-pay auction may coincide.

In these models, there are three players consisting of two interest groups and a two-tier government. One interest group is 'a challenger' who is interested in the approval of the proposed policy. A second interest group is 'a defender' who prefers the status quo and is therefore interested in the rejection of the proposed policy. The government consists of an elected politician who sets the agenda (proposes a policy that along with the status quo constitutes the agenda) and approves or rejects the proposed policy.

We show that within a general class of this public-policy contest, in contrast to Grossman and Helpman (1996), Felli and Merlo (2001) and Epstein and Nitzan (2004 [2008]), lobbying may result in the proposal and implementation of an extreme policy. In other words, lobbying is not necessarily compromise enhancing.

This result crucially depends on the policy maker (the politician in our case) being a 'principal' and on his having an effective incentive to be extreme. The existence of such an incentive hinges on the payoffs (contest stakes) of the interest groups and their dependence on the implemented policy and on the preferences of the policy maker; in

---

[5] The examples that are given by the authors are anti-abortion stands by the Republican Party in the United States, pro-affirmative action positions by the Democratic Party in the United States, adoption of the poll tax by the Thatcher government in the United Kingdom and privatization in former Communist countries of Eastern Europe.

[6] The interest groups can also try to influence the proposed policy. In our setting the proposed policy is not directly affected by the lobbying groups. However, it is indirectly affected by the interest groups in light of the awareness of the politician who proposes the policy to the interest groups and through the effect on the outcome of the contest.

contrast, Epstein and Nitzan (2004 [2008]) and Munster (2006) consider the case where two interest groups compete over the approval of a policy that each of them proposes. When lobbying outlays are positively related to the policy set by the politician, the stronger the political rent-extraction motive, as represented by the weight assigned to the lobbying outlays, the more extreme is the proposed policy.

It is therefore possible that the defender and the challenger of the status quo prefer a policy that is less radical and more efficient than the policy proposed by the politician. In particular, it is possible that more than the calf (challenger of the status quo policy) wishes to suck, the cow (politician) desires to suckle. When this happens, the politician is more concerned than the challenger about enhancing the latter's interest.[7]

An example of policies in which lobbying can give rise to a proposed policy that is more extreme than the proposals preferred by the interest groups is the determination of a minimum wage, where the proposed minimum wage is more extreme than the union's most preferred wage. Another example is migration quotas: governments can determine quotas that may well exceed the quota preferred by the capital owner who takes part in the political contest over the quota, and this quota can be lower than the capital owner's sought number of immigrants in a situation in which the quota is approved with certainty (or there is no political contest involved in the determination of the quota).[8]

We begin by presenting the micro-foundations for a contest created by a politician and then discuss the self-restraint in policy set by a specific interest group. We proceed by considering policy restraint in a model of two interest groups, each restraining their proposed policy and finally consider the government as an active player determining the public policy contest. The results presented in this chapter are to be found in Epstein and Nitzan (2003, 2004 [2008], 2006a, 2006c) and other cited papers.

4.2 THE POLICY CONTEST

Suppose that a policy I is proposed by the government. Two interest groups, contestants i and j, compete on the approval or rejection of I. Approval is the preferred policy for player i, whereas rejection of the proposed policy is the preferred policy for player j. Approval implies that player i wins the contest. The present discounted value of the preferred outcome to player i is equal to u_i and the value of this outcome to his oppo-

---

[7] Esteban and Ray (1999) observe that in a classical contest game where the two players not only have to decide on how much lobbing effort to provide but also for which alternative they want to lobby, all lobbyists will always invest their effort in favor of their most preferred policy alternative. Hence we would have expected that agenda setting does not harm the interest groups while enhancing a compromise. As mentioned above, we show that this is not the case and that the proposed policy may well be more extreme even relative to the ideal certain proposal of the challenger. Note that if the proposed equilibrium policy is approved, it is also implemented because, *ex post*, the challenger prefers it to his *ex ante* most preferred policy.

[8] See, for example, Boeri et al. (2002). The price determined for a regulated monopoly – Peltzman (1976), Congleton (1988), Baik (1999), Epstein and Nitzan (2003) or the degree of restriction of bank branching (Kroszner and Strahan 1999) – is also, by the reasoning above, an example in which the proposed policy can be more extreme than the policy that would have been proposed by the relevant interest groups. See also the policies in Glazer et al. (1998).

nent, player j, is equal to v_j. Approval of the proposed policy is associated with a positive payoff for player i, since, by assumption, $u_i > v_i$. Similarly, rejection is associated with a positive payoff for player j, since, $u_j > v_j$. Note that the players' payoffs corresponding to the approval and rejection of the policy I depend on I. Player i's preferred contest outcome, namely, the approval of I, is reached in probability Pr_i. The probability of player j's preferred contest outcome is $\Pr_j$, $\Pr_j = 1 - \Pr_i$. These winning probabilities depend on the efforts made by the two contestants, x_i and x_j. The efforts of the players, x, affect the winning probability since they are directed at the government/politicians affecting their decision making. Examples for such transfers to the politicians could be efforts invested in advertisements and public relations that benefit the politician, campaign contributions, bribes and other benefits for the rent extractor, which he may seek to maximize (see, for example, Congleton 2004; Congleton and Lee 2009).
can be seen as

The expected net payoff of the risk-neutral player i is equal to:

$$E(w_i) = \Pr_i u_i(I) + \Pr_j v_i(I) - x_i\,,\, i \neq j. \tag{4.1}$$

Denote by $n_i = (u_i - v_i)$ the stake of player i (his benefit from winning the contest) (see Baik 1999; Epstein and Nitzan 2002, 2007; Nti 1999). The expected net payoff of interest group i can be rewritten as follows:

$$E(w_i) = v_i(I) + \Pr_i n_i(I) - x_i\,. \tag{4.2}$$

In general, the stakes of the contestants may differ, one of them having an advantage over the other in terms of his benefit from winning the contest. In such cases, we will refer to the advantageous higher stake contestant as player H and to his opponent, the lower stake contestant, as player L, so $n_L \leq n_H$.

Since $v_i(I)$ is the minimum benefit obtained by interest group/contestant i, regardless of the outcome of the contest, we can concentrate on his expected net payoff, disregarding this value. Such a simplification will no longer be legitimate when changes in the proposed policy I are allowed to affect the different contest outcomes. At this stage, however, the objective function of the contestant can be written as

$$E(u_i) = \Pr_i n_i(I) - x_i\,. \tag{4.3}$$

We shall refer to this expression as the net payoff of the contestant.

4.2.1 Contest Equilibrium

The function that specifies the winning probabilities of the contestants corresponding to their efforts, the CSF, is an important component of the policy contest. In this section we focus on contest equilibrium under two specific CSFs. These CSFs are the most commonly assumed functions in the contest literature. The first is the logit CSF, first studied by Tullock (1980 [2008]), under which the probability of winning the contest is a continuous function of the efforts invested in the contest. The second CSF, which is not continuous, is often applied in auctions. This CSF is referred to as the all-pay auction (see Hillman and Samet 1987 [2008]; Hillman and Riley 1989 [2008]) and unambiguously determines the contest winner by comparing the expenditures of the contestants. The contest equilibrium outcome derived under the above two CSFs consists of the contestants' efforts (lobbying expenditures, influence activities, rent-seeking outlays) that directly yield their winning probabilities and their expected net payoff.

4.2.2 The Logit (Generalized Lottery) CSF

The logit CSF, which is also referred to as the generalized lottery function (Tullock 1980 [2008]; Lockard and Tullock 2001), is given by:

$$\Pr_i = \frac{g x_i^r}{g x_j^r + x_i^r} \textit{ for } r \leq 2 \textit{ and } g > 0.$$

The return to effort according to this lottery function is captured by the parameter r. The other parameter g is positive. If $g > 1$, then player i has an advantage over player j in terms of ability to affect the contest outcome, that is, in terms of ability to turn effort into winning probability.

4.2.3 The All-pay Auction

Under the all-pay auction the contestant who makes the larger effort wins with probability one. If the two contestants make the same effort, then the winner is chosen randomly. The probability of winning (Hillman and Riley 1989 [2008]) is thus given by

$$\Pr_i = \begin{cases} 1 & \textit{if} \quad x_i > x_j \\ 0.5 & \textit{if} \quad x_i = x_j \\ 0 & \textit{if} \quad x_j > x_i \end{cases}. \tag{4.4}$$

4.3 THE RATIONALIZATION OF A CONTEST

The government could decide to select the policy that results in the realization of the above policy, that is, to select the policy that generates the highest benefit to one of the interest groups: the stake n_H for group H (H for the group with the higher stake). The group with the lower stake is denoted group L. An alternative option for the government is to choose randomly between the two different policies that it faces. Even though the government chooses randomly, the interest groups may affect the choice probabilities. Clearly, if the utility the government derives from the selection of a policy is positively related to the aggregate net payoffs (stakes) of the interest groups, then it would never randomize, that is, it would select the policy that generates the higher stake. The probabilities of realization of the two policies in the complete-information public-policy contest are given by the CSF. This function specifies the relationship between the interest groups' investment in the so-called influence, lobbying or rent-seeking activities and the probability of realization of the two policies. The expected payoff of interest group i is given by $E(u_i)$ and the effort invested by each interest group is denoted by x_i.

As commonly assumed in the political economy literature, let the government's objective function be a weighted average of the expected social welfare and lobbying efforts:

$$G(.) = \alpha(E(u_L)+E(u_H)) + (1-\alpha)(x_L+x_H). \tag{4.5}$$

The parameters a and $(1 - a)$ are the weights assigned to the expected social welfare and the contestants' lobbying outlays. If the government decides not to generate a contest and choose the policy that results in the higher stake n_H, then the value of the government's objective function is equal to αn_H. It is therefore sensible for the government to create a contest if and only if the expected value of its objective function increases as a result of the existence of the contest. As we presented (Epstein and Nitzan 2006c, 2007),

$$\alpha(E(u_L)+E(u_H))+(1-\alpha)(x_L+x_H)>\alpha n_H. \tag{4.6}$$

We show that if the weight assigned to the lobbying outlays is greater than that assigned to the expected stakes, a contest based on a CSF, such as the commonly assumed all-pay auction or Tullock's lottery logit functions, can be preferable to no contest. That is, random government behavior is therefore rational.

Rewriting (4.6), given (4.3), $Pr_L + Pr_H = 1$, $\Pr_i > 0$ (both players participate in the contest) and $n_H = bn_L$, where $b \geq 1$, we obtain:

$$\frac{(1-2\alpha)}{\alpha}\frac{(x_L+x_H)}{\Pr_L} > (b-1)\,n_L. \tag{4.7}$$

Whether this condition is satisfied or not hinges on the CSF, on the parameters n_L, b and α that represent the contestants' stakes and the weights assigned by the governments to its two utility components, and on the resulting equilibrium lobbying efforts of the contestants $x_L + x_H$ and, in turn, on their contest-winning probabilities $\Pr_L$ and $\Pr_H$. Given the CSF and the three parameters, the above condition is satisfied if the lobbying efforts of the interest groups are sufficiently large or the contest-winning probability of the low stake player is sufficiently low. This simple condition has the following straightforward implications regarding the effect of the parameters:

1. When $b \geq 1$, inequality (4.7) requires that $\alpha < 0.5$. That is, a necessary condition for the existence of an effective incentive for a politician to create a contest is that the weight he assigns to social welfare is lower than the weight assigned to the contestants' lobbying outlays, $\alpha < 0.5$. More generally, equation (4.7) highlights which parameter values of $(1 - \alpha)$ make random behavior more attractive to the government. A sufficiently low level of this parameter implies that random behavior is irrational. In such a case the government would not bother to create a contest. If $(1 - \alpha)$ is sufficiently high, namely, the government assigns a sufficiently high weight to the lobbying outlays of the interest groups, then it is sensible to create a contest and act randomly in approving or rejecting the policy it proposes. A rational politician who only cares about the public well-being will never choose to act randomly. If he cares just about extracting tangible rents for himself, as explicitly or implicitly assumed in many studies that followed Tullock (1980 [2008]), that is, if

$(1 - \alpha) = 1$, then acting randomly is his preferred alternative, provided that the contestants' lobbying efforts are positive.

2. If the contest is symmetric in terms of the lobbies' stakes ($n_L = n_H$, that is, $b = 1$ *and* $\alpha < 0.5$), then the government always prefers to act randomly according to the CSF of this contest, rather than select the policy yielding the higher stake with certainty. The reason for this is that when both stakes are identical, $\Pr_H n_H + \Pr_L n_L = n$. The politician therefore always gains αn, regardless of who wins the contest. In such a case any contest that generates positive lobbying efforts is preferred to the 'no contest' alternative, provided that the weight assigned to the lobbying efforts is larger than the weight assigned to the aggregate net payoffs of the interest groups.
3. Rational randomness, that is, preference of a contest, requires the existence of contest equilibrium. In the case of a pure strategy equilibrium, the following first and second order existence conditions: $\frac{\partial \Pr_i}{\partial x_i} > 0, \frac{\partial \Pr_i}{\partial x_j} < 0$ *and* $\frac{\partial^2 \Pr_i}{\partial x_i^2} < 0$ are also required for the government to prefer its seemingly ad hoc random behavior according to the CSF. Notice that these conditions also ensure that as the stake of a player increases, his effort as well as his expected payoff are increased.
4. The left-hand side of (4.7) can be rewritten as: $\beta_1(\Pr_L n_L + \Pr_H n_H) + \beta_2(x_L + x_H)$, where $\beta_1 = \alpha$ and $\beta_2 = 1 - 2\alpha$. To satisfy the inequality $\frac{(1-2\alpha)}{\alpha} > 1$, the weight β_1 assigned to the expected stakes $(\Pr_L n_L + \Pr_H n_H)$ must be smaller than the weight β_2 associated with the lobbying effort $(x_L + x_H)$, that is, $\beta_1 < \beta_2$. In terms of the parameter α, this condition becomes: $\alpha < 1/3$. For $\alpha < 1/3$, which satisfies the necessary condition for the superiority of the random contest behavior, a sufficient condition for (4.7) to hold is that, in equilibrium, $x_L + x_H > n_H - (\Pr_H n_H + \Pr_L n_L)$ or, equivalently, $x_L + x_H > \Pr_L(n_H - n_L) = \Pr_L(b - 1)n_L$. This means that, for $\alpha < 1/3$, the contest should generate outlays that are larger than the expected difference between the contestants' stakes. As is known, when the stakes are equal, so that $n_L = n_H = n$, this condition is satisfied.

It can be shown (see Epstein and Nitzan 2006, 2007) that for $\alpha < 1/3$ the all-pay auction and the logit (generalized lottery) CSF satisfy (4.7). For $\alpha < 0.5$ these CSFs may well satisfy (4.7) depending on the value of the different parameters.

We have argued that the CSF, a basic component in contest theory, has a plausible micro-foundation. That is, the government's behavior can be rationalized both when it acts randomly, as in the standard influence activities, lobbying or rent-seeking models, and when it acts rationally in setting the agenda (making policy proposals) and randomly in approving or rejecting these proposals. Our argument has been illustrated using the most commonly studied CSFs.

The micro-foundation of random government behavior has been provided in a context of lobbying that buys influence, disregarding the possible informational role of lobbying (Grossman and Helpman 2001). Our argument is nevertheless valid in the broader context where lobbying can be of both types. In a more general setting, the rationalization of a lobbying contest and, in particular, of random behavior can be based not only on the government's interest in extracting rents from the lobbies but also its interest in enhancing the aggregate equilibrium well-being of the interest groups. When lobbying takes the form of activities that buy influence, it can clearly induce a government to prefer the existence of a contest. When lobbying takes the form of information transmission, it can also induce the government to prefer contest behavior because such lobbying can be welfare enhancing (Lagerlof 1997; Gradstein 2002). In such a broader context, the effect of the relevant parameters and in particular their relative effect on the incentives of the government to prefer the existence of a lobbying contest certainly deserve a careful study.

4.4 SELF-RESTRAINT

In this section we now consider the case under which one interest group can propose a policy that will be in its favor. After the interest group proposes a policy, both interest groups compete in favor or against the proposed policy. Thus, we describe a two-stage contest in which in the first stage one interest group proposes a policy that benefits that group and then in the second stage both groups compete in favor or against the approval or rejection of the policy. The stakes of the interest groups depend on the proposed policy *I*, as presented by equation (4.3).

The expected net payoff (surplus) of the two groups are $E(u_1)$ and $E(u_2)$ given by

$$E(u_i) = \mathrm{Pr}_i n_i(I) - x_i \quad \textit{for } i = 1,2 \tag{4.8}$$

where Pr_1 and Pr_2 are the winning probabilities of the two contestants.

We assume that the contest is determined by Tullock's (1980 [2008]) simple non-discriminating rule. That is, the consumers' probability of success is given by

$$\mathrm{Pr}_i = \frac{x_i}{x_j + x_i} \quad \textit{for } i = 1,2. \tag{4.9}$$

4.4.1 Equilibrium

It is clear from the structure of the game that both players participate in the contest (x_1 and x_2 are positive) and that one of them wins the contest. We therefore focus on interior Nash equilibria of the contest. The conditions characterizing an interior equilibrium of our two-player contest (sub-game) are[9]

$$\frac{\partial E(u_i)}{\partial x_i} = \frac{x_j}{(x_j + x_i)^2} n_i - 1 = 0 \quad \textit{for } i,j = 1,2 \quad j \neq i. \tag{4.10}$$

By (4.10), we obtain

$$\frac{x_2}{(x_2 + x_1)^2} n_1 = 1 \tag{4.11}$$

and

---

[9] The sufficient (second order) conditions of such an equilibrium are satisfied.

$$\frac{x_1}{(x_2 + x_1)^2} n_2 = 1. \tag{4.12}$$

Solving (4.11) and (4.12) yields the equilibrium investments x_1 and x_2. Rewriting (4.10) we obtain

$$x_2 n_1 = (x_2 + x_1)^2. \tag{4.13}$$

Thus,

$$\sqrt{x_2 n_1} = (x_2 + x_1) \tag{4.14}$$

and we find that x_1 is equal to:

$$x_1 = \sqrt{x_2 n_1} - x_2. \tag{4.15}$$

This is player 1's reaction function to player 2's investment. Taking x_1 as in (4.15) and substituting into the first order condition as determined for player 2 – see (4.12) – we obtain:

$$\frac{\sqrt{x_2 n_1} - x_2}{(x_2 + \sqrt{x_2 n_1} - x_2)^2} n_2 = 1 \tag{4.16}$$

which is equivalent to

$$(\sqrt{x_2 n_1} - x_2) n_2 = x_2 n_1. \tag{4.17}$$

Or

$$\sqrt{x_2 n_1} n_2 = x_2 (n_1 + n_2) \tag{4.18}$$

and

$$x_2 n_1 n_2^2 = x_2^2 (n_1 + n_2)^2. \tag{4.19}$$

Therefore,

$$x_2^* = \frac{n_1 n_2^2}{(n_1 + n_2)^2}. \tag{4.20}$$

In a similar way we can calculate the investment of interest group 1:

$$x_1^* = \frac{n_2 n_1^2}{(n_1 + n_2)^2}. \tag{4.21}$$

As we can see, the investments of the interest groups hinge only on the stakes. As the stake of interest group 1 increases, its investment also increases ($\frac{\partial x_i^*}{\partial n_i} = \, > 0$ for $i = 1, 2$).

Given the results presented in (4.20) and (4.21), we can now calculate the equilibrium winning probability by substituting (4.20) and (4.21) into (4.9) and obtain:

$$\Pr_1 = \frac{n_1}{n_1 + n_2} \quad and \quad \Pr_2 = \frac{n_2}{n_1 + n_2}. \tag{4.22}$$

As we can see, the winning probabilities also depend only on the stakes. As the stake of interest group 1 increases, his winning probability is also increased ($\frac{\partial \Pr_i}{\partial n_i} = \; > 0 \; for \; i = 1, 2$).

Now let us substitute the equilibrium investments and the equilibrium probabilities into the expected net payoff function to obtain the equilibrium net payoffs of the groups (recall that the stakes are a function of the proposed policy):

$$E(u_1^*) = \frac{(n_1)^3}{(n_1 + n_2)^2}; \; E(u_2^*) = \frac{(n_2)^3}{(n_1 + n_2)^2}. \tag{4.23}$$

To simplify our calculations, assume that under the existing status quo interest group 1 is interested in a change while interest group 2 is interested in preserving the status quo. Moreover, assume that as the proposed policy increases, the stake of interest group 2 increases as they have more to lose if interest group 1 wins and its policy is applied $\frac{\partial n_2(I)}{\partial I} > 0$.

4.4.2 Determining the Optimal Policy

Let us first consider the optimal policy that interest group 1 would prefer if this policy were to be applied and implemented without any opposition. Under this assumption, interest group 1 will determine its policy such that it maximizes its stake: n_1. The first order condition will thus be:

$$\frac{\partial n_1(I)}{\partial I} = 0 \tag{4.24}$$

and the second order condition,

$$\frac{\partial^2 n_1(I)}{\partial I^2} < 0. \tag{4.25}$$

Assuming that the second order condition is satisfied, denote the policy that maximizes the stake of interest group 1 by I_1^*.

Now consider the case where interest group 1 knows that the moment it determines its optimal policy and puts it forward as a proposal, interest group 2 will challenge it, investing effort in order to preserve the status quo, that is, prevent approval of the proposed policy. Under this scenario, interest group 1 will present a policy that will maximize its expected net payoff and not its stake since it will take into consideration the probability of the proposed policy being approved (Pr_1) and the effort invested in the contest (x_1). Therefore, interest group 1 will select the optimal policy I_2^* that maximizes

$$E(u_1^*) = \frac{(n_1(I))^3}{(n_1(I) + n_2(I))^2}.$$

The first order condition for determining I_2^* is:

$$\frac{\partial E(u_1^*)}{\partial I} = \frac{3(n_1(I))^2 \frac{\partial n_1(I)}{\partial I}(n_1(I) + n_2(I))^2 - (n_1(I))^3 2(n_1(I) + n_2(I))\left(\frac{\partial n_1(I)}{\partial I} + \frac{\partial n_2(I)}{\partial I}\right)}{(n_1(I) + n_2(I))^4} = 0. \quad (4.26)$$

Thus, I_2^* satisfies equation (26). Since this equation is not straightforward, let us consider the value of this derivative at $I = I_1^*$ where $\frac{\partial n_1(I_1^*)}{\partial I_1^*} = 0$ (note that by the definition of $I = I_1^*$ the stake of contestant 1 is optimal and equation (4.24) is satisfied). Moreover, as described above, $\frac{\partial n_2(I)}{\partial I} > 0$ for any I and this also holds for $I = I_1^*$.

Using the fact that $\frac{\partial n_1(I_1^*)}{\partial I_1^*} = 0$, we can calculate the value of $\frac{\partial E(u_1^*)}{\partial I}$ at $I = I_1^*$: $\frac{\partial E(u_1^*)}{\partial I}\Big|_{I=I_1^*}$ and obtain:

$$\frac{\partial E(u_1^*)}{\partial I}\Big|_{I=I_1^*} = \frac{-(n_1(I))^3 2(n_1(I) + n_2(I))\left(\frac{\partial n_2(I)}{\partial I}\right)}{(n_1(I) + n_2(I))^4}. \quad (4.27)$$

Since $n_1(I) > 0, (n_1(I) + n_2(I)) > 0$ *and* $(\frac{\partial n_2(I)}{\partial I}) > 0$, we obtain that $\frac{\partial E(u_1^*)}{\partial I}\Big|_{I=I_1^*} < 0$. This implies that the policy that maximizes interest group 1's expected net payoff is smaller than the policy that maximizes interest group 1's stake: $I_2^* < I_1^*$.

In Figure 4.1 we can see the graph of the expected payoff function that has one optimal point at I_2^*. At this point $\frac{\partial E(u_1^*)}{\partial I} = 0$. The value of $\frac{\partial E(u_1^*)}{\partial I}$ at the point $I = I_1^*$ is negative, which means that the function $E(u_1^*)$ is decreasing and thus obtains a lower value at $I = I_1^*$ than at $I = I_2^*$.

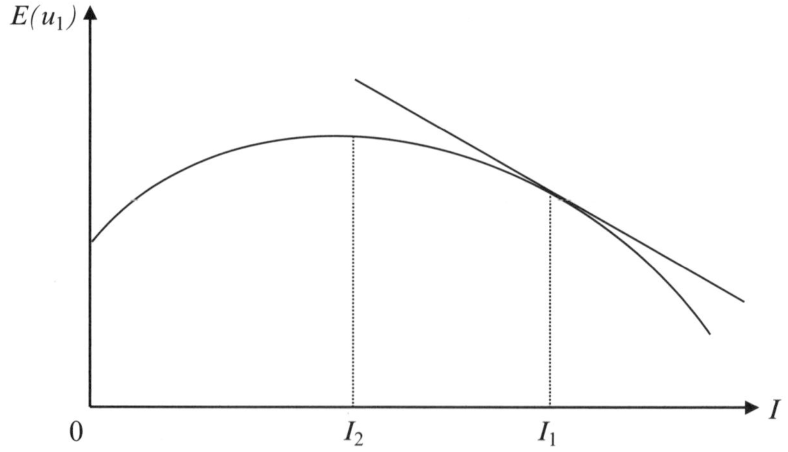

Figure 4.1 The optimal policy

This result is similar to that of Leidy (1994). The intuition for this result is as follows: lowering the proposed policy of interest group 1 slightly below the policy that maximized interest group 1's stake leads only to a second order decrease of the interest group's stake (its profit from winning the regulatory contest), but yields a first order increase in interest group 1's benefit. Since this decreases the stake of interest group 2, interest group 2 will be less aggressive in the contest and, in turn, its probability of winning the contest is reduced. This favorable effect dominates the former unfavorable effect and therefore interest group 1 prefers to lobby for a policy $I = I_2^*$ that is lower than $I = I_1^*$.

In Epstein and Nitzan (2004 [2008]), we generalize this result by enabling two interest groups that each can propose a policy and then compete for it. To understand their framework, suppose that a status quo policy is challenged by one interest group and defended by another group. This policy can be the price of a regulated monopoly, the maximal degree of pollution the government allows or the existing tax structure. The defender of the status quo policy (henceforth interest group *d*) prefers the status quo policy I_s to any alternative policy. The challenger of the status quo policy (interest group *c*) prefers the alternative policy I_a. Without any loss of generality, it is assumed that $I_s \leqslant I_a$ and that the policy I_s (I_a) is the optimal policy proposal of the defender (the challenger), provided that his supported policy gains certain approval. That is, disregarding the possibility that his proposed policy can be rejected, in which case the policy proposed by the rival interest group is assumed to be approved. For example, in the contest over monopoly regulation studied in Baik (1999), Ellingsen (1991 [2008]) and Schmidt (1992), the monopoly firm defends the status quo, lobbying for the profit-maximizing monopoly price (against any price regulation), while consumers challenge the status quo, lobbying for the competitive price (a tight price cap).

The actual implemented policy depends on the contest between the interest groups on the approval of their proposed policies. These proposed policies that are endogenously determined in the extended setting are denoted I_c and I_d. The outcome of the political contest is given in terms of the probabilities Pr_c and Pr_d that the interest groups *c* and *d* win the contest. The outcome of the contest depends on the stakes of the contestants and, in turn, on their proposed policies and on their exerted lobbying or rent-seeking efforts. In contrast to Epstein and Nitzan (2002), the government is not introduced as a player in the policy-determination game. However, the important role of the political environment (the form of the government, its motivation and the decision rule it applies) is represented by the commonly used CSF that specifies the relationship between the outcome of the contest and the proposed policies or the efforts of the interest groups.

In Epstein and Nitzan (2004 [2008]), we establish that competition over endogenously determined policy proposals reduces the polarization between the positions of interest groups. In particular, each group restrains its proposal relative to its optimal proposal under certainty. Although the interest groups voluntarily restrain their proposals, they are nevertheless induced to engage in a wasteful contest as complete agreement is not an equilibrium outcome.

This result has broad applications. It rationalizes the self-restraint of interest groups such as firms investing in pollution control or voluntarily adopting cleaner production processes or environmentalists who do not maintain a zero pollution target. It explains why monopolists are induced to self-regulate their price and why their customer coalitions do not insist on a tight price cap. It also implies that an interest group's support of a welfare program or of any policy that has redistribution effects need not reflect its altruistic preferences but rather its egoistic strategic restraint. This result is somewhat related to the voting literature where two parties choosing platforms may have an incentive to moderate their positions and to converge to the same platform (the median voter's ideal position).

The above analysis applies to a discriminating CSF. Munster (2006) considers the endogenous policy proposals of the defender and the challenger assuming a perfectly discriminating contest, that is, the all-pay auction. The winning probability of interest group i is given by (4.4) and, in turn, the expected net payoff is equal to:

$$E(u_i) = \begin{cases} n_i(I) - x_i & \text{if} \quad x_i > x_j, \forall i \neq j \\ \frac{1}{2}n_i(I) - x_i & \text{if} \quad x_i = x_j, \forall i \neq j\,. \\ -x_i & \text{if} \quad x_j > x_i, \forall i \neq j \end{cases} \tag{4.28}$$

Munster (2006) shows that under the all-pay auction, in equilibrium both players make the same proposal. Since the two interest groups propose the same policy, there will be no need for a contest between the groups.

The difference in outcomes is due to the different nature of the contests. In an imperfectly discriminating contest, the group that chooses the higher lobbying outlay does not necessarily win. There is some 'noise' in the determination of the winner and the winning probabilities are continuous functions of the lobbying efforts.

4.5 PUBLIC POLICY

In the preceding section, the interest groups proposed the policy and then competed for its approval or rejection. In this section, we consider public policy that is proposed by the government and then brought forward before the interest groups. The proposed policy can be approved or rejected. In case of rejection the status quo is preserved.

Suppose that a status quo policy, I_s, is challenged by one interest group and defended by the other. The defender of the status quo policy (henceforth, interest group d) prefers the status quo policy I_s to any alternative policy. The most preferred policy of the challenger of the status quo policy (interest group c) is I_c. With no loss of generality, it is assumed that $I_s < I_c$ and that the policy I_s (I_c) is the optimal policy proposal of the defender (the challenger), provided that his supported policy gains certain approval.[10] That is, each of these policies is optimal for the respective interest group when it disregards the possibility that its proposed policy can be rejected, in which case, by assumption, the policy proposed by the rival interest group is approved.

The interest groups engage in lobbying activities because they wish to increase their probability of winning the public-policy contest, that is, secure the realization of their

[10] Note that assuming that $I_s > I_c$ would not qualitatively change any of our results.

preferred policy.[11] In our model, the lobbying groups do not try directly to affect the policy proposed by the politician. Rather, the lobbying efforts are directed to the politician who approves or rejects the proposed policy and therefore they do affect, indirectly, the policy proposed by the politician. Interest group d wins the contest when the proposed policy is rejected. In such a case the status quo I_s is implemented. Its benefit in such a case is its avoided loss. Interest group c wins the contest when the proposed policy is approved and implemented. The ruling politician is responsible for the existence of the contest, being aware of its direct potential benefit, namely, of the possibility to benefit from all or part of the lobbying outlays. He may also be aware of the effect of his decision on his probability of being re-elected either via the expected campaign contributions of the contestants or via the expected support of the voters whose welfare depends on the policy of the government.

As in (4.3), the expected net payoffs of the two interest groups, d and c, are given by

$$E(u_d) = \mathrm{Pr}_d n_d(I) - x_d \text{ and } E(u_c) = \mathrm{Pr}_c n_c(I) - x_c \tag{4.29}$$

where n_d and n_c denote, respectively, the net benefits or the contest stakes of the interest groups. We assume that for any I in the interval $[I_s, I_c]$, an increase in the proposed policy I increases the stakes of both interest groups, that is, $\frac{\partial n_d(I)}{\partial I} > 0$ *and* $\frac{\partial n_c(I)}{\partial I} > 0$.[12]

By our assumptions, the interest groups participate in the contest, that is, x_d and x_c are positive. We therefore focus on interior Nash equilibria of the second stage of the contest. Solving the first order conditions we obtain:

$$\Delta_i = \frac{\partial \mathrm{Pr}_i(x_i, x_j)}{\partial x_i} n_i(I) - 1 = 0, \ \forall i \neq j \ and \ i, j = d, c. \tag{4.30}$$

In the first stage of the game, the politician selects his strategy, that is, the proposed policy I subject to the political constraint, namely, subject to the lobbying contest on the approval of his proposal. Hence, as indicated above, his objective function $G(.)$ is of the general form[13] $G(E(u_c); E(u_d); (x_c + x_d))$, where $E(u_c)$ and $E(u_d)$ are the expected net payoffs of the challenger and the defender that positively affect G. See equation (4.5) as an example. The contenders' lobbying outlays $(x_d + x_c) = X$ represent either transfers to the government or resources wasted in the contest. Note that taking into account the public interest is consistent with the politician being either benevolent or self-interested in wishing to be re-elected.

The first order condition for an interior maximization of $G(.)$ with respect to I requires that

---

[11] Modeling the rent seekers as single agents presumes that they have already solved their collective action problem. The proposed model thus applies to already formed interest groups.

[12] This condition holds in many situations. In particular, it holds in the context of monopoly-price regulation where I_s is the competitive status quo price and I_c is the profit-maximizing monopoly price, see Epstein and Nitzan (2003). The assumption is also plausible in the context of minimum-wage determination, where I_s represents the existing equilibrium wage and I_c represents the minimum wage preferred by the workers' union or in the context of protective trade policy (by tariff or quota).

[13] See Epstein and Nitzan (2002).

$$\frac{\partial G(.)}{\partial E(u_c^*)}\frac{\partial E(u_c^*)}{\partial I}+\frac{\partial G(.)}{\partial E(u_d^*)}\frac{\partial E(u_d^*)}{\partial I}+\frac{\partial G(.)}{\partial X^*}\frac{\partial X^*}{\partial I}=0. \tag{4.31}$$

A sub-game perfect interior Nash equilibrium of the public-policy contest is thus characterized by the three equalities in (4.30) and (4.31).

The effectiveness of the policy maker's incentive to propose a policy that exceeds I_c^* or is lower than I_d^* depends on the sensitivity of G with respect to its three arguments and on the sensitivity of the equilibrium total lobbying outlays X^* and of the expected utility of the interest groups with respect to the proposed policy. Let I^{**} denote the equilibrium policy that satisfies (4.31). At I_c^*, $\frac{\partial E(u_c)}{\partial I}|_{I=I_c^*}=0$, at I_d^*, $\frac{\partial E(u_d)}{\partial I}|_{I=I_d^*}=0$ and therefore at I^{**}, $\frac{\partial E(u_c)}{\partial I}|_{I=I^{**}}<0$ and $\frac{\partial E(u_d)}{\partial I}|_{I=I^{**}}<0$. By the equilibrium condition (4.31), we therefore get that $I^{**}>I_c^*$ or $I^{**}<I_d^*$ if

$$-\frac{1}{\left.\frac{\partial G}{\partial X}\right|_{I=I^{**}}}\left[\left.\frac{\partial G}{\partial E(u_d)}\right|_{I=I^{**}}\left.\frac{\partial E(u_d)}{\partial I}\right|_{I=I^{**}}+\left.\frac{\partial G}{\partial E(u_c)}\right|_{I=I^{**}}\left.\frac{\partial E(u_c)}{\partial I}\right|_{I=I^{**}}\right]<\left.\frac{\partial X}{\partial I}\right|_{I=I^{**}}. \tag{4.32}$$

Notice that the left-hand side of (4.32) is positive and since its right-hand side is independent of $G(.)$, we obtain that $I^{**}>I_c^*$ or $I^{**}<I_d^*$, if at I^{**}, $\frac{\partial X^*}{\partial I}>0$ and the sensitivity of $G(.)$ with respect to X relative to its sensitivity with respect to $E(u_d)$and $E(u_c)$ is sufficiently large.

Note that $\frac{\partial E(u_d)}{\partial I}|_{I=I^{**}}<0$ *and* $\frac{\partial E(u_c)}{\partial I}|_{I=I^{**}}<0$. Therefore, since $\frac{\partial G}{E(u_d)}|_{I=I^{**}}>0$ *and* $\frac{\partial G}{E(u_c)}|_{I=I^{**}}>0$, if $\frac{\partial X}{\partial I}|_{I=I^{**}}>0$, then for (4.32) to hold, $\frac{\partial G}{\partial X}|_{I=I^{**}}>0$ must be satisfied.

If, for example, $G(E(u_c);E(u_d);(x_c+x_d))=G((x_c+x_d))$, then (both in the perfectly and imperfectly discriminating contests) a sufficient condition for the proposition to hold is that $\frac{\partial X^*}{\partial I}|_{I=I^{**}}>0$.[14] Recall that under the perfectly discriminating contest, the all-pay auction, the total amount of resources invested in the contest under the proposals of the interest groups will be zero. Therefore, if the politician wishes to obtain payments, he or she must propose a policy that is more extreme than that of the interest groups.

As we can see, in the above condition, the effect of a change in the proposed policy on the lobbying efforts of the contenders plays an important role. In general, the effect of a change in the proposed policy I on X^* is ambiguous in the imperfectly discriminating contest while it is positive in the all-pay auction. The role of stake-asymmetry and ability-asymmetry between the interest groups in determining the sign of $\frac{\partial X^*}{\partial I}$ is clarified in Epstein and Nitzan (2006b).[15] A simple sufficient condition ensuring that the total lobby-

---

14 For example, in the case of monopoly price determination, if the demand is given by: $p=1-q$, the marginal cost equals zero and the CSF is Tullock's lottery logit function, the monopoly profit-maximization price is equal to 0.5 while the price that maximizes the total lobbying efforts incurred by the contestants is equal to 0.575426.

15 Note that asymmetry in the contestants' ability depends on the form of the CSF and, in particular, on its second order cross derivatives. However, it also depends on the stakes of the interest groups because these cross derivatives are computed in equilibrium, which is affected by the stakes.

ing outlays are monotone increasing in the policy set by the politician is stated in terms of the relative stakes and the relative stake elasticities of the interest groups.[16]

In the above models, the lobbying efforts of the interest groups are directed to the politicians at the second stage of approval or rejection of the proposed policy. Alternatively, the interest groups could lobby the politician at the first stage in order to influence his proposed policy. In general, the interest groups may wish to influence both the proposed policy and the probability of its approval and therefore allocate their lobbying efforts between the two stages. In such alternative lobbying models, as long as the proposed policy or the approval of the proposed policy remain uncertain from the viewpoint of the interest groups, the main insight of the present study is basically preserved. Uncertainty regarding the contest outcome and a policy maker who is a 'principal' are the basic modeling features necessary for the existence of non-compromising lobbying. The sufficient conditions require appropriate relative commitments of the politician to the enhancement of the well-being of the interest groups and to the increase of the lobbying outlays and appropriate relative stakes and relative stake elasticities of the interest groups that ensure the positive effect of a change in the proposed policy on the total lobbying efforts. Therefore, we find that if the government is not directly involved in the determination of the proposals (as in Epstein and Nitzan 2004 [2008]), then moderation of the proposals will occur; however, if the government is involved directly in determining the proposal, then we have shown sufficient conditions for polarization.

The analysis has been confined to a reduced-form, very simple public-policy contest that has micro-foundations for both the imperfectly discriminating contest and the discriminating contest – the all-pay auction. Despite its simplicity, this stylized setting is sufficient to illustrate that the compromise-enhancing effect of lobbying is not necessarily valid when the policy maker, the politician in our case, is a 'principal' rather than an 'agent'. As is well known from other models of special-interest politics, institutional details – such as the number of candidates, the number of interest groups, the voting rule, the amendment rules, the procedures for government formation and dissolution – can have a marked effect on outcomes. This has been demonstrated here regarding the effect of lobbying on the nature of the equilibrium public policy.

4.6 CONCLUDING REMARKS

This chapter has viewed the creation of a contest between interest groups as endogenous. A government's random behavior can be rationalized both when it acts randomly, as in the standard influence activities, lobbying or rent-seeking models, and when it acts rationally in setting the agenda (making policy proposals) and randomly in approving or rejecting these proposals. We used for illustration the most commonly studied CSFs; the Hillman-Samet all-pay auction and two types of logit functions, Tullock's simple discriminating lottery function and Tullock's generalized lottery function.

[16] In the context of monopoly regulation (Epstein and Nitzan 2003), the sufficient condition is satisfied, so an increase in the proposed price increases the total lobbying expenditure of the interest groups.

This chapter has described how lobbying affects the choice of the agenda – the policies that lobbyists favor or oppose. A two-stage model has shown how a proposed policy is determined and then lobbying takes place. For example, in the first stage, interest groups may choose to lobby for a particular policy and, then, in a second stage, engage in a lobbying contest over the proposed policies.

Using as a benchmark a status quo policy that is the preferred policy of one interest group (the status quo defender) when there is no opposition, we showed that the status quo is not an equilibrium strategy of 'the defender'. Likewise, the equilibrium proposal of 'the challenger' differs from his optimal proposal when he does not face opposition. Both interest groups choose more moderate positions. Hence, competition over endogenously determined policies can reduce polarization and, in turn, wasteful lobbying activities. Such competition would not result, however, in a (strategic) compromise where the two interest groups share the same equilibrium proposal and so entirely avoid the expenditure of wasteful resources.

We considered the case in which a government determines policy subject to lobbying. We showed that the policy determined by the government may increase polarization in a contest, by letting the interest groups determine the policy for which they will compete.

Overall, the policy-contest literature demonstrates that the effects of anticipated rent seeking on the policy proposals put forward by interest groups and governments should not be ignored.

REFERENCES

Aidt, Toke S. (2003), 'Redistribution and deadweight cost: the role of political competition', *European Journal of Political Economy*, **19**(2), 205–26.

Appelbaum, Elie and Eliakim Katz (1986), 'Transfer seeking and avoidance: on the full social costs of rent seeking', *Public Choice*, **48**(2), 175–81.

Appelbaum, Elie and Eliakim Katz (1987), 'Seeking rents by setting rents: the political economy of rent seeking', *Economic Journal*, **97**(387), 685–699, reprinted in Roger D. Congleton, Arye L. Hillman and Kai A. Konrad (eds) (2008), *40 Years of Research on Rent Seeking 1 – The Theory of Rent Seeking*, Heidelberg: Springer, pp. 555–69.

Baik, Kyung H. (1999), 'Rent-seeking firms, consumer groups and the social costs of monopoly', *Economic Inquiry*, **37**(3), 542–54.

Becker, Gary S. (1983), 'A theory of competition among pressure groups for political influence', *Quarterly Journal of Economics*, **98**(3), 371–400.

Besley, Timothy and Stephen Coate (1997), 'An economic model of representative democracy', *Quarterly Journal of Economics*, **112**(1), 85–114.

Besley, Timothy and Stephen Coate (2001), 'Lobbying and welfare in a representative democracy', *Review of Economic Studies*, **68**(1), 67–82.

Boeri, Tito, Gordon Hanson and Barry McCormick (eds) (2002), *Immigration Policy and the Welfare System*, Oxford: Oxford University Press.

Congleton, Roger D. (1986), 'Rent-seeking aspects of political advertising', *Public Choice*, **49**(3), 249–63, reprinted in Roger D. Congleton, Arye L. Hillman and Kai A. Konrad (eds) (2008), *40 Years of Research on Rent Seeking 2 – Applications: Rent Seeking in Practice*, Heidelberg: Springer, pp. 297–311.

Congleton, Roger D. (1988), 'Evaluating rent-seeking losses: do the welfare gains of lobbyists count?', *Public Choice*, **56**(2), 181–4.

Congleton, Roger D. (1991), 'Ideological conviction and persuasion in the rent-seeking society', *Journal of Public Economics*, **44**(1), 65–86, reprinted in Roger D. Congleton, Arye L. Hillman and Kai A. Konrad (eds) (2008), *40 Years of Research on Rent Seeking 2 – Applications: Rent Seeking in Practice*, Heidelberg: Springer, pp. 769–90.

Congleton, Roger D. and Sanghack Lee (2009), 'Efficient mercantilism? Revenue-maximizing monopoly policies as Ramsey taxation', *European Journal of Political Economy*, **25**(1), 102–14.

Ellingsen, Tore (1991), 'Strategic buyers and the social cost of monopoly', *American Economic Review*, **81**(3), 648–57, reprinted in Roger D. Congleton, Arye L. Hillman and Kai A. Konrad (eds) (2008), *40 Years of Research on Rent Seeking 1 – The Theory of Rent Seeking*, Heidelberg: Springer, pp. 399–408.

Epstein, Gil S. and Shmuel Nitzan (2002), 'Endogenous public policy, politicization and welfare', *Journal of Public Economic Theory*, **4**(4), 661–77.

Epstein, Gil S. and Shmuel Nitzan (2003), 'The social cost of rent seeking when consumer opposition influences monopoly behavior', *European Journal of Political Economy*, **19**(1), 61–9.

Epstein, Gil S. and Shmuel Nitzan (2004), 'Strategic restraint in contests', *European Economic Review*, **48**(1), 201–10, reprinted in Roger D. Congleton, Arye L. Hillman and Kai A. Konrad (eds) (2008), *40 Years of Research on Rent Seeking 1 – The Theory of Rent Seeking*, Heidelberg: Springer, pp. 421–30.

Epstein, Gil S. and Shmuel Nitzan (2006a), 'Lobbying and compromise', *Public Choice*, **126**(3–4), 317–30.

Epstein, Gil S. and Shmuel Nitzan (2006b), 'Effort and performance in public-policy contests', *Journal of Public Economic Theory*, **8**(2), 265–82.

Epstein, Gil S. and Shmuel Nitzan (2006c), 'The politics of randomness', *Social Choice and Welfare*, **27**(2), 423–33.

Epstein, Gil S. and Shmuel Nitzan (2007), *Endogenous Public Policy and Contests*, Heidelberg: Springer.

Esteban, Joan and Debraj Ray (1999), 'Conflict and distribution', *Journal of Economic Theory*, **87**(2), 379–415.

Fabella, Raul V. (1995), 'The social cost of rent seeking under countervailing opposition to distortionary transfers', *Journal of Public Economics*, **57**(2), 235–47.

Felli, Leonardo and Antonio Merlo (2001), 'Endogenous lobbying', Working Paper No. 291, CESifo, Munich.

Glazer, Amihai and Henry McMillan (1992), 'Pricing by the firm under regulatory threats', *Quarterly Journal of Economics*, **107**(3), 1089–99.

Glazer, Amihai, Mark Gradstein and Kai A. Konrad (1998), 'The electoral politics of extreme policies', *Economic Journal*, **108**(451), 1677–85.

Gradstein, Mark (2002), 'Can the pursuit of rents grease the wheels of the economy? Allocative benefits of rent seeking', Unpublished paper, Department of Economics, Ben-Gurion University of the Negev, Beer Sheva.

Grossman, Gene M. and Elhanan Helpman (1994), 'Protection for sale', *American Economic Review*, **84**(4), 833–50, reprinted in Roger D. Congleton, Arye L. Hillman and Kai A. Konrad (eds) (2008), *40 Years of Research on Rent Seeking 2 – Applications: Rent Seeking in Practice*, Heidelberg: Springer, pp. 131–48.

Grossman, Gene M. and Elhanan Helpman (1996), 'Electoral competition and special interest politics', *Review of Economic Studies*, **63**(2), 265–86.

Grossman, Gene M. and Elhanan Helpman (2001), *Special Interest Politics*, Cambridge, MA: MIT Press.

Hillman, Arye L. (1982), 'Declining industries and political-support protectionist motives', *American Economic Review*, **72**(2), 1180–87, reprinted in Wilfred J. Ethier and Arye L. Hillman (eds) (2008), *The WTO and the Political Economy of Trade Policy*, Aldershot, UK and Brookfield, VT, USA: Edward Elgar Publishing, pp. 43–50.

Hillman, Arye L. (2013), 'Rent seeking', in Michael Reksulak, Laura Razzolini and William F. Shughart II (eds), *The Elgar Companion to Public Choice*, 2nd edn, Cheltenham, UK and Northampton, MA, USA: Edward Elgar Publishing, pp. 307–30.

Hillman, Arye L. and John G. Riley (1989), 'Politically contestable rents and transfers', *Economics and Politics*, **1**(1), 17–39, reprinted in Roger D. Congleton, Arye L. Hillman and Kai A. Konrad (eds) (2008), *40 Years of Research on Rent Seeking 1 – The Theory of Rent Seeking*, Heidelberg: Springer, pp. 185–207.

Hillman, Arye L. and Dov Samet (1987), 'Dissipation of rents and revenues in small numbers contests', *Public Choice*, **54**(1), 63–82, reprinted in Roger D. Congleton, Arye L. Hillman and Kai A. Konrad (eds) (2008), *40 Years of Research on Rent Seeking 1 – The Theory of Rent Seeking*, Heidelberg: Springer, pp. 165–84.

Hillman, Arye L. and Heinrich W. Ursprung (1988), 'Domestic politics, foreign interests, and international trade policy', *American Economic Review*, **78**(4), 729–45, reprinted in Roger D. Congleton, Arye L. Hillman and Kai A. Konrad (eds) (2008), *40 Years of Research on Rent Seeking 2 – Applications: Rent Seeking in Practice*, Heidelberg: Springer, pp. 113–29.

Kroszner, Randall S. and Phillip E. Strahan (1999), 'What drives deregulation? Economics and politics of the relaxation of bank branching restrictions', *Quarterly Journal of Economics*, **114**(4), 1437–67.

Lagerlof, John (1997), 'Lobbying, information, and private and social welfare', *European Journal of Political Economy*, **13**(3), 615–37.

Leidy, Michael P. (1994), 'Rent dissipation through self-regulation: the social cost of monopoly under the threat of reform', *Public Choice*, **80**(1–2), 105–28.

Lockard, Alan and Gordon Tullock (2001), *Efficient Rent Seeking: Chronicle of an Intellectual Quagmire*, Boston, MA: Kluwer.

Long, Ngo Van (2013), 'The theory of contests: a unified model and review of the literature', *European Journal of Political Economy*, **32**, 161–81, reprinted in Chapter 3, this volume.

Munster, Johannes (2006), 'Lobbying contests with endogenous policy proposals', *Economics and Politics*, **18**(3), 389–97.

Nitzan, Shmuel (1994), 'Modelling rent-seeking contests', *European Journal of Political Economy*, **10**(1), 41–60.

Peltzman, Sam (1976), 'Toward a more general theory of regulation', *Journal of Law and Economics*, **19**(2), 211–40.

Persson, Torsten and Guido Tabellini (2000), *Political Economics: Explaining Economic Policy*, Cambridge, MA: MIT Press.

Schmidt, Torsten (1992), 'Rent-seeking firms and consumers: an equilibrium analysis', *Economics and Politics*, **4**(2), 137–49.

Skaperdas, Stergios (1996), 'Contest success functions', *Economic Theory*, **7**(2), 283–90, reprinted in Roger D. Congleton, Arye L. Hillman and Kai A. Konrad (eds) (2008), *40 Years of Research on Rent Seeking 1 – The Theory of Rent Seeking*, Heidelberg: Springer, pp. 263–70.

Tullock, Gordon (1980), 'Efficient rent seeking', in James M. Buchanan, Robert D. Tollison and Gordon Tullock (eds), *Toward a Theory of the Rent-seeking Society*, College Station, TX: Texas A&M Press, pp. 97–112, reprinted in Roger D. Congleton, Arye L. Hillman and Kai A. Konrad (eds) (2008), *40 Years of Research on Rent Seeking 1 – The Theory of Rent Seeking*, Heidelberg: Springer, pp. 105–20.

5. Asymmetries in rent seeking

Giuseppe Dari-Mattiacci, Eric Langlais, Bruno Lovat and Francesco Parisi

SUMMARY

In rent-seeking contests, players are seldom identical. In this chapter, we review the rent-seeking literature that explores the effects of forms of asymmetry between contestants. We consider Tullock's rent-seeking contests involving two players who differ in strength (marginal returns to effort), motivation (valuations of the sought-after rent) and cunning (bargaining power). The combined interaction of these three forms of asymmetry in rent seeking are described. We examine how these asymmetries affect the rent-seeking contest and investigate the effect of *ex post* trading opportunities on the players' efforts and probabilities of winning and on the social costs of rent seeking.

5.1 INTRODUCTION

In real-world competitive contests, players are rarely identical. Just like other competitive scenarios, rent-seeking contests are seldom symmetric. Players, more often than not, exhibit non-trivial differences with respect to their competitive abilities, resources and costs, motivation, bargaining power and the like. The rent-seeking literature has analyzed the effects of players' asymmetric characteristics in isolation. In this chapter, we review the existing literature, contributing to the understanding of the effect of various asymmetries in rent seeking. We consider the interaction between various forms of asymmetries and we organize ideas around three relevant characteristics: strength, motivation and cunning. We use the term 'strength' to refer to a player's marginal returns to effort: effort by a strong player increases his or her probability of winning more than the effort of a weak player. 'Motivation' refers to a player's valuation of the prize at stake: motivated players value the price more than unmotivated players. Both strength and motivation have relevance for the rent-seeking phase of the game. When rents are tradable, the players enter a second phase in which they can negotiate over who gets the rent. Typically, the motivated player buys the rent from his unmotivated counterpart. In this phase, strength plays no role and is replaced by 'cunning', a player's ability to strike a better deal: his negotiating abilities and bargaining power.

This chapter is organized as follows. In Section 5.2, we discuss various examples of asymmetries in the existing literature. Literature on non-tradable rents has studied the effect of players' asymmetries in strength and motivation (or both), while the literature on tradable rents has focused on the role of cunning for players with asymmetric motivation. In Section 5.3, we look at some of the interactions between various asymmetries, introducing a two-player rent-seeking model with and without opportunity for resale.

We study the players' efforts and probabilities of winning and the social costs of rent seeking. In Section 5.4, we compare the results of the rent-seeking games discussed in the previous sections. More specifically, in Section 5.5 we consider whether the introduction of *ex post* trading opportunities exacerbates or mitigates the effect of asymmetries between players, looking at the effect of *ex post* trade on *ex ante* incentives to exert effort in the primary contest. In Section 5.6, in order to set some landmarks for the study of the combined effects of strength, motivation and cunning, we introduce the notions of balanced rent seeking and fair negotiations. In balanced rent seeking, one player's strength perfectly offsets the other player's motivation. With fair negotiations, a player's cunning in the negotiation phase compensates for his lack of strength in the rent-seeking phase. In Section 5.7, we conclude with some additional analysis and policy considerations.

5.2 ASYMMETRIES IN THE LITERATURE

Tullock's (1980 [2008]) seminal paper and much of the early rent-seeking literature considered a wide array of rent-seeking contests in which contestants were identical to one another. It is only with more recent contributions starting in the late 1980s that the effects of specific forms of asymmetry between the contestants began to draw the attention of rent-seeking scholars.[1]

In the basic rent-seeking setting, players compete for the appropriation of a rent, which cannot be transferred *ex post* between players. In this chapter, we shall refer to this underlying assumption as 'non-tradable rent'. The literature that assumes non-tradable rents focuses its attention on the players' asymmetries in strength and motivation. The reason for this focus is that when rents are non-tradable, the players' motivation is fully at work: a high-valuing player who loses the contest cannot subsequently acquire the rent from the winner. Without an *ex post* trading opportunity, however, differences in the parties' bargaining power have no effect on rent-seeking incentives. Within this body of literature, Allard (1988) is the first contribution to introduce the possibility of differences among players in a rent-seeking game, while an earlier contribution by Harris and Vickers (1985) studied sequential investments by two asymmetric parties in a race. Differences in the parties' strength are generally modeled as parameters added to the rent-seeking return functions or cost functions. These asymmetric parameters can affect the effectiveness of the parties' efforts, denoted by the coefficients preceding their effort levels, and the returns to scale in their efforts, denoted by the exponents of the parties' effort levels. Baik (1994, 2004) is an example of the former formulation of the problem, in which different strength is modeled as a parameter (under the form of a coefficient that multiplies the effort of a party), so that the share of party A is $\frac{sA}{sA+B}$ with $s > 0$. In this model players exhibit different strength, as well as different motivation, which is

[1] Literature on non-tradable rents has studied the effect of players' asymmetries in strength (Allard 1988; Kohli and Singh 1999; Singh and Wittman 2001; Bennour 2009) and motivation (Hillman and Riley 1989; Leininger 1993; Hurley 1998; Nti 1998, 1999 [2008]; Matros 2006) or both (Baik 1994, 2004; Nitzan 1994; Stein 2002), while the literature on tradable rents has focused on the role of cunning for players with asymmetric motivation (Suen 1989; Dari-Mattiacci et al. 2009).

modeled by allowing the value of the rent to vary between the players. One of Baik's results is that more strength can compensate the effect of more motivation.[2] The model developed in Section 5.3 is an example of asymmetries in the parties' returns to scale, denoted by the exponents of the parties' effort levels, such that the share of party A is $\frac{A^a}{A^a + B^b}$ where $a \neq b$. A third way in which differences in the parties' strength have been modeled in the rent-seeking literature can be found in Ryvkin (2007), who models differences in strength as a difference in the cost parameter: asymmetric players face different (constant) marginal costs of effort. Finally, Cornes and Hartley (2005) model different strength, with a general implicit function of effort, to study existence and uniqueness of equilibria and rent dissipation.

The rent-seeking literature has considered the effects of asymmetric players' motivation on rent-seeking behavior, by modeling players with different valuations of the sought-after rents. Most notably, Hillman and Riley (1989) show that asymmetric valuations inhibit the participation of low-valuing contenders. Their application of the model focuses on political-influence contests and provides a possible explanation for several stylized facts in the empirical literature, including the fact that only small numbers of players actively participate in lobbying and that political markets to exercise political influence are similarly concentrated.[3] Leininger (1993) formulated a model with players with different rent valuations, focusing on the effect of sequential moves. Stein (2002) and Matros (2006) subsequently considered the effect of differences in rent valuations on rent-seeking expenditures, in the context of an N-player model. In Matros (2006), valuations of the players varied across players. The author showed that one of the results of Tullock's (1980) analysis did not hold when asymmetries in valuation were taken into consideration. Similar to the conventional result, total rent dissipation increased in N and individual winning probabilities decreased in N. Differently from the conventional result, individual rent-seeking efforts could under certain conditions actually increase (rather than decrease, as in Tullock 1980 [2008]), with the addition of a player. Stein (2002) models rent-seeking contests in which players exhibit different motivation and strength. Strength is modeled as in Baik (1994) and he extends the results to consider N-player contests.[4] The paper shows that rent dissipation increases in the valuation of each player. A player's expenditure increases in his own valuation. Both players' efforts increase in the valuation of the highest-valuing player. An increase in a player's valuation makes his probability of winning and his payoff increase, but makes the probability of winning and the payoff of the other player decrease. A similar effect of strength is

---

[2] Kohli and Singh (1999) model a rent-seeking contest with players with different strength, as in Baik (1994), and combine asymmetry in strength with endogenous rent formation and multiple periods. Bennour (2009) models differences in the parties' strength as in Baik (1994), analyzing the likelihood of conflict in a predator-prey setting. Singh and Wittman (2001) present a model with asymmetric strength, in which the information about strength is private. Their focus is more closely related to the literature on contest design and auctions than to the standard rent-seeking literature. Stein and Rapoport (2004) study asymmetric contests with two stages.

[3] Nitzan's (1994) survey of rent-seeking models includes a review of the prior literature on asymmetric valuations and strength.

[4] Runkel (2006) also models a rent-seeking contest in which players exhibit different valuations of the rent and different strength, but strength is modeled with an implicit function, not with parameters of Tullock's standard return function.

revealed. Nti (2004) develops a model with asymmetric valuations, showing that efforts may be reduced when players with different rent valuations participate in a contest.[5] Nti approaches the problem from the point of view of contest design – aimed at maximizing contestants' effort, rather than minimizing rent dissipation – hence suggesting the use of value-weighted contenders (discounting the effort of the high-valuation player) in order to induce him to make greater effort.[6]

The effect of differences in the parties' valuations is not limited to parties' rent-seeking incentives. When valuations are asymmetric, a new dimension of the rent-seeking context acquires relevance: allocative efficiency. In the absence of *ex post* markets, when a low-valuing contestant appropriates the rent, an allocative loss arises. Hurley (1998) modeled rent-seeking contests with players with different valuations, introducing the notion of contest efficiency as an alternative to the traditional measure of rent dissipation. When examining contests with asymmetric valuations, the criteria for evaluating the outcomes of the contest should also include contest efficiency – defined as the measure of the maximum obtainable benefit captured by the contestants. The allocative gains may offset rent dissipation, such that a contest may be more efficient notwithstanding the greater rent-seeking expenditures incurred by the parties.

In our analysis, we shall extend the standard model to look at the effects of *ex post* transfer opportunities on the parties' rent-seeking incentives. We shall refer to this alternative setting as 'tradable rents'. The literature on tradable rents has instead focused on the role of cunning for players with asymmetric motivation. Suen (1989) considers differences in strength (modeled as a cost of exerting effort) and valuations; the model is not a traditional Tullock contest but a model of waiting; the model also includes a trading phase where trading does not necessarily reduce dissipation. Dari-Mattiacci et al. (2009) analyze the effect of an *ex post* market in Tullock's traditional rent-seeking game by allowing the parties' valuations to differ. In the first stage, contestants compete to appropriate the rent; in the second stage, if a misallocation occurs (that is, the low-valuing contestant wins the rent), the winner can resell the rent to the loser. The authors focus on the *ex ante* effects of a secondary market on efforts, payoffs, rent dissipation and rent misallocation, showing that tradable rents have a double-edge effect. *Ex post* markets correct possible misallocations but may exacerbate rent dissipation. In some situations, the increase in rent dissipation more than offsets the allocative advantage of the *ex post* trade – the availability of a secondary market might actually reduce welfare. In this chapter, we build on their setup to study the interaction of strength, motivation and cunning in the case of asymmetric players with resale opportunities.

The results of the asymmetric rent-seeking literature (and the interaction of different forms of asymmetry) are important for the understanding of real life contests among

---

[5] Nti (1998, 1999 [2008]) had previously developed a model with asymmetric valuations, considering the existence of equilibria in pure strategies.

[6] There is a wide array of related literature that falls outside the traditional framing of the rent-seeking problem, but which is worthy of mention. Donohue and Levitt (1998) model a contest with asymmetric players and imperfect information where parties are allowed to exit the contest. They do not use Tullock's success function, but interestingly highlight the effect of an exit option on players' strategies. Hirshleifer (2001) similarly analyzes several models in which asymmetries between players are important, but often uses a different success function from Tullock's.

asymmetric players, when the players differ in more than one characteristic. We study how these asymmetries affect the rent-seeking game, comparing the outcomes obtained in the presence of secondary markets, or lack thereof, where rents can be reallocated after the contest (tradable versus non-tradable rents). In particular, we focus on the players' efforts and probabilities of winning and on the social costs of the rent-seeking game. With non-tradable rents we consider rent dissipation – the sum of the players' efforts – and rent misallocation – the probability that the unmotivated, low-valuing player wins the contest times the difference in the valuations. With tradable rents, misallocation disappears and only rent dissipation constitutes a social cost. We look at whether opening trade increases or reduces the total social costs. The three characteristics that we consider play different roles in a rent-seeking contest. Strength and cunning are advantages that become relevant at different stages of the game. Strength is relevant in the rent-seeking stage (primary market), while cunning is relevant in the reallocation stage (secondary market). Motivation instead is an advantage that consists of the larger surplus that is obtainable by one of the parties. The effect of motivation is relevant in both stages of the game, although its effect differs depending on whether trade is allowed or not. To put the model used in this chapter in the context of the existing literature, we should note that although strength is usually modeled as in Baik (1994), as a multiplier of the effort of one of the parties, we use Tullock's exponent. Further, asymmetry in valuation is usually said to reduce dissipation (Hillman and Riley 1989); we show that by adding the rent misallocation loss, the maximum total social loss remains constant, with and without asymmetry. We finally show that the maximum total social loss is less with tradable rents in general.

5.3 RENT SEEKING WITH ASYMMETRIC PLAYERS

In the traditional Tullock rent-seeking game,[7] two parties compete to appropriate a rent of common value $V > 0$ (which motivates the parties to play) by investing each a non-negative amount of effort denoted by A (he) and B (she), respectively. The rent is shared according to the now classic Tullock success function $Q_A = \frac{A^r}{A^r + B^r}$ for party A and $Q_B = \frac{B^r}{A^r + B^r}$ for party B. We can alternatively interpret these shares as probabilities to obtain the entire rent. The exponent $r > 0$ indicates the parties' returns to effort (their strength). With $r < 1$ parties have decreasing returns to effort, which implies that the party who exerts more effort obtains a less than proportional increase in his or her share of the rent; that is, if A invests more than B, then the ratio of their shares in the rent is $\frac{Q_A}{Q_B} = (\frac{A}{B})^r < \frac{A}{B}$, giving A a less than proportional return to his or her effort. With $r = 1$ parties have constant returns to effort and the rent is shared proportionally to the parties investments and $\frac{Q_A}{Q_B} = \frac{A}{B}$. Finally, with $r > 1$ parties have increasing returns to effort so that the party exerting more effort obtains a more than proportional advantage; if, for instance, A exerts more effort than B, we have $\frac{Q_A}{Q_B} = (\frac{A}{B})^r > \frac{A}{B}$. The parties' return-to-effort exponent determines their incentives to exert effort and hence the amount of resources that will be dissipated in total in the rent-seeking contest. The standard result is that

[7] Tullock (1980 [2008], 1985), Tollison (1982), Rowley et al. (1988) and Lockard and Tullock (2001).

total rent dissipation – that is, the sum of the parties' investments in rent seeking – will be equal to $\frac{r}{2}V$, that is, it will increase in the parties' return to effort and in their valuation of the rent.[8] Thus, stronger (higher r) and more motivated (higher V) parties exert more effort. Since the sought-after rent has the same value for both contestants, *ex post* resale opportunities are not considered in this framework.

This basic framework considers identical parties and will be extended in three directions in order to consider as many dimensions along which parties can differ. The first dimension concerns the parties' strength. While the traditional Tullock game assumes that parties have the same strength (return-to-effort exponent) r, we will consider here parties with different levels of strength a and b, respectively. Therefore, the rent will be shared according to the parties' strength and Tullock's success functions become $S_A = \frac{A^a}{A^a + B^b}$ and $S_B = \frac{B^b}{A^a + B^b}$. We will say that A is stronger than B if $a > b$ and vice versa.

Note also that with different levels of strength, the interpretation of the exponents a and b as returns to effort is not as straightforward as with r. In fact, in this case the ratio of the parties' shares is $\frac{S_A}{S_B} = \frac{A^a}{B^b}$ and it is no longer true that the share in the rent of the party investing more is more or less than proportional to his or her effort depending on whether that party's strength is greater or less than 1. In fact, this relationship also depends on the other party's strength in a rather complex way. To preserve the traditional interpretation it is therefore necessary to examine how the ratio of the parties' shares in the rent changes if effort changes. For instance, if party A increases his or her effort, the ratio changes in his or her favor at a decreasing rate if $a < 1$, at a constant rate if $a = 1$ and at an increasing rate if $a > 1$. These results hold symmetrically true for party B.[9] Therefore, we can speak of the parties' asymmetric levels of strength in the same way as in the traditional Tullock framework.

The second departure from the traditional framework consists of allowing the parties to have different valuations for the rent, so that party A values the rent at V_A and party B values it at V_B, that is, they have different motivations to exert effort. Introducing differences in motivation has two sizable effects. Motivation changes the parties' incentives to exert effort in a similar way as strength does, so that we expect strong motivated parties to be willing to invest more than weak unmotivated contestants. Yet, motivation has also an additional and possibly more radical effect on the rent-seeking game. Since parties attach different values to the rent, it is in theory possible – and even socially desirable – that a low-valuing winner of the contest will sell the rent to the high-valuing loser. Differences in valuations open the door to a secondary market for rents, which cannot be conceived in the traditional, homogeneous-valuation framework.

Analyzing the case of *ex post* resale of the rent makes it possible to introduce a third dimension of asymmetry: the parties' cunning, that is, their ability to obtain a more

8 The usual condition is $0 < r \leq 2$, which guarantees that the sum of the parties' efforts does not exceed the value of the rent and hence gives pure-strategy solutions.

9 Formally, we have $\frac{\partial}{\partial A}\left(\frac{A^a}{B^b}\right) = \frac{aA^{a-1}}{B^b} > 0$ and $\frac{\partial^2}{\partial A^2}\left(\frac{A^a}{B^b}\right) = (a-1)\frac{aA^{a-2}}{B^b}$, which is less than, equal to or greater than zero depending on whether $a < 1$, $a = 1$ or $a > 1$, respectively. The same holds symmetrically for B: $\frac{\partial}{\partial B}\left(\frac{B^b}{A^a}\right) = \frac{bB^{b-1}}{A^a} > 0$ and $\frac{\partial^2}{\partial B^2}\left(\frac{B^b}{A^a}\right) = (b-1)\frac{bB^{b-2}}{A^a}$. The case with $a = b = r$ can be seen as a special case of this more general framework. See Dari-Mattiacci and Parisi (2014) for a discussion of the possible interpretations of the returns to effort in rent-seeking games.

favorable price during the negotiations. This asymmetry can be easily represented by the resale price P. By hypothesis, the price will have to lie somewhere between the higher valuation – which determines the maximum price that the high-valuing party is willing to pay for the rent – and the lower valuation – which determines the minimum price that the low-valuing party is willing to accept. While strength and motivation were introduced as absolute characteristics of the parties, cunning is necessarily a relative notion: a high price means that the low-valuing seller is more cunning – a more seasoned negotiator – than the high-valuing buyer and, vice versa, a low price indicates that the high-valuing party has the upper hand during the negotiation.

The presence of a trading phase after the rent-seeking phase of the game is important for social welfare as well as for the parties' incentives. Knowing that he can buy the rent *ex post* might reduce the incentives of the high-valuing party, while making the low-valuing party implicitly more motivated by the resale opportunity. In fact, the availability of trade removes the asymmetry in motivation and replaces it with an asymmetry in cunning, which operates in a markedly different way. To anticipate one of the aspects of rent seeking with resale, parties with different valuations play a symmetric game due to the fact that the rent is now implicitly valued at its resale price by both contestants. In the following, we study the consequences of asymmetries in strength, motivation and cunning for the parties and for society. In the analysis we focus exclusively on the characteristics of pure-strategy Nash equilibria. Each subsection is closed with a proposition summarizing the main results. All propositions are restricted to pure-strategy equilibria.[10] We start with non-tradable rents.

5.3.1 Non-tradable Rents

We consider two rent-seeking contestants, A and B, who differ in their strength and motivation. Without loss of generality, throughout this chapter we assume $V_A > V_B$, that is, we assume that player A values the sought-after rent more than player B and is thus the more motivated player. Instead, we allow either player to be stronger than the other; with $a > b$ the more motivated player A is also stronger; with $a = b$ players have equal strength; and with $a < b$ the less motivated player B is stronger than the more motivated A. The contestants earn the following expected payoffs from the game: $U_A = \frac{A^a}{A^a + B^b} V_A - A$ and $U_B = \frac{B^b}{A^a + B^b} V_B - B$, respectively. We denote the parties' probabilities of winning as $S_A = \frac{A^a}{A^a + B^b}$ and $S_B = \frac{B^b}{A^a + B^b}$, so that we can rewrite the parties' payoffs more concisely as $U_A = S_A V_A - A$ and $U_B = S_B V_B - B$. The parties choose their levels of rent-seeking efforts independently of each other in order to maximize their payoffs. The first order conditions for this maximization problem yield the following implicit relationships between the parties' equilibrium levels of effort and their strength and motivation – an asterisk denotes equilibrium values:

$$A^* = aS_A^* S_B^* V_A \tag{5.1}$$

$$B^* = bS_A^* S_B^* V_B$$

[10] On mixed-strategy equilibria, see Dari-Mattiacci et al. (2007) and references therein.

By some simple manipulations of (5.1) we have[11] $S_A^* S_B^* = \frac{A^*}{aV_A} = \frac{B^*}{bV_B} \leq \frac{1}{4}$, which confirms a well-known result in the symmetric case: in a pure-strategy equilibrium, the players' efforts are bounded by $A^* \leq \frac{a}{4}V_A$ and $B^* \leq \frac{b}{4}V_B$. Yet, levels of effort satisfying first order conditions constitute a pure-strategy equilibrium only if they lead to non-negative payoffs for the parties, since it is always possible for a party to exert no effort and earn a payoff equal to zero.[12] This condition[13] yields an upper boundary for the parties' shares in equilibrium:

$$S_A^* \leq \frac{1}{b}$$

$$S_B^* \leq \frac{1}{a} \tag{5.2}$$

Since $S_A = 1 - S_B$, these conditions imply that in a pure-strategy equilibrium the parties' shares cannot be excessively far away from each other. In a sense, for parties to play a pure-strategy equilibrium the outcome must be somewhat fair. The conditions above are satisfied for any value of A and B if both a and b are less than 1, that is, when both parties have decreasing marginal returns to effort (no economies of scale in rent-seeking effort), the first order conditions are sufficient to identify a pure-strategy equilibrium.[14] Yet, if this is not the case, some outcomes that satisfy the first order conditions lead to too extreme a sharing of the rent and do not constitute a pure-strategy equilibrium.[15]

A player's equilibrium payoff increases in his own valuation and strength but decreases in the valuation and strength of the other player;[16] hence the conditions above put some limits to the values of the strength parameters. Since the sum of the parties' shares in the rent is equal to 1, the conditions in (5.2) can be simultaneously satisfied only if $\frac{1}{a} + \frac{1}{b} \geq 1$, which can be rewritten as

---

11 The inequality follows from the fact that $S_A^* + S_B^* = 1$ and hence the maximum of $S_A^* S_B^*$ is reached when players face equal probabilities of winning, $S_A^* = S_B^* = \frac{1}{2}$.

12 $\frac{\partial U_A}{\partial A} = \frac{a}{A} S_A S_B V_A - 1 = 0$ and $\frac{\partial U_B}{\partial B} = \frac{b}{B} S_A S_B V_B - 1 = 0$. An alternative way to define Nash equilibria is to assume that there are minimum levels of the parties' efforts and to look for mixed-strategy equilibria. See Dari-Mattiacci et al. (2007).

13 Using (5.1) and noting that $S_A = 1 - S_B$, we have that payoffs are non-negative ($U_A \geq 0$ and $U_B \geq 0$) if and only if $S_A^* V_A \geq a S_A^* S_B^* V_A \Leftrightarrow S_B^* \leq \frac{1}{a}$ and $S_B^* V_B \geq b S_A^* S_B^* V_B \Leftrightarrow S_A^* \leq \frac{1}{b}$.

14 Yet, this condition does not guarantee the existence of values of the parties' efforts that satisfy the first order conditions. For the case in which A is stronger and obtains the rent with a greater probability than B, the general condition for the existence and uniqueness of a pure-strategy Nash equilibrium is $(\frac{aV_A}{4})^a \geq (\frac{bV_B}{4})^b$, if $b < a \leq 1$; if $a > 1$, an additional condition needs to be satisfied, which depends on two subcases: with $b < 1 < a$, the additional condition is $(bV_B)^b a^{2(a-b)} < (aV_A)^a (a-1)^{a-b-1}$; with $1 < b < a$, the additional condition is $(bV_B)^b b^{2(a-b)} > (aV_A)^a (b-1)^{a-b-1}$. The proof is involved and is available with the authors.

15 Note that the conditions imposed by the non-negative payoff restriction are more stringent than the second order conditions, which, therefore, never bind. The second derivatives of the parties' payoffs are $\frac{\partial^2 U_A}{\partial A^2} = \frac{a}{A^2} \frac{A^a B^b}{A^a + B^b} (aA^a - aB^b + A^a + B^b) V_A$ and $\frac{\partial^2 U_B}{\partial B^2} = -\frac{b}{B^2} \frac{A^a B^b}{(A^a + B^b)^2} (bB^b - bA^a + A^a + B^b) V_B$. Some simple manipulations yield $\frac{b+1}{b-1} > \frac{S_A^*}{S_B^*} > \frac{a-1}{a+1}$, which can also be rewritten as $S_A^* < \frac{b+1}{2b}$ and $S_B^* < \frac{a+1}{2a}$. Note that these two conditions are always satisfied if the conditions in (5.2) are satisfied.

16 This is a straightforward consequence of the envelope theorem. See also Stein (2002).

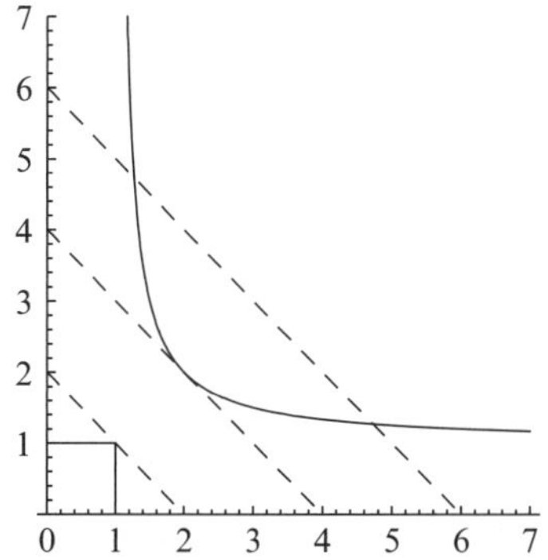

Figure 5.1 *Necessary condition for pure-strategy equilibria with asymmetric strength (the solid curve depicts $ab = a + b$, while the dashed lines depict $a + b = 2$, $a + b = 4$ and $a + b = 6$, respectively)*

$$ab \leq a + b \tag{5.3}$$

The condition in (5.3) represents an absolute limit to the admissible values of the strength parameters that can support a pure-strategy equilibrium. If the parties' strength parameters sum up to less than 4 ($a + b \leq 4$), then the condition in (5.3) is always satisfied. However, above this threshold ($a + b > 4$), the condition in (5.3) can be satisfied only if there is a large asymmetry between the parties, that is, if a and b are sufficiently different. This point is illustrated by Figure 5.1, where the admissible values are contained in the region below the curve. The straight lines depict three cases. The line $a + b = 2$ lies entirely within the region, indicating that the product of any combination of a and b summing up to 2 will be less than 2, hence satisfying the condition in (5.3). The case of $a + b = 4$ represents the boundary case. Above this boundary, as, for instance, with $a + b = 6$, there are values of a and b whose product exceeds their sum. For instance, with $a = 3$ and $b = 3$, we have $ab > a + b$. In this case the necessary condition in (5.3) can only be satisfied if the values of a and b are sufficiently different, thus never for $a = b$. For instance, with $a = 5$ and $b = 1$, we have $ab < a + b$, as required by condition (5.3). The interpretation of this result is that the stronger the parties are, the more they must differ in strength in order for a pure-strategy equilibrium to emerge.

Yet, values below the curve only satisfy a necessary condition on the strength parameters. This condition is not sufficient. In general, not all the points below the curve in Figure 5.1 correspond to pure-strategy equilibria. Outside the unit square in Figure 5.1, the existence of an equilibrium will depend both on the parties' motivation and on the first order conditions. Instead, inside the unit square, the existence of an equilibrium only depends on the first order conditions because the equilibrium payoffs will always be non-negative irrespective of the parties' valuations.[17]

---

17 A more precise characterization of the existence conditions yields some additional restrictions on the parameters for both strength and motivation. See note 14.

Proposition 1: With non-tradable rents, an increase in a player's motivation or strength increases that player's payoff and reduces the payoff of his or her opponent.

5.3.2 Tradable Rents

The difference in the parties' valuations of the rent creates trading opportunities. If resale is feasible, rents that are appropriated by an unmotivated (low-valuing) player will be transferred to the motivated (higher-valuing) player. The possible contract space for the *ex post* transfer of the rent is bounded by the players' respective threat points: player B's minimum willingness to accept, V_B, and player A's maximum willingness to pay, V_A. The actual price paid for the rent, P, will be determined by the players' cunning, which results among other things from their ability to negotiate and their bargaining power. The presence of a secondary market affects not only the final allocation of the rent but also players' strategies, since *ex post* trading opportunities change the *ex ante* stakes of the game.

Player A expects to obtain the rent if he succeeds in the rent-seeking contest and to obtain the difference between his valuation and the price to be paid to buy the rent from B if she succeeds in the rent-seeking contest. Therefore, the payoff of party A is $U_A = S_A V_A + S_B(V_A - P) - A = S_A P - A + (V_A - P)$. As before, S_A and S_B can be interchangeably interpreted as shares in the rent or as probabilities of success. Note that the term in brackets is a fixed amount, which does not change with the effort exerted by player A and hence does not affect his incentives. Therefore, player A plays the game as if the rent had a value equal to the price P. Party B also takes into account the fact that if she succeeds in the contest, she will not keep the rent but rather she will sell it to A and obtain the price P. Therefore, the payoff of party B is $U_B = S_B P - B$. Also party B plays the game as if the rent had a value equal to P. The presence of a secondary market makes the difference in motivation irrelevant for the parties' incentives. Yet, cunning affects the price at which the rent will be sold *ex post* and hence implicitly determines the overall stakes of the rent-seeking contest. Quite intuitively, if a player's strength or cunning increases, that player's payoff will increase to the detriment of his or her opponent's payoff.[18]

As before, the first order conditions[19] determine an implicit relationship between the levels of effort exerted by the parties and the strength and cunning parameters of the game. Differently from motivation, cunning has the same effect on both parties. Here we indicate equilibrium values with a double asterisk:

$$A^{**} = aS_A^{**} S_B^{**} P \tag{5.4}$$

$$B^{**} = bS_A^{**} S_B^{**} P$$

from which we can obtain again a boundary condition, $S_A^{**} S_B^{**} = \frac{A^{**}}{aP} = \frac{B^{**}}{bP} \leq \frac{1}{4}$, so that the players' levels of effort in a pure-strategy equilibrium are bounded by $A^{**} \leq \frac{a}{4} P$ and

18 As in the previous subsection, this follows from the envelope theorem.

19 The first order conditions are $\frac{\partial U_A}{\partial A} = \frac{a}{A} S_A S_B P - 1 = 0$ and $\frac{\partial U_B}{\partial B} = \frac{b}{B} S_A S_B P - 1 = 0$.

$B^{**} \leq \frac{b}{4}P$. Second order conditions and the conditions for non-negative payoffs are as in the previous subsection.

Proposition 2: With tradable rents, an increase in a player's strength or cunning increases that player's payoff and reduces the payoff of his or her opponent.

5.4 EFFORT IN ASYMMETRIC CONTESTS

In this section we further study the parties' choices of efforts and their probability of winning the contest.

5.4.1 Non-tradable Rents

We have already seen in the previous section that an increase in motivation or strength increases a player's payoff and reduces the payoff of his or her opponent. Similarly, an increase in motivation or strength makes a player's effort increase relative to the effort of the other party: from (5.1) we obtain the following relationship between the players' efforts $\frac{A^*}{B^*} = \frac{aV_A}{bV_B}$, which also indicates that in equilibrium the player exerting more effort must have an advantage in terms of strength, motivation[20] or both. Strength and motivation have a comparable impact on the parties' decisions to invest in rent-seeking effort, so that a party's lack of motivation might be compensated by a greater strength and vice versa.[21] Note also that the ratio of the parties' idiosyncratic rent dissipation – that is, the ratio of the portion of the parties' idiosyncratic valuations that is invested in the rent-seeking contest – is equal to the ratio of the strength parameters $\frac{A^*}{V_A}\frac{V_B}{B^*} = \frac{a}{b}$, that is, it does not depend on the parties' valuations,[22] so that an increase in motivation will not change the parties' relative idiosyncratic dissipation, while an increase in a player's strength will.

Yet, these results concern the parties' relative efforts and say very little about their absolute levels of rent-seeking investments. The ratio of the parties' rent-seeking efforts might remain unchanged even if both parties' efforts went up or if both went down. An inspection of the parties' first order conditions reveals some interesting patterns of behavior. If a party's valuation of the rent increases, that party has stronger incentives to exert effort[23] and hence his or her level of effort will tend to increase. The incentives of the other party depend on his or her position in the game: a party that is winning with a high probability will tend to increase his or her effort, while a losing party will tend to give up and reduce his or her effort.[24] This effect will feed back into the contestant's effort level, so that the final outcome is difficult to determine in a general way. The effect of an

---

[20] See also Nti (1999).

[21] See also Baik (1994).

[22] Baik (2004) finds that the rent dissipation ratios are independent of the strength parameters. This is due to a different way of modeling strength, thanks to which the strength parameter cancels out in the first order conditions.

[23] The first order conditions in note 12 increase in V_A and V_B, respectively.

[24] We have $\frac{\partial^2 U_A}{\partial A \partial B} = \frac{ab}{AB} S_A S_B (S_A - S_B) V_A$ and $\frac{\partial^2 U_B}{\partial B \partial A} = \frac{ab}{AB} S_A S_B (S_B - S_A) V_B$, where the sign depends on whether $\frac{S_A}{S_B}$ is greater or less than one.

increase in strength on the absolute levels of the parties' effort is even more involved, as it also depends on whether the returns to effort are increasing or decreasing.[25]

If a party's effort increases due to a boost in motivation or strength, it is not a priori clear whether his or her probability of winning the contest will also improve. In fact, in equilibrium, we have $\frac{S_A^*}{S_B^*} = \frac{(A^*)^a}{(B^*)^b}$. Since $S_A^* = 1 - S_B^*$, a relative improvement in a party's success probability corresponds to an absolute increase is such probability. Yet, a relative increase in a party's effort does not necessarily translate to an increase in his or her probability of winning since the final effect will also depend on the values of the strength parameters.

Proposition 3: With non-tradable rents, an increase in a player's motivation or strength increases the ratio of that player's effort relative to the effort of his or her opponent; an increase in a player's strength also increases the ratio of that player's idiosyncratic dissipation relative to the idiosyncratic dissipation of his or her opponent; the effects on the players' success probabilities are ambiguous.

5.4.2 Tradable Rents

We shall now consider how the results derived above are changed when players have *ex post* trading opportunities. As discussed in the previous section, with tradable rents subjective valuations of the rent are rendered immaterial by the presence of resale opportunities. Both players, whether they subjectively value the prize or not, face the same stakes in the rent-seeking contest given by the resale value of the prize in the secondary market, P. From (5.4) the relationship between the players' efforts thus becomes $\frac{A^{**}}{B^{**}} = \frac{a}{b}$, which indicates that when a player exerts more effort this is because of his advantage in terms of strength, not because of his motivation. Motivation does not affect effort in this case, because the possibility of trade makes the game symmetric with respect to the stakes. *Ceteris paribus*, high-valuing and low-valuing players will exert the same amount of effort in the game. It is clear that, in this case, only strength can drive differences in effort and a stronger player will thus exert relatively more effort.

Note, however, that the ratio of the players' idiosyncratic dissipation is now $\frac{A^{**}}{V_A}\frac{V_B}{B^{**}} = \frac{aV_B}{bV_A}$, which suggests that a player is willing to invest a relatively larger share of the expected prize if his or her strength is large relative to his or her valuation. This is due to the fact that resale opportunities are more profitable for higher-valuing players and therefore lower-valuing players will focus more heavily on the initial rent-seeking phase of the game rather than rely on the trading phase and vice versa.

The success probability of the stronger player might, however, be lower than the success probability of his or her opponent, as in the case of non-tradable rents, since we have $\frac{S_A^{**}}{S_B^{**}} = \frac{(A^{**})^a}{(B^{**})^b}$. Cunning, determining the price of the rent at the resale phase, will determine the absolute levels of the parties' effort but does not have an effect on a party's effort relative to his or her opponent.

---

25 We have $\frac{\partial^2 U_A}{\partial A \partial a} = \frac{1}{A} S_A S_B (1 - a(S_A - S_B)\log A) V_A$ and $\frac{\partial^2 U_A}{\partial A \partial b} = \frac{a}{A} S_A S_B (S_A - S_B)(\log B) V_A$ for party A, and $\frac{\partial^2 U_B}{\partial B \partial b} = \frac{1}{B} S_A S_B (1 - b(S_B - S_A)\log B) V_B$ and $\frac{\partial^2 U_B}{\partial B \partial a} = \frac{b}{B} S_A S_B (S_B - S_A)(\log A) V_B$ for party B.

Proposition 4: With tradable rents, an increase in a player's strength increases the ratio of that player's effort relative to the effort of his or her opponent; an increase in a player's strength also increases the ratio of that player's idiosyncratic dissipation relative to the idiosyncratic dissipation of his or her opponent; an increase in a player's motivation decreases the ratio of that player's idiosyncratic dissipation relative to the idiosyncratic dissipation of his or her opponent; cunning does not affect relative efforts and idiosyncratic dissipations; the effects on the players' success probabilities are ambiguous.

5.5 THE SOCIAL COST OF ASYMMETRIC RENT SEEKING

5.5.1 Non-tradable Rents

In the presence of asymmetries, the social cost of rent seeking consists of the traditional rent dissipation and an additional cost, rent misallocation, due to the fact that the parties value the rent differently.[26] Dissipation costs are given by the sum of the players' efforts in equilibrium. Misallocation costs arise when players have different valuations of the rent and are given by the difference in the players' valuations weighted by the probability that the lower-valuing player actually appropriates the rent. Using (5.1), these costs can thus be written as follows in the no-trade scenario:

$$D^* = A^* + B^* = S_A^* S_B^* (aV_A + bV_B) \tag{5.5}$$

$$M^* = S_B^* (V_A - V_B)$$

Since the less motivated (lower-valuing) player B does not necessarily exert a lower level of effort to appropriate the rent, nor is she less likely to win the contest than her motivated (higher-valuing) opponent, rent misallocation costs can be particularly relevant. Increasing asymmetries in strength can have ambiguous effects on social welfare when motivation is also at stake. Consider rent dissipation. If A is stronger, then there is more weight on V_A, which is larger, thus we have more dissipation. However, the players' probabilities of winning become more divergent due to the fact that A will invest more in the contest and, hence, the term $S_A^* S_B^*$ becomes smaller, thus reducing dissipation. Moreover, if player A is stronger, we have a smaller S_B^*, thus misallocation is reduced. Asymmetry with respect to motivation also has ambiguous effects when players with asymmetric strength are involved. A large difference in the players' valuations leads to a decrease in $S_A^* S_B^*$, hence reducing dissipation, but exacerbating misallocation costs.

It is interesting to expand on the notion of full dissipation. When the rent is commonly valued, full dissipation occurs when the sum of the parties' efforts equals the value of the rent. In our setting, however, the rent is valued differently by the two parties, so that an

[26] Hurley (1998) introduced the notion of context efficiency, which measures the ability of the highest-value player to obtain the rent, net of the total rent dissipation. Rent misallocation is a somewhat analogous concept, but it only focuses on the allocation of the rent, while leaving aside considerations of the resources spent to obtain it, which are captured by the notion of rent dissipation.

additional social loss will derive from the misallocation of the rent, occurring when the low-valuing party B wins the contest. Yet, as in the traditional setting, also with asymmetric valuations the total social loss is bounded in equilibrium. Since in equilibrium the parties must earn non-negative payoffs, the sum of the parties' investments in rent seeking cannot exceed the sum of their expected gains from rent seeking and we must have: $D^* = A^* + B^* \leq S_A^* V_A + S_B^* V_B$. Since the rent misallocation is $M^* = S_B^*(V_A - V_B)$, summing up, we have that the total social loss cannot exceed the highest rent valuation: $D^* + M^* \leq V_A$.[27]

Within this overall limit, both dissipation and misallocation are also individually bounded. Using (5.2), rent dissipation can be at most a weighted average of the parties' valuations, $D^* \leq \frac{aV_A + bV_B}{ab} \leq V_A$. Similarly, the rent misallocation is also bounded: $M^* \leq \frac{1}{a}(V_A - V_B) \leq V_A$.

The worst-case scenario in which the highest rent valuation is entirely lost due to the rent-seeking game arises when both parties obtain a payoff equal to zero.[28] We have seen above[29] that this can be the case only if $S_A^* = \frac{1}{b}$ and $S_B^* = \frac{1}{a}$. Since the sum of the parties' shares is necessarily equal to 1, then we must have that $\frac{1}{a} + \frac{1}{b} = 1$, which can be rewritten as $ab = a + b$. This means that the total social cost of rent seeking will be equal to the highest rent valuation only along the curve in Figure 5.1. Looking at Figure 5.1, it is also clear that this condition can be verified only if $ab \geq 4$ and if both a and b are greater than 1. Also the opposite is true: if a point lies on the curve in Figure 5.1, then it must be the case that the parties' payoffs are both zero, parties spend $A^* = \frac{V_A}{b}$ and $B^* = \frac{V_B}{a}$ in rent seeking.[30] Any other value of the strength parameters that supports a pure-strategy equilibrium will leave some social value untouched.

This result generalizes the traditional full dissipation result in Tullock's framework. In fact setting $a = b = r$, the condition becomes $r^2 = 2r$, which yields $r = 2$, as in the traditional analysis. The fact that the asymmetry in the parties' valuations does not appear in the definition of the maximal social cost of rent seeking should not be surprising. In fact, such difference enters the calculus of the total social loss in two offsetting ways. On the one hand, rent dissipation is somewhat diminished by the fact that valuations are asymmetric, in that the sum of the parties' efforts will not reach the highest valuation. On the other hand, rent misallocation comes about precisely because of the asymmetric valuations, picking up the remaining loss and bringing the total social loss to a level that, at the limit, equals the highest valuation.

Proposition 5: With non-tradable rents, the total social cost of rent seeking is equal to the highest valuation of the rent if and only if the product of the parties' strength is equal to their sum.

---

27 Compare to Hillman and Riley's (1989) result that asymmetries in rent valuations reduce the rent dissipation. We add that if one considers rent misallocation, asymmetries do not affect the maximal social loss.

28 To clarify, $D^* + M^* = V_A$ occurs if and only if $D^* = S_A^* V_A + S_B^* V_B$.

29 See note 13 and accompanying text.

30 This is because if $\frac{1}{a} + \frac{1}{b} = 1$ the conditions in (5.2) must hold strictly. The parties' rent-seeking expenditures are derived substituting (5.2) into (5.1).

5.5.2 Tradable Rents

Ex post trading opportunities will correct any initial misallocation of the rent, bringing misallocation costs to zero, but retain the potential for dissipation through rent-seeking expenditures:

$$D^{**} = A^{**} + B^{**} = S_A^{**} S_B^{**}(a+b)P \tag{5.6}$$

$$M^{**} = 0$$

Also in this case, the rent dissipation (and hence the total social loss of rent seeking) is bounded and cannot exceed the price $D^* \leq P$. Yet, although the opportunity to trade rents after the initial contest eliminates possible misallocation costs, it can exacerbate rent dissipation. This is due to the fact that resale opportunities raise the stakes for low-valuing contestants making the contest more symmetrical and thus increasing the value of $S_A S_B$. As seen below, the net effect of *ex post* trading opportunities on social welfare is ambiguous. We could repeat here what has already been observed in the previous subsection about the total social loss. Yet, the problem here is simpler, in that the rent misallocation is always zero and social loss is confined to rent dissipation. Thus, full dissipation occurs when $D^{**} = V_A$, which can occur only if $P = V_A$. The results obtained in the previous subsection need to be slightly adapted to the new setting:

> *Proposition 6: With tradable rents, the total social cost is equal to the highest valuation of the rent if and only if the product of the parties' strength is equal to their sum and if the resale price is equal to the valuation of the high-valuing party.*

5.6 TRADING AWAY ASYMMETRIES

5.6.1 The Effect of Trade on Effort

The possibility to trade the won prize in a secondary market aligns the players' motivation. Although they attach different subjective valuations to the prize, both players engage in the rent-seeking context facing similar stakes. Low-valuing players know that rents can be sold after the contest at price *P*; similarly, high-valuing players know that rents can be bought; thus, both players play the rent-seeking game facing symmetric stakes, *P*, rather than asymmetric stakes V_A and V_B. The effect of this aligned motivation on the players' efforts can be studied by comparing (5.1) and (5.4), which gives $\frac{A^*}{B^*} = \frac{aV_A}{bV_B} > \frac{a}{b} = \frac{A^{**}}{B^{**}}$. Yet, this inequality does not offer any determinate answer to the question under consideration. In fact, it may be the case that $A^* > B^*$ without trade and $A^{**} < B^{**}$ with trade, satisfying the inequality but leaving open the question as to the effect of *ex post* trade on parties' *ex ante* efforts. To answer this question, let us first define an indifference criterion with respect to efforts: $\frac{A^*}{B^*} = \frac{B^{**}}{A^{**}}$. If this equality is satisfied, opening trade triggers a perfect switch in the players' effort choices. Without trade the motivated player would exert more effort, while with trade the unmotivated player would exert more effort, perfectly inverting the ratio between the efforts. The equality is satisfied if the following holds:[31]

$$\frac{V_A}{V_B} = \left(\frac{b}{a}\right)^2 \tag{5.7}$$

The latter condition implies that we must have $a < b$, given that $V_A > V_B$. This means that such a reversal of effort strategies will occur only in rent-seeking games where a strong but unmotivated player plays against a weak but motivated player. Without trade the motivated, weak player exerts more effort, inasmuch as the rent-seeking contest provides for him the only opportunity for appropriating the sought-after rent. Once trade opportunities are introduced, this relationship could be reversed. Trade opportunities remove motivation-driven asymmetries, leaving only strength-driven differences between the players' incentives. Whether the resulting effort levels are more or less asymmetric when trade is introduced depends on the relative importance of motivation-driven and strength-driven incentives on the parties' strategies. We can restate the problem in light of the above considerations, distinguishing three possible cases.

First, with $\frac{V_A}{V_B} > (\frac{b}{a})^2$, player A's advantage in motivation weighs more heavily than player B's advantage in strength. In this case, trade removes the greater of the two sources of asymmetry, leading to a convergence between the parties' effort levels. This case includes two scenarios. In the first scenario, player A has greater motivation as well as greater strength than player B. Trade leads to a convergence between the players' efforts by removing one of the two advantages for player A. In the second scenario, we might observe player A with greater motivation and player B with greater strength, with a heavily dominating effect of motivation-driven incentives. By introducing trade and eliminating the effect of motivation, we would replace the large asymmetry driven by motivation with a smaller asymmetry driven by strength, leading again to a convergence between the parties' effort levels.

Second, with $\frac{V_A}{V_B} = (\frac{b}{a})^2$, we have the special case considered in (5.7) where the two sources of asymmetry perfectly balance one another. In this case, introducing trade leads to an inversion of the ratio of the players' efforts.

Finally, with $\frac{V_A}{V_B} < (\frac{b}{a})^2$, player B's advantage in strength generates a greater asymmetry than player A's advantage in motivation. Without trade, these two advantages operate in opposite and partially offsetting directions. Trade removes the advantage in motivation, upsetting this balance, thus increasing the asymmetry between the players' efforts.

Concluding, the effect of trade on the players' success probabilities is ambiguous because it depends on the absolute values of the players' efforts and on their strength levels as we have seen in the previous section.

Proposition 7: Trade reduces (increases) the asymmetry of the rent-seeking contest and leads to a convergence (divergence) between the players' rent-seeking efforts if and only if a player's advantage in motivation is greater (less) than the other player's squared advantage in strength. In the special case where a player's advantage in motivation is

---

[31] Note that $\frac{A^*}{B^*} = \frac{B^{**}}{A^{**}} \Leftrightarrow \frac{aV_A}{bV_B} = \frac{b}{a} \Leftrightarrow \frac{V_A}{V_B} = (\frac{b}{a})^2$.

equal to the other player's squared advantage in strength, trade keeps the asymmetry of the rent-seeking contest unchanged, but inverts the ratio of players' rent-seeking efforts. The effect of trade on the success probabilities is ambiguous.

5.6.2 The Effect of Trade on the Social Loss of Rent Seeking

In general, trade does not necessarily reduce rent dissipation,[32] but puts a lower limit on the maximal total social loss that can materialize, which is V_A without trade and only $P \leq V_A$ with trade. In this subsection we introduce the two notions, which will be useful to study the effect of trade on the social loss of rent seeking. As observed above, strength, motivation and cunning play different roles in asymmetric rent-seeking contests. Strength and motivation are only relevant in the rent-seeking phase, while cunning is only relevant in the resale phase when secondary markets are introduced. Unlike strength, which is always relevant in the rent-seeking phase of the game, regardless of the presence of resale opportunities, motivation is only relevant in the rent-seeking phase when resale opportunities are unavailable. In order to refine our understanding of the combined effects of strength, motivation and cunning, we shall now introduce the notions of 'balanced rent seeking' and 'fair negotiations'. In balanced rent seeking, one player's strength perfectly offsets the other player's motivation. With fair negotiations, a player's cunning in the negotiation phase compensates his lack of strength in the rent-seeking phase. Both notions crucially depend on the asymmetry in motivation.

The notion of balanced rent seeking applies to the rent-seeking phase and is characterized by $aV_A = bV_B$. In a balanced contest, the players exert the same levels of efforts notwithstanding their differences in both strength and motivation. In these situations, a player's advantage in one dimension is balanced by a disadvantage in the other dimension. The notion of fair negotiations considers instead the correlation between a player's disadvantage in the rent-seeking phase and his advantage in the *ex post* trading phase. Imposing a restriction on the trading phase, a contest with fair negotiations is characterized by $P = \frac{aV_A + bV_B}{a + b}$, that is, the price is a weighted average of the players' valuations, where the weights are given by the strength exponents. The condition of fair negotiations is verified when a player's advantage in strength translates into a disadvantage in bargaining power and vice versa. In fact, it is in a player's interest that the price be close to the other player's valuation and not his own. If player A is strong (large a) in the rent-seeking phase, then he will be disadvantaged in the trading phase, since the price will be relatively high and in fact close to V_A. Conversely, if player B is strong (large b) in the rent-seeking phase, then she will be disadvantaged in the trading phase, since the price will be relatively low and close to V_B.

In a balanced contest, the players' efforts without trade are the same, $A^* = B^*$ and the stronger player always wins with a higher probability. Since we are assuming that A is more motivated, then B must be stronger for the contest to be balanced, thus we have $\frac{a}{b} < 1$ and hence $\frac{S_A^*}{S_B^*} < 1$. With trade, the players' efforts depend on their relative strength,

---

32 See also Suen (1989) showing that trading does not necessarily reduce rent dissipation.

with the stronger player exerting more effort, $\frac{A^{**}}{B^{**}} < 1$,[33] and hence winning more often, $\frac{S_A^{**}}{S_B^{**}} < \frac{S_A^*}{S_B^*} < 1$.[34]

If the contest is characterized by fair negotiations, we can write the ratio of the rent dissipations with and without trade as follows:

$$\frac{D^*}{D^{**}} = \frac{S_A^* S_B^*}{S_A^{**} S_B^{**}} \frac{aV_A + bV_B}{(a + b)P} = \frac{S_A^* S_B^*}{S_A^{**} S_B^{**}}$$

Note that if the context is balanced, we have $\frac{S_A^* S_B^*}{S_A^{**} S_B^{**}} > 1$.[35] Thus, combining fair negotiations with a balanced context, we obtain the following result: rent dissipation decreases with trade. We can further compare total social loss in the two scenarios. Recall that in the case of rent seeking without trade, total social loss is given by the sum of dissipation and misallocation costs, whereas in the case of rent seeking with trade, misallocation losses are eliminated, yielding total social loss equal dissipation.[36] When the parties' motivation, strength and cunning are balanced, while trade decreases dissipation, the total social loss might be greater or less than without trade.

Proposition 8: Trade reduces the maximal social loss of rent seeking. In a balanced contest with fair negotiations trade also reduces dissipation.

5.7 CONCLUSIONS

Rent-seeking contests, more often than not, involve players who differ with respect to one or more characteristic. In this chapter we marked a pathfinder through the relevant literature on asymmetric rent seeking, considering the effect of asymmetries between the parties' competitive abilities, motivation and bargaining power. These characteristics play different roles and become relevant at different stages of a rent-seeking contest. Strength, for example, acquires relevance in the rent-seeking stage, while cunning becomes relevant in the reallocation stage. Motivation is an advantage (larger surplus that is obtainable from the rent) that plays different roles on the parties' incentives. The effect of motivation differs depending on whether rent is tradable *ex post* or not and the bargaining ability of the parties. We looked at whether the possibility of tradable rents increases or reduces the total social cost of rent seeking. This bird's eye view on asymmetric rent-seeking problems provides a valuable lens through which to analyze real life conditions of rent-seeking competition.

---

33 As it is intuitive, in a balanced contest, we have $\frac{V_A}{V_B} < (\frac{b}{a})^2$: trade increases the asymmetry of the contest in terms of incentives to exert effort.

34 See Proposition 2.

35 Note that $\frac{S_A^{**}}{S_B^{**}} < \frac{S_A^*}{S_B^*} < 1$ implies that the difference between the winning probabilities increases with trade. Since the winning probabilities sum up to 1, their product decreases if the difference between the two increases, this implies $\frac{S_A^* S_B^*}{S_A^{**} S_B^{**}} > 1$.

36 The ratio of the total social losses in the two scenarios is $\frac{D^* + M^*}{D^{**}} = \frac{S_B^*}{S_A^{**} S_B^{**}} \frac{V_A(1 + aS_A^*) - V_B(1 - bS_A^*)}{(a + b)P}$. By simulating the results it is possible to verify that the ratio can be greater or less than 1.

REFERENCES

Allard, Richard J. (1988), 'Rent seeking with non-identical players', *Public Choice*, **57**(1), 3–14.

Baik, Kyung Hwan (1994), 'Effort levels in contests with two asymmetric players', *Southern Economic Journal*, **61**(2), 367–78.

Baik, Kyung Hwan (2004), 'Two-player asymmetric contests with ratio-form success functions', *Economic Inquiry*, **42**(4), 679–89.

Bennour, Khaled (2009), 'The value of rents and the likelihood of conflicts', *International Review of Economics*, **56**(2), 163–73.

Cornes, Richard and Roger Hartley (2005), 'Asymmetric contests with general technologies', *Economic Theory*, **26**(5), 923–46.

Dari-Mattiacci, Giuseppe and Francesco Parisi (2014), 'Returns to effort in rent-seeking games', *Public Choice*, **159**(1–2), 99–104

Dari-Mattiacci, Giuseppe, Eric Langlais, Bruno Lovat and Francesco Parisi (2007), 'Crowding-out in productive and redistributive rent seeking', *Public Choice*, **133**(1–2), 199–229.

Dari-Mattiacci, Giuseppe, Sander Onderstal and Francesco Parisi (2009), 'Seeking rents in the shadow of Coase', *Public Choice*, **139**(1–2), 171–96.

Donohue, John J. III and Steven D. Levitt (1998), 'Guns, violence and the efficiency of illegal markets', *American Economic Review*, **88**(2), 463–7.

Harris, Christopher and John Vickers (1985), 'Perfect equilibrium in a model of a race', *Review of Economic Studies*, **52**(2), 193–209.

Hillman, Arye L. and John G. Riley (1989), 'Politically contestable rents and transfers', *Economics and Politics*, **1**(1), 17–39.

Hirshleifer, Jack (2001), *The Dark Side of the Force*, Cambridge: Cambridge University Press.

Hurley, Terrance M. (1998), 'Rent dissipation and efficiency in a contest with asymmetric valuations', *Public Choice*, **94**(3–4), 289–98.

Kohli, Inderjit and Nirvikar Singh (1999), 'Rent seeking and rent setting with asymmetric effectiveness of lobbying', *Public Choice*, **99**(3–4), 275–98.

Leininger, Wolfgang (1993), 'More efficient rent seeking – a Münchhausen solution', *Public Choice*, **75**(1), 43–62.

Lockard, Alan and Gordon Tullock (eds) (2001), *Efficient Rent Seeking: Chronicle of an Intellectual Quagmire*, Boston, MA: Kluwer.

Matros, Alexander (2006), 'Rent seeking with asymmetric valuations: addition or deletion of a player', *Public Choice*, **129**(3–4), 369–80.

Nitzan, Shmuel (1994), 'Modelling rent-seeking contests', *European Journal of Political Economy*, **10**(1), 41–60.

Nti, Kofi O. (1998), 'Effort and performance in group contests', *European Journal of Political Economy*, **14**(4), 769–81.

Nti, Kofi O. (1999), 'Rent seeking with asymmetric valuations', *Public Choice*, **98**(3–4), 415–30, reprinted in Roger D. Congleton, Arye L. Hillman and Kai A. Konrad (eds) (2008), *40 Years of Research on Rent Seeking 1 – The Theory of Rent Seeking*, Heidelberg: Springer, pp. 149–64.

Nti, Kofi O. (2004), 'Maximum efforts in contests with asymmetric valuations', *European Journal of Political Economy*, **20**(4), 1059–66.

Rowley, Charles K., Robert D. Tollison and Gordon Tullock (eds) (1988), *The Political Economy of Rent Seeking*, Boston, MA: Kluwer.

Runkel, Marco (2006), 'Optimal contest design, closeness and the contest success function', *Public Choice*, **129**(1–2), 217–31.

Ryvkin, Dmitry (2007), 'Tullock contests of weakly heterogeneous players', *Public Choice*, **132**(1–2), 49–64.

Singh, Nirviker and Donald Wittman (2001), 'Contests where there is variation in the marginal productivity of effort', *Economic Theory*, **18**(3), 711–44.

Stein, William (2002), 'Asymmetric rent seeking with more than two contestants', *Public Choice*, **113**(3–4), 325–36.

Stein, William and Amnon Rapoport (2004), 'Asymmetric two-stage group rent seeking: comparison of two contest structures', *Public Choice*, **118**(1–2), 151–67.

Suen, Wing (1989), 'Rationing and rent dissipation in the presence of heterogeneous individuals', *Journal of Political Economy*, **97**(6), 1384–94.

Tollison, Robert D. (1982), 'Rent seeking: a survey', *Kyklos*, **35**(4), 575–602.

Tullock, Gordon (1980), 'Efficient rent seeking', in James M. Buchanan, Robert D. Tollison and Gordon Tullock (eds), *Towards a Theory of the Rent-seeking Society*, College Station, TX: Texas A&M University Press, pp. 97–112, reprinted in Roger D. Congleton, Arye L. Hillman and Kai A. Konrad (eds) (2008), *40 Years of Research on Rent Seeking 1 – The Theory of Rent Seeking*, Heidelberg: Springer, pp. 105–20.

Tullock, Gordon (1985), 'Back to the bog', *Public Choice*, **46**(3), 259–63.

6. Prize-sharing rules in collective rent seeking

Sabine Flamand and Orestis Troumpounis

SUMMARY

In this chapter, we review our knowledge as to how different ways of sharing a prize among the members of a group in collective rent seeking affect individuals' incentives to contribute to their group's aggregate effort. Starting with Nitzan in 1991, the literature has considered both exogenous and endogenous sharing rules, while it has assumed that the choice of such rules may occur under either public or private information. In turn, group sharing rules affect the extent of total rent dissipation, the occurrence of the group size paradox, group formation and the choice between productive and appropriative activities.

6.1 INTRODUCTION

Collective contests where group members organize and compete for a prize are a common phenomenon: research and development races, procurement contests, funds to be allocated among different departments within a university, regions within a country or countries in the European Union (EU), prizes and projects allocated among different divisions of a firm or party members that participate in pre-electoral campaigns.

This survey aims at reviewing our knowledge on a particular aspect of collective rent seeking: prize sharing.[1] Starting with Nitzan (1991a), the literature on sharing rules has analysed how different ways of allocating the contested prize among group members affect individual incentives to contribute to the group's aggregate effort. If such sharing rules embed some degree of meritocracy they account for individuals' relative contributions to some extent.[2] Alternatively, egalitarian sharing rules split the prize equally among group members regardless of their individual effort. The intra-group sharing rules, the size of the competing groups and the nature and valuation of the prize jointly

---

[1] For a recent survey on collective rent seeking one can refer to Kolmar (2013). For surveys of the literature on rent seeking in general, see Nitzan (1994), Corchón (2007), Konrad (2009), Hillman (2013) and Long (2013).

[2] Naturally, the crucial importance of different types of sharing rules in the general context of a competition between players has been stressed earlier, as any rule determining the winners and losers of a competition (such as Tullock's (1980 [2008]) classical contest success function) in fact can be understood as a way of allocating a prize among contestants. For instance, Congleton (1984 [2008]) has compared what he calls 'all or nothing' rules to the traditional rule based on relative individual contributions in terms of their effect on rent-seeking expenditures (see also Congleton 1980 [2008]). Another related contribution in this context is Long and Vousden (1987 [2008]), who stress the fact that agents may be competing for a share of a (divisible) rent rather than for its totality.

determine individual incentives to contribute to collective rent seeking. In turn, sharing rules affect both the extent of rent dissipation and the potential occurrence of the group size paradox (GSP henceforth), a situation in which smaller groups outperform larger ones in terms of their winning probability (Olson 1965).

Before proceeding, it is worth mentioning that we focus on group contests where individual contributions to their group's aggregate effort in order to win the inter-group contest are also the ones determining the allocation of the prize within the victorious group.[3] Our narrative is structured as follows. We first present a standard model of collective rent seeking where exogenous group sharing rules apply. We then allow these rules to be endogenously determined by the competing groups prior to the choice of individual efforts, considering both the cases of public and private information regarding the sharing rules.

6.2 EXOGENOUS SHARING RULES

Consider n groups competing for a private prize V. Group i has size $n_i \geq 2$ and $N = \sum_{i=1}^{n} n_i$ is the total number of individuals. Group i's probability of success π_i in the inter-group contest is given by

$$\pi_i(X_1, \ldots, X_n) = \frac{X_i}{\sum_{j=1}^{n} X_j} = \frac{X_i}{X} \tag{6.1}$$

where x_{ki} is the effort exerted by member k in group i and $X_i = \sum_{k=1}^{n_i} x_{ki}$ is the total effort of group i. Notice that we focus on contests where group members' efforts are perfect substitutes and the contest among groups is ruled by a standard contest success function (CSF henceforth) that can be essentially understood as a lottery (Tullock 1980 [2008]).[4]

[3] The alternative scenario where group members exert two different types of efforts devoted to the between- and within-group contest, respectively, is not covered in this survey. While Münster (2007) assumes such contests to take place simultaneously, most authors assume a two-stage procedure (for example, Katz and Tokatlidu 1996 [2008]; Konrad 2004 [2008]). In the first stage, several groups compete for a prize. Once the prize is shared among these groups, the members of each group compete for receiving what the group won in the inter-group contest. Several applications such as Wärneryd (1998), who considers resource allocation within federations, Inderst et al (2005, 2007), who consider the allocation of free cash flow within organizations or Müller and Wärneryd (2001), who consider distributional conflict between shareholders of corporations also rely on such two-stage procedures. A central result is that the coordination problem within groups in the inter-group contest and the fact that the prize will be subject to the future intra-group contest can reduce total effort (Konrad 2004).

[4] The literature on collective rent seeking started with groups competing for a public good with a CSF such as (6.1) and perfectly substitutable member efforts (Katz et al. 1990). As the choice of sharing rules is irrelevant whenever the contested prize is a pure public good, important contributions in this context are not reviewed here (for example, Baik 1993, 2008; Riaz et al. 1995 [2008]; Ursprung 1990 [2008]; Dijkstra 1998; Baik et al. 2001; Cheikbossian 2008; Epstein and Mealem 2009, 2012 among several others). More recently, several authors have departed from the assumption of perfect substitutability of members' efforts. D. Lee (2012) assumes that efforts are perfect complements, so that groups are represented in the group contest by the member exerting

The literature on sharing rules starts with the seminal contribution of Nitzan (1991a), who introduces a sharing rule that allocates part of the prize V in an egalitarian manner among group members, while the remaining part is allocated among group members based on relative contributions.[5] Formally, member k in group i receives a share of the prize V, given by

$$(1 - \alpha_i)\frac{x_{ki}}{X_i} + \alpha_i \frac{1}{n_i} \tag{6.2}$$

where $\alpha_i \in [0, 1]$. Nitzan (1991a) considers the case of a linear cost of effort, hence the objective function of member k in group i is given by

$$U_{ki} = \frac{X_i}{\sum_{j=1}^{n} X_j}\left[(1 - \alpha_i)\frac{x_{ki}}{X_i} + \alpha_i \frac{1}{n_i}\right]V - x_{ki} \tag{6.3}$$

The first-order condition for maximizing (6.3) is given by:

$$\frac{\alpha_i V}{n_i}\left(\frac{X - X_i}{X^2}\right) + (1 - \alpha_i)V\left(\frac{X - x_{ki}}{X^2}\right) = 1 \tag{6.4}$$

In a symmetric Nash equilibrium, identical members of the same group receive the same payoff, hence $x_{ki} = x_i$ for all $i = 1, \ldots, n$ and $k = 1, \ldots, n_i$. For illustrative purposes we first consider the two polar cases in which the prize is allocated solely on the basis of relative contributions (that is, $\alpha_i = 0$) and on an egalitarian basis (that is, $\alpha_i = 1$), respectively. We then consider linear combinations of these two sharing rules, that is, the allocation of the prize involves both a meritocratic and an egalitarian component.

6.2.1 Relative Effort Sharing Rule

If $\alpha_i = 0$ for all $i = 1, \ldots, n$, the prize is allocated according to relative effort within the winning group. Notice from (6.3) that the nominator of the inter-group contest cancels out with the denominator of the group relative effort rule, so that the N individuals eventually compete in a standard Tullock contest. For $\alpha_i = 0$, (6.4) reduces to

$$V(X - x_i) = X^2 \tag{6.5}$$

Consequently, in equilibrium under prize sharing according to the relative effort rule, $x_i = x$ for all $i = 1, \ldots, n$, which yields

the lowest effort. Kolmar and Rommeswinkel (2013) use a constant elasticity of substitution function embedding varying degrees of complementarity, while Chowdhury et al. (2013) consider that groups are represented in the group contest by the member exerting the highest effort.

[5] Vazquez (2014) has recently studied the parallel notion of 'cost sharing rules' and stressed the importance of cost sharing for inducing higher levels of individual effort in collective rent seeking. Nitzan and Ueda (2014) show that heterogeneous prize valuations across the members of a group tend to lower the degree of cost sharing within the group.

$$x^* = \frac{(N-1)V}{N^2} \tag{6.6}$$

The equilibrium effort in (6.6) reproduces the one of a standard Tullock contest among N identical players. Observe that in this case, a larger group is more likely to win the prize. Indeed, a larger size is advantageous for the group since in equilibrium its probability of winning is equal to n_i/N. Furthermore, neither the distribution of individuals among the groups nor the number of groups affects the total amount of rent seeking.

6.2.2 Egalitarian Sharing Rule

If $\alpha_i = 1$ for all $i = 1, \ldots, n$, the prize is divided on an egalitarian basis within the winning group regardless of individual contributions. In such a case, (6.4) reduces to

$$\frac{X - X_i}{X^2} = \frac{n_i}{V} \tag{6.7}$$

which yields the following equilibrium:

$$X_i^* = \frac{(n-1)[N-(n-1)n_i]V}{N^2} \tag{6.8}$$

Furthermore, total rent dissipation is given by

$$X^* = \frac{(n-1)V}{N} \tag{6.9}$$

Notice that the individual effort levels are undetermined. Indeed, as in this case the first-order conditions do not determine how the aggregate effort of each group is allocated between its members, the equilibrium is unique regarding group efforts, but a multiplicity of equilibria arises regarding individual contributions to group effort.

Contrary to the relative effort sharing rule, a smaller group outperforms a larger group in terms of its winning probability. Indeed, with an egalitarian sharing rule, free-riding intensifies and dominates the positive group size effect. Furthermore, total rent seeking is increasing in the number of groups and decreasing with the total population. Finally, the reduced dissipation rate is due to the stronger free-riding incentives within the groups.

S. Lee (1993) analyses competition between two groups for a prize shared according to the egalitarian rule, using the general form of the inter-group CSF in (6.1):

$$\pi_i(X_1, \ldots, X_n) = \frac{X_i^r}{\sum_{j=1}^{n} X_j^r} \tag{6.10}$$

When $r > 1$ (< 1), rent-seeking activities exhibit characteristics of increasing (decreasing) returns to scale. In such a case, total rent seeking for $n = 2$ is given by

$$X^* = \frac{r\left[\dfrac{n_1^r n_2^r}{n_1} + \dfrac{n_1^r n_2^r}{n_2}\right]V}{(n_1^r + n_2^r)^2} \tag{6.11}$$

If $r > 1$ (< 1), an increase in disparity of the group sizes decreases (increases) the extent of rent dissipation, while if $r = 1$, as can be seen from (6.9), group size asymmetry has no effect on the extent of rent dissipation. Using a group CSF such as (6.10), S. Lee (1992) studies group formation among N individuals in a two-stage game, assuming that both the prize and the costs of group formation are shared on an egalitarian basis among the group members. He shows that allowing for (equal size) group formation among the N individuals reduces total rent-seeking expenditures.

Esteban and Ray (2001) study the occurrence of the GSP considering the possibility of the prize V being a mixture between a private and a public good and assuming a convex cost of effort. The objective function of member k in group i is now given by

$$U_{ki} = \frac{X_i}{\sum_{j=1}^{n} X_j}\left[p\frac{1}{n_i} + (1 - p)\right]V - x_i^{\beta} \tag{6.12}$$

where $p \in [0, 1]$ denotes the degree of privateness of the prize to be shared on an egalitarian basis, and $\beta \geqslant 1$. They show that the smaller group exerts more effort than the larger group if and only if $p + 1 > \beta$. Intuitively, the GSP cannot occur if costs rise very quickly with effort. Clearly, the most favourable case for the GSP to arise is when $p = 1$ (that is, the prize is a pure private good), but even in this case the cost cannot have an exponent larger than two. If the cost of effort is linear ($\beta = 1$), the GSP arises for all values of p except for the extreme case of a pure public good (that is, $p = 0$).

6.2.3 Mixed Sharing Rule

If $\alpha_i \in (0, 1)$ for all $i = 1, \ldots, n$, the group sharing rule is a mixture between the relative effort and egalitarian rules. If sharing rules are identical across groups ($\alpha_i = \alpha$ for all $i = 1, \ldots, n$), summing (6.4) over i yields total rent dissipation in equilibrium:

$$X^* = \frac{[(1 - \alpha)N + \alpha n - 1]V}{N} \tag{6.13}$$

Total rent seeking is increasing in the number of groups (n) and decreasing in the proportion of the prize distributed equally among group members (α). That is, total rent dissipation is lower in societies applying egalitarian sharing rules for distributing rents than in societies incentivizing effort by compensating individuals according to their relative contributions.[6]

---

6 Hausken (1995) applies Nitzan's (1991a) sharing rule to a different setup in which each group $i = 1, \ldots, n$ is involved in a within-group contest which determines the provision of a within-group public good that is then used as an input in the contest between groups for an external prize V. The

For $n = 2$ and using symmetry, (6.4) yields the following equilibrium individual level of effort in group i:

$$x_i^* = \frac{[n_i - \alpha(n_i - n_j)][n_i + n_j - 1 - \alpha(n_i + n_j - 2)]\,V}{n_i(n_i + n_j)^2} \tag{6.14}$$

And thus in equilibrium a member of the small group exerts higher effort than a member of the large group (that is, $x_i^* > x_j^*$ if and only if $n_i < n_j$). Furthermore, the GSP occurs if and only if the group sharing rules put relatively more weight on egalitarianism than on relative effort (that is, $\alpha > 1/2$).

Nitzan (1991b) further considers the possibility of non-identical sharing rules across groups, that is, $\alpha_i \neq \alpha_j$ for all $i \neq j$, and $\alpha_i \in [0, 1]$ for all i. Davis and Reilly (1999) and Ueda (2002) characterized the corner equilibria that arise in this problem for two and n groups, respectively. In particular, Ueda (2002) provides the conditions for what he calls oligopolization and monopolization to arise in equilibrium, that is, situations in which one or more groups are inactive in equilibrium.

- **Oligopolization:** All groups in $A \subset \{1, \ldots, n\}$, and only these groups, exert positive effort in a pure strategy Nash equilibrium if and only if

$$\alpha_i < \frac{\sum_{h \in A} \alpha_h (n_h - 1) + 1}{\sum_{h \in A} n_h} \frac{n_i}{n_i - 1} \text{ for all } i \in A \tag{6.15}$$

and

$$\frac{\sum_{h \in A} \alpha_h (n_h - 1) + 1}{\sum_{h \in A} n_h} \frac{n_i}{n_i - 1} \leqslant \alpha_i \text{ for all } i \notin A \tag{6.16}$$

As it appears from the previous two conditions, it is the combination of sharing rules and group sizes that determines which groups exert positive effort in equilibrium and which ones remain inactive. Other things equal, a group is more likely to be active the lower its α, meaning that its sharing rule is relatively more meritocratic (from 6.15). Conversely, the more egalitarian the sharing rule of a group, the more likely that (6.16) is satisfied, so that the group remains inactive. Observe that an extreme situation in which (6.16) is satisfied for all but one group may arise, which means that only one group is active in equilibrium:

- **Monopolization:** Only one group, say i, exerts positive effort in a pure strategy Nash equilibrium if and only if

$$\alpha_h \geqslant \frac{\alpha_i (n_i - 1) + 1}{n_i} \frac{n_h}{n_h - 1} \text{ for all } h \neq i \tag{6.17}$$

---

author develops an algorithm illustrating how the interaction within and between groups proceeds through time.

or, equivalently,

$$B_i = (n_i n_h - n_i)\alpha_h - (n_h n_i - n_h)\alpha_i - n_h \geqslant 0 \text{ for all } h \neq i \tag{6.18}$$

Monopolization is a peculiar possibility in collective rent seeking, as it requires one group to exert a large enough amount of effort so as to make all other groups inactive. Such behaviour is never a best response in rent seeking among individuals. In collective rent seeking, however, members of a single group may be willing to exert great effort even when other groups are inactive, because they are still competing within the group.[7]

Let $n = 2$ and suppose that group one shares the prize in a more egalitarian way than group two (that is, $0 \leqslant \alpha_2 < \alpha_1 \leqslant 1$). As shown by Davis and Reilly (1999), if $B_2 < 0$ then a Nash equilibrium exists with both groups being active (that is, $x_1^* > 0$ and $x_2^* > 0$). If $B_2 \geqslant 0$ then a Nash equilibrium exists with only the second group being active:

$$x_1^* = 0 \text{ and } x_2^* = \frac{(1 - \alpha_2)(n_2 - 1)V}{n_2^2} \tag{6.19}$$

Consider the polar two-group case in which group one shares the prize in a fully egalitarian way while group two uses the relative effort rule (that is, $\alpha_1 = 1$ and $\alpha_2 = 0$). Observe that $B_2 \geqslant 0$ whenever group sizes are non-trivial (that is, $n_i > 1$ for $i = 1, 2$), hence in equilibrium only members of group two are active (that is, $x_1^* = 0$ and $x_2^* > 0$). As free-riding incentives are overwhelming in group one, efforts of its members drop to zero. Indeed, the members of the group that allocates the prize according to merit (that is, group two) are far more willing to exert effort than the members of the group that allocates the prize on an egalitarian basis (that is, group one). When contributing to the group effort, members of group two make it more likely that their group will win, while also increasing their own share of the prize in case of victory. In turn, this induces high levels of individual effort within the meritocratic group even though it does not face any serious competition from the egalitarian group.

Ueda (2002) also allows for different valuations across groups (that is, $V_i \neq V_j$ for all $i \neq j$), and shows that groups with low valuation of the prize are also likely to retire from the contest. From the modified conditions for oligopolization of rent seeking by a set of groups A, one can show that if every group contains only one member, then $\alpha_i = 0$ for all i and we have

$$V_i \leqslant \frac{A - 1}{A} \frac{A}{\sum_{h \in A} \frac{1}{V_h}} \text{ for all } i \notin A \tag{6.20}$$

[7] Balart et al. (2014) derive condition (6.18) for $n = 2$ and the case of a mixed public-private prize with $p \in [0,1]$ denoting the degree of privateness of the prize (see also equation (6.29) in the next section). As B_i is increasing in p for $\alpha_i \in [0, 1]$ $(i = 1, 2)$, it follows that the higher the degree of privateness of the prize, the more likely that one group is inactive in equilibrium. For a pure public good ($p = 0$), $B_i < 0$ for $i = 1, 2$, hence both groups are always active (recall that sharing rules are irrelevant in that case).

This is the rule by Hillman and Riley (1989), which limits entry to an imperfectly discriminating contest with asymmetric valuations of the prize. Hence, the analysis of Ueda (2002) can be seen as the generalization of this rule for collective rent seeking.

6.3 ENDOGENOUS SHARING RULES

Given the crucial effects sharing rules have on group performance several authors have proceeded to endogenize their choice. Collective rent seeking now takes place as a two-stage procedure. In the first stage, the representative of each group i determines the value of α_i to maximize the group's joint welfare, taking the other groups' sharing rules as given. In the second stage, every member of each group decides his level of individual effort. The sharing rules α_i are endogenously determined as a solution to this two-stage Nash game. The solution is subgame perfect and is obtained by backward induction.

In the second stage of the game, individual k in group i chooses x_{ki} to maximize (6.3), which yields the first-order condition given in (6.4). In the first stage of the game, the problem of the representative of each group can be written as

$$\max_{\alpha_i} \sum_{k=1}^{n_i} U_{ki} = \frac{X_i V}{X} - X_i \text{ such that (6.4) holds, and } \alpha_i \in [0,1] \text{ for all } i = 1,\ldots,n \quad (6.21)$$

Ueda (2002) provides the equilibrium sharing rules for the unique subgame perfect equilibrium of this two-stage game, in which every group puts in positive expenditure:

1. When no group has a greater size than half of the total population, we have $\alpha_i^* = 0$ for all $i = 1, \ldots, n$, or every group adopts the relative effort rule as its intra-group sharing rule.
2. When a group j has a size greater than half of the total population, all the remaining (small) groups adopt the relative effort rule (that is, $\alpha_i^* = 0$ for all $i \neq j$), while the large group sets

$$\alpha_j^* = \frac{n_j - \sum_{h \neq j} n_h}{2(n_j - 1)\sum_{h \neq j} n_h} \quad (6.22)$$

For $n = 2$, this yields (S. Lee, 1995):[8]

1. If $n_1 > n_2$, the equilibrium sharing rules are given by

$$\alpha_1^* = \frac{n_1 - n_2}{2n_2(n_1 - 1)} \text{ and } \alpha_2^* = 0$$

[8] Recently, S. Lee and S.K. Lee (2014) have explicitly examined the boundary conditions for this problem, providing the correct way of deriving the equilibrium identified by S. Lee (1995). Furthermore, they allow for the possibility of one group consisting of a single member.

The smaller group applies the relative effort rule to encourage voluntary contributions, while the larger group can spare some of the rent to be distributed according to the egalitarian rule. However, the two groups devote the same amount to rent seeking, as

$$X_1^* = X_2^* = \frac{(2n_2 - 1)V}{4n_2}$$

Thus, both groups are equally likely to win. Furthermore, the larger group two, the greater the amount of rent-seeking expenditures.

2. If $n_1 = n_2$, the equilibrium sharing rules are given by $\alpha_1^* = 0$ and $\alpha_2^* = 0$, that is, the two groups distribute the prize according to the relative effort rule. Hence, we are back to the equilibrium in (6.6), the two groups are equally likely to win, and total rent dissipation coincides with the one of the standard Tullock contest with N individuals.

Baik and S. Lee (1997) allow for more flexibility in the choice of group sharing rules by lifting the restriction that α_i must belong to the interval [0, 1].[9] A negative value of α_i implies that group i's sharing rule places great emphasis on members' relative contributions. In this case, group i collects $(-\alpha_i V/n_i)(X_i/X)$ from each of its members, and then distributes $(1 - \alpha_i)V(X_i/X)$ among them in proportion to relative effort. Conversely, when $\alpha_i > 1$, voluntary contribution is discouraged. In such a case, group i collects $(\alpha_i - 1)V(X_i/X)$ from its members according to relative effort, while distributing $\alpha_i V(X_i/X)$ equally among them.

For $n = 2$, the equilibrium (unrestricted) sharing rule in group i is given by

$$\alpha_i^* = \frac{n_i - n_j}{(n_i - 1)(n_i + n_j)} \tag{6.23}$$

Note that the small group distributes more than the rent in proportion to relative effort in order to overcome its size disadvantage. On the other hand, the large group can spare some of the rent to be distributed on an egalitarian basis, while its sharing rule places more emphasis on relative effort than when it is restricted.

Total rent seeking in group i is given by

$$X_i^* = \frac{n_j(n_i + n_j - 1)V}{(n_i + n_j)^2} \tag{6.24}$$

and thus the small group is more likely to win the prize than the large group, which suffers from the negative size effect due to free-riding. Finally, total rent dissipation coincides with the one of the standard Tullock contest with N individuals.

Baik and S. Lee (1997) go on to introduce inter-group mobility into the model by adding one more stage to the game. In the first stage a chance to move to the other group

---

9 Baik and Shogren (1995) have also noted this possibility.

is given to every member of each group. Each member takes all the other members' membership decisions as given and makes his own membership decision. No cost is incurred with movement of members across groups. In the second stage, each group selects its sharing rule. All the members choose their efforts simultaneously and independently in the third stage.

The payoff of each member of group $i = 1, 2$ can be written as a function of n_1 and n_2. Let $n_1 \geq n_2$. If $U_1(n_1, n_2) < U_2(n_1 - 1, n_2 + 2)$, a member of group one has an incentive to move to group two. Likewise, a member of group two will move to group one if $U_1(n_1 + 1, n_2 - 1) > U_2(n_1, n_2)$. When equality holds, an individual is indifferent between staying in his group and moving to the other one. The equilibrium is such that no one can increase his payoff by moving to the other group.

1. Let $\alpha_i \in [0, 1]$ for $i = 1, 2$. If $N \geq 5$ and N is an odd number, then $(n_1^*, n_2^*) = ((N + 1)/2, (N - 1)/2)$. If $N \geq 5$ and N is an even number, then $(n_1^*, n_2^*) = ((N/2) + 1, (N/2 - 1)$. Hence, for a large population, the two groups are of almost the same size, with a difference of only one or two members. Each group adopts a sharing rule that places great emphasis on relative effort.
2. Suppose there is no restriction on α_i for $i = 1, 2$. If $N \geq 6$ and N is an odd number, then $(n_1^*, n_2^*) = ((N + 1)/2, (N - 1)/2)$. If $N \geq 6$ and N is an even number, $(n_1^*, n_2^*) = (N/2, N/2)$. Hence, for a large and even N, the two groups are of the same size, and they adopt the relative effort rule. For a large and odd N, the two groups are of almost the same size, with a difference of only one member. The sharing rules of both groups are very close to the relative effort rule.

In a later contribution, Baik and S. Lee (2001) allow for the endogenous formation of strategic groups prior to the choice of group sharing rules and individual effort decisions. In strategic groups, group members compete individually for a prize and the winner keeps a part of the prize, while dividing the rest among group members. In this context, the choice of sharing rules thus amounts to specifying the share of the group's winner.[10] In this alternative formulation, if a member of group i wins the prize, he takes $\sigma_i V$ and each losing group member takes $(1 - \sigma_i) V/(n_i - 1)$, where $\sigma_i \geq 1/n_i$ is the winner's fractional share in group i. If $\sigma_i = 1/n_i$, group i's members share the prize equally when the winner belongs to group i. If $\sigma_i \in [1/n_i, 1)$, the winner takes less than the prize. If $\sigma_i = 1$, the winner takes all the prize. Finally, if $\sigma_i > 1$, the winner takes more than the prize.

The authors find that when only one strategic group is formed in equilibrium, if a group member wins the prize, he helps the losers in the group and thus the winner's share is less than the prize. When two strategic groups are formed and N is even, the winner takes all the prize. Finally, when more than two strategic groups are formed, the winner takes all the prize and receives 'bounties' from the losers in his group. Thus, in this case, the winner's share is more than the prize.

Baik et al. (2006) have established the strategic equivalence of competitive-share groups and strategic groups in collective rent seeking, the former corresponding to Nitzan's (1991a) original formulation, that is, groups compete for a rent and the winning

10 See also Baik (1994).

group's members share the prize according to a weighted average of the relative effort and egalitarian rules.[11] In particular, they show that[12]

$$\alpha_i = \frac{n_i(1 - \sigma_i)}{n_i - 1} \tag{6.25}$$

The authors show that the contest with strategic groups and the one with competitive-share groups yield the same individual efforts, expected payoffs and total rent dissipation, provided that the number of individuals, the number of groups and their size distribution are the same.

From Baik and S. Lee (2001) and using (6.25), we get the general unrestricted equilibrium sharing rule for group $i = 1, \ldots, n$:

$$\alpha_i^* = \frac{2n_i - N}{N(n_i - 1)(n - 1)} \tag{6.26}$$

This yields total effort in group $i = 1, \ldots n$:

$$X_i^* = \frac{(N - n_i)[N(n - 1) - 1]V}{[N(n - 1)]^2} \tag{6.27}$$

Finally, total rent dissipation is independent of the group size distribution, while it is increasing in both the number of individuals in the contest and the number of groups:

$$X^* = \frac{N(n - 1) - 1}{N(n - 1)} \tag{6.28}$$

For the two groups case, Balart et al. (2014) allow for the contested prize to have both private and public good characteristics. In such a case, the objective function of member k in group i is given by

$$U_{ki} = \frac{X_i}{(X_i + X_j)}\left\{p\left[(1 - \alpha_i)\frac{x_{ki}}{X_i} + \alpha_i\frac{1}{n_i}\right] + (1 - p)\right\}V - x_{ki} \tag{6.29}$$

where, as in (6.12), $p \in [0, 1]$ is the degree of privateness of the prize. They show that when the sharing rules α_i are unrestricted, the larger group uses its sharing rule as a coordination device among its members so as to make the small group inactive for most intermediate degrees of privateness. In particular, the small group (group two) is active

11 Baik and Shogren (1995) study voluntary competitive-share group formation, where the group is treated as a single player competing with the non-members to win the prize. They show that the competitive-share group is always formed voluntarily. Furthermore, with voluntary group formation, total rent dissipation is less relative to individual rent seeking. Note that with the competitive-share groups formulation, the members of the winning group need to know how much effort each member exerted when they share the prize, whereas this is not the case with the strategic groups formulation.

12 The restriction that $\sigma_i \geqslant 1/n_i$ is thus equivalent to $\alpha_i \leqslant 1$.

in equilibrium if and only if $p > \frac{n_2(n_1 - n_2 - 1)}{1 + n_2(n_1 - n_2 - 1)}$, which is very close to one. Remarkably, an arbitrarily small and negligible degree of privateness of the prize is sufficient to allow the large group to prevent any activity by the small group. Such a coordination mechanism among the members of the large group is possible to the extent that α_i can be negative, in which case an inactive group member has to pay a transfer to the other (active) group members. As a result, selecting a highly meritocratic sharing rule allows the large group to address free-riding among its members even for low degrees of privateness, thereby leading to high levels of individual effort and ultimately to the inactivity of the small group.

Further, the authors introduce the possibility of a sequential choice of sharing rules by the two groups. Regardless of the leader's size, and as in the simultaneous case, the small group is inactive for most values of privateness of the contested prize. If the prize is sufficiently private, so that both groups are active in equilibrium, the sequential choice of sharing rules yields the following insights: the large group acting as the leader adopts a sharing rule putting more emphasis on relative effort than in the simultaneous case, thereby increasing the level of competition between groups. Conversely, the small group acting as the leader chooses to lower competition between groups, hence it chooses a more egalitarian rule than it does in the simultaneous case. In turn, this follows from the fact that the sharing rules are strategic substitutes from the perspective of the small group, while they are strategic complements from the perspective of the large group.[13] Finally, while the GSP may occur when the choice of sharing rules is simultaneous, it always vanishes when such choice is sequential regardless of the leader's size.

Contrary to the literature presented so far, Noh (1999) makes the distinction between productive and appropriative activities when two groups compete over the common pool of output. He explores the interactions among intra-group sharing rules and the allocation of resources between the two types of activities. Member k of group $i = 1, 2$ is endowed with resources r_{ki} that can be used for productive purposes, b_{ki}, or for appropriative purposes, x_{ki}. The budget constraint of each individual is thus given by $r_{ki} = b_{ki} + x_{ki}$ for $k = 1,\ldots,n_i$ and $i = 1, 2$. and $i = 1, 2$. The productive technology is assumed to be

$$Y = B_1 + B_2 \tag{6.30}$$

In contrast to the literature we have reviewed so far, where the contestable prize is fixed, (6.30) explicitly captures the fact that appropriable output is determined endogenously and that appropriative activities are costly in terms of consumable output. Noh (1999) assumes the following timing: in the first stage, the two groups determine their sharing rules $\alpha_i \in [0, 1]$ either simultaneously or sequentially. In the second stage, given the sharing rules, each individual makes decisions on resource allocations

[13] This can also be seen from the first-order condition of the problem defined in (6.21) for $n = 2$ and a pure private good ($p = 1$), which yields the following reaction function:

$$\alpha_i = \frac{(n_i - n_j)[1 + \alpha_j(n_j - 1)]}{2n_j(n_i - 1)}$$

and thus we have $\frac{\partial \alpha_i(\alpha_j)}{\partial \alpha_j} > 0$ if and only if $n_i > n_j$.

simultaneously. Solving the second stage of the game yields the appropriative expenditures in group i:

$$X_i^* = \frac{(1 + K_i + K_j)(1 + K_i)}{(2 + K_i + K_j)^2}(R_i + R_j) \tag{6.31}$$

where $K_i = (1 - \alpha_i)(n_i - 1)$. As before, let $n_1 \geqslant n_2$. If the choice of sharing rules is simultaneous and for $\alpha_1 \in [(n_1 - 1)/(n_2 - 1), 1]$, any pair of sharing rules that satisfy $K_1 = K_2$ can be an equilibrium. That is, in contrast to Lee S. (1995), both groups may adopt the fully egalitarian rule (that is, $\alpha_i = 1$ for $i = 1, 2$). At the other extreme, the larger group selects a partially egalitarian rule whereas the smaller group distributes all the group income according to the relative (appropriative) effort rule. The sequential choice of intra-group sharing rules yields the adoption of fully egalitarian sharing rules in both groups, thereby minimizing the amount of resources allocated to appropriate activities.

In Noh (2002), the author adds endogenous group formation to the model for $N = 3$, assuming that the probability of winning the prize of the group formed by individuals i and j is given by $\pi_{ij} = \gamma X_{ij}/(\gamma X_{ij} + X_k)$ where $\gamma \geqslant 1$. That is, if a group is formed, its members' appropriative activities become more effective relative to those of the outside adversary. The author shows that either the two better endowed or the two less endowed agents may form a coalition, depending on the extent to which the effectiveness of the alliance's appropriative activities is enhanced as a result of alliance formation. If the two better endowed agents form an alliance, they adopt the egalitarian rule, thereby maintaining the size of the common pool at its maximum while keeping the share of the outside adversary at its minimum.[14]

Lee and Kang (1998) analyse collective contests with endogenous sharing rules in the presence of externalities, in the sense that each player's real cost of effort is affected by the aggregate amount of rent-seeking expenditures.[15] Specifically, the real cost of effort of player k is given by $x_k - \beta X$ where $\beta < 1/N$. Let $n = 2$ and $n_1 \geq n_2$. The expected payoff of individual k in group i is now given by

$$U_{ki} = \frac{X_i}{X}\left[(1 - \alpha_i)\frac{x_{ki}}{X_i} + \alpha_i\frac{1}{n_i}\right]V - (x_{ki} - \beta X) \tag{6.32}$$

The equilibrium sharing rule for group i is given by

[14] In a very different setting consisting of a hedonic game of coalition formation Barberá et al. (2014) examine the consequences of letting group members vote between egalitarianism and meritocracy when groups of a certain size must be formed in order for individuals to become productive. The authors study the existence of core stable partitions and show that the inability of voters to commit to one distributional rule or another is a potential source of instability. Nevertheless, when stable organizational structures exist, they may be rich in form, and different from those predicted by alternative models of group formation, while stability is compatible with the coexistence of meritocratic and egalitarian groups.

[15] See also Gürtler (2005).

$$\alpha_i^* = \frac{(n_i - n_j[1 - \beta(n_i + n_j)]}{(n_i - 1)(n_i + n_j)} \tag{6.33}$$

Therefore, the smaller group adopts an extremely effort-based incentive scheme ($\alpha_2 < 0$), while the larger group always remunerates its members partly on an egalitarian basis ($\alpha_1 > 0$). Rent seeking in group $i = 1,2$ is then given by

$$X_i^* = \frac{(n_i + n_j - 1)[n_j + \beta(n_i^2 - n_j^2)]V}{(1 - \beta)(n_i + n_j)^2} \tag{6.34}$$

Therefore, total rent dissipation is given by

$$X^* = \frac{(N - 1)V}{(1 - \beta)N} \tag{6.35}$$

which coincides with total rent seeking in the standard Tullock contest with N individuals. Furthermore, total expenditures are increasing in the strength of externalities.

Recently, Ursprung (2012) introduced the notion of cooperation among group members, under which not only the prize is split in an egalitarian fashion but so is the cost. The expected payoff of individual k in group $i = 1, 2$ is then given by

$$U_{ki} = \frac{X_i}{X_i + X_j}\frac{V}{n_i} - \frac{X_i}{qn_i}$$

where $q \in [0, 1]$ denotes the fraction of group members that cooperate and is equal for both groups. Groups can choose among the three sharing rules described earlier (that is, relative effort, egalitarian or mixed rule) and full cooperation. In a standard game theoretic two-stage model with endogenous sharing rules, and provided the two groups are of equal size, the subgame perfect equilibrium is such that they both adopt the relative effort rule. However, the author points out that such games do not provide any intuition regarding the dynamics of incentives in organizations, nor are they consistent with empirical evidence supporting a gradual increase in individual incentives. The author explains such a mechanism through an evolutionary narrative where groups start from a status quo characterized by egalitarian sharing. Suppose that one group is innovative and capable of introducing new incentive schemes while the other group simply mimics the opponent if its strategy proved to be successful. The author shows that the groups can gradually evolve from the egalitarian rule to full cooperation, followed by the adoption of the mixed rule that eventually leads to the relative effort rule through gradual adjustments of α. Nevertheless, this process requires time and incentives tend to crowd out cooperation.

6.3.1 Private Information

The studies reviewed so far assume that each group's sharing rule is observable by its rivals, thereby making sharing rules work as strategic variables. However, as the decision regarding the sharing rules is made within the groups, another likely possibility is that when expanding their effort, members of each group do not observe the sharing rules selected by their rivals.

Baik and S. Lee (2007) introduce private information regarding the group sharing rules for two groups of the same size (that is, $n = 2$ and $n_1 = n_2 = N/2$) and consider the following timing: first, the players make a binding agreement on the value of their sharing rule α_i. Next, all the players in both groups choose their effort level simultaneously and independently. When expending their outlays, the players in each group know the sharing rule of their own group, but do not know the one of the rival group. Furthermore, the authors allow for different group abilities in the contest by assuming that the winning probability of group one is given by

$$\pi_1 = \frac{\gamma X_1}{\gamma X_1 + X_2} \tag{6.36}$$

where $\gamma \geq 1$. Each group has two sequential moves, the first of which is hidden from the players in the other group, the second moves of the groups are chosen simultaneously, and payoffs to each group's members do not depend directly on the first move of the rival group. When solving the game, the authors treat it as a simultaneous-move game between the two groups, as each group chooses its two moves without observing the ones of the other group.

In the symmetric equilibrium with private information sharing rules, group one and two respectively select

$$\alpha_1^* = \frac{\gamma}{\gamma + 1} \quad \text{and} \quad \alpha_2^* = \frac{1}{\gamma + 1} \tag{6.37}$$

Individual effort is the same across groups and individuals, and given by

$$x^* = \frac{\gamma V}{(N/2)(\gamma + 1)^2} \tag{6.38}$$

The group sharing rules depend only on the ability asymmetry parameter γ. If $\gamma = 1$, both groups choose the same sharing rule, and they give equal weight to the relative effort and egalitarian rules (that is, $\alpha_i = 1/2$ for $i = 1, 2$). If $\gamma > 1$, the strong group (group one) gives more weight to the egalitarian rule than to the relative effort one, whereas the weak group (group two) does the opposite (that is, $\alpha_1 > 1/2$ and $\alpha_2 < 1/2$).

If $\gamma = 1$, given that the two groups are of equal size, we know from (6.23) that with public information they both adopt the relative effort rule (that is, $\alpha_i = 0$ for $i = 1, 2$). In such cases, all individuals exert the same level of effort given in (6.6). Thus, with public information regarding the sharing rules, each group gives more weight to relative effort compared to the case of private information. Indeed, with public information, each group can make a strategic commitment for the second stage inter-group competition by announcing its sharing rule in the first stage. In turn, to achieve their competitive advantage in the second stage, the members of each group have an incentive to behave 'aggressively', and do so by giving a large weight to relative effort when selecting their sharing rule. As a result, individual effort is larger when information regarding sharing rules is public than when it is private.

Generalizing to the case of n groups, Baik (2014) shows that all groups adopt the same sharing rule given by $\alpha_i^* = 1/n$. Thus, the higher the number of groups, the more emphasis they put on the relative effort rule. In turn, total equilibrium effort is the same across groups, and is given by

$$X_i^* = \frac{(n-1)V}{n^2} \tag{6.39}$$

and thus total rent dissipation is increasing in the number of groups, and is given by

$$X^* = \frac{(n-1)V}{n} \tag{6.40}$$

Similar to Baik and S. Lee (2001), Baik (2014) also allows for the endogenous formation of strategic groups prior to the choice of group sharing rules and individual effort decisions, this time under the assumption that information regarding the sharing rules is private. He shows that when the number of players is five or greater, and contrary to the case with observable sharing rules, group formation does not occur. As the author argues, the unobservability of sharing rules lowers individual incentives to form groups given that there is no more strategic advantage that the players could gain by forming groups and announcing their sharing rules.

In complement to the analysis of Esteban and Ray (2001), who study the occurrence of the GSP assuming a mixed public-private prize and an exogenous egalitarian sharing rule in each group (see equation (6.12)), Nitzan and Ueda (2011) endogenize the choice of such a rule in a setup of private information.[16] More specifically, the authors assume private information regarding the group sharing rules, while allowing for a mixed public-private prize and different marginal costs of effort across groups. As when making a decision on how much to contribute, each individual is required to infer the sharing rules in the other groups, the authors apply the perfect Bayesian equilibrium notion.

Let the total prize be normalized to unity, and denote the ratio of the private good part by γ, where $\gamma \in (0, 1]$. The expected payoff of individual k in group i is given by

$$U_{ki} = \frac{X_i}{\sum_{j=1}^{n} X_j} V\left(\lambda\left[(1-\alpha_i)\frac{x_{ki}}{X_i} + \alpha_i \frac{1}{n_i}\right], 1-\lambda\right) - c_i(x_{ki}) \tag{6.41}$$

where $c_i(0) = 0$, $c_i'(x_{ki}) > 0$ and $c_i''(x_{ki}) \geq 0$ for all $x_{ki} > 0$. The authors assume away oligopolization by assuming that $\lim_{x_{ki} \to 0} c_i'(x_{ki}) = 0$. Denote by q the amount of the private good distributed to the individual and by G the amount of group-specific public good provided to the group to which the individual belongs. The function $V(q, G)$ is twice

[16] For the case of public information regarding the group sharing rules and the consequences in terms of the GSP, see Balart et al. (2014).

differentiable and $V(q, G) > 0$ unless $(q, G) = (0, 0)$. Furthermore, $V_q > 0$, $V_G \geq 0$ and $V_{qq} \leq 0$ hold for all $q > 0$ and $G > 0$.

As before, at first the decision on the value of the group sharing rule is made simultaneously in each group. After observing the sharing rule chosen by his group, each member of the competing groups chooses his effort level individually. In the unique pure strategy perfect Bayesian equilibrium, all members of a given group choose a symmetric equilibrium effort, and attain a symmetric utility level. An interior equilibrium sharing rule of group i is given by

$$\alpha_i^* = 1 - \frac{(1 - \pi_i)}{\eta(n_i, \lambda)} \tag{6.42}$$

where π_i is given by (6.1) and $\eta(n_i, \lambda)$ is the elasticity of the benefit from the private part of the prize, that is,

$$\eta(n_i, \lambda) = \frac{\partial}{\partial q} V\left(\frac{\lambda}{n_i}, 1 - \lambda\right) \frac{\frac{\lambda}{n_i}}{V\left(\frac{\lambda}{n_i}, 1 - \lambda\right)} \tag{6.43}$$

The authors show the following: if two groups i and j have the same size and $c_i'(x) < c_j'(x)$ for all $x > 0$, then $\pi_i > \pi_j$ and thus $\alpha_i^* > \alpha_j^*$. Furthermore, if $\eta(n_i, \lambda)$ is non-decreasing with respect to n_i (and if $\lambda \neq 1$ holds), then the sharing rule selected by a larger group is more egalitarian.

In a contest for a mixed private-public good where $\lambda \neq 1$, a larger group always attains a higher winning probability. That is, a larger group always outperforms a smaller group unless the prize is purely private. However, the group attaining the lower winning probability is actually the one choosing the rule giving higher incentives to its members.

6.3.2 Information Revelation

A natural question that arises at this point is whether the groups have an interest in revealing their sharing rule to their rivals. Baik and D. Lee (2012) answer this question by analysing rent seeking between two strategic groups of equal size (that is, $n = 2$ and $n_1 = n_2 = N/2$) in which each group has the option of releasing or not its sharing rule information. They consider the following three-stage game: in the first stage, each group decides and announces whether it will release the information about its sharing rule to the rival group. In the second stage, the members of each group jointly choose their sharing rule, and then each group releases the information about its sharing rule if it decided to do so in the first stage. In the third stage, all individuals choose their effort levels simultaneously and independently.

The winning probability of individual k in group one is given by

$$\pi_{k1} = \frac{\gamma x_{k1}}{\gamma X_1 + X_2} \tag{6.44}$$

where $\gamma > 0$. As in Baik (1994, 2014) and Baik and S. Lee (2001), the authors focus on collective rent seeking in which the prize is awarded to one of the players (that is, strategic groups). Again, as shown by Baik et al. (2006), this alternative model yields exactly the same results as the ones of Nitzan's (1991a) original formulation. As we saw, in the former, if a member of group $i = 1, 2$ wins the prize, he takes $\sigma_i V_i$ and each losing member of the group takes $(1 - \sigma_i)V_i/(N/2 - 1)$, where $\sigma_i \geqslant 2/N$ is the winner's fractional share in group i. The expected payoff of individual k in group i is now given by

$$U_{ki} = \pi_{ki}\sigma_i V_i + \frac{(1 - \sigma_i)V_i}{(N/2 - 1)}\sum_{j \neq k}^{N/2}\pi_{ji} - x_{ki} \tag{6.45}$$

Let $V_1 = \delta V_2$, where $\delta > 0$. The authors show the following. First, the case where both groups release their sharing-rule information never occurs in equilibrium. Second, the case where neither group releases its sharing-rule information occurs only if the players are evenly matched (that is, $\delta\gamma = 1$). Finally, when the players are unevenly matched (that is, $\delta\gamma \neq 1$), one group releases its sharing-rule information and the other does not. In turn, the former group becomes the leader, while the latter group becomes the follower.

6.4 CONCLUSION

We reviewed how different ways of sharing a prize among group members in collective rent seeking affect individuals' incentives to contribute to their group's aggregate effort, and the consequences regarding the extent of rent dissipation, the occurrence of the GSP, group formation and the choice between productive and appropriative activities.

While in several contexts efforts devoted to rent-seeking activities are considered as wasteful, in collective rent seeking effort can be desirable. Think, for instance, of a team within an organization sharing a bonus depending on the productivity of its members, or research funds allocated among departments according to their research outputs. Therefore, the reviewed literature on prize sharing in collective rent seeking relates to the broader labour economics literature regarding bonus allocations and payment schemes in order to incentivize workers. Given that experimental evidence in slightly different setups tends to confirm the idea that sharing rules based on relative effort induce higher effort levels than more egalitarian rules (Gunnthorsdottir and Rapoport 2006; Sutter 2006; Kugler et al. 2010), the literature we reviewed clearly has important implications.[17]

REFERENCES

Baik, Kyung Hwan (1993), 'Effort levels in contests: the public-good prize case', *Economics Letters*, **41**(4), 363–7, reprinted in Roger D. Congleton, Arye L. Hillman and Kai A. Konrad (eds) (2008), *40 Years of Research on Rent Seeking 1 – The Theory of Rent Seeking*, Heidelberg: Springer, pp. 347–52.

---

17 For an exhaustive review of the experimental literature on contests see Dechenaux et al. (2012).

Baik, Kyung Hwan (1994), 'Winner-help-loser group formation in rent-seeking contests', *Economics & Politics*, **6**(2), 147–62.
Baik, Kyung Hwan (2008), 'Contests with group-specific public-good prizes', *Social Choice and Welfare*, **30**(1), 103–17.
Baik, Kyung Hwan (2014), 'Endogenous group formation in contests: unobservable sharing rules', Unpublished manuscript, available at http://www.kelley.iu.edu/BEPP/documents/EGF.pdf (accessed 14 November 2014).
Baik, Kyung Hwan and Dongryul Lee (2012), 'Do rent-seeking groups announce their sharing rules?', *Economic Inquiry*, **50**(2), 348–63.
Baik, Kyung Hwan and Sanghack Lee (1997), 'Collective rent seeking with endogenous group sizes', *European Journal of Political Economy*, **13**(1), 121–30.
Baik, Kyung Hwan and Sanghack Lee (2001), 'Strategic groups and rent dissipation', *Economic Inquiry*, **39**(4), 672–84.
Baik, Kyung Hwan and Sanghack Lee (2007), 'Collective rent seeking when sharing rules are private information', *European Journal of Political Economy*, **23**(3), 768–76.
Baik, Kyung Hwan and Jason F. Shogren (1995), 'Competitive-share group formation in rent-seeking contests', *Public Choice*, **83**(1–2), 113–26.
Baik, Kyung Hwan, In-Gyu Kim and Sunghyun Na (2001), 'Bidding for a group-specific public-good prize', *Journal of Public Economics*, **82**(3), 415–29.
Baik, Kyung Hwan, Bouwe R. Dijkstra, Sanghack Lee and Shi Young Lee (2006), 'The equivalence of rent-seeking outcomes for competitive-share and strategic groups', *European Journal of Political Economy*, **22**(2), 337–42, reprinted in Roger D. Congleton, Arye L. Hillman and Kai A. Konrad (eds) (2008), *40 Years of Research on Rent Seeking 1 – The Theory of Rent Seeking*, Heidelberg: Springer, pp. 323–8.
Balart, Pau, Sabine Flamand and Orestis Troumpounis (2014), 'Strategic choice of sharing rules in collective rent seeking', Lancaster University Economics Working Paper Series 2014/005, available at http://eprints.lancs.ac.uk/70687/1StratagicChoice.pdf (accessed 14 November 2014).
Barberá, Salvador, Carmen Beviá and Clara Ponsatí (2014), 'Meritocracy, egalitarianism and the stability of majoritarian organizations', Barcelona GSE Working Paper Series, Working Paper 737.
Cheikbossian, Guillaume (2008), 'Heterogeneous groups and rent seeking for public goods', *European Journal of Political Economy*, **24**(1), 133–50.
Chowdhury, Subhasish M., Dongryul Lee and Roman M. Sheremeta (2013), 'Top guns may not fire: best-shot group contests with group-specific public good prizes', *Journal of Economic Behavior & Organization*, **92**, 94–103.
Congleton, Roger (1980), 'Competitive process, competitive waste, and institutions', in James M. Buchanan, Rober D. Tollison and Gordon Tullock (eds), *Toward a Theory of the Rent-seeking Society*, College Station, TX: Texas A&M University Press, reprinted in Roger D. Congleton, Arye L. Hillman and Kai A. Konrad (eds) (2008), *40 Years of Research on Rent Seeking 1 – The Theory of Rent Seeking*, Heidelberg: Springer, pp. 69–96.
Congleton, Roger D. (1984), 'Committees and rent-seeking effort', *Journal of Public Economics*, **25**(1), 197–209, reprinted in Roger D. Congleton, Arye L. Hillman and Kai A. Konrad (eds) (2008), *40 Years of Research on Rent Seeking 1 – The Theory of Rent Seeking*, Heidelberg: Springer, pp. 279–91.
Corchón, Luis C. (2007), 'The theory of contests: a survey', *Review of Economic Design*, **11**(2), 69–100.
Davis, Douglas D. and Robert J. Reilly (1999), 'Rent seeking with non-identical sharing rules: an equilibrium rescued', *Public Choice*, **100**(1–2), 31–8.
Dechenaux, Emmanuel, Dan Kovenock and Roman M. Sheremeta (2012), 'A survey of experimental research on contests, all-pay auctions and tournaments', available at http://ssrn.com/abstract=2154022 or http://dx.doi.org/10.2139/ssrn.2154022 (accessed 14 November 2014).
Dijkstra, Bouwe R. (1998), 'Cooperation by way of support in a rent seeking contest for a public good', *European Journal of Political Economy*, **14**(4), 703–25.
Epstein, Gil S. and Yosef Mealem (2009), 'Group specific public goods, orchestration of interest groups with free riding', *Public Choice*, **139**(3–4), 357–69.
Epstein, Gil S. and Yosef Mealem (2012), 'Cooperation and effort in group contests', *Economics Bulletin*, **32**(1), 624–38.
Esteban, Joan-Maria and Debraj Ray (2001), 'Collective action and the group size paradox', *American Political Science Review*, **95**(3), 663–72, reprinted in Roger D. Congleton, Arye L. Hillman and Kai A. Konrad (eds) (2008), *40 Years of Research on Rent Seeking 1 – The Theory of Rent Seeking*, Heidelberg: Springer, pp. 379–88.
Gunnthorsdottir, Anna and Amnon Rapoport (2006), 'Embedding social dilemmas in intergroup competition reduces free-riding', *Organizational Behavior and Human Decision Processes*, **101**(2), 184–99.
Gürtler, Oliver (2005), 'Collective contests with externalities: corrigendum', *European Journal of Political Economy*, **21**(2), 533–6.

Hausken, Kjell (1995), 'The dynamics of within-group and between-group interaction', *Journal of Mathematical Economics*, **24**(7), 655–87.
Hillman, Arye L. (2013), 'Rent seeking', in Michael Reksulak, Laura Razzolini and William F. Shughart II (eds), *The Elgar Companion to Public Choice*, 2nd edn, Cheltenham, UK and Northampton, MA, USA: Edward Elgar Publishing, pp. 307–30.
Hillman, Arye L. and John G. Riley (1989), 'Politically contestable rents and transfers', *Economics & Politics*, **1**(1), 17–39, reprinted in Roger D. Congleton, Arye L. Hillman and Kai A. Konrad (eds) (2008), *40 Years of Research on Rent Seeking 1 – The Theory of Rent Seeking*, Heidelberg: Springer, pp. 185–208.
Inderst, Roman, Holger M. Müller and Karl Wärneryd (2005), 'Influence costs and hierarchy', *Economics of Governance*, **6**(2), 177–97.
Inderst, Roman, Holger M. Müller and Karl Wärneryd (2007), 'Distributional conflict in organizations', *European Economic Review*, **51**(2), 385–402.
Katz, Eliakim and Julia Tokatlidu (1996), 'Group competition for rents', *European Journal of Political Economy*, **12**(4), 599–607, reprinted in Roger D. Congleton, Arye L. Hillman and Kai A. Konrad (eds) (2008), *40 Years of Research on Rent Seeking 1 – The Theory of Rent Seeking*, Heidelberg: Springer, pp. 537–46.
Katz, Eliakim, Shmuel Nitzan and Jacob Rosenberg (1990), 'Rent seeking for pure public goods', *Public Choice*, **65**(1), 49–60.
Kolmar, Martin (2013), 'Group conflicts. Where do we stand?', University of St Gallen, School of Economics and Political Science, Discussion Paper 2013-31.
Kolmar, Martin and Hendrik Rommeswinkel (2013), 'Contests with group-specific public goods and complementarities in efforts', *Journal of Economic Behavior & Organization*, **89**, 9–22.
Konrad, Kai A. (2004), 'Bidding in hierarchies', *European Economic Review*, **48**(6), 1301–08, reprinted in Roger D. Congleton, Arye L. Hillman and Kai A. Konrad (eds) (2008), *40 Years of Research on Rent Seeking 1 – The Theory of Rent Seeking*, Heidelberg: Springer, pp. 547–54.
Konrad, Kai A. (2009), *Strategy and Dynamics in Contests*, Oxford: Oxford University Press.
Kugler, Tamar, Amnon Rapoport and Asya Pazy (2010), 'Public good provision in inter-team conflicts: effects of asymmetry and profit-sharing rule', *Journal of Behavioral Decision Making*, **64**(3), 421–38.
Lee, Dongryul (2012), 'Weakest-link contests with group-specific public good prizes', *European Journal of Political Economy*, **28**(2), 238–48.
Lee, Sanghack (1992), 'Optimal rent-seeking group', *American Economist*, **36**(2), 58–60.
Lee, Sanghack (1993), 'Inter-group competition for a pure private rent', *Quarterly Review of Economics and Finance*, **33**(3), 261–6.
Lee, Sanghack (1995), 'Endogenous sharing rules in collective-group rent seeking', *Public Choice*, **85**(1–2), 31–44.
Lee, Sanghack and J. Hyeong Kang (1998), 'Collective contests with externalities', *European Journal of Political Economy*, **14**(4), 727–38.
Lee, Sanghack and Sung-Kyu Lee (2014), 'Endogenous sharing rules in collective rent seeking: a graphic characterisation', *Journal of Economic Research*, **19**(3).
Long, Ngo Van (2013), 'The theory of contests: a unified model and review of the literature', *European Journal of Political Economy*, **32**(4), 161–81, reprinted in Chapter 3, this volume.
Long, Ngo Van and Neil Vousden (1987), 'Risk-averse rent seeking with shared rents', *Economic Journal*, **97**(388), 971–85, reprinted in Roger D. Congleton, Arye L. Hillman and Kai A. Konrad (eds) (2008), *40 Years of Research on Rent Seeking 1 – The Theory of Rent Seeking*, Heidelberg: Springer, pp. 293–308.
Müller, Holger M. and Karl Wärneryd (2001), 'Inside versus outside ownership: a political theory of the firm', *RAND Journal of Economics*, **32**(3), 527–41, reprinted in Roger D. Congleton, Arye L. Hillman and Kai A. Konrad (eds) (2008), *40 Years of Research on Rent Seeking 2 – Applications: Rent Seeking in Practice*, Heidelberg: Springer, pp. 679–93.
Münster, Johannes (2007), 'Simultaneous inter- and intra-group conflicts', *Economic Theory*, **32**(2), 333–52.
Nitzan, Shmuel (1991a), 'Collective rent dissipation', *Economic Journal*, **101**(409), 1522–34, reprinted in Roger D. Congleton, Arye L. Hillman and Kai A. Konrad (eds) (2008), *40 Years of Research on Rent Seeking 1 – The Theory of Rent Seeking*, Heidelberg: Springer, pp. 309–22.
Nitzan, Shmuel (1991b), 'Rent seeking with non-identical sharing rules', *Public Choice*, **71**(1–2), 43–50.
Nitzan, Shmuel (1994), 'Modelling rent-seeking contests', *European Journal of Political Economy*, **10**(1), 41–60.
Nitzan, Shmuel and Kaoru Ueda (2011), 'Prize sharing in collective contests', *European Economic Review*, **55**(5), 678–87.
Nitzan, Shmuel and Kaoru Ueda (2014), 'Cost sharing in collective contests', CESifo Working Paper Series.
Noh, Suk Jae (1999), 'A general equilibrium model of two group conflict with endogenous intra-group sharing rules', *Public Choice*, **98**(3–4), 251–67.
Noh, Suk Jae (2002), 'Resource distribution and stable alliances with endogenous sharing rules', *European Journal of Political Economy*, **18**(1), 129–51.
Olson, Mancur (1965), *The Logic of Collective Action*, Harvard, MA: Harvard University Press.

Riaz, Khalid, Jason F. Shogren and Stanley R. Johnson (1995), 'A general model of rent seeking for public goods', *Public Choice*, **82**(3–4), 243–59, reprinted in Roger D. Congleton, Arye L. Hillman and Kai A. Konrad (eds) (2008), *40 Years of Research on Rent Seeking 1 – The Theory of Rent Seeking*, Heidelberg: Springer, pp. 361–78.

Sutter, Matthias (2006), 'Endogenous versus exogenous allocation of prizes in teams – theory and experimental evidence', *Labour Economics*, **13**(5), 519–49.

Tullock, Gordon (1980), 'Efficient rent seeking', in James M. Buchanan, Robert D. Tollison and Gordon Tullock (eds), *Toward a Theory of the Rent-seeking Society*, College Station TX: Texas A&M University Press, pp.97–112, reprinted in Roger D. Congleton, Arye L. Hillman and Kai A. Konrad (eds) (2008), *40 Years of Research on Rent Seeking 1 – The Theory of Rent Seeking*, Heidelberg: Springer, pp. 105–20.

Ueda, Kaoru (2002), 'Oligopolization in collective rent seeking', *Social Choice and Welfare*, **19**(3), 613–26.

Ursprung, Heinrich W. (1990), 'Public goods, rent dissipation, and candidate competition', *Economics & Politics*, **2**(2), 115–32, reprinted in Roger D. Congleton, Arye L. Hillman and Kai A. Konrad (eds) (2008), *40 Years of Research on Rent Seeking 1 – The Theory of Rent Seeking*, Heidelberg: Springer, pp. 329–46.

Ursprung, Heinrich W. (2012), 'The evolution of sharing rules in rent-seeking contests: incentives crowd out cooperation', *Public Choice*, **153**(1–2), 149–61.

Vazquez, Alexis (2014), 'Sharing the effort costs in collective contests', available at http://ssrn.com/abstract=2439828 or http://dx.doi.org/10.2139/ssrn.2439828 (accessed 14 November 2014).

Wärneryd, Karl (1998), 'Distributional conflict and jurisdictional organization', *Journal of Public Economics*, **69**(3), 435–50.

7. Rent seeking and organizational structure

Karl Wärneryd

SUMMARY

A hierarchically structured rent-seeking contest may be associated with lower equilibrium expenditure than a corresponding flat contest. In this chapter we discuss how this fact may be used to explain the structure of organizations such as firms, including why firms commonly have outside owners.

7.1 INTRODUCTION

Conventional wisdom used to have it that the structure of organizations, such as firms, is dictated by technological concerns (see, for example, Chandler 1962). Thus, for example, as American firms faced expanding markets after around 1850, it successively became necessary to hire administrative experts to specialize in various functions such as production and marketing. As firms diversified, the unitary firm structure came to be replaced by the multidivisional firm, with each product line essentially its own organization. And so on.

From a rent-seeking perspective, however, each decision-maker in an organization is also a locus of influence. If decisions affect the fortunes of others in the organization, those others will have an incentive to try to exert influence to have decisions made in their favor. To the extent that such influence activities are about purely distributional concerns, and involve the spending of resources or efforts that could have been deployed productively instead, they may represent a cost to the organization – and, indeed, ultimately to society. (See Tullock 1967 [2008].) In this chapter we shall investigate how different organizational structures give rise to different levels of these costs.

Intuition might suggest that the more levels, and thus the more nodes of decision-making, a hierarchical organization has, the more resources will necessarily be wasted on rent seeking. Indeed, this seems to be taken for granted in such writings on influence activities in organizations as Meyer et al. (1992), Milgrom and Roberts (1990) and Scharfstein and Stein (2000 [2008]). A central message of this chapter, in contrast, will be that hierarchy can help to decrease rent-seeking costs, thus providing an explanation for its existence in the first place.

Neoclassical economics provides no hints as to why there are firms and organizations in the economy in the first place, let alone why they should be structured in a particular way. The firm of general equilibrium theory is just a black-box production function, and all transactions take place in the market. In his famous paper in 1937, Coase argued that real-world firms owe their existence to what is now commonly known as 'transaction costs,' costs of transacting in the market that can be avoided within a firm. Coase exemplified transaction costs by such things as the search cost of finding somebody to transact with, the cost of drafting a contract once a partner has been found and the cost of enforcing contracts. According to Coase, these costs do not arise within the firm because the firm is characterized by the fact that one party, the firm's owner, has the power simply to decree the terms of any within-firm transaction.

Quite apart from how this explanation for the firm's rationale seems to attribute too much authority to the firm's owner, it does not shed any light on the most common form of ownership of firms today, that of separation of ownership and control. As we shall see, the rent-seeking perspective can provide an explanation for why it may be optimal for a firm to have outside owners, rather than operate as a partnership or cooperative.

7.2 RENT SEEKING AND HIERARCHY

7.2.1 The Flat Organization

Consider an organization comprised of n identical participants, who produce something together that is worth Y. Suppose it is not possible to write an enforceable contract that specifies how Y should be split among the participants; instead, each individual may exert effort or spend resources on obtaining a larger share, in competition with the others. Let x_i be the level of such appropriative effort engaged in by individual participant i. We shall assume that the share of the surplus that accrues to individual i, given everybody's rent-seeking expenditures, is

$$p_i(x_1,x_2,\ldots,x_n) := \begin{cases} x_i/\sum_j x_j & \text{if } \sum_j x_j > 0 \\ 1/n & \text{otherwise.} \end{cases}$$

This particular 'contest success function' was introduced by Tullock (1980 [2008]) explicitly for the study of rent seeking, and has become very popular in the literature. As such, it has a somewhat ad hoc flavor, as it is not immediately clear why the rent-seeking process should be of this specific nature. It was axiomatized by Skaperdas (1996).

Assuming rent-seeking expenditures come at unit cost, individual i's objective or utility function is then

$$u_i(x_1, x_2, \ldots, x_n) := p_i(x_1, x_2, \ldots, x_n)\, Y - x_i.$$

First, note that it cannot happen in equilibrium that nobody expends anything. For assume everyone except individual i expends nothing on rent seeking. If individual i then also expends nothing, he gets Y/n. If instead he expends some very small amount he gets all of Y, less that small amount. Hence there must be some such small amount that individual i could profitably spend.

Taking everyone else's expenditures as given, the first-order condition for a best reply expenditure on the part of individual i is therefore

$$\frac{\partial u_i}{\partial x_i} = \frac{\Sigma_j x_j - x_i}{(\Sigma_j x_j)^2} Y - 1 = 0.$$

To solve for equilibrium expenditures, we can make use of the fact that we have a symmetric situation. Inspection of the first-order condition reveals that each individual best-reply expenditure depends only on the total of expenditures. Hence in equilibrium it must be the case that everybody makes the same expenditure x^*. The above expression may then be written as

$$\frac{nx^* - x^*}{(nx^*)^2}Y - 1 = 0.$$

The solution is therefore

$$x^* = \frac{n-1}{n^2}Y.$$

Hence individual equilibrium utility is Y/n^2. Aggregate expenditure in equilibrium is

$$nx^* = \frac{n-1}{n}Y.$$

Defining the rate of rent dissipation as the ratio of total expenditure to the value of the surplus, we have that

$$\delta := \frac{nx^*}{Y} = \frac{n-1}{n}.$$

With a finite number of participants, therefore, less than the value of the rent is invested in equilibrium. But as n approaches infinity, aggregate expenditure approaches Y and the rate of dissipation approaches 1. Hence 'perfect competition' in rent seeking in this model leads to perfect dissipation.

7.2.2 The Two-tier Organization

Suppose now that the previously studied organization is split into two divisions, with n_1 and n_2 members, respectively, where $n_1 + n_2 = n$.

We shall assume that rent seeking at the top level takes a similar form to that at the divisional level, but that individual rent-seeking efforts increase the divisional share. That is, an increased divisional share is now a public good to members of the division. Specifically, if S_{di} is the top-level rent-seeking expenditure of individual i in division d, we shall assume the share of Y that goes to division 1 is

$$\alpha := \begin{cases} \Sigma_i s_{1i}/(\Sigma_i s_{1i} + \Sigma_j s_{2j}) & \text{if } \Sigma_i s_{1i} + \Sigma_j s_{2j} > 0 \\ 1/2 & \text{otherwise.} \end{cases}$$

As the division-level contest has the same structure as before, each member of division 1 expects to get $\alpha Y/n_1^2$ in the end. In the top-level contest, the objective function of a member of division 1 is therefore

$$v_{1i} := \frac{\alpha Y}{n_1^2} - S_{1i}.$$

For reasons similar to before, it cannot happen that nobody expends anything in equilibrium. Hence the optimal top-level expenditure of member i in division 1 is given by the first-order condition

$$\frac{Y}{n_1^2}\frac{\Sigma_j s_{1j}}{(\Sigma_k s_{1k} + \Sigma_j s_{2j})^2} = 1.$$

The corresponding condition for a member of division 2 is

$$\frac{Y}{n_2^2}\frac{\Sigma_k s_{1k}}{(\Sigma_k s_{1k} + \Sigma_j s_{2j})^2} = 1.$$

Inspection of these conditions reveals that they do not uniquely determine individual contributions in equilibrium, as only aggregate divisional expenditures matter. This is, of course, because of the public good nature of expenditure at the top level. Hence there are many equilibria, all of them with the property that a division's aggregate expenditure has the same level.

Having noted this multiplicity problem, we now focus on within-division symmetric equilibrium. That is, we now look for an equilibrium such that all individuals in a division make the same equilibrium expenditure. Let S_1 be the common equilibrium expenditure level in division 1, and S_2 that in division 2. The conditions for equilibrium are then that

$$\frac{Y}{n_1^2}\frac{n_2 s_2}{(n_1 s_1 + n_2 s_2)^2} = 1$$

and

$$\frac{Y}{n_2^2}\frac{n_1 s_1}{(n_1 s_1 + n_2 s_2)^2} = 1.$$

Defining $\theta := n_1^2 + n_2^2$, the solution to this system of equations is

$$s_1 = \frac{n_2^2 Y}{n_1 \theta^2}$$

and

$$s_2 = \frac{n_1^2 Y}{n_2 \theta^2}.$$

This implies that in equilibrium we have $\alpha = n_2^2/\theta$, that is, the division with fewer members gets the larger share of the top-level pie. The intuition for this is that a dollar increment of the share at this stage is worth more to agents in the less populated division, since less of it will be dissipated in the internal divisional contest than would be the case if it ended up in the more populated division. Therefore individuals in the smaller division are willing to expend relatively more resources to get such an increment.

Note that resources are now expended at both of the two contest levels. Total aggregate expenditure in the hierarchical two-tier organization is therefore

$$X^H := n_1 s_1 + n_2 s_2 + n_1 x_1 + n_2 x_2 = \frac{Y}{\theta} + \frac{n_1 - 1}{n_1} n_2^2 \frac{Y}{\theta} + \frac{n_2 - 1}{n_2} n_1^2 \frac{Y}{\theta}.$$

The corresponding aggregate equilibrium expenditure in a flat organization with the same total number of participants is

$$X^F := \frac{n_1 + n_2 - 1}{n_1 + n_2} Y.$$

The difference in total conflict costs between the two organizations is therefore

$$X^F - X^H = \frac{n_1^4 + n_2^4 - n_1^2 n_2 - n_1 n_2^2}{n_1 n_2 (n_1 + n_2)(n_1^2 + n_2^2)} Y.$$

The denominator of the fraction is always positive. The numerator may be written $\theta^2 + 2n_1^2 n_2^2 - n_1^2 n_2 - n_1 n_2^2$, which is also always positive.

Hence the two-tier hierarchical organization is always associated with lower equilibrium rent-seeking expenditure than the corresponding flat organization.

The intuition for this result is the following. There are two effects at work lowering equilibrium expenditure under hierarchy relative to the flat organization.

- In equilibrium, the larger share of the surplus will end up in the less populated division, where it will be dissipated less.
- There is a free-rider problem at the top level of the game. Since the divisional share, given the contest structure, is a public good to the agents in a division, they will each spend relatively less than they would if the entire increment due to an individual contribution fell to the individual agent.

Wärneryd (1998) first showed this result, in the context of a discussion of federalism. Inderst et al. (2007) consider its generalization to a larger class of contest success functions, while Inderst et al. (2005) discuss optimal hierarchies. Münster (2007) analyses the role of decision order and endogeneity of the prize. For an early discussion of rent seeking in hierarchies, see Hillman and Katz (1987 [2008]).

7.3 LEVIATHAN AND THE NATURE OF THE FIRM

It seems natural to view the firm as a group of agents who produce something together. So why are not all firms organized as partnerships or cooperatives, that is, owned by all the participants together? Certain types of firms, for example, law firms and medical practices, are, indeed, typically organized like this. But why is the most common form of ownership to have outside owners? As we shall see, the rent-seeking or conflict perspective can shed some light on the issue.

As already noted, Coase argued that the firm avoids certain costs of transacting in the market, since transactions within the firm can be carried out by decree to fit the wishes of its owner. That is, the Coasian firm is characterized by the use of power or authority.

Alchian and Demsetz (1972) pointed out that this view of the firm overstates the power normally wielded by the owner. In reality, the firm seems to have no power beyond threatening to fire an employee. Since, similarly, an employee of the firm may threaten to leave it, this perspective does not explain how firm transactions are different from market transactions. Instead, Alchian and Demsetz argue, the existence of firms is explained by the monitoring problems that arise in joint production. Externalities in production give rise to problems of observing and measuring the individual contribution to a collective undertaking. Since participants cannot then be rewarded on the basis of individual efforts, the monitoring problem in turn leads to a free-riding problem. Hence there may be a need for an outsider, not directly involved in production, who performs monitoring of individual efforts. To have the correct incentives, this outsider should be a residual claimant, and thus becomes the firm's owner.

Holmström (1982) developed this reasoning further by pointing out that there will always be a free-riding problem if the entire surplus generated by the organization has to be shared among the participants. If the budget has to balance, as would normally be the case with the partnership model, it cannot be the case that each agent receives the value of his marginal contribution. Hence such an organization cannot provide the correct incentives for efficient production. In Holmström's view, the owner is an outsider who credibly threatens to remove resources in case the efficient production target fails to be met.

But from the point of view of the insiders of the firm, outside owners can also be viewed as a 'common enemy' in the struggle to appropriate individual shares of the firm's surplus. Much like how Thomas Hobbes's Leviathan by presenting a greater threat causes citizens to behave more peacefully toward one another, the outside owner can contribute to lowering the aggregate amount of resources spent on rent seeking in the firm, even though effort must now also be taken to prevent the outsider from confiscating the entire surplus. In the following, we shall consider this conflict perspective on firm ownership (based on Müller and Wärneryd 2001).

If managers in a firm cannot commit to a sharing rule in advance, there will be wasteful distributional conflict *ex post*. Introducing outside owners, whose only role is to take part in the distributional conflict against the managers as a collective, may be optimal, because it lessens the within-firm conflict. Unlike, for example, the arguments of Holmström, this theory can explain why it may be optimal to have more than one outside owner. Furthermore, the analysis will suggest a framework for explaining why some firms are nevertheless partnerships.

7.3.1 Partnerships

Consider a firm that has m managers, which we shall sometimes also refer to as the insiders. The firm may also have workers, whose productive efforts are completely contractible. The production activity of the firm gives rise to a surplus Y after the workers have been paid. We shall assume that

$$Y := (1 - \theta)\bar{y} + \theta \sum_{i=1}^{m} e_i,$$

where $\bar{y}$ is a constant, e_i is a firm-specific investment of manager i and $\theta \in [0,1]$ is a parameter that measures the relative importance of managerial investments for the value of output.

For now (indeed throughout), we shall assume we have $\theta = 0$, that is, managerial investments have no effect on output.

We assume enforcement of property rights is imperfect and costly. Hence when the surplus Y first arrives, it is owned by nobody in particular, and each individual manager has to take costly action to acquire or safeguard a share of it. Such activities, for concreteness, may take the form of, for example, on-the-job consumption. That is, we assume the managers cannot agree in advance on a sharing rule, or, if they can agree on a sharing rule then it is still contestable. Consider the case of, for example, a law firm organized as a partnership. Empirically, such firms often officially have an egalitarian sharing rule, according to which the partners share what remains of the surplus, after deducting costs, equally among themselves. The cost-deduction part is key here. By manipulating costs, a partner in such a firm could in effect increase his relative share of the surplus, even though on the face of it everyone gets the same share – for instance, by reporting private consumption as costs associated with working with a client.

In particular, we assume that the utility of manager *i*, given safeguarding or rent-seeking expenditures r_j, is

$$u_i := \alpha_i Y - r_i,$$

where

$$\alpha_i := \begin{cases} r_i / \Sigma_j r_j & \text{if } \Sigma_j r_j > 0 \\ 1/m & \text{otherwise} \end{cases}$$

is manager *i*'s surplus share. Note that if nobody expends anything on rent seeking, then the default split is egalitarian.

By analogy with the previous discussion, there is a unique symmetric equilibrium where each manager expends

$$r^* := \frac{m-1}{m^2} Y.$$

Hence total expenditures are $mr^* = ((m-1)/m)Y$, and each manager gets utility Y/m^2 in equilibrium under the partnership model.

7.3.2 Outside Ownership

Next assume the original partners of the firm could instead sell shares to one or more outside owners. Owning shares in a corporation does not directly entitle you to anything other than the right to go to shareholders' meetings. Since managers initially control the surplus, they can retain all of it through, for example, accounting measures taken to hide it and internal diversions of resources leading to its consumption. Hence share ownership is most realistically thought of as the right of the outside owner to participate in a contest with the original managers for a slice of the cake. In order to get anything at all out of the firm, shareholders must exert costly effort.

As with the partnership, it is still the case that managers must take costly action to guarantee themselves a share of whatever remains in the firm, but under outside ownership they must also fight as a collective against the outside owner in order to retain as large a fraction as possible of the surplus within the firm.

That is, we are considering replacing the organizational structure of the partnership, which looks like Figure 7.1:

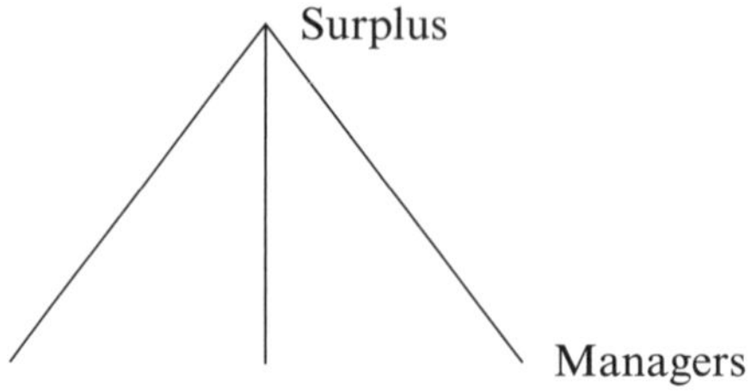

Figure 7.1 Organizational chart for the partnership

with one with an outside owner (or owners) that looks like Figure 7.2:

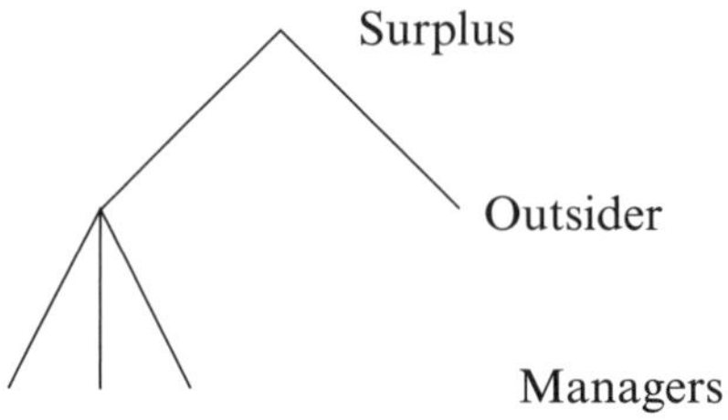

Figure 7.2 Organizational chart for the corporation

Hence if βY, with $\beta \in [0,1]$, is what remains in the firm after the outsiders get theirs, the final contest between insiders will yield each individual manager $\beta Y/m^2$, by straightforward analogy with the partnership case discussed above.

It seems natural to model the higher-level contest between outsiders and insiders analogously with the inside contest, with the single difference that the share retained by the firm is a public good to the managers. We therefore assume that

$$\beta := \begin{cases} \Sigma_j s_j / (\Sigma_j s_j + \Sigma_k t_k) & \text{if } \Sigma_j s_j + \Sigma_k t_k > 0 \\ 1 & \text{otherwise,} \end{cases}$$

where s_i is the expenditure of manager i in the contest with outsiders and t_j is the corresponding expenditure of outside owner j. Note that, as seems reasonable, if the outsiders exert no effort at all, all of the surplus remains with the firm.

We assume the n owners own one share each. Each receives $1/n$ of the uncovered surplus of $(1 - \beta) Y$ as a dividend payment. Hence owner i's objective function, given the contest expenditures of the insiders and the other owners, is

$$u_i^o := \frac{1}{n}(1 - \beta) Y - t_i,$$

and his first-order condition for an optimal expenditure level is

$$\frac{\partial u_i^o}{\partial t_i} = \frac{\Sigma_j s_j}{(\Sigma_j s_j + \Sigma_k t_k)^2} \frac{Y}{n} - 1 = 0.$$

We note that since the surplus share is a public good to the owners, the first-order condition only determines aggregate owner expenditure.

Similarly, the objective function of insider i is

$$u_i^m := \frac{\beta Y}{m^2} - s_i,$$

with corresponding first-order condition

$$\frac{\partial u_i^m}{\partial s_i} = \frac{\Sigma_k t_k}{(\Sigma_j s_j + \Sigma_k t_k)^2} \frac{Y}{m^2} - 1 = 0.$$

As with the owners, we note that this condition only determines aggregate equilibrium expenditure on the part of the insiders.

As in the previous section, however, we shall focus on within-group symmetric equilibrium. That is, we shall assume all owners make the same expenditure t and all managers the same expenditure s. Hence the conditions for equilibrium expenditure reduce to

$$\frac{ms}{(ms + nt)^2} \frac{Y}{n} - 1 = 0$$

and

$$\frac{nt}{(ms + nt)^2} \frac{Y}{m^2} - 1 = 0.$$

Solving this system of simultaneous equations for s and t, we have that

$$s = \frac{n}{m(m^2 + n)^2} Y$$

and

$$t = \frac{m^2}{n(m^2 + n)^2} Y.$$

Total expenditure on rent-seeking activities by all agents, taking into account the expenditures made by the managers in fighting for individual shares of the surplus retained in the firm, is then

$$ms + nt + \frac{m - 1}{m} \frac{n}{m^2 + n} Y = \frac{m - n + mn}{m(m^2 + n)} Y.$$

This quantity is strictly less than total rent-seeking costs under inside ownership, $((m - 1)/m) Y$, for all $m > 1$ and $n \geq 1$. In the limit, however, as n approaches infinity, it approaches the cost of inside ownership. Thus having many owners is just like having none, as free-riding among the outsiders completely cancels their efforts.

Much like before, the intuition for the drop in rent-seeking costs as a result of outside ownership lies in two interacting effects.

- The public good nature of the firm's share of surplus induces a free-rider problem for the managers, leading to under-contribution relative to what would have been collectively optimal.
- Since the outsiders will always make positive expenditure in equilibrium, less than the entire surplus will be retained in the firm. Hence each individual manager's share will be worth less in the end, making for lower expenditure in the internal fight among managers.

Assuming capital markets are competitive, potential outsiders can be made to pay exactly their expected value for a share in the firm, taking into account the subsequent distributional conflict. Hence each share is sold at a price of $(m^2(m^2 + n - 1))\,Y/(n(m^2 + n)^2)$. Assuming the insiders split the proceeds from share sales equally, they each have an *ex ante* utility (adding the share proceeds to the utility of the two levels of ensuing contests) of $(m^3 - m + n)\,Y/m^2(m^2 + n))$, which, as expected, is strictly greater than their total individual utility Y/m^2 under inside ownership.

We have seen how introducing outside owners may lower rent-seeking costs in the firm. This happens even though we assume outside owners have no control rights, and, indeed, only serve to remove part of the surplus from the firm.

So far, however, we have assumed that the size of the firm's surplus is fixed and independent of any activities on the part of managers. Things may be different if managers have to be provided with incentives to make firm-specific investments *ex ante*. Since managers receive a smaller share of the total surplus when there are outside owners, their incentives to make firm-specific investments are dulled. There is a 'holdup' problem. Hence in choosing an optimal ownership structure, there is a tradeoff between minimizing rent-seeking costs and providing investment incentives.

Empirically, the partnership or cooperative form of firm organization is often found in, for example, law firms and medical practices. What these industries have in common may be the importance of incontractible human capital investments by partners. It is precisely in such cases that the rent-seeking theory of firm ownership suggests that the tradeoff between minimizing conflict costs and providing incentives should favor the partnership model.

REFERENCES

Alchian, Armen A. and Harold Demsetz (1972), 'Production, information costs, and economic organization', *American Economic Review*, **62**(5), 777–95.

Chandler, Jr, Alfred D. (1962), *Strategy and Structure: Chapters in the History of the American Industrial Enterprise*, New York: Doubleday & Co.

Coase, Ronald H. (1937), 'The nature of the firm', *Economica*, **4**(16), 386–405.

Hillman, Arye L. and Eliakim Katz (1987), 'Hierarchical structure and the social costs of bribes and transfers', *Journal of Public Economics*, **34**(2), 129–42, reprinted in Roger D. Congleton, Arye L. Hillman and Kai A. Konrad (eds) (2008), *40 Years of Research on Rent Seeking 1: The Theory of Rent Seeking*, Heidelberg: Springer, pp. 523–36.

Holmström, Bengt (1982), 'Moral hazard in teams', *Bell Journal of Economics*, **13**(2), 324–40.

Inderst, Roman, Holger M. Müller and Karl Wärneryd (2005), 'Influence costs and hierarchy', *Economics of Governance*, **6**(2), 177–97.

Inderst, Roman, Holger M. Müller and Karl Wärneryd (2007), 'Distributional conflict in organizations', *European Economic Review*, **51**(2), 385–402.

Meyer, Margaret, Paul Milgrom and John Roberts (1992), 'Organizational prospects, influence costs, and ownership changes', *Journal of Economics & Management Strategy*, **1**(1), 9–35.
Milgrom, Paul and John Roberts (1990), 'Bargaining costs, influence costs, and the organization of economic activity', in James E. Alt and Kenneth A. Shepsle (eds), *Perspectives on Positive Political Economy*, Cambridge: Cambridge University Press, pp. 57–89.
Müller, Holger M. and Karl Wärneryd (2001), 'Inside vs outside ownership: a political theory of the firm', *RAND Journal of Economics*, **32**(3), 527–41, reprinted in Roger D. Congleton, Arye L. Hillman, and Kai A. Konrad (eds) (2008), *40 Years of Research on Rent Seeking 2 – Applications: Rent Seeking in Practice*, Heidelberg: Springer, pp. 679–93.
Münster, Johannes (2007), 'Simultaneous inter- and intra-group conflicts', *Economic Theory*, **32**(2), 333–52.
Scharfstein, David S. and Jeremy C. Stein (2000), 'The dark side of internal capital markets: divisional rent-seeking and inefficient investment', *Journal of Finance*, **55**(6), 2537–64, reprinted in Roger D. Congleton, Arye L. Hillman and Kai A. Konrad (eds) (2008), *40 Years of Research on Rent Seeking 2 – Applications: Rent Seeking in Practice*, Heidelberg: Springer, pp. 621–48.
Skaperdas, Stergios (1996), 'Contest success functions', *Economic Theory*, **7**(2), 283–90, reprinted in Roger D. Congleton, Arye L. Hillman and Kai A. Konrad (eds) (2008), *40 Years of Research on Rent Seeking 1: The Theory of Rent Seeking*, Heidelberg: Springer, pp. 263–70.
Tullock, Gordon (1967), 'The welfare costs of tariffs, monopolies, and theft', *Western Economic Journal*, **5**(3), 224–32, reprinted in Roger D. Congleton, Arye L. Hillman and Kai A. Konrad (eds) (2008), *40 Years of Research on Rent Seeking 1: The Theory of Rent Seeking*, Heidelberg: Springer, pp. 45–53.
Tullock, Gordon (1980), 'Efficient rent seeking', in James M. Buchanan, Robert D. Tollison and Gordon Tullock (eds), *Toward a Theory of the Rent-seeking Society*, College Station, TX: Texas A&M University Press, pp. 269–82, reprinted in Roger D. Congleton, Arye L. Hillman and Kai A. Konrad (eds) (2008), *40 Years of Research on Rent Seeking 1: The Theory of Rent Seeking*, Heidelberg: Springer, pp. 105–20.
Wärneryd, Karl (1998), 'Distributional conflict and jurisdictional organization', *Journal of Public Economics*, **69**(3), 435–50.

8. Contest effort

Yosef Mealem and Shmuel Nitzan

SUMMARY

This chapter compares effort with contest-success functions of the Tullock logit-lottery type and the all-pay auction. We describe the circumstances in which combinations of the parameters in the general contest give rise to greater effort. Our presentation encompasses in principle two types of contests. In rent-seeking contests, the social objective is to minimize effort because effort is used unproductively. In the contest-design literature, the objective of the designer of the contest can be to maximize effort because effort is privately beneficial to the contest designer, as when 'effort' takes the form of a monetary bribe. The bribes then become rents to be contested.

8.1 INTRODUCTION

A contest-design literature (Gradstein and Konrad 1999 [2008]) has considered how a contest might be designed to maximize effort of contestants when the effort is beneficial to the contest designer, as in the case of bribes. The bribes entail creation and extraction of rents that are ultimately contestable (Hillman and Katz 1987 [2008]; Hillman 2013). In this chapter, we describe how choice of the contest-success function (CSF) affects the total 'effort' in a contest or the value of bribes. We compare outcomes with the two most common CSFs, the logit Tullock-type lottery (Tullock 1980 [2008]) and an all-pay auction or APA (Hillman and Samet 1987 [2008]; Hillman and Riley 1989 [2008]). We shall use the general terminology 'effort' in expositing the models, where effort can be understood to encompass bribes made to influence the outcome of a contest.

Fang (2002) initiated the study of the comparison between efforts in contests based on the CSFs. He focused on a simple lottery and clarified the effect of asymmetry in contestants' valuations of prizes on the outcome of the comparison regarding social loss. In this chapter, we describe generalizations of the comparison between the CSFs allowing for asymmetry in valuations of prizes; any Tullock-type lottery; any overt structural bias among contestants (Lien 1986, 1990; Clark and Riis 2000; Epstein et al. 2011, 2013; Nti 2004); and any pattern of differential prize taxation satisfying the balanced-budget constraint (Mealem and Nitzan 2012, 2014). In some of the cases, we also allow for any number of contestants N (Mealem and Nitzan 2012; Franke et al. 2013, 2014).

The conclusions of the comparison between a Tullock lottery and the APA depend on whether the lottery is simple or not; on the asymmetry between the contestants' valuations; on the number of the contestants; and on the form of the allowed bias between the contestants. The comprehensive clarification of the role of these parameters in influencing effort evoked (or bribe revenue provided) in contests is the purpose of this chapter.

A detailed summary of the conclusions is presented in the final section. A less specific brief summary of the primary conclusions is presented below, assuming asymmetric prize valuations.

- In a fair (unbiased) two-player contest, the APA yields larger total effort at persuasion than a simple lottery, if the contestants' prize valuations are not too asymmetric.
- In a fair two-player contest, the effort-maximizing lottery for the contest designer yields larger total effort at persuasion than the APA.
- In a fair contest allowing overt discrimination as well as differential taxation of the prize subject to a balanced-budget constraint, the effort-maximizing lottery for the contest designer yields larger total effort at persuasion than an APA, for any number of contestants.
- In an unfair contest allowing overt discrimination, but not differential prize taxation, the effort-maximizing simple lottery for the contest designer yields smaller total effort at persuasion than the effort-maximizing APA, for any number of contestants.
- When overt discrimination is allowed, but differential prize taxation is not allowed, there is a lottery that yields total effort with certainty that is equal to the expected total effort under the effort-maximizing APA.

8.2 THE EXTENDED CONTEST AND THE CSFs

8.2.1 The Setting

In the basic one-stage contest setting, there are two risk-neutral contestants, the high and low-benefit contestants, 1 and 2.[1] The valuations of the prize of the contestants are denoted by v_i, $v_1 > v_2$ or $k = \frac{v_1}{v_2} > 1$. Assuming common knowledge of the contestants' prize valuations, we are concerned with the conditions that give rise to maximal contest effort, which is a rational objective for the contest designer who is the beneficiary of the efforts of contenders. Given the contestants' fixed prize valuations and the CSF, which is the function that specifies the contestants' winning probability given their effort $\Pr_i(x_1, x_2)$, the expected net payoff (surplus) of contestant i is:

$$E(u_i) = \Pr_i(x_1, x_2)\, v_i - x_i, \; (i = 1,2) \tag{8.1}$$

where $x_1 \geq 0$ and $x_2 \geq 0$ denote the contestants' respective efforts (if $x_1 = x_2 = 0$, then $\Pr_i = 0.5$). The total expected effort of the contestants in equilibrium is denoted by:

$$G = E(x_1 + x_2) \tag{8.2}$$

---

[1] The general case of an N-player contest will be discussed later.

That is, the function (8.2) specifies the Nash-equilibrium efforts of the contestants in the equilibrium of the contest when the applied CSF is $Pr_i(x_1,x_2)$ and the payoff functions of the contestants are given by (8.1). We focus on the widely studied logit CSFs that include APAs and Tullock's lotteries.[2]

8.2.2 Differential Prize Taxation Under a Balanced-budget Constraint

Direct discrimination via differential taxation of the contested prize that affects the contestants' actual prize valuations, v_1 and v_2, is a pair of (positive or negative) amounts, ε_1 and ε_2 that changes the prize valuations to $(v_1 + \varepsilon_1)$ and $(v_2 + \varepsilon_2)$. A contest designer who applies such a taxation scheme must ensure that the transformed prize valuations are positive; otherwise the contestants will not voluntarily take part in the contest and the designer's revenue will be equal to zero. We assume that the contest designer faces a balanced-budget constraint, that is, ε_1 and ε_2 must satisfy the requirement that the designer's expected expenditures are equal to zero, that is, $p_1\varepsilon_1 + p_2\varepsilon_2 = 0$.[3] This *ex ante* balanced-budget constraint is reasonable when the designer is 'risk neutral' in the sense that he or she is willing to face an *ex post* deficit after the outcome of the contest has been revealed. The balanced-budget constraint is plausible when the designer controls a series of identical contests that are held during a fixed period (weekly, monthly or quarterly contests that are held during the budget year). In such a case, the designer tries to ensure that during the relevant period the net transfers between the contestants are cancelled out such that his budget is balanced.

8.2.3 All-pay Auctions

In our setting, winning with certainty means that the CSF leaves no residual winning uncertainty after the revelation of the contestants' efforts. In such a case, the certain winner is the contestant who makes the largest effective effort, where a unit of effort by one contestant is not necessarily equally effective as a unit of effort of his rival, as first suggested in the context of a bribery game by Lien (1986, 1990) and later by Clark and Riis (2000). That is, the CSF for $\delta > 0$ is an APA given by:

$$p_1(x_1,x_2) = \begin{cases} 1 & \text{if} \quad x_1 > \delta x_2 \\ 0.5 & \text{if} \quad x_1 = \delta x_2 \\ 0 & \text{if} \quad x_1 < \delta x_2 \end{cases} \tag{8.3}$$

2 In Epstein et al. (2011), when the weight assigned to the expected welfare of the contestants is sufficiently high, in equilibrium there is no contest (and so no efforts are made) and the winner is the contestant with the higher valuation. In contrast, in our model, such an equilibrium cannot emerge because the weight assigned to the expected welfare of the contestants is zero. Therefore, any equilibrium is an interior one: there is real competition and 'meaningful' winning (each contestant makes an effort with a positive winning probability).

3 The possibility of a balanced-budget constraint faced by the contest designer was first considered in Mealem and Nitzan (2012, 2014). The possibility of caps on the contestants' efforts has been examined, for example, by Che and Gale (1998) and Ujhelyi (2009).

and for $\delta = 0$, $p_1(x_1, x_2) = 1$. By (8.3), a reduction in δ increases the overt structural bias in favor of the more motivated contestant 1. Furthermore, $0 \leq \delta < 1$ implies a bias in favor of contestant 1. When $\delta = 1$ the contest is fair and there is no bias. When $\delta > 1$ the bias is in favor of contestant 2.[4]

8.2.4 The Logit Lotteries

When winning is uncertain, the CSF leaves some residual winning uncertainty after the revelation of the contestants' efforts. In such a case, in equilibrium every contestant has some positive winning probability. Sufficiently large effort can secure a high probability of winning, but not certain winning.

Our analysis is confined to the well-studied logit Tullock-type lotteries. For $\delta > 0$, these lotteries are given by:[5]

$$p_1(x_1,x_2) = \frac{x_1^{\alpha}}{x_1^{\alpha} + (\delta x_2)^{\alpha}} \tag{8.4}$$

where $0 < \alpha < \infty$ and for $\delta = 0$, $p_1(x_1, x_2) = 1$, where α and δ are selected by the contest designer. The interpretation of δ is as previously indicated.

8.3 UNBIASED APA VERSUS THE SIMPLE UNBIASED LOTTERY

With asymmetric prize valuations, $k > 1$ and $\alpha = 1$, Fang (2002) (see Subsection 8.6.2) has shown that a simple lottery can yield more effort than an APA. Specifically, in equilibrium, the total effort in a contest based on a simple lottery, $G_L = \frac{v_1 v_2}{v_1 + v_2}$, is larger than the expected efforts in a contest based on an APA, $G_A = \frac{v_2(v_1 + v_2)}{2v_1}$,[6] provided that the gap between the contestants' stakes is sufficiently large, that is, $k > 1 + \sqrt{2}$.[7] The intuitive

4 For alternative additive modeling of the bias, see Konrad (2002) and Li and Yu (2012).

5 As is well known (see Konrad 2009 and references therein), when $0 < \alpha \leq 2$, the contest has a pure-strategy equilibrium. Since, one can easily see that for $\alpha = \infty$ the logit lottery takes the form (8.3). The form in (8.4) is slightly different from the form of the logit lottery in Epstein et al. (2011) because in the present chapter, as will become clear, it is important to make a meaningful comparison between the degree of discrimination under the two types of CSFs. Such a comparison requires that discrimination be defined in a similar way in the two cases.

6 In equilibrium of the unbiased APA (δ=1) (Hillman and Riley 1989 [2008]; Konrad 2009), the expected efforts are $x_1^* = 0.5v_2$ and $x_2^* = \frac{v_2^2}{2v_1}$. In turn, the expected net payoff of the player with the lower prize valuations is zero, namely, when $k > 1$, only the player with the higher prize valuation enjoys some surplus. The expected net payoff of the player with the higher prize valuation is equal to $E(u_1^*) = (v_1 - v_2)$. In equilibrium, the value of the designer's objective function (the expected aggregate efforts of the contestants in the mixed-strategy equilibrium) is equal to $G_A = \frac{v_2(v_1 + v_2)}{2v_1}$,.

7 This condition is derived from the general condition obtained by Fang (2002) for any number of contestants N. Matros and Duffy (2012) study a model of public-good provision assuming that the good is provided if the total amount of contributions made in a contest exceeds the common value of the public good. We present conditions for the superiority of the unbiased

explanation of this result is as follows: The intensity of rent-seeking competition in the APA game is largely determined by the gap between the valuations of the contestants. As this gap becomes more substantial, competition becomes weaker and the politician gains less in expected effort or revenue. In contrast, the politician's revenue from the lottery is less dependent on this gap. Furthermore, since $G_A = \frac{v_2(v_1 + v_2)}{2v_1}$ is the expected revenue for the APA, while for the lottery $G_L = \frac{v_1 v_2}{v_1 + v_2}$ is a certain revenue, assuming risk neutrality, the politician will strictly prefer the lottery even when $k = 1 + \sqrt{2}$. Undoubtedly, the significance of this result is that it paved the way for the comparison between the two prototypical CSFs that are sometimes called the discriminating and the simple non-discriminating CSFs (see Hillman and Riley 1989 [2008]).

8.4 UNBIASED APA VERSUS THE UNBIASED LOTTERY

As mentioned above, Fang (2002) has shown that, with asymmetric prize valuations, a simple lottery can yield more effort (or in a rent-seeking context be more wasteful) than an APA (yielding larger total efforts) provided that the gap between the contestants' stakes is sufficiently large. Epstein et al. (2013) have considerably strengthened this finding by establishing that in a fair contest ($\delta = 1$), if $k > 1$, then a designer who can select the exponent α *always* prefers a logit lottery because it yields larger efforts relative to the APA, even when the sufficient condition $k > 1 + \sqrt{2}$ is not satisfied. In fact, the exponent of the preferred lottery satisfies $0 < \alpha < 2$, which means that the corresponding contest game has a unique pure-strategy equilibrium.

The result of Epstein et al. (2013) implies that in a fair contest, if $k > 1$, then a Tullock-type lottery is always preferred to the APA for a risk-neutral or a risk-averse designer.[8] Alcalde and Dahm (2010) have shown that for any $\alpha \geq 2$ there exists an equilibrium in mixed strategies that is equivalent to the equilibrium of the APA. However, so far a characterization of the complete set of mixed-strategy equilibria is not available. Since Epstein et al. (2013) show that there exists α, $0 < \alpha < 2$, which yields efforts that are larger than those obtained under the APA, it is clear that this conclusion remains valid (at least partly) when the parameter α satisfies the requirement $0 < \alpha < \infty$.

8.5 APA VERSUS LOTTERY WITH $\alpha \leq 1$: THE CASE OF ENDOGENOUS δ

Epstein et al. (2011) have shown that, with overt discrimination, the effort-maximizing APA is the designer's preferred CSF (it yields larger efforts than the effort-maximizing lottery) as long as $0 < \alpha \leq 1$. For $\alpha = 1$ and any number of contestants, this result

simple lottery relative to the unbiased APA (the good is supplied under the simple lottery but not under an APA).

[8] This result differs from that obtained in Epstein and Nitzan (2006, section 4.2.2). In fact it corrects that result, which did not take into account the non-negativity constraints of the contestants' utilities.

remains valid, as shown by Franke et al. (2014), in the general N-player contest. This contest has a two-stage structure: In the first stage, the administrator decides on the specific personal prices that determine the winning probabilities or the weights assigned to the agents that might result in a biased contest rule. In the second stage, the contestants choose effort, taking as given the specified price/weight structure of the administrator and the efforts of opponents. Although the underlying two-stage game is highly stylized and simple, its analysis is rather complex: it requires a solution of a bilevel program or, more precisely, a mathematical program with equilibrium constraints.

8.6 APA VERSUS LOTTERY WITH $0 < \alpha < \infty$: THE CASE OF ENDOGENOUS δ AND $N = 2$

In a Nash equilibrium of the contest, every contestant determines effort, given the parameters of the CSF. In the unconstrained environment that allows overt structural discrimination, anticipating the effort of the contestants, the contest designer sets the parameters of the CSF such that effort is maximized. When considering the APA, we take into account the degree of discrimination δ set by the designer. When considering the logit lottery, we take into account both δ and the exponent α selected by the designer. Note that in a rent-seeking context, the preferred parameters for the designer are the socially most wasteful ones.

Most of the literature studying Tullock lotteries and the APA disregarded deliberate discrimination between the contestants and control of the exponent α. However, in the context of an APA, Lien (1986, 1990) and Clark and Riis (2000) studied a bribery game in which an official (designer of the contest) can engage in overt structural discrimination in a multiplicative form. Nti (2004) examined the effect of the exponent α on the contestants' efforts in Tullock lotteries disregarding discrimination between the contestants and focusing on pure-strategy equilibria. He thus initiated the study of effort-maximizing contest design through control of the exponent α for Tullock CSFs. As noted, Epstein et al. (2011) presented a complete analysis of the designer's effect on contestants' efforts through control of the degree of discrimination both for the APA and the logit lotteries, assuming that in the case of the lotteries the exponent α is given and restricted to the range $0 < \alpha \leq 1$. They thus reshifted the emphasis in the study of effort-maximizing contest design to control through overt discrimination.

In this section the two approaches are combined allowing the control of both the exponent α and the degree of discrimination between the contestants. In addition, the analysis is generalized by allowing any value of the exponent α in the logit CSFs that gives rise to a Tullock-type lottery associated with a pure-strategy or a mixed-strategy equilibrium, $0 < \alpha < \infty$, or to an APA that is associated with a mixed-strategy equilibria where $\alpha = \infty$.[9]

---

[9] Note that under the logit CSF, where $0 < \alpha < 2$, the exerted efforts are certain whereas under the APA, the meaning of effort is expected effort.

8.6.1 The Effort-maximizing APA

Under the APA, aggregate effort (8.2) is maximized by determining the effort-maximizing value of δ. The effort-maximizing δ is equal to k (for a proof, see Epstein et al. 2011, proposition 1, assuming that no weight is assigned to the expected welfare of the contestants). This effort-maximizing bias maximizes the extent of competition between the contestants. In fact, such bias eliminates the advantage of contestant 1, creates actual equality between the competitors and completely eliminates their surplus. The corresponding value of the expected aggregate effort of the contestants in the mixed-strategy equilibrium of the contest is $G_A = 0.5(v_1 + v_2)$. Thus, in equilibrium, the expected total effort is equal to the average prize valuation.

8.6.2 The Effort-maximizing Lottery

Under the logit CSF, we take into account the effort-maximizing level of α, $0 < \alpha < \infty$ and δ, $\delta \geq 0$. Let us partition the range of the parameter α into $0 < \alpha \leq 2$ and $2 < \alpha < \infty$. For $0 < \alpha \leq 2$, where a unique pure-strategy equilibrium exists, the effort-maximizing values of δ and α are equal to $\delta^* = k$ and $\alpha^* = 2$ (see Epstein et al. 2013). The corresponding value of the designer's objective function (the certain aggregate efforts of the contestants in the pure-strategy equilibrium of the contest) is $G_L = 0.5(v_1 + v_2) = G_A$. We therefore obtain:

> *Proposition 1: If we take into account the effort-maximizing values of both the degree of discrimination* δ, $\delta \geq 0$, *and the exponent* α, *then the maximal contestants' efforts under a lottery are larger than or equal to the expected efforts obtained in the mixed-strategy equilibrium of the effort-maximizing APA.*

The combined effect of the designer's preferred discrimination $\delta = k$ and his selection of the exponent α in the logit CSF

$$p_1(x_1,x_2) = \frac{x_1^\alpha}{x_1^\alpha + (\delta x_2)^\alpha} = \frac{1}{1 + (\delta x_2/x_1)^\alpha}$$

that gives rise to a pure-strategy equilibrium when $0 < \alpha \leq 2$, results in equal (expected) effort and elimination of the surplus of both of the contestants. This result implies that, from the designer's viewpoint, the effort-maximizing logit lottery (which need not satisfy the constraint $0 < \alpha \leq 2$) cannot be dominated by the APA. In other words, in terms of rent seeking, the endogenously selected lottery cannot be socially less wasteful than the endogenously selected APA.

Proposition 1 establishes that the intuition that a larger exponent α induces greater effort is not valid. Under discrimination, even the use of an effort-maximizing APA that is maximally receptive to the contestants' efforts would not induce greater effort than when one is less receptive to the contestants' efforts, $\alpha^* = 2$, allowing random winning. Recall that in both cases, bids are subject to effort-maximizing discrimination, the effort-maximizing degree of discrimination being equal to k. Nevertheless, the valid part of the above intuition is that a larger exponent α indeed induces greater effort under the logit lottery provided that the exponent α gives rise to a pure-strategy equilibrium.

8.7 APA VERSUS LOTTERY WITH $0 < \alpha \leq 2$: THE CASE OF $\delta = 1, N = 2$ AND DIRECT DISCRIMINATION

If the designer faces a balanced-budget constraint, then his preferred taxation under the APA yields total effort that is equal to the average of the initial stakes. In Mealem and Nitzan (2014), we have shown that these efforts are larger than those obtained under almost any Tullock-type lottery and, in any event, they are always larger than or equal to those obtained under any lottery.

> *Proposition 2: The total effort of the contestants corresponding to the designer's preferred taxation scheme under the APA is equal to the average prize valuation,* $G_A = 0.5(v_1 + v_2)$. *The total effort is larger than or equal to that obtained under any Tullock-type lottery with* $0 < \alpha \leq 2$.

The maximal effort under an APA can also be secured under a Tullock-type lottery with the exponent α being equal to 2. In other words, the maximal effort under differential taxation can be attained in the mixed-strategy equilibrium of the extreme logit CSF where $\alpha = \infty$ (the APA) or in the pure-strategy equilibrium of the extreme logit CSF where $\alpha = 2$. Note that such equivalence has the flavor of the neutrality result obtained in Alcalde and Dahm (2010). However, in Mealem and Nitzan's (2012) setting of contest design, the contestants' maximal efforts are larger than those obtained in the setting of Alcalde and Dahm (2010) because of the allowed discrimination between the contestants via the application of the designer's most effective scheme of differential taxation of the prize.

8.8 THE CASE OF ANY N AND THE EFFORT-MAXIMIZING LOTTERY (THE APPROPRIATE α, δ AND DIRECT DISCRIMINATION)

Examining direct and overt discrimination, Mealem and Nitzan (2012) clarify the effectiveness of discrimination that can take the form of both differential prize taxation and structural discrimination. The first claim in this study is:

Claim 1: For $k > 1$ *and* $0 < \alpha < 2$, *the combination of direct and overt discrimination yields larger efforts than those obtained just by direct discrimination.*[10]

---

[10] In section 4 of Mealem and Nitzan (2012), we show that direct discrimination is more effective than overt discrimination. This implies that the combination of direct and overt discrimination yields larger efforts than those obtained just by overt discrimination.

The proof of this claim uses the following idea: the designer increases polarization between the contestants' stakes by reducing the stake of contestant 1 and increasing the stake of contestant 2. The increase in polarization is associated with an increase in the sum of the contestants' prize valuations. But to enable the increased polarization, the balanced-budget constraint requires creating a structural bias in favor of contestant 1, the contestant whose stake has been reduced, by selecting δ that is smaller than 1. In the proof of the claim, the required reduction in δ results in the preservation of the contestants' winning probabilities while increasing the sum of their stakes, and this causes the increase in their exerted efforts. This idea raises the following question: what happens to the total effort if the designer 'maximizes' the extent of polarization between the contestants' stakes by reducing the stake of contestant 1 almost to zero ($\varepsilon_1 \to -v_1^+$) and by increasing the stake of contestant 2 to a 'very large' level. Clearly, to ensure that the balanced-budget constraint is satisfied, the designer must create an appropriate bias in favor of contestant 1 by selecting a very small δ. That is, $p_1\varepsilon_1 + p_2\varepsilon_2 = 0$ or

$$\delta = \left(\frac{v_1 + \varepsilon_1}{v_2 + \varepsilon_2}\right)\left(-\frac{\varepsilon_1}{\varepsilon_2}\right)^{\frac{1}{\alpha}} \tag{8.5}$$

The two types of discrimination exerted in this case are somewhat different than those described in the proof of claim 1, because the designer does not confine himself to preserving the winning probabilities of the contestants. It turns out that for $\alpha = 1$, this combined discrimination with maximal polarization, that is, $\varepsilon_1 \to -v_1^+$ and $\varepsilon_2 \to \infty$, is an effort-maximizing strategy yielding efforts that are almost equal to v_1, the initial higher prize valuation of contestant 1. For example, for $\alpha = 1$, $v_1 = 100$ and $v_2 = 2$, if the designer considerably increases the polarization between the contestants' stakes by selecting $(\varepsilon_1, \varepsilon_2) = (-99.9, 100000)$ and δ according to (8.3), $\delta \cong 9.9898 \cdot 10^{-10}$, the total effort is equal to $G = 99.7$. This example illustrates the more general finding obtained in the first part of proposition 1 presented in Mealem and Nitzan (2012). That is, when $0 < \alpha \leq 1$, combined discrimination with maximal stake polarization and selection of δ that satisfies (8.5) yields efforts that are almost equal to αv_1. When $\alpha = 1$ these efforts are equal to those obtained under the most effective 'take it or leave it' mechanism. However, in our setting v_1 is almost obtained using a standard simple lottery that allows structural bias between the contestants, without setting a minimal effort for contestant 1, without disregard for the balanced-budget constraint and without deterring the participation of one of the contestants.

Undertaking the extreme combined discrimination that maximizes polarization, $\varepsilon_1 \to -v_1^+$ and $\varepsilon_2 \to \infty$, while choosing δ according to (8.5), such that the balanced-budget constraint is satisfied, is possible for $0 < \alpha \leq 1$. But it is not possible for $1 < \alpha \leq 2$. The reason is that the designer's selection of $(\varepsilon_1, \varepsilon_2, \delta)$ must ensure that the utility of the contestants is not negative, to prevent their abandonment of the competition and, in turn, the decline of the contestants' efforts to zero. In this case ($1 < \alpha \leq 2$), when $k > 1$, $\varepsilon_1 \to -v_1^+$, $\varepsilon_2 = \frac{\varepsilon_1}{1-\alpha}$ and δ is set according to (8.5). The corresponding total effort converges to $\frac{1}{\alpha}v_1 + (1 - \frac{1}{\alpha})v_2$, which is smaller than v_1. This result appears in the second part of proposition 1 in Mealem and Nitzan (2012).

The special appeal of the dual polarized discrimination strategies presented in the above discussion is highlighted by the following result.

Proposition 3: For any $0 < \alpha \leq 2$, the dual polarized discrimination strategies applied in the discussion above yield the maximal equilibrium total effort of the contestants.

The relationship between the exponent α of a lottery and the maximal attainable effort G is presented in Figure 8.1. It turns out that under any lottery exhibiting constant or increasing returns to scale, $1 \leq \alpha < 2$, and under lotteries exhibiting decreasing returns to scale, such that $0.5 + \frac{1}{2k} < \alpha < 1$, the combined effects of the extreme polar modes of discrimination increase effort (or the designer's revenue) beyond the average value of the initial prize valuations, $0.5(v_1 + v_2)$, which is the maximal effort obtained by either direct or overt discrimination under any possible lottery. Proposition 3 implies that when the designer applies two modes of discrimination, overt and direct discrimination, each type of discrimination has a positive 'added value' that enhances the exertion of efforts relative to the situation in which the designer resorts to just one mode of discrimination. That is, the two modes of discrimination are supportive or 'complementary' – the combination of overt and direct discrimination yields larger effort than obtained by separate application of one of these modes of discrimination for almost any given level of overt discrimination ($0 < \alpha < 2$). Furthermore, under lotteries with increasing or constant returns to scale, as well as under some lotteries with decreasing returns to scale, such combined discrimination yields efforts that are larger than the average prize valuation (see ABC in Figure 8.1), which is the largest possible total effort under separate application of overt or direct discrimination. The advantage of combining these two types of discrimination relative to the use of a single mode of discrimination is due to the distinctive features of the contribution of each of these modes of discrimination to exerted effort as described below.

1. Direct discrimination increases as much as possible the initially lower prize valuation while reducing the initially higher prize valuation almost to zero. This increases the sum of the contestants' prize valuations to infinity and makes the 'income effect' (associated with a scheme that increases the sum of the final stakes from $(v_1 + v_2)$ to $(v_1 + \varepsilon_1 + v_2 + \varepsilon_2)$) of direct discrimination the dominant effect.[11]
2. The maximal possible increase in the sum of the contestants' prize valuations is not the result of direct discrimination alone. It is rendered possible by overt discrimination that ensures that the balanced-budget constraint is satisfied. Specifically, overt discrimination counterbalances the above 'income effect' by almost completely ensuring that the winning probability of candidate 1 converges to zero.

The moderating effect described in (8.2) is necessary to attain the maximal effort. While overt discrimination has a 'second order' effect on effort that moderates the income effect of the direct discrimination, it also enables the dominance of this 'first order' income effect on effort described in (8.1), namely, the increase in effort due to the

---

[11] For a clarification of the meaning of the income effect, see the discussion following proposition 2 in Mealem and Nitzan (2014).

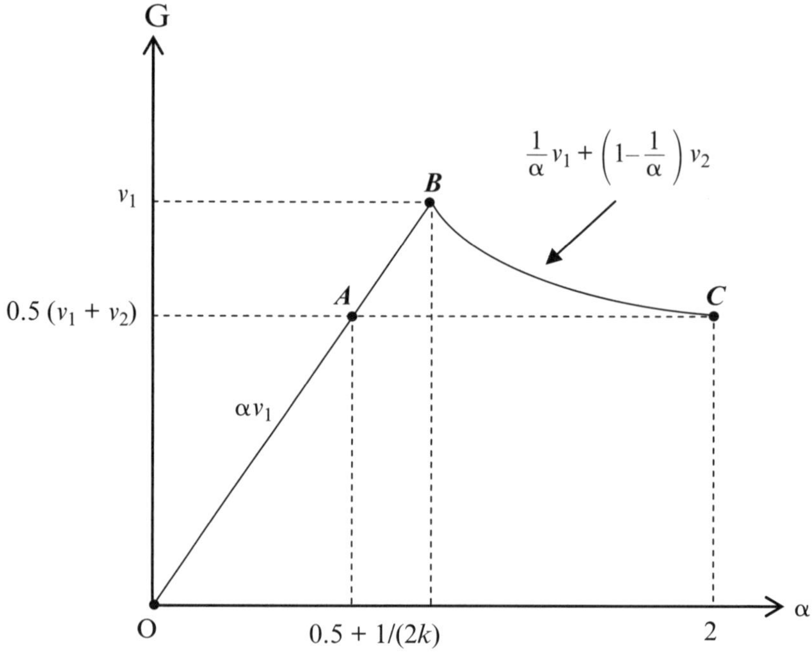

Figure 8.1 The relationship between the exponent α and the maximal attainable efforts G

increase in the sum of the contestants' prize valuations. The dominance of the effect of direct discrimination means that the more extreme the direct discrimination, the higher the total effort and this requires the extremity of overt discrimination.

The discussion before Proposition 3 also implies that if the designer can control δ, ε_1, ε_2 as well as α, he can secure almost the largest possible effort v_1 by selecting $\alpha = 1$ (recall that according to part 2 of Proposition 3 the effort exerted when $1 < \alpha \leq 2$ converge to a value that is smaller than v_1). Any lottery with $\alpha \neq 1$ is therefore inferior to a simple lottery where $\alpha = 1$, when in both cases the designer applies the effort-maximizing discrimination strategy, viz, the dual polarized discrimination strategy. The superiority of $\alpha = 1$ is in marked contrast to its non-effort-maximizing consequence when the designer is not allowed to discriminate between the contestants overtly or directly, or when the designer is allowed to discriminate between the contestants, but just overtly or just directly.

Two important conclusions can be drawn from the results. First, for $k > 1$, when the designer applies the (most effective) dual polarized discrimination strategy (the strategy that maximizes the contestants' efforts), an increase in α from $\alpha = 1$ to $\alpha = 2$ reduces efforts. Second, when $\alpha = 1$ and the designer applies a dual polarized discrimination strategy, he can attain the maximal efforts (almost v_1) given any number of contestants N. In the more general multi-player contest, the designer has to reduce the stakes of $N - 2$ contestants to zero, making sure that contestant 1 with the highest stake is not included among them. Applying the dual polarized discrimination strategy with respect to the two remaining contestants, the designer can induce efforts that are almost equal to v_1.

8.9 SUMMARY

The outcome of a comparison between total effort or revenues received with the APA and a lottery is equivocal. The basic comparison by Fang (2002) for N-player contests implies that in a two-player, fair, simple contest, with $\alpha = 1$ and $\delta = 1$, the APA yields larger total effort than the simple lottery if and only if $k < 1 + \sqrt{2}$. Epstein et al. (2013) considerably strengthen this finding by establishing that in a fair contest ($\delta = 1$), if $k > 1$, then a contest designer who can select the exponent α (regardless of whether the designer is risk neutral or risk averse) always prefers a logit lottery, which yields larger total effort relative to the APA, even when the sufficient condition $k > 1 + \sqrt{2}$ is not satisfied. In fact, the exponent of the preferred lottery satisfies $0 < \alpha < 2$, which means that the corresponding contest game has a unique pure-strategy equilibrium. Alcalde and Dahm (2010) have shown that for any $\alpha \geq 2$ there exists an equilibrium in mixed strategies that is equivalent to the equilibrium of the APA. However, so far, a characterization of the complete set of mixed-strategy equilibria is not available. Since Epstein et al. (2013) show that there exists α, $0 < \alpha < 2$, which yields total effort that is larger than that obtained under the APA, it is clear that this conclusion remains valid when the parameter α has to satisfy the requirement $0 < \alpha < \infty$.

Che and Gale (1997) point out that intuition suggests that contest designers who are receptive to effort of contenders (a large exponent α) would induce greater effort, all else equal. Epstein et al. (2013) establish that this intuition is not valid when we move from the range $0 < \alpha \leq 2$ to $\alpha = \infty$. In particular, when $\delta = 1$ and $k > 1$, the parameter α in the logit CSF that yields the largest total effort is not $\alpha = \infty$, since there is some α that is smaller than 2 that yields larger total effort.

In Mealem and Nitzan (2012), we show that for any number of contestants, if $\alpha = 1$ and dual overt and direct discrimination is allowed, then the effort-maximizing lottery yields larger total effort than the effort-maximizing APA. In such a case, total contest effort is maximal and equal almost to the highest prize valuation (the intuition behind this result was clarified in the preceding section).

Epstein et al. (2011) show that for two contestants under effort-maximizing overt discrimination (choice of δ) and a lottery with $0 < \alpha \leq 1$, the effort-maximizing APA yields larger total effort than the lottery. Franke et al. (2014) have generalized the result of Epstein et al. (2011), but only for a simple lottery with $\alpha = 1$, establishing that for any number of contestants and effort-maximizing overt discrimination (choice of δ), the effort-maximizing APA yields larger total effort than the effort-maximizing simple lottery. The results of Epstein et al. (2011) and Franke et al. (2013, 2014) that establish the superiority of the effort-maximizing APA for the contest designer are not valid when the parameter α defining the lottery is allowed to satisfy $0 < \alpha \leq 2$. Epstein et al. (2013) show that for two contestants under effort-maximizing overt discrimination (choice of δ) and, in the lottery case, also choice of covert discrimination (choice of α) such that $0 < \alpha \leq 2$, the effort-maximizing APA yields the same total effort as the effort-maximizing lottery.

Finally, Mealem and Nitzan (2014) show that for two contestants, $\delta = 1$ and effort-maximizing direct discrimination subject to a balanced-budget constraint, for $0 < \alpha < 2$, the effort-maximizing APA yields larger total effort (is socially more wasteful in a rent-seeking context) than the effort-maximizing fair lottery; and for $\alpha = 2$, the effort-maximizing APA and the effort-maximizing fair lottery are equivalent (yield the same total effort).

REFERENCES

Alcalde, José and Matthias Dahm (2010), 'Rent seeking and rent dissipation: a neutrality result', *Journal of Public Economics*, **94**(1–2), 1–7.

Che Yeon-Koo and Ian Gale (1997), 'Rent dissipation when rent seekers are budget constrained', *Public Choice*, **92**(1–2), 109–26.

Che Yeon-Koo and Ian Gale (1998), 'Caps on political lobbying', *American Economic Review*, **88**(3), 643–51.

Clark, Derek J. and Christian Riis (2000), 'Allocation efficiency in a competitive bribery game', *Journal of Economic Behavior and Organization*, **42**(1), 109–24.

Duffy, John and Alexander Matros (2013), 'All-pay auctions vs. lotteries as provisional fixed-prize fundraising mechanisms: theory and evidence', Working Paper, Department of Economics, University of Pittsburgh.

Epstein, Gil S. and Shmuel Nitzan (2006), 'The politics of randomness', *Social Choice and Welfare*, **27**(2), 423–33.

Epstein, Gil S., Yosef Mealem and Shmuel Nitzan (2011), 'Political culture and discrimination in contests', *Journal of Public Economics*, **95**(1–2), 88–93.

Epstein, Gil S., Yosef Mealem and Shmuel Nitzan (2013), 'Lotteries vs. all-pay auctions in fair and biased contests', *Economics and Politics*, **25**(1), 48–60.

Fang, Hanming (2002), 'Lottery versus all-pay auction models of lobbying', *Public Choice*, **112**(3–4), 351–71.

Franke Jörg, Christian Kanzow, Wolfgang Leininger and Alexandra Schwartz (2013), 'Effort maximization in asymmetric contest games with heterogeneous contestants', *Economic Theory*, **52**(2), 589–630.

Franke Jörg, Christian Kanzow, Wolfgang Leininger and Alexandra Schwartz (2014), 'Lottery versus all-pay auction contests – a revenue dominance theorem', *Games and Economic Behavior*, **83**(1), 16–126.

Gradstein, Mark and Kai Konrad (1999), 'Orchestrating rent-seeking contests', *Economic Journal*, **109**(458), 536–45, reprinted in Roger D. Congleton, Arye L. Hillman and Kai A. Konrad (eds) (2008), *40 Years of Research on Rent Seeking 1 – The Theory of Rent Seeking*, Heidelberg: Springer, pp. 571–80.

Hillman, Arye L. (2013), 'Rent seeking', in Michael Reksulak, Laura Razzolini and William F. Shughart II (eds), *The Elgar Companion to Public Choice*, 2nd edn, Cheltenham, UK and Northampton, MA, USA: Edward Elgar Publishing, pp. 307–30.

Hillman, Arye L. and Eliakim Katz (1987), 'Hierarchical structure and the social costs of bribes and transfers', *Journal of Public Economics*, **34**(2), 129–42, reprinted in Roger D. Congleton, Arye L. Hillman and Kai A. Konrad (eds) (2008), *40 Years of Research on Rent Seeking 1 – The Theory of Rent Seeking*, Heidelberg: Springer, pp. 523–36.

Hillman, Arye L. and John G. Riley (1989), 'Politically contestable rents and transfers', *Economics and Politics*, **1**(1), 17–39, reprinted in Roger D. Congleton, Arye L. Hillman and Kai A. Konrad (eds) (2008), *40 Years of Research on Rent Seeking 1 – The Theory of Rent Seeking*, Heidelberg: Springer, pp. 185–207.

Hillman, Arye L. and Dov Samet (1987), 'Dissipation of contestable rents by small numbers of contenders', *Public Choice*, **54**(1), 63–82, reprinted in Roger D. Congleton, Arye L. Hillman and Kai A. Konrad (eds) (2008), *40 Years of Research on Rent Seeking 1 – The Theory of Rent Seeking*, Heidelberg: Springer, pp. 165–84.

Konrad, Kai A. (2002), 'Investment in the absence of property rights: the role of incumbency advantages', *European Economic Review*, **46**(8), 1521–37.

Konrad, Kai A. (2009), *Strategy and Dynamics in Contests*, Oxford: Oxford University Press.

Li, Sanxi and Jun Yu (2012), 'Contests with endogenous discrimination', *Economics Letters*, **117**(3), 834–6.

Lien, Donald (1986), 'A note on competitive bribery games', *Economics Letters*, **22**(4), 337–41.

Lien, Donald (1990), 'Corruption and allocation efficiency', *Journal of Development Economics*, **33**(1), 153–64.

Mealem, Yosef and Shmuel Nitzan (2012), 'Differential prize taxation and structural discrimination in contests', CESifo Working Paper No. 3831, Munich.

Mealem, Yosef and Shmuel Nitzan (2014), 'Equity and effectiveness of effort-maximizing taxation in contests under an all-pay auction', *Social Choice and Welfare*, **42**(2), 437–64.

Nti, Kofi O. (2004), 'Maximum efforts in contests with asymmetric valuations', *European Journal of Political Economy*, **20**(4), 1059–66, reprinted in Roger D. Congleton, Arye L. Hillman and Kai A. Konrad (eds) (2008), *40 Years of Research on Rent Seeking 1 – The Theory of Rent Seeking*, Heidelberg: Springer, pp. 581–8.
Tullock, Gordon (1980), 'Efficient rent-seeking', in James M. Buchanan, Robert.D. Tollison and Gordon Tullock (eds), *Toward a Theory of the Rent-seeking Society*, College Station, TX, Texas A&M University Press, pp. 97–112, reprinted in Roger D. Congleton, Arye L. Hillman and Kai A. Konrad (eds) (2008), *40 Years of Research on Rent Seeking 1 – The Theory of Rent Seeking*, Heidelberg: Springer, pp. 105–20.
Ujhelyi, Gergely (2009), 'Campaign finance regulation with competing interest groups', *Journal of Public Economics*, **93**(3–4), 373–91.

9. Sabotage in contests

J. Atsu Amegashie

SUMMARY

This chapter reviews the literature on sabotage in contests. In such cases, contenders expend resources in contests to hinder or impede the efforts of other contenders. Resources used in sabotage are wastefully used and add to the resources used unproductively by rent seekers to win a rent. The theory of sabotage in contests is more general than rent seeking and includes any contest in which the opportunity is available to impede competitors. A basic feature of sabotage is that if there are more than two contenders in a contest, resources used by any one contender to sabotage any other contender have attributes of public-good benefits for other contenders. The review in this chapter encompasses the formal game-theoretic, empirical and experimental literature. The formal model is in the chapter Appendix.

9.1 INTRODUCTION

Contests are an important and pervasive aspect of economic life. A contest is a game in which players compete over a prize by making irreversible outlays. Election campaigns, rent-seeking games, research and development races, competition for monopolies, litigation, wars and sports are all examples of contests.[1] The fact that the players' outlays are sunk or irreversible is important because it implies that both winners and losers forfeit their bids.

Efforts in a contest can take two forms: (1) effort that directly increases a player's own probability of success or payoff without affecting the capacity of other players to exert effort and (2) effort that indirectly increases a player's own probability of success because it reduces the capacity of other players to exert effort. The first type of effort may be referred to as 'productive' effort while the second type of effort may be referred to as 'sabotage' effort or 'destructive' effort.[2] As Konrad (2000, p. 156) observed,

> Instead of producing information that supports their favored policy outcome, interest groups may use resources to produce negative information on the attractiveness of particular alternative decisions or try to reduce the effectiveness of a competing interest group's activities. More generally, interest groups may use effort for two different purposes: for promoting their own project or for sabotaging the activities of a specific competing interest group.

---

1 The literature on the contests is large; see, for example, Congleton et al. (2008a, 2008b) and Konrad (2009).

2 See, for example, Amegashie (2012) and Konrad (2000).

The seminal work on sabotage in contests is Lazear (1989). In his model of internal labor tournaments, he referred to sabotage as 'industrial politics' and defined it as 'any (costly) actions that one worker takes that adversely affect output of another'. Lazear (1989) and Carpenter et al. (2010) refer to sabotage as 'office politics'.

Examples of sabotage are negative campaign ads in political campaigns and dirty and illegal tricks (fouls) in a game of soccer or basketball and time-wasting techniques to make it impossible for one's opponent to exert effort. In internal labor tournaments, contestants may go out of their way to hide valuable effort-enhancing information from each other that is supposed to be shared. For example, based on a survey of Australian manufacturing, Drago and Garvey (1998) found that when the gains from promotion are high, workers are less willing to help their fellow workers. According to Harbring et al. (2007, endnote 1, p. 385):

> When commenting on the possibility of sabotage at Merck, having introduced forced ranking in 1986, Murphy (1992, endnote 4) refers to John Dvorak, PC Magazine editor, who reports on how a friend attained promotion: This friend cracked the network messaging system which allowed him to read all memos. He sabotaged the workgroup software and manipulated the appointment calendars. According to Dvorak, stealing passwords and destroying important data is an easy task for many employees.

In this chapter, I review some of the main theoretical works in the literature on sabotage in contests and the insights gained from them.[3] I also look at a few experimental and empirical studies of sabotage in contests. The treatment will be intuitive with minimal use of technical jargon. The goal is to make the survey very accessible to readers. The chapter Appendix briefly presents a technical analysis of contests with sabotage.

9.2 MODELING SABOTAGE IN CONTESTS

9.2.1 Categories of Models

Modeling sabotage can take various forms. It can be modeled as directly reducing the effectiveness of one's opponent's efforts or output, which translates into a direct reduction in the opponent's probability of success (for example, Lazear 1989; Konrad 2000; Chen 2003; Münster 2007; Gürtler and Münster 2010, Carpenter et al. 2010) or a direct reduction in one's opponent's valuation of the prize (for example, Amegashie and Runkel 2007). It can also be modeled as an increase in one's opponent's unit cost of producing output or effort (for example, Amegashie 2012) which then leads to a decrease in (or destruction of) the opponent's output; this increase in one's opponent's unit cost of effort is analytically equivalent to an increase in the opponent's valuation of the prize as modeled in Amegashie and Runkel (2007).[4]

---

[3] Chowdhury and Gürtler (2013) have also reviewed the literature on sabotage in contests.

[4] Making it difficult for an opponent to exert effort is clearly evident in the above quote by Harbring et al. (2007) where an employee 'sabotaged the workgroup software and manipulated the appointment calendars' of his co-workers. 'Stealing passwords and destroying important data' and examples mentioned above illustrate this point.

It is important to note that standard rent-seeking effort may itself be wasteful or socially useless and is therefore not different from effort invested in sabotage. This is how rent-seeking effort in contests is viewed in the literature pioneered by Tullock (1967 [2008]) and extended and applied by others (see Congleton et al. 2008a, 2008b).[5] Other than Konrad (2000) who is ambivalent about whether a player's non-sabotage effort is productive or socially valuable, all other models of sabotage in a contest assume that one type of effort is productive or socially valuable while the other effort is destructive (sabotage).[6] This may stem from the fact that almost all models of sabotage in contests use the labor tournament model pioneered by Lazear and Rosen (1981). This model assumes that employees compete by producing valuable output. Therefore, in his seminal paper on sabotage in contests, Lazear (1989) interpreted sabotage as the destruction of productive effort or valuable output. He observed that:

> Relative comparisons imply that individuals can increase their wealth in two ways. Competition encourages increased effort, which has a positive effect on output. This is the idea of Lazear and Rosen (1981). But competition also discourages cooperation among contestants and can lead to outright sabotage. (Lazear 1989, p. 562)

In this review, I follow the interpretation in Lazear (1989) and in the majority of papers on sabotage in the sense there is a productive effort and destructive effort in the contest. Obviously, this does not lead to a conflict between standard rent-seeking models and tournament models because sabotage is equivalent to use of resources in socially wasteful rent-seeking activities.

9.2.2 Game-theoretic Models: Why Study Sabotage in Contests?

Is it useful to model sabotage when it ultimately has the same effect as standard rent-seeking effort? Like standard rent-seeking effort, doesn't sabotage increase a player's probability of success or his payoff? How then can modeling sabotage in a contest lead to any useful insights? Surprisingly, a contest with sabotage leads to insights that cannot be gleaned from a contest without sabotage. For example, sabotage crowds out productive effort and thereby reduces output. It also leads to adverse selection in contests.

Consider a labor tournament (a contest) with no sabotage and risk neutrality. In this environment, the standard result is that an increase in the prize (that is, high-powered incentives) will lead to an increase in effort and therefore aggregate output. In this framework, it is difficult to explain the observation that wage compression among workers can be efficient. However, as Lazear (1989) showed in a contest in which sabotage is possible, wage compression (that is, a lower-powered incentive because the spread between the wage of the winner and the wage of losers is smaller) may increase output because it reduces the workers' efforts in uncooperative or sabotage activities. But as Lazear (1989)

[5] Austin-Smith and Wright (1992), Lohmann (1995) and Lagerlof (1997) have argued that rent-seeking efforts need not be socially wasteful because they provide valuable information to help the rent-giver decide the winner of the contest.

[6] In fact, Konrad (2000) uses the term 'standard rent-seeking effort' for what we refer to here as 'productive effort'.

also notes, wage compression also decreases productive effort, so the effect on output is not guaranteed. However, in organizations with high levels of destructive behavior, the fall in sabotage as a result of wage compression is likely to be sufficiently big and this will make the policy optimal for the organization.

A standard result in the theory of rent-seeking contests is that an increase in the number of contestants increases aggregate rent-seeking efforts; the 'competition effect'. But as Konrad (2000) showed, this standard result may no longer hold if there is sabotage. This is because unlike the standard rent-seeking effort, sabotage has a public-good characteristic. When a player in a contest increases his rent-seeking effort, it increases his probability of winning and all the benefits accrue to him alone. In contrast, when a player weakens a specific player by sabotaging him, all other players (including the saboteur) benefit. Konrad (2000) refers to this as the 'dispersion effect' of sabotage. Because of this effect, the benefit per player is smaller, the higher the number of players in the game. Accordingly, players have a weaker incentive to invest more effort in sabotage if the total number of players is large. Therefore, it is no longer the case that an increase in the total number of players necessarily leads to an increase in the aggregate sum of efforts.

Chen (2003) and Münster (2007) found that it is the most able contestant who is sabotaged heavily because he poses the greatest threat to the other contestants.[7] This has a perverse implication for the composition of players in a contest. More able contestants may stay out because of the fear of excessive sabotage. If the field is dominated by less able contestants, then this will lead to a result akin to adverse selection wherein the bad drives away the good. There is some anecdotal evidence for this phenomenon where in some countries, the politics of insults and character assassination suggests that politics is dominated by people with inferior outside options.

It turns out that a model in which competition is between teams as opposed to individuals may lead to a result that is in contrast to the aforementioned result in Chen (2003) and Münster (2007). In particular, Gürtler (2008) shows that in a contest between teams, each team directs all its sabotage activities at only the opponent's least able members. This is due to the fact that a player's productive contribution to his team's success is subject to diminishing marginal returns. Given that the total contribution of a less able teammate is smaller than the total contribution of a more able teammate, diminishing marginal returns to contributions imply that less able teammates have a higher marginal contribution. Also, given an assumption that the contributions of teammates are complements, it follows that the marginal contribution of a member of a team is increasing in the contribution of other team members and therefore is highest for the least able members. These two effects imply that the least able team members are, on the margin, most productive and so that it is most attractive to sabotage them.[8]

---

[7] Gürtler and Münster (2010) and Gürtler et al. (2013) also find that contestants who exert high effort in the first stage of a two-stage contest are sabotaged more than those who exert low effort. Hence there is less incentive to exert high effort.

[8] In a model of a team production, Bose et al. (2010) and Krakel and Muller (2012) find that it may be optimal for a team member to sabotage the team. These models do not consider contests between teams because there is only one team. They are also not contests among members of a team because the principal cannot reward agents according to their relative performance since individual contributions to team performance are not contractible.

Amegashie and Runkel (2007) find that the most able contestant may be the only player who invests in sabotage. Unlike standard models of sabotage, a player in Amegashie and Runkel (2007) cannot sabotage his current opponent but can instead potential or future opponents. Then, given that the most able player has the highest valuation of advancing to the next stage of the contest, there is an equilibrium in which he engages in sabotage while the other less able players do not.

In a two-stage contest with sabotage, Amegashie (2012) finds that productive effort is increasing in the prize when the prize is below a certain threshold and then stays constant thereafter. There is no investment in sabotage below the threshold. Beyond the threshold, the players invest in only sabotage effort, which is increasing in the value of the prize. Therefore, the ratio of productive effort to sabotage effort falls as the value of the prize increases beyond a certain threshold. After some point, it is not profitable to increase productive effort even if the value of the prize increases. As in Chen (2003) and Münster (2007), being productive invites too much sabotage but, unlike their models, this result in Amegashie (2012) is obtained in a model with identical contestants.

It is important to note that in Lazear's (1989) framework and other models of sabotage in contests, both productive and sabotage efforts are monotonically increasing in the prize (that is, the players' valuation). In these models, sabotage only partially crowds out productive effort. The result in Amegashie (2012) implies that beyond a threshold value of the prize, sabotage fully crowds out any additional productive effort that would have been put forth by the players in the absence of sabotage.[9] To the best of my knowledge, Amegashie (2012) is the first paper to show that in a contest with identical players, productive efforts and/or destructive efforts of the contestants need not be monotonically increasing in the value of the prize.[10]

The important point is that personal effort in a contest provides personal benefit only whereas sabotage is a case of private provision of a public good (see Hillman 2009, chapter 3). Hence results concerning sabotage parallel conclusions regarding private incentives to provide public goods. Thus, Konrad (2000) and Amegashie (2012) find that there is no investment in sabotage (no private provision of the public good) if the number of contestants is sufficiently high.

9.3 EMPIRICAL AND EXPERIMENTAL STUDIES OF SABOTAGE IN CONTESTS

Since sabotage is typically an illegal and hidden activity,[11] it does not easily lend itself to empirical tests. This makes it difficult to assess its extent and its victims. To avoid this problem, researchers have used experimental methods.

Consistent with Lazear (1989), a number of experimental studies show that sabotage

---

9 In Chen (2003), the equilibrium productive effort is increasing in the value of the prize while sabotage effort is independent of the prize. Hence, there is no additional crowding out of productive effort as the prize increases. This result is not general and it is driven by a linearity assumption.

10 This non-monotonicity result has been shown in the case of non-identical contestants (for example, Epstein and Nitzan 2006).

11 Not all sabotage is illegal. For example, negative campaigning in elections is not illegal.

activities increase as the spread between winner and loser prizes widens (Harbring and Irlenbusch 2005, 2008, 2011; Vandegrift et al. 2010). The latter also find that the contest designer responds to this behavior by reducing the spread in the prizes.[12]

In Harbring and Irlenbusch (2005), groups of four agents compete in a rank-order tournament. In one of the treatments, there is a principal who determines winner and loser prizes. In this treatment, subjects play a two-stage game in which the principal offers a wage contract to the four agents in the first stage and then, in the second stage, the four agents choose their effort levels simultaneously in a rank-order tournament. In a benchmark treatment with an exogenous prize structure, the contestants engage in a simultaneous move rank-order tournament. The results of the experiment indicate that both productive effort and sabotage increase in the winner's prize. Furthermore, sabotage is higher when the prize structure is not exogenous but chosen by the principal.

Harbring and Irlenbusch (2011) allow for communication between the contestants and the principal. They find that communication helps curb sabotage because the principal and the agents manage to agree to small prize spreads in exchange for high output. They also find that sabotage is lower when the instructions frame the experimental tasks as an employer–employee relationship and refer to the action of lowering other participants' effort as 'sabotage'.

Harbring et al. (2007) compare sabotage behavior in symmetric contests to behavior in asymmetric contests wherein low-ability players compete with high-ability players. They find that high-ability contestants tend to sabotage each other's effort more than they sabotage low-ability contestants.[13] They also find that revealing the identity of the saboteur leads to less sabotage relative to treatments in which the saboteur's identity is hidden. One may interpret the revelation of the saboteur's identity as an increase in the private cost of engaging in sabotage through identity or esteem and expressive utility (Brennan and Pettit 2004; Hillman 2010).

In Carpenter et al. (2010), agents can influence the performance measurement of their competitors in a real-effort experiment. In particular, agents engage in a clerical task whose output is measured along two dimensions: quantity and quality. Agents privately evaluate each other's performance along these two dimensions. Under-reporting both the performance of one's opponent quantity and/or quality is sabotage and is costless in the experiments. It turns out that the anticipation of the harmful influence of competitors discourages agents to exert effort in the first place. Therefore, consistent with the models of Chen (2003), Münster (2007), Gürtler et al. (2010, 2013) and Amegashie (2012), sabotage may not only lead to the destruction of output but will also discourage agents from exerting productive effort.[14]

Balafoutas et al. (2012) rely on a natural experiment in Judo World Championships

---

12 This result is also obtained in the experiments of Falk et al. (2008).

13 This does not contradict the result in Gürtler (2008) because in his model two teams compete and each team member sabotages the effort of the least able contestants of his opponent's team. Harbring et al.'s (2007) is a model with no teams.

14 In an experiment on contests for status, Charness et al. (2014) find that sabotage opportunities have a strong detrimental effect on performance and that inducing group identity discourages sabotage among peers but increases in-group rivalry.

to study sabotage in contests. They looked at the effects of a rule change in 2009 that effectively reduced the cost of engaging in sabotage (that is, breaking an opponent's attack in an unsportsmanlike manner, an act seen as sabotage). Based on a dataset of 1422 fights and consistent with theoretical findings, the authors found (1) a considerable increase in the use of sabotage following the rule change in 2009; (2) strong evidence that sabotage is more likely to be used by relatively less competent individuals, and to be targeted at more competent individuals; and (3) that sabotage reduced the welfare of spectators based on a survey administered on 115 spectators of a Judo Grand Prix.

Brown and Chowdhury (2014) examine a contest in which contestants can be handicapped. In particular, they consider horse races in which in handicap races, horses within a range of abilities are permitted to take part, but superior horses are given heavier weights. Using data on 9646 UK horse races in 2010, they find that participants in handicap races are substantially more likely to commit sabotage[15] than those competing in non-handicap races. That is, leveling the field increases the likelihood of sabotage in contest environments.

Using the increase in points for winning a game from 2 to 3 as a measure of an increase in the prize (value) of winning a game in the Spanish football league, Garicano and Palacios-Huerta (2014) and del Corral et al. (2010) find an increase in sabotage (fouls) as a result of this rule change.[16]

9.4 POLICIES TO REDUCE SABOTAGE

Since sabotage effort crowds out productive effort and can discourage highly able people from competing in a contest, it is important to think of ways of mitigating it. As noted earlier, in labor tournaments, Lazear (1989) recommends wage compression as an optimal response to the counterproductive behavior of contestants.

Lazear (1989), Lazear (1995) and Chen (2003, 2005) recommend external recruitment in labor tournaments because someone who is yet to join an organization is more difficult to sabotage. Lazear (1989, p. 577) and Lazear (1995, chapter 3) document that before the break-up of AT&T, its president was usually chosen from its subsidiaries as opposed to choosing someone from the head office. This was because there appeared to be more sabotage activities if the competition was among people who were in the head office than among people from different subsidiaries.

Related to the preceding point, Lazear (1989) suggested that organizations should take the personalities of their workers into account. Some workers are too aggressive (hawks) while others are not (doves). He makes the insightful point that in organizations in which winning is crucial for promotion, the upper echelons of the organizations will be dominated by hawks. If so, bonuses based on only individual or firm output may be

[15] Sabotage takes the form of interference. This may include one horse knocking into another horse, a horse forcing another off their racing line and a jockey stealing another jockey's whip during the race. According to Brown and Chowdhury (2014), in 2010 there were 2564 instances of alleged sabotage, with 847 leading to a guilty verdict.

[16] Deutscher et al. (2013) undertake a similar exercise using German data.

better for high-level management because – compared to payments based on relative performance – payments based on only individual performance do not induce sabotage.

In a two-stage contest in which contestants sabotage those who are high performers, Gürtler et al. (2013) show that the disincentive effect of sabotage can be mitigated by concealing information about performance in the first stage.

Based on their experimental findings, Harbring and Irlenbusch (2011) suggest that organizations should use terms that refer to the immoral character of the sabotage activity in their newsletters or codes of conduct.

9.5 CONCLUSION

The literature on sabotage in contests is small and relatively new. In this chapter, I have presented an overview of this literature. Based on both theoretical and empirical studies, the general consensus is that sabotage in contests crowds out productive effort.

The literature on contests began with models of complete information about the types or abilities of players. Subsequent models studied contests with incomplete information. These latter models do not study the incentives of players to sabotage one another. This will be a useful direction in which to move the literature on sabotage in contests.

REFERENCES

Amegashie, J. Atsu (2012), 'Productive versus destructive efforts in contests', *European Journal of Political Economy*, **28**(4), 461–8.

Amegashie, J. Atsu and Marco Runkel (2007), 'Sabotaging potential rivals', *Social Choice and Welfare*, **28**(1), 143–62.

Austin-Smith, David and John R. Wright (1992), 'Competitive lobbying for legislators' votes', *Social Choice and Welfare*, **9**(3), 229–57.

Balafoutas, Loukas, Florian Lindner and Matthias Sutter (2012), 'Sabotage in tournaments: evidence from a natural experiment', *Kyklos*, **65**(4), 425–41.

Bose, Arup, Debashis Pal and David E.M Sappington (2010), 'Equal pay for unequal work: limiting sabotage in teams', *Journal of Economics and Management Strategy*, **19**(1), 25–53.

Brennan, Geoffrey and Philip Pettit (2004), *The Economy of Esteem: An Essay on Civil and Political Society*, Oxford: Oxford University Press.

Brown, Alasdair and Subhahish M. Chowdhury (2014), 'Sabotage in handicap contests', Working Paper, University of East Anglia.

Carpenter, Jeffrey, Peter Hans Matthews and John Schirm (2010), 'Tournaments and office politics: evidence from real effort experiment', *American Economic Review*, **100**(1), 504–17.

Charness, Gary, David Masclet and Marie Claire Villeval (2014), 'The dark side of status', *Management Science*, **60**(1), 38–55.

Che, Yeon-Koo and Ian Gale (2000), 'Difference-form contests and the robustness of all-pay auctions', *Games and Economic Behavior*, **30**(1), 22–43.

Chen, Kong-Pin (2003), 'Sabotage in promotion tournaments', *Journal of Law, Economics and Organization*, **19**(1), 119–40.

Chen, Kong-Pin (2005), 'External recruitment as an incentive device', *Journal of Labor Economics*, **23**(2), 259–77.

Chowdhury, Subhahish M. and Oliver Gürtler (2013), 'Sabotage in contests: a survey', Working Paper, University of East Anglia.

Congleton, Roger D., Arye L. Hillman and Kai A. Konrad (eds) (2008a), *40 Years of Research on Rent Seeking 1 – The Theory of Rent Seeking*, Heidelberg: Springer.

Congleton, Roger D., Arye L. Hillman and Kai A. Konrad (eds) (2008b), *40 Years of Research on Rent Seeking 2 – Applications: Rent Seeking in Practice*, Heidelberg: Springer.

del Corral, Julio, Juan Prieto-Rodrigeuz and Rob Simmons (2010), 'The effect of incentives on sabotage: the case of Spanish football', *Journal of Sports Economics*, **11**(3), 243–60.
Deutscher, Christian, Bernd Frick, Oliver Gürtler and Joachim Prinz (2013), 'Sabotage in tournaments with heterogeneous contestants: a field study', *Scandinavian Journal of Economics*, **115**(4), 1138–57.
Drago, Robert and Gerald T. Garvey (1998), 'Incentives for helping on the job: theory and evidence', *Journal of Labor Economics*, **16**(1), 1–25.
Epstein, Gil S. and Shmuel Nitzan (2006), 'Reduced prizes and increased effort in contests', *Social Choice and Welfare*, **26**(3), 447–53.
Falk, Armin, Ernst Fehr and David Huffman (2008), 'The power and limits of tournament incentives', Working Paper, University of Bonn.
Garicano, Luis and Ignacio Palacios-Huerta (2014), 'Sabotage in tournaments: making the beautiful game a bit less beautiful', in Ignacio Palacios-Huerta (ed.), *Beautiful Game Theory: How Soccer Can Help Economics*, Princeton, NJ: Princeton University Press, chapter 8.
Gürtler, Oliver (2008), 'On sabotage in collective tournaments', *Journal of Mathematical Economics*, **44**(3), 383–93.
Gürtler, Oliver and Johannes Münster (2010), 'Sabotage in dynamic tournaments', *Journal of Mathematical Economics*, **46**(2), 179–90.
Gürtler, Oliver, Johannes Münster and Petra Nieken (2013), 'Information policy in tournaments with sabotage', *Scandinavian Journal of Economics*, **115**(3), 932–66.
Harbring, Christine and Bernd Irlenbusch (2005), 'Incentives in tournaments with endogenous prize selection', *Journal of Institutional and Theoretical Economics*, **127**(4), 636–63.
Harbring, Christine and Bernd Irlenbusch (2008), 'How many winners are good to have? On tournaments with sabotage', *Journal of Economic Behavior and Organization*, **65**(3), 682–702.
Harbring, Christine and Bernd Irlenbusch (2011), 'Sabotage in tournaments: evidence from a laboratory experiment', *Management Science*, **57**(4), 611–27.
Harbring, Christine, Bernd Irlenbusch, Matthias Krakel and Reinhard Selten (2007), 'Sabotage in corporate contests – experimental analysis', *International Journal of the Economics of Business*, **14**(3), 367–92.
Hillman, Arye L. (2009), *Public Finance and Public Policy: Responsibilities and Limitations of Government*, 2nd edn, New York: Cambridge University Press.
Hillman, Arye L. (2010), 'Expressive behavior in economics and politics', *European Journal of Political Economy*, **26**, 403–18.
Jia, Hao, Stergios Skaperdas and Samarth Vaidya (2013), 'Contest functions: theoretical foundations and issues in estimation', *International Journal of Industrial Organization*, **31**(3), 211–22.
Konrad, Kai A. (2000), 'Sabotage in rent-seeking contests', *Journal of Law, Economics and Organization*, **16**(1), 155–65.
Konrad, Kai A. (2009), *Strategy and Dynamics in Contests*, Oxford: Oxford University Press.
Krakel, Matthias and Daniel Muller (2012), 'Sabotage in teams', *Economics Letters*, **115**(2), 289–92.
Lagerlof, Johan (1997), 'Lobbying, information, and private and social welfare', *European Journal of Political Economy*, **13**(3), 615–37.
Lazear, Edward (1989), 'Pay equality and industrial politics', *Journal of Political Economy*, **97**(3), 561–80.
Lazear, Edward (1995), *Personnel Economics*, Cambridge, MA: MIT Press.
Lazear, Edward and Sherwin Rosen (1981), 'Rank-order tournaments as optimal labor contracts', *Journal of Political Economy*, **89**(5), 841–64.
Lohmann, Susanne (1995), 'Information, access, and contributions: a signaling model of lobbying', *Public Choice*, **85**(3), 267–84.
Münster, Johannes (2007), 'Selection tournaments, sabotage, and participation', *Journal of Economics and Management Strategy*, **16**(4), 943–70.
Murphy, Kevin J. (1992), 'Performance measurement and appraisal: motivating managers to identify and reward performance', in W.J. Bruns, Jr (ed.), *Performance Measurement, Evaluation, and Incentives*, Boston, MA: Harvard Business School Press, pp. 37–62.
Tullock, Gordon (1967), 'The welfare economics of tariffs, monopolies, and theft', *Western Economic Journal*, **5**(3), 224–32, reprinted in Roger D. Congleton, Arye L, Hillman and Kai A. Konrad (eds) (2008), *40 Years of Research on Rent Seeking 1 – The Theory of Rent Seeking*, Heidelberg: Springer, pp. 45–53.
Tullock, Gordon (1980), 'Efficient rent seeking', in James M. Buchanan, Robert D. Tollison and Gordon Tullock (eds), *Toward a Theory of the Rent-seeking Society*, College Station, TX: Texas A&M University Press, pp. 97–112, reprinted in Roger D. Congleton, Arye L. Hillman and Kai A. Konrad (eds) (2008), *40 Years of Research on Rent Seeking 1 – The Theory of Rent Seeking*, Heidelberg: Springer, pp. 105–20.
Vandegrift, Donald, Abdullah Yavas and Paul Brown (2007), 'Incentive effects and overcrowding in tournaments: an experimental analysis', *Experimental Economics*, **10**(4), 345–68.

APPENDIX: A MATHEMATICAL MODEL OF SABOTAGE IN CONTESTS

For simplicity, consider a contest with two risk-neutral players, 1 and 2. Suppose that player j can choose productive effort, e_j, and sabotage effort, s_j, $j = 1, 2$. Let the total cost of effort for each player be $C(e_j + s_j)$, which is an increasing and strictly convex function and $C(0) = 0$. Suppose that the players have the same valuation, $V > 0$, of the prize. In a labor tournament, the player's valuation is equal to the difference between the winner's wage and loser's wage.

Let player j's output be $q_j = e_j - s_k + \varepsilon_j$, where ε_j is a continuous random variable and $k \neq j, j = 1, 2; k = 1, 2$. Assume that ε_1 and ε_2 are identically and independently distributed with a known density. These random variables are intended to capture luck, noise or measurement error in output.

The player with the higher output wins the contest. Note that player j's output is increasing in his productive effort but decreasing in his opponent's sabotage effort.

Player j's payoff function is

$$\Omega_j = prob(q_j > q_k)V - C(e_j + s_j), \qquad k \neq j, j = 1, 2; k = 1, 2 \tag{9.1}$$

The payoff in (9.1) can be written as:

$$\Omega_j = F[(e_j - s_k) - (e_k - s_j)]V - C(e_j + s_j) \tag{9.2}$$

where $F(\cdot)$ is the cumulative distribution function of $\varepsilon_k - \varepsilon_j$. Given $F'(\cdot) = f(\cdot) > 0$, it follows that player j's probability of success, $P_j = F[(e_j - s_k) - (e_k - s_j)]$, is increasing in his productive effort and sabotage effort but decreasing in his opponent's productive effort and sabotage effort.[17] Player j chooses his productive and sabotage efforts to maximize the payoff function in (9.2).

The above approach to modeling contests was pioneered by Lazear and Rosen (1981) in a model without sabotage. It was the approach used by Lazear (1989), Chen (2003), Münster (2007) and other papers discussed in this chapter to model sabotage in contests. An equivalent but reduced-form approach is to define player j's success probability as:

$$P_j = \frac{g(e_j - s_k)}{g(e_j - s_k) + g(e_k - s_j)} \tag{9.3}$$

where $g'(\cdot) > 0$. One may argue that this assumes that there exists a distribution function for which (9.3) holds.[18] The reduced-form function in (9.3) is called

[17] Note, for example, that if ε_k and ε_j are each normally distributed with a given mean and variance, then the convolution $f(\varepsilon_k - \varepsilon_j)$ will also be a normal distribution with a given mean and variance.

[18] The function in (9.3) can be derived by assuming that the output takes the multiplicative form, $q_j = (e_j - s_k)\varepsilon_j$ and ε_k and ε_j have an exponential distribution. For a review of the microfoundations of this approach, see Jia et al. (2013).

the contest-success function.[19] In a model without sabotage, this approach was pioneered by Tullock (1980 [2008]) in his study of rent seeking and it is the approach used by Konrad (2000), Amegashie and Runkel (2007) and Amegashie (2012).[20]

Returning to the payoff function (9.2), the first-order conditions for player j's problem are:

$$\frac{\partial \Omega_j}{\partial e_j} \le 0,\ e_j \ge 0,\ e_j \frac{\partial \Omega_j}{\partial e_j} = 0 \tag{9.4}$$

and

$$\frac{\partial \Omega_j}{\partial s_j} \le 0,\ s_j \ge 0,\ s_j \frac{\partial \Omega_j}{\partial s_j} = 0, j = 1, 2 \tag{9.5}$$

A pure-strategy Nash equilibrium must satisfy equations (9.4) and (9.5) for both players and second-order conditions must be satisfied as well. Consider an interior solution for both productive effort and sabotage effort: $e_j > 0$ and $s_j > 0, j = 1, 2$. This gives

$$\frac{\partial \Omega_j}{\partial e_j} = f[(e_j - s_k) - (e_k - s_j)]V - C'(e_j + s_j) = 0 \tag{9.6}$$

and

$$\frac{\partial \Omega_j}{\partial s_j} = f[(e_j - s_k) - (e_k - s_j)]V - C'(e_j + s_j) = 0, j = 1, 2 \tag{9.7}$$

Assume that second-order conditions hold.

In a symmetric equilibrium, equations (9.6) and (9.7) become

$$f(0)V - C'(\hat{e} + \hat{s}) = 0 \tag{9.6a}$$

and

$$f(0)V - C'(\hat{e} + \hat{s}) = 0 \tag{9.7a}$$

Equations (9.6a) and (9.7a) are the same. Therefore, we cannot determine unique values for the individual efforts, $\hat{e}$ and $\hat{s}$. But the aggregate effort, $\hat{e} + \hat{s}$, is unique.

When sabotage is not possible, the optimal productive effort, $e^* > 0$, in a symmetric equilibrium satisfies

$$f(0)V - C'(e^*) = 0 \tag{9.8}$$

---

[19] Another reduced-form function used is the difference-form contest-success function, $F[(e_j - s_k) - (e_k - s_j)] = (e_j - s_k) - (e_k - s_j)$; see Che and Gale (2000).

[20] However, in Amegashie (2012), productive effort directly enters the contest-success function (CSF) while destructive effort does not. Instead, destructive effort directly increases one's opponent's marginal cost of productive effort and hence indirectly reduces the opponent's success probability.

Then comparing (9.8) to (9.6a) or (9.7a) and rearranging gives

$$e^* = \hat{e} + \hat{s} \tag{9.9}$$

Total effort remains the same as in Chen (2003). Given $\hat{s} > 0$, equation (9.9) implies that $\hat{e} < e^*$. Productive effort is smaller if sabotage is positive. Therefore, sabotage crowds out productive effort.

10. Behavioral dimensions of contests

*Roman M. Sheremeta**

SUMMARY

The standard theoretical description of rent-seeking contests is that of rational individuals or groups engaging in socially inefficient behavior by exerting costly effort. Experimental studies find that the actual efforts of participants are significantly higher than predicted in the models based on rational behavior and that over-dissipation of rents (or over-bidding or over-expenditure of resources) can occur. Although over-dissipation cannot be explained by the standard rational-behavior theory, it can be explained by incorporating behavioral dimensions into the standard model, such as (1) the utility of winning; (2) relative payoff maximization; (3) bounded rationality; and (4) judgmental biases. These explanations are not exhaustive but provide a coherent picture of important behavioral dimensions to be considered when studying rent-seeking behavior in theory and in practice.

10.1 INTRODUCTION

The variety of economic and political contests that can be described as rent seeking has attracted attention from economic theorists and applied economists (see the papers in Congleton et al. 2008a, 2008b). Rent seeking describes socially inefficient but personally profitable behavior (Tullock 1967 [2008]; Krueger 1974 [2008]). People can engage in productive behavior (creating income and wealth) and unproductive behavior (such as contesting for already existing resources). The unproductive behavior is known as rent seeking. The two most commonly used models to describe rent seeking are the probabilistic contests of Tullock (1980 [2008]) and the all-pay auction (Dasgupta 1986; Hillman and Samet 1987 [2008]; Hillman and Riley 1989 [2008]). The models provide many important theoretical results (see, for example, the overview by Long 2013).

The rent-seeking contest models have been extensively tested in controlled laboratory settings (for a comprehensive review of this literature, see Dechenaux et al. 2015). Most laboratory studies find support for the comparative statistics predictions of the theory of rent-seeking contests. However, the studies also uncover important behavioral phenomena not predicted by the rational-behavior theory. One such

* This chapter is mostly based on joint research with various co-authors over the course of seven years. I gratefully acknowledge and thank Anya Samak, Cary Deck, Curtis Price, Dan Kovenock, Emmanuel Dechenaux, Erik Kimbrough, Jingjing Zhang, Shakun Mago, Subhasish Chowdhury, Ted Turocy and Tim Cason, who worked with me on various projects on contests. I retain responsibility for any errors.

phenomenon is over-dissipation of rents (Sheremeta 2013). This phenomenon is also known as over-bidding or over-expenditure of resources. Participants in laboratory experiments exert effort significantly higher than predicted by the standard Nash equilibrium.

The standard rational-behavior theory cannot explain over-dissipation, but it can be explained by incorporating behavioral dimensions into the standard model, such as (1) the utility of winning; (2) relative payoff maximization; (3) bounded rationality; and (4) judgmental biases. This chapter describes these behavioral dimensions of contests in detail. Attention is restricted mostly to rent-seeking contests of the Tullock (1980 [2008]) type, since such contests have attracted most attention from experimental researchers (Dechenaux et al. 2015) and the over-dissipation phenomenon for these contests has been extensively explored (Sheremeta 2013).

I begin by introducing a standard theoretical contest model. Then, I provide a short overview of the experimental literature on rent-seeking contests and discuss the over-dissipation phenomenon. Then, in order to explain over-dissipation, the theory of contests is extended to the behavioral dimensions of the utility of winning, relative payoff maximization, bounded rationality and judgmental biases. I conclude by suggesting directions for future research and discussing potential mechanisms that can reduce over-dissipation.

10.2 THE STANDARD THEORETICAL CONTEST MODEL

Perhaps the simplest model of rent seeking is a lottery contest model proposed by Tullock (1980 [2008]). In such a contest, there are n identical risk-neutral individuals competing for a prize value of v. The probability that individual i wins the prize depends on individual i's effort e_i and the efforts of all other individuals. Specifically, individual i's probability of winning the prize is defined by a contest-success function (Skaperdas 1996 [2008]):

$$p_i(e_i, e_{-i}) = \frac{e_i}{\sum_{j=1}^{n} e_j} \tag{10.1}$$

Given (10.1), the expected payoff for individual i is equal to the expected benefit, that is, the probability of winning the prize $p_i(e_i, e_{-i})$ times the prize value v, minus the cost of effort $c(e_i) = e_i$. That is,

$$\pi_i(e_i, e_{-i}) = p_i(e_i, e_{-i})v - e_i \tag{10.2}$$

Differentiating (10.2) with respect to e_i and accounting for the symmetric Nash equilibrium leads to an equilibrium effort:

$$e^* = \frac{(n-1)}{n^2}v \tag{10.3}$$

There are no asymmetric equilibria in the lottery contest and the symmetric equilibrium (10.3) is unique (Szidarovszky and Okuguchi 1997 [2008]).[1] Therefore, each individual has an equal probability of winning in equilibrium $p(e^*) = 1/n$. The equilibrium expected payoff can be calculated by substituting (10.3) into (10.2), which gives

$$\pi(e^*) = \frac{1}{n^2}v \tag{10.4}$$

The dissipation rate, measured as a ratio of the total expenditures ne^* to the value of the prize v, is

$$d(e^*) = \frac{(n-1)}{n} \tag{10.5}$$

The economic intuition behind this model is straightforward. A higher value of prize v implies higher equilibrium effort e^*, that is, $\partial e^*/\partial v > 0$, and a higher payoff $\pi(e^*)$, that is, $\partial \pi(e^*)/\partial v > 0$. On the other hand, a higher number of competitors n implies lower equilibrium effort e^*, that is, $\partial e^*/\partial n < 0$ (due to so-called 'discouragement effect'), and lower payoff $\pi(e^*)$, that is, $\partial \pi(e^*)/\partial n < 0$.[2]

The classic formulation of a Tullock contest demonstrates the tension between the socially optimal and the individually rational behavior. The socially optimal level of effort is zero. In such a case, no effort is wasted, that is, $e = 0$, and all individuals have equal probability of winning $p(e) = 1/n$. The expected payoff is $\pi(e) = v/n$ and the dissipation rate is $d(e) = 0$. However, in equilibrium, the rational economic agent engages in an unproductive competition by exerting costly effort $e^* = (n-1)v/n^2$, thus causing rent dissipation $d(e^*) = (n-1)/n$. Each individual earns a positive expected payoff $\pi(e^*) = v/n^2$, and, as in the socially optimal case of no effort, all individuals have equal probability of winning $p(e^*) = 1/n$.

10.3 EXPERIMENTAL FINDINGS ON CONTESTS

Millner and Pratt (1989) were the first to examine a lottery contest using a laboratory experiment. In their experiment, participants were placed in groups of two, that is, $n = 2$, and group composition changed from period to period. In each period, participants could submit their bids (efforts) in order to win a prize of \$8, that is, $v = 8$. Given these parameters, the unique equilibrium effort is \$2 $e^* = v(n-1)/n^2 = 2$, the expected payoff

---

[1] Multiple equilibria may arise if one formally introduces behavioral spillover (Chowdhury and Sheremeta 2011a, 2011b, 2015) or risk preferences (Cornes and Hartley 2012).

[2] Theoretically, the 'discouragement effect' arises because when facing a stronger individual (or more individuals), a weaker individual cuts back on his costly expenditures (Baik 1994; Gradstein 1995; Stein 2002). The discouragement effect has been well documented by numerous experimental studies (Fonseca 2009; Anderson and Freeborn 2010; Deck and Sheremeta 2012; Kimbrough et al. 2014).

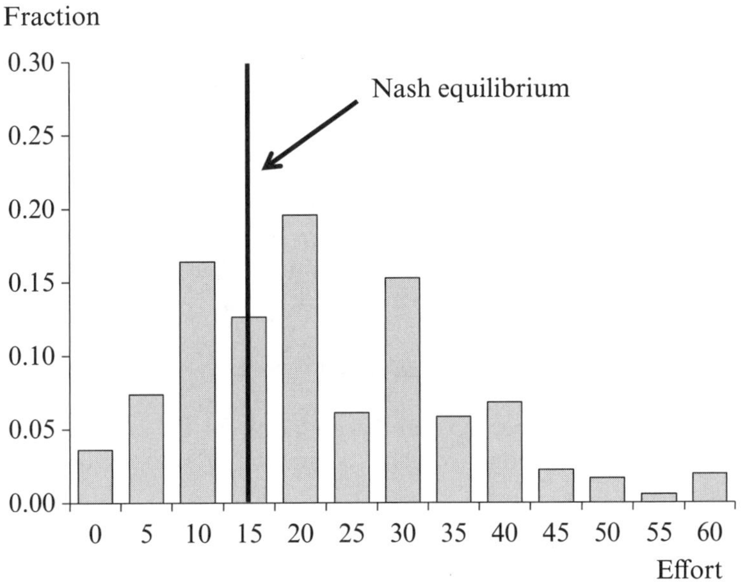

Source: The data are taken from Sheremeta (2011).

Figure 10.1 Distribution of efforts

is \$2 $\pi(e^*) = v/n^2 = 2$, and the dissipation rate is 0.5 $d(e^*) = (n - 1)/n = 0.5$. The results of the experiment showed the actual average effort of \$2.24 and the dissipation rate of 0.56 as significantly higher than predicted. The magnitude of over-dissipation was about 12 percent.

Since Millner and Pratt (1989), many other experiments have replicated the phenomenon of over-dissipation (for a review, see Dechenaux et al. 2015). Based on a sample of 30 contest experiments examined by Sheremeta (2013), the median over-dissipation rate is 72 percent. The magnitude of over-dissipation in some studies is so high that on average participants receive negative payoffs (Sheremeta and Zhang 2010; Price and Sheremeta 2011, 2015; Chowdhury et al. 2014; Mago et al. 2015). Figure 10.1 shows a typical distribution of effort in lottery contests. The data are taken from Sheremeta (2011), where $n = 2$ individuals compete for a prize of $v = 60$. According to the theoretical prediction, the equilibrium effort is 15. Nevertheless, most participants exert effort that is significantly higher than predicted, with average over-dissipation of about 31 percent.

Why do participants over-dissipate relative to the standard Nash equilibrium prediction? In the next section, I extend the theory of contests to behavioral dimensions to explain the phenomenon of over-dissipation.

10.4 BEHAVIORAL DIMENSIONS OF CONTESTS

10.4.1 Utility of Winning

The standard theoretical contest model is based on the assumption that individuals care only about the monetary value of the prize, that is, v. However, participants in actual contests also may care about winning itself. One way to incorporate the utility of winning into a contest model is to assume that in addition to the prize value v, individuals also have an additive non-monetary utility of winning w (Sheremeta 2010). Therefore, the updated expected payoff of individual i can be written as

$$\pi_i^w(e_i, e_{-i}) = p_i(e_i, e_{-i})(v + w) - e_i \tag{10.6}$$

Differentiating (10.6) with respect to e_i and accounting for the symmetric Nash equilibrium gives a new equilibrium effort, which is a function of both a monetary value v and a non-monetary value w:

$$e_w^* = \frac{(n-1)}{n^2}(v + w) \tag{10.7}$$

The corresponding dissipation rate is

$$d(e_w^*) = \frac{(n-1)}{n}\frac{(v + w)}{v} \tag{10.8}$$

It is easy to verify that the new equilibrium effort (10.7) increases in the non-monetary utility of winning w, that is, $\partial e_w^*/\partial w > 0$. Moreover, for any $w > 0$, the dissipation rate $d(e_w^*)$ described by (10.8) is higher than the standard dissipation rate $d(e^*)$ described by (10.5). Therefore, if in addition to the prize value v, individuals indeed have a non-monetary utility of winning w, we should observe over-dissipation in rent-seeking contests.

Although the utility of winning is an appealing behavioral explanation for the over-dissipation phenomenon, it is not trivial to test whether economic agents indeed have such utility. In Sheremeta (2010), I designed a method to elicit the utility of winning by having individuals participate in the contest with a monetary prize and then in the contest with no prize. The results of the experiment showed that individuals who exert significant effort just to be recognized as winners also behave overly competitively in the contest with the monetary prize. In the experiment, students participated in 30 periods of play in a four-individual contest $n = 4$, with a prize value of $v = 120$. At the end of the experiment, participants were asked to submit their efforts for a prize value of 0 $v = 0$. Participants were explicitly told that they would have to pay for their effort and that they would not receive any monetary benefit in case they won. If participants value only monetary payoffs, they should not exert any effort when the monetary prize value is zero. However, if participants derive utility from winning, they may choose to exert positive effort even when there is no monetary prize.

I found that more than 40 percent of economically motivated participants exerted

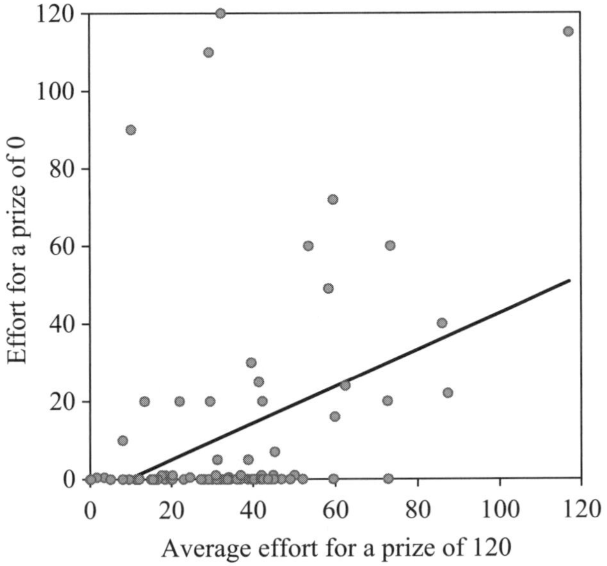

Source: The data are taken from Sheremeta (2010).

Figure 10.2 Utility of winning

positive effort in the contest with a prize value of zero. Moreover, effort in a contest with a zero prize was correlated with effort in contests with a strictly positive prize. Figure 10.2 displays the correlation between an effort for a prize of $v = 0$ and an average (over 30 periods of play) effort for a prize of $v = 120$. According to the theoretical prediction (10.3), the equilibrium effort is 22.5 when the prize is 120 and 0 when the prize is 0. Figure 10.2 shows that there is substantial heterogeneity in effort, and participants who exert higher effort for the prize of 0 also exert higher effort for the prize of 120 (Spearman's correlation coefficient is 0.31, p value < 0.01). Therefore, it appears that, in addition to monetary utility, many participants derive non-monetary utility of winning and such utility can partially explain over-dissipation in rent-seeking contests.

The findings in Sheremeta (2010) have been replicated by other studies (Price and Sheremeta 2011, 2015; Cason et al. 2013; Brookins and Ryvkin 2014; Mago et al. 2015). This suggests that the utility of winning is a robust behavioral regularity that should be incorporated into theoretical models of rent seeking. However, the exact specification of the utility of winning is still an open question. For example, it is possible that the utility of winning is not additive and is not invariant to the value of the monetary prize v, in which case, the correct specification of the utility of winning would be $w = w(v)$. It is also possible that the utility of winning may depend on the number of contestants n, in which case, the correct specification of the utility of winning would be $w = w(n)$. Disregarding the exact functional form, the utility of winning is an important behavioral factor that can help explain over-dissipation.

10.4.2 Relative Payoff Maximization

Related to the utility of winning, studies show that over-dissipation may be driven by spiteful preferences and relative payoff maximization (Fonseca 2009; Cason et al. 2013; Eisenkopf and Teyssier 2013; Mago et al. 2015). In Mago et al. (2015), co-authors and I propose a theoretical model in which individuals care not only about the utility of winning w but also the weighted average payoff of other group members. In such a case, the expected utility of individual i can be written as

$$U_i(e_i, e_{-i}) = \pi_i^w(e_i, e_{-i}) + s\frac{1}{n}\sum_j \pi_j^w(e_j, e_{-j}) \tag{10.9}$$

where s is a relative payoff parameter representing a measure of how individuals weigh their payoffs relative to others: $s > 0$ reflects preferences of pro-social individuals seeking to increase the payoff of others, while $s < 0$ reflects preferences of status-seeking individuals striving to obtain a higher relative payoff than others. The exact origin of the relative payoff parameter s is ambiguous. First, it may be the case that individuals simply have other-regarding preferences (Fehr and Schmidt 1999). Second, evolutionary game theory would argue that individuals care about their 'survival' payoff (Leininger 2003; Hehenkamp et al. 2004 [2008]; Riechmann 2007). Finally, the quest to seek higher expected payoffs than others is also consistent with the 'spite effect' (Hamilton 1970) and status (Congleton 1989 [2008]). Despite the origin of the relative payoff maximization, there is substantial research indicating that individuals care about their payoff relative to others (Frey and Stutzer 2002).

Differentiating (10.9) with respect to e_i and accounting for the symmetric Nash equilibrium gives the equilibrium effort

$$e^*_{ws} = \frac{(n-1)}{n(n-s)}(v+w) \tag{10.10}$$

The corresponding dissipation rate is

$$d(e^*_{ws}) = \frac{(n-1)}{(n-s)}\frac{(v+w)}{v} \tag{10.11}$$

It is easy to verify that the equilibrium effort (10.10) increases in the utility of winning w, that is, $\partial e^*_{ws}/\partial w > 0$, and increases in the relative payoff parameter s, that is, $\partial e^*_{ws}/\partial s > 0$. Moreover, for $w > 0$ and $s > 0$, the dissipation rate $d(e^*_{ws})$ described by (10.11) is higher than the standard dissipation rate $d(e^*)$ described by (10.5).

In Mago et al. (2015), we found that 51 percent of participants have positive utility of winning, that is, $w > 0$, replicating the findings in Sheremeta (2010). Moreover, we found that 67 percent of participants behave as status seekers, that is, $s > 0$. These findings suggest that over-dissipation in contests can be explained by a combination of a utility of winning and relative payoff maximization.

10.4.3 Bounded Rationality

The two explanations discussed so far are based on the behavioral facts that individuals participating in contests care about winning itself (w) and their relative payoffs (s).

Another well-documented behavioral fact is that people are prone to mistakes and instead of behaving rationally, use bounded rationality (Camerer 2003).

One way to introduce bounded rationality into a contest model is to assume that participants make mistakes, which adds noise to the Nash equilibrium solution. McKelvey and Palfrey (1995) suggested an elegant method of incorporating mistakes into strategic environments, naming the corresponding solution a quantal response equilibrium (QRE). In the Nash equilibrium (10.3), each individual plays a pure strategy e^*, given that others are playing the equilibrium strategy e^*. In the QRE, each individual plays a mixed strategy σ^* in which the probability of playing a pure strategy e is increasing in the expected payoff $\pi(e, \sigma^*)$ of that strategy, given that others are playing the equilibrium mixed strategy σ^*. The most commonly used specification of the QRE is the logistic QRE, where the equilibrium probability of choosing e is given by:

$$\sigma^*(e) = \frac{\exp(\pi(e, \sigma^*)/\mu)}{\int_x \exp(\pi(x, \sigma^*)/\mu)} \tag{10.12}$$

where $\mu > 0$ is an error parameter describing the level of noise in the decision-making process. If $\mu \to 0$, then the Nash equilibrium effort e^* is chosen with probability one, that is, $\sigma^*(e^*) = 1$. If $\mu \to \infty$, then each effort e between 0 and the maximum allowed effort level is equally likely to be chosen.

One implication of the QRE is that if individuals are unconstrained and are allowed to exert any effort between 0 and the value of the prize v, then any level of mistakes, that is, $\mu > 0$, will lead to over-dissipation (Sheremeta 2011; Chowdhury et al. 2014; Lim et al. 2014). The intuition is simple. Consider an individual who is completely confused and does not understand the rules of the game, that is, $\mu \to \infty$. According to the QRE, such an individual will make his or her decision by randomly choosing any effort level e between 0 and the value of the prize v. Therefore, such an individual on average will exert an effort of $v/2$, which is higher than the Nash equilibrium effort $e^* = v(n-1)/n^2$, for any $n \geq 2$.

In Sheremeta (2011), I explicitly tested the predictions of the QRE model by conducting two experimental treatments. In each treatment, four participants $n = 4$, competed in a lottery contest for a prize value of $v = 120$. In one treatment, participants were constrained to choose their efforts between 0 and 60 and in the other treatment, participants were constrained to choose their efforts between 0 and 40. Constraining participants to choose their efforts not higher than either 60 or 40 is not binding relative to the Nash equilibrium of $e^* = v(n-1)/n^2 = 22.5$. Figure 10.3 displays the expected average effort at the QRE as a function of μ and *constraint*. When $\mu \to 0$, the behavior is consistent with the Nash equilibrium. When $\mu \to \infty$, individuals move closer to a random play, and thus the average effort approaches 30 (over-dissipation) for the constraint of 60 and it approaches 20 (under-dissipation) for the constraint of 40. Therefore, if participants make substantial levels of mistakes, then the average effort should be significantly higher in the treatment with the constraint of 60. I found that the actual average effort is 29.3 when the constraint is 60 and 21.0 when the constraint is 40, consistent with the predictions of the QRE.

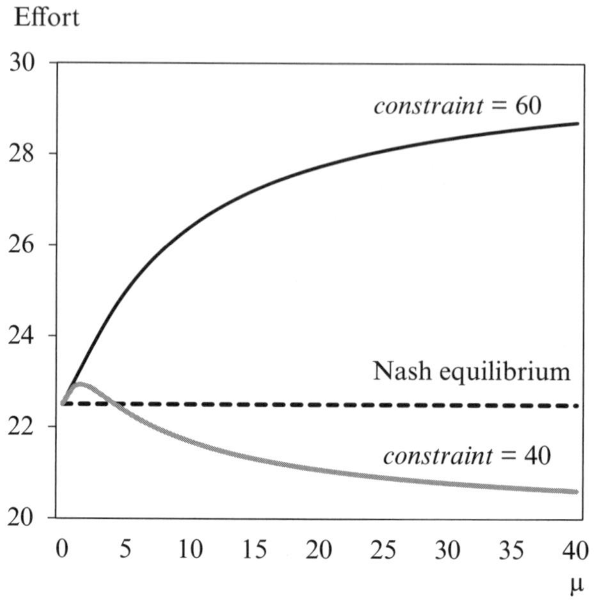

Figure 10.3 Expected average effort at the QRE

The findings in Sheremeta (2011) suggest that participants indeed make mistakes when participating in rent-seeking contests and the mistakes can explain over-dissipation. There are two potential explanations as to why participants make mistakes. First, it is possible that participants hold incorrect beliefs about the actions chosen by their opponents. Second, participants may simply make errors in their own actions. The first explanation is less likely to be true. The main reason is that the best-response functions in lottery contests are structured in such a way that if a participant believes that the opponent is going to either make higher or lower than equilibrium effort, his best response is to always exert lower than the equilibrium effort.

10.4.4 Judgmental Biases

It is well documented in the behavioral economics literature that people not only make random mistakes (as in the case of the QRE) but they also exhibit systematic 'judgmental biases' (Camerer et al. 2011), which can explain behavior in rent-seeking contests (Baharad and Nitzan 2008; Sheremeta and Zhang 2010; Chowdhury et al. 2014; Price and Sheremeta 2015).

Baharad and Nitzan (2008) apply the idea of a distorted probability weighting function from the 'prospect theory' of Kahneman and Tversky (1979) to prove that over-dissipation of rents is theoretically possible. Following Tversky and Kahneman (1992), they assume that individuals assign a distorted (biased) inverse S-shaped probability weighting function $b(p)$ to the objective probability p. Thus, instead of contest-success function (10.1), the individual's perceived probability of winning is given by

$$b(p) = \frac{p^\beta}{(p^\beta + (1 - p)^\beta)^{1/\beta}} \tag{10.13}$$

Given the distortion function (10.13), the expected payoff for an individual i can be written as

$$\pi_i^d(e_i, e_{-i}) = b(p_i(e_i, e_{-i}))v - e_i \tag{10.14}$$

Differentiating (10.14) with respect to e_i and accounting for the symmetric Nash equilibrium gives the equilibrium effort

$$e_b^* = \frac{(n - 1)}{n^\beta(1 + (n - 1)^\beta)^{1/\beta}}\left(\beta - \frac{1 - (n - 1)^{\beta-1}}{1 + (n - 1)^\beta}\right)v \tag{10.15}$$

The corresponding dissipation rate is

$$d(e_b^*) = \frac{n(n - 1)}{n^\beta(1 + (n - 1)^\beta)^{1/\beta}}\left(\beta - \frac{1 - (n - 1)^{\beta-1}}{1 + (n - 1)^\beta}\right) \tag{10.16}$$

When comparing the dissipation rate $d(e_d^*)$ described by (10.16) to the standard dissipation rate $d(e^*)$ described by (10.5), we find that for certain configurations of parameters it is possible to observe over-dissipation, that is, $d(e_b^*) > d(e^*)$. For example, with $n = 15$ and $\beta = 0.61$, the dissipation rate described by (10.16) is $d(e_b^*) = 1.05$, while the standard dissipation rate described by (10.5) is $d(e^*) = 0.9$. The magnitude of over-dissipation is about 16 percent, which is close to the magnitude of over-dissipation observed in many experimental studies (Sheremeta 2013; Dechenaux et al. 2015).

Although there is substantial evidence for the distorted probability weighting function both in the laboratory and in the field (Wu and Gonzalez 1996; Bruhin et al. 2010), there are currently no experimental studies directly relating the phenomenon of over-dissipation to distorted probability weighting.[3] Closely related studies have examined how the behavior of participants in rent-seeking contests changes when the contest-success function (10.1) is replaced by a share function (Cason et al. 2010, 2013; Fallucchi et al. 2013; Shupp et al. 2013; Chowdhury et al. 2014). In Chowdhury et al. (2014), for example, co-authors and I designed a two-by-two experiment, by varying whether the prize is assigned probabilistically (that is, efforts determine the probabilities of winning the prize) or proportionally (that is, efforts determine the shares of the prize) and whether the cost function is linear or convex. Although in all treatments the risk-neutral Nash equilibrium effort level was constant, we found that compared to the probabilistic contest-success function, the proportional rule results in effort levels that are closer to the

[3] Parco et al. (2005) and Amaldoss and Rapoport (2009) apply the distorted probability weighting function, combined with a utility of winning, to explain the pattern of the data observed in their contest experiments. However, in their experiments participants are budget constrained, making it impossible to observe over-dissipation.

risk-neutral prediction (with almost no over-dissipation).[4] Combining the proportional rule with a convex cost function further strengthens these results. Therefore, it appears that even though there is no direct evidence as to whether distorted probability weighting causes over-dissipation in rent-seeking contests, related studies show that even a slight modification to the contest-success function plays a major role in determining individual behavior.

In Price and Sheremeta (2015), we applied another idea from the prospect theory of Kahneman and Tversky (1979) to explain over-dissipation in contest experiments. We designed an experiment in which some participants had to earn their income before participating in a laboratory rent-seeking contest experiment. We found that participants who earn their income exert lower effort in subsequent contests than participants who receive their income directly from the experimenter. The main reason for this result is that participants who earn their income and participants who receive their income for free have different reference points. Participants who earn their income operate in the domain of losses, while participants who receive income for free operate in the domain of gains.

In two other studies (Sheremeta and Zhang 2010; Chowdhury et al. 2013), co-authors and I pointed out yet another judgmental bias that may partially explain over-dissipation in repeated contests. Specifically, we found that, participants who win in period $t - 1$ are more likely to make higher effort in period t. In Sheremeta and Zhang (2010), we point out the similarities in correlation between winning in period $t - 1$ and higher efforts in period t to a 'hot hand' phenomenon found in the gambling literature – belief in a positive autocorrelation of a non-autocorrelated random sequence (Gilovich et al. 1985; Chau and Phillips 1995; Croson and Sundali 2005). Therefore, it appears that a hot hand response by participants may help in explaining over-dissipation in repeated contest settings.[5]

10.5 DISCUSSION AND CONCLUSION

One of the main findings from experimental studies on contests is that participants exert effort that is significantly higher than predicted by the standard Nash equilibrium (Sheremeta 2013). This phenomenon is referred to as over-dissipation of rents, overbidding or over-expenditure of resources. The standard rent-seeking contest model, based on the assumption of rational economic agents, cannot explain over-dissipation. The over-dissipation phenomenon can be explained by incorporating behavioral dimensions into a standard contest model, such as (1) the utility of winning; (2) relative payoff maximization; (3) bounded rationality; and (4) judgmental biases.[6]

---

[4] Note that the proportional rule eliminates the utility of winning and thus lower over-dissipation also might be due to the absence of the utility of winning.

[5] Most experimental studies use repeated designs in order to give participants enough time for learning.

[6] One may add to this list other candidates such as regret, overconfidence and risk aversion. It is important to emphasize, however, that risk aversion cannot explain over-dissipation in contests (Dechenaux et al. 2015). Although theoretically it is possible for risk aversion to cause over-

There are several fruitful avenues for future research. First, it is still an open question as to which behavioral dimensions are the most important in explaining individual behavior in rent-seeking contests. It is possible that some of the factors explaining over-dissipation are correlated. For example, the relative payoff maximization may be driven by the utility of winning or judgmental biases may be driven by systematic mistakes. The relative impact of these factors on individual behavior remains unknown.

Second, given the prevalence of over-dissipation in laboratory experiments, it is important to know whether over-dissipation occurs in field settings with real effort and high stakes. Do field experiments offer insights into whether over-dissipation is a robust phenomenon? Are the explanations for over-dissipation in the field similar to the explanations for over-dissipation in the laboratory? These questions are important and answering them would significantly advance our understanding of the over-dissipation phenomenon.

Finally, given that rent-seeking behavior is unproductive and costly (even more so than predicted by the rational-behavior theory), it is important to develop and investigate mechanisms aimed at avoiding unproductive competition.[7] Since the seminal book by Schelling (1960), a number of mechanisms for avoiding conflict have been proposed, ranging from deterrence via extensive armament to contractually binding side-payments. Recent experimental studies have examined different conflict resolution mechanisms including side-payments (Kimbrough and Sheremeta 2013, 2014), random devices (Kimbrough et al. 2014, 2015), communication (Cason et al. 2012, 2014), cooperative spillovers (Savikhin and Sheremeta 2013) and social identification (Mago et al. 2015). Whether these mechanisms are effective in the field remains an open question.

REFERENCES

Amaldoss, Wilfred and Amnon Rapoport (2009), 'Excessive expenditure in two-stage contests: theory and experimental evidence', in F. Columbus (ed.), *Game Theory: Strategies, Equilibria, and Theorems*, Hauppauge, NY: Nova Science Publishers, pp. 241–66.

Anderson, Lisa R. and Beth A. Freeborn (2010), 'Varying the intensity of competition in a multiple prize rent seeking experiment', *Public Choice*, **143**(1–2), 237–54.

Baharad, Eyal and Shmuel Nitzan (2008), 'Contest efforts in light of behavioural considerations', *Economic Journal*, **118**(533), 2047–59.

Baik, Kyung Hwan (1994), 'Effort levels in contests with two asymmetric players', *Southern Economic Journal*, **61**(2), 367–78.

Brookins, Philip and Dmitry Ryvkin (2014), 'An experimental study of bidding in contests of incomplete information', *Experimental Economics*, **17**(2), 245–61.

Bruhin, Adrian, Helga Fehr-Duda and Thomas Epper (2010), 'Risk and rationality: uncovering heterogeneity in probability distortion', *Econometrica*, **78**(4), 1375–412.

---

dissipation (Treich 2010; Cornes and Hartley 2012), experimental contest studies show that more risk-averse subjects choose lower efforts than less risk-averse subjects (Millner and Pratt 1991; Anderson and Freeborn 2010; Sheremeta and Zhang 2010; Sheremeta 2011; Mago et al. 2013; Shupp et al. 2013).

[7] Over-dissipation is of course not desirable. In the context of research and development and labor tournaments, there may be positive externalities generated from increased research spending (Cason et al. 2010).

Camerer, Colin F. (2003), *Behavioral Game Theory: Experiments in Strategic Interaction*, Princeton, NJ: Princeton University Press.
Camerer, Colin F., George Loewenstein and Matthew Rabin (2011), *Advances in Behavioral Economics*, Princeton, NJ: Princeton University Press.
Cason, Timothy N., William A. Masters and Roman M. Sheremeta (2010), 'Entry into winner-take-all and proportional-prize contests: an experimental study', *Journal of Public Economics*, **94**(9), 604–11.
Cason, Timothy N., Roman M. Sheremeta and Jingjing Zhang (2012), 'Communication and efficiency in competitive coordination games', *Games and Economic Behavior*, **76**(1), 26–43.
Cason, Timothy N., William A. Masters and Roman M. Sheremeta (2013), 'Winner-take-all and proportional-prize contests: theory and experimental results', Working Paper, Economic Science Institute, Chapman University.
Cason, Timothy N., Roman M. Sheremeta and Jingjing Zhang (2014), 'Asymmetric and endogenous communication in competition between groups', Working Paper, Economic Science Institute, Chapman University.
Chau, Albert W. and James G. Phillips (1995), 'Effects of perceived control upon wagering and attributions in computer blackjack', *Journal of General Psychology*, **122**(3), 253–69.
Chowdhury, Subhasish M. and Roman M. Sheremeta (2011a), 'A generalized Tullock contest', *Public Choice*, **147**(3–4), 413–20.
Chowdhury, Subhasish M. and Roman M. Sheremeta (2011b), 'Multiple equilibria in Tullock contests', *Economics Letters*, **112**(2), 216–19.
Chowdhury, Subhasish M. and Roman M. Sheremeta (2015), 'Strategically equivalent contests', *Theory and Decision*, forthcoming.
Chowdhury, Subhasish M., Dan Kovenock and Roman M. Sheremeta (2013), 'An experimental investigation of Colonel Blotto games', *Economic Theory*, **52**(3), 833–61.
Chowdhury, Subhasish M., Theodore L. Turocy and Roman M. Sheremeta (2014), 'Overbidding and overspreading in rent-seeking experiments: cost structure and prize allocation rules', *Games and Economic Behavior*, **87**, 224–38.
Congleton, Roger D. (1989), 'Efficent rent seeking: externalities and the evolution of status games', *Journal of Economic Behavior and Organization*, **11**, 175–90, reprinted in Roger D. Congleton, Arye L. Hillman and Kai A. Konrad (eds) (2008), *40 Years of Research on Rent Seeking 2 – Applications: Rent Seeking in Practice*, Heidelberg: Springer, pp. 697–712.
Congleton, Roger D., Arye L. Hillman and Kai A. Konrad (eds) (2008a), *40 Years of Research on Rent Seeking 1 – The Theory of Rent Seeking*, Heidelberg: Springer.
Congleton, Roger D., Arye L. Hillman and Kai A. Konrad (eds) (2008b), *40 Years of Research on Rent Seeking 2 – Applications: Rent Seeking in Practice*, Heidelberg: Springer.
Cornes, Richard and Roger Hartley (2012), 'Risk aversion in symmetric and asymmetric contests', *Economic Theory*, **51**(2), 247–75.
Croson, Rachel and James Sundali (2005), 'The gambler's fallacy and the hot hand: empirical data from casinos', *Journal of Risk and Uncertainty*, **30**(3), 195–209.
Dasgupta, Partha (1986), 'The theory of technological competition', in Joseph E. Stiglitz and G. Frank Mathewson (eds), *New Developments in the Analysis of Market Structure*, Cambridge, MA: MIT Press.
Dechenaux, Emmanuel, Dan Kovenock and Roman M. Sheremeta (2015), 'A survey of experimental research on contests, all-pay auctions and tournaments', *Experimental Economics*, forthcoming.
Deck, Cary and Roman M. Sheremeta (2012), 'Fight or flight? Defending against sequential attacks in the game of Siege', *Journal of Conflict Resolution*, **56**(6), 1069–88.
Eisenkopf, Gerald and Sabrina Teyssier (2013), 'Envy and loss aversion in tournaments', *Journal of Economic Psychology*, **34**, 240–55.
Fallucchi, Francesco, Elke Renner and Martin Sefton (2013), 'Information feedback and contest structure in rent-seeking games', *European Economic Review*, **64**, 223–40.
Fehr, Ernst and Klaus M. Schmidt (1999), 'A theory of fairness, competition, and cooperation', *Quarterly Journal of Economics*, **114**(3), 817–68.
Fonseca, Miguel A. (2009), 'An experimental investigation of asymmetric contests', *International Journal of Industrial Organization*, **27**(5), 582–91.
Frey, Bruno S. and Alois Stutzer (2002), 'What can economists learn from happiness research?', *Journal of Economic Literature*, **40**(2), 402–35.
Gilovich, Thomas, Robert Vallone and Amos Tversky (1985), 'The hot hand in basketball: on the misperception of random sequences', *Cognitive Psychology*, **17**(3), 295–314.
Gradstein, Mark (1995), 'Intensity of competition, entry and entry deterrence in rent seeking contests', *Economics and Politics*, **7**(1), 79–91.
Hamilton, William D. (1970), 'Selfish and spiteful behaviour in an evolutionary model', *Nature*, **228**, 1218–20.
Hehenkamp, Burkhard, Wolfgang Leininger and Alexandre Possajennikov (2004), 'Evolutionary equilibrium in Tullock contests: spite and overdissipation', *European Journal of Political Economy*, **20**(4), 1045–57,

reprinted in Roger D. Congleton, Arye L. Hillman and Kai A. Konrad (eds) (2008), *40 Years of Research on Rent Seeking 1 – The Theory of Rent Seeking*, Heidelberg: Springer, pp. 473–85.
Hillman, Arye L. and John G. Riley (1989), 'Politically contestable rents and transfers', *Economics and Politics*, **1**(1), 17–39, reprinted in Roger D. Congleton, Arye L. Hillman and Kai A. Konrad (eds) (2008), *40 Years of Research on Rent Seeking 1 – The Theory of Rent Seeking*, Heidelberg: Springer, pp. 185–207.
Hillman, Arye L. and Dov Samet (1987), 'Dissipation of rents and revenues in small numbers contests', *Public Choice*, **54**(1), 63–82, reprinted in Roger D. Congleton, Arye L. Hillman and Kai A. Konrad (eds) (2008), *40 Years of Research on Rent Seeking 1 – The Theory of Rent Seeking*, Heidelberg: Springer, pp. 165–84.
Kahneman, Daniel and Amos Tversky (1979), 'Prospect theory: an analysis of decision under risk', *Econometrica*, **47**(2), 263–91.
Kimbrough, Erik O. and Roman M. Sheremeta (2013), 'Side-payments and the costs of conflict', *International Journal of Industrial Organization*, **31**(3), 278–86.
Kimbrough, Erik O. and Roman M. Sheremeta (2014), 'Why can't we be friends? Entitlements and the costs of conflict', *Journal of Peace Research*, **51**, 487–500.
Kimbrough, Erik O., Roman M. Sheremeta and Timothy W. Shields (2014), 'When parity promotes peace: resolving conflict between asymmetric agents', *Journal of Economic Behavior and Organization*, **99**, 96–108.
Kimbrough, Erik, Jared Rubin, Roman Sheremeta and Timothy Shields (2015), 'Commitment problems in conflict resolution', *Journal of Economic Behavior and Organization*, forthcoming.
Krueger, Anne O. (1974), 'The political economy of the rent-seeking society', *American Economic Review*, **64**(3), 291–303, reprinted in Roger D. Congleton, Arye L. Hillman and Kai A. Konrad (eds) (2008), *40 Years of Research on Rent Seeking 2 – Applications: Rent Seeking in Practice*, Heidelberg: Springer, pp. 151–63.
Leininger, Wolfgang (2003), 'On evolutionarily stable behavior in contests', *Economics of Governance*, **4**(3), 177–86.
Lim, Wooyoung, Alexander Matros and Theodore L. Turocy (2014), 'Bounded rationality and group size in Tullock contests: experimental evidence', *Journal of Economic Behavior and Organization*, **99**, 155–67.
Long, Ngo Van (2013), 'The theory of contests: a unified model and review of the literature', *European Journal of Political Economy*, **32**, 161–81, reprinted in Chapter 3, this volume.
Mago, Shakun D., Roman M. Sheremeta and Andrew Yates (2013), 'Best-of-three contest experiments: strategic versus psychological momentum', *International Journal of Industrial Organization*, **31**(3), 287–96.
Mago, Shakun, Anya Samak and Roman Sheremeta (2015), 'Facing your opponents: social identification and information feedback in contests', *Journal of Conflict Resolution*, forthcoming.
McKelvey, Richard D. and Thomas R. Palfrey (1995), 'Quantal response equilibria for normal form games', *Games and Economic Behavior*, **10**(1), 6–38.
Millner, Edward L. and Michael D. Pratt (1989), 'An experimental investigation of efficient rent-seeking', *Public Choice*, **62**(2), 139–51.
Millner, Edward L. and Michael D. Pratt (1991), 'Risk aversion and rent-seeking: an extension and some experimental evidence', *Public Choice*, **69**(1), 81–92.
Parco, James E., Amnon Rapoport and Wilfred Amaldoss (2005), 'Two-stage contests with budget constraints: an experimental study', *Journal of Mathematical Psychology*, **49**(4), 320–38.
Price, Curtis R. and Roman M. Sheremeta (2011), 'Endowment effects in contests', *Economics Letters*, **111**(3), 217–19.
Price, Curtis R. and Roman M. Sheremeta (2015), 'Endowment origin, demographic effects and individual preferences in contests', *Journal of Economics and Management Strategy*, forthcoming.
Riechmann, Thomas (2007), 'An analysis of rent-seeking games with relative-payoff maximizers', *Public Choice*, **133**(1–2), 147–55.
Savikhin, Anya C. and Roman M. Sheremeta (2013), 'Simultaneous decision-making in competitive and cooperative environments', *Economic Inquiry*, **51**(2), 1311–23.
Schelling, Thomas C. (1960), *The Strategy of Conflict*, Cambridge, MA: Harvard University Press.
Sheremeta, Roman M. (2010), 'Experimental comparison of multi-stage and one-stage contests', *Games and Economic Behavior*, **68**(2), 731–47.
Sheremeta, Roman M. (2011), 'Contest design: an experimental investigation', *Economic Inquiry*, **49**(2), 573–90.
Sheremeta, Roman M. (2013), 'Overbidding and heterogeneous behavior in contest experiments', *Journal of Economic Surveys*, **27**(3), 491–514.
Sheremeta, Roman M. and Jingjing Zhang (2010), 'Can groups solve the problem of over-bidding in contests?', *Social Choice and Welfare*, **35**(2), 175–97.
Shupp, Robert, Roman M. Sheremeta, David Schmidt and James Walker (2013), 'Resource allocation contests: experimental evidence', *Journal of Economic Psychology*, **39**, 257–67.
Skaperdas, Stergios (1996), 'Contest success functions', *Economic Theory*, **7**(2), 283–90, reprinted in Roger D. Congleton, Arye L. Hillman and Kai A. Konrad (eds) (2008), *40 Years of Research on Rent Seeking 1 – The Theory of Rent Seeking*, Heidelberg: Springer, pp. 263–70.

Stein, William E. (2002), 'Asymmetric rent-seeking with more than two contestants', *Public Choice*, **113**(3–4), 325–36.
Szidarovszky, Ferenc and Koji Okuguchi (1997), 'On the existence and uniqueness of pure Nash equilibrium in rent-seeking games', *Games and Economic Behavior*, **18**(1), 135–40, reprinted in Roger D. Congleton, Arye L. Hillman and Kai A. Konrad (eds) (2008), *40 Years of Research on Rent Seeking 1 – The Theory of Rent Seeking*, Heidelberg: Springer, pp. 271–6.
Treich, Nicolas (2010), 'Risk-aversion and prudence in rent-seeking games', *Public Choice*, **145**(3–4), 339–49.
Tullock, Gordon (1967), 'The welfare costs of tariffs, monopolies, and theft', *Western Economic Journal*, **5**(3), 224–32, reprinted in Roger D. Congleton, Arye L. Hillman and Kai A. Konrad (eds) (2008), *40 Years of Research on Rent Seeking 1 – The Theory of Rent Seeking*, Heidelberg: Springer, pp. 45–53.
Tullock, Gordon (1980), 'Efficient rent seeking', in James M. Buchanan, Robert D. Tollison and Gordon Tullock (eds), *Towards a Theory of the Rent-seeking Society*, College Station, TX: Texas A&M University Press, pp. 97–112, reprinted in Roger D. Congleton, Arye L. Hillman and Kai A. Konrad (eds) (2008), *40 Years of Research on Rent Seeking 1 – The Theory of Rent Seeking*, Heidelberg: Springer, pp. 105–20.
Tversky, Amos and Daniel Kahneman (1992), 'Advances in prospect theory: cumulative representation of uncertainty', *Journal of Risk and Uncertainty*, **5**(4), 297–323.
Wu, George and Richard Gonzalez (1996), 'Curvature of the probability weighting function', *Management Science*, **42**(12), 1676–90.

PART III

APPLICATIONS AND OUTCOMES

11. Regulatory rent seeking

William F. Shughart II and Diana W. Thomas

SUMMARY

This chapter views the theory of rent seeking in the context of governmental regulation of prices and conditions of market entry. Such policies create economic rents for the regulated firms and put in place incentives for rent seeking through use of real resources to contest and gain access to the rents. Evidence from the history of economic regulation and deregulation in the United States is marshaled to show that regulatory intervention does not add to society's wealth, but, consistent with the logic of collective action, instead redistributes existing wealth from unorganized, politically weak groups ('the many') to well-organized, politically effective groups ('the few').

11.1 INTRODUCTION

The term 'rent' refers to the income earned by the owner of a resource over and above that resource's value in its next best alternative use. A pure economic profit, which may materialize temporarily in a hypothetical, textbook perfectly competitive market or persist in the long run if competition is imperfect, is one example of a rent. So, too, is the bulk of the compensation of a superstar athlete, artist, or entertainer, whose scarce talents cannot easily be replicated.

One must be cautious in drawing parallels between rent and profit, however, in order to avoid conflating the social welfare implications of the conditions that give rise to them and, what is more important, the consequences of the activities rationally undertaken in their pursuit (Buchanan 1980a). Returns in excess of normal are lures to alert entrepreneurs who see and then seize opportunities to position themselves for earning rents by redeploying resources from less highly valued to more highly valued uses. Rents can arise naturally in ordinary market settings following unanticipated increases in demand, which signal consumers' greater willingness to pay for existing products; from discoveries of new technologies or more efficient ways of combining labor, capital, raw materials and other productive inputs, which lower suppliers' costs; from exploiting previously untapped product or geographic markets; or from taking advantage of wholly novel, creatively destructive ideas (Schumpeter 1942 [1950]). When rents emerge in those ways, the prospect of collecting them triggers the entry of new profit-seeking enterprises or expansions of capacity by incumbent producers. Supply to the market increases, prices fall and, in the limit, rents (extraordinary economic profits) are fully competed away (driven down to normal levels), thereby ensuring that the benefits of market exchanges accrue to consumer-buyers.

But the story of the social benefits of rent seeking is changed entirely if rents are created artificially. Returns in excess of normal also can be made available by any policy adopted by the public sector that offers limited rights for producing a good that is consumed within a defined geographic area and that bars the entry of rivals other than a favored few. Examples of such policies are legion and include licensing requirements for accountants, lawyers, cosmetologists, taxicab drivers, medical doctors and other professionals; exclusive franchises for the suppliers of electric power, natural gas, garbage collection and cable television services; import tariffs and other controls on international trade; and acreage restrictions on the growers of agricultural crops as well as minimum prices at which their produce can be sold. Such constraints, enforced by the police powers of the state that can lead to the imposition of monetary fines and other penalties on violators, plainly create rents and, as is true of ordinary profit opportunities, elicit competition for access to the rents.

But such competition generates none of the benefits of rivalry for naturally occurring rents. As a matter of fact, rent seeking, as construed herein as competition for returns in excess of normal associated with artificial, government-created profit opportunities, wastes society's scarce resources in whole or in part because the contestants' investments of time, effort and money serve only to determine the winner of the rent on offer. In order to elicit rivalry for a rent, the output of the good or service in contention must remain fixed below the otherwise competitive level and so, too, must final product price and the favored producer's profit remain above competitive levels. Rent seeking therefore does not lead to expansions of output or reductions in price or profit. Consumers do not benefit from such competition – the benefits accrue solely to the winner of the contest and to its organizers, in the form of bribes or other forms of political support.

The rent-seeking insight arose from the fertile mind of Gordon Tullock (1967 [2008]), although Anne Krueger (1974 [2008]), by all accounts unaware at the time of Tullock's seminal contribution, coined the by now widely accepted term later. The literature spawned by Tullock, especially the specific form of the contest-success function that he proposed (Tullock 1980 [2008]), is immense and has been surveyed many times, beginning with Tollison (1982), followed by Nitzan (1994) and Hillman (2013), among others. Papers since Tullock's insight have been reprinted in Congleton et al. (2008a, 2008b), who also review the literature.

In this chapter, we summarize Tullock's model of rent seeking as it applies to governmental intervention in the commercial affairs of the private sector in the form of economic regulation. Generally speaking, public regulation of industry falls into two broad categories, the first and original rationale for which was to intervene in markets characterized by the conditions of 'natural monopoly' or as being touched by some version of the 'public's interest'. In the United States, at least, such a public-interest color was first applied to the operation of a private business entity engaged in the storage of grain and then later extended to public utilities as well as to the railroads and other so-called common carriers. 'Economic regulation' typically is defined as the imposition of governmental controls on the prices charged by privately owned business entities and on the conditions of entry into markets subject to such regulation. A second, more recent type of governmentally mandated controls, falls into the broad category of 'social regulation', which applies to rules on workplace health and safety, consumer protection, environmental air and water quality and to regulations applying to marriage contracts, childbirth and to other aspects of non-market collective decision-making, such as health insurance and public pension programs. In this chapter, we focus on the former, but mention the latter from time to time as circumstances warrant.

The chapter is organized as follows. We begin in Section 11.2 with a brief review of the standard theory of economic regulation and then present the interest-group theory of government. The former is concerned with the theory and practice of 'optimal' regulation, that is, determining the prices regulated firms are allowed to charge, along with monitoring other business decisions, such as production capacity and service quality, so as to restrain the exercise of the market power that firms otherwise would enjoy. As such, the standard theory assumes that regulation benefits the regulated firm's customers at the owners' expense. The interest-group theory, in contrast, predicts that public intervention into specific private markets and regulatory regimes that apply more generally – such as antitrust or competition policy (Shughart 1990; McChesney and Shughart 1995) – tend to favor 'concentrated' (that is, small and well-organized) interests at the expense of 'diffuse' (that is, large and poorly or less well-organized) groups. Consistent with the logic of collective action (Olson 1965), George Stigler (1971) observed that narrow interests almost always dominate broader interests in the political process, leading to the 'capture' of regulatory agencies by the very firms subject to governmental oversight. Regulation, in other words, benefits the owners of regulated business entities at their customers' expense. Economic regulation creates rents for the regulated firms and triggers wasteful rent seeking both before and after the onset of regulation. Indeed, rather than being thrust on unwilling producers, regulation often is sought by the producers.

The evidence related to regulatory rent seeking is summarized in Section 11.3. Paradoxically, perhaps, the conclusion that economic regulation operates to promote the interests of regulated firms and industries is confirmed by events following episodes of deregulation in the United States and other corners of the globe. We end, in Section 11.4, with an overview of Gordon Tullock's contributions to our understanding of the purposes and effects of public regulation of private business entities.

11.2 TWO THEORIES OF ECONOMIC REGULATION

11.2.1 'Natural' Monopoly and Beyond

In an older way of thinking, economic regulation was intended to prevent private for-profit enterprises from abusing their 'market power', defined customarily as a seller's ability to raise the price charged to its customers above marginal cost without losing so many sales at that higher price that the price increase becomes unprofitable. The classic example of market power thought to require public regulation occurs under circumstances of so-called natural monopoly. If the production of a good or service, electric power, say, is characterized by substantial economies of scale over a wide range of possible rates of output, the producer's long-run average costs decline continuously over that range and if, in addition, the market demand curve intersects the long-run average cost curve at a point where average costs are still falling, then it is economically efficient in a production-cost sense for one firm to supply the entire market. That single firm can achieve a lower cost per unit of output than two or more firms filling the same market demand.[1]

---

[1] The existence of scale economies up to the level of market demand is sufficient for establishing

Left to its own devices, however, the natural monopolist will not produce and sell the quantity of output at which demand is equal to long-run average cost. It will produce somewhat less than that quantity, determining its output by, as every student of price theory learns, equating marginal revenue with marginal cost. And by reducing its rate of output below that at which demand intersects long-run average cost, the natural monopolist can raise price above marginal (and average) cost, charging the maximum amount consumers are willing to pay for the quantity on offer. That above-marginal-cost price reduces consumers' surplus, transferring some of it to the seller in the form of a pure economic profit and, at the same time, creates a deadweight social welfare loss triangle (Harberger 1954) that impairs the economy's allocative efficiency: Compared to the ideal of perfect competition, less than a socially optimal amount of scarce resources is deployed in the production of the natural monopolist's good or service. Potential gains from trade are lost because some consumers would be willing to pay more for some of the unproduced units than it would cost the seller to supply.[2]

Hence, the impetus for economic regulation: if a public regulatory agency mandates that in return for its exclusive franchise, the natural monopolist charges a price below the one that would otherwise maximize its profits, the regulated firm will expand its output and its economic profits will decline without sacrificing (much of) the productive efficiency of single-firm supply. Such a Goldilocks result, however, requires the regulatory agency to have very precise information both about market demand and the regulated firm's costs of production. The price the regulators allow the firm to charge its customers cannot be 'too low' – it must satisfy a break-even constraint such that the regulated firm is able to earn at least a normal rate of return and thereby remain viable in the long run.[3] If the price is set 'too high', the allocative inefficiency of monopoly either will not be reduced materially or may be magnified.

Construed narrowly, the natural monopoly justification for regulation rests on some very specific assumptions about the configurations of market demand and production cost; as such, it applies only to a limited set of 'public utilities'. Water and sewer systems, electric power grids and telecommunication networks, which have been subject

---

natural monopoly when the firm produces a single product. In modern parlance, scale economies are a strong form of 'cost sub-additivity', meaning that there is no feasible way of subdividing the firm's total quantity of output, *Q*, having each subpart produced by separate firms, without incurring higher total costs. In other words, 'the cost of producing the whole is less than the sum of the costs of producing the parts' (Baumol et al. 1982, p. 17). Strict cost sub-additivity (and, hence, natural monopoly) in the multi-product case requires both economies of scale and economies of joint production, the latter representing situations in which the total cost of producing the individual products by separate firms is greater than the total cost of having all of them produced by the same firm (Tirole 1988, pp. 19–20; also see Sherman 1989; Spulber 1989).

2 Such comparisons commit what Harold Demsetz (1969) calls the 'nirvana fallacy', evaluating the performances of actual markets, not in light of other, necessarily imperfect alternatives, but judging them instead by the outcomes that would materialize in some idealized and unattainable, perfectly competitive textbook world.

3 The regulated price cannot be set equal to the producer's marginal cost (even if the regulators could determine it) because marginal cost lies continuously below average cost when the latter is declining. A regulatory marginal-cost price thus would cause the firm to incur losses (sustain negative economic profits), thereby requiring a subsidy of some sort for the producer to remain viable in the long run.

to regulation by local, state and national governments in the United States and Europe, are prime examples. Even in these textbook cases, however, the theoretical rationale for regulation is weak.

Competition *for* the field can substitute for competition within it (Demsetz 1968; Williamson 1976). Additionally, a regime of 'access pricing', whereby rival suppliers pay for the right to utilize the large-scale infrastructure necessary to serve public utility customers, can avoid duplicative investments in production capacity and promote efficient utilization of that capacity (Shy 2001, p. 8). It also turns out that if an unregulated natural monopolist operates under conditions of contestability,[4] it will charge Ramsey (1927) optimal prices in all markets (that is, prices that are inversely proportional to the elasticity of demand in each market), subject to a minimum profit constraint that ensures viability (Baumol et al. 1977, 1982; Tirole 1988, pp. 308–9). Hence, while the particular market conditions defining unregulated natural monopoly prevent the attainment of first-best outcomes, they may not preclude second-best optimums even in the absence of regulation (Coase 1959, 1960).[5]

Public regulation of industry in the United States began at the federal level in 1887 with passage of the Act to Regulate Commerce, which established the Interstate Commerce Commission (ICC) and delegated to that agency authority to ensure that railway rates were 'just and reasonable'. The ICC's regulatory powers ultimately were expanded to include control over most surface (and some subsurface) interstate transportation modes, including inland water carriers, trucks, buses and crude oil pipelines – industries to which the natural monopoly label does not obviously apply.

Public regulation of industry in the United States in fact predates the Act to Regulate Commerce by a decade. In 1877, the US Supreme Court ruled that when private property is 'affected with a public interest', regulation is constitutionally permissible despite the Fourteenth Amendment's guarantee that 'no State shall . . . deprive any person of life, liberty, or property without due process of law'. That ruling was handed down in *Munn* v. *Illinois*, 94 U.S. 113 (1877), a case challenging a provision of the Constitution of the State of Illinois designating privately owned grain elevators as public warehouses as well as a law passed by the Illinois legislature in 1871 prescribing maximum rates for grain storage. Munn and Scott, two grain-elevator operators, had been convicted of charging rates higher than the law allowed; the Supreme Court upheld their conviction. In the following years, the Court construed the 'public-interest' standard strictly, approving state regulation of only a select group of industries, including in addition to grain storage, banks, fire insurance companies and insurance agents. Limited as the early extensions of regulation may have been, none of the newly regulated industries conceivably were monopolies, natural or otherwise.

But the Court rejected even the narrow construction of *Munn* in 1934, declaring that 'the phrase "affected with a public interest" can, in the nature of things, mean no more than that an industry, for adequate reason, is subject to control for the public good' and furthermore that 'there can be no doubt that on proper occasion and by appropriate measures the

---

[4] A 'contestable' market is one characterized by the absence of barriers to entry and to exit; see Baumol et al. (1982) for a more formal definition.

[5] The discussion in this and the following four paragraphs is based on Shughart (2003 [2008]).

state may regulate a business in any of its aspects, including the prices to be charged for its products or the commodities it sells'. *Nebbia* v. *New York*, 291 U.S. 502 (1934), upheld the right of New York's Milk Control Board to regulate milk prices in the state; the Court in effect ruled that there is no constitutional distinction between public utilities and other industries. The states thereafter were free to regulate any business operating within their jurisdictions for any reason public officials plausibly could justify as promoting the public interest, so long as the regulation was 'neither arbitrary nor discriminatory'.

Many of the regulatory agencies still operating at the state and federal levels of government in the United States are the children of Franklin Delano Roosevelt's (FDR) New Deal. The Federal Communications Commission, the Food and Drug Administration, the Federal Power Commission, the Civil Aeronautics Board and the Securities and Exchange Commission, among others, were created in response to the perceived failings of unfettered markets, to which the unprecedented economic collapse of the Great Depression popularly was traced and which private market forces seemed incapable of reversing. Investor-owned electric power companies, farms and dairies, manufacturing and labor relations, including the setting of minimum wages and maximum hours of work, all were brought within the ambit of governmental regulatory control in order to counter ostensible chronic overproduction by the private sector and the low prices and wages to which such overproduction gave rise.

Although it subsequently was declared to be unconstitutional by the US Supreme Court, one of the legislative ornaments of FDR's famous first 100 days was the National Industrial Recovery Act. That law established the National Recovery Administration (NRA), which oversaw the writing of codes of 'fair competition' by the members of hundreds of American industries, the purpose being the forging of agreements to limit production and to 'stabilize' prices so as to promote employment and, hence, economic recovery.[6] Thus, given the evidence we report below on the actual effects of economic regulation, regulatory intervention was born and flourished at a time when its aim was thought to be to reduce the outputs of the regulated industries and to keep their prices and profits high.

It is important to emphasize that the information regulators require to achieve regulation's stated goals by and large must be obtained from the regulated industry itself. Depending on how methodically regulatory rate hearings are conducted and how aggressively the regulatory agency adjusts allowable prices over time to take account of changing conditions of cost and demand, the regulated firm may strategically be able to exploit its superior knowledge to benefit owners and managers at customers' expense.

In the end, and in spite of a large and elegant scholarly literature prescribing mechanisms for dealing with the complexities of economic regulation in settings where information about demand and cost is distributed asymmetrically between the regulated industry and its regulators, commentators associated with the Chicago School conclude that regulation's

> contribution to social and economic welfare is very possibly negative. The benefits of regulation are dubious, not only because the evils of natural monopoly are exaggerated but also because

[6] See Couch and Shughart (1998) for a detailed history of the regulatory, output-reducing initiatives of the New Deal, along with analyses of their origins and effects.

the effectiveness of regulation in controlling them is highly questionable. (Posner 1969 [1999], p. 106)[7]

In what follows, we ignore the huge literature on 'optimal' economic regulation (see, for example, Train 1991) in order to focus on the public-choice questions it raises.

11.2.2 The Interest-Group Theory of Regulation

Leaving aside the complex scientific problem of choosing the appropriate price or prices the regulated firm will be allowed to charge,[8] the orthodox approach to regulation poses a puzzle. If economic regulation of price actually reduces the profits of regulated firms to normal levels, there would be no need also to block entry into the regulated market. 'Normal' profits do not invite new entry because the returns to the incumbent firm equal the returns to investments elsewhere in the economy.[9] A more nuanced analysis of the issue therefore is demanded.

The positive economic analysis of regulation began with George Stigler (1971). Stigler's important contribution to the literature is consistent with the work of Mancur Olson (1965) insofar as it suggests that economic regulation will tend to favor the few over the many.

Stigler's theory of regulatory 'capture' drew on the evidence he had amassed on the basis of his own analyses of the actual – as opposed to the 'intended' – effects of several

---

[7] Another reason for doubting economic regulation's purposes and effects is that even otherwise staunch supporters of active government intervention into the private economy admit that arguments based on 'trumped-up claims of monopoly' (Scherer 1980, p. 482) frequently have been advanced in order to widen regulation's scope far beyond the limited set of industries for which public-sector controls might theoretically be defensible.

[8] The necessity of creating a schedule of allowable rates arises whenever customers differ in their marginal valuations of the good or service supplied by the regulated firm. Under such quite common circumstances, requiring the regulated firm to charge the same price to all buyers generates allocative inefficiency even if that price is set at the proper break-even level that allows the firm to earn a normal profit. Price discrimination is the standard solution to this problem. Following this approach, customers are segregated into different classes based on their elasticities of demand for the regulated firm's product and a separate rate is set for each class that is inversely proportional to its demand elasticity (Ramsey 1927). The result of price discrimination is charging higher rates for those customers having less elastic demands and lower rates for those customers having more elastic demands. It is not unusual, for example, for industrial customers to be required to pay more for electric power than commercial (small business) customers, who are in turn required to pay more than residential customers. Such discriminatory rate structures help achieve regulation's twofold objective of mitigating allocative inefficiency while preserving productive efficiency, at least in principle.

[9] Posner (1971) supplies an important exception to the conclusion that regulatory restrictions on new entry are not needed if regulators limit prices and profits to normal levels. Suppose that the regulated firm is required to offer services to customers who would not otherwise be served because the allowable price is less than the regulated firm's marginal cost of doing so. That circumstance arises when a 'universal service' mandate requires that all customers be served regardless of cost. In order for the regulated firm to fulfill that requirement, it must be permitted to charge above-cost prices in its more remunerative service areas to subsidize below-cost prices in other service areas. Blocking entry by competitors into the former service areas thus is necessary to prevent overall profit erosion so that the regulated firm satisfies the break-even constraint. Also see Posner (1969).

US state and federal regulatory interventions. His study of electric utility regulation, in collaboration with Claire Friedland, for instance, found that it had had little or no impact on the prices consumers paid or on the rates of return to investments in that industry (Stigler and Friedland 1962). In another study, investors were found to have obtained few benefits from the regulatory oversight of new stock issues by the US Securities and Exchange Commission (Stigler 1964). Indeed, a survey of the early empirical literature supporting the 'capture' theory of regulation suggested that while regulatory intervention was not always as ineffective as Stigler and Friedland had found – as a matter of fact, they were later shown sometimes to have been wrong (Peltzman 1993) – in those industries where regulation did affect prices and profits, the effects actually were perverse (Jordan 1972). In particular, when applied to otherwise competitive industries, such as air and surface transportation, regulation uniformly was found to have reduced the number of firms serving specific markets and to have raised prices (and profits) above competitive market levels. On the other hand, when applied to industries more plausibly characterized by natural monopoly conditions, regulation had little or no effect on prices.

These empirical findings raised two important questions. If consumers' interests are not materially advanced by regulation, why is regulation adopted in the first place? Given the very real costs of regulation – the costs to taxpayers of defraying the expenses of the regulatory agencies as well as the costs to society in the forms of the resources misallocated by poorly crafted regulatory constraints and the resources consumed in attempts to influence the regulatory process – why does regulation persist?

Stigler's (1971) answer was that public regulation is designed for and operated to benefit the firms subject to regulatory controls on allowable prices and conditions of entry. Politicians, in an effort to fill their campaign war chests and to enhance their re-election prospects, offer regulatory interventions that promise rents to the producers in the industry that is to be regulated. In exchange, the members of the regulated industry offer votes and campaign contributions to their political benefactors. The amount of support a particular set of producers can offer to any given politician is constrained by the group's ability to overcome the inevitable collective action ('free rider') problem (Olson 1965); the costs of organizing to demand regulatory intervention must then be weighed in the balance against the benefits the producer group expects to receive from regulation. By conceiving the regulatory process as pitting the interests of producers against those of consumers, Stigler concluded that the former would almost always dominate the latter since consumers generally are disorganized and the per capita cost of economic regulation to them typically is small, whereas producers are positioned to supply effective political pressure (because they are already organized into trade associations, for example) and have much larger individual stakes in regulatory decisions.

Sam Peltzman (1976) formalized and extended Stigler's original theory by incorporating the idea that utility-maximizing politicians optimally allocate the benefits and costs of regulation such that no one interest group is likely to capture all of the potential gains. Such an outcome requires that the groups whose interests are harmed by regulation be utterly impotent politically. Peltzman's model therefore is more general than Stigler's in the sense that it accommodates the interests of groups seeking regulatory favors as well as the interests of groups that oppose granting them. The politician-suppliers of regulation thus face a tradeoff between the support (votes and campaign contributions) offered to them by regulation's beneficiaries and the support they will lose from those who bear regulation's costs. The point at which the political balance is struck depends on the relative political effectiveness of the interest groups on the opposing sides of a proposal to enact a new regulatory regime or to modify an existing one, but neither group will get all that it wants from the regulatory process: the benefits and costs of regulation will tend to be shared.

Applied to Stigler's model of producer versus consumer interests, Peltzman's more general theory predicts that pure protection of producer interests will not materialize as long as consumers can moderate regulatory decisions by offering at least some votes or campaign contributions to regulating politicians – or by threatening to withdraw such political support. Hence, consumers are not necessarily the only group that gets the short end of the regulatory stick.

Producer interests are not monolithic and so regulatory interventions can redistribute wealth within a particular industry, as, for example, from firms using labor-intensive production methods to those using capital-intensive methods following the negotiation of a collective bargaining agreement that raises wage rates industry wide (Williamson 1968), or from water-powered textile mills to steam-powered mills as the result of regulations limiting hours of work or prohibiting child labor (Marvel 1977). The short political life of the tariff imposed on imported steel by President George W. Bush supplies a more recent example. That policy decision, which created rents for US steel producers, was quickly rescinded, not because of opposition by masses of American consumers but because of the political pressure brought to bear on the Bush administration by the domestic manufacturers of automobiles, household appliances and other steel-using industries that were harmed by a tariff-ridden increase in the price of a key input.

Peltzman's model is important in that it predicts regulatory intervention into sectors that otherwise would be competitive, such as agricultural and surface transportation markets, as well as those that approach conditions of monopoly. If prices and profits are close to monopoly levels, the political benefits to regulators from redistributing wealth away from producers in favor of consumers are plain. But, unlike Stigler, Peltzman's theory additionally predicts that redistributing wealth from consumers to producers by mandating higher prices is also salient for politicians and regulators in cases where unregulated market outcomes would approach the perfectly competitive ideal. Fewer such gains are available to regulators confronting oligopolistic market conditions, wherein most theoretical models conclude that unregulated prices and profits will lie somewhere between the extremes of perfect competition and pure monopoly.

A few of the examples of regulatory rent seeking that we discuss in the next section support Peltzman's insight that rents will be distributed among many rival interests. Railroad regulation, for example, not only benefited the railroads themselves but also short-haul ground shippers (who, because unregulated before 1935, took business away from the higher priced railroads) and, more specifically, agricultural interests. More surprisingly, however, many episodes of deregulation also lend support to the interest-group theory of regulation. Tullock (1975 [2008]) and, in his wake, Tollison and Wagner (1991) had argued that regulation, once in place, would be difficult to reverse because the transitional gains from regulation, which accrue to the regulated industry, would be fully capitalized in asset prices. With fully capitalized regulatory gains, regulation creates a 'trap' in the sense that deregulation would impose large capital losses on the entrenched members of the industry and, moreover, those losses necessarily exceed the potential gains from deregulation to society as a whole, leading to political 'disinterest in deregulation' (McCormick et al. 1984; Shughart 1999).

Peltzman (1989]) suggested that erosion of rents could trigger deregulation; he and Thomas (2009) argued furthermore that in addition to rent erosion, the opportunity cost of a particular regulatory scheme to a previously regulated industry may rise as a result of technological innovation that promises larger potential rents in a deregulated market. In the following section, we discuss a subsample of regulatory episodes as well as deregulation initiatives that offered new opportunities for earning rents to various special interest groups.

11.3 EVIDENCE SUPPORTING THE INTEREST-GROUP THEORY OF REGULATION

The empirical literature on rent seeking in practice is vast and includes applications to most spheres of human activity, including but not limited to rent seeking inside firms, rent seeking to gain protection from foreign competition, as well as rent seeking in the context of public-sector budgets, political elections, the legal system, economic development, faculty governance and civil society (Hillman 2013). Gordon Tullock's (1967 [2008]) original description of the social cost of rent seeking included applications of his rent-seeking insight to the social costs of tariffs, monopoly and theft. The main implication of his model is that any resources 'invested' in rent seeking reduce the wealth of nations by redirecting scarce resources from productive to unproductive uses.[10]

Subsequent contributions have focused on the resource waste associated with rent seeking by describing and estimating its social costs. Krueger (1974 [2008]) estimated that roughly 15 percent of Turkish gross domestic product (GDP) and 7 percent of Indian GDP were wasted in the competition for limited numbers of licenses permitting their holders legally to import goods from producing nations for which tariff and non-tariff barriers to international trade had been erected. Posner (1975) was the first scholar to estimate the social cost of regulation for a number of US industries, including crude oil, airlines and eyeglasses. He found that between 1.7 and 3.5 percent of gross national product (GNP) had been lost through regulatory monopolies.

In the same article, Posner also supplies a straightforward hypothetical example of how rent seeking creates such resource waste. Suppose that an artificially created rent worth \$100 000 is on offer, that ten risk-neutral rent seekers compete for it and that their 'bids' are not refundable. If the contest is unbiased (that is, the winner is chosen randomly), each rent seeker will bid the contest's expected individual value, namely \$10 000,

[10] In developing his rent-seeking idea, Tullock seems to have been influenced by experiences as an employee of the US foreign service during a posting to China early in his career (Tullock 1984), specifically by observing the huge investments undertaken by college students preparing for competitive national examinations that would qualify them for selection to highly desirable jobs in the Chinese civil service. While studying for the exam undoubtedly created some private benefits in the form of a general knowledge of Chinese history, the contests elicited (wasteful) investments of time and effort in pursuing a prize that only a very few participants would win.

which follows from observing that any one contestant has a 10 percent chance of winning \$100 000. Participation in the contest is rational because the winner will net \$90 000. But summed over all participants, \$100 000 is spent to capture \$100 000 – the rent is fully dissipated in the process of seeking it and, so, from society's point of view the rent may as well never have been offered in the first place. Rent seeking is wasteful because the rent seekers' time and effort are redirected in an opportunity cost sense from potentially socially more productive investments into socially unproductive ones.

More specific evidence confirming the theoretical insights of the interest-group theory of regulation is plentiful and includes episodes of regulation as well as deregulation. We begin by reviewing the literature on initial regulatory capture and then provide an overview of examples of deregulation that support this theory.

11.3.1 Regulatory Capture by Special Interests

Regulation of surface transportation modes (especially short-haul trucking) is a clear case in point supporting the interest-group theory as opposed to an alternative 'public-interest' theory. In the United States, the onset of economic regulation of railroads by the ICC in 1887 morphed into regulation of the trucking industry after passage of the Transportation Act of 1935, which established minimum freight rates and imposed conditions of entry (licensing requirements) on common-carrier truckers. The adoption of such regulations strongly implies that the railroads had initially been able to charge above-cost prices for shipments tendered to them (and thereby to capture above-normal profits) and, moreover, that those prices were being undercut by truckers, especially on short-haul routes. The mode-specific benefits from the public regulation of railway rates therefore were unsustainable unless truckers were brought under the ICC's regulatory umbrella.

In support of that interpretation, Moore (1978, p. 342) estimates that the regulatory rents to unionized drivers of over-the-road trucking companies and the owners of trucking 'certificates of convenience and necessity' amounted in 1972 to between \$2.5 and \$3.3 billion, which translates into a conservative estimate of a 37 percent wage premium for unionized over non-unionized drivers. Similar rate and entry restrictions existed in some European countries and, in particular, the former West Germany (Moore 1976).

Railroad regulation is one of the earliest examples of a public policy that seems to confirm the idea that regulation is designed to benefit the regulated industry at the expense of consumers. The 1887 Act to Regulate Commerce required railroad rates to be 'reasonable and just' and prohibited discrimination between short-haul and long-haul shipping rates. The Transportation Act of 1920, which reprivatized US railroads after a short period of nationalization in support of the nation's socialist policies during the First World War, strengthened railroad regulation further. Peltzman (1989, p. 21) identifies the following three essential elements of railroad regulation after 1920: (1) cross-subsidization of short-haul shippers by adopting a rate structure that penalized long-haul shippers; (2) commodity-based price discrimination, which penalized the relatively inelastic demands for high-value-to-weight commodities in favor of more elastically demanded, low-value-to-weight shipments; and (3) entry and exit controls on both freight and passenger service. That scheme protected existing producers from competition and furthermore provided benefits to other groups, in particular agricultural interests, who were beneficiaries of the cross-subsidization of short-haul and low-value-to-weight freight rates. (Posner 1971 calls such cross-subsidies 'taxation by regulation'; see footnote 9.)

The regulation of US commercial airlines by the Civil Aeronautics Board (CAB), much like trucking regulation, protected incumbents from potential new entrants by setting minimum fares and blocking entry into the industry. Various studies have estimated the benefits to the airline industry from regulation that existed until 1978, when the CAB was disbanded by then-President Jimmy Carter as one of his administration's policy initiatives to counter then-rampant price inflation.[11] Keeler (1972) finds, for example, that fare markups on regulated routes in 1968 ranged from 20 percent to 95 percent of unregulated fares on intrastate routes over the same distance. Peltzman (1989, p. 27, table 2) provides an overview of the airline industry's operating cash flows as a percentage of revenue (an estimate of the industry's price-cost margin), which declined slowly from 23.2 cents per dollar in 1950–54 to 7.1 cents per dollar in the post-deregulation period, 1980–86. That evidence suggests that regulatory rents to the industry declined over time and eventually fell to such low levels that the industry no longer supported regulation. The reason for the airlines' change of heart can be traced to the profit-reducing effects of non-price competition, more on which below (Douglas and Miller 1974, 1976).

The healthcare industry similarly is regulated primarily to benefit producer interests. Paul (1982) finds that in 1976 states wherein licensing boards for the medical profession are controlled directly by their members, physicians' incomes were on average $2800 higher than in other states. In related work, Shepard (1978) contends that dental licensing boards, empowered by state legislatures and professional licensing boards to regulate the practice of dentistry, limited entry by non-resident (out-of-state) practitioners as well as newly trained dentists and thereby protected established (in-state) licensed dentists from competition. He estimates that licensing boards raised dentists' fees-for-service and annual incomes by between 12 percent and 15 percent.

As yet one more example, the regulation of farming is also usually designed to benefit producer interests. It is important to reiterate in that regard that such regulation cannot be explained either by the so-called public-interest theory or by Stigler's 'capture' theory of regulation. In consequence of rising productivity (yield per acre), the agricultural sectors of most western nations are in steep decline as fractions of GDP. Farmers nevertheless continue to wield substantial political influence on public policies respecting their parochial interests. That political power is consistent with Olson's (1965) law of the few. On the other hand, the political effectiveness of the expanding cohort of aging 'baby boomers', whose influence swamps that of younger wage earners, who are taxed to finance massive income transfers to their parents and grandparents, seems to be inconsistent with Olson's logic of collective action.[12]

---

[11] President Carter or his advisers apparently confused a change in the relative price of one service (commercial airfares) with a change in the relative prices of all goods. Jimmy Carter was trained in engineering, not economics.

[12] Olson (1965) proposes a 'selective incentive' theory of collective action that plausibly explains the political effectiveness of relatively large groups, such as the American Association of Retired Persons (AARP), which represents the interests of its members in taxpayer-financed entitlement programs, such as Social Security and Medicare. Group membership offers access to low-

Salhofer et al. (2000) estimate the rents to Austria's agricultural sector from existing regulation. They find that not only farmers but also the producers of inputs used in farming and the downstream food industry benefited from Austrian agricultural policy before European Union accession. Wise and Sandler (1994) report empirical evidence of rent seeking by different coalitions in two votes on pesticide regulation by the US House of Representatives in 1986 (the Panetta amendment and the Roberts amendment). Kamath (1989) provides evidence for substantial rent-seeking activities in the Indian sugar sector between 1967 and 1982. Using 1973 US data, Ippolito and Masson (1978) estimate the social cost of milk regulation at roughly $60 million a year.

The interest-group theory likewise has been shown to be helpful in explaining the adoption of workplace safety rules (Maloney and McCormick 1982) and environmental quality regulations (Pashigian 1985; Bartel and Thomas 1987). Requiring all producers to employ the same technologies for reducing the risk of on-the-job injuries or for controlling the emission of pollutants can benefit some firms at the expense of others. Dolar and Shughart (2007, 2011, 2012) report evidence that the anti-money laundering provisions of the USA PATRIOT Act benefited large financial institutions at the expense of their smaller rivals. The actual (as opposed to the stated) purposes of regulation frequently are cloaked in high-minded ideals.

11.3.2 Evidence for the Interest-group Theory of Deregulation

In seeking to explain why a regulatory policy has been adopted, the economic theory of regulation 'tells us to look, as precisely and carefully as we can, at who gains and who loses, and how much . . .' (Stigler 1975, p. 140). In seeking to explain why a regulatory policy persists, especially in the face of evidence that its actual effects are 'unrelated or perversely related' to its announced goals, the interest-group theory tells us that 'the *truly intended effects should be deduced from the actual effects*' (Stigler 1975, p. 140, emphasis in original). Errors are of course possible, but in the Stigler-Peltzman framework,

> errors are not what men live by or on. If an economic policy has been adopted by many communities, or if it is persistently pursued by a society over a long span of time, it is fruitful to assume that the real effects were known *and desired.* Indeed, an explanation of a policy in terms of error or confusion is no explanation at all – anything and everything is compatible with that 'explanation.' (Stigler 1975, p. 140, emphasis added)

Hence, if it is found that the regulatory policies of the US CAB placed the interests of the commercial airlines over those of the flying public, or that the regulatory policies of the ICC placed the interests of the railroads and motor carriers over those of their customer-shippers, then the interest-group theory teaches that it is reasonable to conclude that regulation was intended to have precisely those effects.

But what of deregulation? An important barrier to regulatory reform is what Gordon Tullock (1975 [2008]) calls 'the transitional gains trap': the promise of above-normal returns motivates resource owners to seek regulatory privileges from the state. But these

---

cost automobile insurance and other benefits not available to non-members, thereby supplying incentives to join the organization.

gains are only transitory. First, the present value of the available rents is in some cases dissipated upfront in the form of expenditures incurred in the pursuit of monopoly rights. To the extent that these rent-seeking investments are 'sunk', deregulation will not necessarily increase society's welfare (McCormick et al. 1984; Shughart 1999). Second, regulatory rent streams may be eroded *ex post* by non-price competition among the privileged franchisees. Last, if the monopoly franchise is subsequently sold, the rents will be capitalized in the purchase price of the monopolist's assets.

In all such cases, the rate of return to investments in the regulated industry is driven to normal levels. As a result, there seems to be no politically acceptable way of abolishing a regulatory program that is inefficient both from the standpoint of consumers, who pay artificially high prices, and from the standpoint of producers, who no longer make exceptional profits: 'those persons and groups who have established what they consider to be entitlements in the positive gains that have been artificially created will not agree to change, and those persons and groups who suffer losses will not willingly pay off what they consider to be immoral gainers' (Buchanan 1980b, p. 365). The controversy over compensation for the 'stranded costs' of regulated electric utilities – investments made under regulation that are not viable in a competitive market environment – is illustrative (McChesney 1999).

From a theoretical perspective, the uncomfortable fact of the matter is that the grip of the 'dead hand' of monopoly (Buchanan and Tullock 1968) has been loosened in the airline industry, the trucking industry and elsewhere. While economists have not yet fully fleshed out a general theory of institutional change, at least some of the episodes in what has thus far been a highly selective deregulation movement seem amenable to explanation by the economic theory of regulation (Keeler 1984; Peltzman 1989).

While it is relatively easy, after the fact, to identify the winners and losers from regulation's adoption, how is it possible to explain policies freeing an industry from regulatory control, thereby presumably confiscating its hard-won rents? One theory appeals to regulation's 'unintended consequences': designed to ensure that regulated firms would earn profits in excess of normal levels, some regulatory regimes were in practice unable to deliver on that promise. Two theories have been advanced to explain those failures: (1) the erosion of regulatory rents owing to regulatory agencies' inability to control competition between regulated firms on margins other than price and (2) technological innovations that created unsustainable regulatory regimes.

Airline rate regulation under the auspices of the CAB, for instance, has been described as 'sporadic, casual, and uninformed' (Wilcox 1966, p. 424). The agency's failure in that regard has been attributed to a number of factors, not the least important of which was the problem of determining 'the' cost of a seat on a particular flight, given the industry's complex mix of routes, traffic schedules and capital equipment (Douglas and Miller 1976). Lacking sufficient flexibility in the fares they were permitted to charge under regulation, the airlines rationally competed for passengers by a variety of non-price means, including safety records, quality of in-flight meals, comfort of aircraft cabin interiors and the attractiveness of cabin attendants. The scheduling of frequent flights on major routes, offering passengers convenient departure and arrival times, was one of the more important margins of competition.

The consequence of the last was chronic overcapacity: 'for all flights by all major airlines in 1977, the composite load factor stood at only 55.5 percent, which meant that on average each plane was flying a little more than half full' (McGraw 1984, p. 261). Thus, despite regulatory rate fixing, which generated markups ranging from 20 percent to 95 percent over the fares charged on unregulated intrastate flights of equal distance (Keeler 1972), the airlines' profits were driven down by the costs of inefficient scheduling and other forms of non-price competition. Indeed, the airlines hardly ever earned what the CAB considered to be a 'fair' rate of return (Douglas and Miller 1974; Moore 1986).

The railroad industry exemplifies a case in which 'support for . . . regulation eroded along with the rent' (Peltzman 1989, p. 307). Even though federal regulators kept prices artificially high, a secular decline in the demand for rail transport and a regulatory rate structure that accommodated the interests of motor carriers, the ICC's other major constituency, ultimately squeezed railroad profit margins. A spate of bankruptcies in the early 1970s produced a situation in which the only viable political options were nationalization or deregulation. The commercial airline industry, where, as we have seen, profits were dissipated over time by non-price competition between the major carriers and inefficient capacity utilization, is another instance in which the demand for deregulation seems to have originated from the regulated firms themselves. A demand-side theory of deregulation based on the interests of producers, who expected costs to fall faster than prices, is broadly consistent with the Stigler-Peltzman model. Other examples of deregulation (for example, stock brokerage, bank deposits, oil) also seem to fit that model, while some (for example, telecommunications, trucking) do not (Peltzman 1989).

Erosion of regulatory rents is one of the main explanations for deregulation from the perspective of the interest-group theory of regulation. As described above, the erosion of rents in the airline industry following the emergence of non-price competition in a price-regulated transportation market can be one trigger for deregulation. Other industries experienced similar kinds of rent erosion. While regulation benefited at least some of the railroads initially, regulatory rents declined over time, especially after the Motor Carrier Act of 1935 brought over-the-road truckers under the ICC's regulatory purview. Peltzman (1989, p. 23) explains that as a result of the unionization of truck drivers, an event encouraged by passage of the Wagner Act in 1935, trucking interests came to dominate federal regulation of surface transportation modes and the railroads' rents began slowly to fall. That loss of regulatory rents weakened the railroads interest in continued regulation and ultimately turned them into champions of deregulation. Those efforts eventually bore fruit in the passage of the Railroad Revitalization and Regulatory Reform Act of 1976 and the Staggers Rail Act of 1980, which eliminated exit restrictions and widened the band of carriers' rate-setting discretion.

Jarrell (1984), along with Peltzman (1989), argue that the regulation of minimum brokerage rates by the Securities and Exchange Commission came under pressure from regulators in the late 1960s after stockbrokers' rents had already declined owing to the rising importance of larger institutional investors who were undermining traditional brokers' extra-normal profits through competition by non-price means.

Thomas (2009) provides another explanation for deregulation in line with the interest-group theory of regulation. Using the example of beer market regulation in late fifteenth-century Germany, she shows that the regulated industry favored deregulation when innovation in brewing technology increased the opportunity cost of adherence to the existing regulatory regime. Technological change in the form of the development of microwave transmission of voice and data signals, which freed such communications from land-bound lines, also precipitated deregulation of long-distance telephone services in the United States. The rates paid by long-distance telephone customers, supposedly kept high by federal regulators in order to subsidize local telephone customers, fell dramatically after MCI and other competitors began entering the industry. (Deregulation initially was opposed by the incumbent regulated monopolist AT&T on the basis that if MCI were allowed to 'skim the cream' from its most profitable market, AT&T's ability to fulfill its universal local telephone service obligations would be severely compromised.) Local telephone rates also fell as competition emerged in those markets.

To be sure, lower local telephone rates are explained in part by the rapid pace of technological change in the telecommunications industry since the early 1980s – events that themselves owe much to the competitive market forces unleashed by deregulation. It is nevertheless reasonable to conclude from this and similar experiences in the commercial airline industry, the trucking industry and the natural gas transmission industry, among others, that prices (and profits) under regulation tend to exceed normal levels.

Supply-side forces may also be at work. Politicians serve as brokers of wealth transfers in a public-choice interpretation of the economic theory of regulation as well as in an interest-group theory of government more generally (McCormick and Tollison 1981). If wealth transfers, not social welfare, are all the brokers care about – that is, they are 'factionalist reformers' rather than 'utilitarian reformers' (Tollison and Wagner 1991) – then in the face of changes in underlying economic conditions or coalitional strength (producing corresponding changes in relative political prices), they may take advantage of opportunities to advance their own interests by deregulating selected industries, thereby redistributing wealth to newly important constituencies, even though the costs to society of doing so exceed the benefits.

11.4 CONCLUSIONS

> The 'protection of the public' theory of regulation must say that the choice of [oil] import quotas is dictated by the concern of the federal government for an adequate supply of petroleum in the event of war – a remark calculated to elicit uproarious laughter at the Petroleum Club. (Stigler 1971, p. 4)

This chapter has summarized the evidence supporting the interest-group theory of regulation and contrasted it to an alternative 'public-interest' theory. That evidence, taken both from cases in which economic regulation of industry was initially adopted as well as in those rare cases in which formerly regulated industries have been deregulated, is ample and spans the globe. It supports the Tullockian idea of rent seeking as being the principal driver of governmental intervention into markets that otherwise would be workably competitive and thereby ultimately refutes the contention that the public sector's regulation of prices and conditions of entry into the private production of certain goods and services was designed to mitigate the untoward exercise of market power or otherwise improve the efficiency of private market outcomes. It turns out that by imposing minimum prices on the sale of products touched by some conception of the public's interest and limiting the entry of producers into the markets for those products, economic regulation benefited producers at the expense of consumers. Prices and profits after the onset of regulation uniformly were higher, not lower, than beforehand.

Although he may not have known it at the time, George Stigler (1971) was indebted intellectually to Gordon Tullock (1967 [2008]) for supplying the theory that underpins his (Stigler's) economic theory of regulation. If rents (rates of return in excess of normal) artificially are made available by governmental regulatory action to alert entrepreneurs in the private sector, those entrepreneurs rationally will invest scarce resources in their pursuit. Bribes, campaign contributions, investments in lobbying and efforts to mobilize votes for compliant politicians are the currencies for obtaining favorable treatment by regulators and the politicians who sponsor them. And if the returns to such investments exceed those available from allocating resources to inventing new products, exploiting new markets or financing new research and development projects, no profit-maximizing entrepreneur will bypass them (Baumol 1990). But society is made worse off by such investments.

Rent seeking squanders scarce resources. Lawyers and marketing professionals become lobbyists, corporate chief executive officers spend more time in Washington and in state capitals than they devote to maximizing the wealth of their shareholders and elected politicians devote more time to selling favors than they do to tending to their constituents' interests.

Given that some or all of (and perhaps more than) the value of artificially created regulatory rents are dissipated by expenditures undertaken in their pursuit, society would be better off if such rents never were made available in the first place. But such an ideal world is not possible when the police powers of the state can be mobilized to help or hurt private interests.

REFERENCES

Bartel, Ann P. and Lacy G. Thomas (1987), 'Predation through regulation: the wage and profit effects of the Occupational Safety and Health Administration and the Environmental Protection Agency', *Journal of Law and Economics*, **20**(2), 239–64.

Baumol, William J. (1990), 'Entrepreneurship: productive, unproductive, and destructive', *Journal of Political Economy*, **98**(5), 893–921.

Baumol, William J., Elizabeth Bailey and Robert D. Willig (1977), 'Weak invisible hand theorems on the sustainability of prices in a multiproduct monopoly', *American Economic Review*, **67**(3), 350–65.

Baumol, William J., John C. Panzar and Robert D. Willig (1982), *Contestable Markets and the Theory of Industry Structure*, New York: Harcourt Brace Jovanovich.

Buchanan, James M. (1980a), 'Rent seeking and profit seeking', in James M. Buchanan, Robert D. Tollison and Gordon Tullock (eds), *Toward a Theory of the Rent-seeking Society*, College Station, TX: Texas A&M University Press, pp. 3–15, reprinted in Roger D. Congleton, Arye L. Hillman and Kai A. Konrad (eds) (2008), *40 Years of Research on Rent Seeking 1 – The Theory of Rent Seeking*, Heidelberg: Springer, pp. 55–67.

Buchanan, James M. (1980b), 'Reform in the rent-seeking society', in James M. Buchanan, Robert D. Tollison and Gordon Tullock (eds), *Toward a Theory of the Rent-seeking Society*, College Station, TX: Texas A&M University Press, pp. 359–67.

Buchanan, James M. and Gordon Tullock (1968), 'The "dead hand" of monopoly', *Antitrust Law and Economic Review*, **1**, 85–96.

Coase, Ronald H. (1959), 'The Federal Communications Commission', *Journal of Law and Economics*, **2**(1), 1–40.

Coase, Ronald H. (1960), 'The problem of social cost', *Journal of Law and Economics*, **3**(1), 1–44.

Congleton, Roger D., Arye L. Hillman and Kai A. Konrad (eds) (2008a), *40 Years of Research on Rent Seeking 1 – The Theory of Rent Seeking*, Heidelberg: Springer.

Congleton, Roger D., Arye L. Hillman and Kai A. Konrad (eds) (2008b), *40 Years of Research on Rent Seeking 2 – Applications: Rent Seeking in Practice*, Heidelberg: Springer.

Couch, Jim F. and William F. Shughart II (1998), *The Political Economy of the New Deal*, Cheltenham, UK and Lyme, NH, USA: Edward Elgar Publishing.
Demsetz, Harold (1968), 'Why regulate utilities?', *Journal of Law and Economics*, **11**(1), 55–65.
Demsetz, Harold (1969), 'Information and efficiency: another viewpoint', *Journal of Law and Economics*, **12**(1), 1–22.
Dolar, Burak and William F. Shughart II (2007), 'The wealth effects of the USA Patriot Act: evidence from the banking and thrift industries', *Journal of Money Laundering Control*, **10**(3), 300–317.
Dolar, Burak and William F. Shughart II (2011), 'Enforcement of the USA Patriot Act's anti-money laundering provisions: have regulators followed a risk-based approach?', *Global Finance Journal*, **22**(1), 19–33.
Dolar, Burak and William F. Shughart II (2012), 'The Patriot Act's differential impact on large and small banks: evidence from California's high-risk money laundering and related financial crime areas', *Journal of Banking Regulation*, **13**(2), 127–46.
Douglas, George W. and James C. Miller III (1974), 'Quality competition, industry equilibrium, and efficiency in the price-constrained airline market', *American Economic Review*, **64**(4), 657–69.
Douglas, George W. and James C. Miller III (1976), *Economic Regulation of Domestic Air Transport: Theory and Policy*, Washington, DC: Brookings Institution.
Harberger, Arnold C. (1954), 'Monopoly and resource allocation', *American Economic Review Papers and Proceedings*, **44**(2), 77–87.
Hillman, Arye L. (2013), 'Rent seeking', in Michael Reksulak, Laura Razzolini and William F. Shughart II (eds), *The Elgar Companion to Public Choice*, 2nd edn, Cheltenham, UK and Northampton, MA, USA: Edward Elgar Publishing, pp. 307–30.
Ippolito, Richard A. and Robert T. Masson (1978), 'The social cost of government regulation of milk', *Journal of Law and Economics*, **21**(1), 33–65.
Jarrell, Gregg A. (1984), 'Change at the exchange: the causes and effects of deregulation', *Journal of Law and Economics*, **27**(2), 273–312.
Jordan, William A. (1972), 'Producer protection, prior market structure and the effects of government regulation', *Journal of Law and Economics*, **15**(1), 151–76.
Kamath, Shyam J. (1989), 'Concealed takings: capture and rent seeking in the Indian sugar industry', *Public Choice*, **62**(2), 119–38.
Keeler, Theodore E. (1972), 'Airline regulation and market performance', *Bell Journal of Economics and Management Science*, **3**(2), 399–424.
Keeler, Theodore E. (1984), 'Theories of deregulation and the deregulation movement', *Public Choice*, **44**(1), 103–45.
Krueger, Anne O. (1974), 'The political economy of the rent-seeking society', *American Economic Review*, **64**(3), 291–303, reprinted in Roger D. Congleton, Arye L. Hillman and Kai A. Konrad (eds) (2008), *40 Years of Research on Rent Seeking 2 – Applications: Rent Seeking in Practice*, Heidelberg: Springer, pp. 151–63.
Maloney, Michael T. and Robert E. McCormick (1982), 'A positive theory of environmental quality regulation', *Journal of Law and Economics*, **25**(1), 99–124.
Marvel, Howard P. (1977), 'Factory regulation: a reinterpretation of early English experience', *Journal of Law and Economics*, **20**(2), 379–402.
McChesney, Fred S. (1999), 'Of stranded costs and stranded hopes: the difficulties of deregulation', *Independent Review*, **3**(4), 485–509.
McChesney, Fred S. and William F. Shughart II (eds) (1995), *The Causes and Consequences of Antitrust: The Public-choice Perspective*, Chicago, IL: University of Chicago Press.
McCormick, Robert E. and Robert D. Tollison (1981), *Politicians, Legislation and the Economy: An Inquiry into the Interest-group Theory of Government*, Boston, MA: Martinus-Nijhoff.
McCormick, Robert E., William F. Shughart II and Robert D. Tollison (1984), 'The disinterest in deregulation', *American Economic Review*, **74**(5), 1075–9.
McGraw, Thomas K. (1984), *Prophets of Regulation: Charles Francis Adams, Louis D. Brandeis, James M. Landis, Alfred E. Kahn*, Cambridge, MA: Belknap Press of Harvard University Press.
Moore, Thomas Gale (1976), *Trucking Regulation: Lessons from Europe*, Washington, DC: American Enterprise Institute for Public Policy Research.
Moore, Thomas Gale (1978), 'The beneficiaries of trucking regulation', *Journal of Law and Economics*, **21**(2), 327–43.
Moore, Thomas Gale (1986), 'U.S. airline deregulation: its effects on passengers, capital, and labor', *Journal of Law and Economics*, **29**(1), 1–28.
Nitzan, Shmuel (1994), 'Modelling rent-seeking contests', *European Journal of Political Economy*, **10**(1), 41–60.
Olson, Mancur (1965), *The Logic of Collective Action: Public Goods and the Theory of Groups*, Cambridge, MA: Harvard University Press.
Pashigian, B. Peter (1985), 'Environmental quality regulation: whose self-interests are being protected?', *Economic Inquiry*, **23**(4), 551–84.

Paul, Chris W. (1982), 'Competition in the medical profession: an application of the economic theory of regulation', *Southern Economic Journal*, **48**(3), 559–69.
Peltzman, Sam (1976), 'Toward a more general theory of regulation', *Journal of Law and Economics*, **19**(2), 211–40.
Peltzman, Sam (1989), 'The economic theory of regulation after a decade of deregulation', *Brookings Papers on Economic Activity. Microeconomics*, **1**, 1–59.
Peltzman, Sam (1993), 'George Stigler's contribution to the economic analysis of regulation', *Journal of Political Economy*, **101**(5), 818–32.
Posner, Richard A. (1969), *Natural Monopoly and its Regulation*, Washington, DC: Cato Institute, reprinted in 1999.
Posner, Richard A. (1971), 'Taxation by regulation', *Bell Journal of Economics and Management Science*, **2**(1), 22–50.
Posner, Richard A. (1975), 'The social costs of monopoly and regulation', *Journal of Political Economy*, **83**, 807–27.
Ramsey, Frank P. (1927), 'A contribution to the theory of taxation', *Economic Journal*, **7**(145), 47–61.
Salhofer, Klaus, Markus F. Hofreither and Franz Sinabellz (2000), 'Promotion of the agricultural sector and political power in Austria', *Public Choice*, **102**(3–4), 229–46.
Scherer, Frederic M. (1980), *Industrial Market Structure and Economic Performance*, 2nd edn, Boston, MA: Houghton Mifflin.
Shepard, Lawrence (1978), 'Licensing restrictions and the cost of dental care', *Journal of Law and Economics*, **21**(1), 187–201.
Sherman, Roger (1989), *The Regulation of Monopoly*, Cambridge and New York: Cambridge University Press.
Shughart, William F. II (1990), *Antitrust Policy and Interest-group Politics*, New York: Quorum Books.
Shughart, William F. II (1999), 'The reformer's dilemma', *Public Finance Review*, **27**(4), 561–5.
Shughart, William F. II (2003), 'Regulation and antitrust', in Charles K. Rowley and Friedrich Schneider (eds), *The Encyclopedia of Public Choice*, Vol. I, Dordrecht, Boston, MA and London: Kluwer Academic Publishers, pp. 263–83, reprinted in Charles K. Rowley and Friedrich Schneider (eds) (2008), *Readings in Public Choice and Constitutional Political Economy*, Dordrecht: Springer, pp. 447–80.
Shy, Oz (2001), *The Economics of Network Industries*, Cambridge: Cambridge University Press.
Spulber, Daniel F. (1989), *Regulation and Markets*, Cambridge, MA: MIT Press.
Stigler, George J. (1964), 'Public regulation of the securities market', *Journal of Business*, **2**(2), 117–42.
Stigler, George J. (1971), 'The theory of economic regulation', *Bell Journal of Economics and Management Science*, **2**(1), 3–21.
Stigler, George J. (1975), 'Supplementary note on economic theories of regulation (1975)', in George J. Stigler (ed.), *The Citizen and the State: Essays on Regulation*, Chicago, IL: University of Chicago Press, pp. 137–41.
Stigler, George J. and Claire Friedland (1962), 'What can regulators regulate? The case of electricity', *Journal of Law and Economics*, **5**(1), 1–16.
Thomas, Diana W. (2009), 'Deregulation despite transitional gains', *Public Choice*, **140**(3–4), 329–40.
Tirole, Jean (1988), *The Theory of Industrial Organization*, Cambridge, MA: MIT Press.
Tollison, Robert D. (1982), 'Rent seeking: a survey', *Kyklos*, **35**(4), 575–602.
Tollison, Robert D. and Richard E. Wagner (1991), 'Romance, realism, and economic reform', *Kyklos*, **44**(1), 57–70.
Train, Kenneth E. (1991), *Optimal Regulation: The Economic Theory of Natural Monopoly*, Cambridge, MA: MIT Press.
Tullock, Gordon (1967), 'The welfare costs of tariffs, monopolies, and theft', *Western Economic Journal*, **5**(3), 224–32, reprinted in Roger D. Congleton, Arye L. Hillman and Kai A. Konrad (eds) (2008), *40 Years of Research on Rent Seeking 1 – The Theory of Rent Seeking*, Heidelberg: Springer, pp. 45–53.
Tullock, Gordon (1975), 'The transitional gains trap', *Bell Journal of Economics and Management Science*, **6**(2), 671–78, reprinted in James M. Buchanan, Robert D. Tollison and Gordon Tullock (eds) (2008), *Toward a Theory of the Rent-seeking Society*, College Station, TX: Texas A&M University Press, pp. 211–21.
Tullock, Gordon (1980), 'Efficient rent seeking', in James M. Buchanan, Robert D. Tollison and Gordon Tullock (eds), *Toward a Theory of the Rent-seeking Society*, College Station, TX: Texas A&M University Press, pp. 97–112, reprinted in Roger D. Congleton, Arye L. Hillman and Kai A. Konrad (eds) (2008), *40 Years of Research on Rent Seeking 1 – The Theory of Rent Seeking*, Heidelberg: Springer, pp. 105–20.
Tullock, Gordon (1984), 'The backward society: static inefficiency, rent seeking, and the rule of law', in James M. Buchanan and Robert D. Tollison (eds), *The Theory of Public Choice: II*, Ann Arbor, MI: University of Michigan Press, pp. 224–37.
Wilcox, Clair (1966), *Public Policies Toward Business*, 3rd edn, Homewood, IL: Irwin.

Williamson, Oliver E. (1968), 'Wage rates as a barrier to entry: the Pennington case in perspective', *Quarterly Journal of Economics*, **82**(1), 85–116.
Williamson, Oliver E. (1976), 'Franchise bidding for natural monopolies – in general and with respect to CATV', *Bell Journal of Economics and Management Science*, **7**(1), 73–104.
Wise, Sherry Jo and Todd Sandler (1994), 'Rent seeking and pesticide legislation', *Public Choice*, **78**(3–4), 329–50.

12. Rents and international trade policy

*Arye L. Hillman**

SUMMARY

Whether the presence of politically created rents is acknowledged has distinguished two approaches to the study of international trade policy. A model that excludes politically created rents proposes that: (1) governments' efficiency objectives give rise to protectionist policies; (2) social welfare can be increased by a government providing subsidies to firms competing in international markets; (3) tariffs are used by governments to improve the terms of trade, with the population benefitting through distribution of tariff revenue; and (4) trade liberalization takes place to reduce or eliminate the trade restrictions that were imposed to improve the terms of trade. A second model that includes politically created rents offers quite different interpretations of governments' trade policy decisions. The latter rent-inclusive model is consistent with revealed political preference for using trade policy to provide private benefits and with the political insignificance of tariff revenue. McCloskey (1998) has proposed that we view economists as storytellers. Given the evidence that governments' trade policy decisions create rents for private benefit, we can ask why the story without rents has been told.

12.1 INTRODUCTION

Rents associated with international trade policy were present at the outset in expositions of rent seeking. Gordon Tullock (1967 [2008]) included tariffs along with monopoly and theft in examples of social losses from rent seeking. Anne Krueger (1974 [2008]) used data from Turkey and India to compute estimates of rent-seeking losses due to import quotas. In both cases efficiency losses were described as incurred because of the use of otherwise productive resources in contesting rents. Governments were however also doing policy favors through rent creation. Import quotas could, for example, have been auctioned to provide revenue for the government budget but instead governments preferred to create rents for private beneficiaries.

The basic rent-seeking model describes the contesting of a predetermined rent and excludes the motives of government decision makers who create and assign rents.[1] Government decision makers are also absent from a genre of contest model that

* An earlier version of this chapter was presented at the conference Trade and the Organization of Production in the Global Economy in Honor of Wilfred Ethier, Vanderbilt University, 25–26 October 2013. I thank Wilfred Ethier, Bernard Hoekman, Henrik Horn, James Markusen, Steve Matusz, and Kamal Saggi for their comments and observations.

[1] The policy maker is present implicitly through the contest-success function that determines the identity of successful rent seekers (Congleton et al. 2008; Hillman 2013; Long 2013).

describes determination of who transfers rents to whom ('transfer contests' in Hillman and Riley 1989 [2008]).

Political-economy models of policy determination, on the other hand, include policy makers who have electoral concerns and value political support (Hillman 1982 [2008], 1989 [2001]; Cassing and Hillman 1985, 1986 [2008]; Grossman and Helpman 1994 [2008]). Policy can be the outcome of political competition for public office (Young and Magee 1986; Hillman and Ursprung 1988 [2008]; Ursprung 1991). In all these cases, interest groups seek to benefit from politically created rents at the expense of the population at large and there can be voter opposition to the special-interest policies (Grossman and Helpman 2002).[2]

In the international trade literature, rents appear prominently in the 'specific-factors' model. In this model mobile factors of production such as labor can readily change employment between industries or sectors and immobile factors such as land and capital are restricted to employment in a particular industry and have returns that are rents. Protectionist policies reassign rents, which increase in a protected import-competing sector and decline in an export sector. Trade liberalization has the converse effect on rents. The effect of trade policies on the real incomes of mobile factors depends on the weight of goods in consumption, with the position of mobile labor on trade policy therefore depending on the goods that labor consumes. Grounds for a presumption have been proposed that labor gains from free trade.[3] Policy decisions associated with politically created rents and political support can be readily included in the specific-factors model (Hillman 1982 [2008], 1989 [2001]; Grossman and Helpman 1994 [2008]). Under representative democracy, with asymmetric information because of 'rational ignorance' of voters (or the disincentive of non-decisive voters to be informed), with benefits or rents concentrated in interest groups and losses dispersed over the population – and with the number of issues exceeding the number of political candidates – policies can arise that the majority of voters – if informed and having the opportunity – would reject.[4]

---

2 Policy is 'endogenous' with an institutional background of representative democracy. Direct democracy has been described by Wolfgang Mayer (1984). The voting model was extended to representative democracy by Cheng-Chen Yang (1995). In general, trade policy has not been a salient issue in elections. A case in which trade policy was a salient issue is the UK 'corn laws'. See Cheryl Schonhardt-Bailey (2006).

3 The specific-factors model described by Ronald Jones (1971) was further developed by Wolfgang Mayer (1974) and Michael Mussa (1974). Robert Baldwin (1984) placed rent-seeking incentives within the model and noted that, with two sectors, labor and immobile capital in one sector would have a common policy interest, whereas in the other sector there would be a conflict of interest. This observation is important when labor is 'partially' mobile and incurs costs of changing employment. In general, the income of labor has an industry-specific human-capital component. If the mobile factor labor gains from free trade (see the presumption by Ruffin and Jones 1977), there will be policy conflict in import-competing sectors and policy consensus in export sectors.

4 On the principal-agent problems of representative democracy, see Hillman (2009, chapter 2). Mancur Olson (1965) emphasized the organizational and political advantages of small over large groups under representative democracy. How beneficiaries of policy-created rents express gratitude depends on the political culture (Hillman and Swank 2000). In autocracies or 'weak' democracies (where the rule of law and political accountability are not assured), political decision makers can create rents directly for their own benefit and for the benefit of family and friends, or for elites

A 'popular model' of international trade policy has excluded reference to politically created rents. Sections 12.2 and 12.3 describe the two variants of the model. Section 12.4 describes the model in which politically created rents have a role in policy determination. Section 12.5 introduces the terms of trade and budgetary revenue. Section 12.6 describes models of trade liberalization. McCloskey (1998) in 'the rhetoric of economics' described economists as using models to tell stories that reflect inclinations and backgrounds of the storytellers. The final section addresses the question why alternative stories with and without a role for politically created rents have been told about international trade policy.

12.2 THE 'DISTORTIONS' MODEL

12.2.1 The Model

The 'distortions' model of international trade policy, proposed by Bhagwati and Ramaswami (1963), Bhagwati et al. (1969) and Bhagwati (1971), describes an economy that has been 'distorted' away from an efficient outcome. The distortions introduce the theory of the second best and allow the conclusion that closure of an economy to trade can be efficient, if other sources of inefficiency are also present.[5]

The 'distortions' explanation for trade policy is not set within the specific-factors model that identifies industry rents but within the Heckscher-Ohlin model of international trade. The distinction is between the short and long run. If all factors of production can be regarded as intersectorally mobile in the long run, there are in the long run no 'industry interests'.[6]

---

from associated tribes and clans, without the need for the more roundabout process of political exchange that takes place in democracies. When rents are extracted directly by the creators of the rents, rent seeking can occur through competition to occupy the positions in government and bureaucracy to which rents accrue. See Hillman and Katz (1987 [2008]).

[5] The theory of the second best states that, once there has been a departure from a first-best efficient equilibrium, another policy that on its own would reduce efficiency can be efficiency-improving. On second-best or distortions-based policy recommendations and antecedents, see Peter Lloyd (1974). Another second-best conclusion is that rent seeking – with proposed renaming as 'directly unproductive profit-seeking activities' (Bhagwati 1982) – can be efficient because of use of resources with negative shadow prices.

[6] Factors of production can be viewed as adjusting over time by losing industry specifity. See Peter Neary (1978) and Gene Grossman (1983). The association of individuals with industry-specific income is also relaxed when capital or stock markets allow portfolio diversification, in which case a model can include conditions under which earners of industry-specific incomes (or rents) would support free trade (Feeney and Hillman 2004 [2008]). The policy-relevant coalitions in the long-run Heckscher-Ohlin model are domestic intersectorally mobile factors of production. Labor and capital benefit from protection or free trade depending on which factor is relatively scarce or abundant in the economy. The conflicting interests of labor and capital in trade policy are expressed in the Stolper-Samuelson theorem (Stolper and Samuelson 1941), which states that a country's relatively scarce factor of production gains from protection at the expense of the relatively abundant factor. Wilfred Ethier (1974) provides a statement of the theorem beyond a two-good two-factor model.

Suppose that, in a Heckscher-Ohlin model, a government in a relatively labor-abundant country has set a minimum wage that artificially increases the domestic relative price of labor, making it seem that the country has a comparative disadvantage in labor-intensive production. Because of the minimum wage, the direction of international trade is contrary to true comparative advantage, resulting in efficiency losses through trade. With the minimum wage in place, the policy recommendation is to achieve efficiency and to maximize social welfare by closing the economy to international trade.[7]

In another example, for which a Ricardian model suffices (one intersectorally mobile factor of production, generally identified as labor), the presence of a market 'distortion' due to an externality – call it pollution – causes the domestic social cost of producing a good to be greater than the cost based on market prices. As a consequence, international trade can again be contrary to true comparative advantage and a government can again achieve efficiency and increase social welfare by protectionist policies that close the country to international trade.

Child labor in a foreign country may be a concern for the population of a high-income country. Protectionist policies increase the domestic price of imports that are produced using child labor and provide disincentives to use child labor in the foreign country where the children work rather than go to school.[8]

In another example, imports are resulting in destruction of rain forest in a foreign country. The destruction of the rain forest ceases when foreign exports cease. In a case that changed US trade policy, in some regions dolphins were being inadvertently caught in tuna fishing nets and imports of tuna from such regions were banned. Another source of externality is biological diversity, for example, the threat to rhinos because of the belief that ingested ground-up rhino horns are a cure for sexual inadequacy.[9]

12.2.2 Protection and the Distortions Model

The 'distortions' model is logically consistent. Market 'distortions' can justify protectionist policies as being second-best efficiency-enhancing and social-welfare improving. The 'distortions model' appears in particular to be applicable to low-income countries in which significant costs and benefits might be excluded from domestic market valuations. The distortions can be due to planning and government regulatory controls as were, for example, in place in India when the distortions model appeared in the literature.[10]

The scope for the influence of 'distortions' on trade policies in high-income countries appears more limited. A minimum wage, for example, would not prevent trade according to comparative advantage in high-income countries, which tend to be capital-abundant.

---

[7] See Brecher (1974a, 1974b).

[8] The policy is based on the presumption that the children have a school to attend or that their not working will result in schools being provided.

[9] On dolphins, see Körber (1998); on rhinos, see Ellis (2005).

[10] On the policies in India, see Eckhaus (1965) and Bhagwati and Chakravarty (1969). Negative externalities from lax environmental standards for foreign investment in India are evident in the 1984 Bophal environmental disaster. See http://www.ehjournal.net/content/4/1/6 (accessed 14 July 2014). The opportunities for rent creation and rent seeking – and corruption – are enhanced when planning and government controls coexist with private property. See Gupta and Mishra (2007).

A minimum wage would make labor appear relatively scarcer than it in fact is, so reinforcing comparative advantage.

The 'distortions' relevant for policies of high-income countries are thus often to be found in foreign markets. The distortions reflect the inability or lack of will of governments in low-income countries to prevent child labor and provide schooling opportunities, to stop degradation of the environment and to protect threatened wildlife.[11]

The protectionist policy proposals based on 'distortions' are derived from a long-run model with no rents. In the short run, domestic producers seeking policy-created rents benefit from protectionist policies for which the distortions model gives a long-run social-welfare justification. The case of protection of dolphins is an example. Consumers in the United States initially could express pro-dolphin preferences by buying tuna labeled dolphin-friendly but, in the end, US trade policy prohibited imports of tuna from regions of the oceans in which dolphins swim above tuna shoals and become entrapped in tuna fishing nets. A study of the case of the dolphins by Achim Körber (1998) revealed that consumer sentiment favoring dolphins was insufficient to evoke policies to prevent imports of 'dolphin-unfriendly' tuna and that 'dolphin-friendly' trade policy was enacted only when there was producer interest in the policies. Consumer sentiment was 'captured' by rent-seeking producers but consumers benefitted. Körber (1998) titled his study 'Why everyone loves Flipper'. Quite generally, producer and environmental interests in trade policy can coincide (Hillman and Ursprung 1992, 1994). In another example, domestic producers gain from prohibition of competitive imports from countries in which child labor is used and people who object to child labor also benefit from the policies.

Protectionist rents are not present in the distortions model. Superimposing a political-economy structure on the distortions model, however, brings to the fore the producer rents that are not present in the long run but are present in the short run.

12.3 STRATEGIC TRADE POLICY

12.3.1 Social Benefit from Profit Shifting

'Strategic trade policy' describes social benefits from shifting profits from foreign to domestic firms. Assuming a Cournot-Nash equilibrium in a choice of quantities sold, the model shows how governments can increase social welfare by subsidizing domestically owned firms competing with foreign firms in oligopolistic international markets.[12]

---

[11] Demonstrations and protests therefore should not be directed against international agencies such as the World Trade Organization (WTO) and the World Bank that seek more open trade policies but against the governments in low-income countries that allow the policies against which the protesters protest. On against whom protests should be directed, see Hillman (2005).

[12] The 'strategic trade policy' model was proposed by Brander (1985), Spencer (1985) and Brander and Spencer (1985). See also Krugman (1985). A subsidy lowers the domestic firm's costs, resulting in a new equilibrium with a greater market share and greater profits for the domestic firm. The case for the subsidy rests on choice of quantities. With Bertrand price competition, the social-welfare maximizing policy is an export tax and depending on 'conjectures' (the assumption of a firm regarding the response of competitors to its own decisions), the optimal policy can be free trade (Eaton and Grossman 1986).

12.3.2 Framing and Capture

A first response to the proposal of 'strategic trade policy' is that foreign governments can also subsidize 'their' firms – but let us leave retaliatory policies aside. Criticisms of 'strategic trade policy' have not questioned the assumption that government is motivated by a quest for efficiency alone.[13] The recognition of political interest in rent creation however converts 'strategic trade policy' to a rent-seeking model. The criterion for eligibility for subsidies is broad, in including any domestic firm competing with a foreign firm in a market with non-competitive profits. Not all eligible firms can be expected to be subsidized. Rent-seeking contests would therefore be expected to take place to determine which firm will receive the subsidies. Moreover and importantly, the subsidies can be expected to provide private benefit and not benefit for society at large. Successful rent-seeking firms receive the subsidies that taxpayers finance. 'Framing' subsidies to producers as socially beneficial allows 'capture' of the strategic trade policy argument for political rent creation.[14]

12.4 BACK TO RENTS AND POLITICAL ECONOMY

12.4.1 The Common Basis for Distortions and Strategic Trade Policy Theories

The theory of 'strategic trade policy' fits well with the 'distortions' theory. The common basis for both theories is imperfect markets and an efficiency-seeking social-welfare maximizing government rather than a government with electoral and political-support concerns.[15]

12.4.2 How to Explain Trade Policy in Practice?

The distortions and strategic trade-policy models might be regarded as normative abstractions that do not – and perhaps were not intended to – explain trade policy in practice. Explaining trade policies in practice returns us to political rent creation.

---

[13] Gene Grossman (1985) questioned the feasibility of the information requirements for 'strategic trade policy'. The strategic trade policy recommendations were also in violation of the General Agreement on Tariffs and Trade (GATT) and the subsequent World Trade Organization (WTO), which disallowed subsidizing exports. Taking the 'strategic trade policy model' at face value, once the existence of stock markets is acknowledged, it is no longer meaningful to distinguish 'domestic' from 'foreign' firms because investors can internationally diversify portfolios. The subsidies proposed by strategic trade policy introduce extraneous uncertainty for diversified shareholders. See Feeney and Hillman (2001).

[14] In the spirit of the 'strategic trade policy', Kai Konrad (2000) describes a contest model without rent seeking in which governments have only efficiency objectives and a domestic and a foreign firm compete in a third market. The interventionist equilibrium in this model can be preferable to free trade. Governments are assumed to place equal weight on firm profits and tax revenue.

[15] On the two different views of government and motives for policies, see Hillman (1992).

12.4.3 Rents and Political Support

Sam Peltzman (1976) described a regulator as trading off political support from a regulated industry and the public at large. The regulator chose a compromise policy between the maximal monopoly rent sought by the regulated industry and the competitive outcome sought by the public. The equilibrium regulated price equalized the marginal political loss from increasing price to consumers and the marginal political gain from increasing the rents created for the regulated industry. The outcome was summarized by Jack Hirshleifer (1976) as 'share the gain and share the pain', meaning that regulators politically moderate market-determined benefits or losses.

The Peltzman model can be applied to explaining protectionist policies – with amendment (Hillman 1982 [2008]). In models of international trade policy, the origin for measuring political support is free trade. The free-trade no-intervention outcome changes with world prices. The question posed to the policy maker by the beneficiaries of policies is: 'what have your policies done for me, compared to no-intervention free trade?' Political support is therefore determined by changes from free-trade income or rents.

The policy response (Hillman 1982 [2008]) when the world price of imports declines (when the terms of trade improve) is increased protection for an import-competing industry, but the increased protection is insufficient to prevent a decline in the domestic price. Consumers therefore benefit but not by as much as had there been no policy response of increased protection. Jack Hirshleifer's (1976) principle of 'share the gain and share the pain' applies. Consumers 'share the pain' of the domestic import-competing industry through a domestic price that does not provide the full benefits of the decline in the world price. Domestic producers lose, but not by as much as if there had not been a political response to the decline in the world price. The model describes rent creation through increased protection and rent extraction through policies chosen to maximize political support.

12.4.4 Responses to Lower World Prices of Imports

In the Hillman (1982 [2008]) model, governments increase protection when the terms of trade improve, that is, when the relative price of imports declines in the world market. A social-welfare maximizing government views a decline in the world relative price of imports or an improvement in the terms of trade as socially beneficial. A government concerned with political support faces the consequence that an improvement in the terms of trade diminishes rents of domestic import-competing producers and responds by compensating the producers through increased protection.

The response of forestalling declines in rents in income-competing industries occurs in the case of anti-dumping policies. Rather than anti-dumping duties being imposed, foreign producers can be invited to avoid imposition of the duties by 'undertaking' to increase price (Tharakan 1991). The offer of 'undertakings' suggests that governments do not view revenue from trade taxes as important. We shall return to this point.

12.4.5 Rent Seeking as Political Competition

The political competition that is implicit in the political-support model of trade policy can be modeled explicitly as a form of rent seeking that takes place when candidates compete for political office (Young and Magee 1986; Hillman and Ursprung 1988 [2008]). In Hillman and Ursprung (1988 [2008]), the policy-instrument choice is between tariffs and 'voluntary export restraints', which are import quotas assigned to foreign producers. Again, politically created rents displace budgetary revenue. The government of the importing country is overseeing the creation of rents through a foreign cartel, while domestic producers do not act collusively and are not in violation of anti-trust or anti-monopoly laws.[16] The Hillman-Ursprung (1988) model of political competition results in divisive policies when the tariff is the means of protection (one candidate proposing a prohibitive tariff and the other free trade).[17] With a voluntary export restraint, there is convergence to a common policy in which the rents created are shared between domestic and foreign producers. Because imports are permitted, the equilibrium policy does not maximize domestic firms' profits, but nor is the quantity of imports necessarily that which maximizes joint foreign profits.[18]

12.4.6 'Protection for Sale'

Grossman and Helpman (1994 [2008]) describe a political decision maker who creates rents by 'selling' protection. In this elegant model, the politician chooses protection to maximize a political-support function that accounts for campaign contributions received from industry interests and voter support. Equilibrium policy outcomes depend on which groups are organized to pay the politician. If all groups were organized, there would be no deviation from free trade. There is complete rent extraction: the politician extracts all rents from the rent-creating policies that are offered. The rent-extracting politician has a monopoly in offering 'policies for sale' and makes take-it-or-leave-it offers that allow the complete rent extraction. A policy outcome of protection occurs because opponents of protection, who are the voters or the public at large, are not organized. Grossman and Helpman derive a Ramsey-type rule that determines the levels of protection that the rent-extracting politician will set for different industries. The model is in principle similar to models of contest design for maximal rent extraction, except that rent extraction is contained by discontent of voters.

---

[16] In itself, the restraint of trade was illegal under international trade law, but there were no complaints because of rent creation and rent sharing, and hence the policies could persist.

[17] Announced policies and campaign contributions depend on the differences between industry profits associated with candidates' respective policies.

[18] In the model, consumers are not involved in seeking to influence policies. The policy contest is between domestic and foreign producers. Also, the model yields no tariff revenue in the tariff political equilibrium and no campaign contributions in the quantitative-export-restraint political equilibrium because of the convergence to a common policy. There are incentives in the latter case to diverge, to differentiate the candidates and therefore to obtain positive campaign contributions (Ursprung 1990 [2008]).

12.5 THE TERMS OF TRADE AND GOVERNMENT REVENUE

Models of international trade have quite generally made the assumption that the country being studied is 'small' relative to the total world market. The terms of trade are then exogenous. The assumption is one of convenience and can be found when the institutional background is that of a 'large' country (see, for example, Grossman and Helpman 1994 [2008]).

When the terms of trade improve, aggregate welfare increases (fewer exports are required to provide any amount of imports). A case for using tariffs (or trade restrictions in general) to improve the terms of trade, the 'optimum tariff' argument, has been part of international trade theory for more than a century (see Kahn 1947). The 'optimum tariff' maximizes a country's aggregate welfare through terms of trade improvement.[19]

Social benefit from terms of trade improvement is tied to tariff revenue (James and Hillman 1970). A tariff reduces the relative world price of imports because of the decrease in domestic demand in a 'large' country when the tariff increases the relative domestic price. Domestic consumers have lost insofar as the tariff has made imports (and domestic import-competing production) more expensive.[20] The gain to domestic consumers is through the distribution of tariff revenue. Governments must therefore be relied upon not to consume the tariff revenue and not to use the tariff revenue to create rents and cater to rent seeking through the government budget (on which, see Park et al. 2005). Regardless of revenue assignment, tariff revenue can be expected to be a negligible part of a government's budget, in particular in high-income countries, in which government revenue derives principally from taxation of incomes, corporate profits and consumer spending. For political decision makers, additions to revenue from tariffs therefore can be expected to have negligible political weight, because of the small contribution to total government revenue. Also, however, importantly, with tariff revenue part of the general pool of government revenue, it is difficult to benefit politically from assigning tariff revenue through the government budget.

The political-economy model of trade policy emphasizes the political gain from converting tariff revenue to private rents. The quota rents described by Anne Krueger (1974 [2008]) provided private benefit whereas tariffs could have provided revenue for the government budget. In Hillman and Ursprung (1988 [2008]), quota rents likewise provide private benefits. The 'undertakings' offered in response to anti-dumping complaints also show unimportance of tariff revenue. Because distribution of tariff revenue to consumers is required to obtain the benefits to the population from improvement in the terms of trade, if tariff revenue does not matter for governments, nor do the terms of trade.

---

[19] An example is that a country with a domestic market that is large relative to the world market imports coffee and the country's government levies a tariff on imports of coffee. The tariff increases the domestic price of coffee and reduces domestic demand for coffee, thereby reducing demand in the world market for coffee, and so reducing the world price of coffee. The tariff has therefore improved the terms of trade of the tariff-imposing country. The 'optimum tariff' is one of two of the classical cases for protection (the other is the infant-industry argument; see Kemp 1960; Baldwin 1969). The optimum tariff, which is based on monopsony power in international markets, was incorporated in the 'general theory of distortions' (Bhagwati 1971).

[20] In general equilibrium, it is in principle possible for the domestic relative price of the imported good to fall notwithstanding the tariff. We abstract from this possibility.

12.6 TRADE LIBERALIZATION

12.6.1 Trade Liberalization Without Rents

When a government levies an optimum tariff, the trading partner disadvantaged by the change in the terms of trade has an incentive to retaliate, by also levying a tariff on imports and thereby undoing the terms of trade deterioration or at least improving its terms of trade. Successive retaliatory tariffs reduce the volume of trade. Governments can improve aggregate social welfare by agreeing to reduce tariffs and restore trade. Following Harry Johnson (1953–54 [2008]), negotiations by governments to liberalize international trade have been viewed as a means of return from the mutually disadvantageous consequences of tariffs that have been levied to improve the terms of trade. Game theory has been applied to describe trade liberalization (McMillan 1984). Rents are absent from the game-theoretic model. If governments do not care about tariff revenue, they do not care about the tariff revenue lost when trade is liberalized. Without the role of tariff revenue as distributed to increase social welfare, there would have been no terms of trade improvement as the motive for tariffs. The difficulty for the optimum-tariff cum tariff-revenue distribution model is that there is no evidence that governments have ever justified tariffs on optimum-tariff grounds. There is also no evidence that governments have ever, conversely, justified trade liberalization as removal of optimum tariffs.

12.6.2 The Most-favored-nation Clause and Trade Liberalization

Trade liberalization is the converse of protectionism but there is an asymmetry. Whereas protectionism is unilateral (unless a country is a member of a customs union), trade liberalization has in general been multilateral. The multilateralism involves the most-favored-nation (MFN) clause, which requires that any reductions in protectionist barriers – or 'concessions' – granted to one trading partner apply to all trading partners. The universality of the MFN clause protects the benefits of negotiated reductions in trade barriers and so provides the incentive to negotiate trade-liberalization agreements. Benefits that a foreign government has offered through reduced protection will not be diminished by more advantageous benefits being given to another trading partner (Ethier 2001, 2002 [2008], 2004 [2008]).

12.6.3 Trade Liberalization with Rents

In Hillman et al. (1995) and Hillman and Moser (1996 [2008]), reciprocal trade liberalization is modeled as 'politically optimal exchange of market access'. Income and rents are determined according to the specific-factors model. Trade liberalization based on 'exchange of market access' implies a conception of property rights to markets. A government proposes that 'your exporters can sell in *my* domestic market if you allow my exporters to sell in *your* domestic market'.

A unilateral policy of subsidizing exporters would contravene international trade law. Governments wishing to use trade policy to offer benefits to exporters therefore face institutional constraints on subsidization. This in turn constrains the incentives of exporters to engage in rent seeking. The exchange-of-market-access model describes the escape from this situation. Exporters can seek rents that can be obtained through lower trade-partner tariffs. Exchange of market access allows political decision makers in different countries to cooperate to create rents in their respective export sectors by liberalizing trade. There are, at the same time, efficiency benefits. Consumers gain from the more liberal trade policies.

12.6.4 The Terms of Trade and Trade Liberalization

Models of the political economy of trade liberalization differ according to whether, as a carryover from the optimum tariff, the terms of trade have a central role in influencing policy decisions. Governments may be politically motivated to use trade policy to influence domestic incomes and rents but at the same time trade policy influences world prices. A 'terms-of-trade externality' is therefore imposed on trading partners because of a government's politically determined trade policy.

In Bagwell and Staiger (2002), the terms-of-trade externality is the only reason for negotiated trade liberalization. If governments did not care about the terms of trade, there would be no role for trade negotiations. Because of rent creation for domestic industry interests, governments engaged in the trade negotiations are not maximizing social welfare. A domestic political equilibrium that governments cannot improve upon is achieved through negotiated trade liberalization involving the terms of trade.

A premise of political-economy models of choice of trade policy is, however, that rents created for private interests are politically important, whereas tariff revenue for the general government budget is not a consideration in policy decisions.[21] Hence the prediction is that governments will not be concerned with the terms of trade, because benefits through the terms of trade come through the contribution of tariff revenue to the government budget, which is of no political consequence.

Ethier (2004 [2008]) makes the confirming observation regarding the terms of trade, that if the terms of trade were important for policy, export taxes, which are allowed under the rules of the WTO, would be used. Export taxes are, however, not observed – at least not in high-income countries.

There are therefore two alternative ways of modeling the political economy of trade liberalization. In both cases, governments seek rent creation for exporters but the models differ with regard to the purpose of negotiated trade liberalization. Bagwell and Staiger (2002) focus on the terms-of-trade externality. Ethier (2004 [2008], 2013) and Regan (2006, 2015) view the terms of trade as unimportant.

To determine the relevance of the two views, we can look to actual trade negotiators. As proposed by Hillman et al. (1995) and Hillman and Moser (1996 [2008]), trade negotiators focus on 'concessions' offered through exchange of market access. Negotiators do not show concern with the terms of trade. Consistently, when 'punishment' or retaliation

---

[21] Government revenue does not, for example, appear in the Hillman (1982 [2008]) political-support function according to which protectionist policy is determined nor in Hillman et al. (1995) and Hillman and Moser (1996 [2008]) describing the exchange-of-market-access motive for reciprocal trade liberalization.

occurs in trade disputes, the form of retaliation is denial of previously granted market access – again without concern for the terms of trade.

12.7 THE RHETORIC OF ECONOMICS

12.7.1 Different Stories

Deirdre McCloskey (1998) proposed that economists are storytellers who tell different stories. This chapter has described themes of different stories told about international trade policy. The story that includes rents is 'short run'. For political decision makers, the short run is defined by time horizons that may not extend beyond the date of the next election. For executives and managers, the short run can be even shorter because of remuneration linked to stock prices and reporting of corporate profits.[22]

12.7.2 The Switch to Rents

Until approximately the mid 1990s, the story told about protection and trade liberalization excluded politically created rents. Then the story told through the model with politically created rents became prominent.[23]

12.7.3 Concluding Questions

We conclude with questions.

- The distortions model is logically correct. Why however would a model that told a story of efficiency gains from protectionism be given a mainstream role, when the challenge has been rather to exposit and publicize the gains from trade, to assist in resisting the rent seeking of interest groups whose benefits are at the expense of society at large?[24]

---

[22] James Cassing (1996) made the point that investors who can diversify their portfolios through mutual funds are disadvantaged when executives and managers seek protectionist policies. A diversified investor benefits from the efficiency of free trade.

[23] Conjectures can be offered about why the change occurred when it did. Because of the implied character and behavior of politicians, political correctness is a possible reason for excluding rents and rent seeking from economic models (Hillman 1998 [2008]). The end of communism around 1990 may have changed politically correct and therefore acceptable descriptions in economic models of behavior of democratic government. Perhaps there was a change from the ideology and personal identity (Hillman 2010) implicit in the model that had no role for political rent creation. The model without politically created rents had protected human capital in allowing academic economists to work with models with which they were familiar. Protection of a paradigm is a form of rent seeking (on rent seeking in academia, see Brennan and Tollison 1980 and Hillman 2013).

[24] Allowance can be made for the *force majeure* of departure from free trade because of security and refusal of others to trade. See Mayer (1977), Arad and Hillman (1979), Hillman and Long (1983) and Bergström et al. (1985).

- The strategic trade-policy model is also logically correct. Again, however, why emphasize a story about how a society benefits from publicly financed subsidies to firms, when, with recognition of the incentives for political rent creation, the subsidies become prizes in rent-seeking contests?
- Why were optimum tariffs given prominence in academic models when governments do not seem to care about tariff revenue and when the conduct of trade-policy negotiators makes clear that terms of trade effects and accompanying tariff-revenue consequences are not a primary influence on liberalization agreements?

Models without politically created rents describe a sought-after world to be achieved through recommended government policy. Politically-created rents compromise the sought-after world. The denial of the reality of politically created rents can lead to confusion between the perfect world sought and the understanding of why the world and governments are not perfect.

REFERENCES

Arad, Ruth W. and Arye L. Hillman (1979), 'Embargo threat, learning and departure from comparative advantage', *Journal of International Economics*, **9**(2), 265–75.

Bagwell, Kyle and Robert W. Staiger (2002), *The Economics of the World Trading System*, Cambridge, MA: MIT Press.

Baldwin, Robert E. (1969), 'The case against industry-industry protection', *Journal of Political Economy*, **77**(3), 295–305.

Baldwin, Robert E. (1984), 'Rent seeking and trade policy: an industry approach', *Weltwirtschaftliches Archiv*, **120**(4), 662–7.

Bergström, Clas, Glenn C. Loury and Mats Persson (1985), 'Embargo threats and the management of emergency reserves', *Journal of Political Economy*, **93**(1), 26–42.

Bhagwati, Jagdish N. (1971), 'The generalized theory of distortions and welfare', in Jagdish N. Bhagwati, Ronald W. Jones, Robert A. Mundell and Jaroslav Vanek (eds), *Trade, Balance of Payments, and Growth: Essays in Honor of Charles P. Kindleberger*, Amsterdam: North-Holland, pp. 69–90.

Bhagwati, Jagdish N. (1982), 'Directly unproductive, profit-seeking (DUP) activities', *Journal of Political Economy*, **90**(5), 988–1002.

Bhagwati, Jagdish N. and Sukhamoy Chakravarty (1969), 'Contributions to Indian economic analysis: a survey', *American Economic Review*, **59**(4), Part 2, Supplement, Surveys of National Economic Policy Issues and Policy Research, 1–73.

Bhagwati, Jagdish N. and V.K. Ramaswami (1963), 'Domestic distortions, tariffs, and the theory of the optimal subsidy', *Journal of Political Economy*, **71**(1), 44–50.

Bhagwati, Jagdish N., V.K. Ramaswami and T.N. Srinivisan (1969), 'Domestic distortions, tariffs, and the theory of the optimal subsidy: some further results', *Journal of Political Economy*, **77**(6), 1005–10.

Brander, James A. (1985), 'Rationales for strategic trade and industrial policy', in Paul R. Krugman (ed.), *Strategic Trade Policy and the New International Economics*, Cambridge, MA: MIT Press, pp. 23–46.

Brander, James A. and Barbara J. Spencer (1985), 'Export subsidies and international market share rivalry', *Journal of International Economics*, **18**(1–2), 83–91.

Brecher, Richard A. (1974a), 'Minimum wage rates and the pure theory of international trade', *Quarterly Journal of Economics*, **88**(1), 98–116.

Brecher, Richard A. (1974b), 'Optimal commercial policy for a minimum-wage economy', *Journal of International Economics*, **4**(2), 139–50.

Brennan, H. Geoffrey and Robert D. Tollison (1980), 'Rent seeking in academia', in James M. Buchanan, Robert D. Tollison and Gordon Tullock (eds), *Toward a Theory of the Rent-seeking Society*, College Station, TX: Texas A&M University Press, pp. 344–56.

Cassing, James H. (1996), 'Protectionist mutual funds', *European Journal of Political Economy*, **12**(1), 1–18.

Cassing, James H. and Arye L. Hillman (1985), 'Political influence motives and the choice between tariffs and quotas', *Journal of International Economics*, **19**(3–4), 279–90.

Cassing, James H. and Arye L. Hillman (1986), 'Shifting comparative advantage and senescent industry collapse', *American Economic Review*, **76**(3), 516–23, reprinted in Wilfred J. Ethier and Arye L. Hillman (eds) (2008), *The WTO and the Political Economy of Trade Policy*, Aldershot, UK and Brookfield, VT, USA: Edward Elgar Publishing, pp. 516–23.

Congleton, Roger D., Arye L. Hillman and Kai A. Konrad (2008), '40 years of research on rent seeking: an overview', in Roger D. Congleton, Arye L. Hillman and Kai A. Konrad (eds), *40 Years of Research on Rent Seeking*, Vols 1 and 2, Heidelberg: Springer, pp. 1–42.

Eaton, Jonathan and Gene M. Grossman (1986), 'Optimal trade and industrial policy under oligopoly', *Quarterly Journal of Economics*, **101**(2), 383–406.

Eckhaus, Richard S. (1965), *Planning in India*, New York: National Bureau of Economic Research, available at http://pdf.usaid.gov/pdf_docs/pnadu284.pdf (accessed 25 May 2014).

Ellis, Richard (2005), *Tiger Bone and Rhino Horn*, Washington, DC: Island Press.

Ethier, Wilfred J. (1974), 'Some of the theorems of international trade with many goods and factors', *Journal of International Economics*, **4**(2), 199–206.

Ethier, Wilfred J. (2001), 'Theoretical problems in negotiating trade liberalization', *European Journal of Political Economy*, **17**(2), 209–32.

Ethier, Wilfred J. (2002), 'Unilateralism in a multilateral world', *Economic Journal*, **112**(479), 266–92, reprinted in Wilfred J. Ethier and Arye L. Hillman (eds) (2008), *The WTO and the Political Economy of Trade Policy*, Cheltenham, UK and Northampton, MA, USA: Edward Elgar Publishing, pp. 567–93.

Ethier, Wilfred J. (2004), 'Political externalities, nondiscrimination, and a multilateral world', *Review of International Economics*, **12**(3), 303–20, reprinted in Wilfred J. Ethier and Arye L. Hillman (eds) (2008), *The WTO and the Political Economy of Trade Policy*, Cheltenham, UK and Northampton, MA, USA: Edward Elgar Publishing, pp. 370–87.

Ethier, Wilfred J. (2013), 'The trade agreement embarrassment', *Journal of East Asian Economic Integration*, **17**(3), 243–60.

Feeney, JoAnne and Arye L. Hillman (2001), 'Privatization and the political economy of strategic trade policy', *International Economic Review*, **42**(2), 535–56.

Feeney, JoAnne and Arye L. Hillman (2004), 'Trade liberalization through asset markets', *Journal of International Economics*, **64**(1), 151–67, reprinted in Wilfred J. Ethier and Arye L. Hillman (eds) (2008), *The WTO and the Political Economy of Trade Policy*, Cheltenham, UK and Northampton, MA, USA: Edward Elgar Publishing, pp. 173–89.

Grossman, Gene M. (1983), 'Partially mobile capital: a general approach to two-sector trade theory', *Journal of International Economics*, **15**(1), 1–17.

Grossman, Gene M. (1985), 'Strategic export promotion: a critique', in Paul R. Krugman (ed.), *Strategic Trade Policy and the New International Economics*, Cambridge, MA: MIT Press, pp. 47–68.

Grossman, Gene M. and Elhanan Helpman (1994), 'Protection for sale', *American Economic Review*, **84**(4), 833–50, reprinted in Roger D. Congleton, Arye L. Hillman and Kai A. Konrad (eds) (2008), *40 Years of Research on Rent Seeking 2 – Applications: Rent Seeking in Practice*, Heidelberg: Springer, pp. 131–48.

Grossman, Gene M. and Elhanan Helpman (2002), *Interest Groups and Trade Policy*, Princeton, NJ: Princeton University Press.

Gupta, Rahul and Santap Sanhari Mishra (eds) (2007), *Corruption: The Causes and Combating Strategies*, Hyderabad: Icfai University Press.

Hillman, Arye L. (1982), 'Declining industries and political-support protectionist motives', *American Economic Review*, **72**(2), 1180–7, reprinted in Wilfred J. Ethier and Arye L. Hillman (eds) (2008), *The WTO and the Political Economy of Trade Policy*, Cheltenham, UK and Northampton, MA, USA: Edward Elgar Publishing, pp. 43–50.

Hillman, Arye L. (1989), *The Political Economy of Protection*, Chur: Harwood, reprinted in 2001, London: Routledge.

Hillman, Arye L. (1992), 'International trade policy: benevolent dictators and optimizing politicians', *Public Choice*, **74**(1), 1–15.

Hillman, Arye L. (1998), 'Political economy and political correctness', *Public Choice*, **96**(3–4), 219–39, reprinted in Roger D. Congleton, Arye L. Hillman and Kai Konrad (eds) (2008), *40 Years of Research on Rent Seeking 2 – Applications: Rent Seeking in Practice*, pp. 791–811 (Presidential Address, European Public Choice Society, Prague, April 1997).

Hillman, Arye L. (2005), 'Globalization and the political economy of international trade policy', in Sisira Jayasuriya (ed.), *Trade Policy Reforms and Development: Essays in Honor of Professor Peter Lloyd*, Vol. II, Cheltenham, UK and Northampton, MA, USA: Edward Elgar Publishing, pp. 3–22.

Hillman, Arye L. (2009), *Public Finance and Public Policy: Responsibilities and Limitations of Government*, 2nd edn, New York: Cambridge University Press.

Hillman, Arye L. (2010), 'Expressive behavior in economics and politics', *European Journal of Political Economy*, **26**(4), 404–19.

Hillman, Arye L. (2013), 'Rent seeking', in Michael Reksulak, Laura Razzolini and William F. Shughart II (eds), *The Elgar Companion to Public Choice, Second Edition*, Cheltenham UK and Northampton MA: Edward Elgar Publishing, pp. 307–30.

Hillman, Arye L. and Eliakim Katz (1987), 'Hierarchical structure and the social costs of bribes and transfers', *Journal of Public Economics*, **34**(2), 129–42, reprinted in Roger D. Congleton, Arye L. Hillman and Kai Konrad (eds) (2008), *40 Years of Research on Rent Seeking 1 – The Theory of Rent Seeking*, Heidelberg: Springer, pp. 523–36.

Hillman, Arye L. and Ngo Van Long (1983), 'Pricing and depletion of an exhaustible resource when there is anticipation of trade disruption', *Quarterly Journal of Economics*, **98**(2), 215–33.

Hillman, Arye L. and Peter Moser (1996), 'Trade liberalization as politically optimal exchange of market access', in Matthew Canzoneri, Wilfred J. Ethier and Vittorio Grilli (eds), *The New Transatlantic Economy*, New York: Cambridge University Press, pp. 295–312, reprinted in Wilfred J. Ethier and Arye L. Hillman (eds) (2008), *The WTO and the Political Economy of Trade Policy*, Cheltenham, UK and Northampton, MA, USA: Edward Elgar Publishing, pp. 290–307.

Hillman, Arye L. and John G. Riley (1989), 'Politically contestable rents and transfers', *Economics and Politics*, **1**(1), 17–39, reprinted in Roger D. Congleton, Arye L. Hillman and A. Kai Konrad (eds) (2008), *40 Years of Research on Rent Seeking 1 – The Theory of Rent Seeking*, Heidelberg: Springer, pp. 185–207.

Hillman, Arye L. and Otto Swank (2000), 'Why political culture should be in the lexicon of economics', *European Journal of Political Economy*, **16**(1), 1–4.

Hillman, Arye L. and Heinrich W. Ursprung (1988), 'Domestic politics, foreign interests, and international trade policy', *American Economic Review*, **78**(4), 729–45, reprinted in Roger D. Congleton, Arye L. Hillman and Kai A. Konrad (eds) (2008), *40 Years of Research on Rent Seeking 2 – Applications: Rent Seeking in Practice*, Heidelberg: Springer, pp. 113–29.

Hillman, Arye L. and Heinrich W. Ursprung (1992), 'The influence of environmental concerns on the political determination of international trade policy', in Richard Blackhurst and Kym Anderson (eds), *The Greening of World Trade Issues*, Ann Arbor, MI: University of Michigan Press, pp. 195–220.

Hillman, Arye L. and Heinrich W. Ursprung (1994), 'Greens, super greens, and international trade policy: environmental concerns and protectionism', in Carlo Carraro (ed.), *Trade, Innovation, Environment*, Heidelberg: Springer, pp. 75–108.

Hillman, Arye L., Peter Moser and Ngo Van Long (1995), 'Modeling reciprocal trade liberalization: the political-economy and national-welfare perspectives', *Swiss Journal of Economics and Statistics*, **131**(3), 503–15.

Hirshleifer, Jack (1976), 'Toward a more general theory of regulation: comment', *Journal of Law and Economics*, **19**(2), 241–4.

James, David and Arye L. Hillman (1970), 'A note on the distribution of tariff proceeds', *Economic Record*, **46**(1), 117–19.

Johnson, Harry G. (1953–54), 'Optimum tariffs and retaliation', *Review of Economic Studies*, **21**(2), 142–53, reprinted in Wilfred J. Ethier and Arye L. Hillman (eds) (2008), *The WTO and the Political Economy of Trade Policy*, Cheltenham, UK and Northampton, MA, USA: Edward Elgar Publishing, pp. 3–14.

Jones, Ronald W. (1971), 'A three factor model in theory, trade, and history', in Jagdish N. Bhagwati, Ronald W. Jones, Robert A. Mundell and Jaroslav Vanek (eds), *Trade, Balance of Payments, and Growth: Essays in Honor of Charles P. Kindleberger*, Amsterdam: North-Holland, pp. 3–21.

Kahn, Richard F. (1947), 'Tariffs and the terms of trade', *Review of Economic Studies*, **15**(1), 14–19.

Kemp, Murray C. (1960), 'The Mill-Bastable infant-industry dogma', *Journal of Political Economy*, **68**(1), 65–7.

Konrad, Kai A. (2000), 'Trade contests', *Journal of International Economics*, **51**(2), 317–34.

Körber, Achim (1998), 'Why everyone loves Flipper: the political economy of the US dolphin-safe laws', *European Journal of Political Economy*, **14**(3), 457–509.

Krueger, Anne O. (1974), 'The political economy of the rent-seeking society', *American Economic Review*, **64**(3), 291–303, reprinted in Roger D. Congleton, Arye L. Hillman and Kai A. Konrad (eds) (2008), *40 Years of Research on Rent Seeking 2 – Applications: Rent Seeking in Practice*, Heidelberg: Springer, pp. 151–63.

Krugman, Paul R. (1985), 'Introduction: new thinking about trade policy', in Paul R. Krugman (ed.), *Strategic Trade Policy and the New International Economics*, Cambridge, MA: MIT Press, pp. 1–22.

Lloyd, Peter J. (1974), 'A more general theory of price distortions in open economies', *Journal of International Economics*, **4**(4), 365–86.

Long, Ngo Van (2013), 'The theory of contests: a unified model and review of the literature', *European Journal of Political Economy*, **32**, 161–81, reprinted in Chapter 3, this volume.

Mayer, Wolfgang (1974), 'Short-run and long-run equilibrium for a small open economy', *Journal of Political Economy*, **82**(5), 955–67.

Mayer, Wolfgang (1977), 'The national defense tariff argument reconsidered', *Journal of International Economics*, **7**(4), 363–77.

Mayer, Wolfgang (1984), 'Endogenous tariff formation', *American Economic Review*, **74**(5), 970–85.
McCloskey, Deirdre N. (1998), *The Rhetoric of Economics*, Madison, WI: University of Wisconsin Press.
McMillan, John (1984), *Game Theory in International Economics*, Chur: Harwood.
Mussa, Michael (1974), 'Tariffs and the distribution of income: the importance of factor specificity, substitutability, and intensity in the short and long run', *Journal of Political Economy*, **82**(6), 1191–203.
Neary, Peter J. (1978), 'Short-run capital specificity and the pure theory of international trade', *Economic Journal*, **88**(351), 488–510.
Olson, Mancur (1965), *The Logic of Collective Action*, Cambridge, MA: Harvard University Press.
Park, Hyun, Apostolis Philippopoulos and Vanghelis Vassilatos (2005), 'Choosing the size of the public sector under rent seeking from state coffers', *European Journal of Political Economy*, **21**(4), 830–50.
Peltzman, Sam (1976), 'Toward a more general theory of regulation', *Journal of Law and Economics*, **19**(2), 211–40.
Regan, Donald H. (2006), 'What are trade agreements for? Two conflicting stories told by economists, with a lesson for lawyers', *Journal of International Economic Law*, **9**(4), 243–60.
Regan, Donald H. (2015), 'Explaining trade agreements: the practitioners' story and the standard model', *World Trade Review*, in press.
Ruffin, Roy and Ronald Jones (1977), 'Protection and real wages: the neoclassical ambiguity', *Journal of Economic Theory*, **14**(2), 337–48.
Schonhardt-Bailey, Cheryl (2006), *From the Corn Laws to Free Trade: Interests, Ideas, and Institutions in Historical Perspective*, Cambridge, MA: MIT Press.
Spencer, Barbara J. (1985), 'What should trade policy target?', in Paul R. Krugman (ed.), *Strategic Trade Policy and the New International Economics*, Cambridge, MA: MIT Press, pp. 69–90.
Stolper, Wolfgang and Paul Samuelson (1941), 'Protection and real wages', *Review of Economic Studies*, **9**(1), 58–73.
Tharakan, P.K. Mathew (1991), 'The political economy of anti-dumping undertakings in the European Communities', *European Economic Review*, **35**(6), 1341–59.
Tullock, Gordon (1967), 'The welfare costs of tariffs, monopolies, and theft', *Western Economic Journal*, **5**(3), 224–32, reprinted in Roger D. Congleton, Arye L. Hillman and Kai A. Konrad (eds) (2008), *40 Years of Research on Rent Seeking 1 – The Theory of Rent Seeking*, Heidelberg: Springer, pp. 45–53.
Ursprung, Heinrich W. (1990), 'Public goods, rent dissipation, and candidate competition', *Economics and Politics*, **2**(2), 115–32, reprinted in Roger D. Congleton, Arye L. Hillman and Kai A. Konrad (eds) (2008), *40 Years of Research on Rent Seeking 1 – The Theory of Rent Seeking*, Heidelberg: Springer, pp. 329–46.
Ursprung, Heinrich W. (1991), 'Economic policies and political competition', in Arye L. Hillman (ed.), *Markets and Politicians: Politicized Economic Choice*, Dordrecht: Kluwer, pp. 1–25.
Yang, Cheng-Chen (1995), 'Endogenous tariff formation under representative democracy: a probabilistic voting model', *American Economic Review*, **85**(4), 956–63.
Young, Leslie and Stephen P. Magee (1986), 'Endogenous protection, factor returns, and resource allocation', *Review of Economic Studies*, **53**(3), 407–19.

13. Rent seeking through public finance*

Michael Brooks

SUMMARY

This chapter reviews the consequences for basic public finance theorems when revenue from various sources is a contestable rent. The basic theorems change because revenue, which is viewed in the orthodox public finance literature as a transfer that facilitates social benefit through public spending, becomes a source of social loss through the wasteful use of resources when that revenue is contestable. In a world of rent seeking, pure rent taxes seem to be a mirage. The Ramsey rule for efficient taxation need no longer apply. Basic theorems about the Pigovian externality-correcting tax and efficient user charges based on peak and off-peak demand are compromised.

13.1 INTRODUCTION

The literature on rent seeking and government revenue is a body of work full of surprises. Despite the voluminous literature on rent seeking – one now so vast and varied that the editors of this volume must have thought it was an opportune time to gather a collection of introductory surveys to the various strands of the diverse literature – and the significant role played by public user charges and taxes on economic activity, the strand of literature devoted to rent seeking and public finance is little more than a couple of handfuls of articles. Nevertheless the small subset of the literature offers a number of significant analytical results that seriously compromise fundamental theorems of orthodox public finance. In the following overview, I offer an entrée to the amazing analytical area of rent seeking and government funding, an area that has been explored, so far, largely by the pioneering efforts of Dwight Lee and Robert Tollison. In orthodox public finance the basic theorems are grounded on the assumption that government revenue is a transfer or a source of funding for valued social expenditure. In the field of public choice, rent seeking in contesting government revenue is a source of social loss. Conclusions can therefore be inverted because corrective taxation and more government revenue are not necessarily socially beneficial.

13.2 A FRAMEWORK

In offering an overview of the extant literature on rent seeking and government revenue, I find it helpful to place the various pieces in a taxonomy that was developed by Geoffrey

* I am indebted to Dwight Lee for a dialogue on one of his papers and Arye Hillman, in particular, for many helpful suggestions.

Brennan (1997) as part of an overview of some of his own work. The vertical dimension sets out the extent to which electoral constraints bind government decision makers, while the horizontal dimension offers a range of motivational assumptions that can be made about government decision makers including the motivations of individuals in their role as voters.

13.3 WHERE IS THE RENT SEEKING?

Nearly 50 years ago Gordon Tullock (1967) wrote the seminal piece on rent seeking and introduced the idea of wasteful completion over rents to the field of public choice. One might have thought that once the idea was put forward that public choice scholars would have been quick to exploit the concept in a range of different areas of research. Curiously, the concept was largely ignored for many years. In this section I comment on some classic works in public choice, where one might have initially thought the rent-seeking concept would have played a greater role than some cameo appearance.

13.3.1 In the Beginning

When Gordon Tullock (1967) set out the seminal paper on the 'The welfare costs of tariffs, monopolies, and theft', in the opening pages, he considers resources expended on trying to capture tariff/tax revenue and with enviable simplicity exposits the central proposition that the welfare costs of a tariff or excise tax exceed the excess burden given by the familiar Harberger welfare triangle. Based solely on a reading of that work, it is not entirely clear where Tullock's initial foray sits in Table 13.1. There is no political

Table 13.1 On the intersection of public finance and public choice

		Motivation			
		Benevolence	→	Self-seeking	→ Malice
Electoral constraints	Not binding	(1) Benevolent Despot		(2) Leviathan	
	Partially binding		(3) Expressive Politics	(4) Interest Group Theory of Government	
	Fully binding			(5) Orthodox Public Choice à la Buchanan vintage 1960s and early 1970s and Downs	

Source: Modified from Brennan (1997, p. 91).

model offered in his seminal contribution. Based, however, on knowledge of his general approach,[1] one can place the initial work in cells 4 and 5.

One might conjecture that once Tullock had toppled the Harberger triangle (Harberger 1964) as the focus of the analysis of wasteful activity, contesting tax revenue would have been a fixture of any subsequent public choice literature on government expenditure and revenue. Curiously, Tullock's argument seems to have been largely ignored by his colleagues[2] for a considerable span of time.[3] Despite the central role of taxation in his colleague's work, there is, for example, no discussion of rent seeking in James Buchanan's *Public Finance in Democratic Process* (1967) or his subsequent work *The Demand and Supply of Public Goods* (1968). Perhaps those works were so sufficiently advanced that it was not possible to rework their arguments in light of the basic rent-seeking proposition. Alternatively, both of these works take an optimistic view of government setting out the generalized gains from exchange that can be achieved by government. Perhaps it was hard to synthesize the optimism of the exchange view of government with the pessimism associated with a rent-seeking perspective.

13.3.2 Leviathan

Over the next decade or so, Buchanan's world view took a dramatic sea change. At the dawn of the 1980s, Buchanan and coauthor Brennan set out the analytical core of a fiscal constitution that was aimed at protecting the citizenry from the ravages of an out-of-control government, which was dubbed Leviathan in their major work *The Power to Tax* (Brennan and Buchanan 2008), a clear reference to Hobbes (1651 [1962]). The theory sits squarely in cell 2 of Table 13.1. One might have expected rent seeking to feature in that work. Once again, rent seeking is largely ignored. Buchanan has acknowledged that around this time period his optimism gave way to pessimism. Significantly, Brennan and Buchanan were no strangers to the concept of rent seeking. In 1979, around the time of the final draft of *The Power to Tax*, both Brennan[4] and Buchanan[5] were working independently on papers on rent seeking. Admittedly, I use the phrase 'largely ignored' advisedly because the concept is there in *The Power to Tax*.

---

1 See Congleton (2004) for an overview of Tullock's analytical approach.

2 Interestingly, in a recent overview of public choice, Buchanan (2003, p. 15) claims that '[g]iven [Tullock's] basic insight, much of modern politics can be understood as rent-seeking activity'.

3 It is not entirely clear how much weight ought to be placed on his colleague's inattentiveness because Tullock himself did not appear to place much store on the insight until the very late 1970s. In the northern autumn quarter of 1977, I was a student in Tullock's class on Collective Choice, which was designed to provide an overview of the central elements of public choice. There Tullock covered the economics of anarchy; economics of bureaucracy; the calculus of consent; the demand-revealing process; income redistribution; economics of legislatures; the paradox of voting and spatial voting. I checked my notes and while the term rent seeking was mentioned in the context of redistribution there was no coverage of the concept.

4 In 1980 Brennan and Tollison published on rent seeking and academia.

5 I seem to recall reading an unpublished draft of Buchanan's important contribution 'Rent seeking and profit seeking' in early 1979 that was subsequently published in November 1980 as part of the collection of papers on rent seeking edited by Buchanan, Tollison and Tullock. The Buchanan line of argument that rent seeking cannot be identified *ex ante* is evident in Tullock (1988).

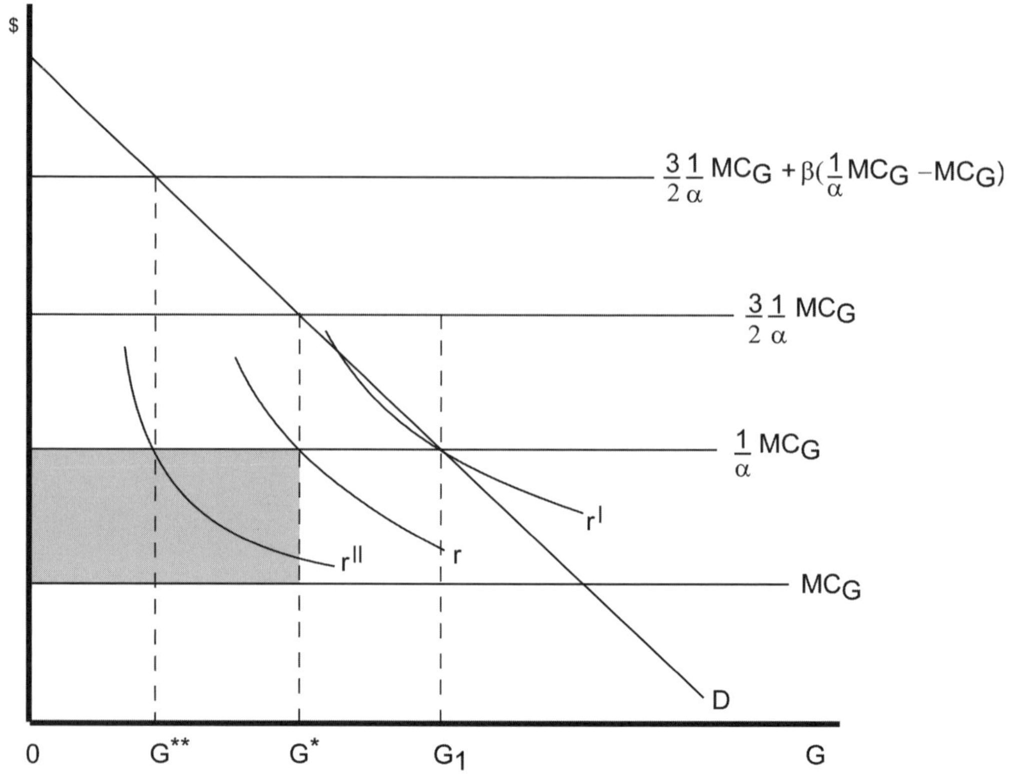

Figure 13.1 A modified version of Leviathan and the choice of tax base

In their account of the choice taxpayers would make at the constitutional forum, Brennan and Buchanan acknowledge rent seeking. In order to see its role, consider Figure 13.1, which, except for one significant refinement,[6] is figure 4.3 from *The Power to Tax*. To simplify the analysis, Brennan and Buchanan assume the veil of uncertainty means all taxpayers possess an identical demand curve for the public good, *G*. The public good is produced under constant costs represented by MC_G. Using a rudimentary model of Leviathan government, Brennan and Buchanan assume that Leviathan captures $(1 - \alpha)$ of any tax revenue for himself. If α equals 0.5, for example, then the amount of revenue that must be collected for a dollar's worth of public provision of *G* must be two dollars. Assuming Leviathan seeks to maximize tax revenue, a single tax rate, and the case where the private good that is subject to taxation exhibits a linear demand and invariant marginal costs, the total excess burden of taxation will be one half of the maximal amount of revenue. In this case the marginal cost will shift to the left by one half to that represented by $(3/2)(1/\alpha)MC_G$. On these analytical foundations Brennan and Buchanan (1980) argue the citizenry will select a

[6] The first three cost curves, from MC_G to $(3/2)(1/\alpha)MC_G$ are analyzed by Brennan and Buchanan (1980, pp. 73–5). I have added the fourth cost curve.

tax base[7] that when exploited to its maximal tax revenue potential, raises the amount represented by the rectangular hyperbola, *r*, thereby achieving the efficient level of provision, G^*.[8]

The acknowledgment of rent seeking by Brennan and Buchanan (1980, p. 33) is limited to the following brief paragraph:

> an element of efficiency cost that has recently emerged under the rubric 'rent seeking' seems to be of particular relevance . . . The existence of profits to be obtained from occupying positions of power in government generates competitive processes to obtain those profits – processes which themselves involve the use of economic resources. The establishment of a completely unconstrained Leviathan under a voluntary constitution would involve the creation of a monopoly franchise of enormous proportions: it would be an example of the creation of potential rents par excellence. Just as the competition for a monopoly franchise in the conventional setting involves the creation of incentives to expend resources to obtain that franchise (conceivably many times larger in value than the value of the monopoly rent involved), so the establishment of powerful monopoly government would create incentives to fight over who will occupy the seat of power. History – military history in particular – is replete with examples. History is also eloquent on the magnitude of the costs. From his disembodied vantage point behind the veil of ignorance, the typical citizen would surely prefer to minimize the expenditure of resources in this utterly wasteful manner. The only way of doing so is, however, to minimize the rents that accrue from 'governing' – that is, by constraining Leviathan so that its surplus is minimal.

I shall return to the implications of rent seeking for the Leviathan theory of government, after explaining some of the theory of rent seeking over contestable tax revenue.

13.4 PUBLIC FINANCE ORTHODOXY UNDER SIEGE

Apart from the brief foray into the theory of Leviathan government, nearly all of the discussion of rent seeking and government funding has been limited to setting out what is the optimal policy in the presence of such wasteful activity, where the underlying analytical framework comprises the view of government represented by cell 4. In the overview of that segment of the literature, I shall show that a number of tax principles of orthodox public finance are in serious need of amendment when account is taken of rent seeking.

13.4.1 The Mirage of a Pure Rent Tax

In a brief note published in *Finanzarchiv* almost three decades ago, Lee and Tollison (1985) raise serious doubts about a government's ability to tax pure rents. Consider[9]

---

7 Orthodox tax theory opts for a broader base tax on the grounds that the given amount of revenue, *r*, could be raised from the application of a lower tax rate on the broader base, which would result in a lower excess burden. The logic of Brennan and Buchanan's model denies the relevance of such an equi-revenue comparison. Leviathan government would exploit the broader tax base, represented by, say, r^l, to its maximal potential revenue, which would result in excessive provision of *G*.

8 I shall come to the reason for adding the fourth cost curve when I have set out Lee's (1985) approach to modeling the cost of rent seeking over tax revenue.

9 The bottom panel, with the addition made here of the demand curve, comes from Lee and

panel (b) of Figure 13.2 in which a perfectly inelastic compensated supply curve is depicted for some private activity Q. It is a widely held theorem of orthodox tax theory that as long as the tax rate does not exceed the line segment $0P$, any tax on Q will be non-distortionary. Lee and Tollison (1985) argue, however, that if individuals devote resources to avoiding the tax, then the neutral properties of the pure rent tax are lost – resources will have been devoted to a distributional struggle between the government treasury and taxpayers without the creation of any new social surplus. Tax avoidance or rent protection activity therefore can represent a wasteful use of resources. Lee and Tollison do not go as far as to state some impossibility result about the pure rent tax, but issue the proviso that if the orthodox economists want to persist with the notion of a pure rent tax, then they must assume zero rent protection activity.

Although Lee and Tollison do not offer any model of the rent-seeking process and significantly fail to discuss the waste that can occur if interest groups devote resources to appropriating the rent tax – a point that needs to be added to their proviso if the orthodox tax result is to hold – it will be useful to the development of a subsequent section, if I push the formal structure a little by introducing here a variant of Lee and Tollison's (1993) simple model of rent seeking over the tax rate as set out in terms of panel *a*.

Suppose the tax rate set in the absence of any rent-seeking or rent-protection effort is T_0 and that the revenue raised from the rent tax is fully earmarked to be spent on an activity sought by an interest group. For simplicity, assume it is possible to speak meaningfully about a group's utility function and that the interest group does not care about activity Q – the interest group's utility is represented by lexicographic indifference curves. The total revenue curve, R, from the pure rent tax here is a linear function of the tax rate, T. The rent-seeking group's outlay on lobbying for an expansion in the tax rate is represented, say, by the curve $C(T - T_0)$ located in the fourth quadrant of panel *a*. The vertical summation of the revenue line and the outlay curve yields the interest group's deterministic net return from rent seeking, $R - C(T - T_0)$. The interest group maximizes its utility by campaigning for and securing the tax rate, T_1. Although simple, the model offers a number of interesting results. First, a rent-seeking group's preferred tax rate is not necessarily equal to the rate that maximizes tax revenue – here the marginal cost of lobbying exceeds the marginal tax revenue before the maximal tax rate is reached. Second, we have a clear account of why the rent tax fails to reach the ideal championed by an orthodox tax theorist. Under the strictures of orthodox theory, the redistribution of tax revenue R_1 from taxpayers to the government treasury represents a pure transfer of resources without almost[10] any cost. The resources used in that transfer here are represented by C_1, which implies that a significant portion of the return from

Tollison (1985). The top panel is based on material drawn from various figures by Lee and Tollison (1991).

[10] I say almost, because even under orthodox tax theory, there are administrative costs associated with the collection of the rent tax. In that limited sense, orthodox tax theory had always offered some accounting for the resources used up in the redistribution from taxpayers to the government treasury. Even so, it would be a mistake to think that orthodox tax theory beat the theorists of rent seeking to the punch – there was no attempt to generalize the proposition beyond the issue that a good tax system should be simple and therefore inexpensive to administer.

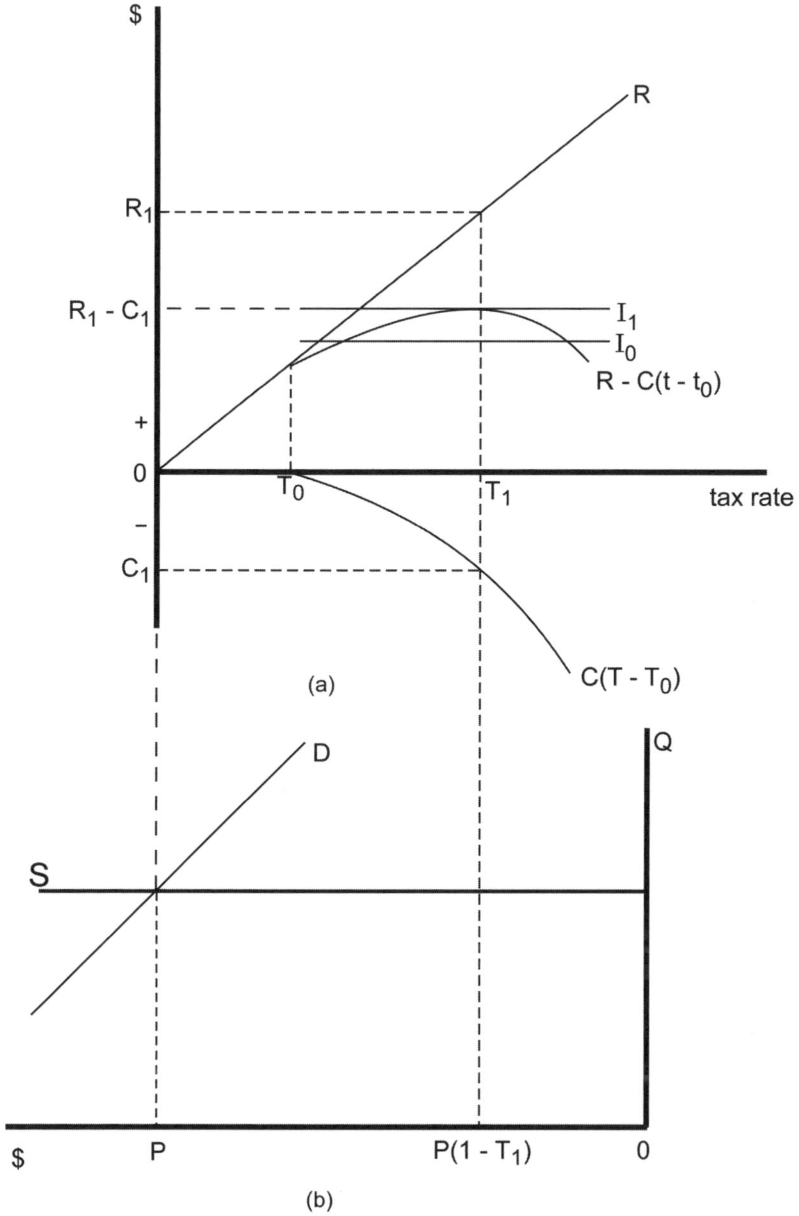

Figure 13.2 On the mirage of a purely neutral rent tax

the tax is dissipated in the redistribution game – the social surplus has diminished by the rent-seeking cost represented by C_1.

As indicated, Lee and Tollison (1985) limit their discussion to the resources expended on trying to avoid the rent tax. Accounting for the contest between taxpayers and various interest groups that stand to benefit from the tax revenue would be an interesting exercise to conduct. A straightforward conjecture from the results of the rent-seeking literature is that the waste from rent seeking and rent protection could easily exceed C_1 and be larger, equal to or less than R_1.

13.4.2 The Ramsey Rule 'Inverted'

A primary result in optimal tax theory is the Ramsey (1927) rule[11] – when cross-price elasticities are zero and marginal costs are constant, the ratio of efficient tax rates equals the inverse of the demand elasticities, $\frac{T_A}{T_B} = \frac{\varepsilon_B}{\varepsilon_A}$. Lee and Tollison (1988) demonstrate that when there is rent seeking, the result need no longer hold. A relatively higher tax rate might need to be imposed on the relatively more elastic good.

In order to provide a simple account of their formal argument it will be useful to modify a simple geometric account of the Ramsey rule, developed by Sobel (1997). In Figure 13.3, the axes represent the tax rates imposed on the two goods. The iso-excess burden curves are concave to the origin because marginal excess burden increases with the tax rate. Assuming the tax rates are set below the revenue-maximizing rates, the relevant segments of the iso-revenue curves are convex because marginal tax revenue declines with the tax rate.

Assume the price elasticity of demand of good *B* exceeds that of good *A*, the goods are supplied under constant costs, and the demands are independent of one another. In the absence of rent seeking and faced with a requirement to raise revenue, R_1, the optimal set of taxes is T_B^O and T_A^O, where the slope of the iso-revenue curve, which represents the ratio of marginal tax revenues, MTR_B/MTR_A, equals the slope of the iso-excess burden curve, EB_0, which, in turn, represents the ratio of the marginal excess burdens, MEB_B/MEB_A. Sobel (1997) shows the tangency condition is identical to the Ramsey rule – at point *J*, the ratio of tax rates equals the inverse of the ratio of price elasticities, $T_A^O/T_B^O = \varepsilon_B/\varepsilon_A$.

Lee and Tollison (1988, p. 344) assume rent seeking increases with the inelasticity of the demand for the goods:

> Purchasers of inelastically demanded products are more vulnerable to exploitation by increased commodity taxation . . . than are consumers of elastically demanded products. Therefore, lobbying against increases or for reduction in excise taxes can be expected to be more intense the less elastic the demand for the product being taxed.

The implication of the assumption is that the iso-waste curve, which represents all the combinations of tax rates that result in an identical level of waste, where waste is now the sum of the excess burden and rent-seeking loss, will be flatter than an iso-excess burden curve, which takes into account only the excess burdens of the taxes. If, for example, the excess burden is the sole source of excess burden, then it is possible to reduce the tax rate on *A to* T_A^{RS} while increasing the rate on *B* to $T_B^{\prime}$ without affecting the total burden. If there is rent seeking, then a tax results in two sources of waste, the conventional excess burden and the resources wasted in lobbying against taxation. The equivalent iso-waste curve w_0 must lie below the measure of loss as represented by the iso-burden curve EB_0 – in the presence of rent seeking a lower rate of tax on *A* generates the same level of loss as

[11] For an exposition of the rule and derivation, see Hillman (2009, chapter 9).

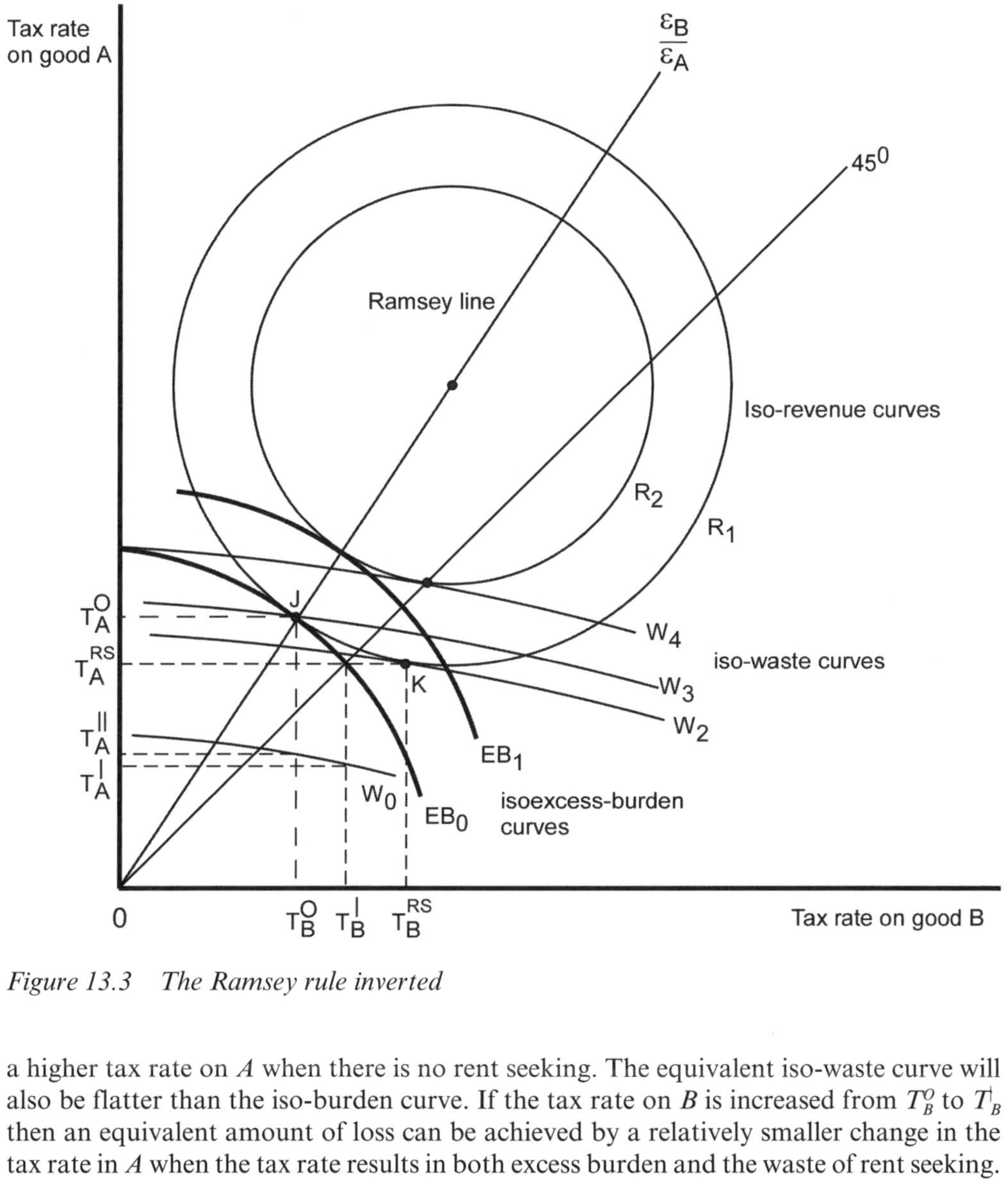

Figure 13.3 *The Ramsey rule inverted*

a higher tax rate on *A* when there is no rent seeking. The equivalent iso-waste curve will also be flatter than the iso-burden curve. If the tax rate on *B* is increased from T_B^O to T_B^I then an equivalent amount of loss can be achieved by a relatively smaller change in the tax rate in *A* when the tax rate results in both excess burden and the waste of rent seeking.

As Lee and Tollison (1988) show formally and as illustrated here, in the presence of rent seeking the possibility exists that the efficiency loss from taxation is minimized by disregarding the Ramsey rule. The efficiency loss from obtaining the revenue objective R_1 is minimized instead by finding the point *K*, where the iso-waste curve, w_2, is tangent to the required iso-revenue curve, R_1. At point *K* the ratio of tax rates lies below the 45 degree line, which means that here a relatively higher tax rate should be imposed on the relatively elastic good, that is, T_B^{RS} should be more than T_A^{RS}. Following the Ramsey rule when there is rent seeking would result in a higher efficiency loss as represented by the iso-waste curve w_3.

13.4.3 The Potential Inefficiency of Pigovian Taxes

Lee (1983) and later with coauthor Paul Wilson (Lee and Wilson 1990, 1991) shows that in the presence of rent seeking over the tax revenue, a Pigovian tax need not be efficient. In the interests of brevity, I do not cover all of the various cases explored by them and confine my attention to providing an alternative[12] simplified version of the formal model and central conclusions.

First, I outline the basic construction of how rent seeking over tax revenue is modeled. Let the *X* axis of Figure 13.4(a) represent a negative externality generating activity. The social/private benefit at the margin from undertaking *X* is represented by the linear demand curve, *P*. Finally, for expositional simplicity, let the marginal private cost be zero.[13] The private equilibrium therefore occurs at the point where the marginal benefit curve cuts the horizontal axis.

Note that a marginal tax revenue curve, *MTR*, identical to the construction of the ordinary marginal revenue, is represented in the first quadrant. The difference between the two curves would be merely one of who is the notional recipient of the revenue resulting from raising the price of the activity above zero. Lee and Lee and Wilson introduce the novel idea that some fraction β, where $0 \leq \beta \leq 1$, of the marginal tax revenue is wasted due to rent-seeking activity. The curve β*MTR*, which represents the marginal cost of rent seeking, is constructed in panel (b) of Figure 13.4, for the case where β is initially assumed to be (1/6). Irrespective of the proportion of the tax revenue wasted due to rent seeking, this curve necessarily cuts the horizontal axis at the point of unitary elasticity, here the mid-point of the line segment between the origin and the market equilibrium. As β increases, the curve β*MTR* pivots clockwise.

In the first quadrant of panel (b), the *MTR* curve takes on positive values, which means that as the rate of the pollution tax is increased (reduced) above T^1 (below the prohibitive tax rate), the marginal cost of rent seeking falls (rises). When the curve β*MTR* is in the fourth quadrant of panel (b), the curve takes on negative values. In that quadrant, when the rate of pollution tax is reduced (increased) below (above) T^1 (a zero tax rate), the total waste from rent seeking over the tax revenue falls (rises).

In the absence of rent seeking, the social optimal occurs where *P* equals $C^{|}$. The net

---

[12] Lee (1985 [1988]) and Lee and Wilson (1991) use a one-panel diagram to illustrate the formal exposition of the effects of rent seeking on the socially optimal rate of the pollution tax. In doing so, they have to construct various line segments between the principal curves to illustrate the optimal tax rate. The technique is somewhat clumsy as it does not allow a straightforward derivation of the optimal tax rate. Here I outline a two-panel construction in which the optimal tax rate in the presence of rent seeking can be easily derived.

[13] The figure is simplified by the assumption of a zero marginal private cost curve but the analysis does not depend on this assumption. If the assumption is relaxed, then the primary differences are that the marginal tax revenue curve would be constructed on the basis of the gross private demand curve rather than here on the basis of the net marginal private benefit curve and the optimal pollution tax would be determined by the vertical difference between the marginal benefit curve and the marginal private cost curve rather than as here by the vertical difference between the demand curve and the horizontal axis. Although the relaxation of that assumption would also change the position of the net marginal private benefit curve in the lower panel, the fundamentals of the analysis would be unchanged.

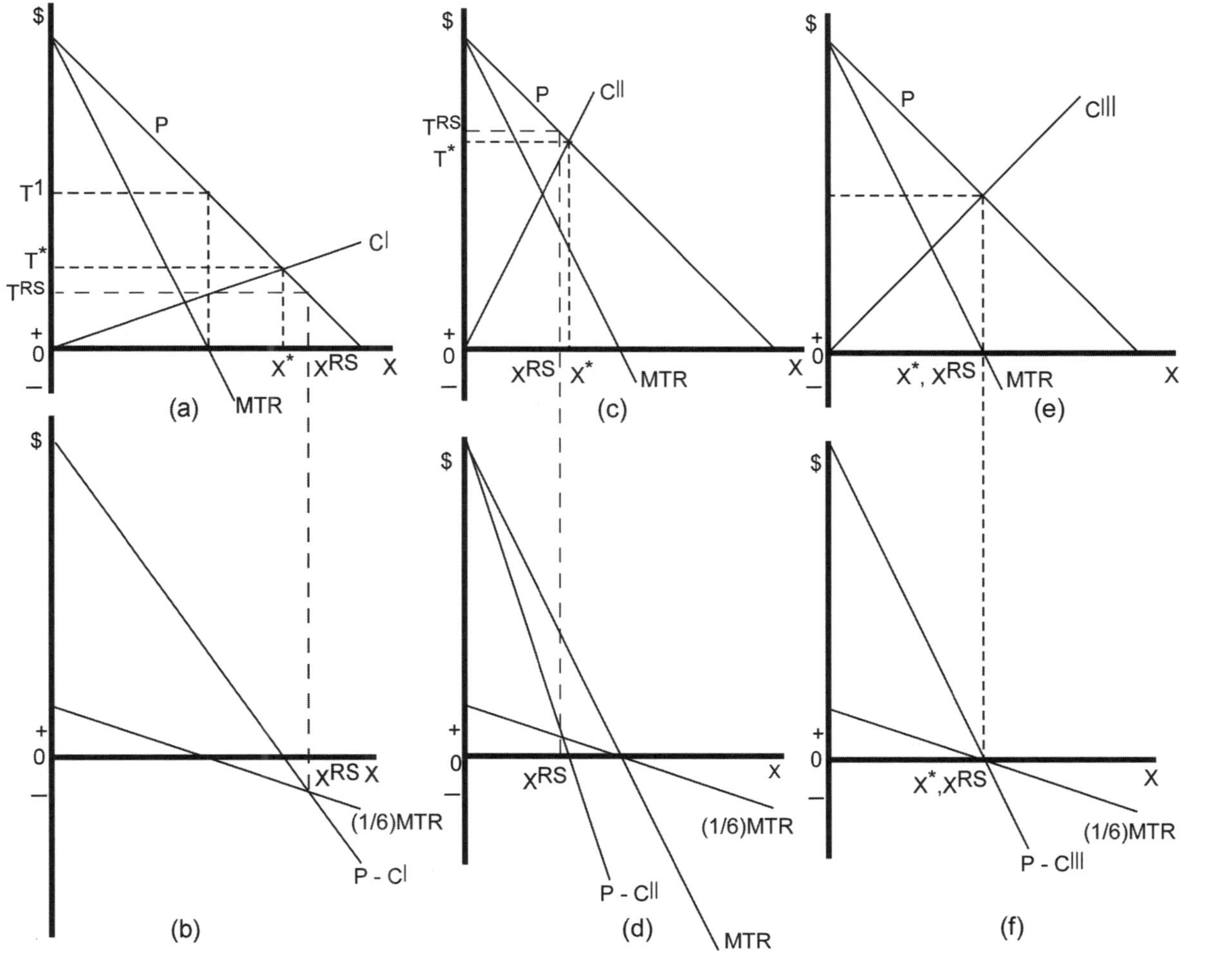

Figure 13.4 Optimal pollution tax

marginal social benefit from reducing X below the market equilibrium is given by the vertical difference between the private benefits and the external cost at the margin and that difference is constructed in the lower panel as the curve $(P - C^{\prime})$. If the net social benefit curve is in the fourth (first) quadrant, then reductions in X below the market equilibrium result in an improvement (deterioration) in social surplus. In the absence of rent seeking, the social optimum occurs where the curve $(P - C^{\prime})$ equals zero or cuts the horizontal axis.

In the presence of rent seeking and assuming there is an interior solution, the social optimal occurs where the net marginal social benefit from X equals the marginal cost of rent seeking, that is, where $(P - C^{\prime}) = (1/6)MTR$.

A moment's reflection will reveal that quite a number of cases, including corner solutions, exist depending on the extent of the rent seeking and the relationship between the marginal benefit and marginal external cost curves. One of the principal determinants of the size of the optimal pollution tax in the presence of rent seeking is whether the marginal external cost curve cuts the elastic or inelastic segment of the marginal benefit curve. As I have indicated, there is insufficient space to cover all the cases. It will suffice, however, to put the model through its paces by examining a select subset.

In the case at hand, the marginal external cost curve cuts the inelastic segment of the demand curve. The extent of rent seeking is such that the net marginal social benefit curve intersects the marginal cost of the rent-seeking curve from below[14] in the fourth quadrant, that is, $(P - C^{\prime})$ cuts $(1/6)MTR$ from below but to the right of the optimal point in the absence of rent seeking.[15] From the associated pollution level, X^{RS}, construct a vertical line to the upper panel and locate where it intersects the demand curve. The efficient pollution tax in the presence of rent seeking is therefore T^{RS}. Consequently, in the presence of rent seeking, the socially optimal level of X here is larger and the optimal pollution rate of tax is smaller than the level spelt out in orthodox public finance where rent seeking is not acknowledged, that is, $X^{RS} > X^*$ and $T^{RS} < T^*$.

By way of contrast, suppose the marginal external cost curve cuts the elastic segment of the demand curve as represented in Figure 13.4(c). The socially optimum level, conventionally interpreted in the absence of rent seeking, therefore equals X^*. In the associated lower panel (d), the net marginal social benefit curve intersects the marginal cost of rent seeking from below in the first quadrant of the lower panel and therefore to the left of the optimal level of X conventionally interpreted. In the presence of rent seeking, the socially optimal level of X^{RS} is relatively smaller and the optimal rate of the pollution tax is relatively larger than is suggested by a non-rent-seeking analysis, that is, $X^{RS} < X^*$ and $T^{RS} > T^*$.

The orthodox public finance analyst, blind to rent-seeking activity, would calculate the socially optimal level of pollution only in the special case in which the marginal

---

[14] If the marginal cost of the rent curve intersects the net marginal benefit curve from below, then the intersection point represents a welfare minimum rather than a maximum. In such a case, the optimal pollution tax is zero, if the net benefits at the private equilibrium – here the integral of the demand curve from zero output to the private equilibrium – are positive.

[15] If the net marginal benefit curve lies everywhere above the marginal cost of the rent-seeking curve, then the socially optimal output is the private equilibrium and the optimal rate of pollution tax is zero.

external cost curve cuts the demand curve at the unitary elastic point as depicted in panels (e) and (f). In all other cases, the conventional analysis misleads by setting out a set of socially inefficient policies.[16]

13.4.4 Leviathan Redux

The general geometrical technique used by Lee to analyze pollution taxation can be used to reconsider the tax base that would be selected behind the veil of ignorance in the Leviathan model when there is rent seeking. If the proportion of Leviathan's surplus that is wasted in the contest to be Leviathan is given by β, then the marginal cost of provision of G in Figure 13.1 must be shifted to the left by the marginal cost of rent seeking over the surplus, denoted here as $\beta[(1/\alpha)MC_G - MC_G]$. If, for example, $\beta = 1$, then the full marginal cost of G is shifted to the left by the full extent of Leviathan's surplus and the full cost curve is represented by $(3/2)(1/a)MC_G + \beta[(1/\alpha)MC_G - MC_G]$. The citizenry when behind the veil, but aware of the waste that will arise due to rent seeking, would not select the tax base that when fully exploited, would result in G^* as the level of the public good but would opt for an even narrower tax base that would, when fully exploited by Leviathan, generate the amount of revenue represented by the rectangular hyperbola r^{II} resulting in G^{**} as the efficient output. Although Brennan and Buchanan (1980) did not explain precisely how rent seeking would affect their argument – that the citizenry at the constitutional forum would opt for an even narrower tax base – their conjecture nevertheless is correct: when rent seeking is taken into account, the appeal of narrowing the tax base is enhanced.

Even so, it is not entirely clear what emphasis should be placed on the rent-seeking insight, at least when Leviathan rules. At the time *The Power to Tax* was written over the late 1970s, much was made of the taxpayer revolutions that had occurred in California. In that setting, *The Power to Tax* was written to proffer advice on how the citizenry might constrain the Leviathan tendencies of modern governments. There is no reason to believe that Buchanan ever withdrew from such a stance. Some 20 years later, Brennan (1997), however, views their joint work more as an exercise in methodology – an attempt to explore the tax implications of changing a despot's motives from benevolence to self-centered wealth maximization, as set out in the move from cell 1 to cell 2. In the case of cell 1, the benevolent despot is an abstraction – an analytical device put in place to implement the policies designed by economists. At the level of such a fictional and omniscient *deus ex machina*, so beloved and relied upon by orthodox public finance economists, rent seeking simply does not have any role to play. It is therefore perhaps not surprising that if *The Power to Tax* was conceived as a methodological comparison of symmetric institutional settings save for a change in motivational assumptions, rent seeking would not feature in such a comparison.

As indicated above, however, Buchanan and Brennan do allow for the possibility of such in their account of Leviathan, which means that, on grounds of comparative institutional analysis, the possibility that real human beings could compete with each other to

---

16 For an analysis of optimal tax rate when there is more than one distortion, see Brooks and Heijdra (1987) who offer an extension of Lee's (1985 [1988]) paper.

be the benevolent despot ought to be accommodated in that notion of government too. The problem here is that the public choice theory and analysis of benevolent individuals competing to be such an entity is largely non-existent.[17] Perhaps public choice economists prejudge the implausibility of such a contest on the basis of a lack of contestants – but surely that is something that needs to be argued rather than simply left as an implicit assumption.

With the interesting tangent on despots and rent seeking broached, I return to exploring how the rent-seeking insight challenges other elements of orthodox public economics.

13.4.5 The Highs and Lows of User Charges Upended

Governments can fund their operations through user charges when excludability is possible.[18] Conventional efficiency analysis maintains that individual users should face a relatively higher user charge in periods of peak demand. In Figure 13.5, for example, in which the off-peak and peak-demand curves are represented by P_L and P_H and the marginal cost of use is represented by C', efficiency requires the off-peak and peak prices should be T_L^C and T_H^C. Note that in Lee and Wilson's (1990, p. 498) model the

> [marginal] cost associated with different levels of use is given by [C'] . . . [and] [f]or analytical convenience it is assumed that the variable portion of the cost of usage results from congestion and therefore does not reduce the net revenue raised by user charges on the facility . . . [T]here is no rent-seeking over the revenue that goes to cover the explicit expense of the facility, which is assumed to consist only of the fixed costs $K\,[< P(X)X]$.

Lee and Wilson (1990) show[19] that in the presence of rent seeking over the revenue raised from the user charges, such a conventional set of relative charges is inefficient: they demonstrate the counterintuitive possibility that the off-peak charge should be relatively larger than the peak-demand charge![20]

Using the geometrical techniques outlined in Subsection 13.4.2, the marginal costs of rent seeking over the funds from the user charges imposed in the off-peak and peak periods can be constructed for the case where $\beta = 0.5$ and are represented as $(0.5)MTR_L$ and $(0.5)MTR_L$. In turn, the net marginal social benefits from reducing the over-use of the facility in the off-peak and peak periods can be constructed and are represented as $P_L - C'$ and $P_H - C'$.

In the presence of rent seeking, the optimal levels of use in the off-peak and peak-demand periods occur at the intersection of the net marginal benefit and marginal costs of rent-seeking curves, namely X_L^* and X_H^*. From these levels, a set of vertical dashed lines are constructed and the optimal user charges in the presence of rent seeking can be read

[17] See Wintrobe (1998,pp. 95–101) for a fledgling analysis of timocracy, the term he has coined for a regime of benevolent leaders.

[18] See Hillman (2009, pp. 185–95) for a discussion of user charges.

[19] Figure 13.5 is based on Lee and Wilson's (1990) figure 3. As in the case of the pollution tax, I opt to represent the marginal cost of rent seeking in a two-panel diagram rather than the one-panel approach followed by Lee and Wilson.

[20] Singh (1992) considers the properties the underlying utility function should possess if Lee and Wilson's counterintuitive argument is to hold.

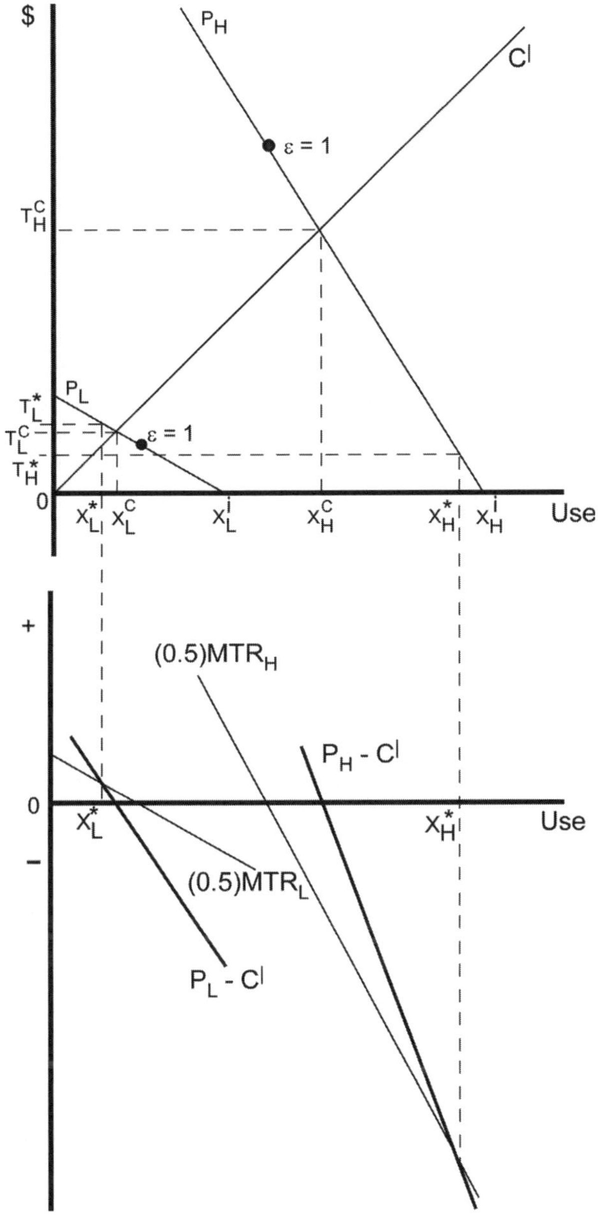

Figure 13.5 Peak and off-peak charges

off the upper panel by locating where these dashed lines intersect the demand curves. In the case at hand, the optimal charges in the off-peak and peak-demand periods are T_L^* and T_H^*. Manifestly, the optimal off-peak charge is relatively larger than the peak-demand charge.

Lee and Wilson (1990, pp. 501–2) are quick to issue a proviso that there is no necessary reason why the strikingly different result should always hold, admitting that the diagram was constructed to offer the surprising result that rent seeking can upend cherished intuitions. Lee and Wilson (1990, 502) consider whether the inclusion of the capacity margin will substantially alter their argument and conjecture that it would not substantially do so.

13.4.6 Tariff Revenue

As indicated, in his original 1967 paper, Tullock refers to tariff revenue. From the perspective of government revenue, tariff revenue is just revenue from an indirect tax. In a novel application of international trade theory, Robert Feenstra and Jagdish Bhagwati (1982) explain that the tariff revenue can be used to compensate losers from liberalization of international trade. Arye Hillman (1988) proposed that if the beneficiaries of the tariff revenue know in advance that any revenue from a tariff will be of benefit to them, then the tariff revenue is not 'compensation' but a further rent to be sought by protectionist interests beyond the increases in income that protectionist policies provide.[21]

13.4.7 Public Debt

The issuing of public debt is another method of financing government programs. Public debt has the principal feature of reducing current rates and increasing future rates. There is an extensive public choice literature on public debt: Brennan and Buchanan (1980, chapter 5), for example, explore a Leviathan government's power to borrow and Buchanan from 1958 to late in his career[22] explored public debt in a wide-ranging set of papers. Despite the extensive treatment of the political economy of public debt there is no extant public choice literature that deals with rent seeking over say the inter-temporal pattern of tax rates.

In Brennan and Buchanan's model of Leviathan government once Leviathan has assumed power there is no role for rent seeking – Leviathan sets tax rates without regard to any pressure groups or lobbying by factions within Leviathan's bureaucratic structure.[23]

In orthodox public choice where the median voter reigns supreme, rationally ignorant individuals might vote in favor of shifting taxes to future generations. Voting from the perspective of the individual voter is an instrumentally insignificant activity. In such a setting, waste can result from the policies chosen collectively but due to its low-cost nature voting itself will not be a significant factor in dissipating the collectivity's social surplus.

If the contest over the inter-temporal pattern of tax rates is to be a significant part of any rent-seeking account of public debt, then future research will need to supplement the Leviathan model with an analysis of Leviathan's supply of regulatory power and/or augment the expressive account of politics with an explicit model of pressure group politics.

---

21 A similar point, in the context of tax compensation schemes, was made by Richard McKenzie (1986).

22 See Brennan et al. (2000) for a collection of some of his papers on public debt.

23 Wintrobe (1998, chapter 7) does consider rent seeking within a dictator's power base but does not extend the discussion to its implications for orthodox tax theory.

13.5 MEASUREMENT OF THE SOCIAL LOSS FROM RENT SEEKING FOR GOVERNMENT REVENUE

The models pinpoint that much of the force of the rent-seeking analysis depends on the extent of the waste. Little headway, however, has been made on measuring the extent of rent seeking in the context of public finances. Eliakim Katz and Jacob Rosenberg (1989), for example, realize that government revenue is contestable and provide empirical estimates of the extent of rent seeking at the margin based on the assumption that changes in the budget mix of a country are solely the consequence of rent seeking.[24] In the context of a formal model of growth, Hyun Park, Apostolis Philippopoulos and Vanghelis Vassilatoss (2005) provide a general equilibrium model of 'rent seeking from state coffers' and use the model to estimate for 108 countries that larger public sectors are associated with their measure of rent seeking. Neither of the papers provides a satisfactory estimate of the extent of rent seeking over government revenues. The Katz and Rosenberg measure assumes that voting is epiphenomenal – plays no role in changes in a country's budget mix. The assumption is under-argued. The Park et al. paper associates rent seeking with government corruption and thereby ignores the perfectly legal role of mass media campaigns and their potential rent-seeking impact on public policies.

13.6 WHAT CAN BE DONE ABOUT RENT SEEKING?

It is not hard to see why rent seeking creates problems for the justification of a case for government intervention. Indeed, one might think that if all government revenue were wasted, then there would be no efficiency case for taxation. The situation is not so clear-cut. There can still be an efficiency case for government taxation, albeit limited relative to a non-rent-seeking setting, if the degree of market failure exceeds the degree of government failure.[25] The waste from rent-seeking activity increases the marginal cost of provision, and thereby limits the efficient level of government activities to those activities that have a higher aggregate willingness to pay. If the market fails completely, then the limited public provision can still represent a social improvement.

The efficiency case of corrective taxation is complex too. If the value of β is 1 in Figure 13.6 – that all the tax revenue is wasted through rent-seeking activity – then the marginal cost of rent seeking from reducing the level of the externality generating activity

---

[24] The initial Katz and Rosenberg (1989) paper resulted in a protracted and largely inconclusive debate in *Public Choice*. See Allard (1995), Scully (1991, 1994) and Schnytzer (1994) for various critiques and Katz and Rosenberg (1994a, 1994b) for their counterarguments.

[25] The analysis of the efficient provision of a public good is more complicated than just shifting to the left the conventional representation of the marginal cost of public funds by the shadow price of rent-seeking costs. Nava Kahana and Doron Klunover (2014) show that the efficiency losses from the excess burden of taxation and from rent seeking are interdependent as a result of an individual's time allocation between work and rent-seeking activity. The conventional measure of the marginal cost of public funds therefore needs to be augmented by the cost of rent seeking and the additional excess burden arising from the interdependency between work and rent-seeking effort. Kahana and Klunover do not provide, however, any measure of how large is the additional excess burden induced by rent seeking.

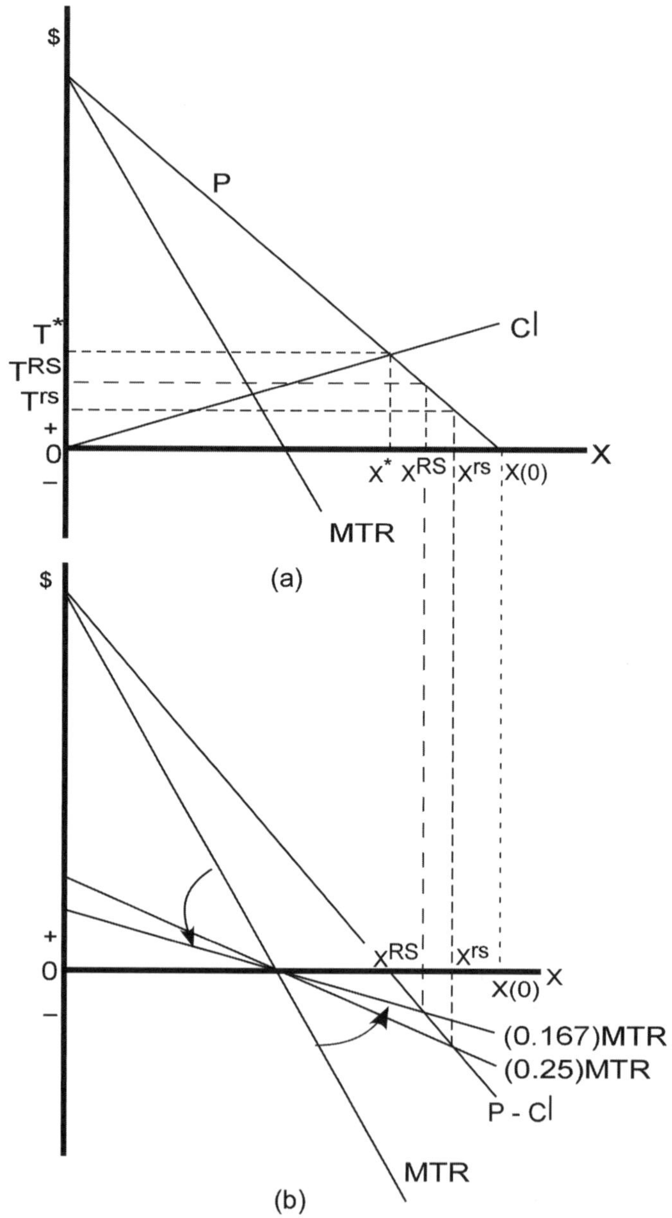

Figure 13.6 Effect of reducing rent seeking

by introducing a pollution tax exceeds the net marginal benefit from reducing the negative externality. In such a case the efficient pollution tax rate is zero.[26] The assumption that β

[26] See Lee and Wilson (1991, p. 371) for a discussion of the point in terms of user charges.

equals 1 does not always result, however, in a case for no tax. Reconsider in Figure 13.4 panels (c) and (d). When β equals 1, the net benefit curve, $P - C^{\|}$, cuts the marginal cost of the rent-seeking curve, *MTR*, from below when the level of the externality generating activity is zero. Here is an efficiency case for a prohibitive pollution tax.

What does remain clear is that if the level of rent seeking can be reduced, then an efficiency gain may be achieved. If β falls from 0.25 to 0.167, then the β*MTR* curve in Figure 13.6 pivots anti-clockwise around the mid-point and the socially preferred level of *X* increases.

There are two sources of the efficiency gain. First, there is a direct gain from the reduction in the wasteful rent-seeking expenditure. Second, there would be an indirect gain resulting from the now permissible further reduction in the extent of excessive levels of pollution, that is, $X^{RS} < X^{rs}$. The issue is: what policies can be put in place to reduce the extent of rent seeking over public revenue?

13.6.1 Taxation of Rent-seeking Activities

Amihai Glazer and Kai Konrad (1999) propose that rent seeking can be reduced by taxing rent-seeking activities. They devote much effort to setting out the mathematical elegance of their proposition but offer little attention to operational issues. In their conclusion, they acknowledge that rent-seeking activities are 'difficult to tax when a firm makes it appear like productive activity' (Glazer and Konrad 1999, p. 70). That way of putting the problem belies the inherent difficulties of taxing rent seeking. As Buchanan (1980 [2008]) argued, rent seeking and profit seeking are indistinguishable *ex ante* and can be discerned only *ex post* on the basis of whether the activity has been negative or positive sum. Admittedly, it is not impossible to form an estimate of whether an activity is rent seeking or profit seeking. Paul Milgrom and John Roberts (1988) provide a plausible account of how influence activities – seemingly just another name coined for rent-seeking activities – can be discerned *ex ante* and reduced in private organizations. The plausibility of their account, however, relies on understanding that influence activities that are part of some redistribution game do not play a productive role in the organization. The difficulty with Glazer and Konrad's analysis is that we do not understand the role of such activities in economy-wide production functions. Lawyers,[27] for example, are sometimes seen as lobbyists for special interest groups, but it is far from clear that efficiency would be promoted by taxing lawyers at a relatively higher rate than other occupations that are prejudged to play little role in distributional struggles. In politics, where rational ignorance reigns, the activity of lawyers representing interest groups can serve the social role of providing information to representative politicians. In private market settings with positive transactions costs and where trustworthiness can be a problem, lawyers serve the useful role of drafting contracts that promote exchange.[28]

---

[27] See Laband and Sophocleus (1988) for an exploration of the hypothesis that the number of lawyers is associated positively with greater rent seeking.

[28] Laband and Sophocleus (1988) attempt to control for the productive role of lawyers but admit their analysis is exploratory.

13.6.2 Earmarking

In an interesting paper, Lee and Tollison (1991) explore the issue of whether tax earmarking can reduce wasteful rent-seeking activity. Although the argument is developed over a series of formal equations and diagrams, the essential policy aspect of their argument can be gleaned from Figure 13.7, which is an amalgam of a modified version of panel (a) of Figure 13.2 and a combination of several of their other diagrams. I have added the convex total excess burden, *EB*, which increases, of course, at an increasing rate with increases in the tax rate.

One of the principal changes to Figure 13.2(a) is that Lee and Tollison assume the interest group derives utility from the taxation of the activity. As a case in point, assume the interest group is a collection of medical practitioners and the taxed activity is cigarette smoking. Initially imagine that none of the tax revenue is earmarked to expenditure of health-improving activities. The interest group maximizes its utility by lobbying for a tax rate higher than that proposed by politicians in the absence of the interest group. As before, the cost of lobbying is represented by $C(T - T_0)$. The interest group maximizes utility at point *N*. The preferred tax rate is $T^*(0)$ and level of rent-seeking costs is represented by the line segment $T^*(0)N$. The excess burden from the tax is represented by $T^*(0)A$. The total revenue from the tax is represented by $T^*(0)K$.

Now let the proportion of tax revenues earmarked to the interest group's activity be, say, $\alpha = 0.5$. The curve $\alpha R(T)$ is therefore the return to the interest group from changing the tax rate aside from the subjective utility from imposing a tax on the activity. The net return from lobbying for a higher tax rate than T_0 is represented by the curve $\alpha R(T) - C(T - T_0)$. The interest group now maximizes utility at point *E* by lobbying for the tax rate, $T'(0.5)$.

Earmarking appears to be Kaldor-Hicks improving.[29] The interest group is better off and the collectivity is better off – when the interest group's optimal tax rate falls relative to the no earmarking case, total excess burden necessarily declines, here to $T'E$. Total rent-seeking losses decline by the amount represented by *MN*.

The result has some intuitive appeal. If a portion of the tax revenue is earmarked to the interest group, then the interest group needs to take into account that lobbying for an increase in the tax rate may yield psychic benefits but it comes here at a pecuniary cost of a decline in net revenue, that is, $T^*(0)G$ is less than $T'(0.5)E$.

Nevertheless, the analysis is incomplete. It does not allow for rent protection activities nor does it explore how any rent seeking over the non-earmarked revenue would impact on the proposed policy.[30]

---

[29] The diagram cannot be used to derive the optimal earmarking rate. It instead sets out some of the comparative statics of one possibility that could emerge when the earmarking rate is increased.

[30] See Lee (1997) for a rudimentary but suggestive account of the political economy of earmarking that goes beyond the assumption that the outcome is determined by the lobbying of just one interest group.

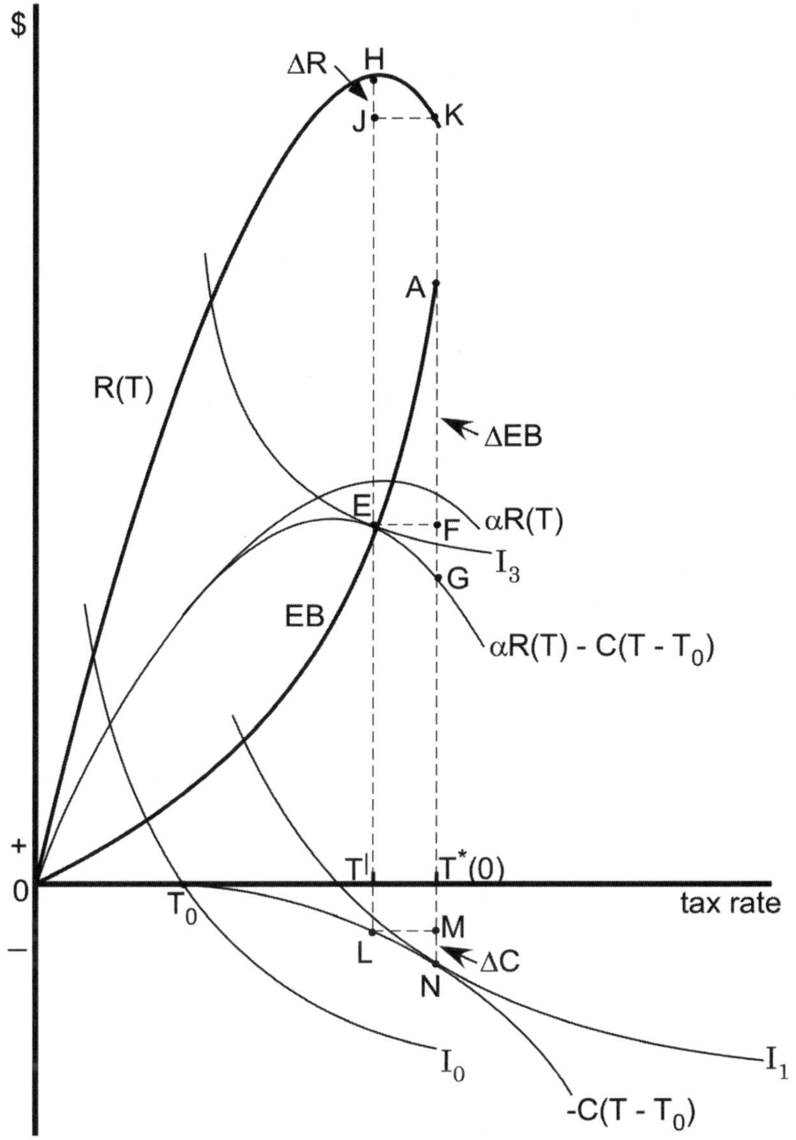

Figure 13.7 Earmarked taxes and an interest group

13.6.3 General versus Specific Taxation

Rent seekers and rent protectors seek differential advantages. Buchanan and Congleton (1998, chapter 8) explore the possibility that such wasteful activities can be reduced if legislation is required to be general rather than allocating differential advantages to one group over another.

13.6.4 Take the Politics Out of Taxation

Most of the analysis of rent seeking and taxation is conducted in terms of the framework described by cell 4 of Table 13.1. Rent-seeking and rent protection activities are a feature of the interest group theory of government. While it is no doubt true that interest groups play a principal role in setting the political agenda, the literature has largely failed to take account of the proposition that interest groups contest policy positions in the shadow of the expressive domain of politics. Voters express their attitudes over the policies lobbied for and against by the interest groups. Consequently, politicians seek to design policies that will appeal to the attitudes of the electorate while appealing to support from various interest groups (see the exposition of the trade-off in Hillman 2009, chapter 2). Just how expressive voting impacts on activities of rent-seeking and rent protection activities is something that needs to be worked out.[31] Nevertheless, it seems reasonable to conjecture that some degree of rent seeking could be reduced if politics were taken out of taxation. Taxes form part of the fiscal constitution and as such should be determined at the constitutional rather than at some in-period stage – the role of politicians, expressively driven voters, interest groups and government bureaucrats in tax reform should be downgraded at the post-constitutional stage, with the prospect of reducing in-period rent seeking.[32]

13.7 CONCLUSIONS

The literature on rent seeking and contesting of government revenue contains many intellectual surprises. In the presence of rent seeking, the domain of taxation principles can represent something of a topsy-turvy world: the Ramsey rule and optimal Pigovian taxes need not hold when tax revenue is wastefully contested. More research is required on estimating the extent of rent seeking over tax revenue.

The political economy models of the tax rate that will eventuate when there is earmarking allow for just one interest group seeking some differential advantage. One line of inquiry would be to examine the tax rate that could emerge when there is a contest between conflicting interest groups and rent seeking over the non-earmarked portion of the tax revenue.

The analysis of the pollution taxes/user charges sidesteps the issue of what rate will emerge and is centered instead on what is the optimal charge when some or all of the revenue is dissipated in a wasteful distributional contest between rent seekers and rent protectors. The analysis largely[33] fails, however, to deal with the supply problem – there is no discussion of why politicians would be motivated or willing to set and maintain the charges and taxes required by the modified optimality conditions. Any analysis of rent seeking and the supply of regulation will have to reckon with the proposition that

---

[31] On expressive voting, see Brennan and Brooks (2013).

[32] See Brennan and Brooks (2010) for a rudimentary appeal to turn over tax reform to independent experts and to take government bureaucrats and politicians significantly out of the drafting process of tax legislation.

[33] See Lee (1997) for some exploratory observations about the rate of taxation that will emerge in the presence of rent seeking.

politicians view taxation and regulation as substitutes[34] – that rent seeking over revenue needs to be modeled in a political economy model in which politicians are designing regulatory/taxation policies to secure the rationally ignorant support of expressive voters and the support of special interest groups seeking particularized policies. Manifestly, despite the voluminous literature on rent seeking, much research remains to be done in the area of rent seeking over public revenue.

REFERENCES

Allard, Richard J. (1995), 'The measurability of budget related rent-seeking', *Public Choice*, **85**(3–4), 389–94.

Brennan, Geoffrey (1997), 'Public choice and taxation: Leviathan after twenty years', in Richard Krever (ed.), *Tax Conversations: A Guide to the Key Issues in the Tax Reform Debate, Essays in Honour of J.G. Head*, London: Kluwer Law International, pp. 87–105.

Brennan, Geoffrey and Michael A. Brooks (2010), 'The Henry tax review: a view from constitutional political economy', in Chris Evans, Richard Krever and Peter Mellor (eds), *Australia's Future Tax System: The Prospects After Henry*, Sydney, NSW: Thomson Reuters (Professional) Australia Ltd, pp. 417–37.

Brennan, G. and Michael Brooks (2013), 'Expressive voting', in M. Reksulak, L. Razzolini and W. Shughart II (eds), *The Elgar Companion to Public Choice*, Cheltenham, UK and Northampton, MA, USA: Edward Elgar Publishing, pp. 111–26.

Brennan, Geoffrey and James M. Buchanan (1980), *The Power to Tax: Analytical Foundations of a Fiscal Constitution*, Cambridge: Cambridge University Press.

Brennan, Geoffrey and Hartmut Kliemt (2008), 'Regulation and revenue', *Constitutional Political Economy*, **19**(3), 249–60.

Brennan, H. Geoffrey and Robert D. Tollison (1980), 'Rent seeking in academia', in James M. Buchanan, Robert D. Tollison and Gordon Tullock (eds), *Toward a Theory of the Rent-seeking Society*, College Station, TX: Texas A&M Press, pp. 344–56.

Brennan, Geoffrey, Hartmut Kliemt and Robert Tollison (eds) (2000), *The Collected Works of James M. Buchanan*, Vol. 14, *Debt and Taxes*, Indianapolis, IN: Liberty Fund.

Brooks, Michael and Ben J. Heijdra (1987), 'Rent seeking with pollution taxation: an extension', *Southern Economic Journal*, **54**(2), 335–42.

Buchanan, James M. (1958), *Public Principles of Public Debt: A Defense and Restatement*, Homewood, IL: Richard D. Irwin, reprinted in Geoffrey Brennan, Hartmut Kliemt and Robert Tollison (eds) (1999), *The Collected Works of James M. Buchanan*, Vol. 2, Indianapolis, IN: Liberty Fund.

Buchanan, James M. (1967), *Public Finance in Democratic Process: Fiscal Institutions and Individual Choice*, Chapel Hill, NC: University of North Carolina Press.

Buchanan, James M. (1968), *The Demand and Supply of Public Goods*, Chicago, IL: Rand McNally and Co.

Buchanan, James M. (1980), 'Rent seeking and profit seeking', in James M. Buchanan, Robert D. Tollison and Gordon Tullock (eds), *Toward a Theory of the Rent-seeking Society*, College Station, TX: Texas A&M University Press, pp. 3–15, reprinted in Roger D. Congleton, Arye L. Hillman and Kai A. Konrad (eds) (2008), *40 Years of Research on Rent Seeking 1 – The Theory of Rent Seeking*, Heidelberg: Springer, pp. 55–67.

Buchanan, James M. (2003), 'Public choice: politics without romance', *Policy*, **19**(3), 13–18.

Buchanan, James M. and Roger D. Congleton (1998), *Politics by Principle Not Interest: Towards Nondiscriminatory Democracy*, Cambridge: Cambridge University Press.

Congleton, Roger (2004), 'The political economy of Gordon Tullock', *Public Choice*, **121**(1–2), 213–38.

Feenstra, Robert C. and Jagdish N. Bhagwati (1982), 'Tariff seeking and the efficient tariff', in Jagdish N. Bhagwati (ed.), *Import Competition and Response*, Chicago, IL: University of Chicago Press for NBER, pp. 245–58.

Glazer, Amihai and Kai A. Konrad (1999), 'Taxation of rent-seeking activities', *Journal of Public Economics*, **72**(1), 61–72.

Harberger, Arnold C. (1964), 'The measurement of waste', *American Economic Review Papers and Proceedings*, **54**(3), 58–76.

[34] See Brennan and Kliemt (2008) for an exploration of the idea that political agents treat regulation and taxation as substitutes.

Hillman, Arye L. (1988), 'Tariff-revenue transfers to protectionist interests: compensation for reduced protection or supplementary reward for successful lobbying?', *Public Choice*, **58**(2), 169–72.
Hillman, Arye L. (2009), *Public Finance and Public Policy: Responsibilities and Limitations of Government*, 2nd edn, New York: Cambridge University Press.
Hobbes, Thomas (1651), *Leviathan*, reprinted in 1962, New York: Collier Books.
Kahana, Nava and Doron Klunover (2014), 'Rent seeking and the excess burden of taxation', *European Journal of Political Economy*, **35**, 158–67.
Katz, Eliakim and Jacob Rosenberg, (1989), 'Rent-seeking for budgetary allocation: preliminary results for 20 countries', *Public Choice*, **60**(2), 133–44.
Katz, Eliakim and Jacob Rosenberg, (1994a), 'More on measuring budget-related rent seeking: a comment', *Public Choice*, **78**(2), 187–91.
Katz, Eliakim and Jacob Rosenberg (1994b), 'Support in the guise of criticism: extraneous observations and the Katz-Rosenberg measure of rent-seeking', *Public Choice*, **79**(3–4), 363–6.
Laband, David N. and John P. Sophocleus (1988), 'The social cost of rent seeking: first estimates', *Public Choice*, **58**(3), 269–75.
Lee, Dwight R. (1985), 'Rent seeking and its implications for pollution taxation', *Southern Economic Journal*, **51**(3), 731–45, reprinted in Charles Rowley, Robert Tollison and Gordon Tullock (eds) (1988), *The Political Economy of Rent Seeking*, Boston, MA: Kluwer Academic Publishers, pp. 353–70.
Lee, Dwight R. (1997), 'The use and abuse of excise taxes', Background Paper, No. 19, Tax Foundation, Washington, DC.
Lee, Dwight R. and Robert D. Tollison (1985), 'There is no such thing as a free tax', *Finanzarchiv*, **43**(3), 451–3.
Lee, Dwight R. and Robert Tollison (1988), 'Optimal taxation in a rent-seeking environment', in Charles Rowley, Robert Tollison and Gordon Tullock (eds), *The Political Economy of Rent Seeking*, Boston, MA: Kluwer Academic Publishers, pp. 339–50.
Lee, Dwight R. and Robert Tollison (1991), 'Rent seeking and tax earmarking', in Richard E. Wagner (ed.), *Charging for Government*, London: Routledge, pp. 125–40.
Lee, Dwight R. and Paul Wilson (1990), 'Rent seeking and peak-load pricing of public services', *National Tax Journal*, **43**(4), 497–503.
Lee, Dwight R. and Paul Wilson (1991), 'Efficient user charges in a rent-seeking model', *Economic Inquiry*, **29**(2), 367–74.
McKenzie, Richard B. (1986), 'Tax compensation schemes: misleading advice in a rent-seeking society', *Public Choice*, **48**(2), 189–94.
Milgrom, Paul and John Roberts (1988), 'An economic approach to influence activities and organizational responses', *American Journal of Sociology*, **96**(Suppl.), S154–S79.
Park, Hyun, Apostolis Philippopoulos and Vanghelis Vassilatos (2005), 'Choosing the size of the public sector under rent seeking from state coffers', *European Journal of Political Economy*, **21**(4), 830–50.
Ramsey, Frank P. (1927), 'A contribution to the theory of taxation', *Economic Journal*, **37**(145), 47–61.
Schnytzer, Adi (1994), 'Changes in budgetary allocations and international comparisons of the social cost of rent seeking: a critical note', *Public Choice*, **79**(3–4), 357–62.
Scully, Gerald W. (1991), 'Rent seeking in U.S. government budgets, 1900–88', *Public Choice*, **70**(1), 99–106.
Scully, Gerald W. (1994), 'Rent seeking: a trivial or serious problem? A reply', *Public Choice*, **78**(2), 193–6.
Singh, Nirvikar (1992), 'Rent seeking and peak-load pricing of public service: an extension', *National Tax Journal*, **45**(4), 443–5.
Sobel, Russell S. (1997), 'Optimal taxation in a federal system of governments', *Southern Economic Journal*, **64**(2), 468–85.
Tullock, Gordon (1967), 'The welfare costs of tariffs, monopolies, and theft', *Western Economic Journal*, **5**(3), 224–32, reprinted in Roger D. Congleton, Arye L. Hillman and Kai A. Konrad (eds) (2008), *40 Years of Research on Rent Seeking 1 – The Theory of Rent Seeking*, Heidelberg: Springer, pp. 45–53.
Tullock, Gordon (1988), 'Rent seeking and tax reform', *Contemporary Economic Policy*, **6**(4), 37–47.
Wintrobe, Ronald (1998), *The Political Economy of Dictatorship*, New York: Cambridge University Press.

14. Rent seeking and the resource curse

Robert T. Deacon and Ashwin Rode

SUMMARY

Many countries receiving natural resource windfalls have had slow growth, low incomes and weak political institutions, an empirical regularity named the resource curse. Patterns in the data suggest a political link: a curse is most likely for countries that have weak institutions initially and for resources that are spatially concentrated. Rent seeking for a resource prize is a prominent theme in theoretical explanations. There is extensive evidence supporting both the curse and a political transmission channel. Three aspects of this chapter are particularly important for rent seeking: (1) political theories of the resource curse consistently predict over-dissipation, a finding at odds with *ex ante* predictions of rent-seeking rational Nash behavior; (2) variations in pre-windfall political institutions can magnify, moderate or overturn the resource curse; and (3) a resource windfall can alter the quality of political institutions.

14.1 INTRODUCTION

The term 'resource curse' derives from the observation that there are resource-rich countries with low per capita incomes whose populations are politically oppressed. Angola, Chad, Sudan and South Sudan, Nigeria, Venezuela and Iraq, where oil has been involved, and Congo, Sierra Leone and Liberia, where the natural resources have been metals and diamonds, are notable examples of places that are rich in natural resources, but also have been plagued in different degrees by low or negative gross domestic product (GDP) growth, widespread poverty, state failure, civil war, corruption and political oppression. Nigeria is an often-cited prime example: its per capita GDP in 2000 was 30 percent lower than in 1965, despite oil revenues of roughly \$350 billion (1995\$) during the intervening period.[1] Lane and Tornell (1996) note that oil-rich Venezuela's terms of trade improved 13.7 percent per year during 1970–90, while per capita output declined at a rate of 1.4 percent per year. They also point out that Saudi Arabia's real per capita GDP declined between 1970 and 1999. Gylfason (2001, p. 848) claims that per capita gross national product (GNP) in the Organization of the Petroleum Exporting Countries (OPEC) fell 1.3 percent per year during 1965–98, while all lower- and middle-income countries were growing at an average rate of 2.2 percent.

Although there is no shortage of countries that support the resource curse hypothesis, several notable counter-examples do exist. Resource-rich countries such as Norway,

[1] The dollar figure represents oil revenues after payments to foreign companies, as reported by Sala-i-Martin and Subramanian (2003, p. 4). Information on income is from Heston et al. (2002).

Chile, Malaysia and Botswana have largely escaped the unfavorable outcomes described above and have experienced rapid economic growth, suggesting that the resource curse phenomenon is neither universal nor inevitable. Whether resource abundance is a curse or blessing appears to hinge on host country institutions and on the particular resource involved. The notion that having more of any natural resource could be disadvantageous in any circumstance is, however, sufficiently counter-intuitive to merit serious study. Indeed there has been a proliferation of research on the resource curse by economists and other social scientists over the past two decades. This chapter focuses on a specific subset of this research – theoretical and empirical research that brings to bear the idea of rent seeking to explain the resource curse phenomenon.

The idea of rent seeking dates back to Tullock (1967) and there has been a substantial subsequent literature (see, for example, the papers reprinted in Congleton et al. 2008b, 2008c). For surveys and overviews of the concept of rent seeking, see Congleton et al. (2008a), Hillman (2013) and Long (2013). The basic idea of rent seeking is that where a contestable benefit or rent is available, resources including time and initiative will be attracted to the unproductive quest to benefit from the rent. The result is a social efficiency loss because the resources used in rent seeking could have been used productively to add to income. The concept of rent seeking was initially applied to the social loss from monopolies, tariffs and discretionary public spending. In these cases, rents are politically created. In the case of natural resources, nature has created the rent that is wastefully contested when property rights are not defined or respected. Rather than undertaking productive activity, groups direct their attention to unproductively contesting natural resource wealth. The outcome in limiting cases has been ongoing civil war.

Anecdotal evidence from Venezuela and Nigeria supports the notion that resource wealth can give rise to rent seeking by political elites. The oil price jump of 1979–81 induced the government of Venezuela to increase public spending on infrastructure and industrial policy, which mainly benefitted political elites; the increase in public spending was so dramatic that Venezuela ran a current account deficit despite the large, favorable shift in its terms of trade (Lane and Tornell 1996, p. 216). In Nigeria, which is rich in oil, income became highly concentrated during the oil price run-up between 1970 and early 2000s. By 2000, the share of income controlled by the richest 2 percent of the population equaled that of the poorest 55 percent; in 1970, the richest 2 percent earned as much as the poorest 17 percent. The fraction of Nigerians who subsist on $1 per day or less rose from 26 percent to 70 percent over the same period (van der Ploeg 2011, pp. 367–8). By contrast, political institutions that have been quite effective in discouraging rent-seeking activity explain the more favorable outcomes in resource-rich countries such as Norway, Chile, Malaysia and Botswana.

Several observers go further and argue that natural resource wealth can change a country's political institutions, for example, by altering property rights, democracy, political stability or amenability to rent seeking. This idea has been incorporated into theories of the resource curse and is also consistent with case-study evidence. Karl (1997) reviewed the history of six resource-rich countries and found that resource wealth and resource rent windfalls can alter the political culture in the host country, particularly if its institutions are precarious at the outset. When wealth is concentrated in minerals and the resulting rents are directed to state coffers, she finds that a government's decision-making framework and the locus of authority can be shifted. Control over mineral rents becomes a basis for political power and institutions evolve to perpetuate existing patterns of control. European colonists who discovered and first exploited mineral resources found it possible to extract mineral rents by controlling only specific mining and export sites, without extending civil authority and the rule of law to the countryside (Karl 1997, pp. 60–61). This was possible because mineral resources tend to be concentrated in space, rather than widely dispersed. A detailed analysis of Venezuela indicates that nationalization, which shifted resource rents to the state, promoted a rent-seeking culture and a patron-client system of governance (Karl 1997). She also notes that the enhanced payoffs to rent seeking enticed individuals with entrepreneurial talent, who otherwise might have been the creators of wealth and future prosperity, to direct their talents to rent seeking. Ross (2001) proposes that a hardwood timber price boom in Southeast Asia impaired governance in similar ways in the Philippines, in Indonesia and in the Malay states of Sarawak and Sabah. Political elites in all three areas altered institutions of governance to capture greater control of timber rents once timber harvesting came to dominate their economies. As political elites channeled rents to supporters, corruption increased and political power became more concentrated.

With this description of the resource curse and its political dimensions as background, the remainder of this chapter reviews research at the intersection of rent seeking and the resource curse. Section 14.2 describes the basic idea of rent seeking and explains why and how rent seeking is central to the resource curse literature; Section 14.3 reviews theoretical models that link rent-seeking behavior to the resource curse; Section 14.4 focuses on purely empirical research on the same topic; Section 14.5 presents conclusions and directions for future research.

14.2 AN OVERVIEW OF RENT SEEKING AND ITS CONNECTION TO THE RESOURCE CURSE

14.2.1 The Efficiency Loss Due to Rent Seeking

Anne Krueger (1974 [2008]) coined the term 'rent seeking' to refer to behavior that had been described by Tullock (1967 [2008]), whereby resources are unproductively used to contest available benefits rather than used productively. The generic idea is displayed in the case of a monopoly depicted in Figure 14.1.[2] The horizontal axis measures the quantity sold of a particular good, while the vertical axis measures price. Consider a given demand curve, D. Under perfect competition, Q^* units of the good will be sold at price P^*. However, if a monopoly were established, it would sell Q^M units of the good at price P^M. According to traditional economic theory, the net social loss (that is, deadweight loss) from the monopoly is the area of the shaded triangle, often referred to as the Harberger triangle (Harberger 1954). This is the consumer surplus that would have been obtained from the purchase of units between Q^M and Q^*, which are neither purchased nor produced under monopoly. On the other hand, the area of the dotted rectangle (that is, monopoly rents) was traditionally regarded as a transfer of surplus from consumers to the monopolist. Because these parties are members of the same society, there is no net social loss involved in this transfer.

---

2 This standard example and the ensuing discussion are derived from Tullock (1987).

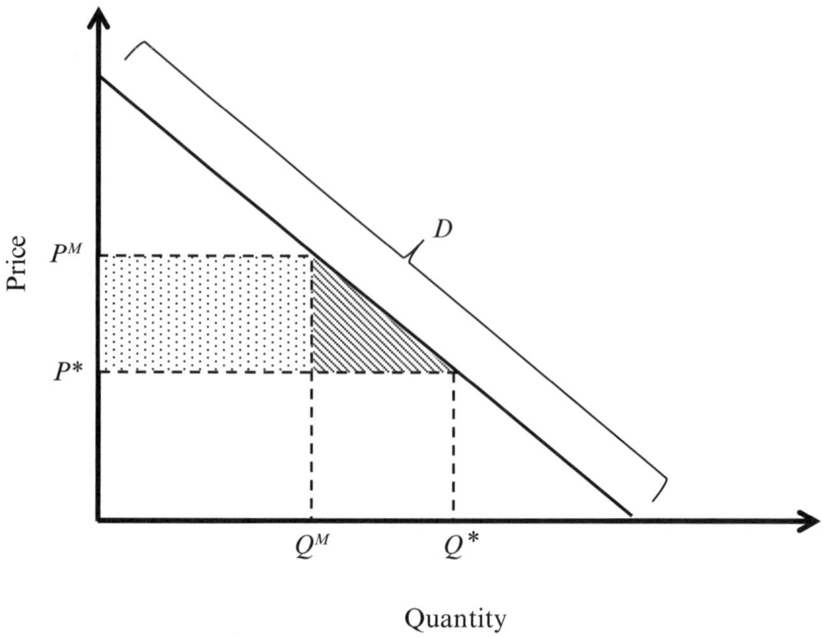

Figure 14.1 *Net social losses from a monopoly*

The rent-seeking idea adds the social loss from contesting the monopoly profits.[3] Firms and individuals could enter the industry and competitively dissipate the monopoly profits by adding to supply, resulting in the socially beneficial competitive outcome, but if entry is impeded and monopoly profits are sustained, resources may be used to displace the incumbent monopolist and secure the monopoly profits. Buchanan (1980 [2008]) distinguished between profit seeking when resources are used to compete with the monopolist and rent seeking when resources are used to displace the monopolist. The first type of competition is socially beneficial, the second is not.[4]

The rent-seeking literature has focused on the extent of rent dissipation in rent-seeking contests, that is, the relation between the value of resources used by rent seekers in contesting a rent and the value of the rent. Because of the efficiency loss from rent seeking, the social loss from monopoly extends beyond the Harberger triangle of traditional economic theory to include the dotted rectangle in Figure 14.1. By a similar argument, with rent seeking present, the social losses due to subsidies, tariffs and other government

---

[3] Monopoly profits of course endure over time. Figure 14.1 is static in describing a point in time. Rent-seeking competition will be for the present value of monopoly profits, discounted by the likelihood that the successful rent seeker will need to contest the monopoly profits again in the future. See Aidt and Hillman (2008).

[4] Contests by groups rather than individuals are also a theme of the rent-seeking literature (see Nitzan 1991; Katz and Tokatlidu 1996 [2008]); in general it is of course groups and not individuals that compete for rent-seeking prizes. If a group is assumed to behave as a single decision-making agent, the results that apply to individuals also extend to groups.

programs exceed the Harberger triangle as well. The general idea of socially unproductive competition for available benefits also extends to natural resource rents.

Because rent seeking is usually not readily observable, models of rent seeking infer rent dissipation and thereby social loss from assumptions about the conditions under which rent seeking takes place. A number of influences, including the nature of the contest-success function, determine the extent of rent dissipation and whether complete dissipation takes place.[5]

The rent-seeking models specify conditions under which complete dissipation occurs based on rational Nash behavior and show that over-dissipation (that is, when the value of resources used in contesting a rent exceeds the value of the rent) is inconsistent with rational Nash behavior. Over-dissipation can, however, occur *ex post* when rent seekers' behavior is described by mixed strategies.[6] Over-dissipation can also occur when behavioral elements are introduced.[7]

The resource curse literature proposes that the over-dissipation outcome can result through general equilibrium effects involving institutional deterioration. A distinguishing aspect of rent-seeking models of the resource curse is a focused concern with political institutions, which provide a set of constraints that may or may not be effective in preventing dissipation of resource rents. At the same time, a resource windfall can itself impair the effectiveness of institutions.

In the next subsection, we provide a brief history of the resource curse literature and examine why it has moved toward political-economy explanations. We then tighten the focus to examine how the resource curse literature has adopted the idea of rent seeking in particular.

14.2.2 Political Economy and the Resource Curse

Research on the resource curse can be broadly divided into two categories based on the type of causal explanations advocated. One category offers market-based explanations, while the other emphasizes political-economy aspects.

Market-based explanations often revolve around a crowding-out phenomenon,

---

5 For a list of influences, see Hillman (2013). Institutions in particular matter in determining how a rent is contested and assigned (Congleton 1980 [2008]). The institutions can be reflected in the rent-seeking contest-success function, which can be a lottery as in Tullock (1980 [2008]) or the highest bidder can win (an all-pay auction) as in Hillman and Samet (1987 [2008]). Hillman and Katz (1984 [2008]) prove complete dissipation for a general contest-success function for risk-neutral rent seekers. In the all-pay auction, Hillman and Samet (1987 [2008]) show that rent dissipation is complete for any number of contenders (two or more).

6 For example, in Hillman and Samet (1987 [2008]), the Nash equilibrium in mixed strategies for two contenders is a drawing from the uniform distribution over the range of the common value of the prize and hence the expected rent-seeking outlay is half the value of the prize for each contender. The sum of the actual *ex post* drawing from the uniform distribution may however exceed the value of the prize. See also Higgins et al. (1985 [2008]).

7 For example, on bounded rationality, see Anderson et al. (1998), on spite, see Hehenkamp et al. (2004 [2008]) and on behavioral influences on contest effort, see Baharad and Nitzan (2008). Sheremeta (2013) provides a comprehensive review of behavioral explanations for overbidding relative to Nash predictions and reviews experimental evidence. See Dechenaux et al. (2012) for a survey of the broader experimental literature on contests, all-pay auctions and tournaments.

whereby a natural resource boom diverts economic activity in ways that are counter-productive.[8] A leading example is the 'Dutch disease' theory formulated to explain the poor economic performance of the Netherlands following the discovery of North Sea oil. This theory postulates that a natural resource boom causes a country's exchange rate to appreciate, making its manufacturing exports less competitive. Dutch disease adherents see manufacturing exports as the engine of growth, while resource exports are not, leading them to conclude that a resource boom that crowds out manufacturing will retard growth. Sachs and Warner (1997, 2001) provided some of the earliest cross-country, cross-sectional empirical evidence that natural resource abundance is associated with lower economic growth. They emphasized the 'Dutch disease' as an explanation.[9] According to Bulte et al. (2005), however, terms of trade effects generally are not significant in economic growth regressions and, overall, there is little empirical support for the Dutch disease argument.[10] The same authors point to an abundance of exceptions to the resource curse and emphasize that the growth experiences of resource-rich countries are highly varied.

These varied experiences and exceptions have motivated researchers to examine the resource curse phenomenon through the lens of political economy. Two empirical regularities have been particularly important in this regard. First, resource abundance or a resource boom tends to generate a resource curse in countries with weak pre-boom institutions, but not in countries where governance and the rule of law are strong initially.[11] Second, a curse is more likely to be associated with resources found in dense concentrations, while other resources seem largely immune.[12] Neither of these regularities is consistent with market-based explanations for the resource curse; they are consistent with theories of how resource extraction and political systems interact, however.

---

[8] For a survey of market-based explanations, see Frankel (2010) and van der Ploeg (2011).

[9] Using a cross-section of countries, Sachs and Warner related growth in per capita income to the importance of primary products in a country's exports, which they interpreted as natural resource abundance, controlling for initial income, openness to trade and the investment to GDP ratio. The coefficient on resource abundance was negative and substantial – seemingly indicating a natural resource curse. Increasing the primary products export share by one standard deviation caused the predicted growth rate to fall by 0.6 to 1.5 percentage points. The use by Sachs and Warner of a country's primary products export share as a measure of natural resource abundance has been criticized on several grounds. Primary products include food, agricultural goods, fuels and minerals, so the goods are heterogeneous. Furthermore, export share is a flow variable, while abundance is a stock variable. Perhaps the most significant criticism is that export share is clearly determined by economic behavior and is therefore endogenous.

[10] Roughly a decade before Sachs-Warner's analysis, Gelb et al. (1988) noted that the poor performance of oil-rich countries after 1970 cannot be explained by conventional economic arguments and concluded that faulty government decision-making was a significant factor.

[11] Sala-i-Martin and Subramanian (2003) were among the first to look for a political link in the connection between resource abundance and reduced economic growth. Adopting the Sachs-Warner cross-sectional empirical strategy, they found that while resource abundance is linked to slow economic growth, the entire effect operates through an institutional channel, operationalized by a rule of law index. If the institutional effect is controlled for, resource abundance has no further direct effect on economic growth.

[12] Leite and Weidmann (1999), Isham et al. (2003) and Boschini et al. (2007) all report this result.

We now turn our attention to the role of rent-seeking behavior in political-economy theories of the resource curse.

14.2.3 The Rent-seeking Context of the Resource Curse

The resource curse is related to rent dissipation through the value of productive inputs drawn into contesting natural resources.[13] In the event of under-dissipation of resource rents, there remain benefits from the natural resources. With complete dissipation, all benefits from natural resources are exactly offset by the resources used to contest the natural resources. There is a true curse if over-dissipation occurs because in that case the social loss due to the existence of the natural resources exceeds the value of the natural resources.[14] The resource curse thus departs from the intuition that greater natural resource wealth can only benefit a society.[15]

As noted previously, models of the resource curse often start from a general equilibrium framework and emphasize questions of economic growth – and routinely predict more than full dissipation of resource rents in equilibrium. The exact mechanism involved varies across models. In the voracity model, government's coercive power is used solely to transfer wealth from the private sector to powerful interests (Lane and Tornell 1996; Tornell and Lane 1999). In the event of a resource price boom or new discovery, a country could experience a more than proportional increase in such transfers, thereby slowing down growth. Another class of models invokes the mechanism of diverted entrepreneurship. A resource windfall becomes a curse by diverting entrepreneurial talent away from increasing returns-to-scale industries and toward non-productive rent seeking (Torvik 2002; Mehlum et al. 2006 [2008]). A model by Hodler (2006) uses a contest function that resembles those of the mainstream rent-seeking literature.[16] More than full dissipation occurs in this model due to a spillover effect whereby property rights are more broadly eroded as a consequence of rent seeking for resource wealth.

The role of political institutions is central to all rent-seeking models of the resource

---

[13] Rent-seeking models are usually specified as rent seekers seeking a rent that is indivisibly assigned to the winner of the rent-seeking contest. Hence, for example, in the monopoly rent case described in Figure 14.1, one successful rent seeker is assumed to capture the entire monopoly rent. Long and Vousden (1987 [2008]) have however described contests in which the prizes are shares of an available rent. The context described by Long and Vousden is applicable to natural resource rents as prizes in rent-seeking contests because the natural resource rents are a common pool to which different groups can establish claims to shares of the rent.

[14] This is all in present value terms. See Aidt and Hillman (2008) for the analogous case of monopoly rents that persist over time.

[15] A qualification is that shadow prices of resources be positive. It has never been demonstrated empirically that this is not the case. Negative shadow prices allow welfare-reducing or 'immiserizing growth.' See Bhagwati (1958).

[16] Contest functions are also used in the model of van der Ploeg and Rohner (2010), which is a model of violent conflict fueled by natural resource wealth. The idea that natural resource wealth can lead to armed conflict constitutes a different kind of resource curse that is exemplified in the experiences of countries such as Angola, Nigeria, Sierra Leone and the Democratic Republic of the Congo (formerly Zaire). We do not cover research on natural resources and armed conflict in this chapter. Interested readers are referred to the survey by Ross (2006) as well as key empirical contributions by Collier and Hoeffler (1998, 2004).

curse. At the very least, the predictions of these models vary depending on how effective political institutions are at preventing rent-seeking behavior. Moreover, institutions are themselves endogenous in many of the models and can be negatively affected by a resource windfall. In addition to the models of Mehlum et al. (2006 [2008]) and Hodler (2006), just described, the following theoretical and empirical contributions all treat institutions as endogenous: Aslaksen and Torvik (2006), Caselli and Michaels (2009), Tsui (2011) and Vicente (2010). This endogeneity of institutions is not present in mainstream rent-seeking models.

In some resource curse contributions, details of government institutions become part of the model and generate theoretical predictions and testable hypotheses. Aslaksen and Torvik (2006) model a democratic government that can descend into anarchy if the prospect of capturing a resource prize is sufficiently attractive to cause one of the political contestants to reject the outcome of an election. Robinson et al. (2006) portray a country with formally democratic institutions in which an incumbent can, nevertheless, sway the outcome of an election by offering public employment benefits to prospective voters. In this treatment, the advent of a resource windfall gives the incumbent both an added incentive and the fiscal means to provide such benefits.

In the next section, we review papers that use rent-seeking theory to explain the resource curse; some of these papers include empirical tests of theoretical predictions. Purely empirical papers on rent seeking and the resource curse are taken up in Section 14.4.

14.3 THEORETICAL MODELS OF RENT SEEKING AND THE RESOURCE CURSE

14.3.1 Voracity, Growth and the Resource Curse

The 'voracity' model describes a situation in which government's coercive power is used solely to transfer wealth from the private sector to powerful interests, possibly by taxation, theft, bribe demands, forced participation, nationalization or expropriation (Lane and Tornell 1996; Tornell and Lane 1999). Government does not appear as a distinct entity in this model, but functions implicitly as a conduit for such transfers. Private sector capital is a common pool in this world and competition for it is constrained only by the transfers of other groups. In a model with a single asset the consequences of such transfers are intuitive: the incentive to accumulate capital is diminished, lowering the economy's growth rate and present value utility. If there were only a single group involved in appropriation, it would internalize the disincentive effect of wealth transfers, enabling the first-best outcome to be achieved. With several groups vying to capture private sector capital, growth is slowed and welfare diminishes, which is consistent with intuition about common pools.

Introducing a second asset that is less productive but functions as a secure wealth haven alters these results dramatically. In a low-income country context, which implicitly is the model's intended application, the wealth haven could be capital in the 'informal' economy, a sector that tax authorities and powerful interests cannot reach. Alternatively, it could be the capital market in a foreign country with rule-of-law institutions that protect assets from arbitrary appropriation. We use the terms 'formal' and 'informal' to indicate sectors in which capital is vulnerable as opposed to invulnerable to transfers. Introducing the informal sector leads to the prediction that capital will flow from the formal to the informal sector, which slows the economy's growth rate.

The counterpart to a resource windfall in this model is an increase in the return to formal sector capital, which could arise from enhanced productivity or a higher output price. Counter-intuitively, a positive shock to formal capital's return causes elite groups to boost the theft of formal capital by an amount that exceeds the productivity gain, so the formal sector capital stock actually shrinks. This is the 'voracity effect' in the terminology of Tornell and Lane (1999). Its strength depends on the number of competing groups in a surprising way. With a small number of groups, each knows that it will receive back a relatively large fraction of any capital transferred from the formal sector stock. With this knowledge, formal sector capital owners are willing to keep capital in the formal sector even if the amount transferred to the informal sector exceeds that which would be required to equalize gross-of-transfer rates of return.

Implications for the resource curse follow from the predicted negative growth response to an increase in productivity. If natural resource wealth is the main form of formal capital, a resource price boom or a new discovery should raise the formal sector's rate of return. The voracity theory predicts that such a windfall will cause capital to flow to the less productive sector, slowing growth. The voracity effect will not operate, however, if there are institutional barriers that prevent rent seeking, since it is rent seeking, particularly theft of formal capital, which causes capital to flow to the less productive sector. We note here that 'rent seeking' is not necessarily the contestable quest for rents on which the rent-seeking models base social losses but refers to the appropriative transfers that take place or rent extraction. According to the voracity theory, a resource productivity windfall will increase growth and welfare if institutional barriers prevent the rent extraction through appropriative transfers. This helps to explain why economic performance following the oil boom of the 1970s was so different in, for example, Norway and Nigeria. It also argues for empirical specifications that allow for different effects of resource windfalls in different institutional contexts.

Informal tests largely bear out the model's key predictions. Tornell and Lane (1999) looked at shifts in government transfers and changes in economic growth in three countries with weak institutions – Mexico, Venezuela and Nigeria – following the oil price shocks of the 1970s and early 1980s. In each country, government transfers as a share of GDP more than doubled between 1970 and the early 1980s; assuming these transfers represent payments to powerful interests, this is consistent with predictions from the voracity model.[17] Over the same period, GDP growth rates in Nigeria and Venezuela were negative and, though positive in Mexico, were well below predicted values from a cross-country growth regression.

More detailed empirical analysis is reported in Lane and Tornell (1996), where the focus is on the institutional conditions required for the voracity effect to operate. The model argues that the presence of powerful rent-seeking groups and an absence of

---

[17] In Mexico the government's share of GDP rose by more than 150 percent between 1970 and the oil price peak of the early 1980s.

institutional restraints on transfers are key enabling conditions. To represent this, a measure of industrial concentration is formed to proxy concentrated political power and interacted with a governance indicator that represents weak institutional barriers.[18] They use positive terms of trade shocks to represent windfalls and rely on a cross-country cross-sectional dataset for testing. In a specification that controls for initial income, education and continent fixed effects, they find that positive terms of trade shocks yield significant improvements in economic growth and investment in non-vulnerable countries, but not in voracity-vulnerable countries. Further, investment responds negatively to positive terms of trade shocks in voracity-vulnerable countries, but this evidence is less robust.

Arezki and Brückner (2010) extended this analysis by examining panel data for 145 countries during 1970–2007. They looked at windfalls, specifically formal sector price booms, with country-specific commodity price indices. They also gave more careful attention to the representation of powerful groups with divergent interests. In a panel specification that includes fixed effects for countries and years, they found that commodity price booms lead to increased domestic and foreign asset investment in countries that are not dominated by polarized groups, which is the conventional response. In countries with polarized groups, however, price booms generally leave foreign investment unchanged, but lead to significant decreases in domestic investment. More directly relevant to the rent-seeking question, commodity price booms are followed by increases in government spending, increased corruption and higher expropriation risk in polarized countries, while less polarized countries exhibit no such effects.

14.3.2 Diverting Entrepreneurial Talent to Unproductive Rent Seeking

If a resource windfall spills into the state's coffers, it may cause some individuals to focus on rent seeking if the country's institutions do not prevent it.[19] If the talent diverted to rent seeking has the potential for entrepreneurship and wealth creation, the results could be slower growth or even reduced income. Torvik (2002) and Mehlum et al. (2006 [2008]) incorporate this intuition into models of the resource curse. Individuals who might otherwise develop 'modern', increasing returns-to-scale industries switch to non-productive rent seeking instead, and switching continues until private returns in the two pursuits are equalized. This leads to 'over-dissipation' (greater than 100 percent loss) because of a demand-linked externality from modern production that these individuals would otherwise have generated. It is therefore the assumed externality that underlies the over-dissipation.

Initial institutional quality enters this model because the payoff to rent-seeking effort depends both on the quality of a country's institutions and the size of the resource rent. For a given level of resource rent, sufficiently high institutional quality will prevent a resource curse from occurring because the return to rent seeking is never high enough to divert entrepreneurs to rent-seeking activity. For institutional quality below some

---

18 The institutional indicator is a dummy variable based on data from the International Country Risk Guide by the PRS Group.

19 Park et al. (2005) describe rent seeking from state coffers more generally.

threshold, however, the same resource rent will divert entrepreneurial talent and generate a resource curse. It is worth emphasizing that the rent dissipation results of Mehlum et al. (2006 [2008]) do not emerge from a contest function and dissipation extends beyond the effort spent trying to capture the prize. Instead, a resource boom combines with weak institutions to discourage entrepreneurship and to put the country onto a lower growth path.

Karl (1997) argues that diverted entrepreneurship contributed to the demise of Spain after its gold discoveries in the New World in the sixteenth century. This episode, arguably the most spectacular natural resource windfall documented historically, was followed by a severe boom and bust cycle in which Spain declared bankruptcy on eight separate occasions between 1557 and 1680. In her view (Karl 1997, p. 35) diverted entrepreneurship played a prominent role:

> [The monarchy] consolidated the loyalty of the lesser aristocracy through political favoritism, especially by selling patents of nobility and ecclesiastical appointments. This practice dramatically expanded the size of a parasitic noble class . . . while simultaneously siphoning off the most productive talent from business and commerce . . . The state bought the talents of those who might have become small entrepreneurs through awarding of offices . . . .

Mehlum et al. (2006 [2008]) present formal empirical evidence based on cross-country growth regressions. In a sharp departure from earlier empirics, they centered their analysis on the proposition that resource wealth is a curse only when institutional barriers to rent seeking are absent. They tested this by adding an interaction term between institutional quality and resource abundance to the Sachs-Warner specification.[20] They found resource abundance to be associated with slow growth when institutional quality is low; significantly, however, they found no evidence for a resource curse in countries with high institutional quality.[21]

A common criticism of cross-country regressions, with one observation per country, is that results may be driven by unobserved country-specific factors that are correlated with resource abundance. Papyrakis and Gerlagh (2007) addressed this concern by testing for a resource curse among states within the United States. Using cross-section data from states within a single country eliminates cross-country heterogeneity. While unobserved cross-state heterogeneity remains, this is arguably less problematic than cross-country heterogeneity. Papyrakis and Gerlagh (2007) took growth in real per capita gross state product (GSP) between 1986 and 2000 as the outcome variable and represented resource abundance by the share of primary products in a state's 1986 GSP. Other control variables included initial income, trade openness, investment rates and schooling, as well as governance institutions, which were represented by political corruption convictions between 1991 and 2007 per 100000 citizens. They found evidence of a resource curse

---

[20] Institutional quality is represented by an index that combines ratings (from the International Country Risk Guide) on corruption in government, risk of contract repudiation, risk of expropriation, bureaucratic quality and rule of law.

[21] The finding that growth rates slow in weak institution countries when a windfall arrives may indirectly be consistent with the over-dissipation hypothesis, if dissipation is construed as a reduction in present value income and the discount rate applied to future income is sufficiently low. Mehlum et al. (2006 [2008]) do not carry out the calculations necessary to determine this, however.

when no control variables other than initial income were included, but the effect became insignificant and small when further control variables, for example, investment rates, schooling levels, openness and institutions were added. From this they concluded that a resource curse does exist among US states, but it operates through indirect channels.

Rode (2013) points out that Papyrakis and Gerlagh (2007) did not incorporate a widely acknowledged regularity – that resource abundance is a curse if institutions are initially weak, but not otherwise. He extended their cross-state analysis to include an interaction term between resource abundance and corruption.[22] Adding the interaction term causes the coefficient on resource abundance to switch from negative to positive, indicating that for US states, resource abundance is a blessing when institutions are strong. The coefficient on the interaction term itself is negative, indicating that poor institutions can erode or overcome the otherwise beneficial effects of resource abundance.[23] This result is consistent with Mehlum et al. (2006 [2008]) and the resource curse story.[24]

14.3.3 Conflict Over Resource Rents and Institutional Decline

Historical accounts indicate that competition among influential groups over resource windfalls can erode a country's political institutions in addition to dissipating rent. Institutional erosion is a strong theme in Ross's (2001) examination of the hardwood timber boom in Southeast Asia and in Karl's (1997) analysis of political events in oil-producing states following the post-1970 price shocks. Hodler (2006) develops a formal model of institutional erosion caused by competition among interest groups for a fixed rent. The equilibrium effect is excess dissipation, so the windfall reduces equilibrium income beyond the value of the rent that initiated the rent seeking. The extent of the loss depends on the number of competing claimants.

Each interest group in Hodler's model decides how to allocate a fixed endowment of effort between ordinary production and rent seeking, and effort spent in rent seeking lowers welfare dollar for dollar. The resource rent is essentially a 'common pool' resource. In line with intuition on common pools, a larger rent leads to greater rent-seeking effort and correspondingly greater waste; the degree of dissipation depends positively on the number of agents competing for the prize, approaching 100 percent as the number of groups increases.

Over-dissipation, the *sine qua non* of a 'resource curse', arises in Hodler's (2006) model because the windfall-induced rent seeking erodes property rights in the non-resource sector. Specifically, a fraction of non-resource assets becomes subject to the same common pool competition that plagues natural resource assets. The result is a true resource curse: a resource windfall causes welfare to decline.[25] The analytical setup is a one-shot, simultaneous move game and the outcome just described is the unique pure

---

22 The data suggest that in the context of US states, corruption and abundance of resources, at least fossil fuel resources may be linked. Several of the high corruption states, such as Oklahoma, Montana, North Dakota, Louisiana and Alaska, have large fossil fuel extraction sectors and are resource-rich more generally (Rode 2013).

23 Both coefficients are only marginally significant.

24 Rode's (2013) empirical strategy does not address possible endogeneity of corruption.

25 This result rests on the key assumption that natural resource rents are allocated only by rent

strategy Nash equilibrium. Unlike other political-economy treatments, institutional constraints cannot limit rent seeking in the model. Hodler (2006) tests the model's predictions with data from a cross-section of countries, where per capita GDP and a property rights security index are the key outcome variables. The number of competing groups is captured by measures of ethnic, linguistic and religious fractionalization.[26] He finds that greater resource wealth and greater fractionalization are associated both with lower income and with weaker property rights. The reliance on cross-country data makes these results subject to caveats mentioned earlier.

The research highlighted in this section has a theoretical orientation, with empirical contributions aimed at testing predictions. In the next section, we turn to research, the contributions of which are entirely empirical.

14.4 EMPIRICAL RESEARCH ON RENT SEEKING AND THE RESOURCE CURSE

Sachs and Warner's (1997) landmark paper was entirely empirical, carried out with cross-country data, and it set the tone for a long list of purely empirical papers to follow. Some of the problems noted earlier with this approach have prompted other researchers to try different empirical strategies.[27] Overcoming empirical problems is important, because certain aspects of the resource curse make it an attractive vehicle for testing political-economy theories. The causal factor is the arrival of a resource windfall and the timing and size of such windfalls often can be pinned down, as when a discovery is made or when a resource price jumps. This feature enables research designs that examine within-country behavior before and after an event, while controlling for untreated (that is, non-windfall) observations. Such strategies have diminished earlier concerns and enabled tests of common resource curse predictions. One such prediction is that a resource boom in a country with weak institutions will increase theft of private assets and capture of government-held wealth by rent seekers. Another is that a resource boom can overwhelm otherwise favorable institutions, making them less effective in curbing rent seeking.

In this section, we discuss leading examples of empirical studies that (a) use more nuanced empirical strategies than cross-country regressions with one observation per country and (b) shed light on the connection between resource wealth and rent seeking. The first of these studies (Collier and Goderis 2009) uses panel data methods to distinguish between short- and long-run responses to resource windfalls in countries with weak versus strong governance. The subsequent three studies focus on oil as a resource and its potential link to governance.

---

seeking, whereas other forms of wealth are, in the absence of institutional impairment, allocated according to the effort provided to produce them.

[26] Fractionalization is the probability that two randomly drawn individuals share a common trait.

[27] There also exist a number of critical appraisals that question whether the resource curse is a real phenomenon or merely a spurious correlation. Readers may refer to Deacon (2011) for a summary of this line of research.

14.4.1 Short- and Long-run Responses to Resource Booms

Collier and Goderis (2009) construct a panel of cross-country observations on resource windfalls, governance institutions and growth outcomes, which they use to examine long- and short-run responses to resource price booms while controlling for unobserved country-level heterogeneity. A resource windfall is represented by a rise in a country's commodity export price index, which the authors construct from data on individual country exports and international price series.[28]

They find support for the resource curse as a long-run phenomenon: higher metal and fuel prices significantly reduce long-run real GDP growth in countries with weak governance. Short-run responses are more in line with conventional economic reasoning, in that higher prices lead to stronger GDP growth, but these effects last only about two years. Long-run effects in countries with strong governance are generally positive, but insignificant.[29]

14.4.2 The Resource Curse in Oil-rich Countries

The preceding study does not directly address key political-economy predictions that a resource windfall will increase rent seeking and cause institutions to erode unless governance is strong at the outset. Other empirical studies have used data on governance indicators and oil booms to address both these predictions. Oil booms are an attractive subject of study due to their economic importance. Further, oil booms can result from price booms or discoveries, both of which are generally easy to observe and measure.

There have been several oil price jumps over the past half-century. Because these jumps occur at points in time and represent a windfall only for oil-endowed economies, empirical tests use a difference-in-difference strategy. The effect of interest can be identified by comparing the outcome variable before relative to after the price boom in an oil-endowed economy, against the same difference in an economy without oil. Oil discoveries provide opportunities for similar tests because they occur at points in time and are geographically isolated. The three studies described next exploit these sources of variation.

14.4.2.1 Oil and municipal corruption in Brazil

Brazil emerged as an important oil producer since production began in the 1940s and in 2012 accounted for 2.7 percent of world output (British Petroleum 2013). The oil industry in Brazil is essentially monopolistic and is heavily regulated. Municipalities

---

[28] Country-specific commodity price indices are constructed using each country's 1990 export levels and treating these as fixed. Collier and Goderis (2009) use panel cointegration methods to separately identify short- and long-run effects. They include country fixed effects and regional time dummies to account for unobserved heterogeneity and include an error correction term to capture short-run responses to shocks. They regard institutions as fixed, unaffected by resource price booms.

[29] Price booms in agricultural commodities are generally beneficial for both weak and strong governance countries.

are entitled to royalties that amount to 3 percent of gross sales value. In prominent oil-producing municipalities, oil royalties account for 30 percent of total revenue.

Caselli and Michaels (2009) exploit this circumstance to examine the political resource curse using data from political subdivisions of a single country, Brazilian municipalities.[30] The authors treat oil royalties as a resource windfall, and test for effects on public spending and service delivery.[31] They find that large royalties tend to increase spending on education and culture, health, sanitation, housing, transportation and social transfers. They find, however, no evidence that the increased spending leads to higher per capita income, better housing or improved public services. Strikingly, royalty receipts are negatively correlated with social transfers for unemployment and poverty assistance. Caselli and Michaels (2009) attribute these discrepancies to theft of royalty revenue by municipal officials. While unable to observe theft, they do show that municipal employees in oil-rich communities have uncommonly high-quality housing and that media in these communities report high levels of municipal corruption. While the results of Caselli and Michaels (2009) support governance-linked predictions about rent seeking and the resource curse, they do not shed light on social costs of rent seeking through rent dissipation.

14.4.2.2 Results from a natural experiment in Africa

Starting in 1997, speculation arose regarding a major oil discovery in Sao Tome and Principe (STP), an island nation off the coast of West Africa.[32] This speculation gained credibility in 1998 when Exxon/Mobil was granted preferential exploration rights. The magnitude of the discovery became evident in 2003 when production rights were auctioned and the high bids amounted to 240 percent of STP's annual GDP. Vicente (2010) exploits the STP oil discovery to study the impact of a resource windfall on one sign of rent-seeking activity – corruption. He uses the neighboring island nation of Cape Verde (CV) as a control. Though the historical and political trajectories of the two countries have been very similar, CV has neither oil reserves nor prospects for future discoveries.[33]

---

30 Other such attempts include Papyrakis and Gerlagh (2007) and Rode (2013), both of which use data from US states.

31 Royalty payments to a municipality are determined by a complex set of rules that take into account the value of a municipality's oil production, as well as its population size and the oil infrastructure situated within its territory. By using oil production as an instrumental variable, Caselli and Michaels (2009) are able to exploit royalty revenue as an exogenous source of a resource windfall. They argue that oil production is a valid instrument because it is seen to be correlated with royalty revenue and is plausibly uncorrelated with a municipality's unobservable characteristics. The latter point is justified by showing that outcome variables did not differ between oil-endowed and non-endowed municipalities prior to oil discoveries. Caselli and Michaels (2009) also find that royalty revenue has no effect on local GDP or the composition of output beyond its direct contribution to petroleum sector output, so resource wealth is not a curse on pure economic grounds.

32 Except where otherwise indicated all of the information in this subsection is taken from Vicente (2010).

33 Both countries were Portuguese colonies for roughly 500 years, before gaining independence in the mid-1970s. Post-independence, both had autocratic socialist regimes until 1989, both conducted their first multi-party elections in 1991 and in each country the incumbent was defeated. In the years since, both have experienced similar electoral cycles and shifts in party dominance. Geographically, both are small island nations located in close proximity to one another, and in

A World Bank Corruption indicator was trending downwards in both countries prior to the discovery. After the discovery, STP's corruption trend turned sharply upward, while CV's continued its downward path. In 2005–06, Vicente (2010) conducted retrospective surveys of corruption perceptions in both STP and CV. Respondents rated the corruption they perceived in pre- and post-discovery periods and stated the forms that it took, as, for example, in the application of customs laws, allocation of college scholarships, financing of schools, public investments in infrastructure, health care provision, public procurements and elections. Using a difference-in-difference strategy, Vicente (2010) showed that perceived corruption increased significantly in STP after the discovery across numerous government functions. His analysis documents institutional erosion, but cannot shed light on rent dissipation.

14.4.2.3 Oil discoveries and trends in governance

Tsui (2011) examined cross-country data on the timing and importance of oil discoveries and a time-varying governance indicator, the Polity IV 'Democracy' Index, to test the prediction that a resource windfall can shift a country's governance away from democracy, particularly if the country is relatively non-democratic when the windfall arrives.[34] The outcome variable in this study is the 30-year change in a country's democracy index following the year of its most prominent oil discovery. The explanatory variables include the amount of oil discovered and its quality, plus interactions between these variables and the democracy level as of the discovery date. The trend in democracy prior to discovery is included as an additional control.[35]

Tsui's (2011) results indicate that institutions decline following a resource windfall in societies that begin with poor institutions. For countries with low democracy scores at the time of discovery, the democracy score 30 years later is found to be 10–20 percentage points lower than it would have been had the pre-discovery trend continued. No such pattern is seen for countries with relatively high democracy scores at the time of discovery, however.[36]

---

recent decades there have been considerable migratory flows between the two countries. Both countries have received similar packages of aid from the International Monetary Fund (IMF) and World Bank and have faced similar conditions from these agencies.

[34] Two papers that make this prediction are Aslaksen and Torvik (2006) and Robinson et al. (2006).

[35] Oil quality (depth and physical characteristics) variables are included to control for variations in the value of oil discovered, as the underlying hypothesis on corruption involves rents derived from petroleum extraction. Tsui (2011) also recognizes that discoveries can be determined by institutions, as Bohn and Deacon (2000) have shown, and uses a two-stage procedure that allows for endogeneity of reserve discoveries.

[36] Adding variables for oil quality to the democracy interactions approximately doubles the estimated negative effect of discoveries on democracy trends. Including fixed effects for decades (to control for temporal effects that may cause democracy shifts worldwide) and for large oil-producing Middle Eastern states affects the size of the estimated effects but does not eliminate their statistical significance.

14.5 CONCLUDING THOUGHTS AND DIRECTIONS FOR FUTURE RESEARCH

In recent years the literature on the resource curse has taken a turn toward political-economy explanations. This turn was motivated by two empirical regularities that are consistent with a political-economy view: (1) resource abundance tends to be a curse only when governance institutions are weak initially and (2) a curse is most likely to plague resources that are found in dense concentrations and are thus easily appropriable. As part of the broad shift toward political-economy frameworks, several authors have relied on the idea of rent seeking to make sense of the resource curse phenomenon. The theoretical and empirical research at the intersection of rent seeking and the resource curse has been surveyed in this chapter.

Rent-seeking models of the resource curse are essentially adaptations of the standard rent-seeking concept but are usually set in a general equilibrium framework. The particular application of the rent-seeking concept is moreover to a common pool problem in which rents are not indivisibly assigned but are shared, as described in the rent-seeking model of Long and Vousden (1987 [2008]).

The theoretical models highlighted in this chapter postulate that common pool competition for shares of resource rents takes place within one of two economic sectors. The alternative sector is implicit in the usual rent-seeking models (because inputs used in rent seeking have alternative productive uses). In the voracity model, the two alternatives are capital invested in a high productivity sector vulnerable to rent seeking versus a low productivity sector that is secure. In models of diverted entrepreneurship, the alternative activities to which effort can be allocated are unproductive rent seeking versus productive wealth creation. In the model of Hodler (2006), productive inputs can either be productively used or used to compete for rents and erode property rights to private capital in the process. In each model, competition for rents from the common pool natural resource can over-dissipate the resource windfall. The large corpus of empirical evidence associating resource wealth with reduced economic growth, particularly in societies with poor governance, gives credence to the prediction of over-dissipation.[37]

A distinguishing feature of rent-seeking perspectives on the resource curse is the explicit treatment of the institutional context within which rent seeking occurs. The mainstream rent-seeking literature has emphasized political rent creation and the contestability of rents through political decisions. Rent seeking would not occur if the political discretion to assign benefits from rents did not exist – or if there were no corruption in securing and assigning benefits through government.[38] Consistently, rent-seeking models of the resource curse are supported by empirical results demonstrating that a resource curse only applies to societies with poor governance, that is, where corruption is extensive.

A prominent departure from the usual rent-seeking literature is the view, now common in the resource curse literature, that institutions are endogenous and can be

---

[37] We are not aware, however, of any direct attempts to verify empirically that dissipation exceeds 100 percent.

[38] Institutions are thus important. See Congleton (1980 [2008], 1984 [2008]) and Sylwester (2001 [2008]).

eroded by competition for a resource prize. The hypothesis on institutional erosion has now been tested several times and generally validated; see, for example, Vicente (2010) and Tsui (2011).

While political-economy theories often are difficult to test empirically, incorporating the resource curse phenomenon into the analysis provides new opportunities for empirical research. The resource curse hypothesis postulates that a resource windfall will set off increased rent-seeking competition, with its attendant consequences. Resource windfalls are generally observable in price shocks or in new discoveries. This provides a source of observable variation in the motivation for rent-seeking competition, which allows political-economy researchers to test hypotheses that to date have been inaccessible to empirical research.

In conclusion, the resource curse phenomenon is an application of the theory of rent seeking, although the two strains of literature have largely proceeded independently. Whereas the rent-seeking models based on rational Nash behavior do not predict *ex ante* over-dissipation of rents, general models of the resource curse phenomenon do make such predictions. Rent-seeking models have emphasized the non-observability of rent seeking and problems of measuring rent-seeking inputs whereas models of the natural resource curse have used empirical inference to detect social losses due to the presence of natural resources that do not have secure property rights, including the property rights of the government as representative of the people.

REFERENCES

Aidt, Toke S. and Arye L. Hillman (2008), 'Enduring rents', *European Journal of Political Economy*, **24**(3), 545–53.

Anderson, Simon P., Jacob K. Goeree and Charles A. Holt (1998), 'Rent seeking with bounded rationality: an analysis of the all-pay auction', *Journal of Political Economy*, **106**(4), 828–53.

Arezki, Rabah and Markus Brückner (2010), 'Commodity windfalls, polarization, and net foreign assets: panel data evidence on the voracity effect', IMF Working Paper WP/10/209, International Monetary Fund, Washington, DC.

Aslaksen, Silje and Ragnar Torvik (2006), 'A theory of civil conflict and democracy in rentier states', *Scandinavian Journal of Economics*, **108**(4), 571–85.

Baharad, Eyal and Shmuel Nitzan (2008), 'Contest efforts in light of behavioural considerations', *Economic Journal*, **118**(533), 2047–59.

Bhagwati, Jagdish N. (1958), 'Immiserizing growth: a geometrical note', *Review of Economic Studies*, **25**(3), 201–5.

Bohn, Henning and Robert T. Deacon (2000), 'Ownership risk, investment, and the use of natural resources', *American Economic Review*, **90**(3), 526–49.

Boschini, Anne D., Jan Pettersson and Jesper Roine (2007), 'Resource curse or not: a question of appropriability', *Scandinavian Journal of Economics*, **109**(3), 593–617.

British Petroleum (2013), *BP Statistical Review of World Energy*, available at http://www.bp.com/content/dam/bp/pdf/statistical-review/statistical_review_of_world_energy_2013.pdf (accessed 11 June 2014).

Buchanan, James M. (1980), 'Rent seeking and profit seeking', in James M. Buchanan, Robert D. Tollison and Gordon Tullock (eds), *Toward a Theory of the Rent-seeking Society*, College Station, TX: Texas A&M University Press, pp. 3–15, reprinted in Roger D. Congleton, Arye L. Hillman and Kai A. Konrad (eds) (2008), *40 Years of Research on Rent Seeking 1 – Theory of Rent Seeking*, Heidelberg: Springer, pp. 55–67.

Bulte, Erwin H., Richard Damania and Robert T. Deacon (2005), 'Resource intensity, institutions and development', *World Development*, **33**(7), 1029–44.

Caselli, Francesco and Guy Michaels (2009), 'Do oil windfalls improve living standards? Evidence from Brazil', NBER Working Paper 15550, National Bureau of Economic Research, Cambridge, Massachusetts.

Collier, Paul and Benedikt Goderis (2009), 'Commodity prices, growth, and the natural resource curse: reconciling a conundrum', Unpublished manuscript, Department of Economics, Oxford University, Oxford.

Collier, Paul and Anke E. Hoeffler (1998), 'On economic causes of civil war', *Oxford Economic Papers*, **50**(4), 563–73.

Collier, Paul and Anke E. Hoeffler (2004), 'Greed and grievance in civil war', *Oxford Economic Papers*, **56**(4), 563–95.

Congleton, Roger D. (1980), 'Competitive process, competitive waste, and institutions', in James M. Buchanan, Robert D. Tollison and Gordon Tullock (eds), *Toward a Theory of the Rent-seeking Society*, College Station, TX: Texas A&M University Press, pp. 153–79, reprinted in Roger D. Congleton, Arye L. Hillman and Kai A. Konrad (eds) (2008), *40 Years of Research on Rent Seeking 1 – Theory of Rent Seeking*, Heidelberg: Springer, pp. 69–95.

Congleton, Roger D. (1984), 'Committees and rent-seeking effort', *Journal of Public Economics*, **25**(1–2), 197–209, reprinted in Roger D. Congleton, Arye L. Hillman and Kai A. Konrad (eds) (2008), *40 Years of Research on Rent Seeking 1 – Theory of Rent Seeking*, Heidelberg: Springer, pp. 279–91.

Congleton, Roger D., Arye L. Hillman and Kai A. Konrad (2008a), '40 years of research on rent seeking: an overview', in Roger D. Congleton, Arye L. Hillman and Kai A. Konrad (eds), *40 Years of Research on Rent Seeking*, Vols 1 and 2, Heidelberg: Springer, pp. 1–44.

Congleton, Roger D., Arye L. Hillman and Kai A. Konrad (eds) (2008b), *40 Years of Research on Rent Seeking 1 – Theory of Rent Seeking*, Heidelberg: Springer.

Congleton, Roger D., Arye L. Hillman and Kai A. Konrad (eds) (2008c), *40 Years of Research on Rent Seeking 2 – Applications: Rent seeking in Practice*, Heidelberg: Springer.

Deacon, Robert T. (2011), 'The political economy of the natural resource curse: a survey of theory and evidence', *Foundations and Trends in Microeconomics*, **7**(2), 111–208.

Dechenaux, Emmanuel, Dan Kovenock and Roman M. Sheremeta (2012), 'A survey of experimental research on contests, all-pay auctions and tournaments', Working Paper, available at http://ssrn.com/abstract=2154022 (accessed 6 November 2014).

Frankel, Jeffrey (2010), 'The natural resource curse: a survey', Discussion Paper 2010-21, Harvard Environmental Economics Program, Cambridge, Massachusetts.

Gelb, Alan H. and associates (1988), *Oil Windfalls: Blessing or Curse?*, New York: Oxford University Press.

Gylfason, Thorvaldur (2001), 'Natural resources, education, and economic development', *European Economic Review*, **45**(4–6), 847–59.

Harberger, Arnold C. (1954), 'Monopoly and resource allocation', *American Economic Review Papers and Proceedings*, **44**(2), 77–87.

Hehenkamp, Burkhard, Wolfgang Leininger and Alex Possajennikov (2004), 'Evolutionary equilibrium in Tullock contests: spite and overdissipation', *European Journal of Political Economy*, **20**(4), 1045–57, reprinted in Roger D. Congleton, Arye L. Hillman and Kai A. Konrad (eds) (2008), *40 Years of Research on Rent Seeking 1 – Theory of Rent Seeking*, Heidelberg: Springer, pp. 473–85.

Heston, Alan, Robert Summers and Bettina Aten (2002), *Penn World Table Version 6.1*, Philadelphia, PA: Center for International Comparisons of Production, Income and Prices, University of Pennsylvania.

Higgins, Richard S., William F. Shughart II and Robert D. Tollison (1985), 'Free entry and efficient rent seeking', *Public Choice*, **46**(3), 247–58, reprinted in Roger D. Congleton, Arye L. Hillman and Kai A. Konrad (eds) (2008), *40 Years of Research on Rent Seeking 1 – Theory of Rent Seeking*, Heidelberg: Springer, pp. 121–32.

Hillman, Arye L. (2013), 'Rent seeking', in Michael Reksulak, Laura Razzolini and William F. Shughart II (eds), *The Elgar Companion to Public Choice*, 2nd edn, Cheltenham, UK and Northampton, MA, USA: Edward Elgar Publishing, pp. 307–30.

Hillman, Arye L. and Eliakim Katz (1984), 'Risk-averse rent seekers and the social cost of monopoly power', *Economic Journal*, **94**(373), 104–10, reprinted in Roger D. Congleton, Arye L. Hillman and Kai A. Konrad (eds) (2008), *40 Years of Research on Rent Seeking 1 – Theory of Rent Seeking*, Heidelberg: Springer, pp. 97–103.

Hillman, Arye L. and Dov Samet (1987), 'Dissipation of contestable rents by small numbers of contenders', *Public Choice*, **54**(1), 63–82, reprinted in Roger D. Congleton, Arye L. Hillman and Kai A. Konrad (eds) (2008), *40 Years of Research on Rent Seeking 1 – Theory of Rent Seeking*, Heidelberg: Springer, pp. 165–84.

Hodler, Roland (2006), 'The curse of natural resources in fractionalized countries', *European Economic Review*, **50**(6), 1367–86.

Isham, Jonathan, Michael Woodcock, Lant Pritchett and Gwen Busby (2003), 'The varieties of resource experience: how natural resource export structures affect the political economy of economic growth', Economics Discussion Paper No. 03-08, Middlebury College, Middlebury, Vermont.

Karl, Terry Lynn (1997), *The Paradox of Plenty: Oil Booms and Petro-states*, Berkeley, CA: University of California Press.

Katz, Eliakim and Julia Tokatlidu (1996), 'Group competition for rents', *European Journal of Political*

Economy, **12**(4), 599–697, reprinted in Roger D. Congleton, Arye L. Hillman and Kai A. Konrad (eds) (2008), *40 Years of Research on Rent Seeking 1 – Theory of Rent Seeking*, Heidelberg: Springer, pp. 537–54.

Krueger, Anne O. (1974), 'The political economy of the rent-seeking society', *American Economic Review*, **64**(3), 291–303, reprinted in Roger D. Congleton, Arye L. Hillman and Kai A. Konrad (eds) (2008), *40 Years of Research on Rent Seeking 2 – Applications: Rent Seeking in Practice*, Heidelberg: Springer, pp. 151–63.

Lane, Philip R. and Aaron Tornell (1996), 'Power, growth and the voracity effect', *Journal of Economic Growth*, **1**(2), 213–41.

Leite, Carlos and Jens Weidmann (1999), 'Does Mother Nature corrupt? Natural resources, corruption and economic growth', IMF Working Paper WP/99/85, International Monetary Fund, Washington, DC.

Long, Ngo Van (2013), 'The theory of contests: a unified model and review of the literature', *European Journal of Political Economy*, **32**(4), 161–81, reprinted as Chapter 3 in this volume.

Long, Ngo Van and Neil Vousden (1987), 'Risk-averse rent seekers with shared rents', *Economic Journal*, **97**(388), 971–85, reprinted in Roger D. Congleton, Arye L. Hillman and Kai A. Konrad (eds) (2008), *40 Years of Research on Rent Seeking 1 – The Theory of Rent Seeking*, Heidelberg: Springer, pp. 293–307.

Mehlum, Halvor, Karl Moene and Ragnar Torvik (2006), 'Institutions and the resource curse', *Economic Journal*, **116**(508), 1–20, reprinted in Roger D. Congleton, Arye L. Hillman and Kai A. Konrad (eds) (2008), *40 Years of Research on Rent Seeking 2 – Applications: Rent Seeking in Practice*, Heidelberg: Springer, pp. 245–64.

Nitzan, Shmuel (1991), 'Collective rent dissipation', *Economic Journal*, **101**(409), 1522–34.

Papyrakis, Elissaios and Reyer Gerlagh (2007), 'Resource abundance and economic growth in the United States', *European Economic Review*, **51**(4), 1011–39.

Park, Hyun, Apostolis Philippopoulos and Vanghelis Vassilatos (2005), 'Choosing the size of the public sector under rent seeking from state coffers', *European Journal of Political Economy*, **21**(4), 830–50.

Robinson, James A., Ragnar Torvik and Thierry Verdier (2006), 'Political foundations of the resource curse', *Journal of Development Economics*, **79**(2), 447–68.

Rode, Ashwin (2013), 'Institutions and the resource curse within the United States', Working Paper, Department of Economics, University of California-Santa Barbara, Santa Barbara, California.

Ross, Michael L. (2001), *Timber Booms and Institutional Breakdown in Southeast Asia*, Cambridge: Cambridge University Press.

Ross, Michael L. (2006), 'A closer look at oil, diamonds, and civil war', *American Review of Political Science*, **9**, 265–300.

Sachs, Jeffrey D. and Andrew M. Warner (1997), 'Natural resource abundance and economic growth', Working Paper, Center for International Development and Harvard Institute for International Development, Cambridge, Massachusetts.

Sachs, Jeffrey D. and Andrew M. Warner (2001), 'The curse of natural resources', *European Economic Review*, **45**(4–6), 827–38.

Sala-i-Martin, Xavier and Arvind Subramanian (2003), 'Addressing the natural resource curse: an illustration from Nigeria', Working Paper 9804, National Bureau of Economic Research, Cambridge, Massachusetts.

Sheremeta, Roman M. (2013), 'Overbidding and heterogeneous behavior in contest experiments', *Journal of Economic Surveys*, **27**(3), 491–514.

Sylwester, Kevin (2001), 'A model of institutional formation within a rent-seeking environment', *Journal of Economic Behavior and Organization*, **44**(2), 169–76, reprinted in Roger D. Congleton, Arye L. Hillman and Kai A. Konrad (eds) (2008), *40 Years of Research on Rent Seeking 2 – Applications: Rent Seeking in Practice*, Heidelberg: Springer, pp. 459–66.

Tornell, Aaron and Philip R. Lane (1999), 'The voracity effect', *American Economic Review*, **89**(1), 22–46.

Torvik, Ragnar (2002), 'Natural resources, rent seeking and welfare', *Journal of Development Economics*, **67**(2), 455–70.

Tsui, Kevin K. (2011), 'More oil, less democracy: evidence from worldwide crude oil discoveries', *Economic Journal*, **121**(551), 89–115.

Tullock, Gordon (1967), 'The welfare costs of tariffs, monopolies, and theft', *Western Economic Journal*, **5**(3), 224–32, reprinted in Roger D. Congleton, Arye L. Hillman and Kai A. Konrad (eds) (2008), *40 Years of Research on Rent Seeking 1 – Theory of Rent Seeking*, Heidelberg: Springer, pp. 45–53.

Tullock, Gordon (1980), 'Efficient rent seeking', in James M. Buchanan, Robert D. Tollison and Gordon Tullock (eds), *Toward a Theory of the Rent-seeking Society*, College Station, TX: Texas A&M University Press, pp. 97–112, reprinted in Roger D. Congleton, Arye L. Hillman and Kai A. Konrad (eds) (2008), *40 Years of Research on Rent Seeking 1 – Theory of Rent Seeking*, Heidelberg: Springer, pp. 105–20.

Tullock, Gordon (1987), 'Rent seeking', in John Eatwell, Murray Milgate and Peter Newman (eds), *The New Palgrave: A Dictionary of Economics*, Vol. 4, 1st edn, London: Macmillan, pp. 147–9.

van der Ploeg, Frederick (2011), 'Natural resources: curse or blessing?', *Journal of Economic Literature*, **49**(2), 366–420.

van der Ploeg, Frederick and Dominic Rohner (2010), 'War and natural resource exploitation', Paper presented at the 2010 American Economic Association Meetings, Atlanta, Georgia.
Vicente, Pedro C. (2010), 'Does oil corrupt? Evidence from a natural experiment in West Africa', *Journal of Development Economics*, **92**(1), 28–38.

15. Rents and the political economy of development aid

*Rune Jansen Hagen**

SUMMARY

Empirical studies suggest little impact of foreign aid on growth on average. As aid can be viewed as a sovereign rent akin to natural resource rents, it is likely that rent seeking plays a role in explaining this disappointing outcome. The analytic starting point of the chapter is the long chain of agents connecting donors in rich countries with beneficiaries in poor countries, making aid a contestable rent for recipients at both the international and domestic levels. Thus, rent seeking can distract attention and divert resources from more important sources of long-term progress in recipients. Moreover, there are serious incentive problems on the donor side of the relationship. Empirically, the effects seem quite heterogeneous and hence more research is needed to further our understanding of this complex system.

15.1 INTRODUCTION

> In these circumstances, the best way to make money is through rent: natural resource rent, aid rent, policy rent. So the private sector will be rent seeking not value creating, it will go for the easy way and make money through rent. (Former Prime Minister Meles Zenawi of Ethiopia, quoted in de Waal 2013, p. 153)

The concept of rent seeking refers to a process in which resources are used to shift wealth instead of creating it.[1] It has been most frequently applied to situations where intervention by the government in the economy creates 'artificial' potential profits that could be appropriated by several different actors, for example, a monopoly established by law, or to lobbying for similar measures. Such profits have been coined rents, in analogy to the surplus that arises in the extraction of natural resources when other inputs have been paid according to their opportunity cost, that is, the economic value generated by the resource itself.

Standard economic analysis of the effects of resource discoveries or booms often starts from the premise that the rent is equivalent to a gift of foreign exchange. On the face of it, foreign aid seems to be another such example.[2] It is by definition an external resource

* I would like to thank Arye Hillman and Kjetil Bjorvatn for comments that substantially improved this chapter. Responsibility for the end product still rests with the author, of course.

[1] The basic idea is usually attributed to Tullock (1967 [2008]), whereas the term rent seeking is due to Krueger (1974 [1980]).

[2] In fact, Collier (2006) dubs both natural resource rents and aid as sovereign rents.

Table 15.1 Top ten recipients of net Official Development Assistance (ODA), 2012

Country	ODA/GNI (%)	Country	ODA per capita (current USD)
Solomon Islands	43.6	Tuvalu	2484
Tuvalu	42.3	Marshall Islands	1446
Liberia	36.1	Micronesia, Fed. Sts.	1113
Marshall Islands	34.7	Tonga	746
Micronesia, Fed. Sts.	33.5	Palau	723
Afghanistan	32.8	Kiribati	642
Malawi	28.4	Samoa	639
Kiribati	25.0	Solomon Islands	555
Burundi	21.2	Cabo Verde	498
Sao Tome and Principe	18.7	West Bank and Gaza	495
Memo		Memo	
Low income	8.0	Low income	49
Least developed	6.2	Least developed	49
Middle income	0.2	Middle income	11

transfer. It is no doubt of importance to quite a few developing countries. At the extreme, the top three recipients in terms of income per capita in the most recent available year (2012) would be middle-income countries even if they produced nothing themselves, as the current World Bank cut-off between low- and middle-income countries is at $1035 (Table 15.1).[3] More generally, it seems reasonable to say that an industry is important if it constitutes more than 5 percent of the economy. According to this standard, aid is important in 49 out of the 131 countries for which the World Bank has current data.[4] On average, it is of significance in both low-income and least developed countries.[5]

While the impact of foreign aid on economic growth in developing countries remains somewhat controversial, the latest empirical studies point to the conclusion that the effect is on average small and probably not significantly different from zero.[6] Needless to say, an insignificant overall effect might mask sizeable heterogeneities across recipient

[3] The source for the data in Table 15.1 and Figure 15.1 is the World Bank's online database, available at http://data.worldbank.org/indicator/DT.ODA.ODAT.GN.ZS and http://data.worldbank.org/indicator/DT.ODA.ODAT.PC.ZS (accessed 15 April 2014).

[4] These are Tajikistan and all the countries to the left of it in Figure 15.1.

[5] The least developed country designation is based on a United Nations (UN) classification that, besides income, takes 'vulnerability' and 'human assets' into account. For these reasons, there have always been some lower middle-income countries in this group. Presently, even two upper middle-income countries (Angola and Tuvalu) and a high-income country (Equatorial Guinea) are categorized as least developed countries (LDCs).

[6] Roodman (2007) demonstrates that the results of the most important studies published in the early parts of the 2000s were not robust, especially with respect to sample changes, and concludes that aid is probably not a decisive factor for development. The meta-studies of Docouliagos and Paldam (2008, 2010, 2011) can be said to generalize this result, establishing aggregate aid ineffectiveness in terms of growth. Rajan and Subramanian (2008) slice the data in many different ways,

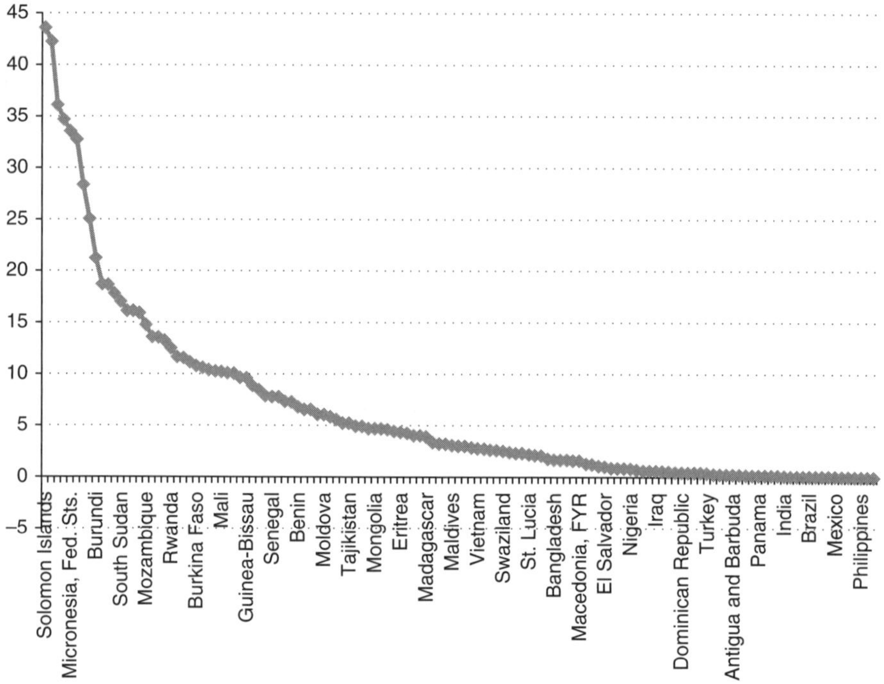

Figure 15.1 Countries ranked by Official Development Assistance/gross national income (ODA/GNI) ratio, 2012

countries and types of aid, and the literature is now heading in the direction of more disaggregated studies that might be able to uncover such variation. Moreover, the welfare effects of such transfers are a wholly different matter. In principle, if all aid is consumed no additional growth could coincide with a higher level of aggregate welfare.

However, supposing that the ineffectiveness of aid in raising growth on average hides some success stories, it follows that there must also be cases where aid has had a negative impact. If no effect is a disappointment in light of the original normative rationale for foreign aid – fostering economic development – backsliding is clearly even worse. Furthermore, there are indications that aid could have perverse effects in other dimensions too. For example, Bjørnskov (2010) finds that in democracies aid worsens the income distribution and Djankov et al. (2008) claim that more aid results in less democracy.

The starting point of this chapter is that it is worthwhile investigating potential reasons why a gift from abroad paradoxically might have no or even a negative effect on the economic development of the recipient. As is the case for natural resource rents, economic mechanisms such as volatility and the Dutch disease could be part of the explanation.[7] However, I focus on the inefficiencies that arise due to the extremely long

including time horizons not previously tested, without finding much of an impact (if anything, it is negative).

[7] Rajan and Subramanian (2011) is one recent study presenting evidence suggesting that aid

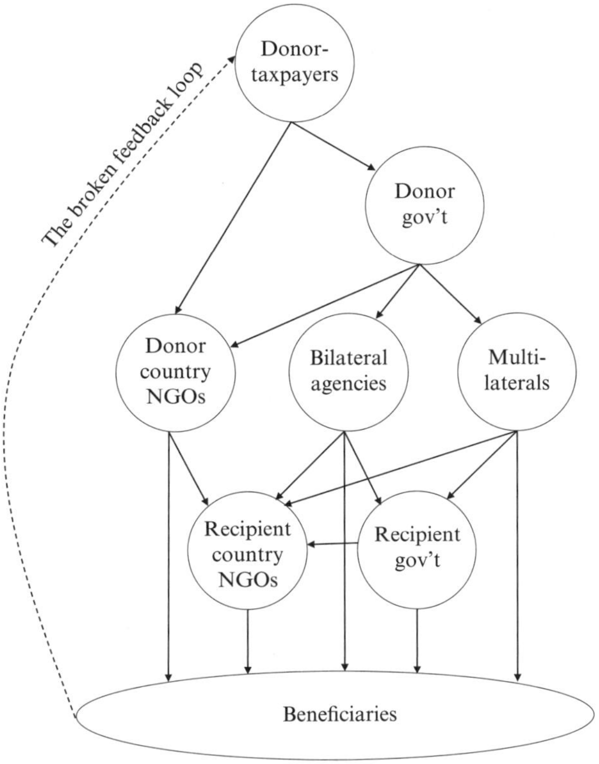

Figure 15.2 The aid chain

'chain' linking the original donors (citizen-taxpayers in rich countries) and the ostensible beneficiaries (poor people in poor countries). Figure 15.2 gives a stylized depiction of this highly complex system. The downward-pointing arrows symbolize flows of 'aid funds', starting at the top with the taxes and private donations of individuals. The aid budget of a donor country government mainly derives from the taxes paid and is in turn divided among different actors, most importantly bilateral and multilateral aid agencies. These channel their funds through recipient country governments and donor and recipient country non-governmental organizations (NGOs), or spend them directly on projects in the field.[8] Resources are consumed in each 'link' of this chain and as a result a substantial

adversely affects the growth rates of industries producing tradable goods by causing an appreciation of the real exchange rate. The simulations of Arellano et al. (2009) demonstrate that the welfare costs of aid volatility can be quite substantial.

8 To avoid cluttering the figure, I have made a number of simplifications. Some of the most important are the following. In recent years, public-private partnerships like the Global Alliance for Vaccines and Immunisation have become important players in the health sector in particular. This is an example of private foundations being major financiers for some purposes. Also note that donor countries use 'international' NGOs as well, mainly from other donor countries. The number and nature of bilateral agencies vary among donors belonging to the Organisation for Economic Co-operation and Development's (OECD) Development Assistance Committee (DAC), and

share of aid never reaches the recipient country, much less the poorest segments of it.[9] Moreover, the beneficiaries have no institutionalized way of reporting back to the citizens of the donor country whether aid works for them or not; in this system, the feedback loop is broken.[10] An important consequence is that accountability for results is much weaker at all stages than in the welfare systems of the donor countries.

In the next section, I analyze the donor part of the chain, discussing citizens, governments, official aid agencies and NGOs in turn. Section 15.3 is devoted to various issues on the recipient side. Section 15.4 contains concluding comments. The main conclusion is that not only is some aid diverted to unproductive activities, such transfers can also distract recipients from the pursuit of development. These effects do not appear to be ubiquitous, however, so there is still plenty of room for research into when aid works, when it does not and why. Still, any progress in our understanding of this system is unlikely to generate strong incentives for change.

15.2 DONORS

15.2.1 Citizen-taxpayers

The aid chain starts with private individuals in donor countries. In some ways, the problematic aspects of aid start here too. The mostly rich-country citizens who are the original source of aid can be said to donate in two ways: through compulsory taxation and through voluntary contributions to NGOs. Their intrinsic motivation for making donations is of course most directly relevant in the second case and can be categorized in terms of whether they are outcome-oriented or not. Reducing world poverty can be viewed as a collective good. In the latest wave of the World Values Survey, more than 50 percent of respondents in major donor countries, such as Germany, the Netherlands and the USA, viewed 'people living in poverty and need' as the most serious problem facing the world.[11]

As is well known from the literature on the private provision of collective goods, in

---

include government ministries as well as executive agencies. The multilateral agencies make up a quite heterogeneous category, ranging from financial institutions like the World Bank to the specialized agencies of the UN. In addition to 'in-house' units and NGOs, official agencies use private contractors to implement projects. For a more detailed view of the complexities of the system as seen from the recipient side, see figure 9 of World Bank (2008).

[9] The administrative costs of aid are not my concern here. A good chunk of these costs are payments to the evaluation 'industry', comprising accountants, auditors, consultants, think-tanks and academic researchers, mostly located in the donor countries.

[10] This was first pointed out in Martens et al. (2002).

[11] http://www.worldvaluessurvey.org/WVSOnline.jsp (accessed 19 May 2014). The complete wording of the question is 'Please indicate which of the following problems you consider the most serious one for the world as a whole?' The survey found that 6.5–13 percent of respondents in these countries considered another development related issue, poor sanitation and infectious diseases as the most pressing. The results are similar in other traditional DAC countries like Australia, Spain and Sweden. The exception is Japan, where more than 40 percent answered that environmental concerns were foremost in their minds.

such situations a free-rider problem arises.[12] It is better for each individual to leave the task of providing the good to other concerned individuals. With the number of potential donors running into hundreds of millions, the free-rider problem is so severe that one would hardly expect any contributions at all. Indeed, Kopczuk et al. (2005) argue that their calculations show that US aid policy is consistent with social preferences that place essentially no value on the welfare of the citizens of the poorest countries or an implicit assumption that all transfers are wasted. On the other hand, we do observe donations that are sizeable enough to sustain thousands of development NGOs, some of which are household names, and are large enough to influence rich-country governments and multilateral institutions. It thus seems likely that a significant part of private contributions to foreign aid can be explained by motivations that are not outcome-oriented.

As noted by Andreoni (2006), fundraisers know most people must be asked to donate. The 'demand' for contributions brings forth the 'supply.' This could be due to the social pressure implicit in the request, especially when someone comes knocking on your door or stands curbside soliciting passers-by. Declining to give in a face-to-face encounter feels a bit like saying 'I'm a mean, non-caring person.' As most fundraising drives are not based on personal interaction, a related inclination is probably even more important in explaining the 'power of the ask', namely, the desire to convince yourself that you are not such an individual. Giving to confirm to oneself that one is a person who cares about others has been labeled expressive giving by Hillman (2010). This notion is closely related to the concept of the warm glow giving of Andreoni (1989). It is the act of contributing that matters to the donor with such motivations, not the outcomes produced.

Why are motivations for giving important? Because they have ramifications for the whole system. If individuals donate to NGOs solely to feel good about themselves, these organizations do not have to deliver results. This is likely to magnify the accountability problems that arise from the peculiar governance structures of NGOs, which per definition have no owners. Similarly, if citizens do not care about outcomes, governments are free to use their aid budgets in pursuit of other goals. Moreover, development in general or aid more narrowly is never the most important topic for voters when deciding which party or candidate to vote for. This observation further strengthens the supposition that the accountability constraint is unlikely to be binding for politicians in this dimension, and implies that special interests such as NGOs and aid bureaucrats, not voters, could be their real principals.

Before we proceed to discuss the roles of these other donor-side actors in more detail, note that assuming expressive behavior on the part of citizen-taxpayers is not a necessary condition for asserting that the latter are unlikely to be demanding results. This is important, for the empirical literature on charitable giving in general finds that government grants to NGOs reduce private donations by a factor of between 0 and 100 percent. As the canonical model of the private provision of a pure public good predicts that crowding out will be complete whereas a model where gifts are only motivated by warm glow suggests there will be no crowding out, the evidence suggest that either people have

[12] The idea originates with Olson (1971). The standard 'technical' reference is Bergstrom et al. (1986).

mixed motives or the population consists of both pure altruists and individuals with an expressive rationale for giving.

However, even if a sizeable number of individual donors 'in principle' are outcome-oriented when it comes to development issues, they are unlikely to be so in practice for the simple reason that they lack the information and knowledge required to judge results. The broken feedback loop in Figure 15.2 illustrates that the aid system does not have an automatic mechanism for the ostensible beneficiaries to report back to the original donors. Analyzing this chain to attribute responsibility for (lack of) results is extremely costly to single citizen-taxpayers. In addition, such information is a collective good and is therefore subject to a second order free-rider problem. Thus, even most outcome-oriented individuals are likely to end up basing their actions with respect to both the voluntary and the compulsory part of their contributions to foreign aid on the emotive appeal of 'doing something' to reduce world poverty. Indeed, Nunnenkamp and Öhler (2012) find that donations to US development NGOs do not seem to be driven by publicly available information about the efficiency with which these organizations allocate funds. Instead, a small crowding-in effect suggests private donors take public funding to be a signal of quality.[13] As I shall now discuss, this is unlikely to be a fool-proof solution as neither politicians nor aid bureaucrats have strong incentives to focus on efficiency in aid allocation and delivery.

15.2.2 Motivations for Official Aid

It follows from the supposition that expressive behavior is likely to be widespread among donor country voters when it comes to development assistance that their governments have considerable slack in delivering results. They could use this space to pursue their own agendas, or find it opportune to adopt the ones pushed by NGOs and official aid agencies. The roles played by the latter two are the subject of the following subsections. Here I focus on the aggregate picture of how official aid is distributed across recipients. Aid allocation is important for at least two reasons. The size of the flow might of course matter for the effects generated. For example, some researchers argue that there are decreasing returns to aid, others that more aid means more rent seeking. There are also studies indicating that donor motives matter for aid impact, with politically driven transfers being less effective.[14] With the notorious lack of robustness of aid-growth regressions in mind and no clear theoretical rationale for these results, one should obviously not jump to conclusions. However, these results suggest that the fine print matters in the aid industry.

It is common to classify donor motives into three categories: recipient need and merit as well as donor interests. The latter is often subdivided into geopolitical and commercial

[13] Naturally, most estimates of crowding out are based on organizations operating domestically. Studies of aid NGOs indicate this sector is different. Ribar and Wilhelm (2002) find little evidence of crowding out, while Herzer and Nunnenkamp (2013) is another study finding crowding in. Unless governments use matching grants to a larger extent in this sector the evidence thus favors warm glow models of private aid, perhaps augmented by official funding serving as a seal of approval.

[14] See, for example, Dreher et al. (2013), Headey (2008) and Kilby and Dreher (2010).

interests. The big picture is that, relative to recipient need, self-interest is on average a more important factor for the bilateral donors than the multilateral institutions. This is due to the large bilaterals, as there is a group of small donor countries that act more like the multilaterals. Nevertheless, the income levels of the recipients influence the allocation decisions of even the most hard-nosed donor countries. The Samaritan's Dilemma suggests that this is not unequivocally a good thing.[15]

The Aid Donor's Dilemma is that what the donor does to alleviate need induces actions by the beneficiaries that counteract the intended effect and quite possibly prolong their dependence upon the donor. The donor might talk tough, but recipients know that actions speak louder than words: aid policy will be dynamically inconsistent as the donor will in the end respond to their needs even if they could have done more on their own account. For concreteness, consider competition for aid among recipient countries.[16] If a fixed aid budget is allocated on the basis of consumption levels, a recipient becoming richer will be given less as the donor redistributes toward the other, now relatively poorer, countries. In effect, the allocation mechanism taxes investment and other efforts raising recipients' own income. This story is consistent with Boone (1996) and Werker et al. (2009), who find that foreign transfers tend to crowd out domestic savings and thus have little impact on investment.[17] As I discuss in Subsection 15.3.2, it is also in line with the ineffectiveness of aid conditionality.

Most studies of aggregate aid allocation reveal a middle-income bias and a small-country bias; both types of recipients tend to receive more aid than their income levels warrant.[18] The standard interpretation is that this is due to geopolitics: middle-income countries tend to be more important strategically and it is argued that it is cheaper to buy the votes of less populous countries in international fora. During the Cold War, pledging allegiance to one of the main protagonists, the Soviet Union or the USA, and supporting them regionally as well as internationally could bring substantial rewards. This seems to be the main explanation for the drop in total aid in the 1990s (Boschini and Olofsgård 2007). The USA has also invested heavily in the peace process in the Middle East over the years.[19] More recently, Afghanistan and Iraq have been major recipients due to the War on Terror. The French support for its former colonies and the Japanese greasing of its relations with various Asian neighbors with whom it has extensive economic ties are relatively stable features of the aid allocation process of DAC donors.

There are arguably cases in which self-interest aid is subject to dynamic inconsistency

---

15 The Samaritan's Dilemma is due to Buchanan (1975) and its application to aid to Pedersen (1996).

16 See, for example, Hagen (2006b), Pedersen (2001) and Svensson (2000b).

17 The main conclusion of Boone (1996, p. 293) is that '[t]he marginal propensity to consume [aid] is insignificantly different from one', whereas '[i]n small countries, or countries where the aid/GNP ratio is extremely large (over 15% of GNP) . . . aid does lead to higher investment'. Werker et al. (2009, p. 227) find 'little measurable effect on growth', as '[a]id substitutes approximately one-for-one for domestic savings and brings little in the way of foreign investment'.

18 Notable studies of aid allocation include Alesina and Dollar (2000), Berthélemy (2006) and Hoeffler and Outram (2011).

19 According to Alesina and Dollar (2000, p. 40), 'Egypt and Israel receive much more aid than other countries with similar characteristics. Egypt receives 481 per cent more and the value for Israel is basically off the scale.'

too. For example, it is hard to deny a strategic ally further aid on the grounds that it has not devoted sufficient resources to the physical and organizational infrastructure that will enable it to fend for itself. One possible explanation why some scholars find that transfers motivated by recipient need produce better results in terms of growth than self-interest aid might be due to the number of applicable recipients. There are many poor countries, and perhaps this limits the extent to which governments can test the patience of 'good' donors. On the other hand, there are fewer countries that are truly important geo-strategically and this could give their governments greater leeway to pursue bad policies, as the main requirement for keeping the money flowing is that they provide military and diplomatic cooperation.

A third factor that potentially matters for aid allocation is 'merit', that is, the quality of policies and institutions. The World Bank and the regional development banks all use subjective measures of policies and institutions when allocating their funds. Among the bilaterals, rule-based distribution of aid is less common.[20] Indeed, Dollar and Levin (2006) show that the multilaterals are more selective than the bilaterals. As most theories of growth predict strong effects of policies (Easterly 2005a) and the dominant position in the literature is that institutions are the main deep determinant of development (Acemoglu et al. 2005), this could explain aid ineffectiveness. Given that the bulk of aid is given bilaterally, it is perhaps not surprising that overall donors do not seem to punish corruption (Svensson 2000a [2008]; Alesina and Weder 2002) or make larger transfers to more democratic recipients (Svensson 1999). On the other hand, it has proved difficult to establish empirical support for the intuitive proposition that aid works better when policies are better.[21] In addition, Rajan and Subramanian (2008) fail to detect any differential effect of multilateral aid on growth. This might be due to the fact that the influence of the largest bilaterals, the USA in particular, extends into the multilateral institutions. Developing countries voting with the USA in the UN Security Council obtaining more and larger International Monetary Fund (IMF) loans with less stringent conditionality is but one consequence.[22]

If allocation criteria have changed for the better after the end of the Cold War we might expect greater aid effectiveness now. Dollar and Levin (2006) conclude that both types of donors have become more selective over time, a finding Claessens et al. (2009) confirm for the bilaterals. In contrast, Easterly and Williamson (2011) contest the existence of a trend toward greater selectivity. It is thus not clear whether foreign aid is now better targeted at countries having better policies and institutions more robust to rent seeking.[23] Moreover, most likely the nitty gritty details of aid policy implementation matter too. Thus, we need to look at what aid agencies do.

---

[20] The Millennium Challenge Corporation of the USA is a notable exception as it tries to take the quality of governance into account when determining with which countries to enter into contracts.

[21] Burnside and Dollar (2000) (in)famously made this claim. However, their results are extremely fragile (cf. Roodman 2007). Of course, growth regressions in general lack robustness. It is also difficult to find good measures of policies, so this does not prove that policies do not matter either.

[22] See Dreher and Vreeland (2011), who also nicely summarize the literature on this topic.

[23] Furthermore, bear in mind that there are studies – some of which are reviewed in

15.2.3 Incentives in Official Aid Agencies

Easterly (2002) describes the aid industry as a 'cartel of good intentions.' We have just seen that good intentions are hardly a complete description of the motivations of donors. Moreover, as Klein and Harford (2005) note, the history of this industry since the end of World War II is one of a steadily increasing number of players as official donors establish new aid agencies, bilateral as well as multilateral, public-private partnerships are formed and the number of humanitarian and development NGOs multiplies. They also point out that there have been no exits to dent the competitive pressures created by the continuous entry of agencies. A more fruitful perspective is therefore to view aid agencies as intermediaries located between donors and recipients in the aid chain (Martens 2005). There has been a growing demand for intermediation in the post-war period due to higher incomes (making donors of Southern European countries like Spain and Portugal, the oil-rich economies of the Middle East and China), the break-up of countries such as the Soviet Union, Czechoslovakia and Yugoslavia (creating both more donors and more recipients) and decolonization (leading to many more recipient countries).

Adopting this analytical point of departure does not mean that Easterly's (2002) list of symptoms is not an accurate description of the health of aid agencies, only that the diagnosis is incorrect. The problems identified stem from well-known problems of bureaucracy, which are amplified in the context of foreign aid by expressive behavior and the broken feedback loop. Like other public agencies, aid agencies suffer from having multiple principals, many goals that are not adequately prioritized and outcomes that are not easily measurable. Organizational theory then prescribes weak incentives, the consequences of which we observe as an excessive focus on inputs or outputs instead of results, an apparent unwillingness to evaluate properly and learn, and the influence of both 'fads and fashions' and media coverage on decision-making.[24]

The argument in short is that in an environment wherein a principal (here the donor country government) wants an agent (for example, a multilateral aid agency) to pursue one or more goals and the former cannot perfectly monitor the actions of the latter, a problem of attribution arises. If the agent is risk-averse, rewards should be less closely tied to performance the more 'noise' there is in the link from effort to (measured) performance. Thus, incentives should be weaker for tasks where outcomes depend to a greater extent on factors beyond the agent's control, or, equivalently, the principal can measure performance less accurately.[25]

Consider the World Bank. It has for a long time expressed its mission in the slogan 'a world free of poverty.' This goal has recently been concretized as ending extreme

---

Section 15.3 – arguing that recipient institutions and policies are changed by donor money. Interpreting interaction effects between aid and some proxy for institutions or policies is a risky business if the latter variables actually are functions of aid.

[24] See Easterly (2001) on the role of fads and fashions in the aid industry. Eisensee and Stromberg (2007) demonstrate that US international disaster relief depends on whether the incident coincides with other newsworthy events, and that the influence of the media creates biases in the response to different types of disasters and the regions in which they occur.

[25] For applications of principal-agent theory to aid, see the contributions in Martens et al. (2002).

poverty, specifically, that the percentage of people living on less than $1.25 a day should be no more than 3 percent globally by 2030 (World Bank 2013). For an aid agency, this target is refreshingly clear. However, the Bank has also adopted a second goal, which is much less precise: promoting 'shared prosperity', which is specified as fostering growth in the incomes of the bottom 40 percent of the population in every country. It is obviously more difficult to hold the institution to account for something as vague as 'fostering growth', and it has a lot of leeway in choosing how to go about this task. Moreover, countless other factors besides the World Bank's decisions influence whether these two objectives are achieved. Its shareholders are therefore well advised not to provide too strong incentives for goal attainment.

A further complication stems from the fact that the Bank has multiple shareholders, which most likely have conflicting objectives. Rich member countries want this institution to be prudent in its lending decisions so as to preserve its good standing with financial markets, as this will minimize the risk that they will have to put up more money. Sometimes they will want it to make exceptions to the rules for important allies. Poor member countries want cheap loans with few conditions. Furthermore, there are a multitude of other actors that would like to influence the Bank to their advantage – staff, private contractors and NGOs, for example – even though they formally play no role. In a situation of common agency, the incentives provided by different actors can easily counteract each other, leaving the Bank with a lot of room to do things its way without being sanctioned.

Selecting intrinsically motivated agents could be a remedy against the ills of weak explicit incentives. It could also mean more cost-effective aid as overall levels of remuneration can be lower when staff shares the goals they are contracted to attain. Casual empiricism suggests there are many such individuals in aid agencies. However, by the standard Olsonian argument, anyone genuinely supporting the goals of a particular aid agency has an incentive to be a free-rider (Francois 2000, 2003). It would be better to work in the private sector, receiving the complete package of monetary incentives your qualifications and experience warrant, and let others do the good deed of working for lower pay in an aid agency. Thus, even if the casual empiricism accurately reflects realities, it is more likely to be a sign of aid agency staff being characterized by expressive behavior. Once again, this matters as they are then not motivated to produce results for the beneficiaries, only to be themselves 'doing something about it.'

One thing aid agencies can do to be perceived as 'doing something' is to spend their budgets. As is the case for other bureaucratic organizations, underspending often appears to be interpreted by political principals as an indication that there is a dearth of programs and projects worth funding. The standard reaction seems to be budget cuts, which are a serious threat to any ambitious bureaucratic czar. With no institutionalized mechanism connecting the two ends of the aid chain, he is under no pressure to demonstrate results either on home ground or foreign soil and has few tools with which to incentivize staff. An exhausted budget does at least keep immediate superiors happy and is often useful when lobbying for further allocations that will boost his power and prestige among his peers.

Given this situation, it is no wonder that critics have been searching for alternatives. One alternative that has had vocal advocates in recent decades is using NGOs. Due to their small size and charitable missions, these private aid agencies are said to be nimbler, more motivated to work in 'difficult environments' and closer to the poor than the official mastodons. Is there any truth to these bold claims?

15.2.4 NGOs in Donor Countries

NGOs are sometimes said to belong to the 'third sector', with the market and the public sector being the other two. As a residual entity, it is very heterogeneous, including foundations, trade unions and other large membership organizations as well as charitable agencies run by a single individual. The tasks they engage in also vary enormously, from local social work to international advocacy. One common denominator has already been mentioned: these organizations do not have any owners in the sense of residual claimants, as they are supposed to be not-for-profit.[26] This raises serious accountability issues, especially for organizations that do not have members either, which are rarely counteracted by regulation by peers or governments. The combination of weak governance and regulation with tax exempt status in many countries (for example, the USA) could tempt entrepreneurs to establish NGOs to profit from overgenerous pay and fringe benefits instead of dividends.

Some researchers argue that NGOs have a competitive advantage over for-profit firms when some aspect of a transaction such as quality is not contractible.[27] *Ex post*, a not-for-profit entrepreneur has a weaker incentive to shirk on quality as remuneration in kind is less valuable than cash, increasing the price consumers are willing to pay *ex ante*. In addition, it is sometimes supposed that if individuals support the mission of a charity, they are willing to work for a wage below their opportunity cost. However, the first argument presupposes that the non-distribution constraint binds to some extent and that consumers know it. Given the generally weak external oversight and numerous examples of fraudulent behavior, this might be questionable. Moreover, even though it is in fact true that many individuals volunteer considerable amounts of time to NGOs, echoing the argument made for the staff of official agencies, anyone intrinsically motivated by the mission of an NGO has an incentive to free-ride. Thus, warm glow utility from expressing a particular image of yourself by volunteering or working for a charitable organization is likely to be a more important motivating factor for staff members than pure altruism. In sum, neither 'only individuals intrinsically motivated by altruism work in this sector' nor 'NGO entrepreneurs are constrained from acting opportunistically by the organizational form' can be assumed without caveats.

In the market, competition usually has positive effects like spurring firms to become more efficient and innovative. The salutary facts are not as obvious in the case of NGOs. Their revenues from user fees or commercial activities usually constitute a minor share of the total. This tends to make them more attentive to the demands of their financiers than to their users. Emotionally charged advertising seems to play an important role

---

[26] Thus, non-profits is another term commonly used for these organizations. A third is voluntary private organization. Each of these captures some, but not all, of the five characteristics that are used by the Comparative Nonprofit Sector Project at Johns Hopkins University: a third sector entity is a self-governing, voluntary and private organization not distributing profits (Salamon et al. 2004). For simplicity, I mostly use the term NGOs.

[27] See, for example, Glaeser and Shleifer (2001) and Hansmann (1980).

in the market for private donations to NGOs in the aid industry, with pictures of poor children or victims of wars and natural disasters featuring prominently in their mass-marketing. As is well known, advertising is a waste of resources to the extent that it merely shifts revenues from one identical actor to another, as opposed to enlarging the market or benefitting more efficient actors disproportionally. While advertising probably raises total donations to some extent, there is little reason to believe that it leads to a reallocation of resources from bad to good NGOs if expressive giving is the dominant driver of contributions. Moreover, Nunnenkamp et al. (2013) show that even though public financiers perform some screening based on administrative overheads – in contrast to private donors – the effect of such costs on the probability of a development NGO exiting the market vanishes when the share of official funding becomes too high. Apparently, beyond some point the positive financial impact on survival cancels out the negative impact of stricter monitoring and evaluation, rendering public funding an imperfect screening mechanism in terms of NGO efficiency.

While donor country NGOs often advocate for larger aid budgets, this is unlikely to be a major activity for the operational ones, as more money in total is a collective good for all NGOs engaged in development work. Lobbying for public funds for their projects and programs and participating in contests for activities designed by official agencies are thus presumably much more important. According to Werker and Ahmed (2008), about half of open United States Agency for International Development (USAID) contracts are awarded to private companies, mostly in infrastructure projects, whereas NGOs tend to obtain contracts in the social sectors, where quality is arguably less easily observable. Similarly, Huysentruyt (2011) finds that the two organizational types rarely compete head-to-head for tenders put out by the UK's Department for International Development (DFID). Moreover, the personnel costs stipulated in bids by non-profits were 60 percent below those of for-profits.

These findings are consistent with the view that NGOs pursue missions providing intrinsic motivation to their staff and/or are constrained from behaving opportunistically by their non-profit status. As is well known, official donor agencies seem to have subscribed to this view as they have channeled more and more aid dollars through these agents (see, for example, figure 1 in Werker and Ahmed 2008). A further impetus to subcontracting aid activities to NGOs has come from the supposition that they are less bureaucratic and more attuned to local needs in recipient countries than bilateral agencies. In addition, since they are private agencies, donor country governments have found them useful in cases where they for various reasons prefer avoiding their own counterparts in recipient countries.

Data on the role played by NGOs in development assistance is rather limited. This not only applies to their own funds but also to the amount of official aid they receive, be it for programs and projects of their own design or as subcontractors. However, the studies that do exist provide little indication that they go where official agencies cannot or will not go. Based on a survey of large international NGOs that do not have an exclusively humanitarian orientation, Koch et al. (2009) conclude that they replicate the location pattern of their official patrons and, moreover, tend to cluster geographically. Econometric analyses of more detailed data from Germany (Nunnenkamp and Öhler 2011), Sweden (Dreher et al. 2010) and Switzerland (Nunnenkamp et al. 2009) confirm this picture of congruence in cross-country allocations for NGOs and official agencies, and reluctance on the part of the former to engage in 'difficult environments.' Furthermore, the more dependent German and Swiss NGOs are on public co-financing, the stronger these tendencies are (Dreher et al. 2012a, 2012b). Hence, there is little basis for viewing development NGOs as a distinct type of aid agency.[28]

Official donors seem to have taken this point. They are increasingly demanding that Northern NGOs have Southern partners in their projects. They have also tried to 'build' civil society in recipient countries by supporting local NGOs directly. As we shall see in the next section, these efforts have been successful in raising the number of such organizations. It is rather more doubtful whether they have managed to lay the foundations for third sectors that are rooted in the concerns of important domestic groups and financially sustainable once the impetus from foreign aid goes away.

15.3 RECIPIENT COUNTRIES

15.3.1 Aid as a Sovereign Rent

Aid can be viewed as a sovereign rent (Collier 2006). This is apt whether it is received for altruistic or strategic reasons; there is some feature of the recipient state that makes it attractive to the donor. This could be poverty, natural resources, cultural ties, a strategic geographical location or a crucial vote in an international body. Some of these assets, such as being a former colony of France, are durable and thus could generate a near-permanent flow. Other rent-producing assets are non-durable, of known (being a non-permanent member of the UN Security Council) or unknown duration (being eligible for International Development Agency (IDA) funding).

In the same way as a natural resource has to be extracted to enjoy the rent today and the size of the rent fluctuates with world market prices, aid rents vary with external circumstances and require some kind of action on the part of the recipient government. Mali is a French colony, but it competes for French aid with other ex-colonies of France, and how much is at stake depends on the French view of the importance of such transfers for its overall foreign policy. As we have seen, some sovereign rent-producing assets (for example, poverty and good governance) are manipulable, inducing inflows in an indirect manner. The point I want to make now is that maybe recipient diplomacy is an underrated part of the aid relationship.

Economic diplomacy could be viewed as international lobbying. Moreover, it consumes resources and is thus a close analogue to standard rent seeking. Consider the example of former President Kikwete of Tanzania (Kamata 2012, p. 298):

> The general disquiet is that the president travels a lot and spends little time at home. Related to this is the money spent on these trips, which many among the public consider to be a misuse of meagre public resources . . . President Kikwete had spent about 120 days and TShs 2.4 billion

[28] The only minor exception is that poverty measures seem to be more important than gross domestic product (GDP) per capita in explaining NGO allocations. Furthermore, the authors of the studies cited caution that they cannot test whether NGOs are better at targeting poor and vulnerable groups within recipient countries.

(about US$ 2 million) on trips abroad between December 2005 and May 2010. Besides the President, other state functionaries, such as ministers, travel abroad for the same reasons.

This story fits with what I heard on the radio in Dar es Salaam one autumn morning in 1999. The news anchor announced that Kikwete's predecessor, Benjamin Mkapa, had gone on a tour of Europe and the USA to prospect for more investment and aid. He also listed the names of the most important individuals accompanying Mkapa. According to my breakfast table companion, this was all the best and brightest permanent secretaries, those who held foreign degrees. My first thought was that this was crazy. Why were they not at home figuring out the best policies for their country to develop? Over the years, I have come to think that even though there might be long-run costs in terms of poor policies, it is perhaps in Tanzania's short-run interests to maximize the foreign resource flow by having the few who in more than one way speak the donors' language travel abroad to lobby. Foreign financial flows are more easily harvested than the returns to long-term domestic investments, particularly if they are unrequited. Unfortunately, this probably makes aid a distraction from the search for prosperity, which ultimately must start at home.

Obviously, not all types of aid are equally attractive to recipients. For example, aid tied to purchases of goods and services from the donor country is less easily appropriated by agents in the recipient country. Similarly, aid earmarked for specific projects, programs and sectors is in general less valuable than transfers that are not 'tagged' in this way, such as general budget support. However, even targeted aid could be fungible. The recipient could reduce its own allocation for that purpose and spend those funds on something else. Hence, the fungible portion of the aid flow may be subject to rent seeking in much the same way as general transfers and other types of public revenues. Determining the degree of fungibility is not straightforward as it depends on the characteristics of the donor, the recipient and the activity, and is in essence a counter-factual exercise.[29] Still, it cautions us against both formalistic distinctions between aid types as well as assertions that any aid dollar is up for grabs, which seems to be the most popular assumption in the literature to which we turn now.

15.3.2 Corruption, Policy Rents, and Rent Seeking

The basic idea of most papers on aid and rent seeking is that the direct positive effect of aid, often taken to be a higher level of some productive public good in the recipient country, is counteracted by a negative indirect effect due to resources being used by individuals or groups to try to appropriate a share of the transfer for their own private benefit.[30] Whether GDP (growth) is larger with aid than without is thus not clear a priori.

[29] See the theoretical analysis and discussion in Hagen (2006a). Feyzioglu et al. (1998) find that the degree of fungibility varies across sectors.

[30] See, for example, Hodler (2007) and Economides et al. (2008). Most authors assume some form of the classic contest function introduced by Tullock (1980 [2008]) applies. There is a small literature surveyed by Mayer and Mourmouras (2008) where the focus is on effects of grants and loans from international financial institutions when vested interests play a major role in recipients. While the approach is useful in many ways, its strong assumptions – that interest groups cannot appropriate any part of the transfer from the multilateral and that the latter can buy reforms – put it beyond the scope of this chapter.

Further complicating the picture is the fact that aid may lead to a reduction in taxation, raising the opportunity cost of rent seeking. The result is a highly non-linear relationship, which cannot in general be expected to be monotonic. Thus, what these models suggest is the possibility of aid having negative effects over some range, most plausibly at high levels, and that the probability of such a perverse outcome is higher where institutions are weak.

While many types of rent seeking such as lobbying for favorable policies or government contracts are hard to measure, proxies for corruption exist.[31] Svensson (2000a [2008]) argues that presumably rent seekers equalize the marginal costs and benefits of different forms of appropriation. If so, the effect of aid on corruption would at least qualitatively inform us about its relationship with rent seeking in general. Whether that is true or not, the topic is of independent interest. Both anecdotes of dictators stuffing bank accounts in tax havens with aid funds and more systematic case studies demonstrating how very large sums are diverted from aid-financed programs indicate that corrupt behavior might be a serious obstacle to aid effectiveness.[32] However, econometric studies paint an ambiguous picture. Whereas Alesina and Weder (2002) tentatively conclude that aid leads to more corruption, Tavares (2003) finds that in his cross-section it is the other way around. The answer of Svensson (2000a [2008]) to the question of whether aid corrupts is 'it depends', as in his data the relationship is positive (negative) above (below) a critical value of ethnic fractionalization. The conflicting results do not seem to be due to a failure to control for the possibility of reverse causality; as already noted, neither Alesina and Weder (2002) nor Svensson (2000a [2008]) detect any tendency for donors to give less to more corrupt regimes.

Both the theoretical literature on aid and rent seeking and empirical studies of aid and corruption are short on specifics when it comes to these appropriative activities. One might argue that measures of policy rents could also be used as proxies for rent seeking, but I do not find this argument persuasive. Rent seeking is only one possible source of inefficient policies. Governments also distort policies because of ideology or for patronage. Moreover, foreign aid could induce policy reforms if properly chosen conditionalities are enforced, but also delay them by soothing the aggregate consequences of distortions.[33] In fact, the mere expectation that donors differentially reward some policies might make governments choose inappropriate policies (Hagen 2015). Empirical studies seem to bear out the 'prediction' that the effects of aid on policies are quite heterogeneous.[34]

To the layman this may seem surprising. Demanding policy changes and institutional

---

[31] A bribe is a transfer, which, viewed in isolation, does not entail social costs. Still, because these transactions are illicit, it is reasonable to argue that resources are wasted in structuring, concealing and enforcing them, as well as in contesting the positions to which the bribes accrue.

[32] For example, Reinikka and Svensson (2004) uncovered that only 13 percent of a donor-financed grant per student reached primary schools in Uganda in the 1990s. The median was zero.

[33] See, for example, Rodrik (1989) and Casella and Eichengreen (1996).

[34] For example, Heckelman and Knack (2008) find that aid slows market-oriented reforms in some areas, but not in others; in sub-Saharan Africa, but not in other regions; and that the effect is much stronger in the 1980s than in the 1990s. Drazen and Easterly (2001) show that whether crises induce reforms depends on the policy instrument, as donors respond positively to extreme values of some policies and negatively to others.

reforms in exchange for aid have been one of the most controversial aspects of aid in recent decades. In the popular discourse, it is often portrayed as mighty donors (usually the IMF and the World Bank) arm-twisting poor country governments into doing things they would rather not do. Frequently the charge has been that recipients are forced to accept a standard package from the aid industry (the so-called Washington Consensus). However, the empirical literature demonstrates that the relationship is not quite as lopsided as the most ardent critics would have it.[35] Compliance is rarely 100 percent. One reason is that there are no institutions for enforcing aid contracts. If they are to be abided by, they must thus be self-enforcing. However, as argued above, aid agencies are under pressure to move money. Halting the flow is unlikely to be a desirable option in the absence of major corruption scandals or a breakdown of diplomatic relations. Threats of doing so are therefore likely to be dynamically inconsistent. Moreover, recipients have many ways in which to counteract the intentions behind the conditions even when they nominally comply. They have long since learned to take advantage of this situation, prompting conclusions like

> All of the case studies agree that economic policy is primarily driven by domestic politics, not by outside agents . . . In the pre-reform phase in which the government is not committed to reform, conditional loans have generally been a farce in which the government agrees to measures it does not believe in as a way to get funding, fail to carry them out, and then receives the funding from donors anyway. (Devarajan et al. 2001, pp. 34–5)

Even though there has been a move from conditionality to selectivity at the rhetorical level, the former has not completely vanished and the latter has thus yet to become the industry standard. Hence, understanding aid (in)effectiveness still requires us to study the political economy of aid within recipients. While the concept of rent seeking often conjures up images of firms lobbying or bribing public officials to obtain favors, in the current context there are also plenty of examples of aid having turned the non-profit sector in recipient countries into an arena for personal gain.

15.3.3 Rent-seeking Entrepreneurs in the NGO Sector

As noted in relation to donor country NGOs, non-profits are a very heterogeneous group. It is thus not surprising that the NGO landscape also varies a lot across countries. Some of the largest NGOs in the world originate in developing countries, for example, BRAC from Bangladesh, home of microfinance. There is also a long tradition in many countries of collective action at the local level, for example, in the form of mutual aid or joint management of village commons. However, while data limitations limit the conclusions that can be drawn, there is evidence suggesting that in many countries receiving aid the outside money has had a significant impact on the number and types of formal not-for-profit organizations. More specifically, there has been a significant increase in the number of NGOs, many of which are only nominally not-for-profit. In the words of Chabal and Daloz (1999, p. 23):

---

[35] See, for example, Dollar and Svensson (1998), Easterly (2005b) and Ivanova et al. (2003) for econometric evidence.

> The use of NGO resources can today serve the strategic interests of the classical entrepreneurial Big Man just as well as state coffers did in the past. Leaving aside those cases where NGOs are used purely for commercial purposes, it is as well to recognize now that there is today an international 'aid market' which Africans know how to play with great skill. Indeed, there is very little doubt that NGOs spend an excessive proportion of their budget on furnishing their members with sophisticated and expensive equipment (from computers to four-wheel-drive vehicles), leaving too little for the development projects which justify the work of the NGO in the first place.

Similar observations have fostered disparaging characterizations such as 'personal' or 'briefcase' NGO, that is, organizations established for personal gain and/or having little activity beyond producing mission statements and funding proposals. One country where we do have insights into such behaviors is Uganda. Religious welfare organizations have a long tradition there, and are important players in the health sector. However, these are not defined as NGOs by Ugandan law. This means that the set of NGOs in the legal sense is particularly well suited to studying the effects of foreign aid. A survey sponsored by the World Bank a decade ago provides detailed information on them that reveal interesting patterns.[36]

Many Ugandan NGOs appear to exist mainly on paper. In the capital, Kampala, the surveyors were only able track down 25 percent of registered organizations, in the countryside less than 50 percent. 93 percent of the organizations investigated claimed to have financial accounts, but only 199 out of 295 could produce statements of revenues and expenditures. Of these, only 62 had revenues approximately equal to expenditures, as a non-profit should. Part of the reason could be that three large organizations accounted for half of total revenues and three quarters of manpower (including volunteers). This gives the impression of a sector populated by a few successful organizations and a tail of smaller ones established in the hope of benefitting from the influx of foreign money, but ultimately failing in their endeavor. The fact that at the time of the survey there were nine times as many registered NGOs as private firms in Uganda only serves to reinforce this impression.

When it comes to funding, in 2001 the average organization received almost 50 percent of its funds from foreign aid agencies (including international NGOs), whereas the weighted sectoral average was 80 percent. This is a common pattern in many recipient countries as donors operate according to the Peter Principle; to those who have shall be given. Concentrating funding on organizations that have already proved themselves of course saves on screening and monitoring costs, but also serves as an entry barrier. This is consistent with the large number of inactive organizations.

Most organizations do not define themselves as suppliers of a specific service, preferring instead to define themselves in terms of target groups or a vague general activity such as 'community development.' The researchers dryly note that this flexibility with respect to activity might be an advantage in terms of attracting funding, but is probably not conducive to achieving gains from specialization. Somewhat surprisingly, client-community assessments were still rather high in general. However, as was noted

---

36 The effort has resulted in a number of papers on which I draw in the following: Barr and Fafchamps (2006), Barr et al. (2005), Fafchamps and Owens (2009) and Burger and Owens (2010).

for donor country NGOs, the Ugandan organizations tend to cluster, resulting in some duplication of effort, and do not seem to reach the poorest segments of society.

In sum, foreign aid has had a significant impact on the size and composition of the NGO sector in Uganda. One potential downside is that the inflow of financing might have drained the private sector of entrepreneurial talent. Such talent is in short supply in any country and they could be of particular importance for countries at low income levels, which need to ignite a growth process.

The theoretical model of Aldashev et al. (2014) illuminates another problem compounding the first. The non-distribution constraint precludes NGOs from having owners rewarded by profits. But even assuming that it holds – a big 'if' in many developing countries where regulation of the charitable sector is both underdeveloped and weakly enforced – it does not by itself stop insiders from benefitting themselves through overly generous wages, plentiful perks or lavish offices. A windfall of foreign aid could then not only attract entrepreneurs wishing to spend this windfall on additional services to the population but also opportunists wanting to maximize their consumption. Thus, as the sector grows, the motivational composition deteriorates too over some range as long as monitoring stays imperfect.[37] This naturally has adverse consequences for the level of sectorial output.

A third problem with having a donor-driven NGO sector is that donor preferences have often proved to be fickle. One year education might be in vogue, the next community development. As seen in the Ugandan case, this tends to favor organizations that are adept at adapting to donor demands, not necessarily those that are good at delivering services in a particular field. At the very least, they are precluded from accumulating gains from specialization and learning-by-doing. Since donors seem to be doing most of the monitoring, the fact that aid agencies often are at least as concerned with spending their budget as they are with outputs or outcomes most likely reinforces this behavior.

A final problem is that when donors call the shots, it is their priorities, which do not necessarily coincide with those of the recipient country population, that are decisive. An extreme example of this is how donor funding for HIV/AIDS has come to dominate the NGO scene in Malawi (Morfit 2011). This disease is a serious problem in Malawi, but it is certainly not the only problem this poor, aid-dependent society has. In countries like Uganda and Malawi, the label 'civil society' hardly seems appropriate for the NGO sector as its activities are directed by foreigners. This naturally brings us to the issue of the relationship between the domestic institutions of aid recipients and foreign aid more generally.

---

[37] Moreover, donors to a large extent started using NGOs because they were dissatisfied with government bureaucracies. The resulting downsizing has probably provided an opportunity for some of the former bureaucrats to become NGO entrepreneurs, a fact that the model of Aldashev et al. (2014) does not address. Individuals do not change motivation when changing sectors, so, if they were corrupt in public service, they are likely to be less than honest in the NGO sector too (though they might face different constraints on behavior).

15.3.4 Aid and the Quality of Governance in Recipients

The empirical literature on the effects of aid on growth is quite sparse when it comes to the issue of whether effects are contingent on the quality of recipient countries' institutions. From a theoretical point of view one would expect such an interaction effect, for example, because of lower corruption. This is what the model of aid and rent seeking by Hodler (2007) implies, for example.[38] In addition, the equivalent interaction variable is in general found to be significant with respect to the economic performance of resource-rich countries.

Rajan and Subramanian (2007) do find that aid reduces the relative growth rates of governance-sensitive industries in recipient countries. Moreover, Svensson (1999) shows that aid has a positive impact on growth in democracies only. He argues that this is due to institutionalized checks and balances preventing democratic governments from channeling funds to non-productive uses. But even if rent seeking is likely to thrive when governance is poor, one cannot simply assume that it is perfectly (negatively) correlated with institutional quality. Bräutigam and Knack (2004), Busse and Gröning (2009), Economides et al. (2008) and Knack (2001) all investigate the effect of aid on a composite index created by summing indices on bureaucratic quality, corruption and rule of law, finding that it is negative. Still, when Knack (2001) looks at the sub-indices separately, he discovers that in contrast to the other two indicators corruption is not significantly related to aid.[39]

These results suggest that there is more going on than easy money inducing corrupt behavior or creating policy rents in the context of weak institutions. Aid may change the quality of governance in recipient countries. This is in fact the purpose of so-called technical assistance. However, while this heavily criticized form of aid has rarely been successful in raising institutional quality in recipient countries, it seems unlikely that it has been responsible for lowering it. A prime candidate for being the cause of such an effect is the transactions costs of aid. As is well known, the average aid recipient has to relate to a double-digit number of official aid agencies and perhaps hundreds of foreign NGOs (World Bank 2008). In combination, these are responsible for a very large number of aid activities, which are usually uncoordinated. In addition, extensive monitoring, reporting and accounting activities accompany aid projects and programs.

The result is that donors often overburden the recipient bureaucracy with uncoordinated requests for meetings, demands for inputs into project planning and onerous reporting requirements. They might also lure the best bureaucrats into their own country offices and project organizations by paying well in excess of civil service pay scales in recipient countries.[40] Even those who stay have their attention diverted by aid activities,

---

38 In Dalgaard and Olsson (2008), the opposite actually applies when the efforts of the government in protecting the rent is less effective than the efforts of rent seekers. However, they stress that they consider this a special case. In Economides et al. (2008) and Svensson (2000a [2008]), aid is a common property resource, that is, rent seekers have access to the total transfer made to the recipient government.

39 There also seems to be some heterogeneity across time as Askarov and Doucouliagos (2013) conclude that aid had a positive effect on governance during the Cold War, but no effect in recent years.

40 Knack and Rahman (2007) present a theoretical model of donor poaching of recipient

as they can collect per diem by attending donor-funded meetings and workshops (see, for example, Smith 2003). Furthermore, donors sometimes circumvent planning processes and oversight mechanisms by cooperating directly with spending ministries and regional authorities instead of coordinating bodies such as ministries of finance or planning. Naturally, these 'transaction costs' are increasing in the number of donors as well as the number of activities they fund. In fact, Djankov et al. (2009) demonstrate that donor fragmentation significantly reduces the growth impact of aid. And while there seems to be some improvement in donor practices in the wake of the Paris Declaration, these problems persist.

The quality of governance matters for economic development as it is a determinant of both the level and efficiency of investment. In a broader perspective, the effects of aid on political institutions have been the subject of a long-standing controversy. Djankov et al. (2008) find that aid is worse than oil in the sense of having a stronger negative impact on the level of democracy, thus furnishing critics with econometric support. On the other hand, the meta-study of Askarov and Doucouliagos (2013) suggests a more cautionary conclusion. While the overall effects are non-positive, aid seems to have fostered democracy in European transition countries. In addition, Kersting and Kilby (2014) argue that foreign transfers can influence the political regime of the recipient country in diverse ways, so careful attention to timing is necessary to tease out the total impact. They conclude that aid works as a positive incentive to democratization, a finding that is supported by the work of Brück and Xu (2012).

A detrimental effect of aid is consistent with the theoretical model of Acemoglu et al. (2004), showing how a kleptocrat can stay in power by skillfully buying off any take-over threats by the opposition using resource rents or aid. However, additional resources are likely to benefit any incumbent leader regardless of regime, at least to the extent that the strings attached are loose. A more general problem transcending the issue of the political regime is therefore that aid makes governments accountable to donors instead of citizens.[41] Of course, if NGOs are captive subcontractors for foreign aid agencies, this accountability problem is aggravated. It is also likely to make it more attractive to be in control over the aid rents that pass through the government.

15.3.5 Contesting the Positions Controlling Aid Appropriation

Violence could be considered the most extreme form of rent seeking. In this case, the rent is the resources that can be commanded by capturing the state. The struggle for power is often modeled in terms of the probability of winning using some form of the Tullock contest function, sometimes adjusted with a parameter quantifying the advantage an incumbent has by commanding the repressive apparatus of the state. In such a setting, aid has several possible effects. First of all, it raises the size of the prize, which

government staff and find that the data is consistent with this story in the sense that aid undermines bureaucratic quality more, the more donors there are.

[41] The classic reference is Moore (1998). Eubank (2012) uses the case of Somaliland, which is not internationally recognized and thus receives no aid, to demonstrate how the need for tax revenues can force unrepresentative governments into concessions in the form of more accountable political institutions.

should lead to more intense competition for power. Secondly, aid channeled through the government could increase any incumbency advantage by allowing for higher military spending. In fact, as aid is fungible, even funds for projects outside the public sector could allow the incumbent to spend more to fight or repress the opposition.[42] Thirdly, if aid fosters growth, thereby raising incomes, the opportunity cost of fighting is increased. As argued in the introduction, the evidence for a growth effect of aid is not very strong. The latter channel can hence probably safely be ignored. We are then left with two effects that counteract one other: aid makes it more attractive to be the sovereign, but also facilitates holding on to power through repression. Which of these prevail is an empirical question.[43]

De Ree and Nillesen (2009) find no significant effect of aid on the onset of civil conflicts in sub-Saharan Africa, the most aid-dependent region, but a negative effect on their duration. Similarly, in the data set of Nielsen et al. (2011), negative aid shocks increase the probability of conflict. In contrast, Nunn and Qian (2012) find that US food aid raises the likelihood as well as duration of civil conflict. This is consistent with the model of Blouin and Pallage (2008). They show that when there is no clear incumbent or rebels control parts of the territory of a state, warring factions can finance their expenditures for arms and soldiers by 'taxing' humanitarian aid organizations.

This further suggests that the geographical distribution of aid within a recipient country matters, as argued by Findley et al. (2011). Investigating Angola, Mozambique and Sierra Leone, they find that aid activities attract conflict. Another mechanism is uncovered by Crost et al. (2014). They study a large-scale intervention in the Philippines financed by the World Bank. Municipalities that were just eligible experienced an increase in conflict as rebels apparently wanted to prevent the program from being successful, fearing this would undermine their support in the population.

Of course, these results do not imply that aid does not lead to social waste when conflicts are quelled and prevented through large-scale expenditures on repression.[44] Moreover, even in countries not prone to (open) violent conflict, foreign transfers could allow rulers to stay in power longer. As I just argued, dictators might use such funds to finance 'divide-and-rule' strategies, but democratic incumbents can also enhance their election probabilities with the help of plentiful patronage spending coming directly or indirectly from fungible aid. Indeed, Kono and Montinola (2009) find that aid helps both autocratic and democratic leaders survive, albeit in slightly different ways.

In turn, as even altruistic donors have an interest in who is allocating their funds in recipient countries, it is unsurprising to find that leadership effects impinge on donor strategies. As shown by Faye and Niehaus (2012), donors give significantly more (less) in election years to more (less) closely aligned governments. US governments of different ideological stripes are also more inclined to fund generously recipient counterparts of

---

42 Collier and Hoeffler (2007) do indeed find that development aid is fungible into military spending.

43 As pointed out by Mehlum and Moene (2006), the issue is actually slightly more complex, for a larger incumbency advantage makes the prize more secure and thus more tempting. This could intensify the fighting.

44 For an analysis of the effects of aid in a model with three possible states – peace, repression and civil war – see Besley and Persson (2011).

similar persuasions (Lskavyan 2014). It seems safe to conclude that the political economies of donors and recipients are inextricably intertwined.

15.4 CONCLUSION

Aid is a sovereign rent much like natural resource rents. As rent seeking is often blamed for the sub-par economic performance of resource-rich countries, it is natural to check whether such unproductive activities can explain why foreign aid on average seems to have little impact on economic development. Theoretically, the comparative statics result is clear: more aid leads to more rent seeking. In recipient countries where governance is poor, this response can be strong enough to outweigh the direct positive effects of the transfer.

Empirically, the picture is less clear. For the two main forms of domestic rent seeking for which we have data, corruption and armed conflict, the jury is still out on the question of whether aid fosters them. This could be due to poor data, but also due to aid being endogenous. However, while some donor organizations condition their transfers on the quality of governance and policies, we have seen that it is not clear whether there is a trend toward greater selectivity on these grounds and the studies of corruption and conflict reviewed here do try to address the endogeneity issue. Moreover, there are other ways in which foreign assistance could have negative effects on economic performance, for example, Dutch disease, large transaction costs and the entrenchment of unaccountable elites. The keyword seems to be heterogeneity, and we need more finely calibrated empirical studies that can pick up variations in aid effects across space and time.

This does not mean that the concept of rent seeking is not relevant to the topic of foreign aid. In a more general sense, there are numerous indications that plentiful aid distracts recipients' attention away from more important sources of progress. Furthermore, I see a number of ways in which more research can further our understanding. First of all, not all aid is equally susceptible to appropriation, but this has so far received scant attention in the literature. Secondly, the main qualification to the analogy between aid and resource rents is that the size and durability of the sovereign rent is to a much larger extent under the control of other agents in the former case. Analyzing dynamic models in which donors have a mix of altruistic and selfish interests, generating a mix of durable and transient rents, is likely to further our insights on aid impact.[45] Thirdly, in the literature on the Samaritan's Dilemma, recipients manipulate some variable of interest to the donor in order to receive more aid. However, anecdotal evidence suggests that aid seeking also occurs directly through economic diplomacy. This close cousin of standard rent seeking has to my knowledge not been explored formally. Finally, international aid seeking and domestic rent seeking could be combined in a hierarchical game.[46] A greater understanding of larger parts of the aid chain might allow for changes that make such

---

[45] A natural starting point for such inquiries would be the general analysis of rents of different and uncertain durabilities by Aidt and Hillman (2008).

[46] Long (2013), reprinted in Chapter 3 this volume, presents an excellent review of rent-seeking contests in general, including hierarchical ones.

transfers more immune to rent seeking at all levels. Unfortunately, given the fact that the ends of the chain are unconnected and that the starting point is donor-taxpayers with expressive behavior, there is little reason to expect major improvements in overall aid effectiveness.

REFERENCES

Acemoglu, Daron, Simon Johnson and James A. Robinson (2005), 'Institutions as a fundamental cause of long-run growth', in Philippe Aghion and Steven N. Durlauf (eds), *Handbook of Economic Growth*, Amsterdam: Elsevier, pp. 385–472.

Acemoglu, Daron, James A. Robinson and Thierry Verdier (2004), 'Kleptocracy and divide-and-rule: a model of personal rule', *Journal of the European Economic Association*, **2**(2–3), 162–92.

Aidt, Toke S. and Arye L. Hillman (2008), 'Enduring rents', *European Journal of Political Economy*, **24**(3), 545–53.

Aldashev, Gani, Esteban Jaimovich and Thierry Verdier (2014), 'When warm glow burns: motivational (mis) allocation in the non-profit sector', CEPR Discussion Paper No. 9963, London.

Alesina, Alberto and David Dollar (2000), 'Who gives foreign aid to whom and why?', *Journal of Economic Growth*, **5**(1), 33–63.

Alesina, Alberto and Beatrice Weder (2002), 'Do corrupt governments receive less foreign aid?', *American Economic Review*, **92**(4), 1126–37.

Andreoni, James (1989), 'Giving with impure altruism: applications to charity and Ricardian equivalence', *Journal of Political Economy*, **97**(6), 1447–58.

Andreoni, James (2006), 'Philanthropy', in Serge-Christophe Kolm and Jean M. Ythier (eds), *Handbook of the Economics of Giving, Altruism and Reciprocity*, Amsterdam: North-Holland, pp. 1201–69.

Arellano, Christina, Aleš Bulíř, Timothy Lane and Leslie Lipschitz (2009), 'The dynamic implications of foreign aid and its variability', *Journal of Development Economics*, **88**(1), 87–102.

Askarov, Zohid and Hristos Doucouliagos (2013), 'Does aid improve democracy and governance? A meta-regression analysis', *Public Choice*, **157**(3–4), 601–28.

Barr, Abigail and Marcel Fafchamps (2006), 'A client-community assessment of the NGO sector in Uganda', *Journal of Development Studies*, **42**(4), 611–39.

Barr, Abigail, Marcel Fafchamps and Trudy Owens (2005), 'The governance of non-governmental organizations in Uganda', *World Development*, **33**(4), 657–79.

Bergstrom, Theodore, Lawrence Blume and Hal Varian (1986), 'On the private provision of public goods', *Journal of Public Economics*, **29**(1), 25–49.

Berthélemy, Jean-Claude (2006), 'Bilateral donors' interest vs. recipients' development motives in aid allocation: do all donors behave the same?', *Review of Development Economics*, **10**(2), 179–94.

Besley, Timothy and Torsten Persson (2011), 'Fragile states and development policy', *Journal of the European Economic Association*, **9**(3), 371–98.

Bjørnskov, Christian (2010), 'Do elites benefit from democracy and foreign aid in developing countries?', *Journal of Development Economics*, **92**(2), 115–24.

Blouin, Max and Stéphane Pallage (2008), 'Humanitarian relief and civil conflict', *Journal of Conflict Resolution*, **52**(4), 548–65.

Boone, Peter (1996), 'Politics and the effectiveness of foreign aid', *European Economic Review*, **40**(2), 289–329.

Boschini, Anne and Anders Olofsgård (2007), 'Foreign aid: an instrument for fighting communism?', *Journal of Development Studies*, **43**(4), 622–48.

Bräutigam, Deborah A. and Stephen Knack (2004), 'Foreign aid, institutions and governance in Sub-Saharan Africa', *Economic Development and Cultural Change*, **52**(2), 255–85.

Brück, Tilman and Guo Xu (2012), 'Who gives aid to whom and when? Aid accelerations, shocks and policies', *European Journal of Political Economy*, **28**(4), 593–606.

Buchanan, James M. (1975), 'The Samaritan's Dilemma', in Edmund S. Phelps (ed.), *Altruism, Morality, and Economic Theory*, New York: Russell Sage Foundation, pp. 71–85.

Burger, Ronelle and Trudy Owens (2010), 'Promoting transparency in the NGO sector: examining the availability and reliability of self-reported data', *World Development*, **38**(9), 1263–77.

Burnside, Craig and David Dollar (2000), 'Aid, policies and growth', *American Economic Review*, **90**(4), 847–68.

Busse, Matthias and Steffen Gröning (2009), 'Does foreign aid improve governance?', *Economics Letters*, **104**(2), 76–8.

Casella, Alessandra and Barry Eichengreen (1996), 'Can foreign aid accelerate stabilization?', *Economic Journal*, **106**(May), 605–19.

Chabal, Patrick and Jean-Pascal Daloz (1999), *Africa Works: Disorder as Political Instrument*, Oxford: James Currey.

Claessens, Stijn, Danny Cassimon and Bjorn Van Campenhout (2009), 'Evidence on changes in aid allocation criteria', *World Bank Economic Review*, **23**(2), 185–208.

Collier, Paul (2006), 'Is aid oil? An analysis of whether Africa can absorb more aid', *World Development*, **34**(9), 1482–97.

Collier, Paul and Anke Hoeffler (2007), 'Unintended consequences: does aid promote arms races?', *Oxford Bulletin of Economics and Statistics*, **69**(1), 1–27.

Crost, Benjamin, Joseph Felter and Patrick Johnston (2014), 'Aid under fire: development projects and civil conflict', *American Economic Review*, **104**(6), 1833–56.

Dalgaard, Carl-Johan and Ola Olsson (2008), 'Windfall gains, political economy and economic development', *Journal of African Economies*, **17**(AERC Suppl. 1), i72–i109.

De Ree, Joppe and Eleonora Nillesen (2009), 'Aiding violence or peace? The impact of foreign aid on the risk of civil conflict in Sub-Saharan Africa', *Journal of Development Economics*, **88**(2), 301–13.

de Waal, Alex (2013), 'The theory and practice of Meles Zenawi', *African Affairs*, **112**(446), 148–55.

Devarajan, Shantayanan, David R. Dollar and Torgny Holmgren (2001), 'Overview', in Shantayanan Devarajan, David R. Dollar and Torgny Holmgren (eds), *Aid & Reform in Africa*, Washington, DC: The World Bank, pp. 1–41.

Djankov, Simeon, Jose G. Montalvo and Marta Reynal-Querol (2008), 'The curse of aid', *Journal of Economic Growth*, **13**(3), 169–94.

Djankov, Simeon, Jose G. Montalvo and Marta Reynal-Querol (2009), 'Aid with multiple personalities', *Journal of Comparative Economics*, **37**(2), 217–29.

Docouliagos, Hristos and Martin Paldam (2008), 'Aid effectiveness on growth: a meta study', *European Journal of Political Economy*, **24**(1), 1–24.

Docouliagos, Hristos and Martin Paldam (2010), 'Conditional aid effectiveness: a meta-study', *Journal of International Development*, **22**(4), 391–410.

Docouliagos, Hristos and Martin Paldam (2011), 'The ineffectiveness of development aid on growth: an update', *European Journal of Political Economy*, **27**(2), 399–404.

Dollar, David and Victoria Levin (2006), 'The increasing selectivity of foreign aid, 1984–2003', *World Development*, **34**(12), 2034–46.

Dollar, David and Jakob Svensson (1998), 'What explains the success or failure of structural adjustment programs?', *Economic Journal*, **110**(466), 894–917.

Drazen, Allan and William Easterly (2001), 'Do crises induce reforms? Simple empirical tests of conventional wisdom', *Economics and Politics*, **13**(2) 129–57.

Dreher, Axel and James R. Vreeland (2011), 'Buying votes and international organizations', Discussion Paper 78, Courant Research Centre, Georg-August-Universität, Göttingen.

Dreher, Axel, Vera Eichenauer and Kai Gehring (2013), 'Geopolitics, aid and growth', Working Paper 4299, CESifo, Munich.

Dreher, Axel, Florian Mölders and Peter Nunnenkamp (2010), 'Aid delivery through non- governmental organisations: does the aid channel matter for the targeting of Swedish aid?', *World Economy*, **33**(2), 147–76.

Dreher, Axel, Peter Nunnenkamp, Susann Thiel and Rainer Thiele (2012a), 'Aid allocation by German NGOs: does the degree of official financing matter?', *World Economy*, **35**(11), 1448–72.

Dreher, Axel, Peter Nunnenkamp, Hannes Öhler and Johannes Weisser (2012b), 'Financial dependence and aid allocation by Swiss NGOs: a panel Tobit analysis', *Economic Development and Cultural Change*, **60**(4), 829–67.

Easterly, William (2001), *The Elusive Quest for Growth. Economists' Adventures and Misadventures in the Tropics*, Cambridge, MA: MIT Press.

Easterly, William (2002), 'The cartel of good intentions: the problem of bureaucracy in foreign aid', *Journal of Policy Reform*, **5**(4), 223–50.

Easterly, William (2005a), 'National policies and economic growth: a reappraisal', in Philippe Aghion and Steven N. Durlauf (eds), *Handbook of Economic Growth*, Amsterdam: Elsevier, pp. 1015–59.

Easterly, William (2005b), 'What did structural adjustment adjust? The association of policies and growth with repeated IMF and World Bank adjustment loans', *Journal of Development Economics*, **76**(1), 1–22.

Easterly, William and Claudia R. Williamson (2011), 'Rhetoric versus reality: the best and worst of aid agency practices', *World Development*, **39**(11), 1930–49.

Economides, George, Sarantis Kalyvitis and Apostolis Philippopoulos (2008), 'Does foreign aid distort incentives and hurt growth? Theory and evidence from 75 aid-recipient countries', *Public Choice*, **134**(3–4), 463–88.

Eisensee, Thomas and David Strömberg (2007), 'News droughts, news floods, and U.S. disaster relief', *Quarterly Journal of Economics*, **122**(2), 693–728.
Eubank, Nicholas (2012), 'Taxation, political accountability and foreign aid: lessons from Somaliland', *Journal of Development Studies*, **48**(4), 465–80.
Fafchamps, Marcel and Trudy Owens (2009), 'The determinants of funding to Ugandan nongovernmental organizations', *World Bank Economic Review*, **23**(2), 295–321.
Faye, Michael and Paul Niehaus (2012), 'Political aid cycles', *American Economic Review*, **102**(7), 3516–30.
Feyzioglu, Tarhan, Vinaya Swaroop and Min Zhu (1998), 'A panel data analysis of the fungibility of foreign aid', *World Bank Economic Review*, **12**(1), 29–58.
Findley, Michael G., Josh Powell, Daniel Strandow and Jeff Tanner (2011), 'The localized geography of foreign aid: a new dataset and application to violent armed conflict', *World Development*, **39**(11), 1995–2009.
Francois, Patrick (2000), 'Public service motivation as an argument for government provision', *Journal of Public Economics*, **78**(3), 275–99.
Francois, Patrick (2003), 'Not-for-profit provision of public services', *Economic Journal*, **113**(486), C53–C61.
Glaeser, Edward L. and Andrei Shleifer (2001), 'Not-for-profit entrepreneurs', *Journal of Public Economics*, **81**(1), 99–115.
Hagen, Rune J. (2006a), 'Buying influence: aid fungibility in a strategic perspective', *Review of Development Economics*, **10**(2), 267–84.
Hagen, Rune J. (2006b), 'Samaritan agents? On the strategic delegation of aid policy', *Journal of Development Economics*, **79**(1), 249–63.
Hagen, Rune J. (2015), 'Dancing to the donors' tune? Policy choice in aid-dependent countries', *Scandinavian Journal of Economics*, **117**(1), 126–63.
Hansmann, Henry B. (1980), 'The role of nonprofit enterprise', *Yale Law Journal*, **89**(5), 835–901.
Headey, Derek (2008), 'Geopolitics and the effect of foreign aid on economic growth: 1970–2001', *Journal of International Development*, **20**(2), 161–80.
Heckelman, Jac C. and Stephen Knack (2008), 'Foreign aid and market-liberalizing reform', *Economica*, **75**(299), 524–48.
Herzer, Dierk and Peter Nunnenkamp (2013), 'Private donations, government grants, commercial activities, and fundraising: cointegration and causality for NGOs in international development cooperation', *World Development*, **46**, 234–51.
Hillman, Arye L. (2010), 'Expressive behavior in economics and politics', *European Journal of Political Economy*, **26**(4), 403–18.
Hodler, Roland (2007), 'Rent seeking and aid effectiveness', *International Tax and Public Finance*, **14**(5), 525–41.
Hoeffler, Anke and Verity Outram (2011), 'Need, merit, or self-interest – what determines the allocation of aid?', *Review of Development Economics*, **15**(2), 237–50.
Huysentruyt, Marieke (2011), 'Development aid by contract: outsourcing and contractor identity', Unpublished paper, London School of Economics.
Ivanova, Anna, Wolfgang Mayer, Alex Mourmouras and George Anayiotos (2003), 'What determines the implementation of IMF-supported programs?', IMF Working Paper 03/8, International Monetary Fund, Washington, DC.
Kamata, Ng'wanza (2012), 'The economic diplomacy of Tanzania: accumulation by dispossession in a peripheral state', *Agrarian South: Journal of Political Economy*, **1**(3), 291–313.
Kersting, Erasmus and Christopher Kilby (2014), 'Aid and democracy redux', *European Economic Review*, **67**, 125–43.
Kilby, Christopher and Axel Dreher (2010), 'The impact of aid on growth revisited: do donor motives matter?', *Economics Letters*, **107**(3), 338–40.
Klein, Michael and Tim Harford (2005), *The Market for Aid*, Washington, DC: International Finance Corporation.
Knack, Stephen (2001), 'Aid dependence and the quality of governance: cross-country empirical tests', *Southern Economic Journal*, **68**(2), 310–29.
Knack, Stephen and Aminur Rahman (2007), 'Donor fragmentation and bureaucratic quality in aid recipients', *Journal of Development Economics*, **83**(1), 176–97.
Koch, Dirk-Jan, Axel Dreher, Peter Nunnenkamp and Rainer Thiele (2009), 'Keeping a low profile: what determines the allocation of aid by non-governmental organizations?', *World Development*, **37**(5), 902–18.
Kono, Daniel Y. and Gabriella R. Montinola (2009), 'Does foreign aid support autocrats, democrats, or both?', *Journal of Politics*, **71**(2), 704–18.
Kopczuk, Wojciech, Joel Slemrod and Shlomo Yitzhaki (2005), 'The limitations of decentralized world redistribution: an optimal taxation approach', *European Economic Review*, **49**(4), 1051–79.
Krueger, Anne O. (1974), 'The political economy of the rent-seeking society', *American Economic Review*,

64(3), 291–303, reprinted in James M. Buchanan, Robert D. Tollison and Gordon Tullock (eds) (1980), *Toward a Theory of the Rent-seeking Society*, College Station, TX: Texas A&M University Press, pp. 51–70.
Long, Ngo Van (2013), 'The theory of contests: a unified model and review of the literature', *European Journal of Political Economy*, **32**, 161–81, reprinted as Chapter 3 in this volume.
Lskavyan, Vahe (2014), 'Donor–recipient ideological differences and economic aid', *Economics Letters*, **123**(3), 345–7.
Martens, Bertin (2005), 'Why do aid agencies exist?', *Development Policy Review*, **23**(6), 643–63.
Martens, Bertin, Uwe Mummert, Peter Murrell and Paul Seabright (2002), *The Institutional Economics of Foreign Aid*, Cambridge: Cambridge University Press.
Mayer, Wolfgang and Alex Mourmouras (2008), 'IMF conditionality: an approach based on the theory of special interest politics', *Review of International Organizations*, **3**(2), 105–21.
Mehlum, Halvor and Karl Moene (2006), 'Fighting against the odds', *Economics of Governance*, **7**(1), 75–87.
Moore, Mick (1998), 'Death without taxes: democracy, state capacity, and aid dependence in the fourth world', in Mark Robinson and Gordon White (eds), *The Democratic Developmental State: Political and Institutional Design*, Oxford: Oxford University Press, pp. 84–121.
Morfit, N. Simon (2011), '"AIDS is money": how donor preferences reconfigure local realities', *World Development*, **39**(1), 64–76.
Nielsen, Richard A., Michael G. Findley, Zachary S. Davis, Tara Candland and Daniel L. Nielson (2011), 'Foreign aid shocks as a cause of violent armed conflict', *American Journal of Political Science*, **55**(2), 219–32.
Nunn, Nathan and Nancy Qian (2012), 'Aiding conflict: the impact of U.S. food aid on civil war', Working Paper 17794, National Bureau of Economic Research, Cambridge, Massachusetts.
Nunnenkamp, Peter and Hannes Öhler (2011), 'Aid allocation through various official and private channels: need, merit and self-interest as motives of German donors', *World Development*, **39**(10), 308–23.
Nunnenkamp, Peter and Hannes Öhler (2012), 'How to attract donations: the case of US NGOs in international development', *Journal of Development Studies*, **48**(10), 1522–35.
Nunnenkamp, Peter, Hannes Öhler, and Tillmann Schwörer (2013), 'US based NGOs in international development: financial and economic determinants of survival', *World Development*, **46**, 45–65.
Nunnenkamp, Peter, Janina Weingarth and Johannes Weisser (2009), 'Is NGO aid not so different after all? Comparing the allocation of Swiss aid by private and official donors', *European Journal of Political Economy*, **25**(4), 422–38.
Olson, Mancur (1971), *The Logic of Collective Action: Public Goods and the Theory of Groups*, Cambridge, MA: Harvard University Press.
Pedersen, Karl R. (1996), 'Aid, investment and incentives', *Scandinavian Journal of Economics*, **98**(3), 423–38.
Pedersen, Karl R. (2001), 'The Samaritan's dilemma and the effectiveness of foreign aid', *International Tax and Public Finance*, **8**(5–6), 693–703.
Rajan, Raghuram G. and Arvind Subramanian (2007), 'Does aid affect governance?', *American Economic Review*, **97**(2), 322–7.
Rajan, Raghuram G. and Arvind Subramanian (2008), 'Aid and growth: what does the cross-country evidence really show?', *Review of Economics and Statistics*, **90**(4), 643–65.
Rajan, Raghuram G. and Arvind Subramanian (2011), 'Aid, Dutch disease, and manufacturing growth', *Journal of Development Economics*, **94**(1), 106–18.
Reinikka, Ritva and Jakob Svensson (2004), 'Local capture: evidence from a central government transfer program in Uganda', *Quarterly Journal of Economics*, **119**(2), 679–705.
Ribar, David C. and Mark O. Wilhelm (2002), 'Altruistic and joy-of-giving motivations in charitable behavior', *Journal of Political Economy*, **110**(2), 425–57.
Rodrik, Dani (1989), 'Promises, promises: credible policy reform via signalling', *Economic Journal*, **99**(September), 756–72.
Roodman, David (2007), 'The anarchy of numbers: aid, development, and cross-country empirics', *World Bank Economic Review*, **21**(2), 255–77.
Salamon, Lester M., S. Wojciech Sokolowski and associates (2004), 'Global civil society: an overview', in Lester M. Salamon, S. Wojciech Sokolowski and associates (eds), *Global Civil Society: Dimensions of the Nonprofit Sector*, Vol. 2, Bloomfield, CT: Kumarian Press, pp. 3–60.
Smith, Daniel J. (2003), 'Patronage, per diems and the "workshop mentality": the practice of family planning programs in Southeastern Nigeria', *World Development*, **31**(4), 703–15.
Svensson, Jakob (1999), 'Aid, growth and democracy', *Economics and Politics*, **11**(3), 275–97.
Svensson, Jakob (2000a), 'Foreign aid and rent seeking', *Journal of International Economics*, **51**(2), 437–61, reprinted in Roger D. Congleton, Arye L. Hillman and Kai A. Konrad (eds) (2008), *40 Years of Research on Rent Seeking 2 – Applications: Rent Seeking in Practice*, Heidelberg: Springer, pp. 165–89.
Svensson, Jakob (2000b), 'When is foreign aid policy credible? Aid dependence and conditionality', *Journal of Development Economics*, **61**(1), 61–84.
Tavares, José (2003), 'Does foreign aid corrupt?', *Economics Letters*, **79**(1), 99–106.

Tullock, Gordon (1967), 'The welfare costs of tariffs, monopolies, and theft', *Western Economic Journal*, **5**(3), 224–32, reprinted in Roger D. Congleton, Arye L. Hillman and Kai A. Konrad (eds) (2008), *40 Years of Research on Rent Seeking 1 – The Theory of Rent Seeking*, Heidelberg: Springer, pp. 45–53.

Tullock, Gordon (1980), 'Efficient rent seeking', in James M. Buchanan, Robert D. Tollison and Gordon Tullock (eds), *Toward a Theory of the Rent-seeking Society*, College Station, TX: Texas A&M University Press, pp. 97–112, reprinted in Roger D. Congleton, Arye L. Hillman and Kai A. Konrad (eds) (2008), *40 Years of Research on Rent Seeking 1 – The Theory of Rent Seeking*, Heidelberg: Springer, pp. 105–20.

Werker, Eric and Faisal Z. Ahmed (2008), 'What do nongovernmental organizations do?', *Journal of Economic Perspectives*, **22**(2), 73–92.

Werker, E., Faisal Z. Ahmed and Charles Cohen (2009), 'How is foreign aid spent? Evidence from a natural experiment', *American Economic Journal: Macroeconomics*, **1**(2), 225–44.

World Bank (2008), *Aid Architecture: An Overview of the Main Trends in Official Development Assistance Flows*, update May, Washington, DC: The World Bank.

World Bank (2013), *The World Bank Group Goals: End Extreme Poverty and Promote Shared Prosperity*, Washington, DC: The World Bank.

16. Rent seeking in international organizations

Roland Vaubel

SUMMARY

The chapter analyzes rent seeking by international organizations and through international organizations. Rent seeking by international organizations is more pervasive than rent seeking by national bureaucracies to the extent that the information cost of politicians and voters is higher but less pervasive to the extent that politicians have less to fear from international bureaucrats than from national bureaucrats. The chapter presents evidence that international organizations charge higher input prices, employ too large quantities of input and demand excessive budgets. Agency slippage is shown to increase with the number of member states. Rent seeking through international organizations is typical of private interest groups. Special interest groups are more powerful at the international than at the national level to the extent that the information cost of voters is higher and international bureaucrats are less controlled by politicians who want to be re-elected. The chapter presents evidence of the power of interest groups in international organizations. It concludes with a number of recommendations on how rent seeking by and through international organizations could be reduced.

16.1 INTRODUCTION

International organizations supply goods and services, subsidies and regulations. Thus, it cannot be surprising that those working in these organizations seek rents for themselves as producers of these goods and services, confer rents on private interest groups demanding subsidies and regulations and try to participate in the rents of these interest groups. To be short, there is rent seeking by international organizations, and there is rent seeking through international organizations. In the following, these types of rent seeking are analyzed in turn – first theoretically, then empirically.

16.2 RENT SEEKING BY INTERNATIONAL ORGANIZATIONS AS PRODUCERS

16.2.1 Theory

International organizations are bureaucracies. Rent seeking by bureaucracies is a major topic in public choice theory. Bureaucrats try to appropriate the consumer surplus of the politicians or citizens who demand their services. The degree to which a bureaucracy can do this depends on whether it competes with other potential suppliers and, if not, whether it has agenda-setting power. If it is competing, it is unlikely to get part of the consumer surplus – it may not even be able to keep its producer surplus. If it is an agenda setter, it can appropriate both producer and consumer surplus. In this case, the politicians (citizens) face a take-it-or-leave-it decision. Among all solutions acceptable to the politicians (citizens), the bureaucratic agenda setter chooses the one that maximizes his utility.

In the economic theory of bureaucracy, most authors (for example, Niskanen 1971; Migué and Bélanger 1974; Wyckoff 1990) assume that the bureaucracy is an agenda setter. There are two possible reasons for this. First, politicians and citizens may lack information about its minimum cost. Second, the incumbent politicians need its support to win re-election. In the case of international bureaucracies, the politicians' and voters' lack of information is even more severe than in a domestic context but politicians, in their quest for re-election, depend less on international bureaucrats than on domestic bureaucrats. Thus, prima facie, it is not obvious whether agenda setting is more widespread among domestic or international bureaucracies.

The staff of the International Monetary Fund (IMF) seems to be an agenda setter, and the Commission of the European Union has gate-keeping power. Martin (2006) reports that the IMF staff effectively presents the Board of Executive Directors with a take-it-or-leave-it decision when suggesting a credit arrangement. The European Commission has the monopoly of legislative initiative. It is true that the Council and the Parliament may amend the Commission's proposals but if the Commission does not make a proposal, Council and Parliament cannot legislate.

There are also instances of competing international organizations. For example, the IMF competes with the World Bank in providing concessionary loans to developing countries, and the European Stability Mechanism (ESM) competes with the IMF in granting subsidized credits to over-indebted European governments and in negotiating and monitoring policy conditions to be implemented by them.

If the bureaucracy is neither competing nor an agenda setter, rent seeking takes the form of a bilateral game between a monopolist (the bureaucrat) and a monopsonist (the incumbent politician).[1] In the case of an international organization, the bureaucracy plays against the government of the decisive member state. If the governments have to agree unanimously, the government least willing to pay is decisive. If the governments decide by simple majority, the median is decisive.

In the economic theory of bureaucracy, there is some disagreement about the form in which the rents are appropriated by the bureaucratic producer. In the pioneering model of Williamson (1964), the bureaucrat is maximizing her staff. Niskanen (1971) assumed that the bureaucrat spends the rent on additional output, arguing that this is the only way in which she can increase her budget. Migué and Bélanger (1974) added the option of consuming rent in the form of 'slack', that is, leisure, amenities and pleasant relationships with one's inferiors. In their model, the typical bureaucrat chooses a combination of excess output and slack. Wyckoff (1990) analyzes a slack-maximizing bureaucrat.

There is also disagreement as to whether bureaucrats produce too much or too little output. Niskanen and Migué and Bélanger conclude that bureaucratic output is too large. Peacock (1983) and Wyckoff (1990) argue that it is too small. All these models

---

[1] See, for example, Gary Miller (1977).

assume an agenda-setting bureaucrat. If the bureaucrat is not an agenda setter but merely an ordinary monopolist, her output is bound to be too small.[2]

Even though, theoretically, it is not clear whether bureaucrats produce too little or too much and whether they appropriate the rents in the form of leisure, amenities, excess staff or excess output, the economic theory of bureaucracy agrees that the per unit cost of production is likely to be too high and higher than in private firms. This is because bureaucracies are rarely competing and, even if they are, they are not selling their output to cost-conscious private buyers in a market. Moreover, they do not have to fear bankruptcy. Finally, as bureaucrats do not earn profits but fixed salaries, they do not cut costs but thrive on them.

In international bureaucracies, these problems are multiplied. Agency slippage increases with the number of principals (Olson 1965, p. 55; Hardin 1982). There are several reasons for this. First of all, as the number of principals grows, each government's financing share and revenue from controlling the bureaucracy decline. The governments, the media and the citizens have little incentive to monitor the performance of an international organization.

Moreover, as the number of member states grows, each government faces rising costs of persuading the others that action has to be taken against bureaucratic rent seeking.

Finally, the principals' cost of information increases because the growth of membership increases the size of the organization, the average distance between principals and agents and the language barrier.

Is there any evidence that supports these hypotheses?

16.2.2 Evidence

A study of 27 international organizations in the years 1950–2001 (Vaubel et al. 2007) reveals that, on average, staff increased at a compound average rate of 3.2 percent per annum, while the number of member states rose by only 2.5 percent per annum. National civilian government employment in the Organisation for Economic Co-operation and Development (OECD) countries expanded even less, namely by 2.1 percent per annum. This evidence may indicate that bureaucratic rent seeking is a serious problem in international organizations and that it is more prevalent in international than in national bureaucracies. But the evidence may also indicate that the voters, the national legislatures or the national governments have preferred to confer more and more tasks on international organizations. In any case, international organizations play an important role in the growth of government.

To demonstrate rent seeking more specific evidence is required. Four types of evidence will be distinguished:

- Input costs are higher in international organizations than in comparable national bureaucracies.

[2] Assume that the politician knows the shape and slope of the cost curve – for example, constant marginal costs – but that he does not know its location and that he is so powerful that he will not consciously give up consumer surplus. Then the bureaucrat maximizes her rent by behaving like a normal monopolist, reducing output until marginal revenue equals minimum marginal cost.

- Input quantities and costs are not significantly related to the size of the task of the international organization.
- Input quantities and costs in international organizations depend significantly on factors that should play no role in an efficient institution and that may be attributed to rent seeking.
- International bureaucrats prefer larger budgets for their organization than the voters do.

16.2.2.1 Higher input prices

The available evidence relates to the cost of labor. Salaries tend to be much higher in international organizations than in comparable national bureaucracies. In 1986, the last year for which the IMF has published the relevant data, net salaries at the IMF exceeded gross salaries at the Federal Reserve Board – also in Washington – by 64 percent (Vaubel 1991). Obviously, the difference in net salaries is even larger. Irwin (1994) reports that in the early 1990s, salaries at the World Bank were almost as high as at the IMF – only 5 percent less. Frey (1985, table 8.3) demonstrated that net salaries at the OECD in Paris exceeded those of comparable German civil servants by 58 percent on average.

The most recent comparison of after-tax salaries relates to the European Commission (Vaubel 2009). The raw data have been compiled and published by the Commission itself – at the request of the Council with which the final decision about salaries rests. The results are shown in Table 16.1.

The net salary of a non-expatriate official (for example, a Belgian working at the Commission in Brussels) is set equal to 100 to control for differences in the cost of living. I have selected three grades (A4/A5, B4/B5 and C4/C5) for which data from all five reference countries and the European Investment Bank (EIB) are available. The

Table 16.1 Relative net salaries at the European Commission and in the central governments of selected member states

EU grade		Commission		EIB	Germany	UK	France	Denmark	Italy
		Non-expatriate	Expatriate						
A4/A5	S	100	123	147	63	74	81	60	27
(councillor)	M	100	121	149	62	61	80	53	24
B4/B5	S	100	120	151	70	84	59	66	41
(secretary)	M	100	119	158	67	67	53	59	43
C4/C5	S	100	120	147	71	57	57	62	46
(security officer)	M	100	117	154	67	44	50	53	37
Average	S	100	121	148	68	72	66	63	38
	M	100	119	154	65	57	61	55	35
	M + S	100	120	151	67	65	63	59	36

Source: European Commission, *Comparative Study of the Remuneration of Officials of the European Institutions*, June 2000, available at ec.europa.eu/reform/pdf/salaries_study_en.pdf.

first line (S) refers to unmarried persons (singles), the second (M) to married couples with two children. The overall average for the five reference countries is 58 percent. This means that an average non-expatriate Commission official earns 72 percent more than a comparable national civil servant. Of course, the salary differential is much larger for nationals of low-income countries who are not covered by the Commission study. In particular, the study, published in 2000, does not include the East European countries that joined in 2004. The study also shows that salaries are somewhat higher at the European Commission than at the North Atlantic Treaty Organization (NATO) Secretariat or UN agencies in Brussels and, moreover, that salaries at the EIB are about 50 percent higher than at the Commission (Table 16.1). The reason usually given to justify this wage differential is that the EIB has to be competitive vis-à-vis private banks. However, its present chairman, a former politician, and most members of its management committee do not have any banking experience.

Rent seeking may also be fraudulent, of course. Some international organizations, for example, the IMF, the World Bank and the European Union (EU), have an independent evaluation office, a court of auditors, an anti-corruption agency or a combination of these. As the dealings and wheelings of international organizations are largely withdrawn from the attention of the voters and media in the member states, irregularities are more likely. In fact, there is evidence of a significantly positive correlation between political centralization and corruption (Fisman and Gatti 2002). A recent and well-known case was the United Nations' (UN) Iraqi oil for food program. An independent commission of inquiry set up in 2005 and chaired by Paul Volcker revealed serious fraud and corruption in its administration.

In the EU, two in three respondents believe that fraud against the EU budget is common and only one in five says that EU institutions are effective in fighting it (Eurobarometer, January 2004). In another survey in the same year, 74 percent agreed with the statement that 'clientelism and corruption are problems in the political institutions of the EU in Brussels' (Haller 2008, p. 345). In 1999, the whole college of Commissioners resigned because an independent committee of inquiry had found evidence of widespread fraud, corruption mismanagement and nepotism. The main culprit was Commissioner Edith Cresson. In 2003, the director of the European Statistical Office, a Frenchman, was involved in a corruption scandal and had to resign. In 2002, the Commission's chief accountant was suspended (and later dismissed) after she refused to sign accounts she believed to be unreliable (Andreasen 2009).

The European Court of Auditors (ECA) and the European anti-fraud office (OLAF) may be doing their best but they do not seem to be very successful. OLAF has less than 20 investigators. The ECA has refused to clear the Commission's accounts each year since 1994, but spending errors continue to abound.[3] OLAF has estimated the damage from fraud at more than 1.5 billion euros per annum.

[3] In 2011, for example, 3.9 percent of EU budgetary spending was found to be erroneous. In the policy areas 'regional policy, transportation and energy' as well as 'rural development' more than one half of the examined expenditures were found to be incorrect. In 2013, even 4.7 percent of overall spending was incorrect.

16.2.2.2 Quantity of inputs unrelated to task

Parkinson (1957) popularized the idea that bureaucracies expand even when their tasks are being reduced. They grow simply because they exist or because they have grown in the past. A possible reason is that each new organization is at the same time an organized interest group employing its resources to increase its budget, power, prestige and amenities. If so, it should be much easier to set up a new international organization than to abolish it. The establishment of the organization alters the political equilibrium. An increase of the demand for its output raises its employment by more than an equal decrease of demand reduces its employment. Thus, its staff expands even if demand merely fluctuates around a constant mean.[4] The theory predicts that staff growth should contain a positive autoregressive component. However, I have been unable to find this.

Parkinson's examples related to national bureaucracies, the British admiralty and the British colonial office. Their staff increased while the number of war ships and colonies, respectively, decreased. However, staff growth unrelated to task has also been observed in international organizations. For instance, the number of IMF staff does not depend significantly on the size of the balance of payments problems or reserve losses of those member states whose international reserves are below average relative to imports (Vaubel 1991, table 6, 1996, table 2A). Similarly, staff size and real administrative expenditure at the International Bank for Reconstruction and Development (IBRD) are not affected by the number of new loans (Vaubel 1996, table 2B).

In normal times, bureaucracies grow gradually. In Tullock's words (1965 [2005], p. 186), 'such progressive building up of a bureaucratic system normally results from a series of individual expansions that are discussed one by one, and each on its own merits independent of the whole structure'. Such 'bureaucratic incrementalism' (Yates 1982) tends to escape the attention of the voters and media in the member states. In times of crisis, the resources of international organizations frequently jump upward. Typically, there is a ratchet effect because the bureaucracy uses its increased power to defend its 'acquis' and because the political actors in the member states lose interest in the international organization once the crisis is over. Peacock and Wiseman (1961) have documented such crisis-induced leaps and ratchet effects for national government spending. Among the international organizations, the history of the IMF and the EU provides the best examples. The IMF has strongly expanded in response to the oil crisis of 1973, the Latin American debt crisis of 1982, the Asian Financial Crisis of 1997 and the financial market crisis of 2008.[5] The EU reacted to the European sovereign debt crisis unfolding from 2010 by establishing a European Financial Stability Facility, a ESM, a Single Supervisory Mechanism and a Single Resolution Mechanism for the euro-states. The German Minister of Finance told the *New York Times* (18 November 2011): 'We can only achieve political union if we have a crisis.'

Thus, the size and structure of an international bureaucracy, at any given point

---

[4] For a formal exposition, see Vaubel (1994, pp. 158ff).

[5] IMF staff grew by 5.9 percent in 1974, 3.9 percent in 1975 and 4.0 percent in 1982 compared with an average compound rate of growth in 1972–88 of 2.3 percent (Vaubel 1991, table 3).

in time, does not represent an equilibrium of current demand and supply. It is path-dependent.

16.2.2.3 Inputs attributable to rent seeking

A panel data analysis for 17 international organizations between 1950 and 2000 reveals that the number of staff members is negatively and significantly affected by the budget share of the largest contributor (almost always the United States), provided that the latter has a conservative government (Vaubel et al. 2007, table 8). Thus, as the financing share of the largest member state dropped due to expanding membership, its incentive to monitor weakened and the international bureaucracies were enabled to extract more rents.

The number of staff also turned out to be significantly larger (all else equal) if the organization's headquarters are outside the United States and if there are many developing countries among its members (Vaubel et al. 2007, table 5).

There is further evidence of rent seeking in specific international organizations. For example, IMF lending has been shown to depend on the quota share of the ten largest contributors and on the date of the next quota review (Vaubel 1991, tables 6 and 7). Once more, the decline of the financing share reduced the incentive to monitor, and 'hurry-up lending' before the next quota review was intended to convey the impression that the Fund was in urgent need of more capital. Similarly, the rate of increase of lending by the International Development Association (IDA), the concessionary branch of the World Bank, rose prior to the date of the next regular replenishment (Vaubel 1996, tables 3B and 4),[6] and IBRD staff was found to depend negatively and significantly on the financing share of the ten largest contributors.

Most governments lack an interest in monitoring the efficiency of the multilateral lending institutions, not only because their contributions are relatively small but also because they expect to be net borrowers. Subsidized loans from these institutions help them to be re-elected. Indeed, there is econometric evidence that the member states draw significantly more on their credit lines with the IMF and the IBRD prior to elections (Dreher and Vaubel 2004). The IMF also commits and disburses significantly more resources immediately after elections (Przeworski and Vreeland 2000; Dreher and Vaubel 2004; Sturm et al. 2005; Moser and Sturm 2011), presumably because the policy conditions agreed in the arrangements can serve as scapegoats for the unpopular measures that often have to be taken after the election to reverse irresponsible expansionary policies adopted before the election.

All these are policies indicating that international organizations seek rents and are successful in doing so. However, it is not only policies but also public proposals and opinion surveys that confirm the hypothesis.

---

6 A former staff member in charge of financing the World Bank told me that this was 'deliberate policy'.

Table 16.2 EU-related opinions of the general public, 50 top Commission officials and 203 members of the European Parliament in nine EU member states (percent)

	General public	Top Commission officials and euro-parliamentarians
The European Union should strengthen its military power in order to play a larger role in the world:		
agree strongly	16	31
agree somewhat	30	34
disagree somewhat	30	17
disagree strongly	21	15
don't know	3	2

Source: European Elite Survey, Centre for the Study of Political Change, University of Siena, May to July 2006 (as published by Ropercenter for Public Opinion Research MCMISC 2006-Elite) and Transatlantic Trends 2006, Topline Data, June 2006, see ropercenter.uconn.edu/CFIDE/cf/action/catalog/abstract.cfm?type=&start=&id=&archno=MCMISC2006-ELITE&abstract=

16.2.2.4 Differences in budgetary preferences

It is well known that the budget proposals of the European Commission always exceed what the Council, that is, the incumbent politicians of the member states, are willing to grant. The same happens in most other international organizations.

For the EU, there are also private opinion polls comparing the preferences of the bureaucrats and the citizens. For example, the pollsters asked whether 'the European Union should strengthen its military power in order to play a larger role in the world'. Table 16.2 reports the results. A larger military role for the EU is desired by a majority (65 percent) of top Commission officials and EU parliamentarians but only by a minority (46 percent) of the citizens. Unfortunately, the responses of the bureaucrats and the parliamentarians cannot be separated.

I now turn to rent seeking by private interest groups through international organizations.

16.3 THE ROLE OF INTERNATIONAL ORGANIZATIONS IN FACILITATING AND EXPLOITING THE RENT SEEKING OF PRIVATE INTEREST GROUPS

16.3.1 Theory

Rent-seeking private interest groups demand subsidies for their products, taxes (tariffs) for their competitors and regulations of price, quantity or quality, which restrict supply. I shall argue that their choice of instrument depends on the strength of their adversaries. If the buyers of the product are also well organized, the interest group prefers subsidies to regulations because subsidies raise the demand for the product and, hence, consumer surplus as well. The subsidies have to be financed by the taxpayers and approved by the national parliaments. If subsidies are difficult to come by because budgetary control is tight, the interest group prefers regulations and tariffs restricting supply and raising producer surplus at the expense of consumer surplus. The rent that can be appropriated in this way is larger, the lower the (absolute) price elasticity of demand for the product. By contrast, the rent that can be attained through subsidies is larger, the higher the (absolute) price elasticity of demand for the product.

Some international organizations, like the World Bank and the IMF, provide mainly subsidies.[7] Even though these are paid to member governments, they may raise the rents of private producers. For example, subsidized IMF and ESM loans to over-indebted governments, as in 1983 and from 2010, raise the rents of the creditor banks. Moreover, ESM loans are used to bail out banks in the euro-zone.

Other international organizations like the International Labour Organization (ILO) and the Bank for Settlements (BIS) produce mainly market regulations.

The EU provides both subsidies (mainly to agriculture, regional development, business research and creditor banks) and regulations (mainly of labor, financial and product markets). However, like the World Trade Organization (WTO), it fights national regulations and tariffs. It also controls national subsidies. Thus, it opposes interest groups at the national level and caters for them at the international level. The catchword is 'integration', which may mean 'market integration' or 'political integration', that is, centralization. 'Integration' is a weasel word that hides the fact that these two types of integration affect rent seeking very differently. While the removal of national subsidies, regulations and tariffs restricting trade and capital movements reduces rent seeking, the provision of EU subsidies, regulations and tariffs (notably anti-dumping duties) increases rent seeking.

Interest groups are likely to exert more influence in international organizations than at the national level. Theory provides two reasons for this. First, as we have seen, international organizations are farther removed from the attention of voters than national policymakers. Interest groups try to bring about policy outcomes that, in their absence, the median voter would not prefer. The median voter is the main adversary of organized interest groups. If the median voter knows little about decision making in international organizations, lobbyists have a field day.

The second reason is that in international organizations, bureaucrats are more influential, and politicians are less influential, than they are in national affairs. Bureaucrats, however, are more responsive to the wishes of lobbyists than politicians are because bureaucrats do not need to be re-elected (Crain and McCormick 1984). Politicians, by contrast, may be punished by the electorate if they take their instructions from interest groups rather than the median voter (Peltzman 1976).

Both considerations run counter to James Madison's view that political centralization weakens lobbyists' influence by establishing constitutional 'checks and balances' that would block one another (Federalist Paper No. 10, 1787 [1987]). In the US context, commercial and financial interests from the East coast, cattle farmers from the Midwest and cotton growers from the South would counteract each other at the federal level.

---

[7] For a recent computation of the *ex post* subsidy in IMF lending, see Urbaczka and Vaubel (2013).

Many Americans, especially in the North, still believe this story (for example, Bollick 1993) because it was the federal government that abolished slavery against the economic interests of the South. What Madison did not take into account is that the more encompassing interests would combine at the federal (and international) level, that organized groups with diverse or even partly conflicting interests would strike deals at the expense of the unorganized groups and that both would become more powerful at the center than they had ever been at the local level because centralization gives the government more power over the citizens. Nevertheless, since the theoretical arguments run both ways, this is an empirical question. Evidence ought to be brought to bear on it.

16.3.2 Evidence

There are two major international organizations that grant formal roles to interest groups in their decision-making processes: the ILO and the EU.

In the General Conference, the Governing Body and the committees of the ILO, each participating state is represented by four delegates: two appointed by the government (the Ministry of Labour), one chosen by the national trade union congress and one selected by the national employers' association. Thus, the member governments cannot adopt conventions against the wishes of both interest groups. Conventions are adopted or revised only if one of the two interest groups can obtain from its government what it cannot obtain from the other interest group in collective agreements. The voting record shows that, in 1975–95, trade union delegates supported more than 70 percent of the conventions or revisions, whereas the employers' representatives voted for only one half of them (Boockmann 2001). The majority requirement in the General Conference is two thirds.

In the EU, a large number of interest groups are formally represented in the Economic and Social Committee (ECOSOC), which, according to the Treaty, must be consulted on all pertinent legislation. Its members receive compensation from the EU. ECOSOC employs a staff of more than 500 persons (half of them translators), who also are paid by the EU. In addition to ECOSOC, more than 100 committees run by the Commission include representatives of organized interest groups (Falke 1996, p. 132). The treaties do not provide for this 'comitologie' but the European Court of Justice approved it in 1970.

Interest group associations also play a formal role in EU 'anti-dumping' policies. The Commission accepts complaints only from EU producers 'acting on behalf of the industry'.[8] In this way, EU legislators have made sure that all major industries are organized in EU-wide associations. The EU is one of the most frequent users of 'anti-dumping' measures and has often been rebuked by the WTO for violating the latter's 'anti-dumping' code. The Commission may either impose 'anti-dumping' duties or negotiate price undertakings. In the latter case, the foreign exporter agrees to raise the price of his exports to the level required by the Commission, and the rent that is caused by the

---

[8] Council Regulation (EC) No. 384/96 on Protection against Dumped Imports, Article 5, No. 1. According to No. 4, 'the complaint shall be considered to have been made by or on behalf of the Community industry if it is supported by those Community producers whose collective output constitutes more than 50 percent of the total production of the like product . . .'.

reduction of supply is shared by domestic and foreign producers while the Commission forgoes the tariff revenue. Thus, foreign exporters prefer price undertakings to duties.

Turning to the internal market, does the EU favor regulations or subsidies in its dealings with private interest groups? One author reports that 78 percent of the pages of the *Official Journal of the European Union* cover special interest legislation (Peirce 1991, table 2). Another study found that about 72 percent of the EU budget is devoted to catering to organized interest groups (Vaubel 1994). Apparently, subsidies and regulations are of almost equal importance. However, there have been major shifts over time. At the beginning, subsidization – namely of agriculture – was the main instrument. This was due to the initial deal that subsidies to French agriculture should largely be paid by Germany. Moreover, the agricultural lobby was well organized, while consumers were not. The system of variable levies raised food prices but the demand for food was fairly inelastic.[9]

The Social Fund provided subsidies as well. After the accession of Great Britain in 1973, the European Regional Fund was added in 1975. Later, the 'Poor Four' countries (Greece, Ireland, Portugal and Spain) made their assent to the Single European Act (1987) and the Treaty of Maastricht (1993) conditional on a doubling of these structural funds and the establishment of the Cohesion Fund, respectively. A large part of the subsidies goes to private producers and interest groups. Under the Treaty of Nice (2003), the Commission began to give large amounts of money to hundreds of nongovernmental organizations including labor unions and the private business sector or professional associations (Mahoney and Beckstrand 2011, table 1). Since the European sovereign debt crisis, the European Financial Stability Facility and the ESM have provided hundreds of billions of subsidized credits to several members of the eurozone, and the European Central Bank has bought hundreds of billions of their bonds, bailing out both the over-indebted governments and their creditor banks.

However, since the early 1970s, the European Community or EU budget relative to the gross domestic product (GDP) of the member states has increased less than the number of European legal acts. While the former doubled, the latter quadrupled (Alesina et al. 2005). For a number of years, the budget/GDP ratio has remained fairly constant at about 1 percent.

The increasing emphasis on regulation can be explained by the decision rules of the Council of Ministers. The size and financing of the budget has to be decided unanimously by the member states in a 'multi-annual financial framework'. The spending decisions are taken either by qualified majority in the Council, if the spending is obligatory as under the agricultural policy, or – ultimately – by simple majority in the European Parliament, if the spending is not obligatory. Since a net contributing country cannot prevent the others from spending its money in a way it dislikes, no net contributor is likely to assent to major budget increases (unless he receives a quid pro quo). Thus, the asymmetry of the decision rule ensures fiscal restraint. Regulations, by contrast, cost the EU institutions very little.

Moreover, with regard to regulation, unanimity has largely given way to qualified

[9] For a public choice analysis of rent seeking in European agriculture see, for example, Josling and Moyer (1991).

majority voting in the Council. With regard to product and labor market regulations, the Single European Act (1987) and the Social Agreement attached to the Treaty of Maastricht (1993) were the main steps. Since 1991, more than 50 labor market regulations have been adopted by the EU (Vaubel 2008, table 1). In addition, the Council has approved at least ten EU-wide labor market agreements between unions and employers, thereby rendering them universally binding (Vaubel 2008, table 2).

Qualified majority voting enables the governments and interest groups of the highly regulated member states to extend their own regulations to the other member states. In the economics literature, this is called 'the strategy of raising rivals' costs'. There is econometric evidence showing that the strategy is also used in the ILO (Boockmann and Vaubel 2009). The common level of regulation imposed on the minority is even higher than the level originally prevailing in the decisive member state because the latter is no longer subject to the competitive pressure from low regulation in the minority of member states.[10]

Does EU lobbying concentrate on the Council or the Commission? Three surveys conducted among about a hundred of the largest European companies in 1984, 1994 and 2004 reveal that the favored venue for lobbying is the European Commission (Coen 1997, 2010). How can this be explained? In choosing among the Commission, the Council, the European Parliament and the Court of Justice, private interest groups use the following criteria:

1. The decision-making body should be small so that few members have to be addressed and won.
2. The majority requirement should be low, ideally at 50 percent, so that the threshold can easily be reached.
3. Since the regulations demanded by private interest groups are likely to harm consumers (Peltzman 1976) and since the subsidies have to be financed by taxpayers, institutions that are far removed from the control of the voters are more likely to yield to pressure groups than decision makers who are directly elected by the people (Crain and McCormick 1984).
4. Private interest groups prefer institutions whose legislative and spending powers are large.

Table 16.3 ranks the Commission, the Council, the Parliament and the Court of Justice with respect to these criteria. Some comments are in order.

- Criterion 1: The Parliament is the largest decision-making body. However, its committees and especially the rapporteurs are attractive targets for lobbyists (Marshall 2010).
- Criterion 2: Only decisions of the Council require more than a simple majority, namely a qualified majority or unanimity.
- Criterion 3: Voters have least control over the selection of the judges; the chain of delegation involves two intermediaries, the parliaments and the governments

10 For a formal exposition, see Vaubel (2008).

Table 16.3 The comparative usefulness of EU institutions to interest groups (ranks)

Criteria Institutions	1 Small number of decision makers	2 Low majority requirement	3 Removed from electoral control	4 Legislative and spending power	Average of ranks
Commission	1	1	2	1	1.25
Council	1	2	3	1	1.75
Parliament	2	1	4	2	2.25
Court of Justice	1	1	1	3	1.50

Note: Rank 1 is the highest rank.

of the member states. Moreover, the Court's decisions are extremely difficult to override. For these reasons, the Court takes rank 1. The Commission takes the second rank after the Court because its members are not only individually selected by the governments of their member states but also collectively confirmed by the European Parliament (one intermediary).[11] The members of the Council rank third because, except for the French President, they are elected by the national parliaments while the European Parliament (rank 4) has been elected directly by the voters since 1979.

- Criterion 4: It is very difficult to determine whether the Commissioners or the members of the Council have more power over spending and legislation. The member states determine the multi-annual financial framework as well as agricultural spending and the Parliament has ultimate control over most of the budget but, within these limits, the final decision on how precisely the money is spent rests with the Commission. With respect to legislation, the Commission possesses the monopoly of initiative but the Council may amend the Commission's proposals (if there are any). The Council has more spending and legislative power than the Parliament because the multi-annual financial framework is more important than the annual budgets and because amendments of the treaties and some important types of secondary legislation, for example, tax harmonization and the conferral of supervisory powers on the European Central Bank, do not require the assent of the European Parliament.

Taking an unweighted average of the ranks, it appears that, on balance, the Commission is the most attractive venue for interest groups, followed by the Court of Justice, the Council and Parliament (in this order).

The Commission assists private interest groups because bureaucrats and lobbyists have common goals. Both are interested in the centralization of policy. Elevating their demands to the European level, they can better escape the attention of voters. The Commission and interest groups form an alliance against the median voter, which in the end undermines democratic control.

There seem to be more than 15000 private lobbyists that attempt to influence the EU's

11 Since 1999, there has also been a separate vote on the president alone.

institutions in Brussels. The total number of EU lobbyists, including those from other governmental and non-governmental organizations, has been estimated at 55000.

Many Commissioners of the EU become private interest representatives after leaving the Commission. A recent study of 92 ex-Commissioners who had left the seven Commissions serving from 1981 to 2009 finds that 36 of them, that is, 39 percent, became private interest representatives – 14 with registered institutions, 22 with non-registered institutions (Vaubel et al. 2012). An ex-Commissioner is significantly more likely to turn lobbyist if he or she is still young and has been in charge of competition, the internal market, industry or taxation. At the 10 percent level of significance, the probability of lobbying is lower if the Commissioner has been proposed by a left wing government, has stepped down after the introduction of the Commission's code of conduct (1999) or has retired from the Delors I Commission, and the probability is higher for Commissioners from central Europe. With regard to the Commissioners' training, 48 percent of the lawyers but only 35 percent of the economists have become lobbyists. Among the private interest representatives, registered lobbyism is significantly more likely than non-registered lobbyism if the ex-Commissioner is a lawyer, has been in charge of competition, the internal market, industry or taxation and – at the 10 percent level – has been proposed by a left wing government.

If Commissioners assume paid positions with private companies or interest group associations or offer their services as independent consultants after leaving the Commission, the prospect of these activities may affect their decisions and voting behavior while they are in the Commission. They may favor subsidies and regulations demanded by industries or particular firms, and they may oppose regulations contrary to these private interests. Even if the outgoing Commissioner offered his or her lobbying services merely with a view to exploiting the human capital acquired at the Commission, the consequences would still be problematic. The Commissioners have accumulated their human capital at the expense of taxpayers, and they then exploit it to obtain subsidies (once more at the expense of taxpayers) or regulations (at the expense of consumers).

A study comparing interest group influence at the European and the national level has concluded that 'the EC system is now more lobbying-oriented than any national European system' (Andersen and Eliasson 1991, p. 178). Madison's prediction does not hold with respect to the EU, and it seems to be a fallacy quite generally.

16.4 CONCLUSION AND RECOMMENDATIONS

Rent seeking plays a major role in international organizations – probably more than in national governments. Rent seeking by international bureaucrats is a cause of excessive costs. Moreover, as international organizations facilitate the rent seeking of private interest groups, they are responsible for excessive subsidization and regulation. Thus, rent seeking in international organizations causes inefficiencies, and it may have undesirable distributional effects. These disadvantages have to be set against the potential benefits of internalizing Pareto-relevant international externalities and of reaping international economies of scale in the production of national public goods. Because of rent seeking, the benefits are not always worth pursuing.

How can the damage from rent seeking be reduced in international organizations?

First, leave more policy competencies to the national and subnational levels of government where they are closer to the citizens.[12] Subsidiarity helps to lower the monitoring cost of the voters and the media. Transparency is the enemy of all rent seekers.

Second, to the extent that policy decisions continue to be taken at the international level, rent seeking can be reduced by giving less power to international bureaucrats and more to elected politicians. For example, an international bureaucracy must not be an agenda setter. In particular, it must not have gate-keeping powers over legislation. The European Commission's monopoly of legislative initiative violates the principle of the separation of powers. Ideally, the executive should not be involved in the legislative process at all.

Third, there is a case for strengthening competition among international organizations (Frey 2008) while reducing their average size.

Fourth, international organizations that have amassed competencies in many different policy areas ought to be split up into several specialized agencies. The deconcentration of international policy conglomerates such as the EU and the IMF would improve transparency and control and help to diffuse political power.

Fifth, international bureaucracies ought to be monitored by specialized bodies that the voters directly elect for this purpose (Vaubel 1999; Frey and Stutzer 2006). Monitoring by the national governments is inadequate because they depend on the support of these bureaucracies and use them to increase their power over the citizens by forming international policy cartels.

Sixth, the salaries of bureaucrats should not be higher in international organizations than in their home country.

Seventh, international bureaucrats ought to be prohibited from dealing with private interest groups.

Eighth, private interest representation by former international bureaucrats ought to be banned. The issue cannot be settled by a 'code of conduct' drafted by the bureaucrats themselves (as in the EU). Rules must not be set by those who later are to abide by them. The 'cooling-off period' for EU ex-Commissioners amounts to merely 18 months even though they may continue to obtain up to 65 percent of their formal salary for three years after leaving. Moreover, the cooling-off period relates only to lobbying within the ex-Commissioner's policy brief even though each Commissioner has the right to vote on all decisions taken by the Commission.

Finally, special interest groups must not play an institutionalized role in legislation or trade policy as they do in the EU.

REFERENCES

Alesina, Alberto, Ignacio Angelloni and Ludger Schuknecht (2005), 'What does the European Union do?', *Public Choice*, **123**(3–4), 275–319.

Andersen, Svein S. and Kjell A. Eliasson (1991), 'European Community lobbying', *European Journal of Political Research*, **20**(2), 173–87.

[12] This is Tullock's main recipe against bureaucratic inefficiency (1965 [2005], p. 236).

Andreasen, Marta (2009), *Brussels Laid Bare*, Yelverton, UK: St Edward Press.
Bollick, Clint (1993), *Grassroots Tyranny: The Limits of Federalism*, Washington, DC: Cato Institute.
Boockmann, Bernhard (2001), 'The ratification of ILO conventions: a hazard rate analysis', *Economics and Politics*, **13**(3), 281–309.
Boockmann, Bernhard and Roland Vaubel (2009), 'The theory of raising rivals' costs and evidence from the International Labor Organization', *World Economy*, **32**(6), 862–87.
Coen, David (1997), 'The evolution of the large firm as a political actor in the European Union', *Journal of European Public Policy*, **4**(1), 91–108.
Coen, David (2010), 'European business and government relations', in David Coen, Wyn Grand and Graham Wilson (eds), *The Oxford Handbook of Business and Government*, Oxford: Oxford University Press, pp. 285–306.
Crain, Mark W. and Robert E. McCormick (1984), 'Regulators as an interest group', in James M. Buchanan and Gordon Tullock (eds), *The Theory of Public Choice – II*, Ann Arbor, MI: Michigan, pp. 287–304.
Dreher, Axel and Roland Vaubel (2004), 'Do IMF and IBRD cause moral hazard and political business cycles? Evidence from panel data', *Open Economic Review*, **15**(1), 5–22.
Falke, Josef (1996), 'Comitology and other committees: a preliminary empirical assessment', in Robin H. Pedler and Günther F. Schäfer (eds), *Shaping European Law and Policy: The Role of Committees and Comitology in the Political Process*, Maastricht: European Institute of Public Administration, pp. 117–65.
Fisman, Raymond and Roberta Gatti (2002), 'Decentralization and corruption: evidence across countries', *Journal of Public Economics*, **83**(3), 325–45.
Frey, Bruno S. (1985), *Internationale Politische Ökonomie*, Munich: Vahlen.
Frey, Bruno S. (2008), 'Outside and inside competition for international organizations – from analysis to innovations', *Review of International Organizations*, **3**(4), 335–50.
Frey, Bruno S. and Alois Stutzer (2006), 'Strengthening the citizens' role in international organizations', *Review of International Organizations*, **1**(1), 27–44.
Haller, Max (2008), *European Integration as an Elite Process*, New York and London: Routledge.
Hardin, Russell (1982), *Collective Action*, Baltimore, MD: Johns Hopkins University Press.
Irwin, Michael H.K. (1994), 'Banking on poverty: an insider's look at the World Bank', in Kevin Danaher (ed.), *50 Years is Enough: The Case Against the World Bank and the International Monetary Fund*, Boston, MA: South End Press, pp. 152–60.
Josling, Timothy and H. Wayne Moyer (1991), 'The Common Agricultural Policy of the European Community: a public choice interpretation', in Roland Vaubel and Thomas D. Willett (eds), *The Political Economy of International Organizations: A Public Choice Approach*, Boulder, CO: Westview Press, pp. 286–305.
Madison, James (1787), 'Federalist Paper No. 10', reprinted in 1987, in Ida Kramnick (ed.), *The Federalist Papers*, Harmondsworth: Penguin.
Mahoney, Christine and Michael J. Beckstrand (2011), 'Following the money: European Union funding of civil society organizations', *Journal of Common Market Studies*, **49**(6), 1339–61.
Marshall, David (2010), 'Who lobby and when: institutional determinants of interest group strategies in European Parliament committees', *European Union Politics*, **11**(4), 553–74.
Martin, Lisa L. (2006), 'Distribution, information and delegation to international organizations: the case of IMF conditionality', in Darren G. Hawkins, David A. Lake, Daniel L. Nielson and Michael J. Tierney (eds), *Delegation and Agency in International Organizations*, Cambridge: Cambridge University Press, pp. 140–64.
Migué, Jean-Luc and Gérard Bélanger (1974), 'Toward a general theory of managerial discretion', *Public Choice*, **17**(1), 27–43.
Miller, Gary (1977), 'Bureaucratic compliance as a game on the unit square', *Public Choice*, **20**(1), 37–51.
Moser, Christoph and Jan-Egbert Sturm (2011), 'Explaining IMF lending decisions after the Cold War', *Review of International Organizations*, **6**(3–4), 307–40.
Niskanen, William A. (1971), *Bureaucracy and Representative Government*, Chicago, IL: University of Chicago Press.
Olson, Mancur (1965), *The Logic of Collective Action*, Cambridge, MA: Harvard University Press.
Parkinson, Cyril Northcote (1957), *Parkinson's Law, or the Pursuit of Progress*, Harmondsworth: Penguin.
Peacock, Alan (1983), 'Public x-inefficiency: informational and institutional constraints', in Horst Hanusch (ed.), *Anatomy of Government Deficiencies*, Heidelberg: Springer, pp. 125–38.
Peacock, Alan and Jack Wiseman (1961), *The Growth of Government in the United Kingdom*, Princeton, NJ: Princeton University Press.
Peirce, William S. (1991), 'Unanimous decisions in a redistributive context: the Council of Ministers of the European Union', in Roland Vaubel and Thomas D. Willett (eds), *The Political Economy of International Organizations: A Public Choice Approach*, Boulder, CO: Westview Press, pp. 267–85.
Peltzman, Sam (1976), 'Toward a more general theory of regulation', *Journal of Law and Economics*, **19**(2), 211–40.

Przeworski, Adam and James R. Vreeland (2000), 'The effect of IMF programs on economic growth', *Journal of Development Economics*, **62**(2), 385–421.
Sturm, Jan-Egbert, Helge Berger and Jakob de Haan (2005), 'Which variables explain decisions on IMF credit? An extreme bounds analysis', *Economics and Politics*, **17**(2), 177–213.
Tullock, Gordon (1965), *The Politics of Bureaucracy*, Washington, DC: Public Affairs Press, reprinted in Gordon Tullock (2005), *Bureaucracy*, The Selected Works of Gordon Tullock, Vol. 6, Indianapolis, IN: Liberty Fund.
Urbaczka, Adrian and Roland Vaubel (2013), 'IMF Subsidies, cancellations and resumptions: new empirical evidence', *Cato Journal*, **33**(1), 155–70.
Vaubel, Roland (1991), 'The political economy of the International Monetary Fund: a public choice approach', in Roland Vaubel and Thomas D. Willett (eds), *The Political Economy of International Organizations: A Public Choice Approach*, Boulder, CO: Westview Press, pp. 204–44.
Vaubel, Roland (1994), 'The political economy of centralization and the European Community', *Public Choice*, **81**(1–2), 151–244.
Vaubel, Roland (1996), 'Bureaucracy at the IMF and the World Bank: a comparison of the evidence', *World Economy*, **19**(2), 195–210.
Vaubel, Roland (1999), 'Enforcing competition among governments: theory and application to the European Union', *Constitutional Political Economy*, **10**(4), 327–38.
Vaubel, Roland (2008), 'The political economy of labor market regulation by the European Union', *Review of International Organizations*, **3**(4), 435–64.
Vaubel, Roland (2009), *The European Institutions as an Interest Group: The Dynamics of Ever Closer Union*, Hobart Paper 167, London: Institute of Economic Affairs.
Vaubel, Roland, Axel Dreher and Uğurlu Soylu (2007), 'Staff growth in international organizations: a principal-agent problem? An empirical analysis', *Public Choice*, **133**(3–4), 275–95.
Vaubel, Roland, Bernhard Klingen and David Müller (2012), 'There is life after the Commission: an empirical analysis of private interest representation by former EU commissioners', *Review of International Organizations*, **7**(1), 59–80.
Williamson, Oliver (1964), *The Economics of Discretionary Behavior*, Englewood Cliffs, NJ: Prentice Hall.
Wyckoff, Paul Gary (1990), 'The simple analytics of slack-maximizing bureaucracy', *Public Choice*, **67**(1), 35–47.
Yates, Douglas (1982), *Bureaucratic Democracy*, Cambridge, MA: Harvard University Press.

17. Litigation as rent seeking

*Francesco Parisi and Barbara Luppi**

SUMMARY

Litigation aims at resolving conflicts. We survey the law and economics literature on litigation to illustrate the scope of application of rent-seeking models and their analytical power in the study of law and procedural issues of litigation, including applications in adversarial and inquisitorial procedures, fee-shifting, consolidation and bifurcation of trials and tort liability. We present a unified model of rent seeking, recasting the various perspectives in the literature, to illustrate the power of rent-seeking models in addressing different dimensions of substantive and procedural legal problems.

17.1 INTRODUCTION

Tullock's concept (1967 [2008]) and model (1980 [2008]) of rent seeking has given birth to an important strand in contemporary economics, game theory, political science and law, with applications spanning from regulatory capture to trade wars and armed conflict. In the field of law and economics, rent-seeking theory has been widely applied to analyze problems both in substantive and procedural law.[1]

The most significant area of application of rent-seeking models in law is probably the field of litigation. As pointed out by Congleton et al. (2008a, p. 41), 'civil law proceedings are rent-seeking contests in which the "prize" is dissipated through conflict'. Similar to a rent-seeking contest, in most litigated disputes, the parties invest effort to win (or to avoid losing) a case. In civil cases, the stakes of the case add up to a fixed amount – one party's winnings are proportional to the other party's losses. Thus, the decision of a plaintiff to file a case, and the defendant's choice to defend it, may be framed as an endogenous decision to participate to a rent-seeking game of the form of a transfer contest (Hillman and Riley 1989 [2008]) in the sense that one side will make a transfer to the other depending on the outcome of litigation. Additionally, the outcome of litigation depends on the objective merits of the case. Litigation in civil cases is affected by institutional features that have no counterparts in other litigation contexts, making civil litigation an interesting and unique field of application for rent-seeking models.

Studies of litigation in the context of civil cases that utilize the rent-seeking framework include Tullock (1975 [2008]), Farmer and Pecorino (1999 [2008], 2012, 2013),

* We are grateful to Daniel Pi for his valuable editorial assistance.

1 See, among others, Buchanan et al. (1980), Rowley et al. (1988) and Congleton et al. (2008a, 2008b) for collections of papers on rent seeking. For surveys of the literature, see Tollison (1982), Nitzan (1994), Hillman (2013) and Long (2013).

Hirshleifer and Osborne (2001), Parisi (2002 [2008]), Baye et al. (2005 [2008]), Luppi and Parisi (2012) and De Mot (2013). The use of rent-seeking models to analyze the plaintiff's and the defendant's incentives to enter litigation has the advantage of providing a tractable framework that allows us to endogenize parties' litigation choices and examine the impact of specific institutional features in civil litigation. Other areas in which rent-seeking models may be applied include evidence law and tort law, inasmuch as the adjudication of substantive and evidentiary rules affect parties' litigation choices. In this chapter, we survey the literature on rent seeking in the law, providing a unified framework within which to analyze substantive and procedural issues, with special attention to litigation.

17.2 TRIALS ON TRIAL: ADVERSARIAL VERSUS INQUISITORIAL SYSTEMS

American systems of discovery and civil procedure are often contrasted with their European counterparts by reference to the adversarial nature of their procedures. Adversarial procedure encompasses a wide range of distinctive elements concerning the functions of judges and lawyers in the discovery process. The proactive role of civil law judges in discovery is often labeled by reference to the inquisitorial role of civil law judges in the fact-finding of the case. Damaska (1986) and Parisi (2002 [2008]) point out that judges can play different roles in the discovery and fact-finding stages of a civil case. In an inquisitorial proceeding, the judge controls discovery of a case, deciding such matters as the admissibility of evidence, the order in which evidence is presented and the relevance of the gathered evidence. In an adversarial system, matters are very different. At the outset of a case, the attorneys manage the discovery phase, with no direct involvement of the judge. The adversarial efforts of the litigants reveal the relevant facts, and it is only at a later stage that the judge or jury evaluates the evidence following the motions presented by the litigants. In the law and economics literature, Tullock (1988) and Posner (1988) have expressed opposing views on the respective merits of the inquisitorial and adversarial systems. As is well known in the law and economics community, Tullock's and Posner's views reflected their underlying differences on the assessment of civil and common law trials.

Parisi (2002, p. 194) summarizes Tullock's and Posner's respective positions as follows:

> Tullock criticized the common law trial system and the adversarial method, as its main characteristic. Posner instead defended the adversarial system pointing out that the adversarial system forced the parties to internalize the costs and benefits of discovery, allowing them to shape the course and extent of litigation. Additionally, he criticized the inquisitorial method for shifting the power to the judges and promoting a de facto expansion of the public sector.

We shall use a rent-seeking model based on Parisi (2002 [2008]) to evaluate the effect of these procedural alternatives on litigation choices. The model, which we recast below, analyzes how the inquisitorial role of the judge affects parties' incentives to invest in litigation.

In a typical rent-seeking framework, the plaintiff and defendant decide on how much effort to invest in litigation to maximize their expected payoffs. If the functional form proposed by Tullock (1980 [2008]) is applied, each party is more likely to be successful in litigation, the more effort each invests in the discovery of evidence relatively to the opponent. In such probabilistic rent-seeking models, the probability of winning the case for one party equals the ratio of the party's effort over the sum of total effort spent by both parties. This simplified framework does not take into consideration the procedural aspects of legal systems. In a typical inquisitorial proceeding, the judge determines the order of the evidence during the trial and evaluates the content of the evidence, assessing the credibility and the relative strength of each piece of evidence discussed in court. When an inquisitorial format is adopted, the probability of the result also depends on the judge's decisions. The traditional framework needs to be enriched to take into account how alternative procedural systems affect the incentives of parties to litigate.

Parisi (2002 [2008]) identifies the critical distinction between adversarial and inquisitorial legal procedures in the extent of control of the judge over the evidentiary process. This distinction, however, cannot be treated as a dichotomous variable, since the allocation of control over the process involves many dimensions, each subject to different evaluations. Parisi (2002 [2008]) models the relative dominance of inquisitorial and adversarial elements in the procedural system as a continuous variable, i, that denotes the weight assigned to the inquisitorial evidence when a judge determines the award size.

Plaintiff and defendant invest in litigation effort, denoted, respectively, by x and y. The cost is assumed linear and equal (for simplicity and without loss of generality) to the effort.[2] In the inquisitorial format, the judge invests effort in e_J the evidence discovery. The return of each party depends on the efforts exerted by each party and the judge's effort, but also on the merits of the case attached to the inquisitorial and adversarial sources of evidence, denoted, respectively, by r_I and r_A. The expected return of each party is a weighted average of the inquisitorial and adversarial components, where the weight is the institutional component i. Note that an institutional change, that is, a change of value of i, should have no effect on the total. In other words, a change of the relative weight of the inquisitorial and adversarial components may change the plaintiff and defendant's returns from litigation, but the overall change should be zero, setting aside litigation costs.

The plaintiff chooses his effort level x in order to maximize the expected return from litigation:

$$S_P^e = ir_I e_J + (1 - i)r_A \frac{x}{x + y} - x \tag{17.1}$$

Similarly, the defendant chooses his effort level y in order to minimize the expected costs from litigation:

$$S_D^e = -ir_I e_J - (1 - i)r_A \frac{y}{x + y} - y \tag{17.2}$$

The Nash equilibrium expenditures are:

[2] Parisi (2002 [2008]) considers a general cost function in the formulation of the model.

$$x^* = y^* = \frac{(1 - i)r_A}{4} \tag{17.3}$$

In the presence of an inquisitorial component ($i > 0$), each party's investment in litigation will be proportional to the award in the adversarial format, r_A. In a purely adversarial system ($i = 0$), each party's effort will be, respectively, one quarter of the full value of the case, and the total litigation cost will be one half the full value of the case. In the general case of N litigants, the total dissipation through litigation increases monotonically in the number of participants in litigation, ranging from one half up to the full value of the case.[3]

A simple analysis of comparative statics shows also that the total litigation expenditures increase when lower weight is assigned to inquisitorially produced evidence, i, or equivalently, when higher weight is assigned to adversarially produced evidence. Not surprisingly, total discovery and litigation costs increase with the value of the case, r_A, assessed on the basis of adversarially produced evidence. Additionally, an increase in judicial scrutiny of the adversary discovery decreases litigation expenditures.

Courts may have some advantages in truth-finding compared to litigants. As Posner (1999) points out, the private incentive to search for evidence provided by the adversarial system may result in too much or too little evidence discovery from an efficiency standpoint. Contrastingly, a judge may have incentives to search for truth until the social marginal benefit of an additional piece of evidence equals the social marginal cost of producing it. Litigation is a zero-sum game from the perspective of litigants, but the efforts directed toward truth-finding may produce social benefits that exceed – or that fall short of – the private benefits, due to externalities that are not captured by litigants. Hence, there may be divergences between the private incentives and social incentives in the discovery of evidence. This may explain why historically legal systems have been converging toward a mix of inquisitorial and adversarial elements. The socially optimal system may require a mix of inquisitorial and adversarial elements.

From a normative perspective, it is therefore interesting to characterize the optimal institutional choice of the legal procedure, summarized by the institutional variable i, measuring the weight assigned to the proactive role of the court in truth-finding. The analytical framework proposed by Parisi (2002 [2008]) allows us to identify the optimal weight to be attached to the inquisitorial efforts of the judge as the value that maximizes the social benefits from truthful adjudication as the net of the private and administrative costs.

Following the analysis proposed by Parisi (2002 [2008]), the social welfare function may be thought of as the benefit from accurate discovery and adjudication, less total costs borne by parties and the judge in the process of discovery and production of evidence:

$$\max_i W = B(x, y, e_J) - x - y - C_j(e_J) \tag{17.4}$$

[3] See Dari-Mattiacci and Parisi (2005) on the mixed-strategy solution to Tullock's paradox. See also Higgins et al. (1985 [2008]) for rent-seeking contests with endogenously determined numbers of litigants.

where the parties adopt the privately optimal effort level and the judge chooses e_J to maximize social welfare.

An interior optimum exists for the institutional variable i,[4] implying that neither a pure inquisitorial system nor a pure adversarial system is socially optimal. An analysis of comparative statics illustrates how the optimal weights placed on the adversarial and inquisitorial elements of the legal proceedings depend on some key characteristics of the litigation contests, affecting the benefit of accurate discovery and adjudication. The key features affecting the optimal value of i are the social relevance of the case under scrutiny, the degree of judicial inspection of the parties' evidence, the litigation investments, the relative efficiency of the court in obtaining and evaluating evidence and the number of litigants involved in litigation (Parisi 2002 [2008]). The judicial scrutiny adopted by the judge in revising the evidence produced by the parties for the adversarial portion may be regarded as an institutional imperfect substitute for i, thereby decreasing the socially optimal weight attached to inquisitorial findings. In the case of multiple litigants, a higher level of i may reduce the level of dissipation created by litigation, since each party faces reduced private incentives to invest in litigation, in light of the higher weight assigned to inquisitorially produced evidence. The same holds true in the face of an increase in the private cost of discovery for the parties.

17.3 FEE-SHIFTING AND CASE SELECTION

Procedural rules may substantially affect the choice of litigation and overall costs of adjudication. Among other procedural rules, fee-shifting rules regulate the allocation of lawyer fees between the litigants. Under the American rule, each party is responsible for his or her own legal costs. Under the English rule, the losing party is required to pay the legal costs of the winning party. Switching from the American to the English rule could discourage frivolous suits, which legal commentators observe to be a problem in the United States.[5] By increasing the burden of legal costs imposed on the losing party, the use of an English rule could reduce nuisance suits and the overall expected cost of litigation.[6] Farmer and Pecorino (1999) addressed this question by using a rent-seeking model to analyze how the choice to enter litigation and the magnitude of legal expenditures are affected by the fee-shifting rule, when litigation choices are endogenously determined in equilibrium.

Farmer and Pecorino (1999) model the probability of success of a party according to the standard Tullock contest function with bias (Tullock 1980 [2008]; Katz 1988). Analytically, the probability that the plaintiff prevails at trial is:

$$P = \frac{e^M x^\alpha}{e^M x^\alpha + y^\alpha} \tag{17.5}$$

---

4 We omit the proof for brevity reasons. See Parisi (2002 [2008]) for the analytical details.

5 See, for a complete discussion, Katz and Sanchirico (2011).

6 See also Braeutigam et al. (1984) for an analysis of fee-shifting rules in a litigation context, without assuming the functional form proposed by Tullock (1980 [2008]) to model the contest success function.

where M denotes the merit of the case: a positive (negative) value of M favors the plaintiff (defendant); α denotes legal technology: the value of α identifies returns to scale in litigation; and x and y denote plaintiff's and defendant's litigation efforts, respectively.[7]

Under the American rule, the plaintiff and defendant invest in litigation efforts in order to maximize their expected return from litigation:

$$max_x S_P^e = pW - x \tag{17.6}$$

$$min_x S_D^e = pW + y \tag{17.7}$$

subject to the participation constraints that expected litigation returns are non-negative, that is, $S_P^e \geq 0$ and $S_D^e \geq 0$.

Under the English rule, the plaintiff and defendant invest in litigation effort, respectively, such that:

$$max_x S_P^e = p(W + x + y) - x - y \tag{17.8}$$

$$min_x S_D^e = p(W + x + y) \tag{17.9}$$

subject to the participation constraints that expected litigation returns are non-negative, that is, $S_P^e \geq 0$ and $S_D^e \geq 0$. Equilibrium litigation choices and litigation expenditures are characterized under both the American and English rules as a function of the parameters α and M.

Farmer and Pecorino (1999) show that neither the American nor the English rule is preferable to the other in an absolute sense, but rather depends on the effectiveness of legal technology, α. In the presence of decreasing returns to scale in the legal investment (that is, $0 \leq \alpha \leq 1$), all cases are filed under the American rule, regardless of the merit of the case, while the English rule fosters efficient litigation in the range $\frac{1}{2} \leq \alpha \leq 1$. In contrast, when legal investment displays increasing returns to scale (that is, for values $1 < \alpha \leq 2$), the American rule is preferable to the English one, since only more meritorious cases are filed, while no case reaches litigation under the English rule (or all cases regardless of the merit reach litigation when a first-mover advantage is given to the plaintiff). In the absence of a reliable estimate of the range of values for the technology parameter α that is empirically relevant, Farmer and Pecorino (1999) conclude that no fee-shifting procedural rule can be meaningfully preferred from a policy perspective.

Farmer and Pecorino (2013) extend their analysis to consider pretrial bargaining in a rent-seeking model and the role of fee-shifting rules in the presence of asymmetric information. When litigation expenditures are endogenously determined and the uninformed party is in charge of a settlement offer in a pretrial stage, Farmer and Pecorino (2013) show that the bargaining position of the uninformed party may be strengthened relative to the other party, leading to surprising results relating to information transmission at the pretrial stage. Contrary to the standard result with exogenous litigation

---

7 Note that Pecorino and Farmer (1999) assume parties have access to the same legal technology, measured by α.

expenditures, the party receiving the settlement offer may find it convenient to make a costly voluntary disclosure when he has a weak case.[8] Other studies investigate the role of fee-shifting rules in a rent-seeking contest. For example, Baik and Kim (2007a) compare the effect of contingent-fee and hourly-fee attorney billing on litigation incentives under American and English rules in a rent-seeking model. They show that the English rule is preferable for the plaintiff, even if it produces overall higher litigation costs.

Farmer and Pecorino (1999 [2008], 2012, 2013) demonstrate that fee-shifting rules affect the choices of plaintiffs and defendants regarding whether to enter litigation,[9] and in turn, affect case selection. Luppi and Parisi (2012) propose using rent-seeking models to investigate case selection from an evolutionary perspective. According to Priest and Klein (1984) and Fon and Parisi (2003), potential litigants base their decisions on whether to enter litigation on the estimated expected return from the case, taking into account the expected probability of success. Rent-seeking models allow us to study the dynamics of legal evolution, looking at cases with both symmetric and asymmetric stakes and costly litigation.

Luppi and Parisi (2012) focus on the impact of alternative fee-shifting rules on the parties' litigation strategies and expenditures. Following Luppi and Parisi (2012), let us consider the following litigation context. A plaintiff suffers a loss $W > 0$ caused by the defendant. The plaintiff sues the defendant, who can raise a possible counterclaim at the trial, equal to $L \geq 0$. In the presence of asymmetric stakes, the plaintiff is awarded W by the defendant, if there is a decision in favor of the plaintiff and the defendant is awarded L by the plaintiff, if there is a decision in favor of the defendant. The litigants face a dispute where p denotes the winning probability for the plaintiff and form a rational expectation of the probability of success in litigation. The plaintiff and defendant invest in litigation effort levels x and y, respectively. The greater the litigation investment of each party compared to the other, the more likely a party will prevail in litigation. The probability that the plaintiff wins the case is equal to $p(x, y)$ and is modeled according to Tullock's contest success function $p(x, y) = \frac{x}{x+y}$. Under the American rule, each party is responsible for their own litigation costs, regardless of who prevails at trial.

Analytically, plaintiff and defendant invest in litigation efforts in order to maximize their expected return from litigation:

$$S_P^e = p(x, y)W - (1 - p(x, y))L - x \tag{17.10}$$

$$S_D^e = (1 - p(x, y))W - p(x, y)L - y \tag{17.11}$$

---

[8] The relevance of fee-shifting rules is very broad. Farmer and Pecorino (2012) develop a model of pretrial bargaining under asymmetric information where both the plaintiff's and the defendant's litigation cost are an increasing function of the measure of judgment in trial. The authors examine the impact of fee-shifting rules in this context, showing that any rule shifting variable costs from the defendant to the plaintiff will decrease the incidence of trial.

[9] See also Baik and Kim (2007b) and Baye et al. (2005 [2008]) for a comparative analysis of litigation choices under alternative fee-shifting rules. See Chen and Wang (2007) for the conjunct effect of fee-shifting rules and contingency fees in a litigation context.

subject to the participation constraints that expected litigation returns are non-negative, that is, $S_P^e \geq 0$ and $S_D^e \geq 0$.

Under the English rule, the prevailing party receives compensation from the losing party for at least a fraction of the litigation costs incurred. Analytically, the winning party receives a fraction, denoted by a, of the litigation costs incurred and a fraction, denoted with b, of the total value of the case, equal to $W + L$.[10] Under the English rule, parties invest in litigation efforts in order to maximize their expected returns from litigation:[11]

$$S_P^e = p(W + b(W + L) + ax) - (1 - p)(L + b(W + L) + ay) - x \qquad (17.12)$$

$$S_D^e = (1 - p)(W + b(W + L) + ax) - p(L + b(W + L) + ay) - y \qquad (17.13)$$

subject to the participation constraints that expected litigation returns are non-negative, that is, $S_P^e \geq 0$ and $S_D^e \geq 0$.

Unsurprisingly, under this set-up, equilibrium litigation efforts are higher under the English rule than under the American rule. However, increased litigation efforts imply that litigation rates will decline for the same type of cases. While cases characterized by the ratio W/L equal to 3 can lead to litigation under the American rule, the ratio W/L required to generate litigation under the English rule has a value of $k > 3$. Hence, under an English rule, litigation rates and total expected litigation costs decrease in the range $3 \leq W/L < k$. These differences in litigation choices affect the selection of cases in common law systems.

Figure 17.1 illustrates how the fee-shifting rules may affect case selection. We depict break-even litigation hyperbolas, along which parties have a zero return from litigation. Note that break-even litigation hyperbolas are steeper under the English rule than under the American one.

From inspection of Figure 17.1, cases characterized by a higher probability of success are more likely to be filed under both fee-shifting rules, compared to cases with a lower probability of success. These cases are identified by region A in Figure 17.1. Despite any differences in procedural rules, cases in region A will be filed under both the American and English rules. In regions B and C, the selection of cases brought to litigation differs across fee-shifting rules. Region B, in the north-west quadrant of Figure 17.1, identifies cases that are filed only under the American rule. These cases are characterized by a very low probability of success, but high stakes. By contrast, region C, in the south-east quadrant of Figure 17.1, identifies cases that are filed only under the English rule. These cases are characterized by a very high probability of success, but low stakes.

Consistent with Tullock's predictions, the size of dissipation of resources caused by litigation is higher under an American rule. In fact, region B illustrates those cases with

---

[10] This explicit formulation is motivated, because in jurisdictions adopting the English rule, courts liquidate litigation costs on the basis of the fees established by the professional bar associations, computed according to the value of the case and the actual litigation costs (reflected by the number of hearings and motions filed and so on).

[11] For clarity, we omit the indication of the dependence of the probability function p on x and y.

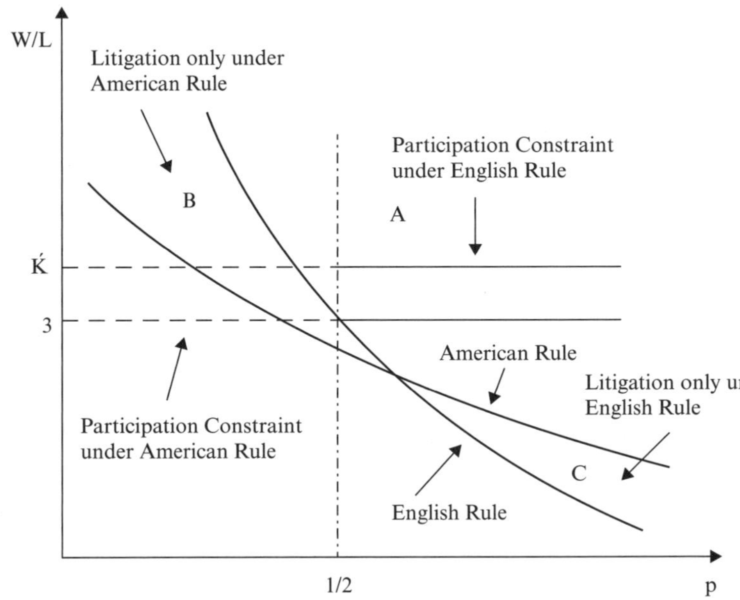

Source: Luppi and Parisi (2012).

Figure 17.1 Case selection under American and English rule

low merit, nevertheless filed under the American rule, while region *C* identifies high merit cases, which are not brought to court due to the incidence of non-recoverable litigation costs. Cases in Region *B* are filed, even if they have a low probability of success, because the plaintiff is not required to compensate the defendant for litigation costs.[12]

17.4 OPTIMAL DESIGN OF TRIALS: BIFURCATION OR CONSOLIDATION

Legal disputes often involve the adjudication of multiple issues, which may be independent claims arising from a single cause of action, or, alternatively, contingent upon one another. There are two ways that a court may manage multiple issues arising from a legal dispute: a judge may opt either for 'unitary litigation' or 'sequential litigation'. In the

12 See Tullock (1997, p. 441) for the plaintiff's externality under the American rule. According to Parisi and Fon (2009) and Luppi and Parisi (2012), the selection of different cases under different fee-shifting rules leads to different paths of evolution of judge-made law. Once adjudicated, these cases will generate a negative flow of precedents, leading to a reduced likelihood of success of similar cases in the future. Region *B* may lead to bubbles of litigation, generating contractionary trends under the American rule, not otherwise observed under the English rule. On the contrary, cases in region *C* will more likely generate a flow of positive precedents and adjudication of these cases will lead to the consolidation of judge-made rules. Region *C* will more likely foster consolidation of remedies and a greater stability of legal protection under the English rule.

context of unitary litigation, all the issues relevant to reaching a decision are addressed in the course of a single proceeding and the judge and/or the jury are called to decide all the issues at once. When sequential litigation is adopted, each issue arising from the dispute is litigated in a separate proceeding. Once a judgment is reached on the first issue, the plaintiff proceeds to the second stage only if he has prevailed in the first stage of litigation and so forth.

Courts are allowed for different degrees of flexibility to separate or join issues in different jurisdictions. In the United States, the Amendment (1966) of FED. R. CIV. P. 42 in 1966 allowed courts to separate issues out into different litigation proceedings when sequential litigation facilitates a faster or less costly deliberation. In the United Kingdom, sequential litigation is allowed under Rule 3.1(2) of the CIVIL PROCEDURE RULES. In Canada, procedural rules vary in each jurisdiction, and most jurisdictions encourage courts to have a strong presumption against sequential proceeding.[13]

In the law and economics literature, Landes (1993) examines litigation disputes involving two issues, analyzing incentives to litigate, when parties have the choice to opt for a unitary versus a sequential trial. Landes (1993) identifies liability and the damages as the two issues arising from the same cause of action as examples in a tort context. When multiple issues arise in a unitary proceeding, parties choose whether to sue or settle for all the issues in the legal dispute at once. In contrast, when the issues are divided out into sequential trials, the plaintiff and the defendant choose whether to sue for the first stage. Parties proceed to litigation on the second issue, contingent upon whether the plaintiff wins at the first stage. For illustrative purpose, we consider a simplified case. A plaintiff sues expecting to win damages V^{eP} with probability p^P. The defendant expects to be found liable for V^{eD} with probability p^D. The plaintiff and defendant may have different subjective expectations, allowing for divergent optimistic views, both on the damage measure and the likelihood of the party prevailing at the trial. Both the plaintiff and defendant face litigation costs, denoted, respectively, as x_t and y_t on issue t, considering the simplest case with only two issues, that is, $t = 1, 2$ and assuming litigation efforts do not differ with respect to unitary versus sequential trial.[14] In a sequential trial, the plaintiff's payoff is $S^e_{S,P} = p^P(V^{eP} - x_2) - x_1$, while the defendant's payoff is equal to the expected cost from litigation $S^e_{S,D} = p^D(V^{eD} + y_2) + y_1$. In a unitary trial, the plaintiff's payoff is $S^e_{U,P} = p^P V^{eP} - x_1 - x_2$, while the defendant's payoff is equal to the expected cost from litigation $S^e_{S,D} = p^D V^{eD} + y_1 + y_2$.

Landes (1993) compares the payoffs of each party in a unitary and a sequential trial, showing that the plaintiff faces an added incentive to sue in a sequential trial, measured by the difference in his or her expected payoff, equal to $S^e_{S,P} - S^e_{U,P} = (1 - p^P)x_2$. The rationale lies in the observation that a sequential trial increases the plaintiff's expected claim because she saves the cost of litigation in stage two, in case she fails to prevail in the first stage of litigation. Sequential trials, in fact, reduce the expected cost of litigation relative to unitary trials, because for a subset of issues adjudication might be avoided (litigation is avoided when the plaintiff loses on a dispositive issue at an earlier stage of

13 See De Mot et al. (2012) for a comparative analysis of legal rules on sequential litigation.

14 De Mot et al. (2012) extend the analysis to consider expenditures that are endogenously determined according to the procedural regime.

the sequential proceeding). At the same time, however, the reduction in expected litigation costs provides a greater incentive for plaintiffs to sue, thereby increasing the total number of lawsuits. This, in turn, causes a contraction of the bargaining space created by litigation costs and a reduction in the out-of-court settlement space.[15]

A number of authors have investigated the issue of bifurcation versus consolidation in other contexts. Landes (1971) examines the choice of unitary versus sequential trials in criminal trials, analyzing the choice to litigate or plead guilty. Gensler (2000) opposes the tendency for issue-consolidation, encouraging federal courts to favor sequential proceedings. De Mot (2012) considered the effects of sequential trials in conjunction with the English rule. De Mot (2012) considers two types of sequential proceedings. The first type corresponds to that considered by Landes (1993), in which parties litigate each issue separately and proceed only when the plaintiff prevails at each stage. The second type of sequential litigation identified by De Mot (2012) is a proceeding in which the defendant raises a counterclaim against the plaintiff and the court decides on it, only if the plaintiff loses his own claim. For example, the defendant may countersue for legal costs as against a frivolous claim, only if the plaintiff loses. Contrary to the standard results in the literature, De Mot (2012) shows that the adoption of an English rule does not always increase the incentive to sue. When courts opt for a sequential proceeding, incentives may actually decrease. Under the English rule, the incentive to sue is greater for sequential trials characterized by sequential litigation of each issue (as modeled by Landes 1993), it is smaller for sequential trials, where defendant's counterclaims are examined only when the plaintiff loses his claim. Additionally, when a sequential trial is adopted, De Mot (2012) shows that the incentive to settle under the American rule decreases by a larger amount than under the English rule.

Further results in the literature show that sequential litigation proves to be superior in reducing expected litigation costs in the presence of asymmetric information. Extending Landes's (1993) framework, Chen et al. (1997) address the superiority of unitary and sequential proceedings, focusing on parties' incentives to settle using non-cooperative bargaining strategies. Contrary to Landes (1993), Chen et al. (1997) showed that settlements may be more likely under sequential proceedings, since the sequential adjudication of multiple issues reveals information stepwise and may foster settlements between the litigants, depending on the information produced in the earlier stages of a sequential legal dispute.[16]

---

[15] Posner (1973) investigates how procedural rules, in both civil and criminal contexts, affect the decision to litigate or settle. Gould (1973) focused on civil disputes and examined the role of risk aversion on the parties' incentives to settle.

[16] Landes (1993) treats litigation expenditures as exogenous, without taking into account the effect of a change in one party's expenditures on the other party's expenditures. De Mot et al. (2012) extend Landes's (1993) framework, by endogenizing the choice of litigation efforts in unitary and sequential proceedings. The authors show that the superiority of sequential litigation hinges upon the tradeoff between the parties' incentive to front-load efforts to the first stage of sequential litigation and the savings in litigation costs in the second stage of the trial.

17.5 LIABILITY RULES AND LITIGATION EXPENDITURES

Rent-seeking models are also a useful analytical tool for characterizing litigation incentives under alternative liability rules. The law and economics literature has extensively investigated the comparative advantages of existing liability rules, focusing primarily on precaution incentives for prospective injurers, while keeping litigation incentives exogenous to the analysis. Rent-seeking models allow us, instead, to study how the litigation incentives vary under alternative liability rules.

From an efficiency perspective, the equivalence of precautionary incentives as between comparative and contributory negligence rules is established only in the presence of perfect knowledge (Shavell 1987). In weighing the relative strengths of comparative versus contributory negligence regimes, the latter appears to be preferable, due to its lower administrative costs, requiring the court to decide only whether parties are negligent but not the relative degree of negligence.[17] Comparative negligence regimes are characterized by higher administrative costs per case in a framework with exogenous litigation costs.[18]

Using a rent-seeking model, De Mot (2013) investigates the relative efficiency of contributory versus comparative negligence by comparing the equilibrium litigation expenditures at trial, endogenously determined in conjunction with the liability rule.[19] De Mot (2013) characterizes equilibrium litigation choices under the two alternative liability regimes when the probability of success of each party is modeled as a function of case merit and litigation efforts, according to the Tullock contest function. Let p_d and p_p denote the probability that the defendant and the plaintiff are found negligent by court, respectively. Let x_1 and x_2 denote the plaintiff's expenditures for proving the defendant's negligence and his own non-negligence, respectively; and let y_1 and y_2 denote the defendant's expenditures for proving his own non-negligence and the plaintiff's negligence, respectively.[20]

In a contributory negligence regime, the plaintiff is entitled to receive compensation in the event that the plaintiff is negligent and the defendant is not. In this case, the plaintiff's objective function is $S_P^{ConN} = p_D(1 - p_P) - x_1 - x_2$, and the defendant's expected loss is $S_D^{ConN} = p_D(1 - p_P) + y_1 + y_2$.

In a comparative negligence regime, the plaintiff receives full compensation when the plaintiff is negligent and the defendant is not, while he receives a share σ of the loss when both parties are found negligent. The share is assumed to be a function of the parties' relative fault, as captured by their probabilities of success. In this case, the plaintiff's objective function is $S_P^{ComN} = p_D(1 - p_P) + p_D p_P \sigma - x_1 - x_2$ and the defendant's expected loss is $S_D^{ComN} = p_D(1 - p_D) + p_D p_P \sigma + y_1 + y_2$.

In contrast with the prior literature, De Mot (2013) shows that comparative negligence is not necessarily more costly than contributory negligence. The intuition behind

---

17 See, for example, Brown (1973), Diamond (1974) and Posner (1977).

18 See Landes and Posner (1987).

19 Note, however, that De Mot (2013) does not address the problem of overall efficiency of the two negligence standards. See Bar-Gill and Ben-Shahar (2003) for an extensive comparative discussion of the efficiency properties of these two liability rules.

20 With no loss of generality, De Mot (2013) normalizes the measure of damages to 1.

this important result can be explained by observing the parties' incentives to invest in litigation efforts under the two alternative liability regimes. First, both parties are more willing to increase litigation expenditures under comparative negligence regimes, because they may affect the court's perception of the relative degree of fault and hence the share of compensation they pay when they are both held liable. Second, parties' expenditures to prove the defendant's negligence are higher under a regime of comparative negligence, since when both parties are negligent, any incremental change in the degree of fault can affect the measure of compensation. At the same time, litigation expenditures aimed at proving the plaintiff's negligence are greater in a contributory negligence regime, because compensation is entirely forgone in that case. De Mot (2013) shows that due to these countervailing effects, litigation expenditures may decrease in a comparative negligence regime for high-quality claims, characterized by a high degree of fault for the defendant relative to the plaintiff.

17.6 CONCLUSIONS

Legal rules play a dual role: one forward-looking, creating incentives for future behavior, and one backward-looking, adjudicating past behavior. When fulfilling their backward-looking role of conflict resolution, legal systems resort to courts, juries and other adjudication mechanisms, reallocating wealth and liability between the litigants. Litigants exert efforts and incur costs to maximize their gains (or minimize their losses) from the case. Rent-seeking models as transfer contests provide a tractable representation of a litigation problem, which can inform the design of substantive and procedural rules, and the organization of courts and legal institutions in general. The adoption of rent-seeking models in the law and economics literature has been – and promises to remain – illuminating, inasmuch as the models provide explicit, but general, comparisons of equilibrium values. In too many cases in the literature, generalizations of problems with the use of an implicit functional form have been employed at the expense of tractability. It is our hope that this chapter will provide a bird's-eye perspective on the existing law and economics literature, the use of rent-seeking models, as well as providing a starting point for future contributions to the field.

A number of research questions remain underexplored in the context of this literature. There has been a growing interest in the impact of fee-shifting rules on parties' litigation choices. However, the role of the burden of proof and its relationship to optimal litigation investments remain largely unexplored. Unlike criminal cases, the burden of proof in civil cases is preponderance of the evidence. It is sufficient that a party proves her claim to be more reasonable than the other party's claim in order to win. A 'loser-pays' fee-shifting rule may or may not be viewed as fair according to the standards of proof adopted by the court. In the contest of rent seeking, it may be worth exploring whether a fee-shifting rule could be adapted, allowing for a proportional recovery based on the strength of the winning claim. A 'proportional loss' fee-shifting rule may, in fact, deter parties from overinvesting in legal expenses at marginally strong cases, as happens when a 'loser-pays' rule is unconditionally adopted. At the same time, this rule would not undermine access to justice for parties with a strong claim, since plaintiffs would receive virtually full compensation when they have a strong case. An additional issue that still remains uninvestigated is the relationship between litigation choices and pretrial settlement decisions. In the presence of information asymmetries and alternative fee-shifting rules, parties may find it convenient to opt for settlements in order to reduce expected litigation costs. The incentive to settle in pretrial bargaining depends, however, substantially on the fee-shifting rules and the burden of proof required in court. In civil cases, when a proportional fee-shifting rule is adopted, not all cases will end up in court. Strong cases will be more likely to be settled, while weak cases will not be filed. From this perspective, the marginal cases that foster legal certainty, where parties have equal merits, will be more efficiently litigated.

REFERENCES

Baik, Kyung Hwan and In-Gyu Kim (2007a), 'Contingent fees versus legal expenses insurance', *International Review of Law and Economics*, **27**(2), 351–61.

Baik, Kyung Hwan and I. In-Gyu Kim (2007b), 'Equilibrium contingent compensation in contests with delegation', *Southern Economic Journal*, **73**(4), 986–1002.

Bar-Gill, Oren and Omri Ben-Shahar (2003), 'The uneasy case for comparative negligence', *American Law and Economics Review*, **5**(2), 433–69.

Baye, Michael, Dan Kovenock and Casper G. De Vries (2005), 'Comparative analysis of litigation systems: an auction-theoretic approach', *Economic Journal*, **115**, 583–601, reprinted in Roger D. Congleton, Arye L. Hillman and Kai A. Konrad (eds) (2008), *40 Years of Research on Rent Seeking 2 – Applications: Rent Seeking in Practice*, Heidelberg: Springer, pp. 421–39.

Braeutigam, Ronald, Bruce Owen and John C. Panzar (1984), 'An economic analysis of alternative fee shifting systems', *Law and Contemporary Problems*, **47**(1), 173–85.

Brown, John Prater (1973), 'Toward an economic theory of liability', *Journal of Legal Studies*, **2**(2), 323–50.

Buchanan, James M., Robert D. Tollison and Gordon Tullock (eds) (1980), *Toward a Theory of the Rent-seeking Society*, College Station, TX: Texas A&M University Press.

Chen, Kong-Pin and Jue-Shyan Wang (2007), 'Fee-shifting rules in litigation with contingency fees', *Journal of Law Economics and Organization*, **23**(3), 519–46.

Chen, Kong-Pin, Hung-Ken Chien and C.Y. Cyrus Chu (1997), 'Sequential versus unitary trials with asymmetric information', *Journal of Legal Studies*, **26**(1), 239–58.

Congleton, Roger D., Arye L. Hillman and Kai A. Konrad (eds) (2008a), *40 Years of Research on Rent Seeking 1 – The Theory of Rent Seeking*, Heidelberg: Springer.

Congleton, Roger D., Arye L. Hillman and Kai A. Konrad (eds) (2008b), *40 Years of Research on Rent Seeking 2 – Applications: Rent seeking in Practice*, Heidelberg: Springer.

Damaska, Mirjan (1986), *The Faces of Justice and State Authority: A Comparative Approach to the Legal Process*, New Haven, CT: Yale University Press.

Dari-Mattiacci, Giuseppe and Francesco Parisi (2005), 'Rents, dissipation and lost treasures: rethinking Tullock's paradox', *Public Choice*, **124**(3–4), 411–22.

De Mot, Jef (2012), 'Sequential trials and the English rule', *European Law and Economics Journal*, **34**(1), 31–43.

De Mot, Jef (2013), 'Comparative versus contributory negligence: a comparison of the litigation expenditures', *International Review of Law and Economics*, **33**(1), 54–61.

De Mot, Jef, Barbara Luppi and Francesco Parisi (2012), 'Are sequential trials really better than unitary trials?', Minnesota Legal Studies Research Paper No. 12-38, available at http://ssrn.com/abstract=2139787 (accessed 30 May 2014).

Diamond, Peter A. (1974), 'Single activity accidents', *Journal of Legal Studies*, **3**(1), 107–64.

Farmer, Amy and Paul Pecorino (1999), 'Legal expenditure as a rent-seeking game', *Public Choice*, **100**(3–4), 271–88, reprinted in Roger D. Congleton, Arye L. Hillman and Kai A. Konrad (eds) (2008), *40 Years of Research on Rent Seeking 2 – Applications: Rent Seeking in Practice*, Heidelberg: Springer, pp. 379–288.

Farmer, Amy and Paul Pecorino (2013), 'Discovery and disclosure with asymmetric information and endogenous expenditure at trial', *Journal of Legal Studies*, **42**(1), 223–47.

Fon, Vincy and Francesco Parisi (2003), 'Litigation and the evolution of legal remedies: a dynamic model', *Public Choice*, **116**(3–4), 419–33.

Gensler, Steven S. (2000), 'Bifurcation unbound', *Washington Law Review*, **75**(3), 705–84.

Gould, John P. (1973), 'The economics of legal conflicts', *Journal of Legal Studies*, **2**(2), 279–300.

Higgins, Richard S., William F. Shughart II and Robert D. Tollison (1985), 'Free entry and efficient rent seeking', *Public Choice*, **46**(3), 247–58, reprinted in Roger D. Congleton, Arye L. Hillman and Kai A. Konrad (eds) (2008), *40 Years of Research on Rent Seeking 1 – The Theory of Rent Seeking*, Heidelberg: Springer, pp. 121–32.

Hillman, Arye L. (2013), 'Rent seeking', in William F. Shughart II, Laura Razzolini and Michael Reksulak (eds), *The Elgar Companion to Public Choice*, 2nd edn, Cheltenham, UK and Northampton, MA, USA: Edward Elgar Publishing, pp. 307–30.

Hillman, Arye L. and John G. Riley (1989), 'Politically contestable rents and transfers', *Economics and Politics*, **1**(1), 17–39, reprinted in Roger D. Congleton, Arye L. Hillman and Kai A. Konrad (eds) (2008), *40 Years of Research on Rent Seeking 1 – The Theory of Rent Seeking*, Heidelberg: Springer, pp. 185–207.

Hirshleifer, Jack and Evan Osborne (2001), 'Truth, effort, and the legal battle', *Public Choice*, **108**(1–2), 169–95.

Katz, Avery (1988), 'Judicial decision-making and litigation expenditure', *International Review of Law and Economics*, **8**(2), 127–43.

Katz, Avery and Chris W. Sanchirico (2011), 'Fee shifting in litigation: survey and assessment', in Chris W. Sanchirico (eds), *Elgar Encyclopedia of Law and Economics*, Volume X, Procedural Law and Economics, Cheltenham, UK and Northampton, MA, USA: Edward Elgar Publishing, pp. 271–307.

Landes, William M. (1971), 'An economic analysis of the courts', *Journal of Law and Economics*, **14**(1), 61–107.

Landes, William M. (1993), 'Sequential versus unitary trials: an economic analysis', *Journal of Legal Studies*, **22**(1), 99–134.

Landes, William M. and Richard A. Posner (1987), *The Economic Structure of Tort Law*, Cambridge, MA: Harvard University Press.

Long, Ngo Van (2013), 'The theory of contests: a unified model and review of the literature', *European Journal of Political Economy*, **32**, 161–81, reprinted in Chapter 3 in this volume.

Luppi, Barbara and Francesco Parisi (2012), 'Litigation and legal evolution: does procedure matter?', *Public Choice*, **152**(1–2), 181–201.

Nitzan, Shmuel (1994), 'Modeling rent seeking contests', *European Journal of Political Economy*, **10**(1), 41–60.

Parisi, Francesco (2002), 'Rent seeking through litigation: adversarial and inquisitorial systems compared', *International Review of Law and Economics*, **22**(2), 193–216, reprinted in Roger D. Congleton, Arye L. Hillman and Kai A. Konrad (eds) (2008), *40 Years of Research on Rent Seeking 2 – Applications: Rent Seeking in Practice*, Heidelberg: Springer, pp. 397–420.

Parisi, Francesco and Vincy Fon (2009), *The Economics of Lawmaking*, Oxford: Oxford University Press.

Posner, Richard A. (1973), 'An economic approach to legal procedure and judicial administration', *Journal of Legal Studies*, **2**(2), 399–458.

Posner, Richard A. (1977), *Economic Analysis of Law*, 2nd edn, Boston, MA and Toronto: Little Brown.

Posner, Richard A. (1988), 'Comment: responding to Gordon Tullock', *Research in Law and Policy Studies*, **2**(1), 29–33.

Posner, Richard A. (1999), 'An economic approach to the law of evidence', *Stanford Law Review*, **51**, 1477–546.

Priest, George L. and Benjamin Klein (1984), 'The selection of disputes for litigation', *Journal of Legal Studies*, **13**(1), 1–55.

Rowley, Charles K., Robert D. Tollison and Gordon Tullock (eds) (1988), *The Political Economy of Rent Seeking*, Boston, MA: Kluwer.

Shavell, Steven (1987), *Economic Analysis of Accident Law*, Cambridge, MA: Harvard University Press.

Tollison, Robert D. (1982), 'Rent seeking: a survey', *Kyklos*, **35**(4), 575–602.

Tullock, Gordon (1967), 'The welfare costs of tariffs, monopolies and theft', *Western Economic Journal*, **5**(3), 224–32, reprinted in Roger D. Congleton, Arye L. Hillman and Kai A. Konrad (eds) (2008), *40 Years of Research on Rent Seeking 1 – The Theory of Rent Seeking*, Heidelberg: Springer, pp. 45–53.

Tullock, Gordon (1975), 'On the efficient organization of trials', *Kyklos*, **28**(4), 745–62, reprinted in Roger D. Congleton, Arye L. Hillman and Kai A. Konrad (eds) (2008), *40 Years of Research on Rent Seeking 2 – Applications: Rent Seeking in Practice*, Heidelberg: Springer, pp. 361–78.

Tullock, Gordon (1980), 'Efficient rent seeking', in James M. Buchanan, Robert D. Tollison and Gordon Tullock (eds), *Toward a Theory of the Rent-seeking Society*, College Station, TX: Texas A&M University Press, pp. 97–112, reprinted in Roger D. Congleton, Arye L. Hillman and Kai A. Konrad (eds) (2008), *40 Years of Research on Rent Seeking 1 – The Theory of Rent Seeking*, Heidelberg: Springer, pp. 105–20.

Tullock, Gordon, (1988), 'Defending the Napoleonic code over the common law', *Research in Law and Policy Studies*, **2**(1), 3–27.

Tullock, Gordon (1997), 'The case against the common law', in Charles K. Rowley (ed.), *The Selected Works of Gordon Tullock*, Vol. 9, Indianapolis, IN: Liberty Fund, pp. 397–455.

PART IV

THE REALITY OF RENTS

18. Profit seeking and rent seeking in the United States and Europe

Dennis C. Mueller

SUMMARY

This chapter describes and compares profit seeking and rent seeking, and rent protection, in Europe and the United States, where historical and cultural differences have resulted in different attitudes to the role of the state. In Europe the state has had an accepted, quite consensual, role as creator and protector of rents for workers and also for producers. In the United States such rent creation and rent protection by government has not been consensual and has been more contested.

18.1 INTRODUCTION

Since Gordon Tullock (1967 [2008]) drew attention to rent-seeking activities and Anne Krueger (1974 [2008]) named and Richard Posner (1975 [2008]) investigated the phenomenon, given the influence of the US public-choice school, much of the descriptive literature has taken as background the United States. European countries, and by this I mean essentially countries in the European Union (EU), resemble the United States in being democracies with market economies. A monopoly rent in Europe is much like a monopoly rent in the United States and efforts to capture it or protect it are similar. There are some important differences with regard to rents, however, on which this chapter focuses.

Rent seeking involves the unproductive use of resources in seeking personal benefits. The benefits sought can have social merit; for example, an association for the blind may convince the government to supply its members with free seeing-eye dogs. Thus, rent seeking, which has efficiency costs, involves attempts at redistribution, but sometimes with merit.

With this consideration in mind, this chapter considers three types of economic rents: the rents accruing to firms, to individuals and to groups of individuals acting together as a kind of cartel protected by the state. I employ the standard definition of a rent as the difference between a person's income from a particular occupation and the person's opportunity costs.

To understand why in some cases rent seeking takes on different forms in the United States and Europe or is of different magnitudes, one must begin by looking at Europe's historical development. This is done briefly in the following section. The chapter then moves on to rents and rent seeking by firms, individuals and groups. Conclusions are in the final section.

18.2 WHY IS EUROPE DIFFERENT FROM THE UNITED STATES?

Throughout much of the last millennium European countries were ruled by monarchs. Although some like Louis XVI were reviled, many like Louis XIV, Elizabeth I, Frederic the Great and Queen Victoria were revered. The Europeans' fondness for monarchy is nicely symbolized by the decision by the Netherlands following Napoleon's defeat to replace the French king Napoleon had installed (his brother) with a Dutch king. Having been a republic without a king for two centuries, the Dutch chose to revert back to monarchy at the beginning of the nineteenth century.

In European languages like German, where nouns have sexes, the expression *der Staat* conjures up a masculine image of a paternalistic ruler. Thus, in Europe historically an attitude toward and trust in the state can be found, which is strikingly different from that in the United States. This difference was succinctly stated by the nineteenth-century German historian, Heinrich von Treitschke:

> For us the state is not, as it is for the Americans, a power to be constrained so that the will of the individual may remain uninhibited, but rather a cultural power from which we expect positive achievements in all areas of national life. (Quoted in Burleigh 2005, p. 327)

Thus, there is a much greater presumption in Europe that the state is acting for the common good than in the United States.

The shift from monarchy to democracy in Europe spanned much of the last millennium culminating at the end of the nineteenth and beginning of the twentieth centuries (Congleton 2011). During much of the nineteenth century the voting franchise was restricted to small fractions of the populations in each country – men owning property or paying taxes. Thus, most voters were relatively well educated and members of the upper class. Imbued with Enlightenment thinking, they sought to introduce a variety of liberal reforms. The Whig Party in Britain was transformed into the Liberal Party and dominated British politics over the second half of the nineteenth century and up until World War I. Mercantilism gave way to free trade and competition and Great Britain became the world's number one economic power of the nineteenth century. In Germany, the National Liberal Party was formed in 1866, and was the major force in German politics until World War I by which time Germany had begun to eclipse Britain as the strongest economy in Europe. Liberal parties also flourished in Austria, the Netherlands and Belgium in the latter half of the nineteenth century and it can reasonably be argued that liberalism reached its zenith in Europe during this period.[1]

Among the reforms the liberals wished to introduce were universal education and the extension of the voting franchise to all classes and both sexes. As the voting franchise expanded to encompass members of the working class, however, the newly enfranchised voters did not reward the liberal parties by voting for them. Instead, they largely opted for religious, socialist and nationalist parties. The socialist parties were obviously against economic liberalism, but so too were the religious parties. As a reaction to the Enlightenment and the excesses of the French Revolution, both the Catholic and

---

1 See discussion and references in Mueller (2009, chapter 9) and Congleton (2011).

Protestant Churches were strongly against liberalism, democracy and 'modernism' in general.[2] Here we have two important differences between Europe and the United States. Except for a few parts of the country in the 1930s, the United States has never had an overtly socialist party that gathered much voter support or an overtly religious party.

By the beginning of the twentieth century, liberal parties in Europe were in severe decline or on their way to extinction.[3] The British Liberal Democrats' entry into government as a junior partner after the last election was its first taste of political power in a hundred years. Thus, the liberal reforms of the nineteenth century in Europe paved the way for the triumph of religious, socialist and nationalist parties at the beginning of the twentieth century.

To summarize, three salient differences between Europe and the United States can be identified – a greater trust in the state in Europe, a more hostile attitude toward economic liberalism (competitive markets, capitalist firms) and a more entrenched and powerful trade union movement with ideological roots anchored in socialistic thinking. This entrenchment extends deeply into both the attitudes of voters and the political process. If a person knowledgeable about the principles of the public-choice school but ignorant of US and European politics were to appear from nowhere and were to be asked to guess whether the Republican Party or the Democratic Party was to the left of the median voter, the answer could be only a wild guess. The parties' names reveal nothing about their ideologies. If asked whether the British Labour Party or the Conservative Party was on the left, the task of answering would be much easier. The German Socialist Party would be evidently identified as to the left of center. Indeed, despite communism being openly discredited after 1989, communist political parties, or their barely disguised replacements, still win seats in some European countries.

18.3 RENT SEEKING BY FIRMS

To have rent seeking, one needs economic rents. Firms with market power earn profits above the levels needed to cover their costs of capital, and if these are protected from dissipation through competitive entry, they become economic rents.

Enterprises with great market power appeared toward the end of the nineteenth and beginning of the twentieth centuries in both Europe and the United States. In Europe one found Karl Benz and Gottlieb Daimler founding an automobile dynasty. In steel there was August Thyssen and Friedrich Krupp, in cosmetics Eugène Schueller (L'Oréal) and so on. There were parallel developments in the United States – Henry Ford in automobiles, Andrew Carnegie and Henry Frick in steel, John D. Rockefeller in oil and many others. Joseph A. Schumpeter (1911 [1934]), observing these developments in Europe, formulated his famous theory of economic development. Economic growth was driven by the innovative activity of entrepreneurs such as Benz and Krupp, whose rewards were the monopoly profits from successful innovations. The inherent competitiveness of

---

2 See Fogarty (1957, pp. 307, 319–20), Zwart (1997) and discussion and references in Mueller (2014).

3 Congleton (2011) and Mueller (2009, chapter 9).

capitalist systems, however, led to the erosion of these profits through what Schumpeter famously called 'the gale of creative destruction', which prevails in capitalist, free-market economies. For Schumpeter, it was not price competition that was the driving force behind the dissipation of monopoly profits, but competition from new products, new production processes, marketing strategies and organizational structures. Innovations such as these require investments. Thus, Schumpeter can legitimately be regarded as the first person to describe profit-seeking activities or the quest for profit through private initiative (Buchanan 1980 [2008]) and not through the quest for privilege from government that underlies the political economy of rent seeking (Tullock 1989).

In the United States, the rise of the giant 'trusts' like Standard Oil, Carnegie Steel and the New York Central Railroad led to a populist movement to constrain their economic power, which resulted in the passage of the Interstate Commerce Act in 1887 to control the railroads, and the Sherman Act in 1990 to prohibit cartels and abuses of monopoly power elsewhere in the economy.[4] No similar movements and legislation took place in Europe. Thus, rent-protecting cartels remained legal across Europe over the first half of the twentieth century, while they were vigorously challenged in the United States. Indeed, there was essentially no antitrust policy of any kind in Europe until well after World War II. The European governments did not prohibit cartels and other anti-competitive behavior that created and sustained rents. Policies provided rent protection in Europe with large enterprises enlisting the state on their behalf.

The advent of the EU had two positive effects on competition in Europe. By creating the Common Market it eliminated many – but not all – tariffs and other impediments to international trade within Europe, thereby eliminating the rents such barriers cause to trade. Secondly, it introduced an EU-wide, vigorous competition policy comparable to that in the United States. Thus, by making cartels and other market power generating activities illegal, the EU indirectly curbed rent seeking by firms and rent protection in Europe.

Contemporary counterparts to the entrepreneurs who founded the industrial dynasties a century ago include Bill Gates (Microsoft), Steve Jobs (Apple), Larry Page and Sergey Brin (Google) and Mark Zuckerberg (Facebook). All of these men founded companies in the United States, and all of these companies are in the new, high-tech industries in which Europe is poorly represented. There are many factors that may account for Europe's lagging in the new, high-tech sectors. One is certainly the much higher tax rates in Europe, which dampen the incentives of those who wish to become rich by founding new firms in Europe. Wealth was however created in the United States. Both Steve Jobs and Steve Wozniak, cofounders of Apple, had estimated wealth of over $6 billion in 2010.[5] Bill Gates, often listed as the richest man in the world, in 2010 had an estimated net worth of some $54 billion.[6] Google was founded in 1998 and went public in 2004, and yet by 2006 its founders, Sergey Brin and Larry Page, then aged 32 and 33, respectively, were ranked 26th and 27th in *Forbes Magazine*'s

---

[4] See the interesting discussion by Mark Roe (2012).

[5] For an estimate of Jobs's net worth, see http://www.tgdaily.com/business-and-law-features/51674-zuckerbergs-wealth-more-than-doubles-in-a-year, for Wozniak, see http://wiki.answers.com/Q/What_is_Steve_Wozniak%27s_net_worth_in_2008 (accessed 14 January 2014).

[6] http://www.billgatesmicrosoft.com/networth.htm (accessed 14 January 2014).

list of the world's richest people, with net worth in each case of nearly $13 billion.[7] An even younger Mark Zuckerberg, founder of Facebook, had amassed a fortune of some $6.9 billion by the age of 26.[8] More broadly, 47 percent of the world's richest people (assets over $1 million) have been estimated to have made their fortunes by starting their own companies.[9] The motives behind the innovative efforts of entrepreneurs such as these are undoubtedly multiple and complex but among these motives, it seems reasonable to guess, has been the desire to become rich. Symbolically, in late 2012 France introduced a tax of 75 percent on incomes over one million euros, thereby fulfilling a campaign promise of its newly elected, Socialist Party President, François Hollande. The message was clear for any future Steve Jobs or Sergey Brin – if you want to become rich, do not found your firm in France.

Larry Page and Sergey Brin met and developed the ideas that led to the founding of Google in a dormitory of Stanford University. Stanford and the other great universities in the United States have spawned many high-tech start-ups. For example, a recent study estimates that MIT graduates have founded 25 800 companies that are still in business, and that these had a total employment of 3.3 million people, and total annual sales of $2 trillion.[10] A quality education costs money, and tuition fees at American universities are the highest in the world. Continental Europe has by and large chosen to socialize the provision of higher education with tuition fees being modest, if not zero across virtually all of Europe. The result, as often happens when a potentially private good is socialized, is a product of mediocre quality. In the QS World University Rankings for 2010, the top ten ranked universities came either from the United States (six) or the United Kingdom (four). The highest ranked university in the EU outside the United Kingdom was France's École Normale Supérieure, Paris, with a rank of 33. Out of the top 100 ranked universities, 31 were located in the United States, 19 in the United Kingdom, and only 18 in the rest of the EU, even though its population is two thirds larger than that of the United States and seven times larger than that of the United Kingdom. Australia, with a population barely a 20th of that of all non-UK EU members, managed to place seven of its universities in the top 100. Moreover, while the United States and United Kingdom dominated the top ranks of the list with 19 of the top 25 spots, the non-UK members of the EU were over-represented in the bottom 25 (8).[11] There are now several international rankings of universities, but each paints a similar picture – the United States and United Kingdom dominating the top rankings, the rest of the EU beginning to appear around rank 30. Thus, the superior education potential entrepreneurs receive in the United States leads to the creation of more wealth.

Saint-Paul (1997) puts some of the blame for Europe's failure to produce more entrepreneurs and new start-ups on its rigid labor markets, to be discussed below. Potential

---

[7] For Page, see, http://www.forbes.com/lists/2006/10/XFXI.html and for Brin, http://www.forbes.com/lists/2006/10/D664.html (accessed 14 January 2014).

[8] http://www.tgdaily.com/business-and-law-features/51674-zuckerbergs-wealth-more-than-doubles-in-a-year (accessed 14 January 2014).

[9] *The Economist* (2011, p. 4).

[10] *The Economist* (2011, p. 14).

[11] http://www.topuniversities.com/university-rankings/world-university-rankings/2010 (accessed 14 January 2014).

entrepreneurs shy away from starting new firms in high-tech, high risk industries, because of the high costs of laying off or firing people should the new enterprise not succeed.

Whatever the cause, the numbers are startling. During the last 25 years of the nineteenth century, Europe and the United States had about equal numbers of firms in the largest 500 of the world. In the last quarter of the twentieth century, the United States had ten times as many firms in the largest 500. Between 1950 and 2007, 12 companies were founded in Europe and grew large enough to enter the largest 500, 57 companies performed the same feat in the United States (Philippon and Véron 2008). In patent filings, the United States was second in the world to Japan in 2005 with almost 400000. In that year there were about 125000 filings at the European Patent Office, another 60000 in Germany and 20000 in France (World Intellectual Property Organization 2007). Microsoft, Apple, Google and Facebook are among the most profitable companies in the world. That fact accompanied by the lawsuit culture in the United States means that they spend hundreds of millions of dollars each year to protect their economic rents. At the same time, their rivals and potential competitors are spending millions to take those rents away. Some of this money is spent in research and development (R&D) laboratories, some in advertising and some in court rooms. Where there are no rents, there is no rent seeking. Thus, as well as leading Europe in patenting, the United States also leads it in litigation. In 2012, for example, there were roughly 1.25 million lawyers in the United States, more than five times as many lawyers per capita as in France (Ramseyer and Rasmusen 2010, p. 5). Thus, a somewhat happy consequence of Europe's failure in recent years to create economic rents by founding new firms is that there is undoubtedly less rent seeking to protect or capture the rents of other corporations in Europe than in the United States.

The large rents earned by leading companies not only spur rent seeking by other firms, they are an incentive for individuals to engage in rent seeking. In an infamous case in 1994, Stella Liebeck sued McDonald's after she spilt hot coffee on her lap at a drive-thru outlet. A jury awarded her $2.86 million in damages, the judge reduced the award to a mere $650000. Had the accident occurred at a single-proprietor coffee shop, Ms Liebeck would probably not have sued, as the expected award would have been much lower. Indeed, probably no lawyer would have taken the case; but giant and profitable companies in the United States, like McDonald's, must anticipate that every customer and every employee is prepared to sue, should a possible case of negligence arise. Here again the litigation-friendly institutions in the United States undoubtedly encourage more rent seeking of this type than takes place in Europe. Ramseyer and Rasmusen (2010, p. 5) record 5806 suits filed in the United States per 100000 citizens as opposed to 1768 in France.

18.4 INDIVIDUAL RENTS

Frank and Cook (1995) describe how globalization has led to large compensation packages for those at the top of their professions. A century ago the sales of most firms were concentrated in their domestic markets. A giant multinational can have a value added greater than the gross domestic products (GDPs) of some small countries. Its managers receive accordingly high compensation packages. Sports teams like Manchester United and the New York Yankees have fans around the world, and make millions of pounds and dollars marketing their 'products' outside their ballparks. Their players share in these revenues. An economic rent is defined as the difference between an individual's income and his or her opportunity cost: if these opportunity costs are defined as the income a person could earn in another profession, then managers, athletes, movie stars, opera singers and others with specialized talents earn substantial individual rents. In this section, I note the rents earned in a few professions. To put the European experience in context, the data for Europe are compared with those of the United States.

18.4.1 Athletes

Football, American soccer, is far and away the most important sport in Europe. Stadiums are filled in many countries, and television contracts are lucrative. In 2012, the three highest paid European football players earned in euros the equivalents of \$15.2 million (Cristiano Ronaldo), \$13.3 million (Lionel Messi) and \$12.7 million (Fernando Torres).[12] These are impressive numbers to be sure, but they pale in comparison to the top salaries of those playing American football – \$37.1 million (Haloti Ngata), \$36.8 million (Larry Fitzgerald) and \$35.3 million (Ndamukong Suh). To these one might add compensation from endorsing products. For example, Peyton Manning's salary was 'only' \$32.4 million, but he earned another \$10 million in endorsements making him the highest paid National Football League (NFL) player in terms of total compensation.[13] I could not find endorsement figures for Europeans, but given the greater importance of television advertising in the United States compared to most of Europe, I expect that these are also much lower for Europeans.

While there is really only one major professional sport in Europe based on total revenues, there are arguably four in the United States – baseball, basketball, hockey and American football. Basketball and hockey are also professional sports in parts of Europe, but are much less popular than football, and the salaries are correspondingly more modest. The two highest paid basketball players in Europe during the 2011–12 season each earned the equivalent of \$4.4 million (Mehmet Okur and Deron Williams).[14] The National Basketball Association's (NBA) Miami Heat, by way of contrast, had three players earning more than \$17 million (Chris Bosh, Dwane Wade and Lebron James).[15]

Average incomes in the United States are higher than in Europe, and the US market is much larger than any single national market in Europe. Television advertising is much higher in the United States. Thus, it is perhaps not surprising that professional athletes receive much higher rents in the United States. These rents go to the athletes with the greatest skills. To develop these skills, athletes must devote countless hours to practicing

---

12 See http://bleacherreport.com/articles/1165767-european-footballs-50-biggest-wage-salaries-of-last-year-are-they-worth-it/page/51 (accessed 23 November 2012).

13 See http://www.nfl.com/photoessays/09000d5d829f6793#photo=5 (accessed 23 November 2012).

14 See http://www.ballineurope.com/european-basketball/top-salaries-european-basketball-3298/ (accessed 23 November 2012).

15 http://www.hoopsworld.com/miami-heat-team-salary (accessed 23 November 2012).

and conditioning. The social costs from this rent seeking include the many wasted hours and efforts of those who try to become superstars, but fail. And what are the social benefits? Do fans watching the Boston Celtics or Manchester United have more enjoyment out of a game played today than fans got 50 years ago? Are Manchester United's players better today than they were 50 years ago? Comparing teams from different eras is difficult, but in golf players play against the course as well as against each other. The Masters golf tournament in Augusta, Georgia, has a glorious history that began in 1934. In 2012, Buba Watson earned $1 440 000 for winning the tournament, shooting 10 under par. Cha Schwartzel earned the same for a 14 under par round in 2011. In contrast, for his winning 14 under par round in 1953, Ben Hogan earned $4000 – $33 800 in 2012 dollars. Rents in golf have also increased over time.[16]

18.4.2 Managers

There has been much controversy on both sides of the Atlantic over the levels of executive compensation. They are indeed quite large. In 2010 in the United States, Philippe Dauman of Viacom received reportedly the highest total compensation of any chief executive – $84.5 million. He was followed by Ray Irani of Occidental Petroleum with a compensation package of $76.1 million. A full 100 US executives reportedly earned ten or more million dollars (New York Times 2012).

Data for executive compensation in Europe are less readily available. One study, which uses an unpublished database, reports that executive compensation in the United States is more than double that of Europe on average (Conyon et al. 2011). This figure corresponds to those appearing in the popular press.[17] There has been quite a debate in the economics and finance community over whether high executive compensation is the outcome of the intersections of supply and demand schedules in the market for managers or is merely a manifestation of the principal-agent problem between managers and shareholders with managers using their discretionary power to inflate their incomes.[18] Even if the first perspective is the correct one, a good portion of executive compensation must be regarded as an economic rent from the perspective of society. Viacom may have to offer Philippe Dauman a huge compensation package to keep him from going to another company, just as Miami Heat must offer Chris Bosh a high salary to prevent him from jumping to another team, but both would earn much less if they had to seek employment in a different occupation.

In basketball, rent seeking takes the form of countless hours spent on the practice court and in the conditioning gym. Rent seeking in corporate management begins with long hours of study and, perhaps, high tuition fees paid at prestige universities. These are followed by long hours spent at the office in an effort to be promoted over the other candidates for promotion, and continue until the executive suite is reached. Assuming that boards of directors know what they are doing, the most capable managers will fill the top

---

16 http://en.wikipedia.org/wiki/Masters_Tournament (accessed 23 November 2012).

17 'The pay at the top', *USA Today*, 14 May 2012, http://usatoday30.usatoday.com/money/companies/management/2008–06–29-europe-ceo-pay_N.htm (accessed 27 November 2012) and 'Pay attention', *The Economist*, 12 June 2008, http://www.economist.com/node/11543665.

18 For a recent survey, see Conyon (2012).

corporate positions. But, as with professional sports, the improvement in a company's performance brought about by the collective struggle for managerial rents may not be very large compared to the effort and outlays expended to secure them.

Corporations are larger and more profitable in the United States than in Europe. Just as the US companies earn larger profits than their European counterparts, it is not surprising to find that the managers of US companies also earn substantially larger rents than managers in Europe.

18.4.3 Other Professions

The same forces leading to high rewards in sports and management are at work in other professions – motion pictures, medicine, law and even to a lesser extent in academia (Frank and Cook 1995). Hollywood remains the motion picture capital of the world despite an increasing tendency for films to be shot 'on location' outside Hollywood. American made films gross many times what films produced on the European continent do, and stars in American films benefit accordingly. In 2010, Johnny Depp was reported to be Hollywood's highest paid actor with an income of $100 million.[19] A survey of European movie stars claimed that Dany Boon, 'the director and star of France's most successful film ever, "Bienvenue Chez Les Ch'tis," has become the best paid European actor in European film history'. In 2008, he earned in euros the equivalent of $33 million.[20] Here it might be noted that many stars in American films, as well as directors, camera operators and others in the motion picture business are, like Ray Irani of Occidental Petroleum, foreign born. Those in the movie business who wish to earn millions gravitate to the United States.

An education at a medical or law school in the United States can cost in the hundreds of thousands of dollars. On the European continent, tuition fees in these areas are modest or even zero. Thus, rent-seeking expenditures in these professions start out much higher in the United States than in Europe. Those studying in the United States would not make these outlays if they did not expect to be highly rewarded for them. A survey of doctors' salaries reported that general practitioners in the United States are the highest paid in the world with mean annual income in 2009 of $161 000. The highest paid general practitioners in Europe were found in the United Kingdom with mean annual incomes of the equivalent of $118 000. The figures for Belgium and France were $61 000 and $92 000, respectively. The highest paid specialist doctors, however, were in the Netherlands (mean of $253 000). Specialists in the United States came in second in the world with a mean of $230 000. In the United Kingdom, Belgium and France the mean incomes of specialists were $150 000, $188 000 and $149 000, respectively (Rampell 2009). Of course, the very highest paid surgeons will earn in the millions, but here too I expect the figures to be smaller for Europeans than for Americans.

Similar differences appear to exist in the legal profession. Not surprisingly, corporate

---

[19] http://www.therichest.org/entertainment/vanityfairtop-40-highest-paid-stars-in-hollywood/ (accessed 28 November 2012).

[20] http://www.asiaone.com/News/Latest%2BNews/Showbiz/Story/A1Story20090227–124860.html (accessed 14 January 2014).

law pays particularly well, with those making it to the top earning almost as much as corporate managers. The top paid general counsel in the United States in 2012 was reportedly Louis Briskman of CBS who had a total compensation of $14611037 (Lat 2012).

We conclude that the individual rents earned by professionals, as for athletes and managers, are higher in the United States than in Europe. The above examples are consistent with a more general literature on high incomes, for example, the studies in Atkinson and Piketty (2007). Bivens and Mishel (2013) note the role of rents as a component of high incomes.

18.5 RENT SEEKING THROUGH THE STATE

As noted above, Europeans put more trust in the state than Americans do, and it is to be expected that the state will play a more important role in facilitating rent seeking and rent protection in Europe. Public sectors in Europe take up roughly half of GDP on average, almost half again as much as in the United States. Thus, there is considerable scope for rent seeking through the state in Europe. In this section, I discuss a few of the more egregious cases.

18.5.1 Farmers

Levels of subsidies for farmers and other forms of benefits like tariffs are decided by the EU. Over the seven-year period ending in 2007, the EU's Common Agricultural Policy (CAP) resulted in transfers to farmers averaging around 50 billion euros per year, roughly 100 euros for every man, woman and child in the EU (National Audit Office 2009). This amounted to some 45 percent of the total EU budget. Although this percentage has fallen considerably over time, it still is a substantial burden on EU taxpayers. To this must be added the losses to consumers from higher prices as a result of the steep tariffs imposed by the EU. One early study estimated the average losses to consumers from the CAP as three times as large as the costs to taxpayers (Buckwell et al. 1982). This would bring the total losses to each EU citizen from the CAP up to 400 euros. A study published by a consumer advocacy group put the total cost of the CAP to a British family at £400 per year with half of that cost coming from higher food prices (Rotherman 2012).

To secure these benefits, EU farmers must engage in considerable lobbying efforts.[21] Beyond these, they occasionally engage in demonstrations, which impose additional costs on EU citizens – such as dumping milk or other agricultural products on streets and blocking traffic with tractors and other farm equipment, which are acts of rent seeking or actually rent protection.

---

[21] For a theoretical analysis of rent seeking fostered by the EU's Common Agricultural Policy, see Nedergaard (2006).

18.5.2 Unions

When US President Ronald Reagan fired the striking air traffic controllers in 1981, he appeared to have broken the backs of all the private sector unions in the United States. Labor unions remain strong in most of Europe, however, and air traffic controllers in France routinely go on strike whenever there are rumors of possible organizational changes to improve efficiency.[22] More generally, strikes are quite common in many European countries. Moreover, the target of a strike is often not a particular company or industry, but the state. Workers in Europe, like its farmers, often hold general strikes stopping traffic and sometimes destroying property to obtain favorable legislation or to prevent legislation threatening labor market reforms. Many countries have laws that make it very difficult or expensive to fire or lay off a worker. These laws deter companies from hiring workers, which helps explain why unemployment rates are generally higher in Europe than in the United States, Canada, Australia and New Zealand.

In addition to job security, workers in many countries have succeeded in having the state adopt laws regulating hours worked, lengths of vacations and retirement ages. Statutory minimum retirement ages are low in many European countries, and penalties for early retirement are often modest. This leads to dramatically low labor force participation rates for older workers in many European countries. Column 2 of Table 18.1 presents the participation rates for 55 to 64 year olds in the United States and several European countries. In 2011, 60 percent of Americans, men and women, aged 55 to 64 were employed. Only one European country – Sweden – had a higher participation rate (72.5 percent). Several countries (Austria, France, Italy) had participation rates around 40 percent. I have included tiny Slovenia in the table, since it had the lowest participation rate of any Organisation for Economic Co-operation and Development (OECD) country – 31.2 percent.

In many European countries, not only do fewer people work than in the United States and other Anglo-Saxon countries, but those who do work often work many fewer hours per year. Thus, while the labor force participation rates in column 2 are comparable for the United States and the Netherlands, the average Dutch worker (all ages) worked almost 400 fewer hours in 2011 than his or her American counterpart – the equivalent of ten 40-hour weeks. Although the number of hours worked in a few countries, such as Italy, comes close to that in the United States, in most European countries it is considerably lower.

Low statutory retirement ages, weak restrictions on early retirements and generous payments to those in retirement combine to produce large state outlays for pensions in several European countries. Column 4 in Table 18.1 reports the percentages of GDP going into state pensions for the United States and selected countries in Europe. In six of the European countries, pensions account for over 10 percent of GDP. Austria, France and Italy devote more than twice as much of their national income to pensions than does the United States. At the same time, we observe that the elderly are not equally successful at garnering transfers from the state in all European countries. Denmark, the

---

[22] http://www.dailymail.co.uk/news/article-123723/Strike-chaos-holidaymakers.html (accessed 14 January 2014).

Table 18.1 Labor market and pension statistics for selected countries

Country	Employment rate 55–64 year olds	Annual hours worked	State expenditures on pensions as percent of GDP
Austria	41.5	1600	12.3
Belgium	38.7	1577	8.9
Czech Republic	47.6	1774	7.4
Denmark	59.5	1522	5.1
France	41.4	1476	12.5
Germany	59.9	1413	10.7
Italy	37.9	1774	14.1
Netherlands	56.1	1379	4.7
Portugal	47.9	1711	10.8
Slovenia	31.2	NR	9.6
Spain	44.5	1793	8.0
Sweden	72.5	1690	7.2
United Kingdom	56.8	1625	5.4
United States	60.0	1787	6.0

Note: Employment rates are percentages of workforce. Figures in columns 2 and 3 are for 2011, in column 4 for 2007. NR = not reported.

Source: OECD statistics, http://www.oecd.org/statistics/ and http://stats.oecd.org/Index.aspx?DatasetCode=ANHRS (accessed 30 November 2012); http://news.bbc.co.uk/2/hi/business/7598467.stm (accessed 6 December 2012).

Netherlands and the United Kingdom spend proportionally less on pensions than does the United States.

With state sectors much larger in Europe than in the United States, taxes are correspondingly higher in Europe. This helps explain why workers in Europe use their bargaining power to obtain more leisure rather than higher wages, which in turn explains why average incomes are lower in most of Europe than in the United States. Europeans often defend low retirement ages and short work weeks as part of the benefits of the European model of the welfare state. The term 'welfare state' also conjures up the notions of social justice and equity. In practice, however, the labor and retirement laws in Europe produce large inequities. If a self-employed jeweler or carpenter in France chooses to work 35 hours a week instead of his or her previous 40 to 48 hours, his or her income falls proportionally, unlike that of the industrial sector workers who succeeded in having the government mandate a 35-hour week for them without a reduction in pay. A jeweler may also find it more difficult to justify early retirement on a state pension by claiming undue stress than, say, a school teacher. The rent-seeking activities of unions in Europe produce great benefits for their members – secure jobs at reasonable pay, short work weeks, long vacations, early retirements. These may be regarded as forms of privileged economic rents, since they are not available to all members of the community, and are the result of the political activity of organized unions. Job protection and the other benefits enjoyed by some workers in Europe also produce large costs for those not fortunate enough to qualify for these benefits – such as the unemployed youths who cannot find jobs – because those having jobs are so well protected, those who cannot or will not in good conscience feign a disability or stress so as to retire early.[23]

18.5.3 Businesses

In the theoretical literature on rent seeking and rent creation, a political decision maker can assign the right to monopolize the sale of a given product. Under a variety of assumptions, much if not all of the rents are competed away or dissipated in the contest for the rent.[24]

While kings once sold or gave away monopoly rights, democratic governments do not generally do so today. They do issue licenses to operate, to import, to practice certain professions and the like, and these licenses can provide their owners with a degree of monopoly power and thereby economic rents. States can also create rents for successful bidders for procurement and construction contracts by paying more than the costs of the goods and services purchased. Thus, government bureaucrats do have opportunities to create rents for companies and professionals, and to benefit from awarding them.

Obtaining private benefits in this way is generally illegal, however. Thus, the amounts of bribes paid to state bureaucrats are not available in published statistics. Transparency International publishes a country index of corruption based on surveys in each country of citizens' and business people's perceptions of the degree of corruption. This index can serve as an indicator of the amount of rent seeking through the state by businesses and professionals. Table 18.2 reports the rankings and scores for the EU countries in 2012, along with those of the four non-EU Anglo-Saxon countries, Australia, Canada, New Zealand and the United States. The highest possible score indicating the least corruption is 100. Three of the four Anglo-Saxon countries are ranked in the top ten with New Zealand tying for first place with Denmark and Finland. The United States ranks only 18th with a score of 73 compared to New Zealand's 90. Below the United States come 19 of the 27 EU countries, however, with Greece being the most corrupt of the 27, tied with India, Moldavia and Mongolia for place 94 on the list with a corruption score of only 36.

The data in Table 18.2 tell a mixed story. While four EU countries are ranked in the top ten with two tied for first, several have corruption levels comparable to those of many developing countries. Italy has a lower score than Romania. Of particular note is Greece, which ranks last among the 27 EU countries in the corruption index, and also ranks last among the 27 in the World Economic Forum's competitive index for 2012–13 – 96th in the world (Schwab 2012). One of the many disadvantages Greece has in terms of competitiveness is that businesses are hampered by onerous and outdated regulations and license requirements. Why do these exist in a country that needs to attract foreign investment and encourage new start-ups to achieve economic growth? Table 18.2 suggests that the answer is related to corruption – and to other related political-economy aspects of rents in Greece (Katsimi and Moutos 2010).

---

23 On the political economy of early retirement, see, for example, Neugart (2009).

24 For surveys of this literature, see Nitzan (1994), Tollison (1997), Mueller (2003, chapter 15) and Hillman (2013).

Table 18.2 Corruption indexes for 2012

Rank	Country	Score	Rank	Country	Score	Rank	Country	Score
1	Denmark	90	18	United States	73	46	Hungary	55
1	Finland	90	22	France	71	48	Lithuania	54
1	New Zealand	90	25	Austria	69	54	Czech Republic	49
4	Sweden	88	25	Ireland	69	54		
7	Australia	85	29	Cyprus	66	62	Latvia	49
9	Canada	84	30	Spain	65	66	Slovakia	46
9	Netherlands	84	32	Estonia	64	72	Romania	44
12	Luxembourg	80	33	Portugal	63	75	Italy	42
13	Germany	79	37	Slovenia	61	94	Bulgaria	41
16	Belgium	75	41	Poland	58		Greece	36
17	United Kingdom	74	43	Malta	57			

Source: Transparency International, Corruption Perceptions Index 2012, http://www.transparency.org/cpi2012/results (accessed 8 December 2012).

18.5.4 The Greens

Concerns about environmental degradation are a part of the political agenda. Numerous interest groups press for legislation to protect the environment. In Europe most countries have a Green Party whose raison d'être is the promotion of environmental issues. Many countries have ministries or other forms of bureaucracies dedicated to environmental policies. Clean air and water and the other environmental issues championed by greens are forms of public goods and the greens are expressing their preferences for these public goods.

Rent seeking arises in the military sphere, if the persons or companies seeking more military spending are part of the defense industry and benefit from a larger military budget. The same is true in the environmental area. The EU and its member states individually have arguably been the world leaders in pressing for international agreements to limit greenhouse gases and in unilaterally adopting policies with this goal. Yet the amount of carbon in the world's atmosphere rises relentlessly, as do predictions of future global temperatures. The main thrust of Europe's attack on global warming has been to promote alternatives to coal, oil and gas as sources of energy. Wind and solar power have been the favored alternatives with respect to electricity generation. Wind and solar power are more expensive sources of energy and so electricity prices in Europe are high. A 2004 study by the Royal Academy of Engineering in the United Kingdom estimated the cost of a kilowatt hour of electricity produced by windmills on land to be 5.4 pence. A kilowatt hour produced by windmills off-shore costs 7.2 pence. The costs of kilowatt hours produced by gas or nuclear energy were in contrast 2.2 and 2.3 pence, respectively.[25] This has made some energy-intensive industries in Europe uncompetitive internationally, and driven their production activities to countries with less stringent

[25] Royal Academy of Engineering, *The Cost of Generating Electricity* (2004), http://www.raeng.

environmental standards such as China and India, which are heavily dependent on coal for generating electricity – the worst source of energy as far as carbon dioxide (CO_2) emissions are concerned. From the year 2000 through 2010, the global demand for coal grew by over 70 percent with China and India accounting for more than 90 percent of this growth (Helm 2012, p. 32). Thus, while the Europeans build windmills and install solar panels at increasing rates, thereby reducing their consumption of coal, they contribute to the increase of CO_2 in the atmosphere by stimulating production in China, India and other developing countries through their importation of goods from these countries. A more misguided set of policies is difficult to imagine.[26]

How could the Europeans make such mistakes? Part of the explanation may come from economic illiteracy of people attracted to the green movement who do not consider cost-benefit calculations or economic incentives. Or perhaps as NIMBYs (not-in-my backyard) they are focused on local consequences. Industries have however arisen – windmill and solar panel producers, wind farm operators, contractors installing solar panels, manufacturers of 'smart' appliances, which save electricity, and so on – which benefit from, or indeed could not exist without, the regulations and state subsidies that constitute the EU's environmental policies (Helm 2012, pp. 94–9). Part of these subsidies are paid by consumers in the form of higher prices, but some half of the operating costs of wind farms in Great Britain is covered by government subsidies, estimated at over £1 billion in 2009, projected to rise to £5 billion in 2020 (Leach and Gray 2010). Through higher prices, German consumers are estimated to subsidize wind-generated electricity by over 14 billion euros per year (Wetzel 2012).

Subsidies impose costs on consumers but can keep production at home. High-cost energy however affects location production decisions. When economists think of the social losses from rent seeking, they usually are looking at the Tullock (1967 [2008]) rectangles created by higher regulated prices. These rectangles exist as a result of EU energy policies but, as noted, these policies carry with them the additional environmental costs in making the global problem they seek to solve worse by shifting energy-intensive production activities from Europe to countries making much greater use of coal as a source of energy.

18.6 CONCLUSIONS

The United States throughout much of its history has been viewed as a land of opportunity by both those who already reside there and those wishing to move there. Many have made their way to the United States – at first largely from Europe, more recently from Latin America and Asia – in the hopes of making great fortunes. Enough have succeeded to make the United States the richest large country in the world albeit with substantial inequality. Private enterprise in the United States has several advantages over Europe – a large market with customers who speak the same language and share the same culture,

org.uk/news/publications/list/reports/Cost_Generation_Commentary.pdf (accessed 5 December 2012).

[26] For a detailed and depressing discussion of these issues, see Helm (2012).

lower taxes, less regulation and superior universities. Thus, the private sector in the United States both creates more profits than in Europe, but, with competition in product markets and competition through innovation, not necessarily more protected rents.

The United States did not experience as great a social upheaval during the Industrial Revolution as Europe did. This upheaval in Europe fostered various socialist movements that became solidified in the socialist and labor parties that formed toward the end of the nineteenth century. This political development, combined with a greater trust in the state across Europe, resulted in the state playing a larger role in facilitating rent seeking and rent protection than in the United States, and meant that the beneficiaries in Europe were more often the organized working class rather than the business and professional class as in America. Greater regulation of product and labor markets, and larger public sectors engaged in income transfers are manifestations of the kind of rent protection and rent seeking in Europe.[27]

Behind every protected rent is the state in one form or another – as patent granter, trademark enforcer, entry barrier producer or regulator. The free-market, individualistic culture of the United States has resulted in the state being pro-business for much of its history and helps explain the greater amount of profit seeking as opposed to rent seeking in the private sector in the United States than in Europe. The persistence of socialist culture of Europe helps account for the forms of rent protection and rent seeking that the state facilitates in Europe.

REFERENCES

Angelopoulos, Konstantinos, Apostolis Philippopoulos and Vanghelis Vassilatos (2009), 'The social costs of rent seeking in Europe', *European Journal of Political Economy*, **25**(3), 280–99.

Atkinson, Anthony and Thomas Piketty (eds) (2007), *Top Incomes Over the Twentieth Century: A Contrast Between Continental European and English-Speaking Countries*, Oxford: Oxford University Press.

Bivens, Josh and Lawrence Mishel (2013), 'The pay of corporate executives and financial professionals as evidence of rents in top 1 percent incomes', *Journal of Economic Perspectives*, **27**(3), 57–77.

Buchanan, James M. (1980), 'Rent seeking and profit seeking', in James M. Buchanan, Robert D. Tollison and Gordon Tullock (eds), *Toward a Theory of the Rent-seeking Society*, College Station, TX: Texas A&M University Press, pp. 3–15, reprinted in Roger D. Congleton, Arye L. Hillman and Kai A. Konrad (eds) (2008), *40 Years of Research on Rent Seeking 1 – The Theory of Rent Seeking*, Heidelberg: Springer, pp. 55–67.

Buckwell, Allan E., David R. Harvey, Kenneth J. Thomson and Kevin A. Parton (1982), *The Costs of the Common Agricultural Policy*, London: Croom Helm.

Burleigh, Michael (2005), *Earthly Powers*, London: HarperCollins.

Congleton, Roger (2011), *Perfecting Parliament*, Cambridge: Cambridge University Press.

Conyon, Martin J. (2012), 'Executive compensation: governance and the financial crisis', in Dennis C. Mueller (ed.), *The Oxford Handbook of Capitalism*, Oxford: Oxford University Press, pp. 371–404.

Conyon, Martin J., Nuno Fernandes, Miguel A. Ferrerira, Pedro Matos and Kevin J. Murphy (2011), 'The executive compensation controversy: a transatlantic analysis', 13 February, available at http://digitalcommons.ilr.cornell.edu/cgi/viewcontent.cgi?article=1004&context=ics (accessed November 2012).

Fogarty, Michael D. (1957), *Citizen Democracy in Western Europe, 1820–1953*, Notre Dame, IN: University of Notre Dame Press.

Frank, Robert H. and Philip J. Cook (1995), *The Winner Take-all Society*, New York: Free Press.

Helm, Dieter (2012), *The Carbon Crunch*, New Haven, CT: Yale University Press.

Hillman, Arye L. (2013), 'Rent seeking', in Michael Reksulak, Laura Razzolini and William F. Shughart II

[27] Angelopoulos et al. (2009) have computed estimates of the social cost of rent seeking in Europe.

(eds), *The Elgar Companion to Public Choice*, 2nd edn, Cheltenham, UK and Northampton, MA, USA: Edward Elgar Publishing, pp. 307–30.
Katsimi, Margarita and Thomas Moutos (2010), 'EMU and the Greek crisis: the political-economy perspective', *European Journal of Political Economy*, **26**(4), 568–76.
Krueger, Anne O. (1974), 'The political economy of the rent-seeking society', *American Economic Review*, **64**(3), 291–303, reprinted in Roger D. Congleton, Arye L. Hillman and Kai A. Konrad (eds) (2008), *40 Years of Research on Rent Seeking 2 – Applications: Rent Seeking in Practice*, Heidelberg: Springer, pp. 151–63.
Lat, David (2012), 'Who are America's best-paid general counsel?', available at http://abovethelaw.com/2012/07/who-are-americas-best-paid-general-counsel-2012-rankings/ (accessed 28 November 2012).
Leach, Ben and Richard Gray, 'Wind farm subsidies top £1 billion a year', *Daily Telegraph*, 23 January 2010.
Mueller, Dennis C. (2003), *Public Choice* III, Cambridge: Cambridge University Press.
Mueller, Dennis C. (2009), *Reason, Religion, and Democracy*, Cambridge: Cambridge University Press.
Mueller, Dennis C. (2014), 'Religious parties', in Francesco Forte, Ram Mudambi and Pietro Navarra (eds), *A Handbook of Alternative Theories of Public Economics*, Cheltenham, UK and Northampton, MA, USA: Edward Elgar Publishing, pp. 177–97.
National Audit Office (2009), *United Kingdom, Financial Management in the European Union*, London, 24 March.
Nedergaard, Peter (2006), 'Market failures and government failures: a theoretical model of the Common Agricultural Policy', *Public Choice*, **127**(3–4), 393–413.
Neugart, Michael (2009), 'Pensions with early retirement and without commitment', *Applied Economics Letters*, **16**(3), 257–60.
New York Times (2012), 'The pay at the top', *New York Times*, 14 May, available at http://projects.nytimes.com/executive_compensation (accessed 27 November 2012).
Nitzan, Shmuel (1994), 'Modeling rent-seeking contests', *European Journal of Political Economy*, **10**(1), 41–60.
Philippon, Thomas and Nicolas Véron (2008), 'Financing Europe's fast movers', Bruegel Policy Brief, available at http://aei.pitt.edu/8321/1/PB200801.pdf (accessed 6 December 2012).
Posner, Richard A. (1975), 'The social costs of monopoly and regulation', *Journal of Political Economy*, **89**(4), 807–27, reprinted in Roger D. Congleton, Arye L. Hillman and Kai A. Konrad (eds) (2008), *40 Years of Research on Rent Seeking 2 – Applications: Rent Seeking in Practice*, Heidelberg: Springer, pp. 45–65.
Rampell, Catherine (2009), 'How much do doctors in other countries make?', *New York Times*, 15 July, available at http://economix.blogs.nytimes.com/2009/07/15/how-much-do-doctors-in-other-countries-make/ (accessed 28 November 2012).
Ramseyer, J. Mark and Eric B. Rasmusen (2010), 'Comparative litigation rates', Harvard Discussion Paper No. 681, 11/2010, Cambridge, Massachusetts, ISSN 1936–5357 (online).
Roe, Mark J. (2012), 'Capital markets and financial politics: preferences and institutions', in Dennis C. Mueller (ed.), *The Oxford Handbook of Capitalism*, Oxford: Oxford University Press, pp. 78–111.
Rotherman, Lee (2012), 'Food for thought', *The Taxpayers Alliance*, available at http://www.taxpayersalliance.com/cap.pdf (accessed 29 November 2012).
Saint-Paul, Giles (1997), 'Is labour rigidity harming Europe's competitiveness? The effect of job protection on the pattern of trade and welfare', *European Economic Review*, **41**(3–5), 499–506.
Schumpeter, Joseph A. (1911, in German), *The Theory of Economic Development*, reprinted in 1934, Cambridge, MA: Harvard University Press.
Schwab, Klaus (ed.) (2012), *The Global Competitiveness Report 2012–13*, World Economic Forum, available at http://www3.weforum.org/docs/WEF_GlobalCompetitivenessReport_2012–13.pdf (accessed 8 December 2012).
The Economist (2011), 'The few', *The Economist*, 22 January, 1–20.
Tollison, Robert D. (1997), 'Rent seeking', in Dennis C. Mueller (ed.), *Perspectives on Public Choice*, Cambridge: Cambridge University Press, pp. 506–25.
Tullock, Gordon (1967), 'The welfare costs of tariffs, monopolies and theft', *Western Economic Journal*, **5**(3), 224–32, reprinted in Roger D. Congleton, Arye L. Hillman and Kai A. Konrad (eds) (2008), *40 Years of Research on Rent Seeking 1 – The Theory of Rent Seeking*, Heidelberg: Springer, pp. 45–53.
Tullock, Gordon (1989), *The Economics of Special Privilege and Rent Seeking*, Dordrecht: Kluwer Academic Publishers.
Wetzel, Daniel (2012), 'Ökostrom-Milliarden sind selbst Erzeugern zu viel', *Die Welt*, 6 December, available at http://www.welt.de/dieweltbewegen/article106483214/Oekostrom-Milliarden-sind-selbst-Erzeugern-zu-viel.html (accessed 6 December 2012).
World Intellectual Property Organization (2007), *WIPO Patent Report*, available at http://www.wipo.int/freepublications/en/patents/931/wipo_pub_931.pdf (accessed 7 December 2012).
Zwart, Rutger S. (1997), 'Christian democracy and political order in the Netherlands', in Emiel Lamberts (ed.), *Christian Democracy in the European Union (1945/1995)*, Leuven: Leuven University Press, pp. 242–53.

19. Rents in a welfare state

Martin Paldam

SUMMARY

This chapter describes rents in Denmark, a developed welfare state in which the private sector is sharply delimitated and kept efficient by secure property rights and markets including free trade. In the public sector, rents in the form of excess costs of provision are difficult to measure, but in a number of cases as described in this chapter, the rents are revealed. The implicit welfare coalition, defined as voters receiving their income from the public budget, is the majority, placing the median voter within the welfare coalition. Rents are created and protected by the welfare coalition. Non-governmental organizations have been coopted to serve large welfare expenditure programs that benefit the welfare coalition.

19.1 INTRODUCTION

The concept of the welfare coalition was proposed in Christoffersen and Paldam (2003) and Christoffersen et al. (2014, pp. 261–3). The 'welfare coalition' is defined as the group of those who receive their income from the public sector, either as a salary or as a social subsidy. This cross-partisan group is not a formal coalition but has common interests through their source of income. In Denmark the median voter is within the welfare coalition, as it probably is in other Northwest European welfare states. In Denmark, the welfare coalition is estimated to be some 55 percent of voters.

19.1.1 The Language Confusion of the Welfare State and its Huge Success

In the language of economics, welfare is a function of the consumption and leisure of the individual, and social welfare is an aggregate of welfare of the people in a society. Economic theory has studied pure public goods such as national defense; broader classes of impure or congestible public goods; and positive and negative externalities with public-good properties such as environmental quality. Also, it has considered social welfare behind a veil of ignorance allowing for the welfare and efficiency consequences of redistribution (see Hillman 2009 for an overview).

The language of the welfare states uses the same words but gives the words different meaning. 'Welfare' is taken to mean public spending. 'Public goods' are the goods supplied by the public sector whether the goods have public-good properties or not. All 'redistribution' is welfare enhancing. The terminology defines politicians as benevolent and policies as implemented by unselfish and loyal civil servants. The theory of rent seeking proposes that this is not the whole story.

The welfare state has been a great success in Denmark: it has obtained the support of the great majority of the population and of the political parties. That includes an acceptance of the high taxes that are required.

No war of attrition is fought around the welfare budget as in the USA and elsewhere. The public debt ratio to gross domestic product (GDP) is below half of that in the USA and the Euro area, so the Danish debt is only about 50 percent of GDP. An important tradition is that in the end all 'responsible' parties vote for the budget,[1] and parties do not want to be classified as 'irresponsible.' During the lengthy budget negotiations, the main macro-model of Statistics Denmark is used by the Ministry of Finance (and the parties) for consistency checks. Normally the negotiating parties start by agreeing on the budget balance, and even though there is often some drift away from the balance, it is rarely large.

It also appears that the standard measures of trust, honesty, and happiness are unusually high in the welfare states – and notably so in Denmark. See Bjørnskov and Paldam (2005), Svendsen and Bjørnskov (2007) and Christoffersen et al. (2014).

The Nordic welfare states are quite efficient and have been consistently in the top decile of the countries in the world as regards wealth (see Subsections 19.5.1 and 19.5.2). Nonetheless it is straightforward to point to cases of rent seeking and rent extraction in the Nordic welfare state.

19.1.2 Immigration as Rent Seeking

This chapter focuses on rents in the public sector in a welfare state. The Danish-type welfare state is 'universal' and the payments given are on a need basis with a small insurance element only. For immigrants, the Danish language is a considerable barrier to productive employment for those who do not learn the local language. Though English is widespread in Denmark, full labor market integration requires a considerable investment in the Danish language. Immigrants with a high labor market value will try to go to a country where the language barrier is smaller. A universal welfare state attracts the needy and less productive – obviously many potential immigrants would like to come and enjoy the rents of the welfare state. There is therefore adverse selection of immigrants.

The adverse selection has made the rules of entry into Denmark increasingly stringent and hence bureaucratic for immigrants from low-income countries. To prevent discrimination, the rules have been extended to all non-EU citizens. A particularly complex and sensitive field to legalize and administrate is family reunification. Cases have been reported where one young (typically male) immigrant gives rise to a large subsequent immigration using the rules of 'family reunification.'[2] That is, first he brings in his family,

[1] The Danish party system is complex, but it is dominated by the red and the blue block, which are the center left and the center right parties, which are the government and the alternative government. It is difficult for a party to convince the voters that it is government-mature if it does not participate in the budget negotiations and in the end vote for the budget, though some parties sometimes refrain from voting.

[2] Immigrants often come to Denmark after a long clandestine journey. Such journeys are expensive and are typically financed by the (extended) family of the immigrants. If an immigrant succeeds in being accepted, he obviously owes his family.

and then he marries a girl in his country of origin and brings her in, and then her family needs to be reunified and so on.

This has led to rather strict rules about family reunification (including DNA testing in some cases). Also, it has been ruled that spouses should be 24 years of age to be eligible for family reunification, and that the couples should have a sufficiently strong connection to Denmark for a spouse to be brought in. Though these rules have been approved by large majorities in the Parliament, it is another matter when stories about concrete cases are reported in the press.

With the enlargement of the EU in 2004, the problem of immigration into the welfare state has increased. With new EU members in low-income East and Southeastern Europe and the EU rules about free mobility, questions of policies regarding 'welfare tourism' arise. Immigration can pose significant problems for the universal welfare state. The problems of immigration subject to adverse selection have been studied and form central issues with regard to rents and rent seeking. A literature has addressed these issues. A good introduction is provided by the papers of the symposium in Paldam (2007), notably Nannestad (2007), and chapters 8 and 9 in Christoffersen et al. (2014). See also Nannestad (2004 [2008]). There has been less written about the domestic dimension of rents in the public sector in the welfare state.

19.1.3 Rents and Efficiency

Rents are privileged unearned benefits. Rents include monopoly profits, but in the public sector rents are excess expenditures above required costs including redundant costs of bureaucracies. In the national accounts, public production is mainly calculated from the cost side, resulting in rents being included in GDP. Thus, in the short run, more rents mean that GDP increases. GDP will have decreased if the rents were contested using time and resources that could have been productively used (Tullock 1967 [2008]). It is difficult to identify the rents in the public sector, but from time to time events occur that reveal the level of rents or show how new rents are created.

A case of revealed rents occurred when the EU liberalized air traffic. This forced Scandinavian Airline System (SAS) (and many other 'pampered' airlines) to cut about half of the budget to survive. Consequently, SAS had managed to consume rents in the order of 50 percent of the budget in the 2–3 decades prior to the liberalization. This example is discussed in Subsection 19.5.3.

A case of new rent generated happened when a law enacted ten years ago turned power at the public universities from a bottom-up to top-down system. This caused the size and relative salaries of the bureaucracy at the top to start growing rapidly. At the university at which the author works, bureaucracy has increased its share of the budget by about 8 percent of the budget since the reform. At the same time, efficiency has fallen (see Paldam 2014).

The chapter proceeds as follows: Section 19.2 reports the numbers for the size of the welfare coalition. Section 19.3 discusses the theory of this coalition. Section 19.4 describes the capture of a protective non-governmental organization (NGO) rim of the coalition. Section 19.5 describes rents, first from a macro perspective, and then through examples. Section 19.6 concludes.

The text uses 'mill' for million (10^6) and 'bill' for billion (10^9). 'Kr' is Danish Crowns that is fixed to the euro at 7.45 Kr for one euro. Names of Danish institutions are translated, and where the Danish name is deemed necessary, it is given in square brackets.

19.2 SOME NUMBERS FOR THE WELFARE COALITION IN DENMARK

The welfare coalition has two parts: (W1) the public employees, (W2) the welfare recipients who receive most of their income from the public sector.[3] Subsection 19.2.1 is an assessment of the share of the welfare coalition of the voters. Subsection 19.2.2 makes an additional point, as it turns out that the group (W1) is overrepresented in the (Danish) Parliament [Folketinget].

19.2.1 The Voters

The size of the welfare coalition among the voters can be inferred from Tables 19.1 and 19.2, both based on the official data from Statistics Denmark. Table 19.1 is the population reached from the Central Personal Registry, which is known for its precision. Table 19.2 is calculated from business polls, which are less precise.

The last row (4) in Table 19.2 divides the numbers in row (3) by the whole of the population from row (4) in Table 19.1. It appears that only 47.0 percent of the population works. Recently it was in the news (see DR, 13 January 2013) that only three of the 98 municipalities have a majority of working people. The population of eligible voters is 4.09 mill persons. The labor force is 2.84/4.09 = 0.695 of the (eligible) voters.

The share of W1, the public labor force as share of the labor force, is about 29 percent, so W1 $\approx$ 0.695·29 percent = 20 percent of the voters.

It is more difficult to calculate W2, the share of the voters receiving their main income as 'welfare.' The Danish welfare state is a 'universal' one where people receive subsidies directly from the state and not indirectly from compulsory insurance arrangements.

Table 19.1 The population of Denmark, 3rd quarter of 2012

	Age group	Whole population		Eligible to vote (age 18)[a]	
		Number	Share (%)	Number	Share (%)
(1)	0–14	981 023	17.6	–	–
(2)	15–24	708 620	12.7	447 241	10.9
(3)	25–64	2 911 143	52.1	2 675 505	65.4
(4)	65 up	986 299	17.7	965 744	23.6
(5)	All	5 587 085	100.0	4 088 490	100.0

Notes:
At the 2011election 87.7 percent voted, though 0.8 percent of the votes were declared invalid.
a. People below the age of 18 and non-citizens are excluded.

3 In a developed welfare state virtually everybody receives something from the state, but for many it is a rather small part of their income.

Table 19.2 The Danish labor force, 3rd quarter of 2012

	Age group	Labor force			Outside the total	Sum
		Working	Unemployed	Labor force		
(1)	15–24	392 000	63 000	455 000	244 000	699 000
(2)	25–64	2 236 000	152 000	2 388 000	521 000	2 911 000
(3)	All	2 628 000	214 000	2 842 000	765 000	3 607 000
(4)	Share (%)[a]	47.0	3.8	50.9	13.7	64.6

Notes:
The missing 100 − (50.9 + 13.7) = 35.4 percent of the population is younger or older.

a. Share of population (5 587 085) from Table 19.1. The unemployment rate is thus 3.8/0.509 = 7.5 percent of the labor force, or 3.8/0.69.5 = 5.4 percent of the voters.

Hence, the state pays benefits to the 5.4 percent unemployed and the 23.6 percent pensioners, all of whom receive a public base pension [folkepension]. Also, the great majority of the 13.7 percent in the 'working ages' outside the labor force receive some welfare payment – this, for example, applies to the students. This all adds up to W2 ≈ 42.5 percent of the voters.

This number is too high for several reasons. Some between the age of 65 and 70 still work; there are still a few in the 'working age' (that is, 'housewives') who do not receive a public subsidy; and many pensioners have a private pension that is larger than their public pension. However, the 7.5 percent unemployed hides about three times as many, who are unemployed for a period during the year.

My assessment is that when all adjustments are made, the number for W2 is still about 35 percent, so that W1 + W2 = 55 percent is a fair assessment of the share of the welfare coalition in the population. Thus, it is clear that the median voter is within the welfare coalition. Note that the group of public employees, W1, is only 20 percent of the voters, while the group of welfare clients, W2, is about 35 percent, so W2 is substantially larger.

19.2.2 The Welfare Coalition in the Parliament

It is not easy to divide the Members of the Parliament (MPs) into the same groups as used in Subsection 19.2.1, as many of the MPs are full-time politicians, with a loose association to the labor market. However, the Parliament issues a small report after each election (Folketinget 2012) with some statistics about the MPs, and each MP has a home page.

The statistics given set the number of (previous) public employees (W1) in the Parliament at 30.9 percent. The public sector allows employees who step out of a job to be a MP to come back to this job, so it is less risky to be a MP for a public employee than for a person working in the private sector. The number of previous welfare recipients (W2) is set at 8.0 percent only. On the face of it, the welfare coalition does not control the Parliament. However, the home pages of the members tell a story giving three major qualifications:

Q1. About 26 percent of the MPs have been members for more than a decade.
Q2. About 14 percent have never held a full-time job outside politics.

The two groups overlap somewhat, but they still amount to about 35 percent of the MPs. How they should be counted is unclear. MPs receive a salary from public funds, so it is arguable that after some time full-time politicians become public employees irrespective of what they did before. Nevertheless, many Danish politicians stress their prior job, much as Abraham Lincoln, who ran his first campaign as the rail splitter he once was (though it seems only briefly), and not as the lawyer he had become.

Q3. Many of the members of the Parliament (previously) working in the private sector actually worked in NGOs that belong to the gray zone between the public and the private sector (see Section 19.4). Often they even worked in the secretariats of the political parties.[4]

The three qualifications allow a range of alternative counts of the past jobs of the MPs. I have made a number of such counts, and it is easy to reach the result that public employees (W1) alone have a majority in the Parliament. Consequently, I view the data as showing that the welfare coalition is rather strong in the Parliament.

From all counts, it is clear that the welfare coalition in the Parliament is dominated by (W1), while (W2) welfare recipients are strongly underrepresented. One reason is that nobody above the age of 70 was elected in 2011. Also, even if a future MP were to enter politics as unemployed, there are many jobs in political NGOs that need to be filled. These jobs are largely financed from public funds. So by the time the MP is elected, he has nearly always worked for a period.

19.3 THE CORE MODEL OF POLITICAL EQUILIBRIUM

This section starts with a model in which the welfare coalition generates a political equilibrium for the size of the public sector. Then it is argued that the equilibrium is not a stable economic equilibrium, that is, it is not a steady state. And finally some empirics are introduced.

19.3.1 A Core Model for a Political Equilibrium

The model builds on two assumptions: (A1) The welfare coalition agrees on its own self-preservation. (A2) The size of the welfare state is the only dimension in politics.

With these assumptions the 'median voter model' applies. It says that a welfare coalition above 50 percent will ensure that it stays above 50 percent. However, the minimum winning coalition means that once the coalition has reached 50 percent of the voters – as it actually has – it will remain only marginally above this level. The two models are well known (see, for example, Mueller 2003, chapters 11 to 13; Hillman 2009, chapter 6), and will not be reviewed here. This will be termed the 'political equilibrium result.' If the size

[4] Danish political parties receive a subsidy aiming at 'freeing' the parties from sponsor interests. The parties still get sponsor money, but hopefully they are not so willing to make murky deals to get it.

of the welfare state is an independent dimension in politics, and there is no logrolling, it still holds.[5]

19.3.2 The Political Equilibrium is Fuzzy: The Coalition Needs a Safety Margin

In practice, each of the conditions giving the theoretical result only holds to some extent. That is, they are true $\pm \varepsilon_i$, where ε_i is a measure of the fuzziness of condition *i*. So the political equilibrium may only apply with some uncertainty, which is an aggregate, $A_i(\varepsilon_i)$ of the fuzziness of each condition.

The fuzziness comes from: (1) The coalition is not explicit, but only a result of common interests. Surely, the permanent secretary and the unemployed shop assistant may not feel a strong solidarity. (2) The size of the welfare state is not the only issue in politics, and nearly all political issues have budgetary consequences. So the size dimension is somewhat dependent on all other dimensions. (3) The size is important for the development of the private sector in many ways. (4) Logrolling is the soul of politics, but if the welfare coalition is strong, it may set the agenda. All of these fuzziness elements aggregate to a general uncertainty $A(\varepsilon)$ in the relation. It is an equilibrium that does not always hold.

The coalition will hold more often if the welfare coalition is made larger, but there are costs to the members of increasing the coalition above its minimum. This gives a typical trade-off. With enough assumptions the model can be solved to yield an optimal size of a 'working' welfare coalition: It is $50 + S$ percent, where S is a safety margin. Above, the size of the welfare coalition in Denmark was assessed to be about 55 percent – so perhaps the safety margin is $S \approx 5$ percent?

19.3.3 The Political Equilibrium is No Economic Equilibrium

Two reasons why the political equilibrium is not an economic equilibrium shall be discussed.

The first follows from the observation that long-run productivity increases in the public sector are smaller than in the private sector. Why this is the case is a long story, but it is confirmed in the Danish national accounts since the late 1930s (see Paldam and Zeuthen 1988; chapter 10 in Christoffersen et al. 2014). It is partly an artifact because it is difficult to calculate productivity in much of the public sector. Hence, production is calculated from the cost side. However, the low productivity increases are confirmed from a number of attempts to measure output. Thus, in the last 85 years, the annual productivity increases have been about 2 percent lower in the public than in the private sector in Denmark.

Given that difference in productivity, Baumol's law applies: the economy has no steady state (see Baumol 1967, 2004). Some ratio must change steadily.[6] If the welfare coalition wants to preserve itself, the share of public employment should remain the

---

5 This is the well-known Arrow condition of independence of irrelevant alternatives.

6 See chapter 10 in Christoffersen et al. (2013), which builds on the detailed calculations in Paldam (2009). The outcomes described in the next few paragraphs are derived in these papers.

same. Given wage parity between the sectors, this will keep the tax pressure constant, but as productivity keeps rising in the private sector, the real share of the welfare state will fall steadily. This is unlikely to be possible.

The overwhelming majority of the Danish political parties agree that the welfare state should be preserved. This should probably be taken to mean that the real share of the public sector should be preserved. It implies that tax pressure will rise steadily. This is even less possible.

The second reason why the political equilibrium is no economic equilibrium follows from the logic of bureaucracy. Both the main theory of bureaucracy from Niskanen (1968, 1994) and various empirical studies show that bureaucracies want to grow (see Mueller 2003, chapters 16 and 21; Hillman 2009, chapter 2). The only non-partial equilibrium in the Niskanen-type model of bureaucracy occurs when the size of the bureaucracy is so large as to appropriate the full consumer's surplus generated by public expenditure. However, a partial equilibrium arises when the political process manages to impose a budget constraint. The argument above suggests that the constraint is relaxed when the welfare coalition is stronger, which of course means that rents increase with the size of the coalition.

Several attempts have been made to stop the expansion before that extreme limit, but with a sufficiently strong welfare coalition such attempts become difficult. It is easy to give examples of reforms sold under the name of rationalizations that have somehow resulted in larger administrative costs.

An example is the large municipal reform in 2004–07 when 271 municipalities were merged into 98. The reform was announced as a rationalization allowing benefit from economies of scale. However, strong political pressures occurred during the process of implementation that caused many of the municipalities to promise voters that nobody was to experience a lower standard of welfare provision, because all merged municipalities were to go to the highest standard of any of the ones merged. Also bureaucrats were informed that there would be no job losses. At the end of the process it was proudly announced that the new municipalities had managed to find jobs for every bureaucrat. So the original purpose of cost savings through scale economies was turned into a triumph for the welfare coalition. The devil is certainly in the details in administrative reforms.

19.3.4 The Zigzag Path of W1

Figure 19.1 shows the path of the share of the Danish public employment as a percentage of total employment. In 1950 the share was at 7.5 percent and then from 1960 to 1980 it grew dramatically at about 1 percentage point a year. The first observation in Figure 19.1 shows the end of the big expansion. Since then the path has been more 'rocky.'

Figure 19.1 shows four rounds of public savings, when governments have tried to reverse the expansion, but as is shown, there has been an underlying upward slide in the share. Thus, saving rounds have been successful in the short run, but in the longer run the welfare coalition has prevailed. The large increase at the end is mainly due to the fall in the denominator during the crisis.

The upward drift is estimated by the two thin lines, where the flattest disregards the first year and the last three years. The steepest line includes all years. It appears that the

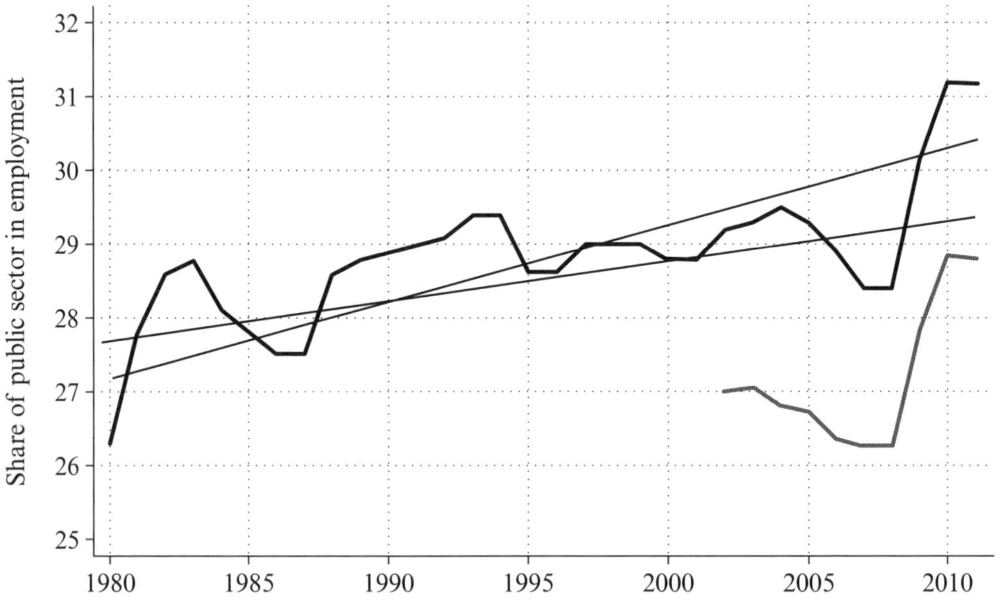

Note: The main series from Statistics Denmark goes back to 1948. The gray line is an adjustment for part-time employment in the public sector. However, the adjustment is not made for the private sector and in the denominator.

Figure 19.1 The share of public employment in Denmark, 1980 to 2011

increase is in the range of 1.5 percent to 3 percent over 30 years. It is a slow drift of 0.05 to 0.1 percent per year.

19.3.5 The Dynamic Path: Some Suggestions

I have not discussed how the internal balance between the two parts of the welfare coalition is formed. However, it has been noted that the welfare recipients, W2, form the largest part of the coalition among the voters, while the public employees, W1, are much stronger in the Parliament. The ones who actually implement the policies are in W1. Consequently, W1 is the most influential in practical decision-making.

It is also interesting that when it comes to the budget, the share of public consumption is larger than the share of transfers – though the difference is not large.

The analysis in Subsection 19.3.4 showed that W1 is sliding upwards, so that if the coalition has to stay at the 'working' minimum (around 55 percent), the share of transfer payments is likely to fall correspondingly to the upward slide in public employment. This is not going to be easy due to demographic developments.

Given the Baumol mechanism, the increase in the share of public employment will slowly increase the tax burden, but the increase will not be enough to prevent a fall in the real share of the public sector in GDP. Thus, the voters will experience: (1) falling transfer payments; (2) a falling share of the real public consumption; and (3) an increasing tax burden. All of these trends will be slow, but they will not be easy for the population to accept, and they will place strains on the welfare coalition.

19.4 INCLUDING THE NGOs BY AN ALLOCATION OF RENT

In comparative studies of social capital, the Northwest European countries – notably the Scandinavian countries – stand out as having unusually high social capital (see Svendsen and Bjørnskov 2007). One of the key dimensions is that the number of voluntary organizations, NGOs, is relatively large. NGOs are supposed to run on voluntary work and members' contributions.

The welfare state extracts a little more than 50 percent of the incomes of people in taxes. This gives a large tax wedge between the primary income of a NGO member and an NGO employee of about $1/0.5^2 = 4$ for the lowest and $1/0.35^2 = 8.3$ for the highest marginal taxpayers. If the value added tax (VAT) of 0.25 is included, it becomes even higher.

This makes it difficult for many NGOs to obtain voluntary contributions that allow them to employ staff.[7] Though many NGOs still run on voluntary work, a system of state subsidies has gradually crept in. This has turned many NGOs into semi-public organizations.

The largest NGO activity is sport, as about 1.8 mill Danes are members of a large number of sports clubs, and here much voluntary work is done. The clubs have an 'umbrella' organization, DIF [Danmarks Idræts Forbund], which spent 997 mill Kr in 2010.[8] Of this, 43 percent were public subsidies, 20 percent were paid by the members and the remaining 37 percent were from sponsorship and gate-fees at sports events. Some of the public subsidy is generated by the public betting organization [Danske Spil]. An interesting symbiotic relation has developed between this organization and organized sports, notably soccer (see Paldam 2008).

The case of sport is probably largely demand driven. People want sport and the large number of voters involved as participants and spectators has gradually led to increased public spending in the field. However, the subsidies are more supply driven in other fields.

19.4.1 The Big Spending Programs: Paying the Piper to Call the Tune

State subsidies to NGOs are especially important in fields in which large public programs exist. Imagine the public budget for an x-purpose, which spends say 1–2 percent of GDP. Imagine further that a large NGO exists in the field.

---

7 The tax wedge makes it difficult to assess the opportunity costs of voluntary work. Also it is a problem to obtain voluntary workers in the NGOs if public employees in the same field receive a salary.

8 The total public spending on sports and leisure activities was about 4 bill in 2010. The funds finance sports facilities, compensation to top sport, a sports hospital and so on. However, it should be mentioned that a recent estimate by DIF is that if all voluntary workers were paid, the going wage it would amount to would be 17 bill Kr.

The NGO has policies that, on the one hand, support public spending in the area and, on the other hand, differ somewhat from those of the 'budget', but the budget will have an 'information' sub-budget, which will have funds to support the NGO, especially if it stresses the one hand and not the other. Also, if the NGO has worked in the field for a long time, it will have some expertise. This will typically give rise to an exchange of personnel, perhaps in the form of the NGO staff working as consultants for the budget, and the budget may outsource some projects to the NGO.

During the process, a great deal of nice words about cooperation and the grassroots support for the public program will be used. When the inflow of public funds starts, the NGO will expand its activity and staff. In order to increase membership, it may also decrease its membership fee, and the modest information sheet of the NGO will become a flashy journal. This, of course, calls for a larger public subsidy. Also, the public program may include special programs to cater to the NGO. In the process, the NGO quickly learns that it has to adjust if it will expand access to public funds. And when public funds pay for most of the activity, a real dependency is created.

The following are two brief case studies of expenditure programs in fields in which NGOs are important.

19.4.2 The Ministry of the Environment and its NGOs

The Danish Ministry of the Environment was established in 1971, and in 2007 a separate Ministry for Energy and Climate was created. The environment issue concerns a number of NGOs. The four main ones are listed in Table 19.3. Column (5) shows that only some of the activity reported in column (4) is financed by the members (3). The two NGOs above the dotted line are from before the Ministry was started. They would exist without public support.

The oldest of the four NGOs is the birdwatchers union, DOF [Dansk Ornitologisk Forening]. Here the share of membership fees in the expenditures has dropped from 100 percent 50 years ago to only 19 percent today.[9] In addition to public funds, several private foundations now support 'nature', but the main part of the finances of DOF is the public subsidy. 50 years ago DOF had only voluntary workers, but now it has about 40 employees and a handful of voluntary workers, mainly on public pension.

The society for Nature Conservation, DN [Danmarks Naturfredningsforening], states that it does not receive public funds, and it appears largely true though it does receive a few mill Kr from funds within the public domain. The expenditure for staff is about 40 mill Kr, and the staff is approximately 70 full-time and about 35 part-time employees.

The two NGOs below the dotted line are very different. Greenpeace is known for its publicity stunts at the borderline of legality, which attracts neither public nor business donors. However, Greenpeace does spend about 8 mill Kr on staff, and it employs 24 people.

The WWF is known as the 'official' NGO, and it certainly does no stunts. It tries, where possible, to have a royal protector (in Denmark, the Prince Consort). It has a staff of 33 and six interns/students. It collects 19 mill Kr in fees – mostly from corporate

[9] The author was a member 50 years ago, and he still is.

Table 19.3 The main environmental NGOs

NGO Data for (2) to (4) from annual accounts	(1) Founded	(2) Number of members	(3) Financed by members	(4) Total spent	(5) Share (%): (3)/(4)
DOF, Birdwatchers	1906	15931	5418	29019	19
DN, Preservation of Nature	1911	133118	59605	90752	65
WWF, Denmark, World Wildlife Foundation	1972	Not clear[a]	19084	52454	36
Greenpeace, Denmark (14.6% of Nordic)	1980	22600[b]	Collections	19600	85

Notes:
WWF has summer/summer year. 2011 is thus 2011/12. The foundation year is for the Danish NGO. Columns (3) and (4) are in 1000 Kr.
a. WWF mainly caters for tax deductable business sponsorships. Individual members pay 360 Kr per year.
b. Greenpeace has activists, who collect campaign contributions, but not regular members.

members.[10] Also, the WWF receives about 36 percent of its funding from the state, mainly for its projects.

These NGOs employ almost 200 people in jobs that are registered as private jobs, though they might also be considered an extension of the public spending program.

19.4.3 Danida (Ministry of Development Aid) and its NGOs

Danida is a part of the Ministry of Foreign Affairs, but it has its own Minister. Its budget for 2012 was 18 bill Kr or close to 1 percent of GDP. Many polls show that Danes support aid to poor countries, but it is given a low priority compared to other spending programs when trade-off items are included in the polls. Also, the aid budget is not a subject of high priority in the Parliament.[11]

Danida finances NGO-run projects in the least developed countries (LDCs), and it also has an information budget to inform the Danish population about the poor countries. Most of this budget finances activities implemented by a net of almost 250 NGOs in the field. Most of these NGOs are small, and the total membership is probably not

---

[10] Firms are offered membership packages from between 4300 Kr to 31000 Kr. The home page of the WWF recommends these packages with the words (my translation): 'Dependent on the sponsorship level, the firm receives a set of advantages. You will network with other firms in the WWF, by participation in Elite Alliance arrangements, and at the annual reception at Fredensborg Castle with HRH the Prince Consort. The membership fee is tax deductible and a good supplement to the CSR policy of the firm.'

[11] The political economy of the Danish 'market' for development aid is discussed in part II of Paldam (1997). A great deal of statistics is reported. Though many big aid reforms have been proclaimed, it is my impression that little has changed since my book was published.

Table 19.4 The four largest development NGOs

NGO, data for (2) to (4) from annual accounts	(1) Founded	(2) Number of members	(3) Financed by members	(4) Total spent mill Kr	(5) Share (%): (3)/(4)
Red Cross, Kr[a]	1876	Unclear	Collections	678.7	23
Church Aid, Kr[b]	1953	Unclear	Collections	528.7	31
ActionAid, Kr (MS)[c]	1949	Ca 8000	6.2	285.3	2.2
IBIS (formerly WUS)[d]	1970	Ca 2000	10.9	208.5	5.2

Notes:
See Table 19.3. Columns (3) and (4) are in mill Kr.
a. Red Cross also working in Denmark, and its non-aid expenditures are perhaps 10 percent not aid.
b. Danish Church Aid started before 1953, but from 1953 it changed to aid to poor countries.
c. ActionAid, MS [Mellemfolkelig Samvirke] gets 1.45 mill from members and collects 4.75 mill.
d. WUS is World University Service. Latest audited accounts are from 2009, so the information used is from a few aggregate numbers. From the older accounts it appears likely that the share of membership fees in column (5) is smaller than 0.5 mill, so the number 10.9 mill given (by IBIS) appears misleading.

above 20000, but about 35000 people help at the 4–5 days a year the organization runs campaigns to collect contributions.

Table 19.4 lists the four main development NGOs, with a combined staff of about 250 employees. They are considerably larger than the rest.[12] The first two are old and have an organization that would survive even without the support from the public budget. The last two have both developed from organizations with another purpose. An unkind interpretation is that they have followed the 'gravy train' to survive. Anyhow, it is obvious that they would collapse without public support.

The examples show that the big spending programs often attract the NGOs. This means that critique of policies from the NGOs becomes rather restrained. It also shows that a considerable element in the opting-in strategy of the public budgets is supply driven.[13] Thus, it can be seen as a policy of building a pressure group by the distribution of rents.

19.4.4 Public Budget Coalitions

The above argument suggests that public spending programs are protected in two ways. One way is through the underlying power structure once the welfare coalition is well above 50 percent of the voters. It does not prevent all rationalizations and trimming programs, but it helps in preventing such policies from being too bad, and it allows trimmed 'branches' to grow back. The second way is through the opting-in of the NGOs around the programs. Instead of having NGOs as organizations that could criticize public

[12] Some large organizations such as the Trade Unions Movement and the Danish Women's Organization have modest offices dealing with international affairs such as development.

[13] When I have publicly criticized policies, I have several times experienced NGO representatives arguing that the critique had a bad timing relative to budget negotiations.

spending programs and take the view of the public interest, they become dependent clients of the programs, almost like extensions of the public relations (PR) departments of the spending programs.

The public budgets have PR departments much like the ones of private companies, and often they also have sector research institutes with 'loyal' researchers.[14] Also, they keep track of 'friendly' journalists, with whom they often develop special relationships. If the Parliament approves a law that moves some expenditure within a budget, so that some subsidy recipients lose and others win, the budget staff can, within a day, organize a number of spots on TV and radio newscasts with deeply wounded losers interviewed by outraged journalists.

Thus, public spending bureaucracies do a great deal to control their political environment.

19.5 RENT ABSORPTION IN THE STATE-OWNED ENTERPRISES

From the above, it would appear likely that the Danish economy may include a lot of well-protected rents. The state-owned enterprise (SOE) sector provides rather neat examples of large rents. But, before these examples are considered, Subsections 19.5.1 and 19.5.2 will make the argument that though the Danish economy is not as efficient as it could be, many other economies are worse.

19.5.1 Comparing Efficiency Over 60 Years

A large literature compares the GDP of different countries and makes lists of the countries that are ahead on one scale or another. Figure 19.2 is a basic version. It compares purchasing power parity (PPP)-GDP per capita with that of the USA and the average of the original six EU (EU6) countries. The figure shows that for the last 40 years rather stable long-run gaps have existed among the three groups.

The two main reasons for the efficiency gap are (a) lower technology and (b) inefficiency generated by protection and bad regulation.

From 1950 to 1970, Figure 19.2 shows the big catch-up after the Second World War. Since then, Denmark has been at 80–85 percent of the US GDP level, while the EU6 have been about 10 percentage points lower. The European countries have lost about 5 percentage points to the USA since the early 1980s.[15] Thus, the Danish economy is rather efficient by European standards. In fact, apart from safe havens such as Luxembourg, Lichtenstein and Switzerland,[16] no European country has been

---

[14] The first rule of research ethics is that sponsors with any 'interest' in the results reached should be mentioned in the first note of the paper. In Denmark this is strictly applied to private sponsors, but not to public sponsors, maybe for the reasons mentioned in the second paragraph of Subsection 19.1.1 above.

[15] Note that Denmark did relatively well from 1995–2008, but has lost this edge during the latest crisis. It is much discussed in Denmark whether this points to a permanent problem.

[16] The excess wealth of safe havens is analyzed in Christoffersen et al. (2013) and Paldam (2013).

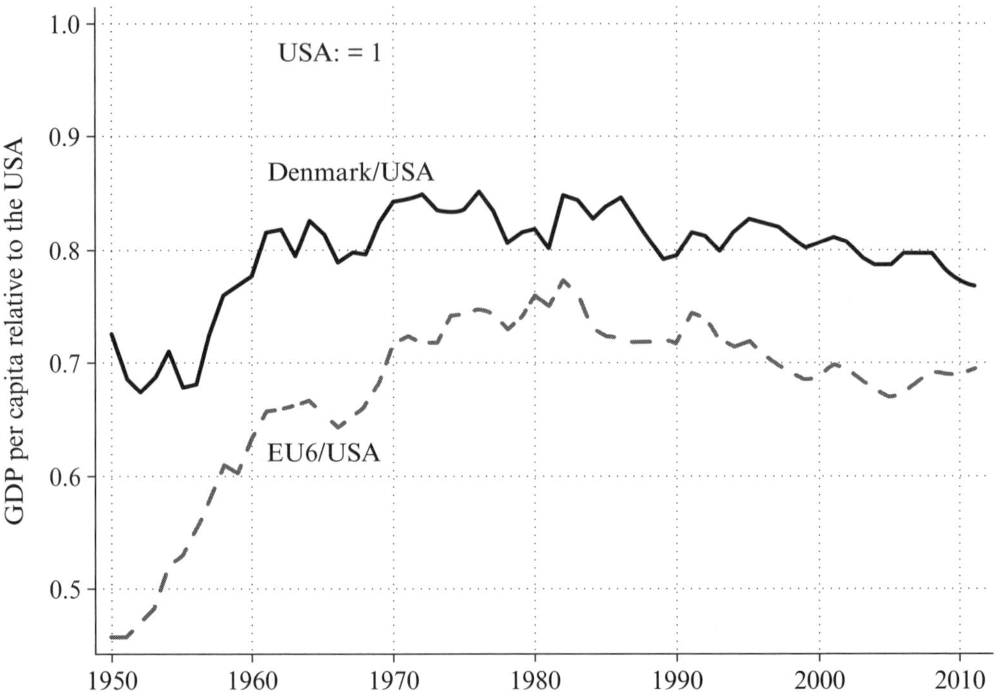

Note: The EU6 countries are Belgium, France, Germany, Italy, Luxembourg and the Netherlands. The weight used to calculate the EU6 series is their average share of the joint GDP, so Luxembourg does not count in the average. The curves are made by dividing the GDP per capita with the one for the USA.

Source: Maddison (2003), updated to 2011 by the PPP series in the World Development Indicators (World Bank n.d.).

Figure 19.2 The relative effectiveness of the Danish economy compared to the USA and the EU6

consistently richer. Sweden has a fairly similar path (and so has Canada), while Norway used to be poorer, but it is now richer, because of oil.

Economic theory suggests that it is the size and competitiveness of the domestic market in the USA that has made its economy so efficient. In Europe a large effort has been made to create a similar sized market. The effort has been rather successful, but not quite as successful as the USA.

19.5.2 The Efficiency/Welfare Trade-off

In the last decade, Sweden has been overtaken by Denmark as the most developed welfare state, and it certainly has the highest tax pressure. It is commonly believed outside Scandinavia that Denmark is a socialist country, but this is wrong.

In order to finance the welfare state, Denmark has a strict protection of property rights and a strong tradition of free trade.[17] One may even say that the extreme size of the welfare state is balanced by an equally extreme 'liberalism' in the private sector. Denmark has no SOEs within trade, industry, agriculture and finance.[18] There has even been a fairly strong movement for outsourcing of traditional public production to private firms.

Christoffersen and Paldam (2003) studied the degree of outsourcing by the Danish municipalities. It turns out that the traditional Left/Right factor has no influence on the degree of outsourcing. However, the size of the welfare coalition in the municipalities has a substantial negative effect.

Figures 19.3 (a) and (b) look at the Fraser Economic Freedom Index for the same countries as in Figure 19.2, though only from 1970, where the index starts. The index aims to measure the regulation regimes of countries. It gives 10 points for laissez-faire. This falls to 1–2 points in extremely regulated states with no freedom to run a private business, such as in the communist bloc before 1990.

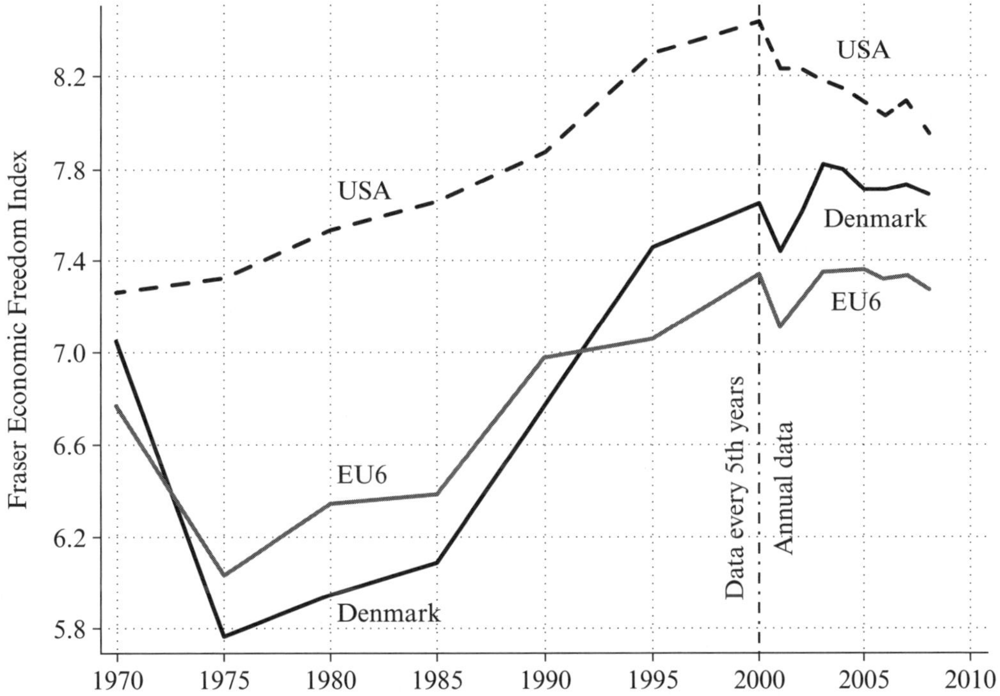

Figure 19.3(a) *The regulation regimes of the USA, EU5 and Denmark according to the Fraser Economic Freedom Index*

---

17 See Bjørnskov and Paldam (2012) for an empirical study of the public support for capitalism versus socialism. The support for capitalism is fairly high in Denmark.

18 See Köthenbürger et al. (2006), for detailed comparisons of the SOE sector in the EU countries. The Danish SOEs are in the network industries and certain traditional services such as Post and Betting. The only big privatization since 1990 has been the telephone company.

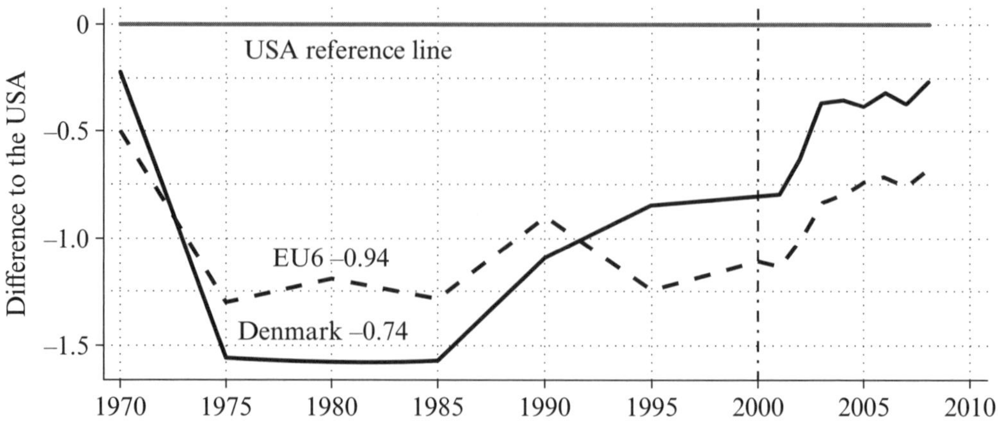

Note: The values compared are the chain-weighted aggregate index. The EU6 and Denmark lines of Figure 19.3(b) are calculated from the data for Figure 19.3(b) by subtracting the US data. The two numbers given, −0.94 and −0.74, are the average deviations from the USA.

Source: Fraser Institute (n.d.).

Figure 19.3(b) The gap between the USA, Denmark and the EU6 countries

It is not surprising that the USA has more economic freedom than the European countries, and one may also have expected to see the fairly large liberalization from 1985 onwards in the (old) EU countries. It is probably surprising to see that Denmark, since 1990, has moved to a position between the USA and the EU6 countries.

The Fraser Index has five components.[19] Denmark has low values for the component of the 'size of government', but scores rather highly in the other components, notably 'the freedom to trade with foreigners' and (absence of) 'business regulations', even during the period from 1975 to 1990 (see Christoffersen et al. 2014, chapter 2.3).

When Figures 19.2 and 3 are compared, it is obvious that there is a connection – the more economic freedom, the wealthier is the country – but it is also clear that the connection is less than perfect. This corresponds rather well to the findings in the literature (see, for example, de Haan 2003).

The two reasons for the 20 percent gap in efficiency between the Danish and the US economy mentioned above were: (a) lower technology and (b) a more sluggish economy due to excessive rents from protection and bad regulation. It is not easy to compare the technology levels. The attempts at comparison in different fields seem to find only a small systematic difference, mainly because the USA does have the world's most advanced technology in some fields, but then there are rather large pockets of fairly low technology. One can suggest that most of the efficiency gap is due to unproductive rents

[19] The five components are: (C1) Government size (−); (C2) Legal quality (+); (C3) Sound money (+); (C4) Freedom to trade with foreigners (+); and (C5) Regulation of business (−). The signs in parentheses show the way the variable affects the Index. Denmark has high scores except for (C1).

in the protected part of the economy. That is mainly in the public sector – notably in the protected semi-public sector.

19.5.3 Rents in the SOE Sector: Transport

The network industries tend to have a natural monopoly. Hence, they have to be regulated. The two examples given are from the two largest transport SOEs. The welfare state wants collective not private transport, so Danish car taxes are the highest in Europe. This gives air and rail transport a large competitive advantage. Both fields have a large SOE: SAS in the air and DSB [Danish State Railways] on rail.

There is no reason to have monopoly in the air, but for a long time Europe had a system of national airlines where most routes were protected from competition. The typical fares were 2–3 times those for similar distances in the USA. One of these airlines was SAS that is jointly owned by the three Scandinavian countries, so it was a triple sheltered public service. But then the market was liberalized, and the pampered family of national airlines started to suffer: Airfares dropped, and big rounds of cost cuts were made to prevent bankruptcies.

When the crunch came, SAS managed to reduce costs by about 50 percent. Thus SAS had managed to absorb rents in the order of 50 percent in the last 2–3 decades before the EU enforced competition. The salaries and frills of pilots were just like those that we all believe we deserve! SAS ran sales offices at the Place de la Concorde, Kurfürstendamm and the like. No expense was too high to secure the absorption of the high ticket prices.

DSB is an old public monopoly that was formed in 1885 after the collapse of several private rail companies, and over the years it has developed its own company culture. Since 2000 a couple of attempts have been made to introduce competition, and some minor lines (with 6 percent of the passenger traffic) are now run by the British company Arriva,[20] which managed to operate with a profit. However, DSB still handles 94 percent of the Danish rail passengers.

In the last 20 years, DSB has built a reputation as having an extraordinarily poor company culture. Frequent deficits (858 mill Kr in 2011) have accumulated rapidly to a debt of 18 bill Kr. DSB is also known for an amazingly high wage level. In January 2013 it was revealed that the salespersons walking the trains with a trolley had a higher salary than a high school teacher, and lo and behold, the trolley sales had large deficits. Similarly high salaries seem to prevail for other staff. The business culture is illustrated by the story of two spin-off companies.

In the late 1990s many bus lines were outsourced after competitive bidding. In order to join the bidding, DSB turned its modest bus company (DSB Bus) into a limited liability company named COMBUS in 1997. It did win a lot of lines by very low bids, and for a short period it was the largest bus company in the country. But it ran most of the lines with a deficit, and already in 1998 the company had consumed most of its equity capital. Both in 1999 and 2000, the state supplied new equity capital, but it gave up in 2001, when the company was sold for a price of 100 Kr to Arriva.

DSBfirst was a company formed in 2009 by DSB and a private British rail company

---

[20] Since 2010 owned by Deutsche Bahn.

(FirstGroup) to run trail traffic in Southern Sweden and Northeast Zealand. FirstGroup managed to leave the company in 2011. Though the final accounts are not in, it appears that it has managed to lose close to 1 bill Kr since its formation.

In addition to these accounts, a 5 bill Kr contract was signed in 2000 with the Italian company AnsaldoBreda for 83 new trains to be delivered before 2005. The last trains were delivered in 2013, but they rarely work. There were never more than ten of these trains actually running on the Danish rails at any time, and it increasingly looks as if DSB has given up on the majority of the trains. How the blame for this business tragedy should be distributed between AnsaldoBreda and DSB will probably be discussed for a good many years.

19.5.4 Culture: The Amazing Story of the Danish Radio and the Royal Theater

The Ministry for Culture had a budget of 20 bill (10^9) Kr in 2011 – local governments spend another 2 bill. The Ministry runs two large SOEs that consume a lot of taxes.

DR [Danmarks Radio] is a Radio and Television SOE, with just above 3000 employees. This is almost the same as the workforce in all the private newspapers added together. DR has special permission to levy a media tax of 4 bill Kr, of which about 12 percent is passed on to other media via the Ministry, but as DR has some other income, its balance is also about 4 bill. In its public accounts it is stated that it owns real estate of a value of 5.3 bill. This is mainly the grand 'DR city', which is a complex of buildings erected between 1999 and 2009 on a former sea-bottom close to the center of Copenhagen. The project involved a 'decision complex' of the Parliament, several ministries, Copenhagen municipality and DR top management. Everybody in the complex is within the welfare coalition, and, of course, so is DR.[21]

The DR city was originally proposed by DR management in 1995–97 as a modest project that could be built from the sales revenue of the previous old buildings, and it was stressed that it would be a big rationalization to move the staff from the scattered old buildings together under one roof! This proved to be one of the sweet songs foxes sing to woo chickens.

Once the decision had been accepted by the complex, the costs and size of the project started to jump. When the design of the architects was in, the scheduled costs had reached 3 bill, and the expected sale revenue for the old buildings had almost evaporated. Then the project started, and before it ended in 2009 the costs went to about 4.5 bill. It did cost about five members of the senior DR management team their job, but some of them would have retired anyhow over the ten years of the project.

I am convinced that if the costs and size of the project had been clear from the start, it would never have been accepted. I also suspect that everybody in the decision complex knew that there would be large cost overruns. Also, of course, the private newspapers and the center-right government (from 2001 to 2011) were critical of the project, and DR

[21] It has often been alleged that the DR staff is to the left of the political center, and it is easy to point to left-wing journalists working in DR, but it is difficult to prove that they dominate. However, in the perspective of the welfare coalition it is clear that DR is the part of the media that is within the public sector.

was repeatedly forced to promise that it would save on the rest of the budget. However, the last budget (covering the five years from 2007 to 2011) shows that it has kept rising by 2 percent per year, though total employment has an unclear trend.

One perspective is that DR is a key part of the PR apparatus of the welfare coalition, and that it has so many friends/clients within the power structure that it has been allowed to proceed with the building of premises that fit with its importance. Also, it has successfully argued that the construction costs are sunk, so that they should have no consequences for future budgets.

The case of the Royal Theater is curiously parallel in the sense that this SOE has also increased its real estate dramatically since the year 2000. Before 2005 the theater had two stages – this has now doubled. In 2005 a private donor (Maersk Foundation) donated a new opera house (to 2.4 bill Kr). While it was being built, the government decided, with virtually no public discussion, that it should also give the theater a new building (to 0.8 bill Kr) with a stage for theater performances. It was inaugurated in 2008, and at that time the smaller of the two old stages was closed, but the number of seats had still increased about three times. It is interesting that neither of the two new buildings had any cost overrun. Now the theater is seeking an increase in its subsidies to tally the increase in seats.

The public budget supports theaters with 1.5 bill Kr annually. Half of this sum goes to the Royal Theater, which has operating costs of 850 mill (of which 130 mill is covered by the sale of tickets). Some money comes from private sponsors. The three theater buildings are all written off, so they are invisible in the accounts, but the annual opportunity costs of the three expensive pieces of real estate must be several hundred mill Kr.[22] So the rent-wedge between the business income and costs is about 8 times. The Royal Theater was founded in 1747. As far as I have been able to find out, the rent-wedge was below 2 a hundred years ago. So the theater has grown in size and has managed to obtain a steadily increasing rent-wedge.

The Royal Theater has a fine statement expressing its goals and values. It provides benefits to the nation and mankind through the art of theater. As may be expected, no mention is made of any 'low' economic matters such as costs. At the risk of being grossly vulgar, one could consider the story of the Royal Theater as a case of a special institution that manages to extract steadily increasing rents. There are other theaters in the country with far smaller rents. The majority of those harvesting rents in the form of cheap tickets seem to be members of the welfare coalition.

19.5.5 Danish SOEs are Like Other SOEs, but Fortunately they are Few

Many studies have been made of SOEs around the world. Some such stories and a good deal of references are given in Köthenbürger et al. (2006). There is also a large literature on the relative costs of outsourced and public production of similar goods and services (see Christoffersen et al. 2007). Denmark is typical in both respects. That is, Danish SOEs extract as much rent as they can: SAS charged the same high prices as other

---

[22] This is a tricky calculation as the three buildings are made precisely for the purpose they are used for. So an assessment demands that the buildings are malleable.

national airlines, when it could. DSB is not more inefficient than other public railway monopolies and so on. Also, the studies of outsourced services in Denmark show much the same efficiency gains as in other countries.

The observation in Subsection 19.5.1 that the Danish economy is fairly efficient thus tallies well with that of Subsection 19.5.2 that there are relatively few SOEs in Denmark.

19.6 CONCLUSION

This chapter is about rent extraction and also rent seeking in the public sector in the most developed welfare state in the world. The rents are relatively well protected, as the median voter is within the informal 'welfare coalition' of those who benefit from the welfare state. The welfare state has built a protecting ring of NGOs around its main spending programs. On the face of it, one should expect that big rents exist in the welfare state.

The comparison of the efficiency of the Danish welfare state with the USA showed that Denmark is 20–25 percent behind. My assessment was that the difference in technology level is less than half of this difference. Most of the rest of the gap is explained by inefficiencies associated with rents. The USA is surely not a society without rents, so rents are substantial in the welfare state. A number of cases in which policy changes caused rents to be visible were given. In these examples rather large rents were revealed.

However, with all of this, it still appears that the Danish economy is rather efficient compared to other European countries, and although the measure of happiness must have some measurement error, the very high Danish happiness scores have been replicated so often that it is clear that the Danes are very satisfied by their life. And they certainly like their welfare state.

REFERENCES

Baumol, William, J. (1967), 'Macroeconomics of unbalanced growth: an anatomy of urban crises', *American Economic Review*, **57**(3), 415–26.

Baumol, William, J. (2004), 'The cost disease of the personal services', in Charles K. Rowley and Friedrich Schneider (eds), *The Encyclopedia of Public Choice, Volume II*, Dordrecht: Kluwer, pp. 132–6.

Bjørnskov, Christian and Martin Paldam (2005), 'Corruption trends', in Johan Graf Lambsdorff, Markus Taube and Matthias Schramm (eds), *The New Institutional Economics of Corruption*, London: Routledge, pp. 59–75.

Bjørnskov, Christian and Martin Paldam (2012), 'The spirits of capitalism and socialism: a cross-country study of ideology', *Public Choice*, **150**(3–4), 469–98.

Christoffersen, Henrik and Martin Paldam (2003), 'Markets and municipalities: a study of the behavior of the Danish municipalities', *Public Choice*, **114**(1–2), 79–102.

Christoffersen, Henrik, Martin Paldam and Allan Würtz (2007), 'Public versus private production: a study of the cost of school cleaning in Denmark', *Public Choice*, **130**(3–4), 311–28.

Christoffersen, Henrik, Michelle Beyeler, Reiner Eichenberger, Peter Nannestad and Martin Paldam (2014), *The Good Society: Denmark and Switzerland*, Heidelberg: Springer.

de Haan, Jakob (ed.) (2003), Special Issue on Economic Freedom, *European Journal of Political Economy*, **19**(3), 395–649.

DR [Danmarks Radio] (2013), 'Andelen af folk i arbejde falder drastisk', 13 January, available at http://www.dr.dk/Nyheder/Indland/2013/01/25/152653.htm (accessed 2013).

Folketinget (2012), *Folketingets medlemmer i tal ved valget 2011*, available at http://www.ft.dk/Demokrati/

media/Pdf_materiale/Pdf_publikationer/Informationsark/Folketingets_medlemmer/medlemmer_i_tal_2011%20pdf.ashx (accessed 2013).
Fraser Institute (n.d.), Home page of the Economic Freedom Index, available at http://www.fraserinstitute.org/ (accessed 2013).
Hillman, Arye L. (2009), *Public Finance and Public Policy: Responsibilities and Limitations of Government*, 2nd edn, New York: Cambridge University Press.
Köthenbürger, Marko, Hans-Werner Sinn and John Whalley (eds) (2006), *Privatization Experiences in the European Union*, Cambridge, MA: MIT Press.
Maddison, Angus (2003), *The World Economy: Historical Statistics*, Paris: OECD. See also the Maddison home page, available at http://www.ggdc.net/maddison/ for updates until February 2010 (accessed 2013).
Mueller, Dennis C. (2003), *Public Choice III*, Cambridge: Cambridge University Press.
Nannestad, Peter (2004), 'Immigration as a challenge to the Danish welfare state?', *European Journal of Political Economy*, **20**(3), 755–67, reprinted in Roger D. Congleton, Arye L. Hillman and Kai A. Konrad (eds) (2008), *40 Years of Research on Rent Seeking 2 – Applications: Rent Seeking in Practice*, Heidelberg: Springer, pp. 281–93.
Nannestad, Peter (2007), 'Immigration and welfare states: a survey of 15 years of research', *European Journal of Political Economy*, **23**(2), 512–32.
Niskanen, William A. (1968), 'The peculiar economics of bureaucracy', *American Economic Review Papers and Proceedings*, **58**(2), 293–305.
Niskanen, William A. (1994), *Bureaucracy and Public Economics*, Aldershot, UK and Brookfield, VT, USA: Edward Elgar Publishing.
Paldam, Martin (1997), *Dansk U-landshælp: Altruismens Politiske Økonomi*, Aarhus: Aarhus Universitetsforlag.
Paldam, Martin (ed.) (2007), 'Symposium: immigration and the welfare state', *European Journal of Political Economy*, **23**(2), 448–532.
Paldam, Martin (2008), 'The political economy of regulating betting – illustrated by the Danish case', in Matti Viren (ed.), *Gaming in a New Market Environment*, Houndmills: Palgrave Macmillan, pp. 184–208.
Paldam, Martin (2009), 'The welfare state and Baumol's Law', Working Paper 2009–05, Department of Economics, Aarhus University.
Paldam, Martin (2013), 'Safe havens in Europe: Switzerland and the ten dwarfs', *European Journal of Comparative Economics*, **10**(3), 377–413.
Paldam, Martin (2014), 'The public choice of university organization: a stylized story with some explanation' *Constitutional Political Economy*, Online First DOI 10.1007/s100602–014–9177–8
Paldam, Martin and Hans. E. Zeuthen (1988), 'The expansion of the public sector in Denmark – a post festum?', in Johan A. Lybeck and Magnus Henreksson (eds), *The Expansion of the Public Sectors in the West*, Amsterdam: North-Holland, pp. 157–86.
Svendsen, Gert T. and Christian Bjørnskov (2007), 'How to construct a robust measure of social capital: two contributions', *Journal of Comparative Policy Analysis*, **9**(3), 275–92.
Tullock, Gordon (1967), 'The welfare costs of tariffs, monopolies, and theft', *Western Economic Journal*, **5**(3), 224–32, reprinted in Roger D. Congleton, Arye L. Hillman and Kai A. Konrad (eds) (2008), *40 Years of Research on Rent Seeking 1 – The Theory of Rent Seeking*, Heidelberg: Springer, pp. 45–53.
World Bank (n.d.), *World Development Indicators*, available at http://data.worldbank.org/data-catalog/world-development-indicators (accessed 2013).

20. Rent seeking through control of the state in Russia

Mark I. Levin and Georgy A. Satarov

SUMMARY

In Russia, rent seeking has involved violence and control of the judiciary. State agencies that formally should protect the state have been used to extract rents through means that are in principle illegal. The end of effective political competition resulted in corruption and expansion of administratively extracted rents. The rent extraction extends throughout the layers of government bureaucracy and local and national levels of government. We provide examples in which rent extraction reaches the individual, through traffic police and a market for academic degrees.

20.1 INTRODUCTION

This chapter describes the complex interplay between rents and rent seeking in post-communist Russia. This interplay involves the political agenda, violence, administrative lawlessness and corruption. The chapter is specifically dedicated to the Russian aspects of rent seeking.[1]

Rent seeking in Russia is deeply rooted in history, whichever historical period we choose to consider: the era of monarchy, the Soviet epoch from 1917 to 1991, Russia in the 'transition' period after the collapse of the Soviet Union or Russia's post-transition political system. Rent seeking during each of these periods has its characteristic features that reflect the institutional structure of the state: the monarchic regime in tsarist Russia; the authoritarian regime and dictatorship in the Soviet years; decentralized government in the period of 'transition'; and weak democracy with increasing authoritarian elements in post-transition Russia. Without significant departure from the pre-revolution years (before 1917), the Soviet era provided vast opportunities for various kinds of rent seeking. Rent-seeking behavior was promoted by the hierarchical system, the planned economy, governmental ownership of all assets and, at the same time, soft budgetary limitations, falsification of plan fulfillment, a considerable shadow economy, 'telephone justice' and cronyism (*blat*).[2]

A form of rent seeking in the planned economy was legal and structured through an

---

[1] For a general description of rent seeking, see the introductory chapters of this book and Buchanan (1980 [2008]), Tullock (1989), Zaostrovtsev (2008, 2014), Congleton et al. (2008) and Hillman (2009, 2013).

[2] On the sources of rents and rent seeking in the different periods and regimes, see Kornai (1980a, 1980b [2008]), Hillman and Schnytzer (1986 [2008]), Hillman (1994, 2002), Anderson and

official system of privileges that included access to financial and non-financial benefits that depended on a person's position in the administrative system and in the hierarchy of the state's only political party. The hierarchy within the Communist Party defined the complete system of distribution of power in the Soviet Union, including control of the management of the national economy, the legal system and its implementation, and to a large extent citizens' private lives.[3]

Within this formal system of privileges there was a second informal form of rent seeking. This included a system of *blat* and mutual services, illegal shadow rent seeking and corruption – all features typical of the Soviet regime from its first day to the last. Causes and forms of these kinds of rent seeking have been described in such works as *Russia's Economy of Favours: Blat, Networking and Informal Exchange* by Ledeneva (1998) and *Institutional Corruption* by Timofeyev (2000), in which *blat* (informal contacts and personal networks used to obtain favors) and corruption are emphasized as necessary elements of the Soviet economic system, because they acted as substitutes for the missing-market features of the economy.

Despite the non-market nature of economy in the Soviet Union, *blat*, corruption and privileges had prices. Soviet economomist, Nobel Prize laureate Kantorovich, proposed a special term to describe shadow prices: 'objectively determined valuations.' These valuations allowed a kind of 'general economic equilibrium' in the presence of non-equilibrium prices, quotas, deficits and impossible-to-fulfill plans. Description of equilibrium in such economic systems can be found in Benassy (1986) and Makarov et al. (1995). Hillman and Katz (1987 [2008]) described a hierarchical rent-seeking system that could correspond to the system that was present; positions of power in the hierarchy created administrative markets (Kordonsky 2006, 2008) that allowed competition for rents, with the prizes in the rent-seeking contests being advantageous positions in the administrative, political or state industrial hierarchy.

After the Soviet economic and political system collapsed and the communist state fell apart, Russia began a transition that generated more types of rents. Along with the administrative and politically extracted rents that had existed in the Soviet period, the transition period introduced new significant rents, arising from private ownership of factory assets and natural resources, as well as from control over the designation of such ownership (Gelb et al. 1998). Rents were obtained by seeking and receiving permits and quotas for international trade. The process of privatization and the contests for politically extracted rents frequently overlapped, which shaped a rent-based political and economic system (Levin and Satarov 2000; Gaddy and Ickes 2002). The development of new social, economic and political institutions paralleled the growth of corruption in a process described by Appelbaum and Katz (1987 [2008]) as 'seeking rents by setting rents.' The results of the empirical studies in this field can be found in Satarov (2013). Since 1991, natural-resource rents from oil and gas have played a major role in private wealth in Russia (Gaddy and Ickes 2005; Zaostrovtsev 2014).

Boettke (1997), Qian and Roland (1998), Hellman et al. (2003), Barsukova (2011) and Levin and Satarov (2000, 2013).

[3] Features of this official system of privileges have been described by Milovan (1957) and Voslensky (1984). Hillman (2009, chapter 2) suggests that, because decisions about benefits were personal rather than made through markets, the scope for rent seeking was maximal.

We identify the following types of rents:

1. Natural-resource rent that derives from mineral wealth or other natural resources, such as water, and that can also arise from a beneficial climate (resorts) or geographical position (for instance, being able to control transportation routes).
2. Monopoly rent that derives from disallowing competition in markets.
3. Politically extracted rents that are assigned by establishing convenient rules of the game, such that some people are permitted to violate existing rules, and allow distributing informal rights through the norm of 'for my friends, anything, for my enemies, the law.'
4. Administratively extracted rents that arise from rent creation through corruption.

Rents are present in Russia through contesting of rents, political or administrative rent extraction, rent creation and rent expansion, and rent granting. Expansion means the broadening of opportunities for rent seeking that already exist. Rent granting is a term frequently used in discussions of the Muscovite model (Kotilaine 2004; Rosefielde 2005; Hedlund 2006; Magomedov and Nikerov 2010), which is the economic model typical of Russia from the fifteenth century. The Muscovite model is based on patrimonial relationships and includes distribution of rents from top to bottom within the ruling coalition or class; privileged rents are granted in exchange for services (primarily military service). It has been proposed that twenty-first-century Russia has returned to this patriarchal model (Rosefielde 2005; Hedlund 2006).

We also distinguish the following categories of rent seeking. 'Situational' rent seeking involves occasional use of an opportunity to extract rent; situational rent seeking is opportunistic and occurs when a person evaluates a rent-seeking opportunity as the most profitable among other opportunities in a given situation. 'Deliberate' rent seeking occurs when the person engages in rent seeking as a priori the most profitable activity, making rent seeking the person's life strategy. 'Systematic' rent seeking occurs when deliberate rent seeking is typical of behavior of many people, who coordinate their efforts in order to build special relationships or institutions aimed at creating and obtaining rents, with the behavior considered natural and acceptable within the dominating system of the society's informal institutions.

Against the background of these classifications, we proceed as follows. Section 20.2 describes transition to political monopoly and consequences for politically assigned rents in Russia. Section 20.3 describes administrative rent extraction. Section 20.4 gives an example of rents and rent seeking in a private market, the market for doctoral dissertations. Section 20.5 is concerned with monopoly rents. Section 20.6 is concerned with natural-resource rents. Section 20.7 describes the process of rent diversification. We set out our conclusions in the final section.

20.2 POLITICALLY ASSIGNED RENTS IN RUSSIA

20.2.1 The Transition

In the 1990s transition period from the communist system, politically assigned rents in Russia were diversified and limited. The rents were divided into a number of relatively small regional rents. On the federal level, parliamentary parties (to a varying degree) would convert their political capital into various kinds of rents but there were insufficient rents to ensure a stable increase in the rents available. Presidential power was limited and used unsystematically, because of strong regional elites and the absence of a large presidential majority in parliament. From a broad perspective, it can be said that in the 1990s there was no major monopoly for politically assigned rents in Russia and extraction of politically assigned rent represented primarily situational or opportunistic behavior.

20.2.2 Political Competition

The contest for politically assigned rents arrived with the new epoch, when, before the parliamentary elections of 1999, two influential political groups – of close political and administrative origin, but relying on different groups of the elite – were each shaping their own political parties to compete in the forthcoming election. The first to arrive was the electoral bloc Fatherland – All Russia (*Otechestvo – Vsya Rossiya*), led by former Prime Minister Evgeny Primakov and Moscow Mayor Yury Luzhkov, the most influential of all the regional leaders. This bloc, like its leaders, was in opposition to President Yeltsin. A little later, the second political bloc emerged, Unity (*Yedinstvo*), established by the presidential administration. In the election, the bloc was represented by popular politicians: Sergey Shoigu (then Russia's Civil Defense and Emergencies Minister), Alexander Karelin (multiple Olympic champion and world champion in Greco-Roman wrestling) and Alexander Gurov (police general lieutenant, fighter against organized crime).

The election campaign was aggressive. The election itself seemed honest. The Communist Party received the most votes but lost its majority in the Duma, the lower chamber of parliament. Unity beat Fatherland. More importantly, however, the newly created political force at the Kremlin involved Yeltsin's 'heir': Vladimir Putin. He was quickly gaining popularity and in March 2000 won the first round of the presidential election. This was sufficient to prompt members of parliament to start joining the ranks of the new authorities' party, which soon was the largest faction of the lower chamber. Shortly afterwards, the presidential administration orchestrated a union of the two previously antagonistic political forces; in the Duma, they were joined by a large group of deputies who had won elections at the single-mandate electoral district. The result of these processes was a new party called United Russia (*Yedinaya Rossiya*) that held the majority of seats in the lower chamber. The new regime started the battle for political control, for political monopoly and for extraction of politically assigned rents.

20.2.3 Political Monopoly

In the process of seeking political monopoly by shaping the pro-Putin Duma majority, United Russia seized all the high-ranking posts in the lower chamber. Then the upper chamber of parliament – the Federation Council – was subjected to a reform. Before the reform, the Federation Council accepted all regional governors and chairs of regional legislative bodies who had won the elections in their regions. The pro-Putin majority in the lower chamber lobbied for a new scheme: now the president would suggest his own regional representatives to the Federation Council and the legislative bodies could approve his suggestions. The Federation Council, too, supported the new scheme, although it was political suicide for its members of the time. The reason behind that was simple: most of the voters in the upper chamber were engaged in corrupt activities, which the presidential administration used against them in order to gain the majority of votes. There was nothing unexpected about this: at the time, many of the posts in the presidential administration were occupied by former special-services officers. Back then, many of the seats in the Federation Council were secured by bribes.

In early September 2004, a group of terrorists seized a secondary school in Beslan, a town in southern Russia. An attempt to free the hostages resulted in major casualties: 334 people dead, including 186 children, and more than 800 injured. In the wake of the national shock, Putin introduced another change that cancelled direct elections of governors. Now the president would present his candidates and the regional legislative bodies could support them.

During these years, Russian regions saw the emergence of symbiosis between regional departments of the pro-governmental party United Russia, regional civil authorities and regional law-enforcement agencies (police, Federal Security Bureau, the Prosecutor's Office and so on). This resulted in monopolistic control over all of the political processes in the regions, and, first of all, the elections. As part of 'counter-terrorist measures', elections to the lower chamber were also subjected to reforms. Ultimately, the reforms presented the Russian electoral system with insurmountable barriers to entry into the political market, and nearly full absence of accountability to the electorate.

In 2001 the authorities launched an attack on two independent public television channels: ORT, controlled by Boris Berezovsky, and NTV, controlled by Vladimir Gusinsky (both of them Russian 'oligarchs'). Ultimately, the authorities established control over federal television broadcasting and could continue to tighten their grip over the regional mass media. At the same time, they were expanding control over large businesses. This process culminated in the arrest of Mikhail Khodorkovsky and Platon Lebedev and the destruction of their oil firm, YUKOS, Russia's most successful company.

In the Soviet Union, the KGB (*Komitet gosudarstvennoy bezopasnosti*) – the all-powerful agency that secured the security of the regime – served as an external controller over the rest of governmental and non-governmental institutions. After Putin's arrival, officers of the Federal Security Bureau (FSB) (the KGB's successor in post-Soviet Russia) started infiltrating the civil bureaucracy, politics, business, mass media and public organizations. This was a new form of total control.

The transition to a harsh political monopoly was brought on by two factors. One was external, a wave of 'color' revolutions in a number of post-Soviet states: in Georgia in 2003, Ukraine in 2004 and Kyrgyzstan in 2005. The Russian ruling elite took these events as a direct threat. It was also clear who the threat came from: the society. As a result, the authorities promptly launched three lines of activity.

In politics three parties that played the part of 'opposition' were allowed to run in elections and received a small share of seats in the federal and regional parliaments. The authorities fully controlled all three of these parties, which was obvious whenever necessity required support for bills that were important for the Kremlin. The other parties were liquidated, and it was virtually impossible to register new ones, unless under the Kremlin's direct control. The same was true for politicians: it was extremely difficult to enter the political arena, be it through elections or through time using the federal mass media. These measures, coupled with growing scope of falsifications during elections, helped the pro-governmental party secure a constitutional majority (over two thirds of votes) in the lower chamber of federal parliament in the 2007 elections; in the upper chamber the problem of securing a majority had already been solved by other means.

The second line of activity was social. First, attacks on public organizations were launched in the mid-2000s. The authorities attempted to compromise the reputation of human rights activists, who were accused of espionage. The Kremlin started putting together public organizations led by 'loyal people' and therefore controllable. These organizations provided 'representatives of society' who, when needed, could be used to initiate dialogue between the authorities and the society.

The decisive attack was launched after an outbreak of public protests in the winter of 2011–12. In the presidential election in the spring of 2012, Putin used a controversial clause in the Russian Constitution to return to the presidential seat after a four-year break, during which he had been prime minister. One day ahead of the inauguration celebration, on 6 May 2012, public activists held a peaceful rally to protest against falsified elections. During that rally, the authorities organized a provocation, broke up the sanctioned protest and arrested hundreds of protesters. The anti-rights activities continued with mock trials that saw dozens of innocent people unlawfully convicted and sent to prison.

In the autumn of 2012, a new law introduced the notion of 'foreign agent', referring to public organizations that received funds from abroad. This law had the effect of allowing many reputable public organizations to be successfully closed. The activities of the surviving organizations became subject to close governmental control. The parliament approved of a number of new laws that introduced harsh limitations in various spheres: from adoption of orphans to the Internet. The pressure on public organizations continued.

In 2013–14 the authoritarian rent-oriented economic model of the previous ten years plunged into crisis. The country was in recession. Even before that, United Russia and Putin had begun to lose popularity. These factors were threatening the regime of political monopoly. The solution was found in the form of channeling the aggression toward an external enemy represented by Ukraine; in fanning up mass quasi-patriotic hysteria or xenophobia.

The third line of the authorities' activity aimed at controlling society was propaganda. Initially, control over the influential media was used only to stop critical voices against the new political regime and to rationalize its actions; but then the Kremlin started using informational channels to popularize quasi-ideological clichés that would support symbolic legitimacy of the regime in order to make up for lack of actual legitimacy. Probably the main cliché, which was introduced before all others, is the notion of 'vertical power.' This term had several functions: to deny constitutional principles of separation of authorities and federalism; to evoke comforting nostalgic associations with Soviet times; and to support new informal institutions of power. However, the new clichés failed to be adopted.

20.2.4 Monopolization of Access to Rents

Dmitry Medvedev's presidential term saw the domination of United Russia in parliament, achieved through a qualified majority. This circumstance was used to amend the Russian Constitution: the members of the lower chamber of parliament were now to be elected for five years instead of four, and the presidential term was increased from four to six years. The anti-constitutional symbolic notion of 'vertical power' was reflected in the formally legal construction of the United Russia party. The party represented the monopoly of bureaucratic power; it was actually more of Vladimir Putin's traditional clientele than a party. In essence, United Russia was an informal institution controlling access to political and administrative rents, as well as distribution of opportunities to enjoy the benefits from these rents.

Access to politically assigned rents simplified access to administrative rent through membership in the United Russia party, in the manner resembling the informal order of organization in the USSR, where the Communist Party used to play the same role. Political monopoly and suppression of civil-society institutions (public organizations, free entrepreneurship and independent media) were preconditions for pocketing the natural-resource rent that emerged in the 2000s; this subject is discussed further in the chapter. The same preconditions allowed the shaping of monopoly rents in various economic spheres. The ruling coalition, established in the early 2000s, relied on politically assigned rents to support transitional rents by blocking full-scale institutional modernization, especially in the area of rule of law. The new social order was supported by law-enforcement institutions that protected the incumbent political regime.

It can be said that, since the mid-2000s, the symbiosis of political power and bureaucracy was the basis for the transition to systematic rent seeking. Thereafter, the authorities expanded, strengthened and preserved the rent-extracting regime of government.

20.3 ADMINISTRATIVE RENT EXTRACTION

In the 1990s, administrative rent extraction in Russia was significant, both in terms of the potential offered by a gigantic, inefficiently run empire and in terms of actual large-scale rent extraction typical of post-communist transition periods. Still, administrative rent extraction was hampered by a number of factors. First, the bureaucracy had been demoralized and torn by the collapse of the Soviet Union and the process of transition. The most enterprising and talented officials had left bureaucratic posts for politics and (or) business, since the same qualities could be used both in organizing corrupt networks and in serving the society. Second, there were limitations similar to those that prevented the development of political monopoly in the 1990s as described above: strong standing of the regions, political competition and influential, independent mass media that thrived on covering corruption scandals on any level. Third, in the 1990s, bureaucracy in Russia stuck to the traditional internal division of officials into two major groups: civil and power structures. Ever since the Soviet Union developed professional secret services, only candidates suggested by the Communist Party were promoted to top positions in the KGB. This policy allowed the Party to maintain political control over the almighty agency. On the other hand, the KGB could control the activities of the civil bureaucracy, including the Communist Party bureaucracy (except for the top-level officials). This principle was sometimes violated, including after the collapse of the Soviet Union, but the border between power and civil bureaucracies persisted. As a result, throughout the 1990s, the prevailing behavior was situational opportunistic rent seeking, but with slow replacement by intentional rent seeking. By the end of the decade, Russia was displaying typical features of systematic rent seeking. This behavior was manifested in the development of the first corruption networks (Rimsky 2007).

When in the 2000s Russia started to develop a new political regime, the limitations on administrative rent extraction gradually faded away. Partly this happened because the border between the civil and power bureaucracies was eroding, destroying the traditional internal mechanism of mutual limitation and control. Another reason was that the establishment of political monopoly, as described above, turned into an uncontrollable monopoly of the ruling bureaucracy, which was controlling the political sphere. This caused a rapid increase of administratively available rents, which was associated with a corresponding increase in corruption. Between 2001 and 2005, business corruption, according to the INDEM Fund, increased by several times over (Levin and Satarov 2013; Satarov 2013). During these years, an average (robust) bribe amount increased by seven times, while the conservative estimate of the corruption market (annual income of state officials from bribes received in the market of business corruption) increased by almost five times.[4]

From the early days of the new regime, its features involved major corruption-related scandals. A telling common feature of two examples presented below is that both scandals involved the successor to the KGB, the FSB.

In September 2000, the Customs Committee of Russia opened an investigation into the smuggling of Italian furniture, sold through the largest furniture stores. The probe was conducted by the Investigative Committee of the Russian Internal Affairs Ministry. The Prosecutor General's Office and the FSB hushed up the case after the investigation revealed that top officials of both these agencies had been protecting the corrupt business through a vast corruption network. As the case was closed, there were casualties: some people were fired, others were charged with fake crimes and some were killed. Whenever the authorities began another short anti-corruption campaign, the investigation would restart. In the end, several people directly involved in the scam received short sentences. Officials from the secret services and law-enforcement agencies, earlier charged as accomplices, were acquitted.[5]

It subsequently became clear that furniture smuggling was only a small source of corruption-related rents supported and protected by the FSB. The corruption was investigated by reporter Yury Shekochikhin, one of Russia's best-known journalists, who was also a member of the lower chamber of parliament and a consultant for the United Nations on organized crime. Shekochikhin died of a mysterious illness, quickly

---

[4] See Satarov (2013, p. 322). The comparison is in relative units, with adjustment for deflators and other time effects; the average bribe amount was measured in purchasing power in the housing market, and the corruption market volume was measured relative to gross domestic product (GDP).

[5] For additional reading, see http://www.rb.ru/inform/30597.html and http://ru.wikipedia.org/wiki/Дело_«Трёх_китов» (accessed 10 July 2014).

and unexpectedly, in July 2003, just as he was finishing his whistle-blowing articles on the FSB-related corruption.[6] The symptoms of his fatal illness were similar to those described in the case of Alexander Litvinenko, a former FSB official previously allegedly poisoned by Polonium-210 in London.

Another major corruption-related scandal began in early May 2005, when someone leaked to the press that the FSB was controlling the smuggling of consumer goods through the port of Nakhodka in Far Eastern Russia, all the way to Moscow, to a military base supervised by the FSB.[7] The scheme was so grand that the scandal could not be hushed up. Many high-ranking officials of the FSB and the Customs Service lost their jobs, and even the Prosecutor General was fired.

Approximately in the mid-2000s, different law-enforcement agencies started battling one another for the right to extract administrative rents. From time to time, some governmental agencies would gain monopolistic control over certain areas; for instance, in some regions the Ministry of Internal Affairs controlled circulation of illegal drugs, while the Prosecutor's Office supervised the illegal gambling industry. However, the agencies would frequently clash over this or that right, for instance, over the right to sell confiscated goods through shadow distribution schemes. Administrative leverage, especially the leverage of law enforcement, was used as a weapon in the battle for corruption markets. One of the major tools used in this battle was the corruption scandal: one agency would initiate an investigation of another's corrupt activities. However, these investigations never ended in actual prison sentences for high-ranking officials.

In a parallel process, the corrupt extraction of administrative rents was also growing at lower levels of interaction between business and the authorities. Studies conducted by the INDEM Fund in the 2000s revealed that smaller business was suffering from new problems stemming from the extraction of administrative rent.[8] In-depth interviews with entrepreneurs in various parts of Russia revealed the popularity of the 'share-based' shadow administrative practice. For instance, if a businessman wanted to build a store, he had to go to the relevant department of the city council and consult the city map showing potential locations for building a store. All of these locations would happen to be in sparsely populated neighborhoods with poor infrastructure, far from popular routes. If the entrepreneur expressed indignation, he would be shown a different map, with very promising locations for his store. However, he would be informed that the map was 'zoned' into areas controlled by different high-ranking city government officials. After choosing a spot, the businessman would find out that in order to build his store there, he needed to 'negotiate' with a certain official, for instance, the deputy

---

[6] A memorial article written ten years after Yury Shekochikhin's death opens as follows, 'Yury Shekochikhin died ten years ago. We know it was murder, but there's no proving it now, because for years the Prosecutor's Office has been doing everything to cover the evidence of the crime.' *Novaya Gazeta*, No. 71, 3 July 2013, http://www.novayagazeta.ru/inquests/58870.html (accessed 10 July 2014).

[7] '68 thousand boxer briefs for the FSB director and the Prime Minister. Special services have been helping smuggle Chinese goods for the Russian government.' *Novaya Gazeta*, No. 36, 23 May 2005, http://2005.novayagazeta.ru/nomer/2005/36n/n36n-s00.shtml.

[8] See, for instance, 'Business and corruptions: communication problems', http://www.anti-corr.ru/cipe/CIPEgid.pdf.

city prosecutor. 'Negotiating' in this context meant offering the deputy prosecutor (or someone in the deputy prosecutor's family) a share in the new business. In exchange for that, the official controlling the zone would help him solve major problems, such as obtaining the multiple permits required in order to legitimately start construction. Moreover, the official in charge could allow the businessman to start construction even before formal permits had been obtained. If instead the businessman opted to take the official route, without a patron, he could easily spend a year or two obtaining permits.

This typical example from daily business life in Russia represents just one case (and rather innocent) of how government officials illegally participate in commercial activities. As we see, illegality does not prevent officials of all levels and areas of government from taking part in business activities. There are two factors that account for such free and ubiquitous breach of the law. First, the system of government turns politicians into a class of bureaucracy; political competition is non-existent; politics per se, in its full meaning, is non-existent. This means that politically assigned rents have become administrative rents. The second factor follows from the first: the disregard of the rule of law is related to the key interests of the ruling coalition. A monopolistic, politically uncontrollable bureaucracy has no interest in starting a fight against itself and its own illegal enrichment through commercial activities.

Administrative extraction of rent is clearly manifested in everyday corruption. An example is corruption in the traffic police. The data collected by the INDEM Fund allow comparison of corruption among traffic police in 2001, 2005 and 2010.[9] The data are presented in Table 20.1.

We can see in Table 20.1 that between 2001 and 2005 the traffic police experienced a decrease in annual income from bribes by approximately 57 percent (in constant prices). This is a humiliating decrease, especially considering that during the same period the

Table 20.1 Traffic police corruption in Russia in 2001, 2005 and 2010

Features of the corruption market	2001	2005	2010
Corruption risk (probability of encountering corruption while interacting with the traffic police) (%)	59.3	59.6	52.4
Inclination to bribe (probability of giving a bribe when encountering corruption) (%)	86.0	68.9	69.3
Average bribe amount, rubles	896	920	2445
Average bribe amount, rubles (adjusted to the prices of 2001 taking into account inflation)	896	559	912
Volume of corruption market (lower estimate of the annual income from bribes received by traffic police), million rubles	11 051	7835	24 436
Volume of corruption market (lower estimate of the annual income from bribes received by traffic police), million rubles (adjusted to the prices of 2001 taking into account inflation)	11 051	4761	9115

9 Satarov (2013).

total market of corruption at the household level expanded. We can easily find the cause for the decrease: Russian drivers became 20 percent less inclined to give bribes. They had two reasons. One was institutional: during the period in question, Russia developed magistrate courts and many drivers chose to settle their arguments with the traffic police in court. The other reason was social and psychological: most often, the people who refused to give bribes had a well-formed anti-corruption attitude. We can further see that between 2005 and 2010, the traffic police's annual income from corruption increased by 48 percent (in constant prices, adjusted for inflation). During the same period, the total volume of everyday corruption (in constant prices) declined. The leap of the traffic police's income from corruption was due to several rounds of amending the traffic rules and the Administrative Violations Code. The amendments included harsher requirements for drivers, higher fines for traffic violations, and hard and fast administrative penalties. For instance, the new regulations introduced the 'zero percent' rule: the level of alcohol in the driver's blood was not to exceed zero. If a blood test revealed a level of alcohol above zero, the driver was severely penalized for driving under the influence. This and other regulations became a reliable source of corruption-related income.

The traffic police example shows that administrative rent extraction may decrease if citizens can resist. Second, this example illustrates our earlier observation on how politically assigned rent in modern Russia is transformed to administratively extracted rent. When the officials of the traffic police were lobbying for the corrupt income sources, they received full support from the legislative organ that is supposed to defend the voters' interests. This is another indication of the presence of systematic rent seeking in Russia.

20.4 RENTS IN A PRIVATE MARKET: DOCTORAL DISSERTATIONS

An interesting and unusual market for corruption-related services is the private market for doctoral dissertations (Kalimullin 2006; Osipian 2009, 2012). In Russia, in order to obtain an academic degree, one has to go through a multiple stage procedure that takes several years to complete and involves the following steps: prepare the dissertation; have it publicly discussed in a small group of experts; defend it in the so-called PhD or Doctorate Degree Awarding Council,[10] which exists in every university or research center; then finally, have it approved by the Higher Attestation Committee at the Ministry for Education and Research.[11]

Defending a dissertation and obtaining an academic degree is more of a socializing factor than anything else. In other words, having a dissertation plays a secondary role in academia, but those who have a PhD or a doctoral degree can build better careers and obtain symbolic power and thus are better socialized. Traditionally, in the Soviet Union, degree-holders would receive additional respect; a dissertation would improve their

[10] With the rarest of exceptions, one needs to be awarded the PhD degree before proceeding to apply for the higher doctoral degree.

[11] This stage is a relic of Soviet times and stems from governmental control over research and development.

image not only among students, teachers and fellow researchers but also among government and Party officials. Having an academic degree presents advantages in the labor market not only in the areas of education and research, as prescribed by relevant regulations, but also in the administrative area, outside of higher education. Therefore, among those who opt to buy a dissertation are politicians, governmental officials (bureaucrats), general officers (for instance, officials of the Interior Ministry), businessmen and top managers, and members of academia aspiring to a scientific career. Having an academic degree is associated with rents and having a dissertation has become a fashionable accessory among businessmen and officials in modern Russia. A degree is a symbol of success that can be converted not only into prestige but also into financial benefits when degree-holders receive the most wanted positions, and when they participate in a corruption market. Dissertations have been bought and sold before, both in Soviet Russia and in Russia before the revolution. However, in the early 1990s, dissertations literally became a commodity sold in a market, even if a somewhat unusual and closed market.

Russia has a vast market that creates and sells dissertation texts to interested applicants. As a rule, dissertations are custom-made to suit the needs of specific customers. Frequently, the customer buys not only the research paper itself but also its favorable reception at all bureaucratic stages described above: the review by university experts, the approval by degree-awarding council, and the final approval by the Higher Attestation Committee. While in the Soviet Union writing dissertations was a shadow area of individual services, in today's Russia it has been taken on by well-organized firms, although individual services are also available on the market.

Depending on the discipline and geographical location (provincial town or big city), the cost of a degree varies from USD $500 to $10,000. Naturally, the price depends on the degree and the package (the research paper and its full support throughout the process cost more than the paper alone). There are rent-earning opportunities in the position of the 'research supervisor', who in principle is supposed to guide the student throughout the research process. The roles of opponents and reviewers also offer rents. Formally, reviewers receive a small remuneration for their services from the government, but frequently they also receive a payment or bribe from the applicant.

At the next level of the process is the degree-awarding council. Its activities are public but, nevertheless, members of some councils receive bribes from the applicant who pays in order to receive the necessary approvals. The final stage of the dissertation being approved at the Higher Attestation Committee is the peak of the corrupt chain. Both officials and the members of the committee (we do not say necessarily all of them) participate in well-paid corrupt activities.

Experience shows that the risk of a penalty is rather low for those who participate in such corrupt activities. Numerous attempts both at the governmental and legislative levels to reform the system of awarding academic degrees have been unsuccessful. However, the authorities did arrest a top official of the Higher Attestation Committee and broke up several degree-awarding councils.

A phenomenon in Russia is the 'Dissergate' movement: a public initiative that uses specialized computer software to reveal plagiarism in dissertations. Dissergate caused several resonant scandals by revealing the illegitimacy of PhD and doctoral degrees of state Duma deputies and top executive officials. Interestingly, the law-enforcement and overseeing organizations did not confront the holders of fake degrees. Judging by the public reaction, we could expect that the flow of plagiaristic dissertations will decrease, but at the same time, the cost of purchasing a dissertation will increase, as will the 'customers' quality requirements. This reflects the dark side of the public hunt for fake dissertations. In reality, plagiarism in the officials' dissertations is just the top of the iceberg: the problem of fake degrees is much deeper. Hundreds of firms offer diplomas and dissertations on demand, and for a price they will write a flawless paper that no software will identify as fake. Dissergate, started by a team of enthusiasts, has accelerated the progress of markets offering fake diplomas and dissertations: quality requirements are now higher, as is the price of dissertations.

20.5 MONOPOLY RENTS

We now return to the Muscovite model that we mentioned at the beginning of the chapter. This model is linked to the era of Ivan the Terrible, the Great Prince and Tsar of All Russia (1533–1584).[12] During the rule of the first Russian tsar, Muscovy started its expansion east and southeast: it conquered and acquired the territories of Kazan and Astrakhan, Bashkiria and Western Siberia. The development of the Muscovite model, which included the system of government based on rent granting, had begun even earlier, under the colonial influence of the Chingisids.[13] During the rule of Ivan the Terrible, the Muscovite model strengthened due to Russia's territorial growth, which made land (the territory with its natural resources) the main source of income, while the developing absolute centralized authority gave rise to the rent-granting system. The constant expansion of territory allowed centralized authorities to use land (together with the serfs assigned to that land) as the basic source of income from rent, which could be distributed in exchange for service.

The extreme centralization of power was also manifested in the economic sphere. The politics of Peter I created influential state monopolies, and included vast dirigisme outside these monopolies. Because the Russian government strongly influenced the economy, and because Russia was falling behind Europe and the USA in developing a competitive market, the monopolies were preserved in Russia up to the beginning of the Bolshevik era. In the early twentieth century, many industries in Russia were controlled by enormous trusts, syndicates and corporations that held 70 to 100 percent of various markets: iron, copper, mirrors, railway carriages, steam engines, agricultural devices and machines, cloth, linen, tobacco and so on. In the early twentieth century, the USA began implementing anti-monopoly or antitrust laws. Perhaps ten or twenty years later, this trend could have reached Russia too, but, in 1917, the Bolsheviks seized power in the country and state monopoly became the foundation of the central planned economy. As a result, Russia was left out of the global anti-monopoly trend that was typical of the market economy of the twentieth century. Thus, when in 1991, at the beginning of market reforms, Russia ratified its first anti-monopoly law, 'On competi-

---

[12] This period approximately corresponds to the British era of Elizabeth I (1558–1603), whose hand Ivan the Terrible asked for.

[13] See, for instance, Vernadsky (2011).

tion and limitation of monopolies in commodity markets', it was a mere legal formality. The monopoly of the Soviet authorities had been so all-encompassing that nobody noticed it, and the negative impacts of monopolies in the new market economy had not had time to develop and convince the public that anti-monopoly efforts were, in fact, necessary and good.

Up to 2003, the anti-monopoly legislation was beneficial for certain fast-growing markets, such as the market for mobile communication, but only because such markets had enough space for multiple players. In the markets for primary commodities, the anti-monopoly legislation made little difference, because prices for carbohydrates were low and diminished incentives to fight for a monopoly. This situation began to change due to several factors. Two have been described above: they were the abrupt expansion of political and administrative rents. The third factor was the increasing price of oil.

20.6 NATURAL-RESOURCE RENTS

World oil prices between 1986 and 2005 are shown in Figure 20.1. Oil prices hit a low point in 1998, and in August of that year Russia defaulted on its debt. Subsequently prices began to increase, and by 2004 this increase had become a major influence on the Russian economy and the politics of the Russian authorities (Gaidar 2006).

Consider the following chain of events, which are not a coincidence: the arrest of Mikhail Khodorkovsky, owner of Russia's most efficient oil company, YUKOS, in October 2003; the sentencing of Khodorkovsky and his business partner Lebedev to nine years in prison on 31 May 2005; the bankruptcy of YUKOS on 28 March 2006; the repurchase of YUKOS' assets by the Russian president's friends. The arrest, investigation and

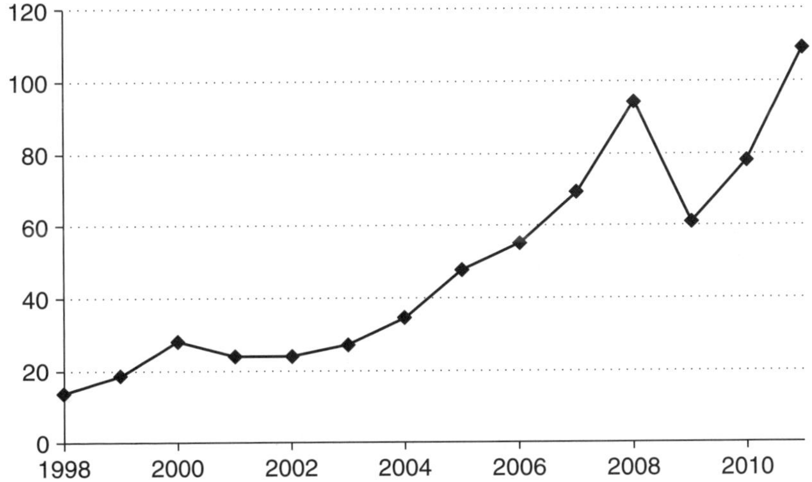

Source: International Financial Statistics (2004) and IMF, quoted in Gaidar (2006).

Figure 20.1 The dynamics of the world oil prices in 1986–2005 (in USD per barrel) deflated by the prices of 2000

sentencing of YUKOS' top managers in the manner that they were carried out became possible due to the merger of political and administrative rent described above. The fate of the company, and the way its assets wound up in the 'reliable hands' of the 'right people', was also facilitated by that merger, as well as by fast-growing oil prices, which made control over natural-resource rents especially desirable.[14] Khodorkovsky's arrest was closely connected with the defense of the newly established symbiosis of political and administrative rents. Oil was not initially a decisive factor. However, during the investigation and the court procedures, the price of oil increased substantially. As a result, the looting of YUKOS' oil assets in 2006 was a direct act of appropriating the sources of oil rent.

The YUKOS case was a turning point, signifying that the Russian authorities had turned to active extraction of political and administrative rents. First, the reassignment of ownership of YUKOS signaled to officials of all levels of authority that it was safe for members of the ruling coalition to seize other people's property. Second, the federal authorities in Russia began actively expanding their control over oil rents. This was manifested in particular in how the tax revenue from natural resources was distributed between regional and federal authorities. Let us consider this topic more closely.

According to the Russian Constitution, the use of natural resources, as well as the assignment of natural-resource rents, should be managed jointly by federal and regional authorities. To exercise such joint management, the federal government and the executive local authorities should enter into agreements on 'delimitation of matters of authority.' Such agreements were primarily signed with regions possessing vast natural resources; they prescribed approved proportions of distribution of income from natural-resource rents. The federal government would invariably receive the larger share. When in the early 2000s oil prices began to increase, federal authorities decided to use delimitation agreements in order to tighten control over natural resources, at the expense of the regions' interests. The share of the federal authorities' income from rents grew and in 2005 this share was nearing 100 percent. These trends can be seen in Table 20.2.

The increasing oil price (see Figure 20.1) was changing the structure of GDP and the budget in a similar manner. The next illustration presents the dynamics of the share of

Table 20.2 The dynamics of share of income from rent (percent) in the oil industry received by the federal budget between 2000 and 2004

Year	2000	2001	2002	2003	2004
Income share (%)	86	82	89	90	94

Source: Calculations were made by Gurvich (2010), who kindly permitted their use for this chapter.

14 YUKOS' main asset, Yuganskneftegaz company, ended up in the hands of Baikalfinansgroup, a company that suddenly emerged from nowhere and vanished again once it resold the prey to the state-owned Rosneft company.

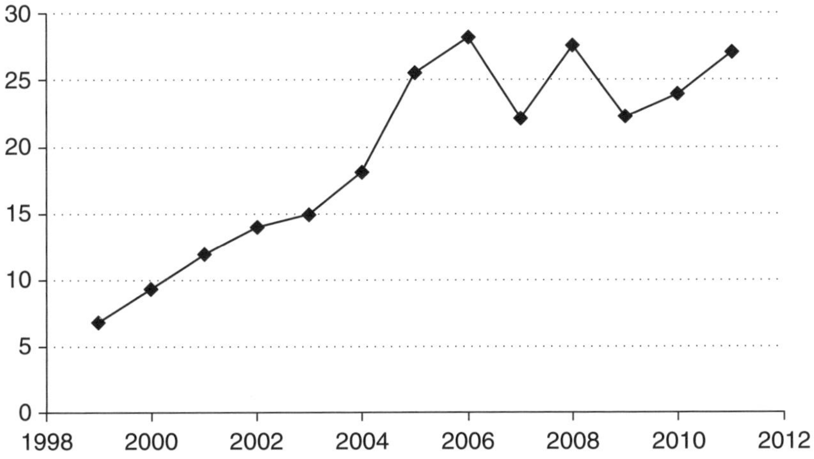

Figure 20.2 The dynamics of share of income from rent in the budget (percent)

income from natural-resource rents in the government budget until 2011. Between 1999 and 2011, this share increased by four times; afterwards, it continued growing.

The growth of income from natural-resource rents per se is less important for rent seeking and rent extraction than its distribution. In 1999 and 2000 Russia did not have any dollar billionaires[15] (in 1997 it had four, but after the default and crisis of 1998 they vanished from the list). In 2008 Russia had a hundred billionaires. The crisis that followed slashed this number to a third, but the number recovered fast, and, by 2014, the poorest Russian billionaire was ranked 111th on the Forbes list of the world's richest people.[16]

For comparison, let us look at Figure 20.4, which shows how GDP changed during the same period.[17] We can see the same dip in the crisis year of 2009 as in Figure 20.2. However, if the number of billionaires went on to recover and even increase, the growth of the economy not only failed to reach the pre-crisis level but kept falling lower and lower.

The statistics on Russian billionaires in Figure 20.3 are supplemented by curious facts in Russian Forbes,[18] which quotes Global Wealth Reports for 2012–13, developed by researchers at Credit Suisse. The report names Russia as having the largest concentration of wealth of billionaires in the world, except for several minuscule states in the Caribbean. On average, there is one dollar billionaire in the world per USD $170 billion

---

[15] The data comes from the Russian edition of *Forbes Magazine*, Mikhail Kozyrev's article dated 12 March 2010, see http://www.forbes.ru/ekonomika/lyudi/46228-russkie-v-spiske-forbes-ot-eltsina-do-medvedeva/slide/1 (accessed 10 July 2014).

[16] http://www.forbes.ru/rating/200-bogateishikh-biznesmenov-rossii-2014/2014 (accessed 10 July 2014).

[17] http://www.ereport.ru/stat.php?razdel=country&count=russia&table=ggecia (accessed 10 July 2014).

[18] 'Russia takes the world lead in income inequality', 10 October 2013, http://www.forbes.ru/news/246002-rossiya-lidiruet-v-mire-po-urovnyu-imushchestvennogo-neravenstva.

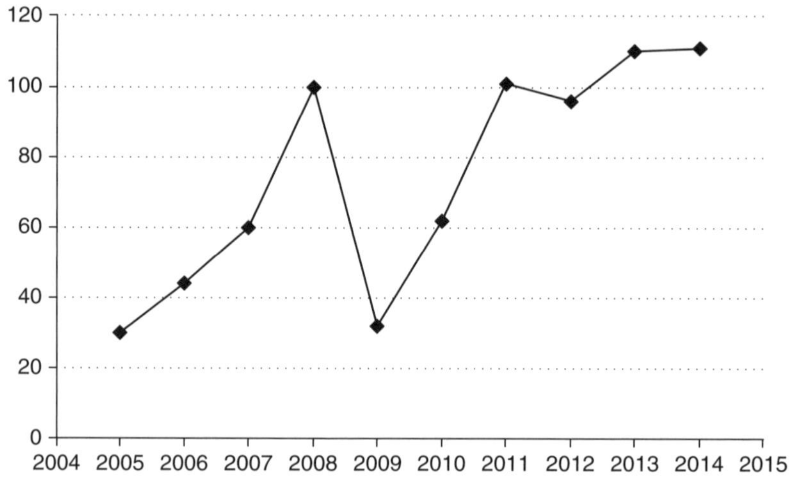

Figure 20.3 The number of US dollar billionaires in Russia as reported by Forbes Magazine *between 2004 and 2015*

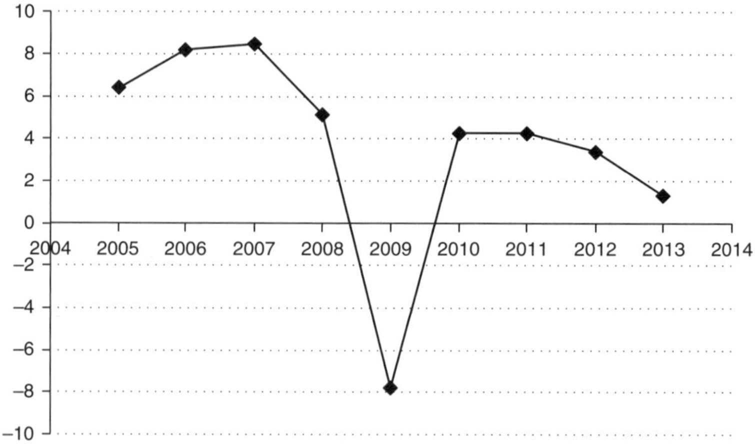

Figure 20.4 Change in GDP in Russia between 2005 and 2013

of global wealth. In Russia there is one billionaire per only USD $11 billion. While in the global economy the total wealth of all billionaires amounts to some 1–2 percent of the global wealth, in Russia 110 billionaires jointly own 35 percent of the country's wealth.

We do not observe the process underlying this concentration of wealth. The theory of rent seeking suggests that contests have taken place. Competition in the contests was however limited by political monopoly and outcomes were determined by asymmetric political power.

20.7 RENT DIVERSIFICATION

By 2007, the authorities had divided and gained control over the oil and gas market. Two corporations were sources of rents: Rosneft and Gazprom.[19] At the same time, the ruling coalition was seeking new rent sources. In 2007, the authorities established several state corporations that in principle assisted the development of various industries, but in fact were mechanisms for gaining control over independent firms and for receiving state funding. Legally, state corporations are considered non-governmental organizations (NGOs). Because of that, state supervisory agencies have only limited control over them. The NGOs manage enormous funds, which makes them a tool for extraction and distribution of rents. In particular, losses are income transfers or in themselves rents. Consider the following examples.

In July 2007, the government established the state-owned corporation Russian Nanotechnologies. The organization's aim was to implement governmental policy in nanotechnology, to assist the development of innovative projects in the industry and invest state funds into the most promising projects. In order to reach these goals, the corporation received 130 billion rubles of budgetary funds for its charter capital. In 2011 the corporation reorganized and became the open joint-stock company RUSNANO, revealed to be a monopoly in the nanotechnology sector. In 2013 RUSNANO reported more than a billion dollars in losses.

In November 2007, the government established Rostec Corporation in order to further the development, manufacture and export of high-tech industrial products. At the government's order, Rostec incorporated hundreds of defense and civil industry firms. In early 2009, it became known that the corporation's enterprises owed more than 625 billion rubles in debts and that one third of the enterprises were displaying signs of bankruptcy. Resolving these problems was expensive for the state budget. After seven years of operations, Rostec had not managed to shift the commodity-oriented focus of the Russian economy, and has not influenced the export structure.

All of this allows for a clear conclusion: the symbiosis between political and administrative rent extraction underlies extraction and distribution of other kinds of rent. It increases the wealth of the ruling coalition members, who control access to all kinds of rents. Since the early 2000s, Russia's political and institutional model has been changing, bringing it back to the Muscovite model.

20.8 CONCLUSION

In their book on *Violence and Social Orders*, North et al. (2009) present a list of 'natural states', in which Putin's Russia stands right next to the Tudors' England. We can point out one more connection between these two states: the Tudor period in England coincided with the Russian period of Vasily III and his son, Ivan the Terrible, which was the epoch that shaped the Muscovite model. There is yet another coincidence: the political

[19] Both had significant debts. In 2013, Gazprom's debts in short-term and long-term credits surpassed one trillion rubles, while Rosneft's debt was nearing two trillion rubles.

dimension of the Muscovite model is based on centralized distribution of rent among the members of the ruling coalition. The natural state as understood by North and colleagues is a social order of limited access that extracts rent and then distributes the rents among the members of the ruling coalition. We have demonstrated that the political regime of Putin's Russia does just that: it appropriates rents and distributes the rents among the members of the ruling coalition. However, these coincidences only concern Putin's Russia and Ivan the Terrible's Russia, while Tudor England has nothing to do with either of them. A major source of rent in England of that time was Spanish gold, which the British corsairs seized in the Atlantic. However, in order to take part in the distribution of this rent, Elizabeth I had to become a shareholder in Francis Drake's pirate expeditions.

Russia's example does not prove that natural-resource rents necessarily lead to degradation of democracy. In Russia's case, the consequences have been especially grim, because a main aim of the ruling coalition has been to preserve a political-monopoly status quo. In order to reach this aim, the authorities had to destroy constitutional institutions of the state and violate civil and political rights and freedom. In particular, the merger of political and administrative rents allowed the authorities to diminish and make virtually extinct independent media, freedom of the press, political competition, free entrepreneurship, federalism, independent local government, division of powers and independent courts. When the critical moment of rent temptation arose in 2003–05, several factors combined to make Russia take the path of institutional degradation bordering on collapse of the institutions of democracy. These factors were: historical tradition, including the 70 years under Soviet rule; weakness of the civil society; and corruptible and corrupted elites.

Below the political control of rents is a culture of corruption and rent seeking that affects ordinary citizens. We have used as illustrations land required by entrepreneurs and bribes to the traffic police. Most worryingly, a meritocracy is inconsistent with the corruption and rent seeking exhibited in the market for academic degrees. 'Experts' are not experts at all and cynicism reaches its highest level, with successful rent seeking having replaced competence in recognition of achievement.

REFERENCES

Anderson, Gary M. and Peter J. Boettke (1997), 'Soviet venality: a rent-seeking model of the Communist State', *Public Choice*, **93**(1–2), 37–53.

Appelbaum, Elie and Eliakim Katz (1987), 'Seeking rents by setting rents: the political economy of rent seeking', *Economic Journal*, **97**(387), 685–99, reprinted in Roger D. Congleton, Arye L. Hillman and Kai A. Konrad (eds) (2008), *40 Years of Research on Rent Seeking 1 – The Theory of Rent Seeking*, Heidelberg: Springer, pp. 555–69.

Barsukova, Svetlana (2011, in Russian), 'The resource economy and social class rents: the approach of S. Kordonsky', *Ekonomicheskaya Sociologiya*, **12**(4), 40–56.

Benassy, Jean-Pascal (1986), *Macroeconomics: An Introduction to the Non-Walrasian Approach*, New York: Academic Press.

Buchanan, James M. (1980), 'Rent seeking and profit seeking', in James M. Buchanan, Robert D. Tollison and Gordon Tullock (eds), *Toward a Theory of the Rent-seeking Society*, College Station, TX: Texas A&M University Press, pp. 3–15, reprinted in Roger D. Congleton, Arye L. Hillman and Kai A. Konrad (eds) (2008), *40 Years of Research on Rent Seeking 1 – The Theory of Rent Seeking*, Heidelberg: Springer, pp. 55–67.

Congleton, Roger D., Arye L. Hillman and Kai A. Konrad (2008), '40 years of research on rent seeking: an overview', in Roger D. Congleton, Arye L. Hillman and Kai A. Konrad (eds), *40 Years of Research on Rent Seeking 1 and 2*, Heidelberg: Springer, pp. 1–44.

Gaddy, Clifford G. and Barry W. Ickes (2002), *Russia's Virtual Economy*, Washington, DC: Brookings Institution Press.

Gaddy, Clifford and Barry Ickes (2005), 'Resource rents and the Russian economy', *Eurasian Geography and Economics*, **46**(8), 559–83.

Gaidar, E.T. (2006), 'Fall of the empire. Lessons for modern Russia', *Russian Political Encyclopedia*, Moscow, p. 448.

Gelb, Alan, Arye L. Hillman and Heinrich W. Ursprung (1998), 'Rents as distractions: why the exit from transition is prolonged', in Nicolas C. Baltas, George Demopoulos and Joseph Hassid (eds), *Economic Interdependence and Cooperation in Europe*, Heidelberg: Springer, pp. 21–38.

Gurvich, Evsey (2010), 'Natural-resource rent in the Russian oil and gas sector', *Voprosy ekonomiki*, **11**, 4–24.

Hedlund, Stefan (2006), 'Vladimir the Great, Grand Prince of Muscovy: resurrecting the Russian service state', *Europe-Asia Studies*, **58**(5), 775–801.

Hellman, Joel S., Geraint Jones and Daniel Kaufmann (2003), 'Seize the state, seize the day: state capture and influence in transition economies', *Journal of Comparative Economics*, **31**(4), 751–73.

Hillman, Arye L. (1994), 'The transition from socialism: an overview from a political-economy perspective', *European Journal of Political Economy*, **10**(1), 191–225, Special issue, Festschrift in honor of Peter Bernholz, ed. Manfred Gärtner and Heinrich W. Ursprung.

Hillman, Arye L. (2002, in Russian), 'On the way to the promised land: ten years in the wilderness without Moses', *Economics and Mathematical Methods – Journal of the Central Economic and Mathematical Institute of the Russian Academy of Sciences*, **38**(1), 78–94.

Hillman, Arye L. (2009), *Public Finance and Public Policy: Responsibilities and Limitations of Government*, 2nd edn, New York: Cambridge University Press, Russian edn 2009 Publishing House, Higher School of Economics, Moscow.

Hillman, Arye L. (2013), 'Rent seeking', in Michael Reksulak, Laura Razzolini and William F. Shughart II (eds), *The Elgar Companion to Public Choice*, 2nd edn, Cheltenham, UK and Northampton, MA, USA: Edward Elgar Publishing, pp. 307–30.

Hillman, Arye L. and Eliakim Katz (1987), 'Hierarchical structure and the social costs of bribes and transfers', *Journal of Public Economics*, **34**(2), 129–42, reprinted in Roger D. Congleton, Arye L. Hillman and Kai A. Konrad (eds) (2008), *40 Years of Research on Rent Seeking 1 – The Theory of Rent Seeking*, Heidelberg: Springer, pp. 523–36.

Hillman, Arye L. and Adi Schnytzer (1986), 'Illegal economic activities and purges in a Soviet-style economy: a rent seeking perspective', *International Review of Law and Economics*, **6**(1), 87–99, reprinted in Roger D. Congleton, Arye L. Hillman and Kai A. Konrad (eds) (2008), *40 Years of Research on Rent Seeking 2 – Applications: Rent Seeking in Practice*, Heidelberg: Springer, pp. 545–57.

Kalimullin, Tagir R. (2006, in Russian), 'The Russian market for dissertation services', Preprint WP4/2006/02, Higher School of Economics, Moscow.

Kordonsky, Simon (2006, in Russian), *Administrative Markets of the USSR and Russia*, Moscow: OGI.

Kordonsky, Simon (2008), *Social Class Structure of Post-Soviet Russia*, Moscow: Public Opinion Foundation.

Kornai, Janos (1980a), *Economics of Shortage*, Amsterdam: North-Holland.

Kornai, Janos (1980b), 'Hard and soft budget constraint', *Acta Oeconomica*, **25**(3–4), 231–46, reprinted in Roger D. Congleton, Arye L. Hillman and Kai A. Konrad (eds) (2008), *40 Years of Research on Rent Seeking 2 – Applications: Rent Seeking in Practice*, Heidelberg: Springer, pp. 569–83.

Kotilaine, Jarmo T. (2004), *A Muscovite Economic Model*, Washington, DC: National Council for Eurasian and East European Research.

Ledeneva, Alena V. (1998), *Russia's Economy of Favours: Blat, Networking and Informal Exchange*, Cambridge: Cambridge University Press.

Levin, Mark I. and Georgy A. Satarov (2000), 'Corruption and institutions in Russia', *European Journal of Political Economy*, **16**(1), 113–32.

Levin Mark I. and Georgy A. Satarov (2013), 'Russian corruption', in Michael V. Alexeev and Shlomo Weber (eds), *The Oxford Handbook of the Russian Economy*, Oxford: Oxford University Press, pp. 286–309.

Magomedov, A. and R. Nikerov (2010), 'Russian oil and rent seeking: towards understanding the nature of political incentives of the Russian authorities', *Izvestija Saratovskogo Universiteta*, new series, **10**(1), 105–8.

Makarov, Valeriĭ L., Mark I. Levin and Aleksandr M. Rubinov (1995), *Mathematical Economic Theory: Pure and Mixed Types of Economic Mechanisms* (Advanced Textbooks in Economics), Amsterdam: North-Holland.

Milovan, Djilas (1957), *The New Class: An Analysis of the Communist System*, New York: Praeger.

North, Douglass C., John Joseph Wallis and Barry R. Weingast (2009), *Violence and Social Orders: A Conceptual Framework for Interpreting Recorded Human History*, Cambridge: Cambridge University Press.
Osipian, Ararat L. (2009), 'Corruption hierarchies in higher education in the former Soviet bloc', *International Journal of Educational Development*, **29**(3), 321–30.
Osipian, Ararat L. (2012), 'Economics of corruption in doctoral education: the dissertations market', *Economics of Education Review*, **31**(1), 76–83.
Qian, Yingyi and Gerard Roland (1998), 'Federalism and the soft budget constraint', *American Economic Review*, **88**(5), 1143–62.
Rimsky, Vladimir L. (2007, in Russian), 'Bureaucracy, clientelism and corruption in Russia', *Politia*, **44**(1), 65–84.
Rosefielde, Steven (2005), 'Illusion of transition: Russia's Muscovite future', *Eastern Economic Journal*, **31**(2), 285–99.
Satarov, Georgy A. (ed.) (2013, in Russian), *Russian Corruption: Level, Structure, Dynamics: An Exercise in Sociological Analysis*, Moscow: Liberal Mission Fund.
Tomofeyev, Lev M. (2000, in Russian), *Institutional Corruption: Essays on the Theory*, Moscow: RSUH.
Tullock, Gordon (1989), *The Economics of Special Privilege and Rent Seeking*, Dordrecht: Kluwer Academic Publishers.
Vernadsky, George V. (2011), *Mongolians and Russia*, Moscow: Lomonosov.
Voslensky, Michael (1984), *Nomenklatura: Anatomy of the Soviet Ruling Class*, London: The Bodley Head Ltd.
Zaostrovtsev, Andrei (2008), 'Oil, rent seeking, and property rights (overview of the conceptions)', in N. Dobronravin and O. Margania (eds), *Oil, Gas and Modernization*, SPb: Economic School, HSE, pp. 3–30.
Zaostrovtsev, Andrei (2014, in Russian), 'The concept of "rent extraction": economic theory of political extortion and Russian practice', *Izvestija Sankt-Peterburgskogo universiteta ekonomiki i finansov*, **3**, 48–63.

21. Rents and development failure in Africa

John Mukum Mbaku and Mwangi S. Kimenyi

SUMMARY

This chapter describes rents and rent seeking in Africa. No description of Africa can be complete without reference to the centrality and pervasiveness of rent seeking and rent extraction. Although there are differences among the many countries, as a general principle, politicians and civil servants have used rent-creating and rent-extracting opportunities to their personal advantage whenever possible. In apartheid South Africa, rent seeking took the form of legislation. In particular under authoritarian regimes but also where there have been elements of democracy, rent seeking has involved rent extraction through corruption. The successful rent-seeking and rent-extracting military and ethnic or tribal groups have marginalized other groups, often resulting in violence. Rent seeking has created incentives for skilled people to forgo their professions to seek rent-extracting positions in government. Business has been in the hands of adept rent seekers rather than necessarily competent businessmen and women.

21.1 INTRODUCTION

Political culture (Hillman and Swank 2000), institutions (Congleton 1980 [2008]) and also whether the rule of law prevails to protect the weak from the strong (Hillman 2004) determine the scope of rent seeking. In Africa, which is the focus of this chapter, the political culture allows use of government for personal benefit. Institutions have facilitated rather than constrained rent seeking and rent creation. Laws and institutions have not protected the weak from the strong who control government and, more particularly, the military. Because of rents, talented skilled people have not made effective use of their comparative advantage and their educational qualifications, but have sought positions in government that allow rent seeking and rent extraction.[1]

In Africa, rent seeking is intertwined with corruption or the use of public office for

[1] A rent is a privileged benefit. Resources used in seeking rents are used in a socially unproductive way, although there are private benefits for successful rent seekers. Rent seeking was noted as a source of social loss by Gordon Tullock (1967 [2008]). Anne Krueger (1974 [2008]) introduced the term in the course of estimating losses from rent seeking in India and Turkey. Rent seeking often involves corruption and bribes. A bribe is a transfer of income without necessary efficiency loss but rent seeking occurs when bribes are contested with the objective of obtaining the political or bureaucratic position at which the bribes are received (Buchanan 1980a; Hillman and Katz 1987 [2008]). Socially unproductive rent seeking is distinguished from socially productive profit seeking (Buchanan 1980a; Kimenyi and Tollison 1999). For surveys of the literature on rent seeking, see Congleton et al. (2008a), Hillman (2013) and Long (2013). Early surveys include Tollison (1982) and Nitzan (1994). The original influential collection of papers was Buchanan et al. (1980). Papers

personal benefit. As Aidt (2003) notes, in the absence of rents to be extracted, there is no basis for corruption. In developed democracies, rent seeking need not entail corruption. Political decision makers may be permitted to create and assign rents with legal bounds of political discretion. In Africa, however, endemic corruption and endemic rent seeking and rent extraction go hand in hand.

The chapter is organized as follows. Section 21.2 introduces the methods of rent creation through government in Africa. Section 21.3 sets out general principles underlying African rent-seeking societies. Section 21.4 describes how rent seeking results in income transfers. Section 21.5 points out the impediments to economic development due to rent extraction and rent seeking. Section 21.6 relates the focus on rents to institutions of governance. Conclusions are in the final section.

21.2 RENT CREATION THROUGH GOVERNMENT

21.2.1 Monopoly

In Africa, rents have been created through government-sponsored monopoly power (Rowley 1999, pp. 223–5). Authoritarian government, common in Africa (Rowley 2000), makes monopoly privileges easier to achieve. It may be sufficient to persuade only the authoritarian ruler to create and assign rents. In a democracy, there are more decision makers to persuade.

21.2.2 Regulation and Bureaucracy

Rents are also associated with regulation and bureaucracy. When entrepreneurs engage in trade, they face three types of costs, namely, (1) identification costs; (2) negotiation costs; and (3) enforcement costs. The costs of searching and securing prospective trading partners are identification costs. After an entrepreneur has identified a trading partner, the parties engage in negotiation to agree on the terms of exchange, involving negotiation costs. Once the terms of exchange have been established, the parties need to agree on an enforcement mechanism that can effectively minimize or prevent post-contractual opportunism and hence there are enforcement costs (Mbaku 2004, p. 125). The cost of exchange includes government regulations. If a government requires business enterprises to keep detailed written records of each transaction, the costs of transacting can be substantial or prohibitive. Civil servants are responsible for enforcing the government regulations and can engage in activities that increase transaction costs faced by private business. An opportunistic civil servant can raise the costs of engaging in exchange by intentionally delaying the approval of projects; the issuance of business, export, import and other types of licenses; and the performance of other services critical to the functioning of enterprises. In African countries, it is common for civil servants to demand bribes from firms seeking approval for business

on rent seeking in the 40 years since Tullock's insight are collected in Congleton et al. (2008b, 2008c).

and investment projects. These rent-extracting activities increase the costs of doing business even before entrepreneurs can seek out and identify partners for eventual exchange.

21.2.3 Economic Policies

Rents are created by economic policies. A case study reveals the general principles of rent creation through economic policies. Shortly after independence from Great Britain in 1957, the Kwame Nkrumah government in Ghana implemented an import-substitution industrialization (ISI) program announced as intended to promote rapid economic growth and provide resources for poverty alleviation. The ISI program was to be anchored on a number of policy instruments, which included (a) the protection of domestic firms through import taxes, exchange rate controls and import quotas; (b) the granting of generous subsidies to foreign firms to establish subsidiaries in Ghana; and (c) the creation of development and investment banks that would grant low-cost or subsidized loans to businesses willing to invest in parts of the economy determined by the government as 'priority development sectors' (Mbaku 2004, pp. 131–2; see also Leith 1974; LeVine 1975). The Nkrumah government also created several parastatals or state-owned enterprises to produce a variety of goods and services. Civil servants, whose job it was to implement the ISI program, used the program to create and extract rents for themselves. Leith (1974, p. 25) observed how the regulatory system, which had been designed to 'meet the apparent national needs and to minimize capricious discrimination among importers, was frequently set aside in favor of Mr. Djin and his associates.' Mr. A.Y.K. Djin was at the time the trade minister. Two important instruments of the ISI program, foreign exchange rationing and import licensing systems, became important for rent creation and rent seeking.

When Mr. Djin was replaced as trade minister by Mr. Kwesi Armah, the regulatory system, as well as its rent-creating potential, remained intact. Shortly after taking office, Mr. Armah began to engage in the same or similar opportunistic activities that had characterized Mr. Djin's tenure in office. He developed and implemented a system that allowed him to benefit personally from all licenses issued by the trade ministry. As stated by a commission of inquiry that investigated rent seeking and corruption during the Nkrumah government,

> He [Mr. Armah] introduced the system whereby all applications for import licenses had to be addressed to him personally under registered cover and he alone was responsible for processing the said applications . . . [T]here was open corruption and malpractices in the matter of grant of import licenses during this period. Import licenses were issued on the basis of a commission corruptly demanded and payable by importers on the face value of the import licenses issued. The commission was fixed at 15 percent, but was in special cases reduced to 7.5 or 5 percent. (Leith 1974, p. 26)

As part of the ISI program, domestic producers lobbied and cajoled the government into imposing tariffs on imported goods. The persons or firms that were granted import licenses were also able to extract rents from consumers (represented by the Tullock rectangle). At the time at which the ISI program was implemented, exchange rate regulation had created a shortage of foreign exchange. The government's solution was to undertake a rationing program. The latter and the import licensing system were sources of rent-creating and rent-seeking opportunities under Nkrumah (see Werlin 1972, 1973; LeVine 1975). Quantitative restrictions on imports, coupled with exchange rate controls, created a parallel market from which significant rents could be extracted. Additionally, restrictive foreign trade policies (foreign exchange controls, high tariff rates, quantitative restrictions on some imports and other non-tariff barriers to trade) created a lucrative 'black market' for imported goods and foreign exchange.[2]

21.2.4 Rent-seeking Ethos

Zaire (now Democratic Republic of Congo – DRC) under Mobutu Sese Seko, who ruled from 1965 to 1997, illustrates a rent-seeking ethos. The ruler personally benefitted.[3] Rent seeking and rent creation were however behavioral principles for the entire population. Opportunities for rent seeking created through Mobutu's regulatory system included: (1) military officers regularly supplemented their compensation packages by 'over-invoicing' – requesting more resources than was justified by the number of troops under their command and illegally appropriating the additional resources for their own personal use; (2) domestic importers exploited the artificial scarcities created by the government to extract rents for themselves and their benefactors; and (3) domestic contractors, protected from competition by government regulations, engaged in over-invoicing, and padded their expense accounts and pay vouchers, in order to illegally enrich themselves from their work on public projects.

In their study of Mobutu's Zaire, Gould and Mukendi (1989, pp. 429–30) concluded that 'the whole bureaucratic structure [had] been converted into an instrument of self-advancement and enrichment by top officials.' They also noted that Mobutu was quite unmoved by or perhaps content with diversion of 'supplies intended for frontline soldiers' for the use of their officers; the 'misuse of judicial machinery for avenging private disputes, selective justice depending on one's wealth and status, smuggling of some exportable products such as coffee and diamonds and the non-repatriation of profits made on them, monthly salary payments to fictitious public officials and teachers, and massive evasion of import duties (by firms which have ties with the ruling elites), etc.'

---

[2] On the means by which individuals and interest groups expend resources to influence governments to create rents and then compete to capture the rents, see Tullock (1993). Kimenyi and Tollison (1999, p. 29) provide a typology of the various forms of government regulation that create opportunities for individuals and groups to compete to capture rents.

[3] Information provided by Transparency International (2004, p. 13) indicates that during his term in power, Mobutu extracted as much as US $5 billion from the country's economy and this, in a very poor country (see Gould 1980; MacGaffey 1983; Gould and Mukendi 1989; World Bank 2014).

21.3 PRINCIPLES

21.3.1 The State and Property Rights

If property rights are secure, there is no rent seeking. Rent seeking can occur when the state controls property rights (Mbaku 1991a) and can assign and transfer rights (Benson 1984, p. 396).[4] A person can purchase a right to ownership from an owner, engage in theft or use physical force to appropriate the right. A further method of appropriation is through government legislation. This method was used in South Africa to create the apartheid system. Land was assigned through legislation for white use and labor-market laws restricted or prevented black labor-market participation. Rents were thereby created for the white population.[5] On a smaller scale, but under the same principle, land was appropriated from white farmers in Zimbabwe, on the grounds that the land had originally been appropriated (Shaw 2003).[6]

---

[4] See also Buchanan (1980a [2008], 1980b, 1980c, 1983).

[5] The Natives Land Act, No. 27 of 1913, enacted by the Union Government in South Africa, transferred land rights of the majority black population to the white minority (Wolpe 1972, pp. 425–6; Feinberg 1993, pp. 65–109). The 1913 statute, together with legislation enacted later (for example, Bantu Trust and Land Act, No. 18 of 1936), limited land ownership by the African majority to 'reserves' in 13 percent of the land. The law was the foundation for apartheid (Davenport 1987, pp. 388–400; Mbaku 1997, pp. 152–65). Color bar legislation enacted in South Africa at the turn of the twentieth century reserved skilled jobs in industry for white labor (Doxey 1961; Hutt 1964). The Transvaal Ordinance, No. 17 of 1907 protected white miners against Chinese competition (Hutt 1964, pp. 61–3; Mbaku 1991a, p. 139). In 1911, in response to lobbying from white labor, the Union Government passed the Mines and Works Act, No. 12 (also known as the Color Bar Act), which involved issuance of certificates of competence for most mining jobs. The law's rent-seeking attribute is that most certificates were issued only to white labor. In the Transvaal and Orange Free State, the law explicitly prohibited the issuance of certificates to Africans and other black groups (Hutt 1964; Williams 1989). The losers were white capital, black labor and the South African economy (Williams 1989; Mbaku 1991a, 1997). In 1922, the decision by mine operators to increase the ratio of blacks to whites in the mines resulted in violent labor strikes sponsored by the all-white Mine Workers' Union. The Afrikaner-dominated Nationalist party, which won the 1924 election, implemented a legislative agenda to limit the labor-market participation of blacks. The 1924 Industrial Conciliation Act, No. 11, outlawed, inter alia, the registration of black trade unions (Nattrass 1981; Hazlett 1988). This and further legislation significantly increased the ability of white labor to extract economic rents by legally preventing black workers from competing in the labor market. In response to a challenge by the Chamber of Commerce (representing mine operators), the courts had effectively attenuated the operational effects of the Mines and Works Act. In 1926, the government resurrected the Mines and Works Act by enacting the Second Color Bar Act (Mines and Works Act, No. 25 of 1926) (Doxey 1961, p. 160; Mbaku 1997, p. 151). The Industrial Conciliation Act, No. 11 of 1924, the Wages Act, No. 27 of 1925 and the Mines and Works Act, No. 25 of 1926 'legally entrenched the concept of white labor supremacy' in South Africa (Nattrass 1981, p. 76).

[6] The severe consequence was that the appropriation was followed by food shortages and overall economic collapse. If the appropriation was just, the cost of justice was high, involving starvation and deprivation of large segments of the population. Willems (2005) has studied the focus of the British press on Zimbabwe, to the exclusion of other countries in the region. She views the focus on Zimbabwe as a 'remnant of empire.'

21.3.2 Post-apartheid South Africa

After the end of apartheid, corruption became pervasive in South Africa. While under apartheid, legislation was used to create rents for the white population and in particular white labor, with the end of apartheid corruption in the government bureaucracy and by politicians became a source of rents. The white apartheid governments had been racist and had created rents for the privileged white population but corruption had not been the primary source of rents. After black-majority rule in 1994, rents were in particular created by regulations obliging black partnership or participation in business. The role of blacks was often no more than nominal participants in a business or investment to allow the black participation criterion to be satisfied. Legislation that was intended to compensate for past injustices emanating from the exclusion of blacks became a source of rents and rent extraction.[7]

21.3.3 Exclusion and Violence

In democracies, the most important methods of persuading a government to create and assign rents are lobbying, the underwriting of the campaigns of public officials, and to a lesser extent corruption. In authoritarian political systems pervasive throughout Africa, incumbent leaders have a monopoly on the creation and disposal of rents. The rents are used for regime security (Mbaku 2004; Bayart 2009). Rents are provided to groups that could challenge the regime. As long as the governance structure continues to deny excluded groups access to rent-seeking or wealth-creating opportunities, the groups may resort to capturing the apparatus of government, to avail themselves of the government-created rents.

Ethnic-based rent seeking under authoritarian regimes benefits primarily the ethno-regional groups affiliated with the regime (Kimenyi 1987). The affiliated ethno-regional groups are akin to permanent interest groups, which are exclusive in that they cannot be penetrated by people who are not born into them. Politically marginalized groups in Africa have, as a consequence of the tribal or ethnic basis of political power, often resorted to violence as a means of rent seeking (Lunde 1991; Mbaku 1991a, 1994, 2004). Throughout the continent, ethnic rent-seeking activities have resulted in military coups d'état, ethnic cleansing, civil wars and other violent confrontations (Kimenyi 1987, 1997, 1998; Kimenyi and Mbaku 1993; Mbaku 1997). Ethnic groups (Igbos of Nigeria; Krahn of Liberia; Hutu of Rwanda) have justified violence on the grounds of permanent exclusion from rents created by governments that are dominated or controlled by politically entrenched ethnic groups (see Mamdani 2001; Williams 2002; Johnson 2003; Uzokwe 2003; Uwechue 2004; Gberie 2005; Turner 2007; Straus and Waldorf 2011).

A most tragic case in scale of violence was the 1994 genocide in Rwanda. The population of seven million of the former Belgian colony of Rwanda in 1994 was composed of 85

---

[7] Despite its very progressive post-apartheid constitution, South Africa continues to struggle to maintain the rule of law. This is evidenced by the high rates of robbery, rape and murder. The conditions that Hillman (2004) describes as Nietzschean (the strong having their way with the weak) have been present. See, especially, Morely (2013).

percent Hutu and 14 percent Tutsi (there was 1 percent population of Twa). The Belgians, as colonialists, had made the minority Tutsi the ruling group. Verwimp (2003 [2008]) proposes an economic rent-related explanation for the genocide in Rwanda, which he attributes to the price of coffee and thereby changes in the price of land. Sargent Samuel K. Doe justified the brutal overthrow of the government of William R. Tolbert in Liberia as ending the more than 100-year old Americo-Liberian hegemony over indigenous peoples, including his Krahn ethnic group, which had been systematically marginalized and excluded from benefits of government (Mutwol 2009). Democracy in Africa provides no assurance of the absence of violence. For example, after elections in Kenya in 2007, there was widespread inter-ethnic conflict and killing (see, e.g., Cheeseman 2008 on the 2007 elections). Goldstein and Rotich (2008) describe how the Internet was used to mobilize forces and organize attacks in the inter-ethnic post-election violence.

It is important to note that not all groups that seek regime change are motivated by rents and rent-seeking opportunities. Groups that fought the European colonialists for independence hoped to establish post-independence institutions that would guarantee the rule of law and economic progress (Mbaku 2013a). Revolutions were, however, hijacked by opportunistic individuals or the revolutionary leaders, who once in power, took autocratic power.

21.3.4 The Military and Other Controlling Groups

The military, which has a comparative advantage in the employment of legitimate violence, has been prominent in rent extraction (Mbaku 1991b, 1994; Tanzi 1998 [2002]). Kimenyi and Mbaku (1995) show that in autocratic regimes, the military is more effective in rent seeking and rent extraction. Gupta et al. (2001) find that higher corruption is associated with higher military spending, which suggests rent extraction through military procurement orders. In African countries, the military has a comparative advantage in violence and has the capability to overthrow a government. Military officers have a role in protecting regime security through policing the rent distribution (Mbaku 1991b, 2004, p. 138). As long as rent flows to military officers (or leaders of other groups with the potential to destabilize the government) are maintained, and as long as the sharing formula is not disturbed, stability can be maintained.

21.3.5 Displacement and Restoration of Rent-sharing Equilibrium

Rent-seeking disequilibrium occurs when there is (1) an interruption in the supply of rents; (2) an increase in the amount of available rents, a situation that may call for a renegotiation of the sharing formula; (3) a severe reduction in the amount of rents available for allocation, requiring that the flow of rents to some groups either be reduced or stopped; and (4) improvements in the bargaining power of some group (for example, an increase in the group's relative population). If the bargaining power of a group increases, that group may attempt to renegotiate the agreement that it has with the government regarding the sharing of rents. Such a process can lead to regime instability. Once negotiations have produced a new sharing formula acceptable to all the parties, a new rent-seeking equilibrium is established and the country returns to political stability. Thus, a military coup and other violent mobilizations against the government are evidence of a rent-seeking disequilibrium that results from a change in the sharing formula that is not favorable to the group initiating the violence.

21.3.6 Rents and Regime Security

To enhance their ability to stay in power, governments in Africa have used the power to legislate to promote economic policies that are not socially desirable but ensure continuous supply of the rents that are needed to bribe military elites and leaders of other groups that are capable of destabilizing the regime (Mbaku 2004, p. 139). As proposed by Robert Bates (1987, p. 129), rents represent resources that can be used to 'organize political support and to perpetuate governments in power.' Thus, instead of providing their countries with the enabling institutional environment for wealth creation – that is, instead of using the regulatory process to improve the functioning of markets and the ability of entrepreneurs to create wealth – African rulers have created rents that have allowed them to placate powerful and politically volatile groups (Mbaku 1991b; Rowley 1999; Kimenyi 1991). Rent creation has been standard in Africa.

21.4 TRANSFERS OF INCOME

21.4.1 Political Wealth Brokers

Income redistribution through rent seeking involves (1) suppliers of wealth; (2) demanders of the wealth transfers; and (3) wealth brokers. The brokering function is performed by government. In countries with democratic political systems, changes in government are undertaken through mechanisms prescribed by the constitution (for example, regular elections) and the wealth brokers in government can be compensated by votes and campaign contributions (that is, electoral support). In the African countries, constitutional methods of regime change either did not exist or did not function effectively.[8] In many of these countries, compensation to brokers usually came in the form of personal payments (bribes) to politicians from entrepreneurs and others seeking access to wealth transfers. If, as has been the case in several countries, the demanders of wealth are military officers, broker compensation may consist of the use of the military's competitive advantage in violence to protect the government from coups d'état and other extra-legal forms of regime change.

Transfers of wealth need not be cash payments. Transfers can be made in the form of special favors that may include (1) legislation specifically designed to protect operators within a domestic industry from external competition; (2) occupational licensing regimes that restrict entry and protect existing practitioners; and (3) laws designed to make foodstuffs 'affordable' in the urban center but which actually force farmers to sell their crops and animals at below market prices (Mbaku 2004, pp. 62–3).

---

[8] This was especially so during the period from independence in the 1960s to the mid 1980s (that is, the period before the third wave of democratization that swept the continent beginning in the early 1990s). See Mbaku and Ihonvbere (2003) and Ihonvbere and Mbaku (2003).

The processes through which individuals and groups organize to seek transfers involve significant transaction and information costs. For an individual to take part in collective action to seek wealth transfers, he or she must determine what the impact will be on his wealth position of engaging in such an activity. Then, others must be found who are similarly inclined and are likely to be interested in being part of the rent-seeking collective. Even after the individual has identified other people with similar interests and who are willing to mobilize for collective action, the new group faces costs of organizing for action. The collective action is of course only worthwhile if expected benefits exceed the expected costs (Mbaku 2004, p. 63). As Shughart (1999, pp. 175–6) has observed, 'the individuals who join together on an issue must reach a consensus on a common course of action, marshal their resources in support of lobbying efforts, overcome free-rider problems, and so on.'

The fact that, throughout Africa, rent seeking through quests for wealth transfers continues indicates that there are groups and individuals with advantages in mobilizing to obtain information about the wealth status of others and seek transfers (Mbaku 2004, p. 63). Asymmetric information is involved. Shughart (1999, p. 176) notes that participants in political markets are likely to 'seek out issues on which the prospective winners are well informed and well organized, while the losers remain rationally ignorant about the effects of transfer activity.'

21.4.2 Rent Extraction as Political Extortion

Fred McChesney (1987 [2008]) added to the rent-seeking model by assigning to the politician an activist entrepreneurial role. Previously, the rent-seeking model had portrayed the politician as serving exclusively as a wealth broker with no personal entrepreneurial talents. McChesney described a politician as extorting rents through threats to impose costs on entrepreneurs or industries. Faced with such a threat, entrepreneurs reward politicians for eliminating or reducing the impact of the policies on their profits (Mbaku 2004, pp. 66–7). McChesney (1997, p. 3) noted that the state can legally appropriate wealth from citizens (also see Rowley 1999, p. 236).

Rent extraction occurs when entrepreneurs make payments to politicians, not to seek 'political favors' but to 'avoid political disfavor' (Rowley 1999, p. 236). Legislators can extort payments from potential victims of proposed legislation (see Tollison 1991; Shughart 1999). Politicians also extract rents from the private sector through 'political fishing.' Politicians pass relatively vague and difficult-to-enforce laws. Following the passage of such laws, individuals and groups mobilize to obtain exemptions or special differential treatment. The fishing process provides politicians with the opportunity to extract benefits from potential victims of their legislative efforts (Tollison 1991).

21.4.3 Centralized Power through One-party Government

During the colonial period in Africa, the European colonialists viewed traditional societal mechanisms for conflict resolution as a threat to their ability to monopolize political and economic control. The colonizers attenuated or abrogated these institutions, which had provided the rule of law in traditional societies (see Kimenyi 1997; Ayittey 2006). In the post-independence period, the new African ruling elites made a concerted effort to eliminate ethnic-based institutions that might have served to harmonize ethnic interests and provide the wherewithal for diverse ethnic groups to articulate their interests and peacefully seek their objectives. Instead, the new elites centralized power, which they captured (Kimenyi 1997). The single political party was the only legal form of political participation and perhaps, more importantly, ethnic-based political organizations were banned (Mbaku 1997, p. 234). In adopting the single political party system, these leaders argued that effective poverty alleviation efforts, national integration and rapid economic growth required centralized power to overcome ethnic-group rivalry and maximize the national well-being (Decalo 1992, pp. 9–10; Mbaku 2004, p. 252).

In Malawi, then President-for-Life Dr. Kamuzu Banda stated that 'there is no Opposition in Heaven. God himself does not want opposition – that is why he chased Satan away. Why should Kamuzu have opposition?' (Decalo 1992, p. 10). According to these dictators, the one-party political system would represent 'all streams of opinions and societal groups' (Decalo 1992, p. 10). Multiparty political systems would, on the other hand, politicize and emphasize ethnic, religious, and other social cleavages, rendering the goals of national integration, nation-building and poverty alleviation unattainable (Decalo 1992, pp. 9–10; Mbaku 2013b).

President Julius Nyerere of Tanzania was one of the many rulers who argued that the most appropriate way to build the nation, both politically and economically, was through a one-party political system. He stated that 'where there is one party, and that party is identified with the nation as a whole, the foundations of democracy are firmer than they can ever be where you have two or more parties, each representing only a section of the community!' (Nyerere 1966, p.196).

21.4.4 Rent Extraction by Civil Servants and Politicians

The political rent extraction model, which was proposed within the framework of democratic political systems (McChesney 1987 [2008], 1997), applies to one-party authoritarian regimes (Rowley 1999). The one-party political system not only concentrated political power in the center but also failed to constrain state custodians (that is, civil servants and politicians). State custodians used their power to regulate economic activities as well as allocate public goods and services to extract resources for their personal use (Rowley 1999). Civil servants distribute access to public goods and services in an arbitrary and capricious manner, threatening to deny or interrupt essential services if bribes are not paid (Mbaku 2004, 2010). Regulators extract rents through regulations that create excess demand for goods and services and the civil servants who control government stocks of the good that is in short supply extract and share the rents created by the artificial excess demand.

Excess demand is created by price controls, which were common in the African countries in the 1960s and 1970s and were eliminated through the structural adjustment programs (SAPs) imposed on the African countries by the International Monetary Fund (IMF) and World Bank beginning in the mid 1980s. Nonetheless, price controls remained a method of rent extraction (Mbaku 1997, p. 119; see also Rowley 1999, pp. 239–40).

Government officials who are granted the power to issue licenses or permits to enter economic sectors that have been closed to competition by government regulations can extract rents. We return to the ISI program of Ghana, where strict control of imported goods allowed the civil servants who administered the ISI program to grant import permits in such a way as to extract rents for themselves. Leith (1974, p. 26) reported that '[i]mport licenses were issued on the basis of a commission corruptly demanded and payable by importers on the face value of the import licenses issued. The commission was fixed at 15 percent, but was in special cases reduced to 7.5 or 5 percent.'

Quite often, civil servants threaten to interpret and enforce complex and vague laws, particularly investment codes, in ways that impose costs on business enterprises.[9] African civil servants also use public procurement to extract rents for themselves.[10] In addition, civil servants have regularly placed compromising documents in the official files of citizens and then have extorted payments from those persons in exchange for removing the documents. State resources could also be requisitioned for private use.[11]

21.4.5 Rent Extraction through Medical Treatment

In public hospitals throughout Africa, medical staff, including doctors, nurses, laboratory technicians and other support staff, extract rents from patients. The rent extraction is not limited to highly skilled staff members. Janitorial staff can also extort payments from patients – a patient who has been assigned to a room needs clean sheets for the bed or toiletries such as soap and tissue; housekeeping is called; housekeeping staff tell the patient that the hospital is out of bed sheets or toiletries, nevertheless, some can be secured if the patient is willing to make a payment directly to the staff. The payment is not used to purchase supplies – the staff keep the money and provide the patient with hospital supplies that were always available. This type of rent extraction is quite common in public hospitals in many countries, including Cameroon, Nigeria and Kenya (see Hope and Chikulo 2000).

Gould and Mukendi (1989, pp. 430–2) concluded that in Zaire (DRC) under Mobutu,

---

[9] For example, when an international insurance company undertook expensive negotiations to purchase a commercial building in the Cameroonian port city of Douala, just before the purchase could be finalized, a top-ranking civil servant, whose signature was required before the sale could be officially approved, refused to sign the necessary documents because the multinational company would not pay a bribe, referred to as a 'commission' by the said official (Mbaku 2010, p. 56). Jua (1991, p. 163) noted that the sale would have provided as much as FCFA 200 million (about US $735 294, at an exchange rate of FCFA 272 to the US dollar) for the Cameroon government.

[10] For example, during the construction of the headquarters of the regional central bank, Banque des états de l'Afrique centrale (BEAC) in Yaoundé, Cameroon, the bureaucrat responsible for determining the winning contract demanded a bribe. As reported in the highly influential *Africa Confidential* (January 1989, p. 5), a bribe (called a 'commission') of FCFA 600 million was paid as a condition for the award of the contract by the company that eventually won the contract (see also Mbaku 2010, p. 56).

[11] Jua (1991, p. 165), in his study of Cameroon, found that the state is sometimes referred to as the 'warehouse,' from which a civil servant can requisition resources for himself, his family, friends and associates: 'An office needs reams of paper. Thus, they are ordered. An agreement is made to pay 8 million or 10 million CFAF for paper that would cost 5 million CFAF. How is the 3 million or 5 million CFAF surplus shared? It is shared between the boss (the linchpin), the store's accountant (the controller) and the businessman (the architect) for sure.'

public hospitals, clinics and dispensaries operated under the mottos that 'unless you pay, you die' and that 'a physician who does not collect illicit payments is foolish.'

21.4.6 Rent Extraction by the Police

In their study of Nigeria, Erero and Oladoyin (2000, p. 280) point out that at each police station in the country, there is a notice that states that 'BAIL IS FREE.' Yet, no person in police custody can be released unless they pay the police the requested bribe. Hence, the bail process is used effectively by the police in Nigeria to extort rents from the public that they are supposed to serve. When someone attempts to bail out an individual in police detention, the 'policemen at the counter will demand money for writing materials with which they claim they will enter the case, whether of a complainant or an accused.' They continue that '[a]t another level, if a policeman effects an arrest, the first thing he or she demands is "chop money" from the suspect. At the level of the inter-relationship between commuter drivers and the police, the situation is a pathetic one. The police of all categories – anti-crime, mobile, or traffic wardens – openly demand and take bribes even in the presence of passengers' (Erero and Oladoyin 2000, p. 280).

21.4.7 Ghost Workers

Ghost workers have been quite common in the public sectors of many African countries. High-level government officials place the names of nonexistent workers on their salary rolls and collect the salaries for themselves (on Cameroon and Zaire, see Gould and Mukendi 1989, p. 432). In Cameroon, a government program for the identification and removal of ghosts from the public payroll eliminated some 20 000 names (Mbaku 2010, p. 60). Baldacci et al. (2004 [2004]) observe that ghost workers are socially more desirable than actual government officials because the ghosts do not extract rents and are not rent seekers. The incomes accruing to the ghost workers, however, make the position of the senior government official who receives the incomes more attractive and thereby increases the resources unproductively used in seeking to displace the official as well as increasing the resources used by the senior official to protect his or her position.

21.4.8 Rent Extraction in Other Public Employment

Erero and Oladoyin (2000, pp. 281–2) found that judicial officers, officials in the Nigerian Railways Corporation, Customs Service clerks, immigration officers and officers of the National Drug Law Enforcement Agency, regularly use their positions to extort extra-legal income from the public. Within the rent-extraction model in Africa, any public office can be exploited for the personal benefit of a civil servant or politician (that is, the holder of the office). An attendant at a public toilet can also extort money from individuals seeking to use the facility. The attendant, whose job is to ensure that the facilities are used properly and only for legal purposes and also to ensure that the appropriate toilet tissue is available, is in a position to extort payments from prospective users of the facility. One extortion scheme is to require that the user provide the attendant with a refundable deposit in order to receive an official roll of toilet tissue, without which entrance is denied – this is justified as making certain that users do not bring foreign materials into the public toilets, which can destroy the proper functioning of these facilities. To retrieve his or her deposit, the public toilet user must travel to another city and undergo a time-consuming ritual. The cost of recovering one's deposit is not worth the benefit and the attendants usually can keep the money.

In a study of corruption in Cameroon by GERDDES-Cameroon and supported by the German Friedrich-Ebert-Stiftung, respondents stated that only a stupid and foolish holder of a public office did not use the office to extract income for himself and his family (Nwel 1999). The study revealed that when an individual or business enterprise applies to the government for services (for example, to obtain a passport to travel abroad; to secure a permit to engage in certain professional activities, such as practicing medicine) or to seek permission to start and run a business, bureaucrats can use their positions to extort money from the applicants. For example, the bureaucrats can 'sit on the applicant's file,' refuse to process the file, remove critical documents from the file so as to render it unfit for processing or misplace the file. None of these events occur if the applicant pays the required bribes (Nwel 1999, pp. 31–3).

Even religious leaders in Cameroon use their positions to extract rent from congregants. The administration of the sacraments and appointments to various offices within the Church often involve the extortion of payments from prospective applicants (Nwel 1999, pp. 33–4).

Government contracts in Cameroon, as they are in many other African countries, provide opportunities for civil servants and politicians to extract or extort rents from the private sector. The award of a contract to provide the government with certain services (for example, construction of a building) is divided into stages and civil servants have the opportunity to extract money or other favors from each stage – call for tenders, award of the contract, signing of the contract, implementation of the contract, certification that the work has been completed and done according to the terms specified in the contract and payment of the contractor for the work done (Nwel 1999, pp. 34–50).

Civil servants in Cameroon and in many other African countries create artificial bottlenecks, which significantly increase transaction costs for business enterprises and can only be removed when bribes are paid. These bottlenecks include but are not limited to delays in (1) issuing travel documents, as well as certificates to qualify for a scholarship; (2) signing documents requested by citizens; (3) clearing goods ordered from abroad; and (4) providing other services requested by members of the entrepreneurial or productive sector and other citizens. For example, a student who has been awarded a scholarship to study abroad needs a passport and applies for one. The officers at the immigration offices, where the travel documents would be granted, can use the process to extort payments from the student – clerks in the office can 'lose' the documents, place them at the bottom of the files to be processed, claim that the director, who has to sign them, will not be available to do so until after the date the student is expected to travel abroad for his or her studies and so on. Once the required payments have been made, all the bottlenecks are gone and the travel documents are provided.

A student who applies to enter an institution of higher learning (for example, the National School of Administration and Magistracy – Ecole Nationale d'Administration et de Magistrature (ENAM)) must either have a 'godfather' or pay the extorted amount. In legal matters, to be granted bail, the detained individual or his benefactors must pay the requested bribe; even after a defendant has bribed his way into a favorable decision, he must still pay in order to have the court decision signed and delivered and so on (Nwel 1999, pp. 51–7; see also Gould and Mukendi 1989, p. 436).

21.5 RENT SEEKING AND ECONOMIC DEVELOPMENT

Behavior associated with rent seeking and rent extraction, including corruption, explains the lack of economic development in Africa.[12] The rent-seeking and rent-extracting behavior of politicians and government officials impedes investment and business activities. Murphy et al. (1993 [2008]) have argued that the firms most vulnerable to political and bureaucratic rent seeking are small innovators. Also, resources are attracted into rent seeking from innovative and productive activities (Kimenyi and Tollison 1999, p. 215; Mbaku and Kimenyi 2003, p. 124). Productive people or people seeking opportunities in life seek to emigrate. Hillman (2007) has determined that rulers and elites may not have incentives to promote economic development because the emergence of a middle class that is associated with higher levels of development will usually result in increased demands for more accountability from government, less impunity and greater protections for individual liberty, all of which will reduce the amount of rents available to governing elites and their benefactors. Economic inefficiency and impediments to economic growth are especially burdensome for African countries, which have had high rates of poverty and deprivation.

21.5.1 Rent Seeking and Comparative Advantage

Rent seeking places the right to enter and operate in the formal sectors of the African economies in the hands of effective rent-seeking entrepreneurs and not necessarily those who are the most efficient and innovative producers. In economies pervaded by rent seeking, political instead of market allocation dominates. As a consequence, inefficient producers who have a comparative advantage in rent seeking can remain in the market indefinitely without facing competition, not because they produce goods and services that are competitive in price and quality but because they are effective in obtaining privileges from the government (Kimenyi and Tollison 1999, pp. 215–16).

The personal incentives to abandon production and innovation and focus on rent-seeking behavior are paralleled by the prominence of rent-seeking behavior in African countries (Mbaku 1992, 1998). Murphy et al. (1993 [2008]) have noted that the most highly skilled and talented individuals seek those professions and occupations characterized by increasing returns to talent. Rent-seeking activities have weak diminishing returns and attract the economy's most talented and skilled human capital. As more of the country's skilled and talented labor resources opt for employment in areas of the economy that have significant rent-seeking opportunities, the productive sector is left

[12] See, for example, Werlin (1973), Leith (1974). LeVine (1975), Kormendi and Meguire (1985), Mauro (1995), Mbaku and Kimenyi (1997), Scully (1988), Grier and Tullock (1989), Kimenyi and Tollison (1999), Easterly (2001, 2006, 2008), Hillman (2002), Abed and Gupta (2002) and Trebilcock and Prado (2011).

with fewer and fewer people to innovate and undertake the activities necessary to create wealth. By a process of self-selection, talented people are not found in the entrepreneurial sector but in government (Acemoglu 1995; Acemoglu and Verdier 1998; Mbaku and Kimenyi 2003).

In many instances, highly skilled Africans thus opt for jobs that do not allow or require them to effectively utilize their skills and talents because other jobs offer enhanced opportunities for rent seeking, and hence extra-legal enrichment (Mbaku 2010, pp. 106–7). A highly trained and skilled graduate with a PhD in chemical engineering may decline a teaching and research position at a local university or research institute and instead seek a job as a clerk – a job that requires only the skills of a high school graduate – in the country's customs and excise department, because the position provides significantly more opportunities for rent extraction. As a customs clerk, he or she can extort money from importers and 'earn' more money in a month than in a year or more of teaching and conducting research at the university. Throughout Africa, highly skilled workers (for example, engineers, nurses, physicians, accountants, pharmacists, university lecturers, dentists, computer programmers and chemists) are in short supply but it is quite common for such highly skilled workers to abandon the professions for which they were trained for positions in government employment, which offer them opportunities for rent extraction. Throughout Africa, many countries depend on skilled expatriate workers to occupy productive positions in the economy as indigenes choose employment in an already bloated and parasitic rent-extracting public sector (Mbaku 2004; Easterly 2006, 2008).

The move away from productive and entrepreneurial activities includes choosing a career in the officer corps of the military because of opportunities for rent extraction (Gould 1980; Gould and Mukendi 1989; Mbaku 1991b; Gupta et al. 2001). Even ordinary enlisted troops use their official positions to engage in economic extortion – they can engage in illegal taxation of economic activities, especially in the rural areas (Mbaku 2010, p. 107).

21.5.2 Emigration and Comparative Advantage in Rent Seeking

Skilled people are also lost to the economy through emigration. Incomes for people with human capital are higher in Western countries, giving rise to emigration that has been described as 'brain drain.' Epstein et al. (1999 [2008]) have explained incentives to emigrate in a rent-seeking context. People are described as distanced from a ruler or king, with those closer benefitting more from privilege through success in rent seeking and those further away providing the source of rents for the successful privileged rent seekers. In a rent-seeking culture, the people with a comparative advantage in rent seeking have advantages in benefitting from rents obtained from closeness to the ruler and the people with a comparative advantage in productive activities supply the rents for privileged distribution. Under these conditions, productive people emigrate if they can, leaving behind the less productive who have a comparative advantage in rent seeking. Epstein et al. (1999 [2008]) describe how an economy can unravel. The departure of productive people places a greater burden on the remaining productive persons who are serving essentially as providers of rents, providing incentives for further emigration. It is also possible to have configurations of rent seeking such that the most productive people become rent seekers and the least productive are most distanced from the source of privilege, as described above, in which low-skilled people have incentives to emigrate. Emigration is by the persons least close to privilege and who provide rather than benefit from rents.

21.5.3 Size of Government and Economic Growth

Baldacci et al. (2004 [2004]) reported that contraction of government debt or public spending in low-income countries, including countries in Africa, increases economic growth. In high-income countries, the explanation for a similar result is that reduced government spending reduces the interest rate and increases private investment. In low-income countries, capital markets are present to provide the same means of increasing growth when the size of government contracts. Growth increases in low-income countries when public spending diminishes, because there are fewer government officials to deter growth through the rent-extracting and rent-seeking activities. Rent seeking in Africa has contributed to the growth of government and thus has had a negative impact on economic growth.

21.5.4 Africa and the Asian Tigers

Ghana, which gained independence from Great Britain in 1957, had a per capita income of US $250 in 1970 (World Bank 1991, p. 2). By 2012, 55 years after independence, per capita income in Ghana had risen only to US $1550 (World Bank 2014). Compare this performance with the so-called Asian Tigers – South Korea, for example, had an income per capita of US $270 in 1970 but by 2012 had a per capita income of US $22 670 (World Bank 2014). South Korea and the other 'tigers,' Taiwan, Hong Kong and Singapore, had governments that were not always democratic but, unlike governments in African countries, encouraged private-sector development through institutions that provided economic freedom, if not always political freedom (Paldam 2003; Mbaku 2004, pp. 96–100).[13]

21.6 RENT SEEKING AND INSTITUTIONS OF GOVERNANCE

21.6.1 Institutional Reform and the Persistence of Rent Seeking

Since the mid 1980s, there have been significant institutional reforms in many African countries (Mbaku and Ihonvbere 2003; IMF 2012; World Bank 2012). In many of these countries, including several in sub-Saharan Africa, there has been significant economic growth (see IMF 2012). Improvements in economic performance in these economies have come primarily from institutional reforms that have (1) reduced government intervention in markets and placed more effective constraints on civil servants and politicians (making it much more difficult for them to engage in rent seeking, act with impunity, or engage in other forms of opportunism); (2) improved the business environment for entre-

[13] For evidence on the relation between economic freedom and entrepreneurship and the creation of wealth, see Stepanek (1999) and Gwartney and Lawson (2000).

preneurial activities (for example, by making it easier for individuals to start and run a business or by improving mechanisms for conflict resolution, including those arising from trade and exchange); and (3) improved the delivery of public goods and services (see IMF 2012; World Bank 2012).

We have also noted that after independence, institutional arrangements facilitated rent seeking and opportunism (Mbaku 2010, 2013a). The wave of democratization that began in the mid 1980s in Africa was expected to bring about institutions that constrained the state and minimized the engagement of state custodians (that is, civil servants and politicians) in corruption, rent seeking and other growth-inhibiting behavior (Mbaku and Ihonvbere 2003). Yet, while there were institutional reforms, rent seeking and corruption did not subside. Rather, there has been an increased incidence of rent seeking and corruption (Mohtadi and Roe 2003, p. 445).

In autocracies rents are critical to the government for ensuring legitimacy or loyalty and stability (Mbaku 1991b; Kimenyi and Mbaku 1993). Why have the continent's young democracies, with significantly improved mechanisms for openness and transparency as compared to the *ancien régimes*, had high levels of rent seeking and corruption?[14]

Newly democratized political systems, such as those in Africa, may have governing processes based on the separation of powers but weak checks and balances. When openness increases, political access and the political culture of rent seeking is sustained, and the greater access to the government increases rent seeking (Hillman and Ursprung 2000 [2008]). In particular, this can involve rent extraction and rent seeking from public funds (Mohtadi and Roe 2003, p. 447). In addition to increased political openness bringing more people into the activity of rent seeking, there has also been an increase in available rents (Mohtadi and Roe 2003, p. 447; Ndulu et al. 2007, 2008; Ologbenla 2012; Akwalefo 2013).

21.6.2 The Rule of Law and Nietzschean Societies

A characteristic of democracy is that political and economic systems are governed by the rule of law.[15] Throughout Africa, rent seeking and other forms of political opportunism have become pervasive notwithstanding democracy because some people, especially those in government or in the military, have considered themselves above the law and have been able to act with impunity (Mbaku 1997, 2004, 2010). Hillman (2004) describes such societies in which power determines public policy outcomes without regard for the rule of law or ethics as Nietzschean, after the philosopher Friedrich Nietzsche.

In a study of corruption in Cameroon, Jua (1991) did not uncover a single case in which the government's anti-corruption organ, the Financial Disciplinary Committee

---

[14] Quite generally, democracy is expected to reduce rent seeking (Calderón and Chong 2005; Crisp and Gwartney 2013).

[15] The rule of law, according to British legal philosopher, Albert Dicey (1885 [1959], p. 181), comprises 'firstly, the supremacy of law as opposed to arbitrariness or even wide discretion by governments.' Legal scholars argue that in order for the rule of law to become pervasive in a country, all citizens, including those who serve in government, and regardless of their political and/or economic positions, must be subject to laws agreed upon in an earlier period (see, for example, Dicey 1885 [1959]; Dickinson 1921, pp. 34–5; Mbaku 2013a, pp. 993–1000). In other words, no one must consider themselves above the law.

of the Ministry of Public Service, had successfully charged any senior civil servant for engaging in corruption or financial malfeasance. According to Jua (1991, p. 162), '[t]hat higher-level bureaucrats are largely immune from trial by the Disciplinary Committee is evidence that Cameroon has an attenuated patrimonial administrative structure in which public discussion and/or criticism of the alleged acts of some members of the ruling class is still taboo.'

21.6.3 Judicial Independence

Judicial independence is critical to the rule of law. Judiciary officers should be granted 'security of tenure,' 'financial security' and 'institutional independence' (Mbaku 2013a, p. 1005). If the judiciary is subservient to the executive, bureaucratic and political corruption, as well as the manipulation of elections, can be serious problems. As an example, in a study of the manipulation of the judiciary in Cameroon, Fombad (2000, pp. 247–8) determined that before the elections of 1996 and 1997, the President of the Republic, Paul Biya, decreed the doubling of the salaries of judicial officers and increased the salaries of the justices of the Supreme Court by almost 200 percent. While judicial officers have a supervisory role to play in national elections, the Supreme Court retains the power to certify the results of each election, including the presidential election. The failure of the Cameroonian judiciary to function independently has contributed to corruption and rent seeking (Fombad 2000; Mbaku 2010; see also Charlier and N'Cho-Oguie 2009).

21.6.4 Rejection of Institutions

Even after significant institutional reforms, some Africans still view their national legal and judicial institutions as externally imposed and designed to benefit the politically privileged ethno-regional elites that rule them. By rejecting the laws and institutions and the civil servants and governmental agencies that enforce them, Africans significantly increase the costs of compliance (Mbaku 2013a, p. 1036). Minority ethnic and religious groups who have argued that they have been marginalized (see, for example, Uzokwe 2003; Uwechue 2004; Mutwol 2009) blame their poverty on public policies that deny them the means to benefit from corrupt and rent-seeking activities (Mbaku 2010). There is a basis for these complaints. Throughout Africa, public goods and services providers usually act arbitrarily and capriciously, favoring individuals and groups that bribe them (Mbaku 2010, pp. 102–5).

21.6.5 Transparency

Openness and transparency in government communication can significantly improve compliance with the rule of law. In fact, transparency is seen as a way to minimize corruption and rent seeking in African economies (Drew and Nyerges 2004, p. 33). Stirton and Lodge (2001, p. 476) have shown that transparency can 'ensure that public service providers respect both the positive and negative rights of individuals' and limit the ability of civil servants and politicians to engage in rent seeking, corruption and other forms of opportunism. This is in line with Bentham's principle for good governance, which states that: 'The more strictly we are watched, the better we behave.' Koppell (2005, p. 96) observes that '[t]ransparency is the literal value of accountability, the idea that an accountable bureaucrat and organization must explain or account for his actions.' If within each African economy, there were legal mechanisms that compel transparency and openness to enhance accountability, corruption, rent seeking and other forms of opportunism would diminish (Gerring and Thacker 2004, p. 316).

21.7 CONCLUSIONS

Hillman and Swank (2000) have tied political culture to behavior of persons in government. In Africa, rent seeking and rent extraction have been central to the political culture. Contact, almost of any sort with government, has resulted in rent extraction from citizens. Moreover, citizens have sought the positions that allow rents to be extracted, resulting in rent seeking. The incomes obtainable from rent seeking entice skilled individuals to forgo their professions for positions that allow rent extraction. The military and politically dominant ethno-regional coalitions have been particularly adept at rent seeking. The success in rent seeking has created marginalized and deprived groups – ethnic and religious minorities, women, rural inhabitants and the urban poor – that have resorted to violence to improve their participation in both rent seeking and rent extraction. Groups that have engaged in violent activities to capture the apparatus of government and improve their political and economic participation have justified their actions on the grounds that existing institutions do not allow for rent sharing or for peaceful regime change. The rent creation and rent seeking have impeded economic development and economic growth. An escape from rent seeking requires institutions that ensure the rule of law and protect citizens from government tyranny. Federalism, by reducing the power of elites associated with the central government, may be part of the solution.

While many African countries, since the mid 1980s, have undertaken institutional reforms that have significantly improved their governing, rent seeking remains pervasive. It is to be hoped that as democracy becomes entrenched and democracies mature, political culture will change and rent seeking and rent extraction will decline.

REFERENCES

Abed, George T. and Sanjeev Gupta (eds) (2002), *Governance, Corruption, and Economic Performance*, Washington, DC: International Monetary Fund.

Acemoglu, Daron (1995), 'Reward structures and the allocation of talent', *European Economic Review*, **39**(1), 17–33.

Acemoglu, Daron and Thierry Verdier (1998), 'Property rights, corruption and the allocation of talent: a general equilibrium approach', *Economic Journal*, **108**(450), 1381–403.

Aidt, Toke S. (2003), 'Economic analysis of corruption: a survey', *Economic Journal*, **113**(491), F632–F52.

Akwalefo, Bernadette D. (2013), *The National Cake: To Bake or To Share?*, Bloomington, IN: AuthorsHouse UK.

Ayittey, George B.N. (2006), *Indigenous African Institutions*, Leiden: Brill Academic Publishers.

Baldacci, Emanuele, Arye L. Hillman and Naoko C. Kojo (2004), 'Growth, governance, and fiscal policy transmission channels in low-income countries', *European Journal of Political Economy*, **20**(3), 517–49, reprinted in Sanjeev Gupta, Benedict Clemens and Gabriela Inchauste (eds) (2004), *Helping Countries Develop: The Role of Fiscal Policy*, Washington, DC: International Monetary Fund, pp. 67–104.

Bates, Robert H. (1987), *Essays on the Political Economy of Rural Africa*, Cambridge: Cambridge University Press.

Bayart, Jean-François (2009), *The State in Africa: The Politics of the Belly*, Cambridge: Polity.

Benson, Bruce L. (1984), 'Rent seeking from a property rights perspective', *Southern Economic Journal*, **51**(2), 388–400.

Buchanan, James M. (1980a), 'Rent seeking and profit seeking', in James M. Buchanan, Robert D. Tollison and Gordon Tullock (eds), *Toward a Theory of the Rent-seeking Society*, College Station, TX: Texas A&M University Press, pp. 3–15, reprinted in Roger D. Congleton, Arye L. Hillman and Kai A. Konrad (eds) (2008), *40 Years of Research on Rent Seeking 1 – The Theory of Rent Seeking*, Heidelberg: Springer, pp. 55–67.

Buchanan, James M. (1980b), 'Reform in the rent-seeking society', in James M. Buchanan, Robert D. Tollison and Gordon Tullock (eds), *Toward a Theory of the Rent-seeking Society*, College Station, TX: Texas A&M University Press, pp. 359–67.

Buchanan, James M. (1980c), 'Rent seeking under external diseconomies', in James M. Buchanan, Robert D. Tollison and Gordon Tullock (eds), *Toward a Theory of the Rent-seeking Society*, College Station, TX: Texas A&M University Press, pp. 183–94.

Buchanan, James M. (1983), 'Rent seeking, noncompensated transfers, and laws of succession', *Journal of Law and Economics*, **26**(1), 71–85.

Buchanan, James M., Robert D. Tollison and Gordon Tullock (eds) (1980), *Toward a Theory of the Rent-seeking Society*, College Station, TX: Texas A&M University Press.

Calderón, César and Alberto Chong (2005), 'Do democracies breed rent-seeking behaviors?', Working Paper No. 534, Inter-American Development Bank, Washington, DC.

Charlier, Florence and Charles N'Cho-Oguie (2009), *Sustaining Reforms for Inclusive Growth in Cameroon: A Development Policy Review*, Washington, DC: World Bank.

Cheeseman, Nic (2008), 'The Kenyan elections of 2007: an introduction', *Journal of Eastern African Studies* (Special Issue on Election Fever: Kenya's Crisis), **2**(2), 166–84.

Congleton, Roger D. (1980), 'Competitive process, competitive waste, and institutions', in James M. Buchanan, Robert D. Tollison and Gordon Tullock (eds), *Toward a Theory of the Rent-seeking Society*, College Park, TX: Texas A&M University Press, pp. 153–79, reprinted in Roger D. Congleton, Arye L. Hillman and Kai A. Konrad (eds) (2008), *40 Years of Research on Rent Seeking 1 – The Theory of Rent Seeking*, Heidelberg: Springer, pp. 69–95.

Congleton, Roger D., Arye L. Hillman and Kai A. Konrad, (2008a), '40 years of research on rent seeking: an overview', in Roger D. Congleton, Arye L. Hillman and Kai A. Konrad (eds), *40 Years of Research on Rent Seeking 1 and 2*, Heidelberg: Springer, pp. 1–42.

Congleton, Roger D., Arye L. Hillman and Kai A. Konrad (eds) (2008b), *40 Years of Research on Rent Seeking 1 – The Theory of Rent Seeking*, Heidelberg: Springer.

Congleton, Roger D., Arye L. Hillman and Kai A. Konrad (eds) (2008c), *40 Years of Research on Rent Seeking 2 – Applications: Rent Seeking in Practice*, Heidelberg: Springer.

Crisp, Alice M. and James Gwartney (2013), 'Institutions and economic, political, and civil liberty in Africa', in James Gwartney, Robert Lawson and Joshua Hall (eds), *Economic Freedom of the World: 2013 Annual Report*, Vancouver, BC: The Fraser Institute, pp. 179–214.

Davenport, T. Rodney H. (1987), 'Can sacred cows be culled? A historical review of land policy in South Africa, with some questions about the future', *Development Southern Africa*, **4**(3), 388–400.

Decalo, Samuel (1992), 'The process, prospects and constraints of democratization in Africa', *African Affairs*, **9**(362), 7–35.

Dicey, Albert V. (1885), *Introduction to the Study of the Law of the Constitution*, reprinted in 1959, London: Macmillan.

Dickinson, John (1921), *Administrative Justice and the Supremacy of Law in the United States*, Cambridge, MA: Harvard University Press.

Doxey, George V. (1961), *The Industrial Color Bar in South Africa*, Cape Town: Oxford University Press.

Drew, Christina H. and Timothy L. Nyerges (2004), 'Transparency of environmental decision making: a case study of soil cleanup inside the Hanford 100 area', *Journal of Risk Research*, **7**(1), 33–71.

Easterly, William (2001), *The Elusive Quest for Growth: Economists' Adventures and Misadventures in the Tropics*, Cambridge, MA: MIT Press.

Easterly, William (2006), *The White Man's Burden: Why the West's Efforts to Aid the Rest have Done So Much Ill and Little Good*, New York: The Penguin Group.

Easterly, William (2008), *Reinventing Foreign Aid*, Cambridge, MA: MIT Press.

Epstein, Gil, Arye L. Hillman and Heinrich W. Ursprung (1999), 'The king never emigrates', *Review of Development Economics*, **3**(2), 107–21, reprinted in Roger D. Congleton, Arye L. Hillman and Kai A. Konrad (eds), *40 Years of Research on Rent Seeking 2 – Applications: Rent Seeking in Practice*, Heidelberg: Springer, pp. 265–79.

Erero, John and Tony Oladoyin (2000), 'Tackling corruption epidemic in Nigeria', in Kempe Ronald Hope, Sr. and Bornwell C. Chikulo (eds), *Corruption and Development in Africa: Lessons from Country Case-Studies*, London: Macmillan, pp. 280–87.

Feinberg, Harvey M. (1993), 'The 1913 Natives Land Act in South Africa: politics, race, and segregation in the early 20th century', *International Journal of African Historical Studies*, **26**(1), 65–109.

Fombad, Charles M. (2000), 'Endemic corruption in Cameroon: insights on consequences and control', in Kempe Ronald Hope, Sr and Bornwell C. Chikulo (eds), *Corruption and Development in Africa: Lessons from Country Case-studies*, London: Macmillan, pp. 234–60.

Gberie, Lansana (2005), *A Dirty War in West Africa: The RUF and the Destruction of Sierra Leone*, Bloomington, IN: Indiana University Press.

Gerring, John and Strom C. Thacker (2004), 'Political institutions and corruption: the role of unitarism and parliamentarism', *British Journal of Political Science*, **34**(2), 295–330.

Goldstein, Joshua and Juliana Rotich (2008), 'Digitally networked technology in Kenya's 2007–2008 post-election crisis', Berkman Center Research Publication 2008–09, Harvard University, Cambridge, Massachusetts.

Gould, David J. (1980), *Bureaucratic Corruption and Underdevelopment in the Third World: The Case of Zaire*, New York: Pergamon Press.

Gould, David J. and Tshiabukole B. Mukendi (1989), 'Bureaucratic corruption in Africa: causes, consequences and remedies', *International Journal of Public Administration*, **12**(3), 427–57.

Grier, Kevin B. and Gordon Tullock (1989), 'An empirical analysis of cross-national economic growth, 1951–1980', *Journal of Monetary Economics*, **24**(2), 259–76.

Gupta, Sanjeev, Luiz de Mello and Raju Sharan (2001), 'Corruption and military spending', *European Journal of Political Economy*, **17**(4), 749–77.

Gwartney, James D. and Robert Lawson (2000), *Economic Freedom of the World: 2000 Annual Report*, Vancouver, BC: The Fraser Institute.

Hazlett, Thomas W. (1988), 'Economic origins of apartheid', *Contemporary Policy Issues*, **6**(4), 85–104.

Hillman, Arye L. (2002), 'The World Bank and the persistence of poverty in poor countries', *European Journal of Political Economy*, **18**(4), 783–95.

Hillman, Arye L. (2004), 'Nietzschean development failures', *Public Choice*, **119**(3–4), 263–80.

Hillman, Arye L. (2007), 'Democracy and low-income countries', in José Casas Pardo and Pedro Schwartz (eds), *Public Choice and Challenges of Democracy*, Cheltenham, UK and Northampton, MA, USA: Edward Elgar Publishing, pp. 277–94.

Hillman, Arye L. (2013), 'Rent seeking', in Michael Reksulak, Laura Razzolini and William F. Shughart II (eds), *The Elgar Companion to Public Choice*, 2nd edn, Cheltenham, UK and Northampton, MA, USA: Edward Elgar Publishing, pp. 307–30.

Hillman, Arye L. and Eliakim Katz (1987), 'Hierarchical structure and the social costs of bribes and transfers', *Journal of Public Economics*, **34**(2), 129–42, reprinted in Roger D. Congleton, Arye L. Hillman and Kai Konrad (eds) (2008), *40 Years of Research on Rent Seeking 1 – The Theory of Rent Seeking*, Heidelberg: Springer, pp. 523–36.

Hillman, Arye L. and Otto Swank (2000), 'Why political culture should be in the lexicon of economics', *European Journal of Political Economy*, **16**(1), 1–4.

Hillman, Arye L. and Heinrich W. Ursprung (2000), 'Political culture and economic decline', *European Journal of Political Economy*, **16**(2), 189–213, reprinted in Roger D. Congleton, Arye L. Hillman and Kai A. Konrad (eds) (2008), *40 Years of Research on Rent Seeking 2 – Applications: Rent Seeking in Practice*, Heidelberg: Springer, pp. 219–45.

Hodler, Roland (2006), 'The curse of natural resources in fractionalized countries', *European Economic Review*, **50**(6), 1367–86.

Hope, Kempe R., Sr and Bornwell C. Chikulo (eds) (2000), *Corruption and Development in Africa: Lessons from Country Case-studies*, London: Macmillan.

Hutt, William H. (1964), *The Economics of the Color Bar: A Study of the Economic Origins and Consequences of Racial Segregation in South Africa*, London: Institute of Economic Affairs.

Ihonvbere, Julius O. and John M. Mbaku (eds) (2003), *Political Liberalization and Democratization in Africa: Lessons from Country Experiences*, Westport, CT: Praeger.

IMF (International Monetary Fund) (2012), *Regional Economic Outlook: Sub-Saharan Africa – Maintaining Growth in an Uncertain World*, Washington, DC: International Monetary Fund.

Johnson, Douglas H. (2003), *The Root Causes of Sudan's Civil Wars*, Bloomington, IN: Indiana University Press.

Jua, Nantang (1991), 'Cameroon: jump-starting an economic crisis', *Africa Insight*, **21**(3), 162–70.

Kimenyi, Mwangi S. (1987), 'Bureaucratic rents and political institutions', *Journal of Public Finance and Public Choice*, **3**, 189–99.

Kimenyi, Mwangi S. (1991), 'Barriers to the efficient functioning of markets in developing countries', *Konjunkturpolitik*, **37**(4), 199–227.

Kimenyi, Mwangi S. (1997), *Ethnic Diversity, Liberty and the State*, Cheltenham, UK and Lyme, NH, USA: Edward Elgar Publishing.

Kimenyi, Mwangi S. (1998), 'Ethnic rent seeking, stability and institutional reform in sub-Saharan Africa', in Silvo Borner, Martin Paldam and Michael Kaser (eds), *The Political Dimension of Economic Growth: Proceedings of the IEA Conference Held in San Jose, Costa Rica*, London: Macmillan, pp. 324–34.

Kimenyi, Mwangi S. and John M. Mbaku (1993), 'Rent seeking and institutional stability in developing countries', *Public Choice*, **77**(2), 385–405.

Kimenyi, Mwangi S. and John Mukum Mbaku (1995), 'Rents, military elites, and political democracy', *European Journal of Political Economy*, **11**(4), 699–708.

Kimenyi, Mwangi S. and Robert D. Tollison (1999), 'Rent seeking, institutions, and economic growth', in Mwangi S. Kimenyi and John Mukum Mbaku (eds), *Institutions and Collective Choice in Developing Countries: Applications of the Theory of Public Choice*, Aldershot, UK: Ashgate, pp. 199–221.

Koppell, Jonathan G.S. (2005), 'Pathologies of accountability: ICANN and the challenge of "multiple accountabilities disorder"', *Public Administration Review*, **65**(1), 94–108.

Kormendi, Roger C. and Philip G. Meguire (1985), 'Macroeconomic determinants of growth: cross-country evidence', *Journal of Monetary Economics*, **16**(2), 141–63.

Krueger, Anne O. (1974), 'The political economy of the rent-seeking society', *American Economic Review*, **64**(3), 291–303, reprinted in Roger D. Congleton, Arye L. Hillman and Kai A. Konrad (eds) (2008), *40 Years of Research on Rent Seeking 2 – Applications: Rent Seeking in Practice*, Heidelberg: Springer, pp. 151–63.

Leith, J. Clark (1974), *Ghana*, New York: National Bureau of Economic Research.

LeVine, Victor T. (1975), *Political Corruption: The Ghanaian Case*, Stanford, CA: Hoover Institution.

Long, Ngo Van (2013), 'The theory of contests: a unified model and review of the literature', *European Journal of Political Economy*, **32**, 161–81, reprinted in Chapter 3, this volume.

Lunde, Tormod K. (1991), 'Modernization and political instability: coups d'état in Africa 1955–85', *Acta Sociologica*, **34**(1), 13–32.

MacGaffey, Janet (1983), 'How to survive and become rich amidst devastation: the second economy of Zaire', *African Affairs*, **82**(328), 351–66.

Mamdani, Mahmood (2001), *When Victims Become Killers: Colonialism, Nativism, and the Genocide in Rwanda*, Princeton, NJ: Princeton University Press.

Mauro, Paolo (1995), 'Corruption and growth', *Quarterly Journal of Economics*, **110**(3), 681–712.

Mbaku, John M. (1991a), 'Property rights and rent seeking in South Africa', *Cato Journal*, **11**(1), 135–50.

Mbaku, John M. (1991b), 'Military expenditures and bureaucratic competition for rents', *Public Choice*, **71**(1–2), 19–31.

Mbaku, John M. (1992), 'Bureaucratic corruption as rent-seeking behavior', *Konjunkturpolitik* (Berlin), **38**(4), 247–65.

Mbaku, John M. (1994), 'Military coups as rent-seeking behavior', *Journal of Political and Military Sociology*, **22**(Winter), 241–84.

Mbaku, John M. (1997), *Institutions and Reform in Africa: The Public Choice Perspective*, Westport, CT: Praeger.

Mbaku, John M. (1998), 'Corruption and rent seeking', in Silvo Borner, Martin Paldam and Michael Kaser (eds), *The Political Dimension of Economic Growth: Proceedings of the IEA Conference Held in San Jose, Costa Rica*, London: Macmillan, pp. 193–211.

Mbaku, John M. (2004), *Institutions and Development in Africa*, Trenton, NJ: African World Press.

Mbaku, John M. (2010), *Corruption in Africa: Causes, Consequences, and Cleanups*, Lanham, MD: Lexington Books.

Mbaku, John M. (2013a), 'Providing a foundation for wealth creation and development in Africa: the role of the rule of law', *Brooklyn Journal of International Law*, **38**(3), 959–1051.

Mbaku, John M. (2013b), 'What should Africans expect from their constitutions?', *Denver Journal of International Law and Policy*, **41**(2), 149–83.

Mbaku, John M. and Julius O. Ihonvbere (eds) (2003), *The Transition to Democratic Governance in Africa: The Continuing Struggle*, Westport, CT: Praeger.

Mbaku, John M. and Mwangi S. Kimenyi (1997), 'Macroeconomic determinants of growth: further evidence on the role of political freedom', *Journal of Economic Development*, **22**(2), 119–32.

Mbaku, John M. and Mwangi S. Kimenyi (2003), 'Rent seeking and economic growth in developing countries', in John Baffoe-Bonnie and Mohammed Khayum (eds), *Contemporary Economic Issues in Developing Countries*, Westport, CT: Praeger, pp. 113–28.

McChesney, Fred S. (1987), 'Rent extraction and rent creation in the economic theory of regulation', *Journal of Legal Studies*, **16**(1), 73–90, reprinted in Roger D. Congleton, Arye L. Hillman and Kai A. Konrad (eds) (2008), *40 Years of Research on Rent Seeking 2 – Applications: Rent Seeking in Practice*, Heidelberg: Springer, pp. 313–30.

McChesney, Fred S. (1997), *Money for Nothing: Politicians, Rent Extraction, and Political Extortion*, Cambridge, MA: Harvard University Press.
Mehlum, Halvor, Karl Moene and Ragnar Torvik (2006), 'Institutions and the resource curse', *Economic Journal*, **116**(508), 1–20, reprinted in Roger D. Congleton, Arye L. Hillman and Kai A. Konrad (eds) (2008), *40 Years of Research on Rent Seeking 2 – Applications: Rent Seeking in Practice*, Heidelberg: Springer, pp. 245–64.
Mohtadi, Hamid and Terry L. Roe (2003), 'Democracy, rent seeking, public spending and growth', *Journal of Public Economics*, **87**(3–4), 445–66.
Morely, Robert (2013), 'South Africa: where corruption, rape and murder are normal', December, available at http://www.thetrumpet.com/article/11050.30898.159.0/society/south-africa-where-corruption-rape-and-murder-are-normal (accessed 8 June 2014).
Murphy, Kevin M., Andrei Shleifer and Robert W. Vishny (1993), 'Why is rent seeking so costly to growth?', *American Economic Review, Papers and Proceedings*, **83**(2), 409–14, reprinted in Roger D. Congleton, Arye L. Hillman and Kai A. Konrad (eds) (2008), *40 Years of Research on Rent Seeking 2 – Applications: Rent Seeking in Practice*, Heidelberg: Springer, pp. 213–18.
Mutwol, Julius (2009), *Peace Agreements and Civil Wars in Africa: Insurgent Motivations, State Responses, and Third-party Peacemaking in Liberia, Rwanda, and Sierra Leone*, Amherst, NY: Cambria Press.
Nattrass, Jill (1981), *The South African Economy: Its Growth and Change*, Cape Town: Oxford University Press.
Ndulu, Benno J., Stephen A. O'Connell, Robert H. Bates, Paul Collier and Chukwuma C. Soludo (eds) (2007), *The Political Economy of Economic Growth in Africa, 1960–2000*, Vol. 1, Cambridge: Cambridge University Press.
Ndulu, Benno J., Stephen A. O'Connell, Robert H. Bates, Paul Collier and Chukwuma C. Soludo (eds) (2008), *The Political Economy of Economic Growth in Africa, 1960–2000, Volume 2: Country Case Studies*, Cambridge: Cambridge University Press.
Nitzan, Shmuel (1994), 'Modelling rent-seeking contests', *European Journal of Political Economy*, **10**(1), 41–60.
Nwel, Pierre T. (1999), *Corruption in Cameroon*, Yaoundé: Friedrich-Ebert-Stiftung.
Nyerere, Julius K. (1966), *Freedom and Unity*, Oxford: Oxford University Press.
Ologbenla, Derin (2012), 'Money-bag politics, rent seeking and flawed elections in Nigeria: a theoretical statement', *Journal of Public Administration and Governance*, **2**(1), 188–211.
Paldam, Martin (2003), 'Economic freedom and the success of the Asian tigers: an essay on controversy', *European Journal of Political Economy*, **19**(3), 453–77.
Rowley, Charles K. (1999), 'Rent seeking and rent extraction from the perspective of Africa', in Mwangi S. Kimeyi and John Mukum Mbaku (eds), *Institutions and Collective Choice in Developing Countries: Applications of the Theory of Public Choice*, Aldershot, UK: Ashgate, pp. 223–54.
Rowley, Charles K. (2000), 'Political culture and economic performance in sub-Saharan Africa', *European Journal of Political Economy*, **16**(1), 133–58.
Scully, Gerald W. (1988), 'The institutional framework and economic development', *Journal of Political Economy*, **96**(3), 652–62.
Shaw, William H. (2003), '"They stole our land": debating the expropriation of white farms in Zimbabwe', *Journal of Modern African Studies*, **41**(1), 75–89.
Shughart, William F. II (1999), 'The interest group theory of government in developing country perspective', in Mwangi S. Kimeyi and John Mukum Mbaku (eds), *Institutions and Collective Choice in Developing Countries: Applications of the Theory of Public Choice*, Aldershot, UK: Ashgate, pp. 169–98.
Stepanek, Joseph F. (1999), *Wringing Success from Failure in Late-developing Countries: Lessons from the Field*, Westport, CT: Praeger.
Stirton, Lindsay and Martin Lodge (2001), 'Transparency mechanisms: building publicness into public services', *Journal of Law and Society*, **28**(4), 471–89.
Straus, Scott and Lars Waldorf (eds) (2011), *Remaking Rwanda: State Building and Human Rights After Mass Violence*, Madison, WI: University of Wisconsin Press.
Svensson, Jakob (2000), 'Foreign aid and rent seeking', *Journal of International Economics*, **51**(2), 437–61, reprinted in Roger D. Congleton, Arye L. Hillman and Kai A. Konrad (eds) (2008), *40 Years of Research on Rent Seeking 2 – Applications: Rent Seeking in Practice*, Heidelberg: Springer, pp. 165–89.
Tanzi, Vito (1998), 'Corruption around the world: causes, consequences, scope, and cures', *IMF Staff Papers*, **45**, 559–94, reprinted in George T. Abed and Sanjeev Gupta (eds) (2002), *Governance, Corruption, and Economic Performance*, Washington, DC: International Monetary Fund, pp. 19–58.
Tollison, Robert D. (1982), 'Rent seeking: a survey', *Kyklos*, **35**(4), 575–602.
Tollison, Robert D. (1991), 'Regulation and interest groups', in Jack C. High (ed.), *Regulation: Economic Theory and History*, Ann Arbor, MI: University of Michigan Press.
Transparency International (2004), *Global Corruption Report, 2004*, Berlin: Transparency International.

Trebilcock, Michael J. and Mariana Mota Prado (2011), *What Makes Poor Countries Poor? Institutional Determinants of Development*, Cheltenham, UK and Northampton, MA, USA: Edward Elgar Publishing.
Tullock, Gordon (1967), 'The welfare costs of tariffs, monopolies and theft', *Western Economic Journal*, **5**(3), 224–332, reprinted in Roger D. Congleton, Arye L. Hillman and Kai A. Konrad (eds) (2008), *40 Years of Research on Rent Seeking 1 – The Theory of Rent Seeking*, Heidelberg: Springer, pp. 45–53.
Tullock, Gordon (1993), *Rent-seeking*, Aldershot, UK and Brookfield, VT, USA: Edward Elgar Publishing.
Turner, Thomas (2007), *The Congo Wars: Conflict, Myth & Reality*, London: Zed Books.
Uwechue, Raph (2004), *Reflections on the Nigerian Civil War: Facing the Future*, Bloomington, IN: Trafford Publishing.
Uzokwe, Alfred O. (2003), *Surviving Biafra: The Story of the Nigerian Civil War*, Bloomington, IN: iUniverse.
Verwimp, Philip (2003), 'The political economy of coffee, dictatorship, and genocide', *European Journal of Political Economy*, **19**(1), 161–81, reprinted in Roger D. Congleton, Arye L. Hillman and Kai A. Konrad (eds) (2008), *40 Years of Research on Rent Seeking 2 – Applications: Rent Seeking in Practice*, Heidelberg: Springer, pp. 191–211.
Werlin, Herbert H. (1972), 'The roots of corruption: the Ghanaian enquiry', *The Journal of Modern African Studies*, **10**(2), 247–66.
Werlin, Herbert H. (1973), 'The consequences of corruption: the Ghanaian experience', *Political Science Quarterly*, **88**(1), 71–85.
Willems, Wendy (2005), 'Remnants of Empire? British media reporting on Zimbabwe', *Westminster Papers in Communication and Culture*, 91–108, available at http://eprints.lse.ac.uk/51155/ (accessed 10 November 2014).
Williams, Gabriel I.H. (2002), *Liberia: The Heart of Darkness*, Bloomington, IN: Trafford Publishing.
Williams, Walter E. (1989), *South Africa's War Against Capitalism*, New York: Praeger.
Wolpe, Harold (1972), 'Capitalism and cheap labor-power in South Africa: from segregation to apartheid', *Economy and Society*, **1**(4), 425–56.
World Bank (1991), *World Tables, 1991*, Baltimore, MD: The Johns Hopkins University Press.
World Bank (2012), *Doing Business 2012: Doing Business in a More Transparent World*, Washington, DC: World Bank.
World Bank (2014), *World Development Report, 2014*, New York: Oxford University Press.

22. Economic development and corruption in China in the shadow of rent seeking

*Chen Kang and Liu Qijun**

SUMMARY

This chapter reviews the role of rents and rent seeking in China, where the transition from a planned economy and economic liberalization proceeded without political liberalization. In an initial phase of transition, markets and decentralization were introduced. Thereafter, a further phase of transition involved recentralization. Both phases created rents and led to rent seeking that was in general associated with corruption. We describe the sources of the rents and present case studies to suggest magnitudes of rents. We show that economic and political activity in Chinese transition cannot be adequately described without reference to rents and rent seeking.

22.1 BACKGROUND

In the transition from a planned economy, China underwent changes that had consequences throughout the world. Remarkably, these changes were brought about, to a great extent, by following closely the three simple and yet profound reform strategies set by Deng Xiaoping, who became the most powerful leader in China in the late 1970s.

The first strategy was to 'let some people be rich first,' which was Deng's secret strategy against conservative forces within the Communist Party of China (CPC) in the early 1980s. When there were few supporters of his market-oriented reforms among China's central leaders in Beijing, Deng resorted to mobilizing grassroot reformers by 'playing to the provinces' (Shirk 1993). The most important element of the 'letting some people be rich first' strategy was to 'let some officials be rich first'. This was an incentive-compatible mechanism that he devised knowing full well that bottom-up reforms would not have succeeded, had local government officials stood in the way (Chen 1998). When officials in Shenzhen and Guangdong became rich by enabling market liberalization in their domain, ripples were sent through China's officialdom that effectively brought thousands of local government officials into the reformist camp through self-interest.

The second strategy was to focus on economic development. Deng argued that 'development is the only hard truth,' and he believed that China's major problems, such as poverty, unemployment and underemployment, could be resolved by economic development. Development was quantified into a number of key performance indicators (KPIs)

* Support from the National Natural Science Foundation of China (Grant No. 71073060) is gratefully acknowledged by the second author.

for local government leaders, including growth rates of gross domestic product (GDP), tax revenue and foreign direct investment (FDI). Fulfilling the KPIs became one of the necessary conditions for promotion for local officials, who were incentivized thereby to do everything they could to meet growth targets, including paying 'helpers' outside the government.

The third and last strategy was to preserve political stability. Deng declared that 'stability is of overriding importance,' for without political stability there would be no economic development. Again, preserving political stability became another necessary condition for promotion for local government leaders, who showed no hesitation in using all means, including money from government coffers, to preserve stability within their localities.

Deng's three strategies worked well in both creating a political-economic environment conducive to market-oriented reforms and unleashing powerful market forces to achieve his goal of moving China toward a 'basically well-off (*xiaokang*) society'. He did not live to see that his strategies continued to work in support of a different development model that emerged from the late 1990s. The government of China adopted recentralization policies and reversed financial reforms in the mid 1990s (Chen et al. 2002; Chen 2004; Huang 2012). Subsequently, the economy of China made a transition, partly intentionally and partly by accident, from the development model in the 1980s and early 1990s (China Model I) in which government played mainly an enabling role to facilitate the growth of market forces and non-state sectors, to a government-led investment-driven development model that emerged in the late 1990s (China Model II), which restricted competition and granted monopoly privileges to state-owned enterprises (SOEs) and those entities well connected with government (Chen 2013). The three strategies mentioned above gave rise to different forms of rent creation and rent seeking under the two China models.

Rent seeking under China Model I served mainly to erode the foundation of central planning and to provide space for the non-state sectors to grow (Chen 1995).There was economic liberalization, although not political liberalization. Looked at from this perspective, the net impact could be efficiency enhancing and wealth creating. In Russia, in contrast, there was initially political liberalization without economic liberalization, which allowed broader participation in rent seeking (Hillman and Ursprung 2000 [2008]). Gordon Tullock (1996) agreed that the recovery from the economic inefficiencies of central planning in China had been faster than that in Russia but was skeptical whether the end result could remain favorable for China because rent seeking would become widespread given that the government of China had decided on economic liberalization with one-party rule maintained. Subsequent developments proved Tullock right: competition was restricted, monopolies were created and protected and corruption was rampant under China Model II.

In this chapter we document rent creation and rent seeking in China during the reform eras. Rents are defined as due to privileges that provide economic transfers artificially created by political and administrative power. We do not include in our discussion those special privileges associated with industrial policies.[1]

---

1 See Tak-Wing Ngo and Yongping Wu (2009) for detailed studies of 'rent allocation' and 'rent-like transfers' associated with industrial policy instruments.

The chapter is organized as follows. Section 22.2 describes rent-seeking activities under China Model I in the 1980s and early 1990s, detailing how rents were created and extracted, and where and by whom. Section 22.3 does the same for rent seeking under China Model II beginning in the mid 1990s. Section 22.4 concludes by commenting on the role of rent creation and rent seeking, and also rent extraction, in explaining economic activity in China.

22.2 RENT SEEKING BETWEEN PLAN AND MARKET

Between 1978 and 1992, market reforms in China followed a pattern of 'two steps forward, one step back' (Naughton 2007). In fact, 'market economy' never appeared in any CPC documents during this period because there was no consensus among the Chinese leaders on whether China should abandon central planning and embrace the market economy. As a compromise, China's economy was allowed to operate under a 'two-tier system' between plan and market. On the one hand, reformist leaders managed to introduce market forces at the margin and opened up space for non-state players outside the sphere of central planning; on the other hand, central planning and public ownership had to be preserved because they had strong support from the 'bird cage group,' which thickly populated the central government (Chen 1998). Deng's strategy of 'letting somebody be rich first' became crucially important in bringing real changes. Rents in this period were mostly created either by reformist leaders through policy initiatives or by local government officials and SOE managers who responded to Deng's signals. Rent-seeking activities by local government officials had a helping-hand nature and served to enable market activities and to erode the foundation of central planning while at the same time benefiting rent creators and rent seekers.

22.2.1 Rents from a Two-tier Pricing System

In the early 1980s, China was under a central planning system in which the planning authority had absolute control over price setting and material allocation. Energy, electricity, raw materials and intermediate goods were all under the control of planners. It would have been impossible for non-state enterprises, such as Township and Village Enterprises (TVEs) or Foreign Funded Enterprises (FFEs), to engage in any productive activities without access to these producer goods.[2] Fortunately, China's reformers inherited a two-tier pricing system from the pre-reform era, with a small share of producer goods allocated through market-like channels among different regions and localities (Chen 1998). The scope of these channels was extended significantly by reformist leaders at the onset of reform when pilot SOEs were allowed to market part of output above the planning quota at 'negotiated prices' and to use the proceeds to pay bonuses to workers

[2] TVEs were previously called 'commune and brigade enterprises', which were set up by local governments with investment from collective funds. Many TVEs, however, were private firms under the disguise of collective ownership. FFEs were set up by foreign investors including those from Hong Kong, Macao and Taiwan.

and managers. Since supplies of the above-plan products were limited compared to market demand, the market price kept increasing and became higher than the planning price in most cases, and rents were created by the gap between the planning and market prices. The larger the gap, the stronger the incentive to bring the product to the market, and the greater the scale of outside-plan market transactions.

The way to seek rents was to obtain products at planning prices and sell them at market prices. Soon 'official profiteering' (*guandao*) became a popular term describing the behavior of government officials, who used their authority to obtain above-quota products at planning prices from SOEs under their supervision and resell them for profit at market prices. Those individuals well connected with the officials also took the opportunity to set up businesses specialized in selling allotment letters authorized by government officials. From 1978 to 1989, especially after 1985 when market prices were no longer under government control, the two-tier pricing system produced a tremendous amount of rents. In 1988 alone, rents from price differentials of producer goods, consumer goods, black market credit and foreign exchange, import quotas and land leases were estimated to be around 400 billion RMB, or 40 percent of the GDP in that year (Hu 1989).

Two interesting observations merit mentioning: (1) rent seekers were the most effective players in defeating planners' efforts to control market prices because they benefited directly from price increases and they had insider information on how to bypass price controls; and (2) as official profiteering became rampant, SOE workers did not benefit much from above-quota production and thus had no incentives to produce more. The way to create more rents was then to reduce plan quota fulfillment rates and bring more producer goods outside planning control (Chen 1998; Wedeman 2003).These efforts certainly served to erode the foundation of central planning, and they were assisted by players on the other side of the market. TVEs and officials from township governments, for example, aggressively persuaded SOE managers to sell them more producer goods. They were willing to pay market prices and did not care whether the products were above or below the plan quota.

Smuggling was a form of rent seeking similar to the two-tier pricing system because rents were created by the gap between prices in foreign and domestic markets. Unlike the small-scale smuggling done by villagers mainly along the southeastern coastline, who shipped bags of grains, barrels of oil, clothing, watches and cigarettes across the border, there were organized groups (including SOEs, government departments and even army units) that smuggled a variety of goods ranging from tape recorders, TV sets, refrigerators, to motorcycles, petroleum products and automobiles (Gong 1997). Some Special Economic Zones (SEZs) also engaged in smuggling-like activities. SEZs were given a special privilege to import goods, free of customs duties, for use within the SEZs. Some SEZs took the opportunity to resell import goods in the domestic market and used the profit to fund infrastructural building inside the SEZ.

22.2.2 Rents and SOE Reforms

Introducing bonuses proved insufficient to improve performance of SOEs when workers succeeded in 'income matching' between SOEs and sharing bonuses evenly within the SOE (Chen 1995). Since the Household Production Responsibility System proved to be a great success in reforming the agricultural sector, the Chinese leaders decided to introduce a similar system under the name of the Contract Management Responsibility System (CMRS) to industrial SOEs in 1986 and hoped it would work equally well. Within 12 months, 78 percent of SOEs managed by the central government adopted this system; and in 1988, CMRS was expanded to over 90 percent of SOEs (Sun et al. 2002). Under this system, SOE managers would sign a contract with the government and receive a significant amount of bonuses at the end of the contract period if the contractual terms were duly fulfilled. However, there were no financial punishments if they failed to discharge contractual obligations because at that time managers did not own commensurate financial assets. The failure of the CMRS to hold SOE managers fully accountable for the performance of the enterprise created an incentive structure that encouraged opportunistic behavior and that started a new wave of rent-seeking activities.

In those days, SOEs never went bankrupt and SOE workers were never laid off because the government was not ready to enforce the bankruptcy law, fearing that high unemployment might cause social instability. SOE workers thus had an 'iron rice bowl' mentality – they felt they had a right to have bonuses as long as workers in other SOEs had them, even if their productivity was low and their firms were incurring losses. Managers faced low-grade labor problems such as absenteeism, breakdowns, low quality of products and wasted materials when they failed to deliver higher bonuses, new housing units or better quality meal services (Walder 1989). Instead of enhancing productivity and efficiency in their firms, SOE managers colluded with workers to reduce the state's share of income by increasing wage income, non-wage income and in-kind payment, and investing in staff living quarters and other non-productive projects (Chen 1995).

SOE managers had additional sources of personal gains, which included kickbacks from sales of products in the market or from provision of credit guarantees for non-state enterprises. Some managers even set up satellite companies registered under the names of their family members or close relatives and used the transfer pricing strategy to shift most of the markups from market transactions to these companies. For example, SOEs holding a steel allotment from the government planning agency came to the steel SOE, only to find the steel they wanted was out of stock. They were told that they could obtain the same type of steel from a satellite company, at the market price. Supply of raw materials operated in a similar way. The steel SOE would only receive supplies from the satellite companies at market prices.

With such transfers and rent-seeking activities, state assets in SOEs, together with forgone profits, found their way into private pockets. In less than ten years, a large proportion of SOEs had negative equity. By 1995, 24 percent of central government controlled SOEs and 72 percent of local government controlled SOEs were in deficit. A tremendous sum of non-performing loans to SOEs was left in state-owned banks (Kanamori and Zhao 2004).[3] There was therefore very little resistance to the SOE ownership reform in the mid 1990s since most local governments wanted to get rid of these losing entities.

---

[3] On the performance of China's SOEs, see also Qian and Roland (1998), Cao et al. (1999) and Shirley and Xu (2001).

22.2.3 Rents through FDI and SEZs

Reform and opening up were the two main approaches adopted by Deng Xiaoping to develop China's economy. One most important early step in opening up was to set up SEZs along the southeastern coastline to attract FDI. Foreign businesses in these zones were offered many special conditions, including tax exemption for the first three years, duty-free imports and exports, and better enforcement of contracts. Benefits from the preferential policies soon became most sought-after rents. Some domestic investors registered a business in a foreign country, which then came back to China to set up a joint venture in the SEZ with their domestic company. 'Round tripping' was used to describe such activity whereby Chinese funds left China and returned back to China as FDI after going through a 'foreign company' registered in Hong Kong, Macau or tax havens such as the Virgin Islands or Cayman Islands. The saying that 'China is the largest source of FDI in China' held certain truth if one adds together FDI from Hong Kong, Macau and those tax havens. Some SOE managers also sought opportunities to set up a joint venture with a foreign investor, which turned out to be a new means of state-assets transfer. Hu (2001) estimated that losses from duty and tax exemption reached 570 to 680 billion yuan each year from 1995 to 1998, equivalent to about 75 percent to 90 percent of total tax revenue of the year, or 7.6 percent to 9.1 percent of GDP.

It should be pointed out that some rent-seeking activities were important breakthroughs for the non-state sector during a time when private companies were not allowed to exist and operate in China. Just as some rural private enterprises were hiding under the hat of 'rural collectives,' some private firms disguised themselves in the form of FFEs and joint ventures. The foreign companies status they had was redistributive, but their contributions to the real economy were certainly wealth creating.

22.2.4 Regional Protectionism

In order for local government officials to benefit personally from market-oriented reforms, the Central-Local Revenue Sharing System was introduced in 1980 to let local governments manage their own budget and 'eat from separate kitchens'. Local governments, after surrendering a fixed amount or a fixed proportion of their revenue to the center, could use the budget surplus to pay for bonuses, subsidies, and fringe benefits of government officials. When Shenzhen SEZ and Guangdong Province ran large budget surpluses by allowing the market to play a larger role, they could afford to pay government officials larger bonuses and let them become rich first. The news traveled fast to other parts of the country, inducing imitation and innovation by other local governments, and spreading market reforms all over China. It led to competition between local governments to enable spontaneous reforms and to test policy innovations. Clearly, China's bottom-up reforms would not have been so successful without the strategy to let some officials become rich first – through rent extraction from the rents that the officials helped create.

Revenue-maximizing local officials also engaged in rent-seeking activities by practicing regional protectionism. They protected, in local markets, locally produced goods with high tax rates such as liquors, cigarettes and detergents. They set up check points at borders to stop raw materials from leaving their domains because these materials, such as tobacco leaves, silkworm, wool, tea leaves and cotton, could be turned into processed goods locally, generating more tax revenues for the local budget than just simply being sold as raw materials in the market. The protectionist behavior of local governments resulted in fragmentation of the domestic market, immobility of resources and lack of industrial specialization and regional integration (Chen 1991; Lu and Chen 2009).

22.3 RENT SEEKING UNDER THE STATIST MODEL

China ended its drift between plan and market in 1992 when the 14th CPC Congress finally adopted a 'socialist market economy' as the goal for its economic transformation. The reformers could then push market-oriented reforms wholesale from the top down. From 1992 to 1998, comprehensive market institutions were created, legal frameworks and social structures established, and SOE ownership reforms and government administrative reforms made significant progress as well.

Reformist leaders at that time felt it necessary to recentralize fiscal resources and administrative power to push for reforms. While recentralization served them well in building the institutional infrastructure at the macro level, this was done at the expense of containing entrepreneurial activities at the micro level (Chen et al. 2002; Huang 2012; Chen 2013).[4] Non-state enterprises were gradually deprived of access to the formal financial system and had to rely on funds from the informal sector, and local governments gradually moved from helping-hand to grabbing-hand behavior when they were no longer residual claimants to fiscal revenues from their localities. When deflation in 1997–2002 threatened to destabilize the country, the technocrat leaders in Beijing, who were good at mobilizing government resources and never had a deep trust in and understanding of market forces, quickly resorted to issuing administrative orders to local governments requiring them to guarantee at least 8 percent annual GDP growth within their region, or simply *baoba* in Chinese.

Baoba had ushered in the statist model of development in China characterized by 'investment hunger' (Kornai 1980a, 1980b [2008]). Four principles underlie *baoba*: (1) government at all levels, not market forces, should be responsible for economic growth; (2) resources, including fiscal and financial resources, should be reserved for governments to generate growth; (3) the SOEs, which are closely linked with central and local governments, are important partners in *baoba* and should be given privileges or preferential treatment; and (4) local governments should guarantee economic growth even if economic, social and environmental costs are high. Indeed, post-1998 China has closely followed these four principles in its economic expansion.

Under the statist model, rents are mainly created by monopolizing resources by governments at various levels and creating monopoly privileges for government agencies

---

[4] On the helping hand of local government in China, see Walder (1995). For a theoretical growth model in the context of a helping and grabbing hand, see Dalgic and Long (2006). They describe a central government that sets the tax rate and the central share of tax revenue and local governments that engage in helping-hand behavior for local enterprises to benefit from an enlarged tax base, while also extracting rents through extortion.

and SOEs (including state-owned financial institutions such as banks, insurance companies and trust companies, which monopolized financial resources). Rents were also created when SOEs underwent ownership reforms in the late 1990s. Rent-seeking activities in this period therefore are mainly redistributive. They reduced economic efficiency and wealth creation, and resulted in misallocation of resources.

22.3.1 SOE Ownership Reform and Asset Stripping

Unable to support so many loss-making SOEs, the central government decided in the mid-1990s to keep only large-scale SOEs in key economic sectors and transform small- and medium-scale SOEs through merger, lease or divestment, which was in fact a process of privatization. The process provided ample opportunities for rent seeking characterized by asset stripping in many cases. The case of Dayu gives a good illustration.

Dayu is a water-conserving tube producer located in Jiuquan, a city in northwestern China. It was a SOE set up by the local government in 1999 with an initial capital of 4.9 million yuan. In subsequent years, the local government expanded the company by more investment, and by the year 2000 the factory had a registered capital of more than 11 million yuan. Wang Dong, an official from Jiuquan Water Authority, was appointed the manager of the company. Due to poor management, the company had negative net assets of 0.2 million yuan only 28 months later. In 2003, the local government decided to sell Dayu. In order to make it more attractive to buyers, the local government packaged the company with the strip of land it occupied and priced the deal at 9.9 million yuan. This strip of land, with an area of 54 000 square meters, was valued at 2.5 million yuan in 2000 but was revalued before the sale at 0.33 million yuan, which was only 13 percent of its original valuation three years earlier. Dayu was finally sold to Wang Dong, the government-appointed legal representative and manager, who paid less than 1 million yuan to become owner of Dayu. In 2009 when Dayu was listed in China's stock market, its market capitalization reached 2.2 billion yuan, making Wang a billionaire in six years. He was president of Dayu, holding 52.8 percent of the total shares of the company.[5]

There were many cases such as Dayu during the SOE ownership reform and the fairness of the state asset assessment and the transparency of the selling process were questioned by the public.

22.3.2 Land Sales

Selling state land is similar to selling state-owned companies. It is also difficult to know who created and extracted rents and who sought rents. The following corruption case, however, sheds some light on this type of rent-seeking activity.

Jiang Renjie was vice mayor of Suzhou City in Jiangsu Province. In 2004, he was detained and interrogated by the Commission for Disciplinary Inspection of the CPC,

---

[5] Lei Liping, 'From a millionaire to a billionaire in six years', *21st Century Business Herald*, Economic Report, 13 November 2009, available at http://finance.sina.com.cn/stock/cngem/gemnews/20091113/00176959497.shtml (accessed 28 September 2012).

and later transferred to the People's Procuratorate.[6] Jiang was sentenced to death for taking bribes of more than 108 million yuan within the 3.5 years during which he served as vice mayor of the city. The investigation revealed a land sale deal in which he served as provider of insider information, partner in rent seeking, adviser to rent seekers and, when the deal ran into problems, the problem solver for the rent seekers.

In 2001, the city government decided to take back a piece of land in Suzhou Industrial Park, which had been sold to a real estate company for 9 million yuan. Jiang came to know about it when the company approached him for help. He suggested to his friend Gu, the owner of another real estate company in Suzhou, to buy the piece of land for 12 million yuan, since he believed the local government would have to pay at least 18 million yuan to buy it back. Gu followed Jiang's advice, but ran into a serious problem when another vice mayor intervened by insisting on buying back the piece of land at its original price of 9 million yuan. Jiang could not reverse this vice mayor's decision as both of them had the same official rank. He then advised Gu to write a letter to the Suzhou Committee of the Communist Party, declaring that his company was a joint venture with a Hong Kong investor. Since Suzhou tried to maintain a good reputation for working effectively with foreign investors, withdrawing the land without proper compensation would tarnish the reputation of the government and affect future investment. When the letter was received, Jiang was sent, as expected, to investigate the case and proposed the land be exchanged for another piece of land of equal area. Gu eventually made a profit of 17 million yuan from the land deal, and shared half of it with Jiang.

Acquisition of land from suburban farmers for city development presents ample opportunities for rent seeking. Farmers, of course, would play simple tricks to increase compensation. However, large rents could be extracted by developers, government officials and village heads. Social unrest and protests are often reported in China because farmers are underpaid in land-related compensations.

22.3.3 Infrastructure Projects

Among the GDP components, local governments can only affect investment. *Baoba* is therefore associated with investment hunger. Naturally, investments in roads, bridges, highways, railways, subways, ports, airports, sewage systems, power and water supply and other infrastructure projects became new opportunities for rent seeking. Seizing big public project contracts becomes a promising way to make a good fortune. It is estimated that the cost of constructing each kilometer of highway in China is much higher than in other countries and the extra cost is due to corruption.[7] For example, in Hunan, a province in central China, four director generals of the provincial transport bureau were convicted, consecutively, for corruption from 1997 to 2010. Interestingly, the amount of bribes they took formed an increasing series. The first director general took 200 000

[6] In China, corruption cases usually undergo two steps. First, the suspected official is detained by the Disciplinary Inspection Committee for enquiries about the details of corrupt activities. This is called 'double specifics' (*Shuanggui* in Chinese) – to report the inspectors at the specific time at the specific place. When corrupt deals are confirmed, the official is transferred to the procuratorate for further investigation and conviction.

[7] For more examples, see Gong (1997, 2002) and He (2000).

yuan, his successor a million, the third nearly 20 million and the last one over 30 million. Ironically, each of them swore to be honest and not to become corrupt in their inaugural address.[8]

How are rents created from infrastructure projects? In principle, rent seeking is impossible under open bidding. In reality, however, rents can be created by manipulation. Bidding for public projects in China often exists only in form but not in substance. The contracts are usually controlled by a few key figures. Contractors and subcontractors form a food chain, and their position in the chain is based on the kind of personal relationship or *guanxi* they have. Once a contract is in the hand of the 'successful bidder,' it is usually resold to a subcontractor who then resells it again to yet another or several sub-subcontractors. When the contract finally comes to the last contractor who actually does the work, there is almost no profit left. He then resorts to performing shoddy work and using inferior materials as substitutes.

Railways in China are state owned, state run and also mainly state invested. With the extension of highways over the country, investment in railway construction has also expanded. From 2003 to 2011, investments in railway construction and facilities totaled 3.3 trillion yuan.[9] This was a golden era for China's railway development, and it was also a period of haymaking for rent seekers. Liu Zhijun was China's Minister of Railways during this period. He did not sell contracts himself, but did so through the hands of a woman who earned 2.4 billion yuan in the process.[10] With the downfall of Liu, more than ten high ranking officials were also detained. It is believed that much more in rents was created and captured through subcontracting. During the eight years, two major railway accidents occurred, taking 110 lives and injuring hundreds.

22.3.4 Budgetary Transfers

After fiscal recentralization in 1994, more than 55 percent of budgetary revenue was collected by the center, which only spent around 25 percent and distributed the rest as budgetary transfers. These transfers became rents subject to rent seeking by local governments, and gave officials in central government agencies good opportunities to become rich too. More than 5000 representative offices were set up in Beijing by provincial, city and county governments to engage in rent-seeking activities so as to secure central transfers. Huang and Chen (2012) found specific-purpose transfers (such as earmarked transfers), which accounted for 69 percent of total transfers by the center in 2009, to be anti-equalizing: rich regions tend to obtain more of the transfers than poor regions. These transfers are typically not rule-based and are subject to political influence and rent seeking.

The representative offices also lobby for preferential policies because they carry rents

---

[8] Available at http://news.sina.com.cn/c/2012-10-13/043925349088.shtml (accessed 16 October 2012).

[9] See the statistical bulletins published by the Ministry of Railways of China, available at http://www.china-mor.gov.cn/zwzc/tjxx/tjgb/ (accessed 10 October 2012).

[10] Available at http://diyizhuye.com/a/baoxian/20120604/4931.html (accessed 10 October 2012).

with them.[11] For example, when a county's GDP per capita is below the line set by the central government, it is called a Poverty County and can thus enjoy many subsidies, tax reductions as well as other privileges. To secure the title of a Poverty County, officials led by the head of a county could stay in Beijing for over a month, with the objective of adding the county to the list of Poverty Counties (Liu 2008).

22.3.5 Regulatory Rents

Government regulations have been used to create regulatory rents, often under a disguise. Here is a typical example from Zhengzhou, the capital city of Henan Province. In 1998, the municipal government set up an office to supervise production and selling of steamed bread (*mantou* in Chinese), a staple food for local people. It required all *mantou* stalls to pay 1100 yuan for a permit issued by the office, and to buy at least 60 sacks of wheat flour every day from shops designated by the office. Any stall that failed to comply would be subject to a fine ranging from 3000 to 20000 yuan. Soon five district governments followed suit to set up their own *mantou* offices. All six offices issued permits, collected fees and gave fines, as well as taking kickbacks from designated flour shops. Competition between the municipal and district offices grew in intensity, culminating in a street fight that broke out in March 2001 when a *mantou* stall was found without a permit from the municipal office. The business owner refused to pay a fine to municipal officials and declared that he had paid for a permit issued by the district office. He gave the office a call for help, which resulted in dozens of officials from both municipal and district offices gathering in the street, all in uniform with equipment, quarreling over who had the right to issue permits and collect fees. The quarrel finally turned into a fight, which was reported in the news and spread through the Internet. *Mantou* offices became a laughing stock and were abolished by the provincial government, not for rent extraction, but for loss of face in public.[12] Ironically, not long after *mantou* offices were abolished, watermelon offices were created. A township government even issued corn-harvesting permits to farmers and demanded a fee of 500 yuan per *mu* (1/15 hectare).

Regulatory rents have become rampant, ranging from designating an audit firm for filing annual audits by the Bureau of Industrial and Commerce, designating a car towing company for emergency road services on highways by the Police Department, to editing yearbooks and selling them to captive buyers by the Department of Culture or Propaganda, or designating a tax consulting firm for filing tax returns by the Tax Bureau. They create side income for government officials in the 'be rich first' pursuit, but stifle the growth of small- and medium-size enterprises when numerous approvals, permits, fees, charges and regulations increase business costs significantly.

---

11 In fact, many institutions, including colleges and universities, have agencies in Beijing. Rent-seeking costs of local governments could be estimated by costs of running the representative offices in Beijing (Liu 2008).

12 Available at http://tieba.baidu.com/p/121659875 (accessed 30 October 2012).

22.3.6 Rents within the Bureaucracy through Promotion

As mentioned in the foregoing discussion, fulfilling KPIs and maintaining stability become the necessary conditions for local government leaders to be promoted to a higher position. There is a type of rent associated with officials' desire to fulfil targets.

In order to fulfil the annual growth target for taxes, some local governments offered to 'buy taxes' from firms located outside their own domains. Here is how it works. Firm A in City A needs to pay tax, but the tax bureau in City A has already met its growth target and does not want to collect more for fear that a higher growth target would be imposed on them next year. City B, on the other hand, could not meet the growth target and needs to collect more taxes. The tax bureau in City B would offer a deep discount to Firm A, collecting 80 000 yuan of taxes but issuing a receipt of 100 000.

Similarly, when FDI is not enough, some local governments would seek help from foreign investors who would then register a few shell companies, wire in funds for a few weeks, receive 'sign-up bonuses' from the local government, and then move the funds out of the country. They could even make some extra money by selling the shell companies to local businessmen who could then carry on enjoying the FFE status.

Maintaining stability (*weiwen*) is another important necessary condition for promotion, and local governments are willing to spend a lot of money to avoid negative publicity from unrest, accidents or appeal at higher offices. Special budgets are set aside to pacify protestors or to send people home from Beijing or provincial capitals free of charge.

A more direct way to promotion is to bribe those officials in charge of promotion (Kahana and Liu 2010). In recent years, quite a few local leaders were convicted for taking bribes in exchange for a promotion, which can be viewed as 'selling official positions'. Ma De, the party secretary of Suihua City in northeastern Heilongjiang Province, is reported to have made a record for position selling in China. From 1995 to 2002, Ma took bribes of 24 million yuan from his subordinates. A total of 265 officials in Suihua were involved in Ma's case, including 50 leaders in ten counties and municipal agencies.[13] Du Xin, another party secretary in Pingdingshan City of Henan Province, took bribes from 148 officials for position seeking. He is special in that each position is clearly priced, varying from 20 000 to 100 000 yuan.[14] Selling official positions provides a major source of income for corrupt officials in poor areas. Hexian County of Anhui Province in eastern China is on the national list of 'Poverty Counties'. Its party secretary, Yang, was convicted in 2006 for taking 106 bribes, of which 87 were from position seekers.[15]

---

[13] Available at http://finance.sina.com.cn/leadership/crz/20050322/17081450964.shtm (accessed 8 October 2012).

[14] Available at http://news.xinhuanet.com/lianzheng/2007-12/26/content_7315532.htm (accessed 8 October 2012).

[15] Available at http://news.sina.com.cn/c/2006-12-05/170611707185.shtml (accessed 8 October 2012).

22.4 CONCLUSIONS

The contesting of rents unproductively uses valuable resources and time (Tullock 1967 [2008]). Rent seeking is also associated with corruption (see, for example, Kahana and Liu 2010). The planned communist economies were intrinsically corrupt rent-seeking systems because all resource allocation and personal benefits derived from political decisions or from personal decisions by some people about benefits to other people (Hillman 2006 [2009], chapter 2). The culture of rent seeking and social losses from rent seeking associated with contesting of ownership of privatized assets continued in the transition from planning in the former Soviet Union and Eastern European countries (Gelb et al. 1998).[16]

Our review in this chapter indicates that in China, rent seeking could give rise to significant positive economic effects. Through 'helping-hand' behavior, regional government officials had incentives to promote growth to benefit from rent extraction or rent sharing. Growth-oriented incremental reforms were often permitted as long as the reforms were consistent with the political interest of the central government (Zhang 2012). Rent seeking, accompanied by profit seeking (Buchanan 1980 [2008]) under the two-tier pricing system, defeated the planners' efforts to control prices and brought goods onto markets for TVEs and other non-state firms. Rent seeking in SEZs and through FDI opened up opportunities for domestic private enterprises that were not legally allowed to exist. Rent seeking accompanied by profit seeking unleashed entrepreneurial energies and released resources for productive use, thereby resulting in shrinkage of the public sector and a rapid increase of the private sector. In 1978, more than 99 percent of China's gross industrial output value was produced by SOEs and collectively owned enterprises. In 1993, the non-state sector contributed 53 percent of gross industrial output value, surpassing SOEs for the first time in the People's Republic of China's history.[17]

We have described how, by the mid-1990s, underlying conditions began to change. Prices were decontrolled, the material allocation system was abolished, private enterprises were legally allowed to exist and market reforms were promoted from the top down by the central government. Rent seeking in this period gravitated toward the more usual model when there is government-led investment. Regulatory rents are created by granting monopoly privileges to government agencies, SOEs or business entities owned by insiders. Other rent-seeking activities, such as asset stripping, contract fixing and official position selling, are just instances of outright corruption.

A new communist leadership that took office in China in 2012 seemed to understand the dire situation that they had inherited. They chose to clean up the mess by cracking down on corruption first, catching more than 20 'tigers' – corrupt minister-ranked officials – in less than two years. They reined in local government debts, stopped wasteful investment projects and ordered large SOEs to give up non-core businesses. They

---

[16] Although not uniformly: see Frye and Shleifer (1997) on helping and grabbing hands in Poland and Russia. For evidence of a grabbing hand in the Ukraine, see Gorodnichenko and Sabirianova Peter (2007).

[17] See China's Statistical Yearbooks, 1981, 1996.

also took steps to clean up regulatory hurdles by requiring government departments to simplify business approval procedures, eliminate unnecessary permits and increase transparency.

Our review of rents and rent seeking in China ends with these policies. We shall not speculate about whether the culture of rent seeking that is associated with the quest for privileged benefit can be brought to an end in China. Accomplishing this may not be easy. Financial liberalization is required and the distributive coalition of insiders would have to be broken up.

REFERENCES

Buchanan, James M. (1980), 'Rent seeking and profit seeking', in James M. Buchanan, Robert D. Tollison and Gordon Tullock (eds) (1980), *Toward a Theory of the Rent-seeking Society*, College Station, TX: Texas A&M University Press, pp. 3–15, reprinted in Roger D. Congleton, Arye L. Hillman and Kai A. Konrad (eds) (2008), *40 Years of Research on Rent Seeking 1 – The Theory of Rent Seeking*, Heidelberg: Springer, pp. 55–67.

Cao, Yuanzheng, Yingyi Qian and Barry R. Weingast (1999), 'From federalism, Chinese style to privatization Chinese style', *Economics of Transition*, **7**(1), 103–31.

Chen, Kang (1991), 'The failure of recentralization in China: interplays among enterprises, local governments and the center', in Arye L. Hillman (ed.), *Markets and Politicians: Politicized Economic Choice*, Boston, MA: Kluwer, pp. 209–29.

Chen, Kang (1995), *The Chinese Economy in Transition: Micro Changes and Macro Implications*, Singapore: Singapore University Press.

Chen, Kang (1998), 'Accidental freedom: economic development experience in post-Mao China', in Kua-Tsai Liou (ed.), *Handbook of Economic Development*, Public Administration and Public Policy Series 69, New York: Marcel Dekker, pp. 611–30.

Chen, Kang (2004), 'Fiscal centralization and the form of corruption in China', *European Journal of Political Economy*, **20**(4), 1001–9.

Chen, Kang (2013), 'China models and local government entrepreneurship', Paper presented at the International Workshop on Local Government Entrepreneurship in China: Dynamics, Achievement and Risks, jointly organized by Lee Kuan Yew School of Public Policy at National University of Singapore and School of Public Policy Management at Tsinghua University, Beijing, 24–26 October.

Chen, Kang, Arye L. Hillman and Qingyang Gu (2002), 'From the helping hand to the grabbing hand: fiscal federalism and corruption in China', in John Wong and Ding Lu (eds), *China's Economy into the New Century: Structural Issues and Problems*, Singapore: Singapore University Press and World Scientific, pp. 193–215.

Dalgic, Engin and Ngo Van Long (2006), 'Corrupt local governments as resource farmers: the helping hand and the grabbing hand', *European Journal of Political Economy*, **22**(1), 115–38.

Frye, Timothy and Andrei Shleifer (1997), 'The invisible hand and the grabbing hand', *American Economic Review*, **87**(2), 354–8.

Gelb, Alan, Arye L. Hillman and Heinrich W. Ursprung (1998), 'Rents as distractions: why the exit from transition is prolonged', in Nicolas C. Baltas, George Demopoulos and Joseph Hassid (eds), *Economic Interdependence and Cooperation in Europe*, Heidelberg: Springer, pp. 21–38.

Gong, Ting (1997), 'Forms and characteristics of China's corruption in the 1990s: change with continuity', *Communist and Post-Communist Studies*, **30**(3), 277–88.

Gong, Ting (2002), 'Dangerous collusion: corruption as a collective venture in contemporary China', *Communist and Post-Communist Studies*, **35**(1), 85–103.

Gorodnichenko, Yuriy and Klara Sabirianova Peter (2007), 'Public sector pay and corruption: measuring bribery from micro data', *Journal of Public Economics*, **91**(5–6), 963–91.

He, Zengke (2000), 'Corruption and anti-corruption in reform China', *Communist and Post-Communist Studies*, **33**(2), 243–70.

Hillman, Arye L. (2006, in Chinese), *Public Finance and Public Policy: Responsibilities and Limitations of Government*, Beijing: Chinese Academy of Social Sciences, reprinted in 2009, New York: Cambridge University Press.

Hillman, Arye L. and Heinrich W. Ursprung (2000), 'Political culture and economic decline', *European Journal of Political Economy*, **16**(2), 189–213, reprinted in Roger D. Congleton, Arye L. Hillman and Kai A. Konrad (eds) (2008), *40 Years of Research on Rent Seeking 2 – Applications: Rent Seeking in Practice*, Heidelberg: Springer, pp. 219–45.

Hu, Angang (2001), 'Corruption and social injustice: estimation and analysis of economic losses from corruption in late 1990s in China' (in Chinese), *Jiangsu Social Science*, **3**, 51–3.

Hu, Heli (1989), 'An estimate of China's rents lost in 1988' (in Chinese), *Comparative Economic and Social Systems*, **5**, 32–7.

Huang, Bihong and Kang Chen (2012), 'Are intergovernmental transfers in China equalizing?', *China Quarterly*, **23**(3), 534–51.

Huang, Yasheng (2012), 'How did China take off?', *Journal of Economic Perspectives*, **26**(4), 147–70.

Kahana, Nava and Liu Qijun (2010), 'Endemic corruption', *European Journal of Political Economy*, **26**(1), 82–8.

Kanamori, Toshiki and Zhijun Zhao (2004), 'Private sector development in the People's Republic of China', Asian Development Bank Institute, Working Paper Series No. 27, Manila, Philippines, available at http://www.adbi.org/book/2004/10/07/602.private.sector.prc/ (accessed 15 May 2014).

Kornai, Janos (1980a), *Economics of Shortage*, Amsterdam: North-Holland.

Kornai, Janos (1980b), 'Hard and soft budget constraint', *Acta Oeconomica*, **25**(3–4), 231–46, reprinted in Roger D. Congleton, Arye L. Hillman and Kai A. Konrad (eds) (2008), *40 Years of Research on Rent Seeking 2 – Applications: Rent Seeking in Practice*, Heidelberg: Springer, pp. 569–83.

Liu, Qijun (2008), *Research on Rent-seeking Behavior* (in Chinese), Wuhan: Huazhong University of Science and Technology Press.

Lu, Ming and Zhao Chen (2009), 'Fragmented growth: why economic opening may worsen domestic market segmentation? (in Chinese)', *Economic Research Journal*, **3**, 42–52.

Naughton, Barry (2007), *The Chinese Economy: Transition and Growth*, Cambridge, MA: MIT Press.

Ngo, Tak-Wing and Yongping Wu (2009), *Rent Seeking in China*, London and New York: Routledge.

Qian, Yingyi and Gerard Roland (1998), 'Federalism and the soft budget constraint', *American Economic Review*, **88**(5), 1143–62.

Shirk, Susan L. (1993), *The Political Logic of Economic Reform in China*, Berkeley, CA: University of California Press.

Shirley, Mary M. and Lixin Colin Xu (2001), 'Empirical effects of performance contracts: evidence from China', *Journal of Law, Economics, and Organization*, **17**(1), 168–200.

Sun, Guanhong, Yuchun Hu and Zhouwang Chen (2002), *On the Government-enterprise Relations in China: A Political-science Perspective* (in Chinese), Nanchang: Jiangxi People's Press.

Tullock, Gordon (1967), 'The welfare costs of tariffs, monopolies and theft', *Economic Inquiry*, **5**(3), 224–32, reprinted in Roger D. Congleton, Arye L. Hillman and Kai A. Konrad (eds) (2008), *40 Years of Research on Rent Seeking 1 – The Theory of Rent Seeking*, Heidelberg: Springer, pp. 45–54.

Tullock, Gordon (1996), 'Book review: the Chinese economy in transition, micro changes and macro implications by Kang Chen', *Public Choice*, **88**(3–4), 425–6.

Walder, Andrew G. (1989), 'Factory and manager in an era of reform', *China Quarterly*, **118**(2), 242–64.

Walder, Andrew G. (1995), 'China's transitional economy: interpreting its significance', *China Quarterly*, **144**(4), 963–79.

Wedeman, Andrew H. (2003), *From Mao to Market: Rent Seeking, Local Protectionism, and Marketization in China*, Cambridge: Cambridge University Press.

Zhang, Yongjing (2012), 'A view from behavioral political economy on China's institutional change', *China Economic Review*, **23**(4), 991–1002.

23. Market liberalization and rent seeking in India

Sugata Marjit and Vivekananda Mukherjee*

SUMMARY

This chapter shows the relevance of rents and rent seeking in post-independence India, where market-oriented reforms have substantially reduced government control over economic activities. Despite the significant economic reforms, rent seeking and corruption have been prevalent. The chapter reviews the research on rent seeking and corruption in India and outlines a theory relating rent seeking to economic reforms. Liberal and conservative economic policies are endogenous in such a framework. We also discuss other possible relationships between reforms and rent seeking in the context of an emerging market.

23.1 INTRODUCTION

India achieved independence from the United Kingdom in 1947. The Indian path to development after the end of British colonial rule was one of command and control with some private participation within a framework of centralized planning, borrowed primarily from the Soviet Union. In the 1980s reforms started to favor incumbent large private firms. In the mid 1980s, imports of technology and capital goods were liberalized to some extent and technology transfer and joint ventures were encouraged. In the 1990s, significant reforms were introduced that removed barriers to trade and to new private investment. As the country began reforming its trade and investment regimes, deregulation of various kinds was implemented or attempted. Tariffs were reduced from an average of more than 200 percent to 25 percent. The so-called license raj, a term for the need for government approval for economic activity, was greatly relaxed. Access to foreign investment was liberalized, financial markets were allowed to function properly, the exchange rate was allowed to depreciate and a regime of managed float was put in place. There are several policies in which the political process was unsupportive of needed reforms but this is not the issue on which this chapter focuses. Deregulation, liberalization, globalization and whatever be the claim to fame as the world's largest democracy, major financial scams with political and bureaucratic involvement reveal a preoccupation with rent creation and the prominence of rent seeking in India.

The idea of rent seeking as explaining behavior proposed by Tullock (1967 [2008]) and applied to India by Krueger (1974 [2008]) was an appropriate characterization of the

* Sugata Marjit acknowledges the RBI endowment and CTRPFP at CSSSC for financial support and the hospitality of the University of Queensland in April 2014 where some of the research was done.

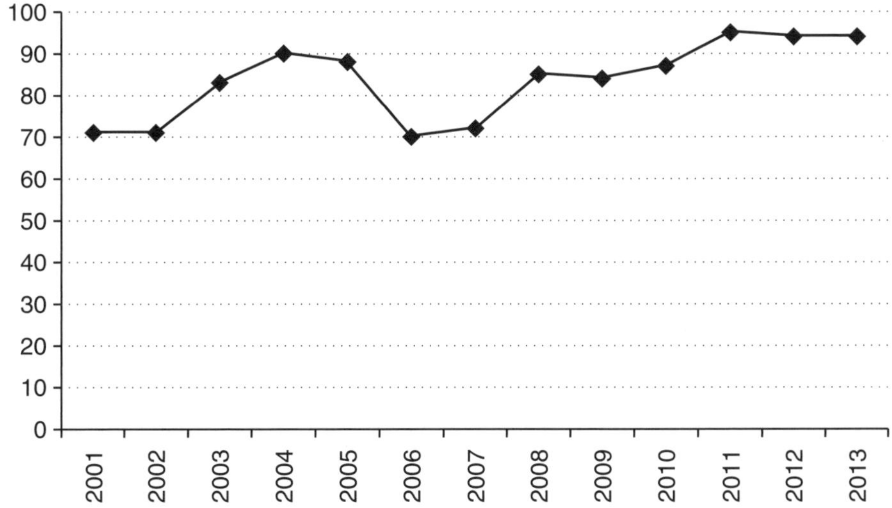

Figure 23.1 CPI ranks of India, 2001–13

Indian economy in the pre-liberalized era of command and control. Bhagwati and Desai (1970) addressed at length the problems related to high tariffs and a license regime that adversely affected allocation of resources in Indian industries. Their research, though not specifically on rent seeking, elaborated situations that created rents due to restrictive trade and industrial policies. In other research, Bhagwati (1971) proposed government intervention in distorted markets in the context of the theory of the second best. The planning and regulatory regime thwarted efficiency and impeded growth and development. Tax evasion, bribery and bureaucratic harassment reduce economic activity and growth.

Introduction of a liberal, market-oriented and deregulated environment is a way of countering rent-seeking behavior by shifting attention from unproductive rent seeking to productive profit seeking (Buchanan 1980 [2008]). Did this happen in India? If so, why did India face a relentless ordeal of scams quite unprecedented in the pre-reform era, yet having experienced very respectable rates of growth?[1]

The corruption perception index (CPI) published by Transparency International shows a consistent downward slide of India in corruption ranking. Figure 23.1 shows the CPI rankings of India over 2001–13. In the CPI, a higher score is an indicator of higher corruption in the economy.

To analyze the issues of a common basis for liberalization and corruption and related rent seeking, a theory can be developed that defines the relationship between rent seeking and reform. The theory is consistent with examples in which reform decisions

---

[1] Samia Tavares (2007) has examined the effect of trade liberalization and political liberalization on corruption from cross-country data in the 1980s and 1990s. The results show that undertaking both types of reforms in quick succession reduces corruption but corruption increases in countries that undertake trade liberalization after five years of democratization. The results appear to be consistent with the Indian case.

are endogenous and guided by motives of rent creation and rent seeking. The inertia inherited from a regulated regime and sustained by the prior colonial ethos of bureaucratic behavior contributes to a relationship between rent seeking and reform that is more complex than rent seeking in usual models of contests (as in Konrad 2009 and Long 2013).

Section 23.2 of the chapter describes the legacy of past rent creation and rent seeking in India as manifested in sustained post-reform rent seeking and corruption. Section 23.3 discusses the underlying theory. Section 23.4 concludes.

23.2 RENT SEEKING IN INDIA

Rent seeking and corruption are expected to be more prevalent in autocracies rather than democracies because democracies have the rule of law and there are more political decision makers who need to be persuaded to do political rent-creating and rent-assigning favors (Hillman 2013). India is, however, a glaring exception to the prediction that democracy moderates rent seeking and corruption. India suffered from corruption under British colonial rule and the tradition of corruption continued and increased in prevalence after independence from British rule in 1947. The first committee appointed by the Government of India on prevention of corruption, in its report submitted in 1964, explored the causes of corruption in India. It observed the following:

> Till about the beginning of the Second World War corruption was prevalent in considerable measure amongst revenue, police, excise and Public Works Department officials particularly of the lower grades and higher ranks were comparatively free from this evil. The smaller compass of State activities, the 'great depression' and lack of fluid resources set limits to the opportunities and capacity to corrupt or to be corrupted. The immense war effort during 1939–45 which involved an annual expenditure of hundreds of crores of rupees over all kinds of war supplies and procurement contracts created unprecedented opportunities for acquisition of wealth by doubtful means. The war time controls and scarcities provided ample opportunities for bribery, corruption, favoritism etc. The then Government subordinated all other considerations to that of making war effort a success. Propriety of means was no consideration if it impeded the war effort. It would not be far wrong to say that the high watermark of corruption reached in India as perhaps in other countries also, during the period of the Second World War. (Government of India 1964, pp. 6–7)

After the War, the British left the country in 1947 with a bureaucracy not competent for controlling burgeoning corruption (Myrdal 1968 [2005]) – or indeed a bureaucracy that was a primary source of corruption.

From post-independence until the beginning of liberal reforms in 1991, India followed a path of development in which the government and public sector enterprises played a dominant role. In the five-year plans starting from 1951, controls over production, prices, investment and foreign trade were deemed essential. Srinivasan (1996, p. 209, emphases in original) summarizes:

> The system involved *industrial licensing* under which the scale, technology and location of any investment project other than the relatively small ones were regulated and permission was needed to expand, relocate, the change of the output or input mixes of operating plants; *exchange control system* which required exporters to surrender their foreign exchange earnings

to Central Bank at the official exchange rate and allocated the exchange earnings to the users through *import licensing*; *capital issues control*, under which access to domestic equity market and debt finance was controlled; *price controls* (complete or partial) on some vital consumption goods (for example food grains, sugar, vegetable oils) and critical inputs (for example fertilizer, irrigation water, fuel); *made-to-measure* protection from import competition, granted to domestic producers in many 'priority' industries, including in particular equipment producers. The agriculture sector was insulated from world markets, subject to land-ceiling and tenancy legislation, and forced to sell part of the output at fixed prices, but it was also provided subsidy on irrigation, fertilizer and electricity. Large commercial banks which were nationalized in 1969 were subject to directed and selective credit controls, controls on deposit and lending rates, and had to lend nearly two-thirds of their loanable funds to government through the operation of reserve requirements of various kinds.

Srinivasan (1996) also points out that all these regulations were discretionary rather than rule-based and automatic. Hence rent seeking was spawned at all layers of administration among politicians and bureaucrats.

Widespread corruption weakens the personal moral cost of being corrupt and contributes to persistence of corruption (Myrdal 1968 [2005]; Andvig and Moene 1990; Gupta and Mishra 2007). On the administrative side, when suspicion of corruption is rampant, a protective device is to spread and share the responsibility for decisions to the maximum extent possible. This makes the bureaucracy slow and sluggish in the delivery of services. Consequently, opportunities are created at the 'low' level of bureaucracy for rent extraction in the name of speeding the delivery of services. Ordinary consumers and firms at all levels pay 'speed money' at the 'low level' of bureaucracy, with rampant use of middlemen for bribing. Large firms including foreign multinationals pay bribes at the 'high level' of bureaucracy for influencing decisions. Small entrepreneurs can avoid formal 'licensing' by operating in an informal sector (or 'shadow' economy).[2]

A publicized case of 'high'-level bribery in the pre-liberalization period was the Bofors scandal in the 1980s, in which the then Prime Minister Rajiv Gandhi and several other ministers were accused of receiving bribes from the Swedish Company Bofors AB in return for a successful bid to provide the Indian military with howitzers (IANS 2007). The value of the bribes was estimated at Rs 640 million (approximately US $1.4 million) (India Today 2009). There were many other similar incidents.

With regard to 'low'-level corruption, a survey comparing the extent of petty bureaucratic corruption across the Indian states found more than 60 percent of Indians to have paid a bribe to receive a government service, amounting to bribes of more than Rs 210 billion (approximately US $4.7 billion) each year across 11 government departments (Transparency International India and Centre for Media Studies 2005). Another survey found that more than one third of people below the poverty line had paid a bribe in the previous year to access government services (Transparency International India and Centre for Media Studies 2007). Bushell (2013) shows that the rents generated at the 'lower' level of bureaucracy have been shared with the higher-level bureaucrats/politicians, with bureaucrats competing among themselves for allotment of prized postings. The picture is consistent with the Hillman and Katz (1987 [2008]) model of

[2] Chaudhuri et al. (2006) estimated the size of the shadow economy in India at the pre-liberalization period of 1974–75 to 1991–92 at 19.97 percent of net state domestic product of India.

hierarchical rent seeking, in which bribes paid at lower levels of government bureaucracy filter upwards to higher-level officials.

Anne Krueger (1974 [2008]) estimated the social loss due to rent seeking because of restrictions on international trade at 7.4 percent of Indian gross national product (GNP). Mohammad and Whalley (1984) estimated that the social cost due to rent seeking was between 35 percent and 50 percent of Indian GNP. This range of values was based on the assumption that rents created at the 'low' level of bureaucracy were not contested; if the 'low'-level bureaucracy rents were also contested, the estimate of social cost of rent seeking of Mohammad and Whalley (1984) of course increases.

Indian federalism is conducive to rent seeking. There are state governments and a central government. The Indian constitution assigns the tax and expenditure responsibilities of these two layers of governments. While the central government has more of the financial power and control over policies, the state governments are responsible for delivery of most of the services at the local level. Though there are statutory provisions of rule-based sharing of central government revenue between the center and the states, the scope of such transfers is limited and the central government has significant discretionary power in allocation of the resources. This leads to lobbying of the center by states for access to a higher amount of funds as well as for favorable national and international policies. Biswas et al. (2010) show that states' lobbying power significantly explains discretionary fund disbursement among Indian states. Using the share of central government consumption expenditure in the combined consumption expenditures of the center and the states as an index of the extent of centralization in Indian federalism, Figure 23.2 shows that the extent of centralization increased over the period 1970–71 to 2009–10, suggesting rent seeking through the type of contest among states correspondingly also increased.

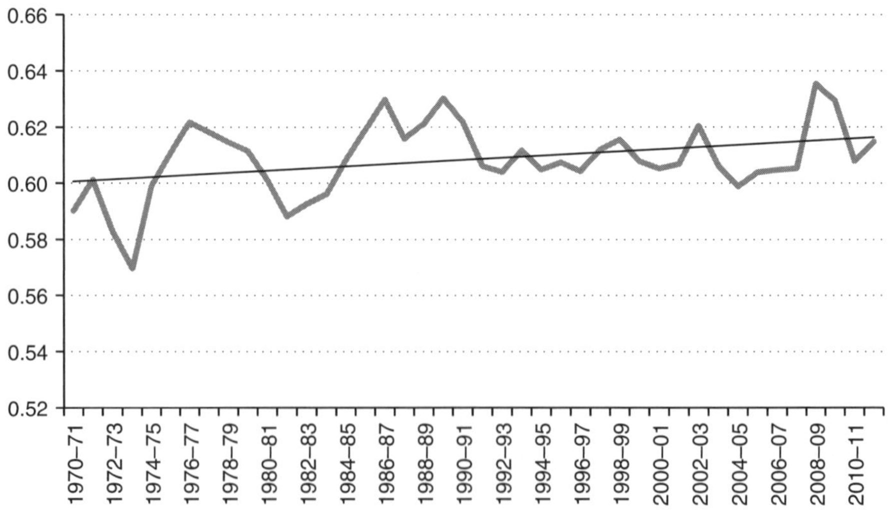

Source: MOSPI (Government of India), http://mospi.nic.in.

Figure 23.2 Share of central government in current consumption expenditure (center and states combined)

Nepotism and common identity in terms of stronger loyalty to less inclusive groups – family, caste, ethnic, religious, or linguistic 'community' and class (Myrdal 1968 [2005]), which are prevalent in a diverse country such as India, influence the distribution of fiscal favors.

Rodrik and Subramanian (2005) distinguish 'internal reforms' that started in the beginning of the 1980s and 'external reforms' that started in 1991. They point out that while the 'internal reforms' were mainly 'pro-business', the 'external reforms' were 'pro-competition'. Salient features of the internal reforms were: (1) elimination of licensing of 25 categories of industries subject to certain fairly onerous conditions; (2) extension of delicensing in 22 industries that were previously restricted by the Monopolies and Restrictive Trade Practices Act and the Foreign Exchange Regulation Act; (3) allowing companies in 28 industries to expand their scope of operation into related activities; and (4) allowing companies that had reached 80 percent capacity utilization to expand their capacity up to 133 percent of that reached in any previous years. Note that except for the first, which allowed entry of new firms in certain industries and promoted competition, all other measures allowed the registered incumbent firms to operate more freely in the market. India did not extensively liberalize trade before 1991. Why did such 'internal reforms' take place?

Kohli (1989) suggested that the reforms were grounded primarily in political calculations rather than in an objective of enhancing efficiency. In Kohli's words: 'in India's political culture . . . two packages of secularism and socialism and Hindu chauvinism and pro-business have tended to offer two alternative legitimacy formulae for mobilizing political support' (p. 308).

After a debacle in the 1977 parliamentary election, Mrs Indira Gandhi, the outgoing prime minister, realized the threat from the pro-business Hindu lobby. In returning to power in the early 1980s, she dropped the first package of secularism and socialism in favor of the second. Rodrik and Subramanian (2005) explain that the private registered manufacturing sector in the Indian economy gained in the process. The productivity of this sector increased. Those states that had higher shares of private registered manufacturing to start with surged ahead of the other states, germinating the seeds of policy-induced regional inequality in India.

The 'external reforms' that started in 1991 were primarily a response to a severe foreign exchange crisis. The Narsimha Rao government that came to power on 26 June 1991 took immediate steps to avoid default on foreign debt but also started reforming the Indian economy in order to cure long-term problems associated with the Indian economic development process. An initial devaluation of the rupee paved the way for market determination of the exchange rate and abolition of import licenses, except on manufactured consumer goods. Restrictions on foreign trade of agricultural commodities also remained in place. Apart from this, as Srinivasan (1996) notes, convertibility (with some notable exceptions) of the rupee on the current account was allowed. The number of tariff lines and tariff rates and excise duty were reduced for a number of commodities. Some limited reforms in direct taxes were initiated. Industrial licensing was abolished. The requirement of environmental clearances, however, was kept for investment in certain locations. The requirements for foreign direct investment were eased. Private investment was allowed in some industries hitherto reserved exclusively for public sector enterprises. The financial sector reforms included simplification of the interest structure with elimination of interest rate floors for large loans, replacement of fixed term deposit rates by an interest rate ceiling, reduction of government pre-emption of loanable funds and recapitalization of banks. In the later years this trend of reforms was pursued further. Ailing public sector enterprises were shut down. Disinvestment took place in good public sector enterprises. Except for arms and ammunitions, almost all the sectors were opened to private sector participation. The state governments followed the lead. The tax structure at the state level was simplified. For delivery of services in many states, e-governance was initiated. Under the overall control of the center, the states were limited in competition in attracting private and foreign investment.

The economic reforms increased competiveness of the economy and efficiency. In the ten-year period ending 2012, the Indian economy maintained a growth rate at an average of 7.8 percent per annum (data source: data.worldbank.org) compared to the pre-liberalization average growth rate, which was below 4 percent in most of the plan periods (Srinivasan 1996).

Was the scope of rent seeking and corruption reduced? The Indian economy has been subject to corruption scandals in the reform period. We report examples. In the state of Karnataka, two cabinet ministers were accused of involvement in illegal mining operations worth an estimated Rs 600 billion (US $13.3 billion) (IANS 2010). There was widespread inflation of contract costs in the preparation of the Delhi Commonwealth Games in 2010, worth an estimated Rs 700 billion (US $15.5 billion) (Times of India 2013). The cost of a 2G spectrum allocation scam was estimated at some US $40 billion (NDTV 2010). A coal license allocation scam was worth Rs 1860 billion (Dnaindia 2013). Chaudhuri et al. (2006), in their estimate of the shadow economy for the years 1992–93 to 1995–96, report an increase to 23.4 percent of net state domestic product of India compared to an average of 19.97 percent of the pre-liberalization period 1974–75 to 1991–92 (see footnote 2).[3]

Reform changed the nature of rent seeking. With greater economic participation of private and foreign firms, the scope of rent seeking increased at the contracting level at which politicians/bureaucrats have discretion. With reform, 'high'-level corruption appears to have increased. It is important to note that the Indian economy is still quite early in its reform process and anti-corruption laws do not yet exist in many cases. The 'first come first served' allocation mechanism that led to the 2G spectrum and coal license allocation scams was replaced by an auction mechanism thought to be transparent, corruption-free and efficient.

Bushell (2012) proposes that the attractions of higher rents in the new era of economic reform led politicians to make various reform decisions. Politicians pursue those reforms that cater to their targeted constituency (which is important for winning the next election) and that offer greater scope for rent seeking through the contracting process. Improving the speed of service delivery leads to sacrifice of the rents to be obtained from

[3] Marjit et al. (2007), in a theoretical model, show that the relation between liberalization and the size of the informal sector of the economy depends on the type of reform pursued. A reduced tariff expands the size of the informal sector, whereas a reduced interest rate, possibly through liberalization of the capital account, reduces the size of the informal sector. Also see Tavares (2007) for empirical cross-country evidence on the relationship between political and economic reforms and corruption.

'speed money' at the lower level of bureaucracy; but the loss is compensated for by higher rent to be obtained at the 'high level' and the electoral benefit. Adoption of information technology enabled one-stop delivery of various services, such as birth certificates, caste certificates, driving licenses, ration cards and so on, eliminating the need for 'speed money'. Bushell (2012) found that the states with higher 'low-level' corruption adopted this scheme at later dates and also offered a smaller range of services. She also shows that the adoption rate was lower when there is a coalition government in a state. In evaluating perceptions of high- and low-level politicians in three states (Bihar, Jharkhand and Uttar Pradesh), in another study, Bushell (2013) found that respondents believed that greater rents are extracted at the policy level, compared to the rents extracted at the contract award level (such as the contract awarded in the construction of roads) and the rent extracted at the service delivery level (such as the delivery of ration cards).

How does Indian democracy react to crime and corruption? While corruption has always been a prominent issue in elections, before 2002 there was no official way to know about criminal records of the candidates for political office. When the Supreme Court of India made a landmark judgment requiring every candidate contesting national and state elections to submit a legal affidavit disclosing his or her educational qualifications, information was revealed about personal wealth and most importantly criminal records.

Dutta and Gupta (2014) analyzed the data for the 2009 Lok Sabha elections and found that voters penalize candidates with criminal records but the magnitude of penalty decreases if there are other candidates in the constituency with criminal records. The vote shares are positively related to candidate wealth, with the marginal effect being higher for candidates with criminal records. The candidates with criminal records also have higher wealth.

The results partly explain why, despite corruption being an important issue, there has been failure to end persistent corruption within Indian democracy. It is also important to realize that the elections are not contested only on the corruption issue. Issues related to inflation, local public good provision, stability of the government and so on are also important. These other issues can eclipse the corruption issue at the time of elections.[4]

23.3 THEORIES OF LIBERALIZATION WITH RENT SEEKING

In principle, market liberalization should increase profit seeking at the expense of rent seeking. In India it appears that liberal economic reform intensified rent seeking.

Hillman and Ursprung (2000) have proposed that sustained political culture can result in increased rent seeking when political liberalization occurs and increases access to rent seeking. In the Hillman and Ursprung model there are initially two contests, a contest among outsiders to be insiders and contest among insiders to secure rents. After political liberalization, insider privilege ends and rent seeking is more open and inclusive, leading

[4] An example from the 2014 parliamentary elections in India illustrates the point: for the first time in India, a party named Aam Admi Party (AAP) contested the election with corruption as the exclusive election issue but could manage to win only three seats out of 541 seats in the parliament, the vote share being 2 percent of the total votes polled (India Today 2014).

to more participation in rent seeking. The relevance of the model is that increased openness in access to political and bureaucratic rent creation has increased rent seeking.

Marjit and Mukherjee (2014) model a rent-extracting rent-maximizing political decision maker who chooses the extent of liberalizing market reform. In contrast to standard models of political support-maximizing regulation (Peltzman 1976) or protection (Hillman 1982 [2007]; Grossman and Helpman 1994 [2008]), the politician is not constrained by political support. The policy chosen affects two firms, one foreign and one domestic, with the foreign firm having a cost advantage. In this model, liberalization of trade policy (a reduced tariff/obstacle to participation of the foreign firm) increases rent seeking because the corrupt political decision maker has access to rent extraction from the foreign firm, the profits of which are increased by reduced protection. The politician is described as extracting a constant fraction of profits of both the domestic and the foreign firm – the former trying to increase the tariff and the latter trying to reduce the tariff – and hence the politician's rent-maximizing policy coincides with maximal joint profit of the two firms. Domestic policy creates the conditions for collusive joint profit maximization of domestic and foreign firms or 'regulation of international industry' (Hillman 1990). The model is consistent with increased political rent seeking and rent extraction when reforms through trade liberalization have occurred.[5]

23.4 CONCLUSIONS

Rents and rent seeking have been central to the Indian economy since independence and were central in the period before independence. The post-independence planning and licensing regime provided incentives for rent creation and rent seeking, but not to the extent of the planned Soviet system. India being a democracy, there were political constraints on high-level corruption but corruption was endemic in the bureaucracy, in particular at lower levels. Economic liberalization has increased rent seeking and the corruption that is the source of rents, specifically high-level corruption. There is, though less discussed, a theoretical basis for predicting that trade liberalization, by increasing rents, will increase rent seeking.

There is a question why democracy in India has not been sufficient to achieve the lower levels of corruption and stringent rule of law found in other democracies. A basic source of difference is of course income. Low incomes influence rent-creating and rent-seeking incentives.

There are also issues of inability of the government to monitor activities that stem from reform. As markets open up and new activities are undertaken, rents can be created, for

[5] As the liberalization progresses, the profit of the foreign firm increases and the profit of the domestic firm falls. Joint profit is non-monotonic in the tariff. In particular, joint profit is convex in the tariff (see also Marjit 1990; Lahiri and Ono 1999). For another model of liberalization with a domestic and foreign firm in a rent-seeking context, involving government procurement, see Long and Stahler (2009). In this model, however, the rent seekers are the firms. In Hillman and Ursprung (2000 [2008]), political candidates choose policies that determine profits of domestic and foreign firms competing in the domestic market and the firms provide campaign contributions that determine the candidates' probabilities of winning the election.

example, through financial opportunism. Stock market-related and bank-related scams in India that occurred in the 1990s have subsided. On the other hand, the mechanism for implementing reforms can be deliberately flawed, such as replacing a properly designed auction process with committee-driven decisions, which is a deliberate route created for rent seeking and rent extraction.

India has a free press and offers the freedom to discuss the behavior of politicians and government officials in seeking and extracting rents. Combined with democracy, this increases the costs of political and bureaucratic opportunism. However, for the cases in which the media is controlled by political parties and big business houses, which are often found in India, it may create some rent seeking as well. Therefore, the effectiveness of a free press on rent seeking and market-oriented reform in India remains uncertain.

REFERENCES

Andvig, Jens C. and Karl O. Moene (1990), 'How corruption may corrupt', *Journal of Economic Behavior and Organization*, **13**(1), 63–76.

Bhagwati, Jagdish N. (1971), 'The generalized theory of distortions and welfare', in Jagdish N. Bhagwati, Ronald W. Jones, Robert A. Mundell and Jaroslav Vanek (eds), *Trade, Balance of Payments, and Growth: Essays in Honor of Charles P. Kindleberger*, Amsterdam: North-Holland, pp. 69–90.

Bhagwati, Jagdish N. and Padma Desai (1970), *India: Planning for Industrialization*, Oxford: Oxford University Press.

Biswas, Rangili, Sugata Marjit and Velayoudom Marimoutu (2010), 'Fiscal federalism, state lobbying and discretionary finance: evidence from India', *Economics and Politics*, **22**(1), 68–91.

Buchanan, James M. (1980), 'Rent seeking and profit seeking', in James M. Buchanan, Robert D. Tollison and Gordon Tullock (eds), *Toward a Theory of the Rent-seeking Society*, College Station, TX: Texas A&M University Press, pp. 3–15, reprinted in Roger D. Congleton, Arye L. Hillman and Kai A. Konrad (eds) (2008), *40 Years of Research on Rent Seeking 1 – The Theory of Rent Seeking*, Heidelberg: Springer, pp. 55–67.

Bushell, Jennifer (2012), *Corruption and Reform in India: Public Services in the Digital Age*, Cambridge: Cambridge University Press.

Bushell, Jennifer (2013), 'Varieties of corruption: the organization of rent-seeking in India', Paper presented at the conference Westminster Model of Democracy in Crisis?, Harvard University, 13–14 May.

Chaudhuri, Kausik, Friedrich Schneider and Sumana Chattopadhyay (2006), 'The size and development of the shadow economy: an empirical investigation from the states of India', *Journal of Development Economics*, **80**, 428–43.

Dnaindia (2013), 'What is the Indian coal allocation scam?', 30 April, available at http://dnaindia.com/New Delhi (accessed 1 June 2014).

Dutta, Bhaskar and Poonam Gupta (2014), 'How Indian voters respond to the candidates with criminal charges: evidence from 2009 Lok Sabha elections', *Economic and Political Weekly*, **49**(4), 43–51.

Government of India (1964), *Report of the Committee on Prevention of Corruption*, New Delhi: Ministry of Home Affairs.

Grossman, Gene M. and Elhanan Helpman (1994), 'Protection for sale', *American Economic Review*, **84**(4), 833–50, reprinted in Roger D. Congleton, Arye L. Hillman and Kai A. Konrad (eds) (2008), *40 Years of Research on Rent Seeking 2 – Applications: Rent Seeking in Practice*, Heidelberg: Springer, pp. 131–48.

Gupta, Rahul and Santap Sanhari Mishra (eds) (2007), *Corruption: The Causes and Combatting Strategies*, Hyderabad: Icfai University Press.

Hillman, Arye L. (1982), 'Declining industries and political-support protectionist motives', *American Economic Review*, **72**(2), 1180–87, reprinted in Wilfred J. Ethier and Arye L. Hillman (eds) (2007), *The WTO and the Political Economy of Trade Policy*, Cheltenham, UK and Northampton, MA, USA: Edward Elgar Publishing, pp. 43–50.

Hillman, Arye L. (1990), 'Protectionist policies as the regulation of international industry', *Public Choice*, **67**, 101–10.

Hillman, Arye L. (2013), 'Rent seeking', in Michael Reksulak, Laura Razzolini and William F. Shughart II (eds), *The Elgar Companion to Public Choice*, 2nd edn, Cheltenham, UK and Northampton, MA, USA: Edward Elgar Publishing, pp. 307–30.

Hillman, Arye L. and Eliakim Katz (1987), 'Hierarchical structure and the social costs of bribes and transfers', *Journal of Public Economics*, **34**(2), 129–42, reprinted in Roger D. Congleton, Arye L. Hillman and Kai A. Konrad (eds) (2008), *40 Years of Research on Rent Seeking 1 – The Theory of Rent Seeking*, Heidelberg: Springer, pp. 523–36.

Hillman, Arye L. and Heinrich W. Ursprung (2000), 'Political culture and economic decline', *European Journal of Political Economy*, **16**(2), 189–213, reprinted in Roger D. Congleton, Arye L. Hillman and Kai A. Konrad (eds) (2008), *40 Years of Research on Rent Seeking 2 – Applications: Rent Seeking in Practice*, Heidelberg: Springer, pp. 219–45.

IANS (Indo-Asian News Service) (2007), 'Chronology of the Bofors scandal', 27 February, available at http://www.dnaindia.com/india/report_chronology-of-the-bofors-scandal_1082262 (accessed 28 May 2014).

IANS (Indo-Asian News Service) (2010), 'Karnataka governor meets Patil, says no "license to corruption"', 13 July, available at http://www.newkerala.com/news/fullnews-145880.html (accessed 28 May 2014).

India Today (2009), 'Key players in Bofors scandal', 28 April, available at http://indiatoday.intoday.in/site/Story/39264/LATEST%20HEADLINES/Key + players + in + Bofors + scandal.html (accessed 28 May 2014).

India Today (2014), 'AAP bags more seats than Shivsena and DMK in Lok Sabha elections', 18 May (accessed 28 May 2014).

Kohli, Atul (1989), 'Politics of economic liberalization in India', *World Development*, **17**(3), 305– 28.

Konrad, Kai A. (2009), *Strategy and Dynamics in Contests*, Oxford: Oxford University Press.

Krueger, Anne (1974), 'The political economy of the rent-seeking society', *American Economic Review*, **64**(3), 291–303, reprinted in Roger D. Congleton, Arye L. Hillman and Kai A. Konrad (eds) (2008), *40 Years of Research on Rent Seeking 2 – Applications: Rent Seeking in Practice*, Heidelberg: Springer, pp. 151–63.

Lahiri, Sajal and Yoshyasu Ono (1999), 'Optimal tariffs in the presence of middlemen', *Canadian Journal of Economics*, **32**(1), 55–70.

Long, Ngo Van (2013), 'The theory of contests: a unified model and review of the literature', *European Journal of Political Economy*, **32**, 161–81, reprinted in Chapter 3, this volume.

Long, Ngo Van and Frank Stahler (2009), 'A contest model of liberalizing government procurements', *European Journal of Political Economy*, **25**, 479–88.

Marjit, Sugata (1990), 'On a non-cooperative theory of technology transfer', *Economics Letters*, **33**, 293–8.

Marjit, Sugata and Vivekananda Mukherjee (2014), 'Rent-seeking and reform: relationship revisited', Working Paper No. 8–14, Centre for Advanced Studies, Department of Economics, Jadavpur University.

Marjit, Sugata, Sudeep Ghosh and Amit Biswas (2007), 'Informality, corruption and trade reform', *European Journal of Political Economy*, **23**, 777–89.

Mohammad, Sharif and John Whalley (1984), 'Rent seeking in India: its costs and policy significance', *Kyklos*, **37**(3), 387–413.

Myrdal, Gunner (1968), *Asian Drama: An Inquiry into the Poverty of Nations*, London: Allen Lane the Penguin Press, Chapter 20, reprinted in Ajit Mishra (ed.) (2005), *The Economics of Corruption*, New Delhi: Oxford University Press, pp. 37–62.

NDTV (2010), '2G Spectrum scam: a Raja meets Karunanidhi', 11 December, available at http://www.ndtv.com/india/article/india/2g-spectrum-scam-a-raja-meets-karunanidhi-71983 (accessed 28 May 2014).

Peltzman, Sam (1976), 'Toward a more general theory of regulation', *Journal of Law and Economics*, **19**(2), 211–40.

Rodrik, Dani and Arvind Subramanian (2005), 'From "Hindu growth" to productivity surge: the mystery of the Indian growth transition', *IMF Staff Papers*, **52**(2), 193–228.

Srinivasan, T.N. (1996), 'Economic liberalization and economic development: India', *Journal of Asian Economics*, **7**(2), 203–16.

Tavares, Samia C. (2007), 'Do rapid political and trade liberalizations increase corruption?', *European Journal of Political Economy*, **23**, 1053–76.

Times of India (2013), 'State Public Accounts Committee indicts Suresh Kalmadi for graft in youth games', 18 April, available at http://timesofindia.indiatimes.com/Mumbai (accessed 1 June 2014).

Transparency International India and Centre for Media Studies (2005), *India Corruption Study 2005*, New Delhi: Transparency International India.

Transparency International India and Centre for Media Studies (2007), *India Corruption Study 2007: With Focus on BPL Households*, New Delhi: Transparency International India.

Tullock, Gordon (1967), 'The welfare costs of tariffs, monopolies, and theft', *Western Economic Journal*, **5**(3), 224–32, reprinted in Roger D. Congleton, Arye L. Hillman and Kai A. Konrad (eds) (2008), *40 Years of Research on Rent Seeking 1 – The Theory of Rent Seeking*, Heidelberg: Springer, pp. 45–53.

24. The democratization of rent seeking in modern Greece

*Thomas Moutos and Lambros Pechlivanos**

SUMMARY

We describe the evolution of the power struggle in Greece among key economic and political stakeholders, who have tried, via strategic positioning and rent-seeking activities, to influence economic policy during the postwar decades. We split the postwar decades into three periods: the catching-up period, the overt populism period of 1973–93 and the 1993–2008 period of stealth populism. In each period, we identify the important players to see how they managed to forge a sustainable winning coalition, and to understand how they shaped policies. The three periods vary substantially in terms of the inherent degree of economic inefficiency that they brought about; the first period was characterized by a concentration of rent seeking mainly among the economic and political elite, whereas the middle period exemplifies the 'democratization' of rent seeking. The middle period's proliferation of rent seeking received some legitimacy from large segments of the population due to widespread, and often ideological, perceptions of long-lasting unfairness in the distribution of economic and political power. The covert populism of the last period used an unsustainable expansion of foreign borrowing to allow for an intensification of rent seeking while providing a semblance of fiscal rectitude.

24.1 INTRODUCTION

This chapter presents a brief synopsis of the economic history in post-Second World War Greece, within a political economy framework. This is done by attempting to explain the evolution of the power struggle among different stakeholders, who try, via strategic positioning and rent-seeking activities, to influence economic policy. In each period, we identify the important players to describe how they manage to forge a sustainable winning coalition, and to understand the efficiency properties of the enacted policies.[1]

Although it is not difficult to find anecdotes in which interested parties directly influence political decisions via sheer power or monetary transfers, we opt to focus on

* Without implicating, we wish to thank Spyros Vassilakis for helpful comments and suggestions.

[1] We refrain from any quantitative assessment of rent seeking in Greece. Angelopoulos et al. (2009) provide estimates of the social costs of rent seeking. Their model-based calculations indicate that Greece exhibits the highest rent extraction and rent seeking among European Union (EU) countries, with about 53 percent of tax revenue extracted by rent seekers. Our discussion of rent seeking covers acts of omission or commission by government officials (for example, regulation) that do not directly impinge on tax revenue.

activities that shape the evolution of public institutions, which are necessary to propagate the power of established interest groups or to nurture the creation of new players.[2]

In the spirit of Stigler (1971) and Peltzman (1976), we try to understand how interest groups attempt to become more effective in exercising their power by guarding against free-riding behavior, through the implantation of protective rules. We then offer a description of different winning coalitions, across time, and explain how their characteristics (broadness, composition and so on) lead to the adoption of policies that give rise to different degrees of inefficiency. Conditions that are external to the analysis, such as scarcity of resources or soft budget constraints due to access to outside financing, are also used to understand different societal tolerance to inefficient public policies.

Nonetheless, even when external conditions are conducive to inefficient outcomes one has to question the reasons why a more efficient outcome does not arise. This is essentially an argument in the tradition of a Coasian–Williamsonian analysis of the evolution of government structures.[3] To address this question we take into account the ideological background within which public discourse on economic policy developed in Greece. Fueled by ancestral feelings of economic inequality and social stratification (that is, deep-rooted perceptions of the illegitimacy of the existing social and economic order), which were exploited in the public arena, a cynical approach has evolved according to which public policy looks more like a zero-sum game, where the redistributive effects play the major role while efficiency reasoning retreats to obscurity.[4]

We split the post-Second World War era into three periods: (a) the 1944–73 period of rapid growth; (b) the 1973–93 period of overt populism and stagnation; and (c) the 1993–2008 period of stealth populism, during which intended declarations of 'modernization' and 'state-rebuilding' coincided with excessive private sector borrowing and a huge increase in the country's (that is, private-cum-public sector) net indebtedness to the rest of the world.

The first period is characterized by a closely knit group of movers and shakers (that we will be calling 'the elite') whose main goal was to propagate and enhance the antebellum economic order. Their grip on the political arena was mainly based on personal relationships with politicians, whose power in turn was based on traditional patron–clientele relations, sometimes still attributed to kinship or local origin. To fabricate social cohesion and galvanize a winning coalition, the corporatist system instituted in the 1930s was kept intact, bringing thus valuable political support from constituents such as professionals and other service sector self-employed. Given the abysmal state of the Greek economy at the end of the Second World War, the goal of the economic

---

2 We focus on key players since we regard it is an oxymoron to assume that the competitive process is distorted by the creation of rents, and yet the process of rent creation is subject to perfectly competitive markets for rent capture.

3 For example, see Coase (1937) and Williamson (1985, 1996).

4 Piketty (1995) argues that perceptions about the unfairness of social and economic outcomes are significant determinants of voters' preferences over redistributive fiscal policies. Moreover, Passarelli and Tabellini (2013) provide a theoretical model in which (privately) costly participation in political unrest (which has been a common occurrence in Greece) may be the result of emotions-motivated perceptions of unfairness. Importantly, they show how such political protests can affect public policy even when the policymaker is benevolent.

elite was to instigate rapid growth policies, and to direct resources to industry, while at the same time keeping its oligopolistic structure. The main strife between the economic elite and the foreign aid donors was the allocation of funds toward the different sectors of the economy and the control of the distributive mechanisms. At bottom, the scarcity of resources and some degree of institutional autonomy of bureaucracy granted by the foreign intervention prevented the adoption of grossly inefficient policies.

The beginning of the second period coincides with the establishment of the Third Greek Republic. Demands for greater political and economic participation grew stronger and received universal acceptance. As a result, a mass of new players (the 'unprivileged', as Andreas Papandreou called them) entered the political arena requesting a larger share of the social surplus. The main vehicle through which their demands were voiced was the creation of a party machine (the Panhellenic Socialist Movement, PASOK) that altered completely the way through which politics could redistribute resources. Now, the ruling party had de facto monopoly power over the allocation of resources and became the conduit through which demands were met. Non-members were effectively foreclosed. The prime goal of party cadres was the perpetuation of their political power. Given that they understood themselves as redistribution facilitators, economic efficiency considerations were ignored. Finally, intra-party competition nurtured a race to the bottom in the sense that different party cadres were trying to ensure that their constituents had the better deal. The results were disastrous as public debt accumulated, growth stalled and the unemployment rate tripled.

The event that introduced the third period was the European Monetary Union (EMU) accession effort. This effort appeared – on the surface at least – to tame the ability of the political machine to cater to its constituents, as economic policy had now to focus on that goal. As a result, the rhetoric in support of overt populist policies was retracted. Somehow, though, this successful bid brought the seeds of the restoration of the previous agenda. Eurozone membership allowed for the first time the Greek economy to have low cost access to finance from the international markets. This was a game changer, as party cadres understood this as a tap to unlimited funding, whose cost would be pushed to future generations. As a result, the raid on public coffers intensified again, the private sector appeared happy with the newly found opportunities for (foreign) credit-driven growth and the Greek economy found itself heavily indebted to the rest of the world in the wake of the global financial crisis.

24.2 ANTECEDENTS OF THE POST-SECOND WORLD WAR ECONOMIC ORDER

By the second decade of the twentieth century it was becoming evident to perceptive Greek politicians that 'the bourgeois state must realize that the danger posed by the lower-classes in the twentieth century can be thwarted only by making sure that the just demands of the workers are swiftly met.'[5] The increasing awareness of mainstream

---

[5] This is our brief summary of what Dertilis (1985) quotes from one of Eleftherios Venizelos's (who was the pre-eminent Greek politician of the first half of the twentieth century) addresses to

decision makers that this could well be a necessary action if liberal democracy was to survive led to the signing by Greece in October 1919 of the six International Labor Conventions, which dealt with hours of work in industry, unemployment, maternity protection, night work for women, minimum age and night work for young persons in industry.[6] The continuing social and economic pressures of the interwar period culminated in the Parliament's decision (Law 5733/1932) to establish the Social Insurance Foundation (IKA) in 1932;[7] however the government was toppled and implementation of the decision was delayed until 1937, a year after the 1936 self-coup that solidified Ioannis Metaxas's rise to power.[8]

Among the alleged intentions of Metaxas's regime (1936–1941) was the abandonment of the existing mercantile/capitalist system and its replacement with a corporatist economic one, in order to promote the national interest. According to Clogg (1987), although the regime had 'superficial trappings of Fascism' and Metaxas did not disguise his admiration for Nazism and Fascism, it is more correctly categorized as paternalist-authoritarian rather than fascist. Trade-unionism came under direct state control and, in parallel, state intervention in the regulation of labor relations widened. Metaxas's avowed aim was to foster 'social and national solidarity' through rejection of individualism and class struggle. It consisted of a scheme for the gradual organization of all 'productive classes' into cooperatives, through a horizontal (according to branches of production) rather than vertical (according to social class), syndicalist organization. Instead of the atomistic (or egotistical) system of interest representation of liberal democracy, Metaxas's regime aim was to generate a system of interest representation in which the constituent units are organized into a limited number of singular, compulsory, non-competitive, hierarchically ordered and functionally differentiated categories, recognized or licensed (if not created) by the state and granted a deliberate representational monopoly in exchange for observing certain 'guidelines' on their selection of leaders and articulation of demands (Schmitter 1974). It appears that the implicit goal of the regime was to use corporatism as a process for both the repression and co-optation of the labor movement and various interest groups.[9]

---

the Greek Parliament in 1911. Venizelos, a century ago, also expressed clearly what appears to be a perennial problem of Greek political economy: 'Before the revolution, it was those connected with the expenditure column of (those feeding on) the budget that mainly governed Greece. Now, its fortunes are mainly in the hands of those who feed the budget's revenue column.'

[6] These were the result of the first International Labor Conference in Washington, which was organized by the newly formed International Labor Office. Among the stipulations of this conference was the eight-hour working day; Greece was allowed to gradually implement this regulation, and by the 1930s the eight-hour day was widely observed.

[7] Both the Confederation of Greek Industrialists (SEV) and the Banks' Union had made their objections to the law known to Prime Minister Venizelos (Liakos 1993).

[8] By the time Law 5733/1932 was implemented, it was subjected to significant amendments that weakened IKA's scope and curtailed the means available to become an effective social insurance organization. This development went in tandem with the establishment of many supplementary social insurance funds, whose number kept growing until the dawn of the twenty-first century.

[9] Some of the 'carrot-and-stick' measures of the Metaxas regime are the 'closure' to outsiders of many professions and the granting of 'employment permits' to 'nationally minded' persons, state control of syndicalism, restrictions on firing workers without the government's approval, the legislation of the minimum wage and legislation rendering all strike activity illegal.

The economic performance of Metaxas's reign was not impressive. According to Maddison (2010), from 1936 to 1940 (Greece did not enter the Second World War until late in 1940), per capita gross domestic product (GDP) (in real terms) declined by 9 percent in Greece, whereas it rose by 10 percent on average in 12 advanced Western European countries. Yet, the regime's influence on subsequent economic developments was impressive and its model of corporatism (albeit under different guises) has retained its influence well into the twenty-first century.

24.3 GREECE ON LIFE SUPPORT: 1944–53

By the end of the Second World War the Greek economy was in ruins. In 1945, GDP was about 36 percent of its pre-war level.[10] Hyperinflation had essentially demonetized the economy that had been reduced to little more than barter. Demand for cash was practically non-existent. Real money balances were 5 percent of the pre-war level (Makinen 1986). Even, in 1946, the sum of all categories of bank deposits, in real terms, amounted to 4.3 percent of the 1938 level.[11] At the same time, demand for gold sovereigns was booming, as gold hoarding became endemic. Big ticket-item transactions were performed solely in gold sovereigns.

Among the first legislative initiatives of the post-liberation government was the 'Currency Arrangement Law' (Law 18/10.11.1944) according to which the 'new drachma' was introduced and all pre-existing contractual obligations, regardless of their denomination (gold or foreign currency), were converted into 'old drachmas' at official exchange rates, and then converted again into 'new drachmas.'[12] As a result, pre-war debt was essentially forgiven, offering a clean slate to households and, more importantly, to firms that survived the World War II occupation period.[13]

In addition, because there was widespread popular resentment that an important group of well-connected individuals and firms collaborated with the occupying forces (German, Italian and Bulgarian), a series of legislative initiatives were undertaken to partially undo such wealth redistribution that allegedly took place during the occupation, but also to stave off popular discontent. Law 182/1945 introduced punitive taxation on 'financial enrichment' during the occupation, and Laws 116/1946 and 1323/1949 allowed for the annulment of most real estate transfers that took place during that period.

However, it is widely believed that these laws were grossly inadequate in addressing popular concerns about collaborators' unethical enrichment, and that a group of collaborators and black-marketeers ascended to the ruling class and managed to further

---

10 The drop in Greek GDP was larger than that experienced by any other country – including Germany, Japan and the USSR (Maddison 2010). It was only in 1953 that Greece managed to surpass the level of GDP per capita it had achieved three decades earlier (in 1924).

11 Actually, if one excludes the mandatory deposits of various semi-public legal entities, it becomes apparent that there was a complete breakdown of the banking sector (Pagoulatos 2006).

12 Each 'new drachma' was worth 50 billion 'old drachmas'.

13 The redistributive properties of such a measure could not pass unnoticed. This forced transfer to borrowers, who often enough were wealthier than average, created a serious dent in the legitimacy of the emerging postwar regime.

gain from their involvement in the Marshall Plan (Kofas 1989). These beliefs, and subsequent political developments until 1973, certainly helped to solidify the widespread perception about the unfairness of capitalism in Greece, and fostered and solidified the latent demands for extensive regulation and redistribution that surfaced in full force after 1973.

Intentionally or not, these policies helped to preserve to a large extent the pre-war economic status quo. Firms and industrialists that succeeded in surviving the war found themselves in relatively good terms. One trend that deserves to be noted is that during the first half of the occupation the banking sector became increasingly intertwined with industry as commercial banks (and by that we essentially mean the National Bank of Greece (NBG) that was by all means a monopoly) were acquiring block holdings in various firms by converting non-performing loans to equity.[14]

The first post-liberation governments were rather unsuccessful in addressing hyperinflation. Three different stabilization programs were initiated, but it was only in 1946 that inflation was finally tamed, possibly due to a greater British involvement. As a result, monetary policy throughout that period was solely focused on fighting inflation. This restrictive monetary policy was further entrenched with the institution of the Currency Committee in 1946, which was effectively responsible for the formulation of monetary, credit and foreign exchange policies. The Currency Committee comprised three cabinet ministers and one representative of the British and one of the US delegation. Because decisions were taken unanimously, foreign aid representatives had veto power. This increased the credibility of the program and finally succeeded in taming inflation (Makinen 1986).

Nonetheless, the tight control over credit policy exercised by the Currency Committee all but eradicated bank lending to industry. As a result, internal financing via retained earnings was the only internal source available to firms.[15] Clearly, this policy favored incumbents by creating barriers to entry, hence maintaining industry structure concentration.

Access to foreign aid funds was essentially the only external source of financing for firms. Indeed, under various guises (the Marshall Plan being the most important of them) Greece received during the period 1944–53 about 2.57 billion USD (Sweet-Escott 1954).[16] The US agencies were rather cautious to extend economic reconstruction funds to the industry as long-term subsidized loans. Loans to manufacturing firms amounted only to 50 million USD over the entire Marshall Plan period (Stathakis 2004). Still, given the complete lack of alternative funding sources and the expectation that these loans would eventually never be repaid in full (as actually happened in many cases), the

---

[14] In 1947, the Governor of NBG reported to the Porter mission that NBG's share on capital in manufacturing firms had risen from 6.4 percent in 1939 to 24.05 percent in 1945 (Historical Archive of NBG, AIΣ32Y1Φ33).

[15] Indeed, in the late 1940s manufacturing firms were operating with extraordinarily large profit margins, often as high as 300 percent (Archives of the United Nations Relief and Rehabilitation Administration (UNRRA) conjectures as reported in Stathakis 2004). This feature of Greek capitalism has proved to be remarkably prescient.

[16] This represented about 20 percent of GDP during this period. Almost half of this aid was channeled toward military purposes, as during the first part of that period the civil war in Greece was still rampant.

program attracted much attention from most firms and funds became a coveted prize. As a result, a frenzy of influence activities took place. The main vehicle through which incumbents lobbied was the NBG, which was pressing the Greek government and the US delegation to relegate the management of the loan program to the commercial banks (in reality to NBG itself). Paul A. Porter, the head of the US delegation in 1946–48, was fending off such involvement; at the end, though, the Currency Committee partially gave in to the demands.[17] Almost 43 out of these 50 million USD were given to just ten 'large' manufacturing firms (operating in cement, steel, chemical and other heavy industries), thus creating a compact group of 'national winners' (Stathakis 2004).

During the Second World War the Greek shipping industry was all but destroyed.[18] Within the auspices of the US aid, 100 'Liberty' ships were offered to the Greek government, which were distributed to the old ship-owners, who then managed to acquire 300 more ships, reviving the Greek shipping industry. Since the shipping industry was the only internationalized sector, it was the only one that had access to foreign finance. As a result, the strong pre-war closely knit group of ship-owners regained its power and its ability to influence policy.[19]

At the same time that the Greek government was reviving a ruined economy, it was also trying to avert a humanitarian crisis, imposed in part by a brutal civil war. Without the humanitarian aid of UNRRA and of the British and US agencies, this crisis would not have been averted. The inability to raise tax revenue and the expressed goal of balancing the budget was precluding the government from instituting any sort of social spending programs.[20] As a result, the government brought back into full force the corporatist system that was instituted in the pre-war period by the Metaxas regime to protect social cohesion and to avoid leakages of the general population toward the communist insurgents' ranks. This created the basis for a coalition involving professionals,

[17] This stand-off took place in late 1948. We believe it is interesting to mention that the Chairman of the Board of NBG, Alexandros Diomidis, stepped down in 1949 to become first Vice-President of the Government and then Prime Minister.

[18] Roughly 80 percent of its pre-war fleet was sunk, while in requisition service for the allied forces.

[19] The ship-owners' power is attested by the following excerpt from an interview given by Paul R. Porter in the 1990s (available at http://www.trumanlibrary.org/oralhist/porterpr.htm), who was Chief of the Economic Cooperation Administration Mission to Greece (1949–50). Porter states: 'one of our big problems was to get the ship-owners to pay taxes. They were about three years in arrears in taxes, and this represented a pretty large sum of money. Finally, we had to insist that the Government refuse shipping documents to any Greek ship-owner who was in arrears in taxes. Now, it took a lot of arm twisting to get the Government to agree to that. Always within the Government were people pressing us to twist their arms even more. It was actually a pretty courageous decision for the Greek Government to make considering how dependent so many of the Government officials were on the ship-owners, and also interlocked with them by marriage, family relationships. The amount of taxes that were collected was about 17 million dollars in one week.' To appreciate how large a sum this was, we note that if it represented today the same share of GDP as it was then, it would be about 2 billion euros.

[20] In 1945, even foreign aid goods were being sold instead of being distributed freely, as this was the only means available to the government to raise revenues. Actually, these sale receipts were expected to comprise 75 percent of government revenues, which was nonetheless not materialized (Makinen 1986; Karatzas 1988).

self-employed and shopkeepers, whose support for the 'liberal' regime (as opposed to communism) hinged on their being granted privileges at the expense of third parties (for example, third-party taxes supporting pension funds or government-sponsored collusive price setting).

24.4 CATCHING UP: 1953–73

The devaluation of 1953 is considered a milestone among researchers of Greek economic history,[21] as it set the stage for a long period of rapid growth. Indeed, in 1973 GDP per capita in Greece was 3.32 times higher than its level in 1953, whereas the corresponding number for the average of 12 advanced Western European (12WE) countries was 2.14, for Portugal 3.07 and for Spain 3.03.[22] To a large extent, this widely quoted, above-average performance of the Greek economy reflects normal catching-up episodes. It also reflects the medium-run successes that often accompany high rates of domestic saving and capital accumulation as the economy shifts from low-productivity sectors (that is, agriculture) to high-productivity ones (that is, manufacturing). During this period, the share of services in GDP remained constant (at 50 percent), whereas the share of the secondary sector increased by 15 percentage points (from 20 percent in 1953 to 35 percent in 1973).[23]

Although the shift away from agriculture to manufacturing has been a feature of many late-developing economies, the constancy of the share of services requires some explanation. This was due to conscious policy exercised by the Currency Committee, which remained an important feature of economic policy until its demise in 1982.[24] The Committee was the pre-eminent manifestation of state autonomy in the sense of rising above the demands of various socioeconomic groups and focusing on a developmental strategy that relied on extensive interventionism in the allocation of credit, the stated aim of which was to encourage manufacturing and exports, and to restrict consumer and trade finance.

In the 1950s industry structure remained rather concentrated.[25] This was a direct result of the fact that most firms were catering to the 'small' domestic market. The few export-oriented firms were established in raw materials related sectors. On top of that, there were substantial barriers to entry. Import substitution policies protected local industry from foreign competition and as a result home-grown 'national winners' were nurtured.

Limited financing opportunities played an equally important role in the propagation

---

[21] The Greek drachma lost 50 percent of its value against the dollar.

[22] All figures pertaining to the evolution of GDP per capita are, unless otherwise stated, calculated from Maddison's (2010) data.

[23] This was the highest share that the secondary sector ever achieved in Greece. Our calculations are based on data drawn from Bank of Greece (1980) and the Ameco Database.

[24] Of course, after the conclusion of the Marshall Plan all foreign representatives had stepped down and the Bank of Greece was playing the prominent role as it was responsible for designing and proposing policy measures that were, usually, adopted by the Committee.

[25] Bourlakis (1996) reports that during the period in question the average 'employment-share Herfindahl Index' in 85 three-digit manufacturing groups was increasing over time, signaling an increase in market concentration.

of oligopolistic structure in most industries as they favored incumbents (that is, 'national winners'). Access to external financing was scarce. Equity financing was in its infancy (way below pre-war levels) and bank financing was the only alternative mode of raising external capital. One has to stress though that banks were not only playing their traditional lending role but, more often than not, also acquiring direct ownership stakes.[26] This created relational vested interests in the banks, which were thinking twice before financing new, possibly competitive, ventures. The extremely concentrated structure of the banking sector (that was essentially a duopoly) exacerbated these 'perverse' incentives.[27] Actually, it has been argued that incumbents had been 'overleveraged' to such an extent that banks were subjected to severe moral hazard risks (Chalikias 1976).

Essentially, internal financing via retained earnings was the only alternative for start-ups to grow. Indeed there were several success stories that managed to grow via this channel in high profit margin sectors, but no doubt it tilted the balance in favor of the incumbents. As a result, almost all firms were essentially family-run. The only significant minority block holdings were owned by banks, which were in a better position to influence management and exercise control than any other minority shareholder. As there was no real demand for the establishment of transparent corporate governance and investor protection rules, the lack of external financing was perpetuated, bootstrapping the evolution of industry structure in many sectors.

Meanwhile, protective regulations in many services allowed most self-employed professionals (lawyers, engineers, doctors and so on) to substantially benefit from the rapid growth path of the economy. The corporatist system of guild-like trade unions and professional associations was kept intact. Through an ever growing web of decrees, they were elevated to a semi-official regulator status, and they were given the authority, for example, to regulate entry (via permits or licenses), to set prices, to impose penalties on their members, and even on the general public through the imposition of taxation, with the revenue earmarked for the benefit (for example, pension funds) of members. As a result, they were able not only to cater to their interests but also to mitigate internal free-riding problems.

The last years of this period (that is, post-1967) were marked by the colonels' junta. By reducing the importance of the Currency Committee, the dictators became unconstrained in the sense that large corporate-welfare handouts were given to many incumbent or regime-affiliated entrepreneurs. The result of this lax credit policy, which was essentially based on arbitrary criteria, was to solidify the widespread feeling that Greek capitalism was of the crony variety (as it later came to be called) that characterized most of the middle-income countries of that era. One may well describe this period as one of 'concentrated or oligopolized' rent seeking.

---

26 As we have already stated, during the Second World War the NBG dramatically increased its share of capital in many 'large firms'.

27 Until 1958 the banking sector in Greece can be described as a monopoly, with a competitive fringe. In that year, Stratis Andreadis (one of the key empire-builders of that era) managed to consolidate in one group three of the most important competitors to NBG and create a second large player in the market.

24.5 OVERT POPULISM: 1973–93

The next 20 years (1973–93) started with the restoration of democracy in 1974 and the establishment of the Third Republic. This period includes the rise of PASOK to power and entry into the European Economic Community (EEC) (as the EU was then called) in 1981, and ends with Greece's decision to aim for accession to the EMU. The rather haphazard way in which the expansion of the public sector took place, along with the careless macroeconomic management that characterized (most of) this period, led to economic stagnation, a rise in the unemployment rate, and culminated in an increase in the public debt to dangerously high levels. The performance of the Greek economy not only weakened considerably relative to the previous 20 years, but it was now worse than the average of the 12WE countries;[28] in 1993 GDP per capita in Greece was only 1.30 times higher than its level in 1973, whereas the corresponding numbers for the average of the 12WE countries was 1.40, 1.58 for Portugal and 1.60 for Spain.

The dismantling of repressive political mechanisms after 1974 meant that governments had to rely on social and economic policy measures in order to garner political support. The growing societal demands, along with the willingness of the then conservative governments to appease an electorate that was all too eager to resume the radicalism of the 1960s, led to a transfer of power from the state to society, or rather, from a moderately effective state bureaucracy (the semblance of a strong state in the Weberian tradition) to groups that claimed to better represent society's interests (Pagoulatos 2003). The growing influence of trade unions and employer associations (especially of public sector state-owned enterprises), in combination with the politicization and weakening of the autonomy of the bureaucratic apparatus after 1981, paved the way for the gradual transformation of the Greek state administration from an almost 'developmental state' to an 'intermediate state'. During this period the older individualistic (or family-based) system of patron-client relationships was supplemented by one dependent on favors bestowed on party members by the party machine (Charalambis 1989).

The conservative (New Democracy) governments of 1974–81 increased spending on social insurance, whose share of GDP rose from 11.3 percent in 1974 to 16.4 percent in 1981. However, these changes did not stem the tide of popular opinion; a broad segment of the public was demanding a change from the post-civil war socioeconomic regime, which, they perceived, had effectively marginalized large segments of the population by conferring undue privileges to a handful of citizens,[29] and which the 1974–81 conservative governments did little to upset. Conspiracy theories about 'the one-hundred families' that run the country acquired an almost religious credo among large segments of the population.[30]

---

28 These are: Austria, Belgium, Denmark, Finland, France, Germany, Italy, the Netherlands, Norway, Sweden, Switzerland and the UK.

29 These were named in the public discourse as the 'privileged'.

30 We are not interested in ascertaining if the public's perception was justified, in any sense. Instead, we take a positivist approach on this matter and try to explain how this 'ideological bias' influenced the public's attitudes toward specific policies. Di Tella and MacCulloch (2009) provide international evidence in support of the notion that citizens' perceptions about corruption reduce their willingness to support 'free-market' policies and induce them to demand more regulation.

The success of this classification (orchestrated by PASOK) was that few could openly identify themselves with the 'privileged', and hence policies aiming to relinquish their economic or political power received wide acceptance. It is thus no wonder that PASOK's declared aspirations of popular sovereignty and social liberation appealed to an electorate eager to experience social participation in order to ensure that 'the basic economic choices are made by the social whole.' It was also believed that by transforming the institutional framework these 'structural reforms' would provide the basis for the modernization and development of the Greek economy (Tsakalotos 1998).

Putting thus an end to 'a long-lasting post-civil-war regime' (Spourdalakis 2008), PASOK managed to express, represent and legitimize a heterogeneous range of collective demands that were excluded from the political arena. However, these demands often failed to satisfy broadly desired social objectives. A particularly poignant example concerns PASOK's intention to create 'decentralized organs of social control', which was essentially a euphemism for its attempt to transfer control over semi-public and even private sector firms to union members affiliated with the party. This was accomplished via the 'socialization' of public enterprises according to which formal authority passed to supervisory councils consisting of representatives of management, workers, local authorities and the state. In addition, several large private sector firms were nationalized via the creation of a new state holding company, whose objective, supposedly, was to restructure these so-called 'ailing' firms, some of which were heavily leveraged, and deemed insolvent. All these efforts failed to achieve their stated objectives of 'social control', but were immensely successful in assigning to party-affiliated union members the real power of redistributing resources. As a result, they were used for furthering PASOK's electoral aspirations, and for 'democratizing' rent-seeking opportunities.

The democratization or proliferation of rent seeking was the main by-product of the infiltration of PASOK into every aspect of economic and social life. This was achieved by replacing the old patron-client relationships in which relatively few policymakers and administrators were able to dispense favors to a select few, to a system in which power was dispersed by allowing a large number of lower-ranked, but party-affiliated, bureaucrats and trade unionists to, effectively, exercise veto power in practically all decisions that required the involvement of any state or quasi-state agency.[31] Such 'bureaucratization of clientelism' (Lyrintzis 2005) and open disregard for the integrity of institutions was aided by public pronouncements of government ministers (including Premier Andreas Papandreou[32]), which encouraged PASOK apparatchiks to colonize the bureaucracy and to control most of the associational activity (for example, trade unions, professional associations, farmer's cooperatives, academic departments, even employer's associations).[33] It was also aided by the proliferation of laws and regulations,

---

[31] A useful ideological construction that PASOK exploited with repeated success was that its predominant aim was to empower precisely the political and social groups whose legitimate representation had been thwarted in the past. For this reason it 'invented' a new historical-political subject, the 'non-privileged', thus appearing as the sole carrier of the 'people's voice', of the people's resentments and frustrated expectations.

[32] Pesmatzoglou (1993) credits Andreas Papandreou with the phrase: 'There are no institutions, there is only the people.'

[33] Board elections in these associations were transformed into party contests, closely monitored

supposedly intended to close the loopholes for unlawful conduct, but which, in effect, were functional in entrenching both clientelistic politics and rent-seeking opportunities.

These developments, along with the decreasing profitability and influence of industrial capital, incentivized existing or aspiring entrepreneurs to form alliances with party functionaries, and to concentrate their activities in sectors in which subsidies and public procurement were relatively plentiful. Worse still, the rent-seeking aspects of clientelistic politics were further enhanced by the gradual weakening of the 'authoritarian' civil-service code, which opened the way for widespread anomie among civil servants, who quickly realized that affiliation with the party in power increased both their chances of promotion and, effectively, guaranteed non-punishment for unlawful conduct. The attraction of PASOK to existing and aspiring public sector employees can be gleaned from the following data: as the number of public sector employees nearly doubled in the 1980s (from about[34] 500000 in 1980 to over 900000 in 1989), the vast majority of new appointments were PASOK supporters; according to a 1986 study (cited by Pridham and Verney 1991), PASOK more than tripled its membership between 1981 and 1986, and 89 percent of PASOK members who joined the party since 1981 were employed in the public sector.

PASOK's policy is more aptly understood as populist, since it was not mainly focused on class cleavages given the absence of a significant cleavage in Greek politics along class lines. This has been due to the relatively small industrial base and small number of industrial workers. Already in the 1980s, public sector employees and the self-employed (about half of which were in agriculture) were making a social majority (Tsoucalas 1987).[35] Moreover, studies of voting behavior in Greece (Gunther and Moreno 2000) suggest that indicators of economic/social class are much weaker as predictors of the vote in Greece along the Left/Right axis than they are in other West European countries.[36] This is not surprising since, in Greece, class structure is less polarized and wealth inequality is small compared to other European countries (Katsimi et al. 2014).[37] This may appear as running counter to the previously described prevalent perception of social injustice; but

---

by the press. For example, even the annual university and high-school student elections became major political events.

[34] The use of the word 'about' is intentional. The government never had (or revealed) any precise knowledge of the number of general government employees – mainly a result of the unwillingness of various ministries to reveal the number of civil servants employed in their core operations and in the public enterprises under their control. In 2010, under the lenders' (EU/European Central Bank/International Monetary Fund) pressure, the Ministry of Interior announced a precise number, which, however, did not go undisputed.

[35] Egalitarian patterns of land ownership resulted from redistribution of agricultural lands seized from the Ottoman Empire in the course of a series of territorial annexations up until the First World War. In addition, aggressive land-reform policies under the governments of Eleftherios Venizelos, especially following the massive influx of Greek refugees from the disastrous Asia Minor campaign of 1919–22, led to nearly universal land ownership among the rural population of Greece. Mavrogordatos (1983) reports that in 1928, 64 percent of the labor force either owned their own businesses or agricultural lands, or were working for other family members, while just over 9 percent of the labor force were employed as manual workers in the industrial sector.

[36] It bears noting that even for the Orthodox Communist Party (KKE) no more than 7 percent of its votes can be explained by objective indicators of social class.

[37] This implies that political polarization in Greece along a Left-Right cleavage was anchored

this may be just one of the instances where the beliefs-driven public discourse is devoid of facts.

These features of Greek society meant that PASOK – in the 1980s – could count on broad political support provided that it supplied society-specific 'public goods.' Among these 'public goods', the most important – in their ability to procure mass political support – were: employment in the wider public sector at relatively high wages; a lax enforcement of tax law for the self-employed; and the granting of (mostly) unfunded pension rights to various groups – these included the provision of public pensions to persons without prior contributions, and the provision of excessively large pension benefits to selected groups of public sector employees (including, especially, those employed in state-owned enterprises and banks) and to the self-employed.[38] In addition, the presence of EU funds allowed the governments since the mid-1980s to secure media support through selective channeling of funds to friendly media moguls – who often enough also happened to be winners of lucrative public procurement contracts.

Ironically, the dismal economic performance of the PASOK governments in the 1980s did not make a large dent in its popularity among the voters. In fact, the rise in the unemployment rate from less than 3 percent in 1981 to 8 percent in 1988 increased PASOK's ability to act as a patron to broad segments of the population, since it became particularly adept in the skillful manipulation of scarcity. PASOK's cadres came to realize that patron-client relationships need not depend on a continuous stream of publicly provided benefits but on sustaining the expectation of rewards in the maximum number of would-be voters for the party with the minimum payoff in concrete benefits. Some of these could be the (relatively) lucrative employment opportunities created by the overstaffing of state-owned enterprises. Naturally, these opportunities were to some extent limited by the lack of government revenue and the inability to borrow from abroad. Yet, there were other means through which patron-client relationships on a large scale could be fostered. Often enough these involved preferential access to scarce public goods and services, which, although in principle were accessible to all citizens, their (timely) availability depended on being able to draw on the goodwill of the party's cadres, or on family and relatives who happened to have been public sector employees at crucial posts.

Borrowing from Olson's (2000) metaphor – and in distinction with the 'stationary bandit(s)' regime of the first three postwar decades that had a stake in growth as long as it afforded its members a portion of the increased output without jeopardizing the survival of the regime – the post-1981 regime could be interpreted as a 'roving bandit(s)' regime, in which, literally, tens of thousands of civil servants and private agents could overtly engage in rent-seeking activities (and covertly in unlikely-to-be-punished outright corruption) without, rationally for each player, too much regard for the detrimental growth effects of such behavior. In essence, a 'growth-without-too-much-trickle-down' regime was replaced by a growth-retarding, 'plough-into-the-public-coffers' regime.[39]

---

in historically constructed political identities, and in the individual welfare consequences of a giant spoils system (Mavrogordatos 1983).

[38] See Matsaganis (2011) for more details regarding the inequities and inefficiencies of Greek social policy.

[39] The 'democratization' of rent seeking became so entrenched that even the Conservative Party (New Democracy) adopted it wholeheartedly while in power (2004–09).

24.6 STEALTH POPULISM: 1993–2008

The final 15 years (1993–2008) before the start of Greece's sovereign debt crisis saw a further expansion (along with some rationalization) of the welfare state, fast growth rates and EMU entry. The Greek economy appeared to perform better as in 2008 Greek GDP per capita was 1.65 times larger than its 1993 level, whereas the corresponding numbers for the 12WE were 1.31, 1.29 for Portugal and 1.61 for Spain.[40]

The parliamentary elections of 1993 returned Andrea Papandreou's PASOK to power after a brief interlude (1990–93) in government of the conservative New Democracy under its more liberal-minded leader Constantine Mitsotakis. New Democracy's return to power followed a series of high-profile corruption cases brought against senior PASOK officials,[41] and in the wake of three consecutive elections, Mitsotakis eventually received enough support to form a government with a very weak parliamentary majority. This seriously compromised the government's ability to carry out its avowed aim of economic liberalization, and it was eventually forced to call early elections, which it lost, in 1993.

PASOK's return to power can only partly be explained by the lackluster economic performance of Mitsotakis's government – after all, PASOK's past performance was equally unimpressive. It can mostly be explained by the widespread perception that, despite its manifest shortcomings, PASOK represented the only alternative if the country was to consolidate the wealth and power redistribution achievements of the last two decades, and to put a brake on the return of the 'unfair capitalism' of the postwar decades. The large decline in income and consumption inequality, which had taken place in Greece since 1974, and especially the rise in the income and consumption shares of the middle of the distribution relative to the top (Mitrakos and Tsakloglou 2012), meant that the mediocre growth record of the 1980s was not compatible with increases in the living standards of the 'median voter.'

Moreover, PASOK was gradually shedding some aspects of its 'third-world populism.' Given the publicly stated objective to aim for participation in the EMU, and under pressure from its 'modernizing wing' – which eventually ruled the country from 1996 to 2004 – PASOK altered its agenda and adopted privatization and liberalization policies.[42] At the same time, it managed[43] to tame budget deficits and inflation, and Greece acceded to the Eurozone on 1 January 2001.

One may have thought that the reduction of budget deficits during this period would have been accomplished by tightening wasteful public spending, thus reducing

---

[40] With the benefit of hindsight we know that the 'growth model' of this period was seriously flawed, as it was predicated on excessive borrowing from abroad; the global financial crisis put the tombstone to this phase, and ushered in the Greek Great Depression, taking the unemployment rate to 27.2 percent (as of January 2013), and returned Greek GDP per capita as a percentage of the corresponding measure for the 12WE to the level it was in 1972.

[41] Even Andreas Papandreou was brought to trial during New Democracy's reign, but he was acquitted in January 1992 after a ten-month trial by a seven-to-six margin.

[42] Ironically, this meant that it ended up adopting some of the policies it fought hard to stop New Democracy from implementing.

[43] We explain below how this was achieved.

opportunities for rent seeking and outright corruption. However, from 1993 to 2000, the share of tax revenue in GDP increased by about 8 percentage points whereas the share of government spending remained intact. More importantly, primary government spending (that is, excluding debt interest payments) was rising during the pre-EMU period, since interest payments were steadily declining as a result of nominal convergence (that is, drop in nominal interest rates) to the rest of the euro area countries. The boost given to the Greek economy by the reduction in real interest rates and the foreign capital inflow allowed for a huge rise in the real value of primary government spending, which increased by 110 percent between 1993 and 2008.

Given the diachronic inability of the Greek state to collect taxes, the rise in tax revenue mentioned above would be no mean achievement if one is interested in meeting a revenue target. Yet, this rise in tax revenue – which managed to arrest the large rise in public debt since 1981 – was partly achieved by allowing an unsustainable string of current account deficits.[44]

For reasons related to the financial liberalization laws enacted in Greece in 1994,[45] international borrowing (mediated through the domestic banking sector) became easier and households started being able to borrow far more in order to finance purchases of consumer durables (and at lower real interest rates as well). This unprecedented (for Greece) credit expansion led to a huge deterioration in the current account balance; from a surplus of 1.3 percent of GDP in 1994 to a deficit of 12.0 percent in 2000.[46] At the same time, (nominal) government revenue tripled during the same period.[47] This was a result of the huge rise in imports; from 24.9 percent of GDP in 1994 to 38.4 percent in 2000. The reason is that imports that suddenly become possible through (international) borrowing need not (necessarily) displace spending on domestically produced goods (they may even increase it!), and create a revenue boon for the government.[48]

The tight time constraints that had to be met if Greece was to be a member of the euro area from the first day of the physical introduction of the euro (1 January 2002) meant that the Greek governments faced a very difficult task if they were to meet the 3 percent budget deficit limit required for gaining accession to the euro area. Leaving aside the charges that Greece 'cheated' in its presentation of budget data, one may well understand

---

[44] Assuming away the Ricardian equivalence hypothesis, it is usually thought that a higher budget deficit leads to a higher current account deficit – the 'twin deficits hypothesis'. (This is not necessarily the case though, since it is the sum of private, government and foreign sector balances that must be equal to zero.) Implicit in this presumption, however, there is, inter alia, another presumption: that causality runs from budget deficits to current account deficits. Nevertheless, the direction of causality can also run from the current account deficit to the budget deficit as we argue in the text.

[45] Financial liberalization was a pre-condition for being admitted to the euro area.

[46] The current account deficit widened further to 16.3 percent of GDP in 2008.

[47] The ratio of government revenue to GDP increased from 34.8 percent in 1994 to 40.1 percent in 2000.

[48] For example, car imports generate immediate tax revenue (VAT, luxury taxes and so on). They also allow for increases in domestic value added (for example, services related to sales, advertising and repairs of automobiles), thus allowing for second-round increases in income tax revenue. In general, the smaller the substitutability between domestically produced and imported goods, the larger will be the rise in domestic output due to higher imports that are financed by capital inflows.

why the Greek governments were willing to allow, temporarily, a large increase in net foreign indebtedness if that helped in achieving the 'national goal' of euro area participation. Unfortunately, even after the EMU accession decision, it proved impossible for the Greek governments to arrest the continuing rise of net foreign indebtedness, since large capital inflows (that is, large current account deficits) continued to be an easy way to keep budget deficits not 'too far' above the 3 percent limit.[49] Thus, a more malign (since it was increasingly mortgaging the country to the rest of the world) and covert populism substituted for the overt populism of the previous period.

That the exigencies of political necessity would make it difficult to reverse the dangerous path of excessive-credit-creation-based budget 'consolidation' became apparent during the pre-election campaign of 2000. In a tightly fought electoral battle, the party in power (PASOK) promised that citizens would receive their due – and delayed – reward of increased 'welfare provisions', since the goal of EMU entry had been achieved.[50] Following their electoral win (by a very small margin), the government proceeded in 'rewarding' citizens (that is, their electoral base) with large increases in public sector wages[51] (Moutos and Tsitsikas 2010) and pensions (Tinios 2012). In effect, in the pre-EMU accession phase, the threat of exclusion acted as a hard budget constraint that forced the Greek government to redress its fiscal imbalances (in the way described). In contrast to the output-driven 'hard-conditionality' of the pre-accession period, the EMU period was characterized by the 'soft-conditionality' of the Stability and Growth Pact, which allowed Greece (even more than other governments) to breach both the letter and the spirit of the Pact.

By this time, successive Greek governments depended not only on their traditional electoral bases but the banking sector. The gradual liberalization of the banking sector, which started in the late 1980s and received a large boost due to the financial liberalization laws of 1994, allowed – until the crisis erupted – for a happy symbiosis between the banking sector and Greek governments. Both government and banks were locked in a growth-on-(foreign) credit-steroids regime, which, as long as foreign credit to both parties was available, allowed Greek governments to continue their clientistic politics and the private sector (mainly the banks) to postpone the consequences of their increasing foreign indebtedness. The banking sector re-entered the nexus of key players who were fatally tied to a regime of (literally) borrowed growth – as any substantial lowering of foreign credit expansion would harm both the government and banking sectors whose revenue and viability depended on an unsustainably large GDP growth rate (due to the huge current account deficits it was producing). The regime could go on only as long as soft budget constraints were allowed to prevail.

---

[49] In fact, Greece violated for every year between 2000 and 2008 the 3 percent limit on budget deficits, frequently being above 5 percent. See Katsimi and Moutos (2010) for a discussion of this and the difference between the 'first release' of the budget deficit and the later estimates of it.

[50] Although the elections were held in April, and the formal decision was taken in June 2000, it was known many months before that the Council would approve Greece's EMU participation.

[51] The cumulative increase over the 1995–2009 period in (gross) nominal private sector wages (excluding the banking sector) was 116 percent, whereas the cumulative increase in civil servants' wages was 159 percent, and in publicly owned enterprises 221 percent (Fotoniata and Moutos 2010; EEAG 2011).

Nothing exemplifies this era's attitude of soft budget constraints more than the way social transfers were wasted. Although in the 2000s Greece managed to catch up with the rest of EU Member States as far as social spending is concerned, it was unable to tilt its social policy toward the categories of the population that receive minimum or no social protection. The waste involved with respect to social transfers in Greece can be gleaned from their (in)effectiveness in reducing poverty risk. EU-SILC data (ELSTAT 2012) indicate that from 2003 to 2008 the average reduction in the at-risk-of-poverty rate was 3 percent in Greece, whereas among the EU15 countries the average reduction in the at-risk-of-poverty rate for the total population was 10 percent. (The poverty rate in Greece before social transfers was about the same as in the EU15.) These data not only underscore the inability of the Greek state to use social policy effectively but also reflect the willingness of Greek policymakers to cater to special interest groups.

A prime example of this inefficiency is the social security system; a highly fragmented pay-as-you-go system that comprised the vast majority of government social expenditure. Between 1980 and 2007, government expenditure on old-age pensions as a share of GDP more than doubled; from 4.6 percent to 10.0 percent. A few examples, which show how pension funds serving 'special interest' groups managed to attain their privileged position – usually achieved by receiving indirect subsidies by the government (often by imposing taxes on third parties) – should suffice. Matsaganis (2011) reports that the same amount of contributions would give a pensioner of IKA, which is the main social insurance fund catering to private sector employees, a pension of €500 at age 65, while it would give a pensioner of TAP-OTE (a fund catering to a telecom firm that was, until recently, publicly owned) €1500 at age 55. Such unequal treatment of pensioners, which was underpinned through the use of public funds, was also responsible for the higher incidence of poverty among pensioners than for the population as a whole. It is thus ironic that social transfers (excluding pensions) in Greece were very effective in reducing the high (relative to EU15) at-risk-of-poverty-rate for persons older than 65, while at the same time government policy was responsible for creating the high poverty risk among pensioners by over-subsidizing through scarce public funds the more 'affluent' pension funds.[52]

The soft budget constraints, due to low-cost access to finance from the international markets, were only one part of the story. The EMU liberalization and privatization agenda was incompatible with the continuation of catering to party cadres' needs via the expansion of an already bloated public sector. The result was to outsource the redistribution-of-resources facility. State-owned enterprises could not be relied upon to be the sole 'intermediaries' available for achieving this objective any longer, as they were coming under scrutiny. The rents redistribution facilitator role was taken by many private entrepreneurs, who were interrelated with the party machine. These private actors became the beneficiaries of lucrative public procurement contracts, and led to widespread graft as it created an 'industry' whose role was to facilitate 'information exchange' and 'matching' between government functionaries and private actors. A

[52] The inequities of social protection in Greece are not restricted to just old-age pensions; they permeate all aspects of it. For example, blind people receive €362 (per month) if they are students or employees, and €697 if they are lawyers; the low-income family benefit is €25 (per month) if the parents are private sector employees, and €236 if they work in the wider public sector or in a bank (Matsaganis 2011).

side-effect of making the redistribution of resources 'private' was probably an increase in the inefficiency of the process, due to the extra effort needed to hide (or legalize) these arrangements. It is probably no coincidence that during this era Greece's ranking in Transparency International's index of corruption declined from 36th in 1998, to 44th in 2002, to 49th in 2004, to 57th in 2008.[53]

We end this section by noting an instance in which well-intentioned attempts to rationalize public sector hiring that were undertaken at the start of this period had unintended consequences. To establish an element of efficiency and/or justice in the hiring decisions, an independent administrative body overseeing public sector hiring (named ASEP) was instituted. Given the cynical social environment within which it was functioning and to avoid accusations of preferential treatment of party affiliates, ASEP tried to establish 'objective' criteria, which were supposed to promote meritocracy. Among these criteria, education was playing the predominant role. Suddenly, a tertiary education degree (no matter what the subject or the quality of the institution) became a valued passport to obtaining a lucrative public sector job.[54] As a result, admission into a university (or even into a technical higher education institute) became a coveted prize – regardless of the actual intrinsic value of the degree. Competitive university entrance exams increased in importance and acquired an almost life-defining role. Not surprisingly, families started preparing their offspring for these exams early on (already from junior high school) by hiring tutors or by attending private crammer schools – most of which operate in the black economy. This meant that secondary education was subordinated to the university entrance exams, leading to a considerable reduction in the quality of education high schools were offering and moreover to costs through family budgets that dissipated the expected university degree rents.[55]

The political hold on the provision of tertiary education in Greece is so unique that it merits some discussion. The Greek Constitution does not allow private (even not-for-profit) universities to operate in Greece.[56, 57] Thus, private spending on tertiary education in

---

53 The inclusion of more countries in the index is only marginally responsible for this deterioration in ranking.

54 For example, 69.5 percent of the new public sector jobs allocated through ASEP in 2004 were earmarked solely for tertiary education graduates. To appreciate the implied increase in the probability of securing a public sector job as a tertiary education graduate, it suffices to say that tertiary graduation rates have never exceeded 35 percent of the relevant age groups.

55 Kanellopoulos et al. (2003) estimate that the share of education expenditures in household budgets (mainly on crammer schools and private tutors) rose from 2.15 percent in 1974 to 4.41 percent in 1999. Recent studies (KANEP-GSEE 2009) estimate that in 2005 this figure had risen to 5.09 percent of household budgets. As a proportion of household spending for families with children in secondary school this can reach more than 20 percent of household income (Psacharopoulos and Papakonstantinou 2005).

56 If, for example, a top US Ivy League University wanted to set up a campus in Greece, the Greek state would not recognize the degrees conferred by it as equivalent to those provided by Greek universities; thus the graduates of any bona fide foreign institution operating in Greece would not be allowed to compete for the coveted public sector jobs, thus diminishing the attractiveness of a degree from such an institution. Even when a degree is gained abroad, such a degree can be recognized as equivalent to a Greek university degree only after the graduate applies for the granting of 'equivalence' to the designated Greek government organization (DIKATSA).

57 In 2007, the latest effort to create a constitutional majority so as to amend the Constitution

Greece as a percentage of total spending on tertiary education was only 0.3 percent in 2009 (OECD 2012) – the lowest, by far, among all Organisation for Economic Co-operation and Development (OECD) countries, whose corresponding average was 22.9 percent. Despite the small (official) presence of the private sector in education in Greece, public spending on education in Greece was only 2.3 percent of GDP for the period 1970–2005, whereas the corresponding number for the OECD average was 5.1 percent.[58]

It is not easy to interpret why Greece appears to underspend on education. For one thing, the numbers mentioned above do not include the considerable spending undertaken by Greeks studying abroad, and the (mostly) unrecorded spending on crammer schools mentioned earlier.[59] Furthermore, one can argue that spending on education may be explained by Greece's specialization in low- to-middle-tech services (for example, tourism and sea transport), which do not require a particularly sophisticated labor force for its operation – thus making the vested interests of these sectors not particularly interested in seeing an improvement in public education.[60] Nonetheless, this argument ignores that the industrial elite intervened and influenced the quality of tertiary and technical education degrees in the 1950s and 1960s when its demand for well-educated employees, especially engineers, boosted the postwar expansion of universities and technical schools. The interest of the industrial elite, though, receded in the post-1973 period. This 'neglect' can be attributed both to the withering importance industrial capital had in the economy from that period onwards, and to the increasing dominance that political parties and other 'social groups' came to exercise over the public university system after the fall of the colonels' junta and the rise of PASOK to power. An important aspect of this over-politicization of tertiary education was the constant scrabble for ideological supremacy (often, but inaccurately, portrayed as a battle between those whose avowed aim was the provision of 'society-benefiting' education and those who wanted a strong linkage between education and the private sector's labor market needs) and control over resources.[61]

Ironically, the avowed aim of insulating educational ideals from labor market needs was effectively reversed with the creation of ASEP. As explained earlier, in the post-1994

---

in this respect was thwarted by George Papandreou's last minute decision to pull PASOK away from such a deal with the then governing New Democracy party.

58 Even in South Korea, that is, a country with similar GDP per capita levels during this period, the corresponding number is 3.6 percent. Furthermore, the above difference can be properly appreciated if one takes into account that in 2000 South Korea had a very large presence of private spending on (all levels of) education, that is, 40.8 percent of the total, while in Greece it was only 6.2 percent.

59 But still, even if these types of private spending are properly accounted for, they would probably raise the 'true' share of private spending on education in Greece from the recorded 6.2 percent of total spending close to the (recorded) OECD average of 12.2 percent, but would certainly keep it far below the recorded 40.8 percent for Korea.

60 Acemoglu and Robinson (2012) provide many historical examples in which the 'elites' showed either 'benign neglect' with respect to the provision of public goods or were openly hostile to their provision – often caring not only about the extra tax burden but also fearing that their provision would diminish their power to influence other types of policies.

61 The Ministry of Education exercised an inordinate amount of control over the allocation of resources, often using public money in order to advance party-political interests and with blatant disregard to the detrimental consequences of these actions.

ASEP period, the public's main interest was to satisfy the increased demand for any tertiary education degree. (Apparently, 'preparing' students for public sector employment was not considered a sacrifice to the ideal of 'society-benefiting' education.) Fittingly, public spending on tertiary education increased from 0.6 percent of GDP in 1995 to become equal to the OECD average of 1.5 percent in 2005. This represents, we believe, another instance of the democratization of rent seeking.

24.7 POST-MORTEM: GREECE'S GREAT DEPRESSION

The global financial crisis of 2007/08 took the Greek growth-on-(foreign) credit-steroids regime apart with a small delay. Once foreign credit to the overextended Greek banking sector collapsed, it took about a year before the 'benefits' of huge current account deficits for the government budget deficit to evaporate. Indeed, for the first time after many years, in 2009 the government budget deficit was larger than the current account deficit. That is, the collapse of foreign lending to the Greek private sector forced, through the channel explained earlier, a large rise in the government budget deficit.

Although it is common to attribute Greece's Great Depression[62] solely to government's profligacy, in fact, the private sector reduced its saving rate at the same time as the government was trying to decrease its own dis-saving from the early 1990s to the mid 2000s. Indeed, it was the decline in the private sector's gross saving rate (from 27 percent in 1988 to 11 percent in 2008) that led to large current account deficits after 1997, which took Greece's net foreign assets' position from negative 3 percent in 1997 to negative 86 percent of GDP by the end of 2009 (Moutos and Tsitsikas 2010). At that point investors started to question the government's ability (and/or willingness) to service its debt to foreigners, since it became clear that the Greek government faced a mission-impossible; on the one hand, to make public debt sustainable, the economy should grow so as to increase tax revenue; on the other hand, to make net foreign debt sustainable, the economy should contract so as to eliminate the huge current account deficit. Under these conditions, foreign creditors started demanding interest rates that embodied a high probability of default, thus forcing the government to resort to the official bailout mechanism to avoid the impending (disorderly) default.

This brought an end to the large expansion of Greek living standards, but it remains to be seen whether the tutelage exercised, once again, by foreign representatives (from the EU/European Central Bank/International Monetary Fund this time) will manage to break the mold that gave rise to the changing political economy coalitions that appear to have been controlling events in Greece during the last decades. Some evidence of the acceptance (albeit grudgingly) of the policies implied by the bailout package can be elicited by the Eurobarometer (2010).[63] There one could sense a change in attitudes by

---

[62] The percentage drop in Greek GDP since 2008 is (circa spring 2013) two-and-a-half times as large as the one experienced from peak to trough in the 1930s.

[63] The Eurobarometer (2010) reports results of interviews conducted between 7 May and 25 May in Greece, when most of the details of the bailout package had already been reported in the press. (For more details along these lines, see EEAG 2011.) In response to the statement 'In an international financial and economic crisis, is it necessary to increase public deficits to create jobs'

the Greek citizens, who have been raised to consider the government as 'employer of last resort.' Given that public sector employment was the main tool through which political parties in Greece dispense favors to partisan voters, as well as a 'redistributive' tool in periods of high unemployment, this change in attitudes is an indication that the foreign lenders (through their tutelage of the post-2009 Greek governments) have succeeded in refashioning the public debate about the role of the public sector in the economy.

Reasons for the absence of a very hostile and open reaction (despite some flurries in June 2011) to the reform package by society at large were, first, the gradual recognition that Greece's predicament was a result of the deep entanglement between political and economic power, and second, that absent the willingness of foreign lenders to accept further increases in debt accumulation it was only fair that the 'entitled' levels of income and social welfare were lowered.[64] There was also some recognition that Greece's predicament had arisen because for a long time powerful key players managed to legitimize and strengthen their position via the democratization of rent seeking, by permitting weaker players to also benefit by a system of inefficient policies (or outright anomie) in which the pilfering of public resources remains largely unpunished. As a result, Greece reached a frightening homeostasis that could be broken only if all the beneficiaries of the current politico-economic equilibrium were to lose their undue privileges. A significant number of voters – let alone the political parties – may not have realized that this was the only way out of the crisis.

REFERENCES

Acemoglu, Daron and James A. Robinson (2012), *Why Nations Fail: The Origins of Power, Prosperity, and Poverty*, New York: Crown Publishers.

Angelopoulos, Konstantinos, Apostolis Philippopoulos and Vanghelis Vassilatos (2009), 'The social cost of rent seeking in Europe', *European Journal of Political Economy*, **25**(3), 280–99.

Bank of Greece (1980), *The Greek Economy: Research Essays and Statistical Series* (in Greek), Athens: Bank of Greece.

Bourlakis, Costas (1996), 'Concentration trends in Greek manufacturing industries 1958–1984: an entropy approach', University of Leicester Discussion Papers No.96/6, Leicester.

Chalikias, Dimitrios (1976), *Potential and Drawbacks of Credit Policy* (in Greek), Athens: Bank of Greece.

Charalambis, Dimitrios (1989), *Clientilistic Linkages and Populism* (in Greek), Athens: Exantas.

Clogg, Richard (1987), *Parties and Elections in Greece: The Search for Legitimacy*, Durham, NC: Duke University Press.

Coase, Ronald H. (1937), 'The nature of the firm', *Economica*, **16**(4), 386–405.

Dertilis, George (1985), *Social Transformation and Military Intervention* (in Greek), Athens: Exantas.

Di Tella, Rafael and Robert MacCulloch (2009), 'Why doesn't capitalism flow to poor countries?', *Brookings Papers on Economic Activity*, **40**(1), 285–322.

EEAG (2011), *The EEAG Report on the European Economy*, 'Greece', Munich: CESifo, pp.97–125.

---

more people in Greece than any other European country have stated that they disagree (for Greece, 37 percent 'Agree' and 53 percent 'Disagree'; for the EU27, 46 percent 'Agree' and 36 percent 'Disagree'). If one takes these responses at face value, then a sea change in attitudes appears to have taken place in Greece during 2010. Unfortunately, previous issues of the Eurobarometer have not dealt with the same issue, and thus we do not have 'direct' evidence of the change in attitudes.

64 Passarelli and Tabellini (2013) explain how the perception of fairness is endogenous, and how as external circumstances deteriorate individuals become resigned to a lower level of welfare. They also show that in such circumstances governments may engage in policy procrastination.

ELSTAT (2012), *Living Conditions in Greece*, available at http://www.statistics.gr (accessed 27 March 2013).
Eurobarometer (2010), *Public Opinion in the European Union*, Eurobarometer 73, Brussels: European Commission.
Fotoniata, Eugenia and Thomas Moutos (2010), 'Greece: neglect and resurgence of minimum wage policy', in Daniel Vaughan-Whitehead (ed.), *The Minimum Wage Revisited in the Enlarged EU*, Cheltenham, UK and Northampton, MA, USA and Geneva: Edward Elgar Publishing and International Labour Office, pp. 213–43.
Gunther, Richard and Jose Ramon Moreno (2000), 'The anchors of partisanship: a comparative analysis of voting behavior in four southern European democracies', Estudio/Working Paper 2000/150, Juan March Institute, Madrid.
Kanellopoulos, Kostas N., Theodore Mitrakos and Kostas G. Mavromaras (2003), *Education and Labour Market* (in Greek), Athens: Center of Planning and Economic Research.
KANEP-GSEE (2009), *Main Figures of Greek Education*, Athens: Center for the Development of Education Policy, General Confederation of Greek Workers.
Karatzas, George (1988), 'The Greek hyperinflation and stabilization of 1943–1946: a comment on Makinen', *Journal of Economic History*, **48**(1), 138–9.
Katsimi, Margarita and Thomas Moutos (2010), 'EMU and the Greek crisis: the political economy perspective', *European Journal of Political Economy*, **26**(4), 568–76.
Katsimi, Margarita, Thomas Moutos, George Pagoulatos and Dimitri Sotiropoulos (2014), 'The (eventual) social hardship of soft budget constraints', in Brian Nolan, Wiemer Salverda, Daniele Checchi et al. (eds), *Changing Inequalities and Societal Impacts in Rich Countries: Thirty Countries' Experiences*, Oxford: Oxford University Press, pp. 299–321.
Kofas, John (1989), *Intervention and Underdevelopment: Greece during the Cold War*, University Park, PA: Penn State University Press.
Liakos, Antonis (1993), *Labour and Politics in Interwar Greece* (in Greek), Athens: Foundation for Research and Education, Commercial Bank of Greece.
Lyrintzis, Christos (2005), 'The changing party system: stable democracy, contested modernisation', *West European Politics*, **28**(2), 242–59.
Maddison, Angus (2010), *Historical Statistics of the World Economy: 1-2008 AD*, Groningen: University of Groningen.
Makinen, Gail E. (1986), 'The Greek hyperinflation and stagnation of 1943–1946', *Journal of Economic History*, **46**(3), 795–805.
Matsaganis, Manos (2011), *Social Policy in Hard Times* (in Greek), Athens: Kritiki.
Mavrogordatos, George T. (1983), *Stillborn Republic: Social Coalitions and Party Strategies in Greece, 1922–1936*, Berkeley, CA: University of California Press.
Mitrakos, Theodore and Panos Tsakloglou (2012), 'Inequality, poverty and material welfare: from regime transition to the current crisis', in Bank of Greece, *Social Policy and Social Cohesion in Greece under Conditions of Economic Crisis* (in Greek), Athens: Bank of Greece.
Moutos, Thomas and Christos Tsitsikas (2010), 'Whither public interest: the case of Greek public finances', *FinanzArchiv: Public Finance Analysis*, **66**(2), 170–206.
OECD (2012), *Education at a Glance 2012*, Paris: OECD.
Olson, Mancur (2000), *Power and Prosperity: Outgrowing Communist and Capitalist Dictatorships*, New York: Basic Books.
Pagoulatos, George (2003), *Greece's New Political Economy: State, Finance and Growth from Postwar to EMU*, London: Palgrave.
Pagoulatos, George (2006), *National Bank of Greece 1940–2000* (in Greek), Athens: NBG.
Passarelli, Francesco and Guido Tabellini (2013), 'Emotions and political unrest', Working Paper No. 4165, CESifo, Munich.
Peltzman, Sam (1976), 'Towards a more general theory of regulation', *Journal of Law and Economics*, **19**(2), 211–40.
Pesmatzoglou, Stephanos (1993), 'The 1980s in the looking glass: PASOK and the media', in Richard Clogg (ed.), *Greece 1981–89: The Populist Decade*, London: Macmillan, pp. 95–113.
Piketty, Thomas (1995), 'Social mobility and redistributive politics', *Quarterly Journal of Economics*, **110**(3), 551–84.
Pridham, Geoffrey and Susannah Verney (1991), 'The coalitions of 1989–90 in Greece: inter-party relations and democratic consolidation', *West European Politics*, **14**(4), 42–69.
Psacharopoulos, George and George Papakonstantinou (2005), 'The real university cost in a "free" higher education country', *Economics of Education Review*, **24**(1), 103–8.
Schmitter, Philippe C. (1974), 'Still the century of corporatism?', *Review of Politics*, **36**(1), 85–131.
Spourdalakis, Michalis (2008), '2007 Greek elections: signs of major political realignment, challenges and hopes for the left', *Studies in Political Economy*, **82**, 171–86.

Stathakis, George (2004), *Truman Doctrine and Marshall Plan: The History of US Aid in Greece* (in Greek), Athens: Vivliorama.
Stigler, George (1971), 'The theory of economic regulation', *Bell Journal of Economics and Management Sciences*, **2**(1), 3–21.
Sweet-Escott, B. (1954), *Greece: A Political and Economic Survey 1939–1953*, London: Royal Institute of International Affairs.
Tinios, Platon (2012), 'Greece: extreme crisis in a monolithic unreformed pension system', *Global Social Policy*, **12**(3), 332–44.
Tsakalotos, Euclid (1998), 'The political economy of social democratic economic policies: the PASOK experiment in Greece', *Oxford Review of Economic Policy*, **14**(1), 114–38.
Tsoucalas, Constantinos (1987), *State, Society, Labour in Postwar Greece* (in Greek), Athens: Themelio.
Williamson, Oliver (1985), *The Economic Institutions of Capitalism*, New York: Free Press.
Williamson, Oliver (1996), *The Mechanisms of Governance*, New York: Oxford University Press.

25. Rent seeking in the democracy of ancient Greece

*George Tridimas**

SUMMARY

This chapter investigates the sources and contests for rents in ancient Athens. After reviewing the institutions of direct democracy invented and practiced during the fifth and fourth centuries BCE, the chapter focuses on the rents derived from controlling citizenship rights, slave labor, subjugation of foreign territories and silver deposits. It then examines the insights that the rent-seeking approach offers to explain the political economy of regulatory policies, tax revenues and public expenditures in Athens. A distinctive structure is revealed that combined free market exchanges, trade taxes but no income taxes, taxation of the rich in the form of property levies and mandatory financing of public services, auctions of public assets, tax farming, wide access to paid public office, where appointment was made by lot, and payment of theatre money to all citizens. Political leaders had opportunities for rent extraction and rent seeking, but they were also closely scrutinized by popular courts. This pattern is broadly consistent with the prediction that under direct democracy large universal benefits are provided to the poor majority of voters. The chapter concludes by proposing that the rent-seeking approach validates the view that economic rationality was prevalent in the ancient economy.

25.1 INTRODUCTION

> where there are revenues men must not do what the popular leaders do now (for they use the surplus for doles, and people no sooner get them than they want the same doles again, because this way of helping the poor is the legendary jar with a hole in it), but the truly democratic statesman must study how the multitude may be saved from extreme poverty; for this is what causes democracy to be corrupt. (Aristotle, Politics, 1320a, 30–35)

Government policies can be the source of considerable privileges through economic rents that would not have been created and obtained in a competitive market. Typical examples include employment in the public sector, public expenditure targeted to specific beneficiaries, tax exemptions and market regulations that favor particular groups. It is rational behavior to compete for the award of such privileges from government, while in the quest for electoral success politicians welcome the support and financial contributions of interest groups in exchange for favorable policy measures. Rent seekers invest resources unproductively to contest rents rather than to create new wealth, and the rents awarded to successful rent seekers are transfers from one group to others. All resources,

* Part of this research was carried out when I was visiting the Center for Study of Constitutional Political Economy, West Virginia University. I would like to thank the Center for its support.

including those of successful and unsuccessful groups, could have been used to produce additional goods and services and are wasted. In addition to inefficiency, rent extraction and rent seeking affect the distribution of income. The creation and sharing of rents and the efficiency losses from rent seeking depend crucially on the political institutions of a society. Neither creation nor competition for rents need bc illegal; but corruption, the use of government authority for private benefit in a way not intended by the law, such as receiving a bribe, is.

Rent seeking transcends time and space. Ancient Athens, hailed for inventing direct democracy and participatory government, was not immune to rent seeking, nor did she shy away from controlling it. Painstaking research by historians has pieced together fragmentary written and archaeological evidence to reconstruct the political and economic structure of the Athenian polis, even though there are no annual records of key Athenian economic variables such as population, gross domestic product (GDP), public expenditure or tax revenue. The picture painted is one of a vibrant democracy, a prosperous economy and a government collecting and disbursing significant sums of money. In what follows I rely on this picture to examine rent extraction and rent seeking in ancient Athens.

Conceptually, the inquiry into rent seeking in ancient Athens requires an understanding of three related issues. First, the definition of citizenship, which defines the identity of those with political rights and the economic and non-economic benefits associated with it. Second, the people who have the power to decide policy; how they are chosen, their decision-making procedures and how they are kept accountable. Third, the sources of rents or means of rent creation, which depend on the structure of property rights, availability of resources, and public policy to regulate economic activity, tax and public expenditure measures. This conceptual framework is applied in the structure of the chapter. Section 25.2 presents the institutions of the Athenian democracy (508–322, all dates are BCE) and their evolution. Section 25.3 offers theoretical predictions on rent extraction and rent seeking in the direct democracy of Athens. Section 25.4 focuses on rent originating outside Athens, namely, slavery and resources extracted from the members of the Athenian League. Section 25.5 examines domestic sources of rent, market regulations, revenues from the silver mines and taxation, and public expenditure and its distribution. Section 25.6 discusses the opportunities for rent seeking open to political leaders who enjoyed discretionary powers. Section 25.7 concludes, arguing that the political-economy insights of rent-seeking behavior support the validity of economic rationality in examining topics of ancient economic history.

25.2 A REVIEW OF THE INSTITUTIONS OF THE ATHENIAN DEMOCRACY AND THEIR EVOLUTION

25.2.1 The Founding of Democracy and its Institutions

Table 25.1 presents the timeline of the Athenian political developments and the subsequent evolution of the democratic constitution in the fifth and fourth centuries, while Table 25.2 summarizes the main organs of the state and their responsibilities. The emergence of democracy in ancient Athens was a long and tortuous process. Athens

Table 25.1 Timeline of the Athenian democracy

632/631	The aristocrat Cylon mounts a failed coup to establish himself as tyrant
621	Draco compiles a written code of laws
594	Solon the lawgiver introduces a wealth-based political dispensation
546–510	Tyranny of Peisistratus and his son Hippias
510	Hippias expelled
508–507	Democracy established: Cleisthenes reforms – citizenship, Council of Five Hundred
502/501	Board of Ten Generals introduced
490	Victory against the Persians at Marathon
483/2	Discovery of silver deposits at Laurion
480	Victory against the Persians at Salamis
478	Foundation of Delian League
c. 467	Victory against the Persians at Eurymedon
462	Powers of Areopagus removed. Introduction of pay for court service
460–446	'First' Peloponnesian War ends with the 30-year peace treaty between Athens and Sparta
454–404	First Athenian League
454	Delian treasury transferred to Athens
451	Pericles' law restricts citizenship to those whose both parents were Athenians
431–404	Peloponnesian War, Athens versus Sparta
411	Athenian defeat in Sicily, Democracy overthrown by oligarchic coup
410	Democracy restored
404	Athenian defeat and surrender, Tyranny of the Thirty
403	Democracy restored
403/402	Introduction of pay for attending the assembly
395–387	Corinthian War – Athens unsuccessful
378–355	Second Athenian League
358–355	Social War – Athens unsuccessful
c. 355	*Theoric* (festival money) fund formalized
355–346	Sacred War – Athens unsuccessful
338	Athenian defeat in Chaeronea by Philip II of Macedon
322	End of the Athenian Democracy after defeats by Macedon in Amorgos and Crannon

was governed by an aristocracy until the laws of archon Solon (594) changed the basis of participation into political decision making from aristocracy (birth right) to wealth holdings. Solon divided the Athenians into four classes according to the size of their annual agriculture produce, the *pentakosiomedimnoi* (500 measures), the *hippeis* (300 measures), the *zeugitai* (200 measures) and the *thetes* (less than 200 measures).[1] In the second half of the sixth century Athens was ruled by the tyrant Peisistratus and his son Hippias (546–510). After the overthrow of tyranny, democracy was established in 508 by Cleisthenes, himself an aristocrat, upon winning a power struggle against Isagoras,

[1] Modern estimates suggest that members of the *pentakosiomedimnoi* needed 30 or more acres of land, the *hippeis* needed 18 or more and the *zeugitai* needed 12 or more (Murray 1993, p. 194). The *zeugitai* were the backbone of the heavy infantry, hoplites, who paid for and owned their armory, but the *thetes*, who did not afford the expense served only as light-armed troops.

Table 25.2 Political institutions in ancient Athens

Institution	Composition and Organization	Function
The Assembly	• Athenian males over 20 years old • Voluntary attendance, Quorum: 6000 • Majority voting rule by show of hands • Remunerated at average daily wage (fourth century)	Supreme decision maker on foreign and domestic policy
The Council of Five Hundred	• Appointed by lot from Athenian males over 30 years old • Remunerated at average daily wage	• Preparation of Assembly agenda • Day-to-day administration
The Ten Generals	• Elected • Remunerated during campaign at three times the average wage, shared war loot and received gifts from foreigners	• Defense, army and navy • Foreign policy • Attended and addressed the Council
The Court of Six Thousand	• Appointed by lot • Panels of 201/501/1001 jurors • Rulings: by secret majority vote • Remunerated at half average wage	• Private party disputes • Public–private disputes • Rulings on indictments against political leaders
1001 Legislators (fourth century only)	• Drawn from the above • Remunerated at half average wage	• Judicial review of policy
The Nine Archons	• Selected from the aristocracy (archaic times) • Appointed by lot (classical times)	• Governing body (archaic times) • Ceremonial duties (classical times)
The Court of Areopagus	• Ex-archons	• Overseer of laws and magistrates and court during archaic times • Homicide trials during classical times
Other Magistrates (Approximately 600)	• Appointed by lot • Typically serving in boards of Ten	• Specific administrative tasks – inspection of markets, public works, judicial administration
Financial Officers	• Treasurer of Military Fund; Board of the *Theoric* Fund; Controller of the Finances	• Public finances (fourth century)

Note: Archaic times: 750–500. Classical times: fifth and fourth centuries.

a rival aristocrat. Cleisthenes reconstituted the population of Athens into ten tribes (*phylae*), each tribe comprising a cross section of citizens from different geographical areas with different economic bases, so that each tribe would be a microcosm of Athens and share the same interests with the rest of the tribes.

Supreme decision making was invested in the Assembly made up of all Athenian male citizens, which decided all external and internal policy issues. Cleisthenes also established the Council of the Five Hundred, whose members were selected by lot, responsible for preparing the agenda of the Assembly and the day-to-day administration of the state.

The board of the ten generals elected by the Assembly by show of hands to command the army and the navy was introduced in 501. In addition, the generals could attend and address the Council and engaged in foreign policy.

A unique feature of direct democracy was the process of ostracism, a mechanism by which the demos in a direct ballot decided whether or not to banish a leading individual, but without any further criminal or financial penalties, to defend the democracy against potential tyrants, with the last recorded such vote in 417. In the fifth and fourth centuries the People's Court (initially set up by Solon to hear appeals against the decisions of the officials), consisting of 6000 jurors selected by lot became a pillar of the power of the demos. It tried civil and penal cases, reviewed the decisions of the Assembly and checked the conduct of political leaders and other officials. In addition, the Athenians were appointing annually by lot another 600 magistrates typically organized in boards of ten members – one per tribe. Their responsibilities covered inspections of market trading, supervision of public and private buildings, roads, water supplies, implementation of spending plans, administration of justice, cult and temples and steering committees for the Assembly.

25.2.2 Developments in the Fifth Century

After defeating the Persians in the sea battle of Salamis (480), the Athenians assumed the leadership of an alliance of Greek islands and coastal city-states, known as the Delian League. When the members of the league switched from ship and manpower contributions to monetary payments, the alliance transformed into an Athenian 'empire' and Athens became the leading center of Mediterranean trade.[2] The preeminent statesman Pericles, who in the middle of the fifth century was elected general for 15 years without interruption, used the newly found wealth to finance an extensive public construction program, including the Athenian long walls and the famous buildings of the Acropolis, an expression of the Athenian success and prosperity at the time. The democratic constitution was completed in the mid fifth century, when Pericles introduced pay for jury service and other magistrates. Pay for public service meant that poor citizens would not lose income for serving as magistrates. But it also guaranteed significant political support for Pericles and the institutions of democracy.[3] At the same time, Pericles also tightened the law of citizenship so that from 451 only those whose both parents were Athenians enjoyed full citizenship rights.

Democracy was interrupted twice by oligarchy. First, in 411 following the defeat of the Athenians in the Sicilian expedition, but was soon reinstated in 410 by the navy after it vanquished the Spartan fleet in Cyzicus. Second, in 404 after defeat by the Spartans in

---

[2] For a detailed account of the prosperity of Athens in the classical age and beyond, the interested reader is referred to Morris (2004) and Ober (2010).

[3] Pericles used the public purse 'as a popular counter-measure against Cimon's [his political opponent] wealth. For as Cimon had an estate large enough for a tyrant, in the first place he discharged the general public services in a brilliant manner, and moreover he supplied maintenance to a number of the members of his deme; for anyone of the Laciadae who liked could come to his house every day and have a moderate supply, and also all his farms were unfenced, to enable anyone who liked to avail himself of the harvest' (Aristotle, AC, 27.1–4).

the Peloponnesian War (431–404), who dissolved the Athenian League. Athens was then ruled by a 30-member strong oligarch commission, known as the 'Thirty Tyrants'. The oligarchic commission was expelled in 403 and democracy was restored. The Athenians set up a new anti-Spartan naval alliance (378–355), but failed to achieve the supremacy attained before the Peloponnesian War.

25.2.3 Developments in the Fourth Century

Blaming the 'demagogues' for leading the people to mistaken choices and defeat in the Peloponnesian War, some of the powers of the Assembly were curtailed; specifically, after 402, the Assembly lost the power to pass laws describing 'general norms without limit of duration' (but continued to elect magistrates, decide foreign policy and pass decrees). Laws that codified earlier constitutional provisions as well as provisions for private contracts, criminal and procedural rules were passed through a special board of legislators, chosen by lot from the same panel of 6000 jurors of the People's Court. From then onwards, when the Assembly decided that a new law code or a revision of an existing one was needed it voted on setting up a board of legislators and authorized their payment.[4] Assembly decrees had to be in accordance with the laws. The distinction between laws and decrees parallels the modern distinction between constitutional charters and ordinary legislation. It also introduced the Court as an additional veto player. In addition, funding of a variety of state functions was fixed by law diminishing the role of the Assembly in deciding public expenditure. More generally, the fourth century witnessed a shift in the relative power of the popular court and against the Assembly because it also held the additional power to nullify Assembly measures deemed contrary to the laws, fine their proposers and impeach politicians accused of attempting to overthrow the constitution, treason, deceiving the people or corruption (see Hansen 2010). A further new feature of the fourth century was that politics were dominated by the orators who unlike the fifth-century statesmen were not elected generals. With the restoration of democracy, pay for attending the Assembly was introduced, which after a 'bidding war' between the proposers (Hansen 1999, p. 150) was set at half the average daily wage. Later, it was doubled for plain meetings and tripled for chief meetings of the Assembly and was restricted to the first 6000 coming to a session (a figure equal to the required quorum).[5] Finally, a number of a new elected financial officers were also introduced, most importantly, the treasurer of the military fund, the board of the *Theoric* Fund (responsible for distributing 'theatre money' – see below) and the controller of the finances. Although unsuccessful in military campaigns, the Athenian economy prospered and so did its public revenue, even though it no longer collected tribute from the allies.

In 322, following the death of Alexander the Great, Athens revolted against the

---

[4] Passing of legislation proceeded like a trial. The author of the proposed law would put the case to the board of legislators; five advocates would speak against the law and the legislators would then vote by show of hands.

[5] Taking into account that Assembly meetings would normally last half a day, pay for attending the Assembly at the average daily wage, between 1.5–2.5 drachmas, compared favorably to jurors' pay at half the daily wage for a full-day service (which according to Jones 1958, p. 80, was 'enough to buy himself food to eat on the day that he sat in court').

Macedonian rule. Her navy was destroyed in the sea battle of Amorgos and the land forces were overwhelmed in Crannon. An oligarchic government was established, which then abolished the People's Court and disenfranchised the lower class citizens, by limiting the franchise to 9000 citizens, out of a total of at least 21 000, namely, those owing property over 2000 drachmae, bringing the end of the democracy.

The brief narrative of the Athenian democracy suggests that its establishment was a slow and gradual process of institutional reforms that culminated with the fall of tyranny and the reforms of Cleisthenes that enfranchised all Athenian males. It was the cumulative result of several steps, some bigger than other, building on each other over a long time. Rather than solidifying, the process of institutional development extended throughout as new arrangements were added to address defects in the system. This suggests that the foundation of ancient democracy paralleled the establishment of western democracy from the industrial revolution to the twentieth century as theorized by Congleton (2011), slow and gradual, building on established arrangements and more peaceful than violent. There was nothing inevitable about its emergence; bargains had to be struck between the elite and the poor majority, chance events influenced subsequent developments, it was shaped from previous experiences, suffered setbacks and was eventually reversed (see Tridimas 2012b for an elaboration).

25.3 CITIZENSHIP, DIRECT DEMOCRACY AND RENT SEEKING

Successful rent seekers take advantage of their economic and political power to increase their wealth at the expense of the rest. On the other hand, rent extraction can be kept in check by establishing political institutions that limit the ability of rent seekers to influence the government and by establishing economic institutions that prevent market-distorting outcomes. In a representative democracy successful rent seeking requires that an interest group is supported by a majority of the legislators. The larger the number of seats in the legislative houses and the more fragmented their partisan composition, the more resources must be invested to secure such a majority. Athens controlled tightly the definition of citizenship and practiced direct participatory democracy where political agency, the delegation of decision making by the voter to the politician, was kept at a minimum. Passing a decree required a simple majority amongst the citizens attending the Assembly, there were no organized political parties, and a large number of public offices were filled by lot from a pool of volunteers amongst those eligible, factors that were inextricably linked and could not have operated independently of each other (for details of this argument, see Tridimas 2011). *Ceteris paribus* such institutional features reduce the potential for rent seeking.

Pericles' law of 451 restricting citizenship only to those born from two Athenian parents had far-reaching implications. It constrained the numbers of those enjoying the political, financial and legal privileges of citizenship (a measure that might have been popular after an influx of foreigners attracted by the economic success of Athens), limited the influence of foreign elites whose offspring were married to Athenian elites, preserved Athenian ethnic purity, elevated the position of Athenian women (who had no political rights), and by formally basing citizenship on birth regardless of wealth put to a final rest Solon's division of Athenians into wealth-based classes. However, Blok (2009) warns against confusing the motives at the time of enacting the law with its subsequent effects. Noting that after military defeats in 451 as well as 403, the number of Athenian citizens was declining, she rules out population pressure as a reason for restricting citizenship. She emphasizes that the essence of citizenship was to participate in the cults of the gods and religious activities according to ancestral tradition. Priests and priestesses officiating in such communal activities were required to be of double Athenian parentage and bequeathed the priesthood office to their offspring. She then interprets the citizenship law and a simultaneous addition of new cults and priesthood offices filled by lot as an attempt to in due course make priesthood offices accessible to all Athenians.[6]

Hansen (1999) estimates that there were about 60000 male citizens in the fifth century but their number stabilized at 30000 in the fourth century as a result of defeat in war, famine and disease. The corresponding total population, including women and children, was estimated at 100000. To those, one must add the free alien residents, called metics, whose number is estimated as between 25000 and 40000 including their families (Finer 1999). There were also large numbers of slaves, over 150000 at times according to Hansen (1999) and their number must have varied over time as the economic fortune of the polis changed.

The hallmark of democracy was appointment to public office by lot (sortition). Appointment by lottery has a number of attractive properties: representativeness of the preferences of the population; horizontal equity (in the sense that when there are no good reasons to favor one candidate over another, it gives them equal chances of success); elimination of rent seeking among candidates for office along with decrease in corruption (for it removed the incentive to spend resources campaigning and otherwise influencing electors); reduction in factionalism and weakening the influence of the elites in appointing post-holders (as no group can be entrenched in office); and the low cost of operating the mechanism. Over and above these desirable attributes commonly discussed in the literature, Tridimas (2012a) shows that when the expected marginal gain from the action of a public official is smaller than the marginal cost of information about the quality of candidates, citizens adopt appointment by lot. The latter condition was satisfied in Athens in the cases where officials performed routine tasks. Nevertheless, posts that required men of ability were not allocated randomly, but by elections, as, for example, the generalships, so that the citizenry could select those that they trusted. With very few exceptions the terms of service for public offices were annual. No citizen could serve more than one term in his lifetime in any magistracy, with the exceptions of the Council where one could serve twice but not in successive years, and the generalship where there were no term limits. Council members, court jurors and the other magistrates were all ordinary citizens without special training for the task undertaken. With such mechanisms in operation, it is no surprise that Athens did not develop classes of professional politicians, lawyers, bureaucrats or any other kind of experts. Citizens in public posts

---

[6] The citizenship law was applied in 445 when Athens received from Egypt a significant gift of grain to be distributed freely among the citizens and the opportunity was taken to de-register 5000 people. However, in view of the loss of citizen numbers in the Peloponnesian War the law was overlooked and citizenship was granted in blocks to the Plataians in 427 and the Samians in 405.

carried out administrative tasks designed for non-specialists 'with reasonable intelligence and motivation' (Hansen 1999, p. 244). Such post-holders were nevertheless helped by a small number of secretaries who presumably made a career by rotating from one task to another as they were not allowed to serve the same magistracy in the same capacity twice.

This setting implied that in the Assembly only policy measures that benefited the poorer median voter passed, and that direct citizen participation acted as an effective check against political agency and rent seeking. In turn, a direct democracy dominated by the poorer median voter will pass measures that benefit a larger number of voters than an indirect democracy dominated by political entrepreneurs more susceptible to pressures from interest groups. The theoretical predictions that follow then are that in the direct democracy of Athens large sums of benefits are disbursed to the poor majority of male Athenian citizens, the benefits provided are general rather than specific and the number of voters benefiting from policy is large but the benefit that each voter receives is small. As shown in the rest of the chapter, these hypotheses are broadly upheld by the pattern of tax and public expenditure policies and even foreign relations of ancient Athens.

25.4 EXTERNAL SOURCES OF RENTS

The present section reviews two sources of rent sanctioned by the prevailing system of property rights that increased the size of total rents available to all Athenians, namely, use of slave labor and the resources of the allies.

25.4.1 Slavery

As already described, there were large numbers of slaves in Athens, but since the Athenians did not keep numerical records, only rough estimates of the number of slaves can be made.[7] Athenian citizens could not be sold as slaves in Athens, and Athenians enslaved in war were bought and freed by the state. No particular race, tribe or nation was singled out for enslavement and Greek war captives were often enslaved. Slaves were used in agriculture, mining, manufacturing, rowing ships, domestic work, banking and the crafts. The Athenian state also owned a number of 'public slaves', working as assistants to the magistrates, as laborers and as enforcers of public orders – a kind of police force. Not surprisingly, large numbers of slaves faced harsh conditions, especially in the mining industry. Yet, the extant sources leave no doubt that during the fourth century there were a number of wealthy slaves playing a leading role in business, especially finance and the crafts (Cohen 2000). In addition, there is evidence that in public building sites, citizens, metics and slaves often worked side-by-side doing the same jobs for the same pay (Hansen 1999, p. 87). Slaves operating their own business paid their owners a fixed sum and kept the profits (a form of first-best levy). The majority of slaves

7 For a recent critical review of the economic impact of slaves, their living conditions and ideological attitudes toward slavery in ancient Greece, see Cohen (2000) and the papers of Cohen (2002), Kyrtatas (2002), Cartledge (2002) and Jameson (2002) in the volume edited by Cartledge et al. (2002).

were probably domestic servants. In military campaigns, a hoplite took with him a slave to carry his armor and food; for this purpose the state paid him a drachma a day. However, there is no evidence that every hoplite had his own slave; many hoplites were hiring slaves for that purpose at the time of hostilities. Slaves could buy their freedom from their owners. It is not clear whether all Athenians owned slaves. On the one hand, as 'the price of a slave was equivalent only to the cost of maintaining him for one to two years, all but the very poor could afford to own at least one slave' (Garnsey 1980, quoted in Cohen 2000, p. xi). On the other hand, 'They were owned in the main by the 1,200 richest families and in decreasing numbers by the next 3,000 or so. It is unlikely that any slaves were owned by two-thirds to three-quarters of the citizen population' (Jones 1958, p. 17). Owning a slave would have facilitated citizen participation in politics. Indeed, the argument often goes that it was slave labor that made the Athenian democracy possible. But as the overwhelming majority of Athenians had to work for a living, Hansen (1999) argues that it was the labor of women (who were denied political rights) rather than slaves that allowed the menfolk to run the polis and practice direct democracy.

We may obviously berate the Athenians for upholding slavery and forcing women to an inferior status. But the point of the present chapter is not to apply modern moral standards to a society at a time when such practices were almost universal and were to continue for more than a millennium. In comparison to her contemporary polities Athens ought to be judged as a political success. Two additional points are of relevance here. First, it bears noting that at times of emergency the Assembly was willing to free the slaves. In 406 all male slaves of military age were freed and granted citizenship to man the ships that won the battle of Arginusae. Similar proposals to free and enfranchise all slaves who fought for the restoration of democracy in 403, and against the Macedonians in the battle of Chaeronea in 338 were defeated. Second, even though the Athenian democracy did not live off slavery, the use of slaves bears rents to their owners, and slavery was, at least partly, responsible for the failure of Athens to establish a system of self-sustaining long-run growth of the kind set in motion by the industrial revolution of the nineteenth century.[8] Slavery is an extractive economic institution that discourages incentives for cost-cutting innovation and wealth creation (Acemoglu and Robinson 2012). Slave holders find it more profitable to increase the use of slave labor than to seek new technologies to increase returns to scale.

25.4.2 Exploitation of the Allies

As we have already described, in the mid fifth century the tribute from the allies was a most significant source of public revenue counting for some 400–600 talents[9] per year (Ober 2008). A related source of Athenian rent was currency seigniorage, that is, the difference between the value of the money and the cost of producing it. The Athenian currency, the drachma, circulated widely outside Athens. Seigniorage power drew not

---

[8] A related reason was the attitude that a free man working in dependent employment for a salary was akin to a slave – see Cohen (2002)

[9] One talent was a significant sum of money. The Athenian currency denomination was 1 talent = 60 minae = 6000 drachmae = 36 000 obols; 1 mina = 100 drachmae; 1 drachma = 6 obols. Finer (1999) reports that a family of four could live off 280 drachmae a year.

only from the dominant position of Athens in international trade but the obligation of her alliance to use the drachma; moreover all Athenian citizens had to hand over foreign coins to be melted and minted into drachmas.

That the tribute paid to Athens by the allies encouraged rent seeking did not escape the fourth-century observers. As Aristotle put it in the 'Athenian Constitution' (AC, 24.2 and 24.3), 'The Athenians took control of the empire, and became more domineering in their treatment of the allies, apart from Chios, Lesbos and Samos . . . In accordance with the Aristides' proposal [a formula to calculate each ally's levy], they provided ample maintenance for the common people, so that more than twenty thousand men were supported from the tribute, the taxes and the allies.'[10]

An equally important source of rent was the system of military cantonments set up in subject territories, known as *cleruchies*. In order to relieve population pressures, poor Athenians were offered plots of land in territories controlled by Athens. Those who took up such offers were called *cleruchs* and rose from the poorest class of *thetes* to the hoplite rank. They did not have to leave Athens as their departure was voluntary, although it was the usual choice. The state provided the *cleruchs* with arms, and paid for their journey. The estates of a settlement were divided among the *cleruchs* by lot. *Cleruchs* retained the rights and duties of Athenian citizens including military service obligations. Unlike colonial settlers, who ceased to be citizens, the interests of the *cleruchs* were tightly aligned with those of the metropolis. Because of their relative small number in the subject territories, and the enforced and unpopular nature of their tenure, their properties depended on the power of the metropolis. Moreover, the metropolis could recall them or reclaim their possessions as a penalty for revolt.

Both the financial tribute and the system of *cleruchies* ended after the dissolution of the empire. Yet, the loss of rent did not signify the demise of Athens. In the fourth century Athens played a leading role in foreign affairs and saw her democracy flourishing, undertaking two of the most expensive outlays, payment for attending the Assembly and the extension of theatre money.

25.5 INTERNAL SOURCES OF RENT: PUBLIC POLICY AND RENT SEEKING

Even though Athens, a polis of free citizens, based her economy on private property, the state assumed a crucial economic role. Concerns about defense, security of imported grain and wealth inequality motivated regulatory, tax and public expenditure policies with implications for rent-seeking opportunities. These are reviewed in the present section.

---

[10] Jones (1958, p. 9) breaks down the total of 20000 as follows: 12000 crew men for 60 triremes that were kept in commission during peace time, along with a navy-borne land force of 1600 archers and 500 shipyard guards. To that total he added the 6000 jurors. However, on each court day only about 2000 out of the 6000 were drawing payment after being selected by lot to serve as jurors.

25.5.1 Market Regulations

Market regulations aim to redress information asymmetries, increase transparency, address externalities and remove monopolies. Athens appointed by lot a number of officials for inspecting product quality standards, prices, measures and weights, overseeing coinage and monitoring the grain trade. The latter was regulated more tightly than other activities, since Athens produced only a small fraction of the grain consumed and depended heavily on imports. There were severe penalties for the Athenian citizens and metics, who imported corn to any place except Athens, and on anyone who lent money to finance a voyage that would not sell the corn cargo in Athens. Hoarding of grain by grain merchants beyond a certain volume was prohibited; special corn-wardens (*sitophylakes*) monitored the grain trade and its products, while foreigners that facilitated sales of grain to Athens at favorable terms were awarded special public honors. Exports of domestically grown grain were prohibited, while specifically appointed officers ensured that ships carrying grain when passing through the port of Piraeus sold two thirds of the cargo to Athens.[11] Moreover, the price of bread was fixed in proportion to the wholesale price of grain, but there is no evidence that the price of the latter was fixed.

An incident in 388 is indicative of the sensitivity of the Athenian authorities to the conditions in the market for grain and the potential for rent seeking. A temporary supply shock caused a severe grain shortage in Athens and a price hike. The price rise was deeply unpopular, leading a group of regulators – *sitophylakes* headed by Anytus to suggest to the grain merchants that they collude to form a monopsony against the grain importers (masters of the ships bringing grain to Athens), so that the import price would fall. To increase the negotiating power of the merchants, prohibitions on grain hoarding were suspended. However, this cartelization of the grain trade led to overzealous hoarding and the consequent restriction in supply handed monopoly power to the traders, resulting in significantly higher consumer prices. The grain traders, who were not Athenian citizens but resident aliens and thus a 'softer' political target (see Dunham 2008), were tried for hoarding and profiteering (the charges carried the death penalty) in what must have been one of the earliest court cases for competition. The incident is known to us from the extant speech for the prosecution 'Against the Corn Dealers' by the orator Lysias, but the court ruling is not.

25.5.2 Revenue

25.5.2.1 The silver windfall

In 483–482 BC, the Athenians discovered an unexpectedly rich vein of silver near Lavrion in Attica. Two motions were put on the Assembly on the use of the public revenue from the royalties (the entire mineral wealth of Attica belonged to the state). The first, supported by the statesman Aristides, was to distribute it as a lump-sum transfer to the citizens (a common practice at the time) paying each recipient ten drachmas at a time

---

[11] They elect by lot ten port-superintendents, whose duty is to superintend the harbor-markets and to compel the traders to bring to the city two thirds of the sea-borne corn that reaches the corn-market' (Aristotle, AC, 51.4).

when a laborer's wage was one drachma a day. The second, advocated by the general Themistocles, was to finance an extensive navy building program to challenge Aegina, an important maritime power at the time. The Assembly, dominated by the poorer voters who saw the opportunities for employment offered by the construction and manning of the warships, decided in favor of building the oars-powered triremes whose number gradually climbed to 200.[12] The Athenian navy proved decisive in defeating the Persians in the 480 sea battle of Salamis, securing thereafter the safety of the sea lanes.[13] In sharp contrast to, for example, the silver wealth that flowed to the Spanish crown from the Americas two thousand years later, the Athenian experience illustrates how democratic institutions may prevent the 'resource curse' that often afflicts countries rich in natural resources. That is, an oligarchy finds it easier to enrich themselves by owning and exploiting natural resources than creating wealth, and may use such rents to buy out opposition groups. However, rival rent seekers may challenge the ownership of the resources destabilizing the economy and the political regime. On the contrary, a democratic polity that established inclusive institutions and distributed widely the revenue from mineral wealth led to political stability and economic prosperity, as well as military success.

Income from the silver mines turned out to be a significant and long-lasting source of revenue. More importantly from the rent-seeking inquiry viewpoint, the revenue was collected in a transparent and open way. The mines were let out in auctions carried out by a board of ten sellers (selected by lot) to the highest bidders on leases of three or ten years at a time. The revenues were collected by a different board of ten receivers (also appointed by lot), and were then allocated to different funds for specific uses.

25.5.2.2 Tax revenue[14]

In addition to the royalties from the silver mines, the Athenian state raised revenues from taxation and from fines and confiscation of property. Tax revenue came from three main sources. (a) Custom duties, with the most important being a 2 percent duty on the value of all imports and exports. (b) Specific poll taxes, most importantly a personal tax for metics, and a license fee paid by all prostitutes to carry out their profession legally. Tax collection of the trade duties and the poll taxes was farmed out to the highest bidder. (c) Property tax, levied by decree of the Assembly first in 428/427 as an occasional duty to finance war efforts, which became a regular tax in the 340s, while the Assembly could always vote for additional levies. It was paid by the wealthiest citizens and resident aliens and levied at 1 percent of the value of all taxable properties. Starting from 378/377 the

---

[12] Herodotus, the ancient historian who describes the event (Histories, Book 7.144), gives few details, some of which are contradicted by Aristotle's account (AC, 22.7). As a result, considerable controversy surrounds the exact size of the annual mining revenue, the number of ships built in its immediate aftermath and the implementation of the funding program; see Wallinga (1993) and Gabrielsen (1994) for details.

[13] For analysis of the navy building program based on the economics of conflict, see Tridimas (2013).

[14] As already described, apart from fragmentary information there are no records of the sums of money involved. As a result, it is not possible to construct the 200-year time profile of public revenue and expenditure. For recent accounts of the Athenian public finances, see Rhodes (2013), Blamire (2001) for the fifth century, and Bitros and Karayiannis (2008) and Kyriazis (2009) for the fourth century.

richest citizens were divided into 100 groups of up to 15 members per group. The 300 richest citizens (those with assets above 15 talents), divided among the 100 groups (called *symmories*), were required to pay in advance the tax due for the whole group, effectively lending free of interest to the state; they could then make their own arrangements for reimbursement from the other members of the group. The number of groups and the size of membership varied in subsequent years, but it appears that the tax fell on the 1200 richest citizens. The advance payment of the property tax by the 300 richest Athenians resolves problems of tax collection for the state, but according to Lyttkens (2013) a more important reason for its introduction was the implicit bargain it involved. The 300 richest who prepay the tax suffer an increased tax burden but at the same time they become a significant economic and political factor since their agreement and cooperation was necessary for the operation of the system.

A final significant source of public revenue came from court fees, fines and confiscations. In court suits both litigants had to pay court fees, while in disputes of citizens against the state, the citizen deposited a percentage of the value in dispute that was kept by the state if the citizen lost. In prosecutions against officials the accuser had to deposit 1000 drachmas that would be forfeited if he abandoned the case or lost by more than four fifths of the votes of the court. The state also received fines from public prosecutions and confiscated goods (that were subsequently sold at public auctions). Hansen (1999) considers that such events were frequent and made a non-negligible contribution to revenue.

25.5.2.3 Revenue collection: tax farming and auctions

In summary, the following features of the tax system stand out. Commodity trade was taxed, no doubt because of the ease of capturing the taxable liability in comparison to other tax bases. Poll taxes were levied on residents who had no citizen rights; they were in Athens by choice rather than force and therefore their motives to leave must have been weak. A progressive tax system operated since only the very rich paid a wealth tax. Tax collection was farmed out by auction to private individuals instead of being carried out by government offices. Clearly, the capacity to raise revenue was constrained by the difficulty to assess the tax liability and the difficulty to collect the tax due. The former related to the general absence of record-keeping in combination with the fact that a sizable part of economic activity took place inside the family farm and the household. To a large extent, the difficulty to collect taxes came from the resistance of Athenians to tax payments; they perceived personal taxation as a sign of servitude.[15] In so far as setting up a bureaucracy is necessary for collecting taxes, light tax treatment of Athenians goes hand-in-hand with the observed absence of bureaucracy.

From the viewpoint of the state, tax farming, where the private individual (tax farmer) appropriates any residual surplus and bears the losses from any revenue shortfall, is an effective form of tax collection when tax revenues are unpredictable and state officials lack the information to assess the tax capacity (which was indeed the case with the 'amateurs' filling Athenian government posts). On the other hand, those individuals that

15 In fact, it was Cleisthenes who with the constitutional changes of 508 also abolished the tax on produce that had been in place before (Harris 2002).

have more information about economic circumstances are in a better position to assess tax capacity and therefore act as tax collectors.[16] However, when there are no controls on the actions of tax farmers, taxpayers may be abused in an attempt to increase the tax farmer's private profits. As the majority of the Athenians were not paying direct taxes, it is not surprising that there are no recorded incidents of mistreatment of taxpayers by tax farmers.

A key feature of auctions may be the presence of asymmetric information. Selling tax farming and mineral rights are common-value auctions where the actual value of the asset sold (the right to collect revenues) is the same for every bidder, but different bidders have different private information about what that value actually is (see Klemperer 1999 for a survey of the economic theory of auctions). For example, the value of the 2 percent trade tax depended on the value of trade through the ports of Attica and bidders may have had access to different information about those sums. Common-value auctions (which differ from private-value auctions where each bidder knows his valuation of the asset but that information is known only to him) are subject to 'the winner's curse', that is, the true value of the asset is unknown to the highest bidder who wins the auction but discovers that he had overestimated the value of the asset and his actual return falls short of the expected. In an ascending-price auction, where the bidder calling the highest price wins the asset, as was the case in Athens, there is no guarantee that the seller (state) will maximize the sale revenue.

Moreover, auctions are vulnerable to collusion: potential bidders restrict competition by agreeing who bids for specific auctions and who abstains so that the price paid to the state for the acquisition of the asset stays low. However, with free entry into the bidding process collusive agreements could not last, as a passage from a surviving court speech by the orator Andocides reveals:

> Last year [402] and the year before our honest Agyrrhius [the disputant of Andocidis] here was chief contractor for the two per cent customs duties. He farmed them for thirty talents, and the friends he meets under the poplar all took shares with him. You know what they are like; it is my belief that they meet there for a double purpose: to be paid for not raising the bidding, and to take shares in taxes which have been knocked down cheap. After making a profit of six talents, they saw what a gold-mine the business was; so they combined, gave rival bidders a percentage, and again offered thirty talents. There was no competition; so I went before the Council and outbid them, until I purchased the rights for thirty-six talents. I had ousted them. I then furnished you with sureties, collected the tax, and settled with the state. I did not lose by it, as my partners and I actually made a small profit. At the same time I stopped Agyrrhius and his friends from sharing six talents which belonged to you. They saw this themselves, and discussed the situation. 'This fellow will not take any of the public money himself', they argued, 'and he will not let us take any either. He will be on the watch and stop our sharing what belongs to the state; and furthermore, if he catches any of us acting dishonestly, he will bring him into the public courts and ruin him. He must be got rid of at all costs. (Mysteries, 1.133–1.135)

In other words, the evidence reveals that in public auctions some bidders colluded, but a system characterized by openness and competition, and court scrutiny of the bidding process, rendered collusion ineffective, securing a higher return for the state.

---

[16] For more details on tax farming, see Lyttkens (1994), who makes the working assumption that the Athenian state maximized tax revenue, and the literature cited therein.

25.5.3 Public Expenditure

25.5.3.1 Public goods and welfare payments

Like all states, the Athenian state provided public goods, administration, defense, law and order, poor relief and benefits-in-kind. Public administration in the form of payments for Assembly, Council, Courts and Boards of magistrates, have already been mentioned.[17] Regarding defense, it is worth noting that Athens did not have a standing army; in times of war citizens were called to arms. Each hoplite (heavy infantry) owned his armor and received a stipend of one drachma per day when in campaign (in addition to a drachma for the slave to carry his arms). Mercenaries were also used. On the other hand, Athens did operate a standing navy that with approximately 200 triremes was a major military force and employer of the poorer Athenians who worked as rowers. Law and order included the powers to police, prosecute, try and punish. Athens had a small paid police force of 1200 slave Scythian archers, who policed the Assembly and the law courts, and enforced the orders of the magistrates. It is perhaps worth reiterating the absence of professional legal experts in the working of the popular court. Hansen (1999) attributes it to a democratic motive in the sense that for all citizens to take part in it, the system had to be designed to be run by amateurs. Extensive capital spending also took place on temples, walls and fortifications, buildings for administration, roads and water fountains and so on.

The state also made a number of welfare payments to the poor and needy. These included war orphans and those who because of disabilities were unable to work and had property below a certain (low) limit. In other words, Athens operated a kind of means-tested system of social insurance, but the sums of money involved are not known. Unlike modern states, Athens was not involved in the provision of publicly funded health or education. Health services were bought privately from physicians and healing cults based in various sanctuaries. Physicians typically acquired their skills by apprenticeships and then traveled from place to place to practice them. Treatment in a religious sanctuary that combined traditional cures, rest, spiritual and ceremonial rituals was also common.[18] The financial bill of health care was met by private means and the notion of publicly funded insurance against the risk of medical expenditure was absent. Education was also seen as an issue of private choice.[19] Individuals were recognized to have different abilities and opportunities and therefore benefit from different levels of education as they saw fit. There was no demand for state-funded schools to provide uniform education. For many families the sensible choice was that their kids first were taught basic reading, writing, arithmetic, music and gymnastics (by highly regulated private tutors),

---

[17] Hansen (1999) estimates that in the 330s the annual cost of running the democratic state was 45 talents for Assembly attendance pay, 15 talents for Council pay, 22–37 talents for jury pay and 10 talents for the Assembly's own budget. If Amemiya's (2007) calculation that fourth-century GDP was 4430 talents is correct, then the share of public administration expenditure was between 21 percent and 24 percent of GDP.

[18] Lyttkens (2011) compares secular and religious medicine in antiquity using modern notions of health economics.

[19] See Bitros and Karayiannis (2011) and the references therein for a recent description of ancient Greek education.

and then learnt how to work in the farm or to practice a craft. Those who could afford it pursued higher education in oration and philosophy. The state was, however, financing the one-year military training (living expenses for students and instructors) of young Athenian males at the age of 18.

25.5.3.2 Theatre money – *Theorica*

On the other hand, a most important benefit conferred by Athenian citizenship was payment of 'theatre money' known as *theorica*. The latter was introduced by Pericles in the mid fifth century to enable poorer citizens to attend the famous theatre plays without losing income during those days (Plutarch, Pericles, 9.1 and 9.2). Theatre was seen as providing important educational functions, teaching morals and history. Each citizen was given the ticket cost of two obols on each day of the three-day Dionysia festival. In the fifth century payments were made on an ad hoc basis as voted by the Assembly, and the sums disbursed would have fluctuated in accordance with the available funds. The *theorica* benefit was gradually extended to other festivals, at the rate of two obols per day up to three days, and in the fourth century was paid to all citizens. Jones (1958) guesses that in the mid fourth century the annual expenditure was 15 talents. In the fourth century the payment was formalized. The *Theoric* Fund (probably established by Eubulus) became a permanent feature of the fiscal landscape receiving fixed funding by law. Over time, the fund acquired additional responsibilities, unrelated to theatre and festivals, including finance of public buildings and roads and the administration of the navy. In the middle of the fourth century it was the overseer of public finances along with the Council of Five Hundred and its members were elected for four years. The Athenians grew accustomed to receiving *theorica* money and proposals by Demosthenes, the famous fourth-century orator, to use them for war purposes were voted down. Demades, a member of the *Theoric* board in the 330s, called *theorica* 'the glue of the democracy' (Plutarch, Moralia – Platonicae Quaestiones 10). On the other hand, the historian Theopompus considered that they had a deleterious effect, rendering citizens most 'cowardly and indolent'.[20]

In modern parlance attendance of theatre and other cultural activities is a merit good, that is, one with private characteristics (rival in consumption and excludable) and social characteristics in the form of spillover effects, which the government decrees must be consumed by the citizens in at least some minimum quantity because the citizens are unable to evaluate the full scale of its benefits. A number of authors, Bitros and Karayiannis (2008), Kyriazis (2009) and Halkos and Kyriazis (2010) amongst others, laud the generosity directed to such cultural pursuits. However, it is doubtful that the only reason for such payment was correction of an externality. There is a major element of rent creation and rent seeking in providing theatre money. There is an obvious, if trivial, aspect, namely, play-writers, theatre performers, theatre leaseholders and theatre-lovers were net beneficiaries of the policy to promote theatre attendance as opposed to other activities. More significantly, Pericles, the general who introduced the payment, and later Eubulus, must have seen that there was popular support to be gained by providing such benefits especially to poorer citizens (in the same way that there were votes to be gained from introducing juror pay). In this light, a more interesting question is why public funds

---

[20] See Roselli (2009) for a detailed discussion of the evolution of *theorica*.

were spent on festivals and theatre rather than other services, like education or health. A possible answer suggested here is as follows. Theatre attendance had indeed an aspect of social education, but more importantly, in the absence of mass media and in the presence of transport difficulties, the Athenians preferred to consume a collective service that involved social interaction, gathering in the same place to talk to one another, to inform and be informed (a process that generated widely shared knowledge that served to solve issues of public interest, an aspect also emphasized by Ober 2008). In addition, perhaps unintentionally, it led to the empowerment of the poorer classes. Payments for attending mass-gathering events, like the popular courts, the Assembly, the theatre and the festivals, not only provided financial assistance to the poorer citizens but perhaps more importantly facilitated communication and reduced their cost of collective action (Olson 1965).

25.5.3.3 Compulsory private finance of public expenditure

Another inventive and distinctive form of public expenditure was the compulsory private finance of public expenditures, the so-called 'liturgies'. The richest citizens, typically those who owned property of three talents and above, as nominated by their demes, discharged various services at their own expense. The services included festivals, like raising choirs, or troops of runners for various competitions, or paying for theatrical plays costing between 300 to 3000 drachmas, and the most expensive one, the command, outfitting, and maintenance of a trireme for one year, called *trierarchy*, costing as much as 6000 drachmas. The trireme-master, *trierarch*, was chosen by the generals among the 300–1200 richest citizens; *trierarchs* were normally exempt from other liturgies. Those performing liturgies in one year were exempt from the obligation of another liturgy in the following year. Even though the liability for liturgy fell on persons, while the liability for the property tax fell on property, it appears that it was the same group of 1200 citizens liable for the property tax who also paid for the festival liturgies.[21] Rich citizens refusing to undertake liturgies faced penalties like fines, loss of property and even loss of citizenship. Since there was no bureaucracy to assess the wealth of citizens, a system partly based on self-assessment and partly on assessment by others operated. Upon successful completion liturgists were awarded golden crowns. Citizens competing for recognition and distinction would willingly offer to undertake liturgies, especially those harboring political ambitions (Lyttkens 2013). Hence, from the viewpoint of the individual liturgist, at a time without mass media paying for a liturgy was a cost-effective way for advertisement and self-promotion (while, in addition, *trierachies* yielded war booty). In other words, there were significant personal gains for a liturgist, over and above his supposed public spiritedness, that made it rational for him to comply with such an obligation, an argument that goes a long way to explain why the arrangement was adopted and survived throughout the era of democracy. On the other hand, the financial burden of liturgies, and especially *trierarchies*, was significant. In order to avoid the expense, rich

[21] 'to be one of the rich citizens who performed liturgies a man would have to have a property of at least 3 or 4 talents. 1 talent equals what an ordinary Athenian could earn in the course of more than ten years, so that the property of any one of the roughly 1200 liturgists would represent a lifetime's ordinary earnings' (Hansen 1999, p. 115).

Athenians would try to hide their wealth in assets that could be concealed from inspection and, when nominated, might argue that there were other wealthier citizens who could afford to pay for it (Engen 2011).

To ascertain whether or not that was the case a procedure of exchange of property (*antidosis*) was established according to which the nominee for a *trierarchy* could challenge another person who in his view ought to perform the liturgy, either to undertake the liturgy or to exchange his property with that of the nominee and then the nominee would perform the liturgy. The challenged citizen could then either accept the liturgy or exchange property with the nominee, or demand that the matter be resolved by a court, which then ruled who would perform the liturgy. In court, the disputants tried to show each one's true wealth to avoid paying for the liturgy. The objective of the exchange-of-properties procedure was to ensure that those who actually were wealthy (rather than those who seemed to be wealthy) would pay for public expenditures with the burden of proof falling on the private actors rather than the state. The mechanism was designed to resolve the conflicting objectives of efficient provision of public goods, voluntary private participation to fund public good provision (feasibility constraint) and budgetary balance constraint. Kaiser (2007) uses a formal game-theoretic framework to analyze its operation. In accordance with economic rationality, her empirical results show that *trierarchs* paid for the liturgy not only for prestige and power but also because by complying with the regulation they protected their assets and long-run financial interests. Out of the surviving records for 492 *trierarchs*, 110 are known to have gone to court for resolving questions of liability. Hansen reports that there is 'not a single example of an exchange of property actually taking place' (1999, p. 112). In view of its high cost, in 358 the system of dividing citizens into 20 groups for advance payment of property taxes was extended to the *trierarchy*. Then the same 300 wealthiest citizens responsible for the advance payment of property taxes became responsible for the advance payment of *trierarchies*. Once more, the Athenians operated a procedure that obviated the need to set up bureaucracies for collecting tax revenue and delivering the relevant service. The system of *trierarchy* ended in 322 with the fall of democracy.

Although at first blush the system of liturgies appears to be a progressive wealth tax combined with hypothecation of the tax revenue to specific uses, on closer inspection its progressivity was less pronounced. Inside the group of taxpayers it was a highly regressive system, since everyone liable for the relevant liturgy was expected to spend approximately the same sum, rather than according to his ability to pay, something that for Demosthenes ruined citizens of moderate fortunes (Jones 1958, p. 87).

25.5.4 Fixed Funding of Public Service by Law

Contrary to modern states, Athens did not have a centralized budget and each spending board had its own funds. In the fourth century the various spending boards were distributing funds by law while additional expenditures required a law passed by the legislators (see Section 25.2), an arrangement that reduced the financial role of the Council and the Assembly. If there were not enough funds to hand over to the spending boards, either the Assembly passed a decree for an extraordinary property tax levied on the richer citizens and free foreigners, or money was drawn out of the temple treasuries whose reserves came from the accumulation of votive offerings, or payments were altogether suspended.

In other words, no explicit public borrowing could take place. For example, 'if we can believe Demosthenes, all private suits were suspended for several years in the 360s, and in 348 the courts were again shut for a shorter period, because there was no money to pay jurors after the Euboian campaign' (Hansen 1999, p. 189). On the other hand, if after all relevant sums had been allocated to the relevant boards there was a surplus, a law required that it would go to the military fund during war time and the *Theoric* Fund during peace times. The long-run assignment of funds to different uses by law had implications for rent seeking. It obviously privileged the recipients of the rent at the time of fixing the sums of money for particular expenditures. It bears noting that by doing so, it made the plans to finance the public services covered by such laws credible. On the other hand, it established a rigid system of public expenditure that privileged the original recipients of the public services and was slow to respond (if at all) to changing economic and political circumstances.

25.6 POLITICAL LEADERS AND RENT SEEKING

So far it has been argued that direct democracy can block rent seeking by subjecting policies and politicians to the control of the demos. Over and above that, Athens put in place a web of arrangements to control rent seeking. As already explained, these included the following. (a) Pay for public service, so that no citizen would lose income for services rendered to the polis. (b) Court scrutiny of the actions of magistrates, especially of those handling public money (before, during and after their term of office), the proposers of Assembly decrees, the military commanders and of the content of policy measures. (c) Opening public office to all citizens who so volunteered, an aspect much derided by aristocratic writers. Open access was achieved by unrestricted entry, meaning no professional qualifications were required for appointment to public office; appointment to office by lot, implying that any citizen might hold office; and non-renewable annual office terms implying that every citizen might hold office at some time, but would not stay long enough to consolidate power. We also saw that as a result of direct democracy, and subject to the economic environment, the preponderance was to pass policies with widely spread benefits.

However, despite the ingenuity of the institutions of direct democracy rent seeking took place. Direct democracy is characterized by high decision costs because of the time, effort and other resource costs that citizens bear to obtain information and negotiate collective decisions.[22] Since information is costly to acquire, the median voter may not be fully informed about the policy issues he is asked to decide. Well-endowed elites and interest groups will then try to manipulate the information available, so that the policy passed confers them rents. Alternatively, when decision making is delegated to political agents, interest groups will try and influence them to implement their favorite policies.

[22] Ober (2008) explains that by and large the Athenians overcame such problems by developing extensive social networks and work teams, putting in place mechanisms for making credible commitments, like taking oaths, and developing media to disseminate information, like public rituals and constructing semi-circle stages that maximized visibility among participants.

No polity can function without delegation of decision-making authority and Athens was no exception.

To begin with, accessibility to paid public office was limited by age. Restricting paid public service in the Council and the Court to citizens over 30 years old implied that younger cohorts were excluded from office rents. The restriction is usually justified by the wisdom of the 'grey beards', that is, older and more experienced people were better suited to hold public posts. An economics consideration suggests, less kindly, financial self-interest as an additional reason. Older people must have found it more difficult to earn a living from their brawn. Serving in public office provided a useful alternative source of income, even something akin to social security. Excluding from office those who were physically stronger served the financial interests of the majority of citizens above the age of 30.

The generals and the orators occupied pivotal positions in the rent-seeking game. The ten generals had the opportunity for rent seeking by virtue of their unlimited access to the Council and could lobby for specific policy measures. They could then be rewarded by the beneficiaries of such policies, since receiving gifts was not forbidden. Moreover, the generals were paid when on active service but not during peace time (Larsen 1946). Given that military campaigning took place from spring to autumn, they were not salaried throughout the year. They could also acquire war spoils as well as gifts from foreign states. Payment for active service may have generated a perverse incentive in favor of war, or at least for prolonging it unnecessarily.

In modern societies legal professionals are counted among the group of successful rent seekers. Indeed, Stiglitz (2012) argues that 'top-flight lawyers' are generously rewarded for helping to design complex laws that allow loopholes for avoiding taxation and for generating monopolies that are then exploited by their clients. Athens, unlike Rome, did not develop a class of legal professionals – jurists, interpreting and commenting on codes and court rulings. Since the legal system was designed to be understood and managed by laypersons, their services were hardly needed. Nevertheless, Athens was a litigious society offering ample opportunities for enrichments to men with rhetorical skills (which in turn could be learnt from private tutors). Litigation was used to contest rents, not only monetary rewards in private disputes but also to hound generals out of office (out of 289 known generals in the period 432–355, 143 of them were taken to court, Hansen 1999, p. 217). Since success in the Assembly and the Court depended on persuasion, a certain rhetorical ability and eloquence was necessary. Rent seekers spent resources on orators to win Court cases and pass favorable motions in Assembly debates. Similar to the generals in peace time, the orators of the fourth century were not remunerated for propagating Assembly decrees, but could receive gifts from interested parties, and so did those preparing Court speeches. Nor was appointment to the Council by lot totally free of manipulation. Jones (1958) discusses how in poor demes with few volunteers for public service, richer citizens could be selected unopposed.

The fourth-century rich elite too engaged in rent seeking in the form of concealing their wealth and avoiding their obligations to perform liturgies and pay property taxes. '[When *trierarchies* were organized by groups] the 300 let the other 900 or so bear more than their fair share . . ., for instead of serving as *trierarchs* themselves they farmed the duty out and obliged five or six or even up to sixteen members of their [groups] to pay the lion's share of the expenses' (Hansen 1999, p. 114). Lyttkens (2013) attributes that development to a breakdown in the implicit contract between the rich and the state. With the loss of the empire, the rich had limited opportunities to acquire estates in conquered lands, while they were still expected to finance public services. In addition, the composition of the elite had changed from the old landed aristocracy to new men of modest background whose wealth was less dependent on land assets and they were less committed to the ideals of public service. Demosthenes, for his own reasons, paints a negative picture of the role of political leaders and rent seeking:

> What is our condition today, thanks to our worthy statesmen? . . . What is the cause of all this, and why, pray, did everything go well then [golden age of the fifth century] that now goes amiss? Because then the people, having the courage to act and to fight, controlled the politicians and were themselves the dispensers of all favors; the rest were well content to accept at the people's hand honor and authority and reward. Now, on the contrary, the politicians hold the purse-strings and manage everything, while you, the people, robbed of nerve and sinew, stripped of wealth and of allies, have sunk to the level of lackeys and hangers-on, content if the politicians gratify you with a dole from the Theoric Fund or a procession at the Boëdromia [a festival], and your manliness reaches its climax when you add your thanks for what is your own. (Demosthenes, 3rd Olynthiac, 27–31)

25.7 CONCLUDING COMMENTS: RENT SEEKING, HOMO POLITICUS AND HOMO ECONOMICUS

In a relatively infertile patch of land, the ancient Athenians invented a truly revolutionary system of government that prevailed for approximately two centuries, providing them with significant wealth, considerable military power, impressive artistic and intellectual achievements and, for their full citizens, political and personal freedoms that had no parallel in the earlier and following millennia of human history until the twentieth century. Equally important, the system set up was not static but evolved over time making important incremental adjustments in the light of previous experiences and new circumstances. The institutions of the state were geared toward direct democracy and citizen rule rather than administrative efficiency. Most prominent were the passing of laws by citizens directly by majority voting, appointment of non-professional citizens to public office by lot, while election was reserved for a few military and financial posts, and wide-reaching scrutiny by the courts. The present study has focused on rent seeking in ancient Athens. While profit-seeking business is subject to consumer sovereignty and conditioned by the market environment, rent seeking rests on the power of the state and depends on how special interests can divert public policy away from the public interest. In Athens significant rents were extracted from slave labor, non-enfranchised resident aliens and women, and the allies. There was natural resource rent extraction as well, through the silver mines that made sizable contributions to the public finances. The picture of rent seeking in Athens that emerges is consistent with the predictions that under direct democracy there will be large general benefits provided to the poor majority of voters: Athenian citizens received payments for attending the Assembly, jury services and theatre money, and only the very rich paid property taxes and funded liturgies. The system of public finances, characterized by collecting revenue through tax farming and auctions, and mandated private payment for public expenditures, is attributed to Athenian aversion to direct taxation, the significant presence of home economic activity, which makes it difficult to record tax liability, and the appointment of non-professionals to public office that resulted in the absence of a specialized bureaucracy. Although it may be difficult to establish clear cause-and-effect links among the above, it is nevertheless plain that they were correlated with each other.

The analysis in this chapter has important implications for the applicability of the model of economic rationality to ancient Athens. Modern scholarship examining ancient civilizations often considers the model of economic rationality as inapplicable to the ancient Athenians, arguing that economic interests were secondary and sometimes incorporated in non-economic interests, like the quest for political and military honors.[23] This is at the crux of the debate between the 'substantivist' and the 'formalist' approaches to the ancient economy. The former, drawing on views that the economy was 'primitive', meaning small-scale, household-based and pursuing the ideal of self-sufficiency at the household and the city-state level, argues that economic activity was embedded in social and political institutions and not pursuing profit maximization (see Finley 1973; Millett 1991). The 'formalist' view is 'modernist' in that it considers the ancient economy as independent of social relations, large-scale and functioning according to market structures with interconnected markets characterized by sophisticated contractual arrangements; see Burke (1992), Cohen (1992) and Morris (1994) for a critical assessment, and Christesen (2003) who provides a recent essay on different concepts of rationality and value systems in ancient economic history.

The rent-seeking inquiry in this chapter can reconcile political objectives with economic rationality. Specifically, rent seeking is a rational act of utility-maximizing actors. As Buchanan (2003, p. 6) put it: 'If an opportunity that promises to yield value arises, persons will invest time and resources in efforts to capture such value for themselves . . . If there is value to be gained through political action, persons will invest resources in efforts to capture this value . . . Once this basic insight is incorporated into the mind-set of the observer, much of modern [and ancient] politics can only be interpreted as rent-seeking activity.' With this insight, we can conceptualize the ancient Athenian quest for honor, the aspect that leads to rejection of economic rationality, as a contest for rents and therefore perfectly compatible with the hypothesis of utility maximization under economic and institutional constraints. Some of those rents can be thought of as pure personal ego-rents, like the satisfaction from gaining and holding public office (which is independent of the ability to decide policy) and winning popularity contests. Such rents may not translate readily to financial rewards but do translate into utility from status as underlying rent seeking (Congleton 1989 [2008]) or expressive utility from confirmation of a sought identity (Hillman 2010). Other rents are of course purely financial. Rent seeking by competing groups entails each group investing resources to contest the 'prize', rather than to produce new valuable goods and services, resulting in a waste of resources and inefficiency. Focusing on the inefficiency, while ignoring the institutional context, may suggest that economic rationality was missing. However, even though rent seeking is a negative-sum game (Tullock 1980), it was perfectly rational for individual actors to seek rents rather than produce.

---

[23] Indeed, ancient thinkers examined as part of politics and ethics issues of production, distribution and organization that today are standard topics of economics.

Indeed, the rent-seeking approach to political economy in combination with direct democracy offers an economic explanation of the high frequency of wars – a case of inefficient outcomes – fought by the Athenians without recourse to non-economic objectives like status honor (although the importance of the latter is not denied). As has been noted, in the 141-year period 479–338, Athens had not had more than ten consecutive years of peace and was on average at war for two out of three years. The Assembly voted for war because the poorer majority benefited by serving in the navy and by allotments of new lands. Military glory, war booty and new lands might also have motivated some of the rich elite, although they were also paying the largest share of the war bill, while many farmers must have worried about being called up into the infantry and about whether their land would be invaded. In the same vein, the expansion of the payments from the *Theoric* Fund after 355 by Eubulus and again by Lycurgus after 338 can be seen as attempts to persuade the majority of poorer Athenians to vote against prolonging war and to accept peace.

Contenders for rents tried not only to win the rents within the rules of the contest game but also sought to change the rules of the game, that is, the political institutions determining rights, organization and decision-making rules, in the hunt for a more favorable and durable outcome that did not require recontesting rents. The collective outcome was full of 'messy' compromises and while it did not maximize the rate of growth of the economy, it was not for lack of rationality.

REFERENCES

Ancient Authors

The original ancient Greek texts referred to in this work can be found along with English translations on the website of the Perseus Project, available at http://www.perseus.tufts.edu.

Andocides, Mysteries

Aristotle, Politics

Aristotle, The Athenian Constitution (referred to as 'AC' in the chapter)

Demosthenes, 3rd Olynthiac

Herodotus, Histories

Lysias, Against the Corn Dealers

Plutarch, Moralia – Platonicae Quaestiones

Plutarch, Pericles

Modern Authors

Acemoglu, Daron and James A. Robinson (2012), *Why Nations Fail: The Origins of Power, Prosperity and Poverty*, New York: Crown Business.

Amemiya, Takeshi (2007), *Economy and Economics of Ancient Greece*, London and New York: Routledge.

Bitros, Georgios C. and Anastassios D. Karayiannis (2008), 'Values and institutions as determinants of entrepreneurship in ancient Athens', *Journal of Institutional Economics*, **4**(2), 205–30.

Bitros, Georgios C. and A.D. Karayiannis (2011), 'Character, knowledge and skills in ancient Greek paideia: some lessons for today's policy makers', *Journal of Economic Asymmetries*, **8**(1), 193–219.

Blamire, Alec (2001), 'Athenian Finance', 454–404 B.C', *Hesperia*, **70**(1), 99–126.

Blok, Josine H. (2009), 'Perikles' citizenship law: a new perspective', *Historia*, **58**(2), 141–70.

Buchanan, James (2003), *Public Choice: The Origins and Development of a Research Program*, Center for Study of Public Choice, Fairfax, VI: George Mason University.

Burke, Edmund M. (1992), 'The economy of Athens in the classical era: some adjustments to the primitivist model', *Transactions of the American Philological Association*, **122**, 199–226.

Cartledge, Paul (2002), 'The political economy of Greek slavery', in Paul Cartledge, Edward E. Cohen and Lin Foxhall (eds), *Money, Labour and Land: Approaches to the Economies of Ancient Greece*, Abingdon: Routledge, pp. 156–66.

Christesen, Paul (2003), 'Economic rationalism in fourth-century BCE Athens', *Greece and Rome*, **50**(1), 31–56.

Cohen, Edward E. (1992), *Athenian Economy and Society*, Princeton, NJ: Princeton University Press.

Cohen, Edward E. (2000), *The Athenian Nation*, Princeton, NJ: Princeton University Press.

Cohen, Edward E. (2002), 'An unprofitable masculinity', in Paul Cartledge, Edward E. Cohen and Lin Foxhall (eds), *Money, Labour and Land: Approaches to the Economies of Ancient Greece*, Abingdon: Routledge, pp. 100–112.

Congleton, Roger D. (1989), 'Efficient status seeking: externalities, and the evolution of status games', *Journal of Economic Behavior and Organization*, **11**(2), 175–90, reprinted in Roger D. Congleton, Arye L. Hillman and Kai A. Konrad (eds) (2008), *40 Years of Research on Rent Seeking 2 – Applications: Rent Seeking in Practice*, Heidelberg: Springer, pp. 697–712.

Congleton, Roger D. (2011), *Perfecting Parliament: Constitutional Reform and the Origins of Western Democracy*, New York: Cambridge University Press.

Dunham, Wayne, R. (2008), 'Cold case files: the Athenian grain merchants 386 B.C.', *Cato Journal*, **28**(3), 495–514.

Engen, Darel T. (2011), 'Democracy, knowledge, and the hidden economy of Athens', *Journal of Economic Asymmetries*, **8**(1), 93–106.

Finer, Samuel E. (1999), *The History of Government I: Ancient Monarchies and Empires*, Oxford: Oxford University Press.

Finley, Moses I. (1973), *The Ancient Economy*, London: Chatto & Windus.

Gabrielsen, Vincent (1994), *Financing the Athenian Fleet: Public Taxation and Social Relations*, Baltimore, MD: Johns Hopkins University Press.

Halkos, George E. and Nickolas Kyriazis (2010), 'The Athenian economy in the age of Demosthenes: path dependence and change', *European Journal of Law and Economics*, **29**(3), 255–77.

Hansen, Mogens H. (1999), *The Athenian Democracy in the Age of Demosthenes: Structure, Principles and Ideology*, London: Bristol Classical Press.

Hansen, Mogens H. (2010), 'The concepts of demos, ekklesia, and dikasterion in classical Athens', *Greek, Roman, and Byzantine Studies*, **50**(4), 499–536.

Harris, Edward M. (2002), 'Workshop, marketplace and household: the nature of specialization in classical Athens and its influence on economy and society', in Paul Cartledge, Edward E. Cohen and Lin Foxhall (eds), *Money, Labour and Land: Approaches to the Economies of Ancient Greece*, Abingdon: Routledge, pp. 67–99.

Hillman, Arye L. (2010), 'Expressive behavior in economics and politics', *European Journal of Political Economy*, **26**(4), 403–18.

Jameson, Michael H. (2002), 'On Paul Cartledge, The political economy of Greek slavery', in Paul Cartledge, Edward E. Cohen and Lin Foxhall (eds), *Money, Labour and Land: Approaches to the Economies of Ancient Greece*, Abingdon: Routledge, pp. 167–75.

Jones, Arnold H.M. (1958), *Athenian Democracy*, New York: Frederick Praeger.

Kaiser, Brooks A. (2007), 'The Athenian trierarchy: mechanism design for the private provision of public goods', *Journal of Economic History*, **67**(2), 445–80.

Klemperer, Paul (1999), 'Auction theory: a guide to the literature', *Journal of Economic Surveys*, **13**(3), 227–86.

Kyriazis, Nicholas K. (2009), 'Financing the Athenian state: public choice in the age of Demosthenes', *European Journal of Law and Economics*, **27**(2), 109–27.

Kyriazis, Nicholas K. and Anastassios D. Karayiannis (2011), 'Democracy, institutional changes and economic development: the case of ancient Athens', *Journal of Economic Asymmetries*, **8**(1), 61–92.

Kyrtatas, Dimitris (2002), 'Domination and exploitation', in Paul Cartledge, Edward E. Cohen and Lin Foxhall (eds), *Money, Labour and Land: Approaches to the Economies of Ancient Greece*, Abingdon: Routledge, pp. 150–55.

Larsen, J.A.O. (1946), 'The Acharnians and the pay of taxiarchs', *Classical Philology*, **41**(2), 91–8.

Lyttkens, Carl H. (1994), 'A predatory democracy? An essay on taxation in classical Athens', *Explorations in Economic History*, **31**(1), 62–90.

Lyttkens, Carl H. (2011), 'Health, economics and ancient Greek medicine', *Journal of Economic Asymmetries*, **8**(1), 165–92.

Lyttkens, Carl H. (2013), *Economic Analysis of Institutional Change in Ancient Greece: Politics, Taxation and Rational Behavior*, Abingdon: Routledge.

Millett, Paul (1991), *Lending and Borrowing in Ancient Athens*, Cambridge: Cambridge University Press.

Morris, Ian (1994), 'The Athenian economy twenty years after the Ancient economy', *Classical Philology*, **89**(4), 351–66.

Morris, Ian (2004), 'Economic growth in ancient Greece', *Journal of Institutional and Theoretical Economics*, **160**(4), 709–42.
Murray, Oswyn (1993), *Early Greece*, Cambridge, MA: Harvard University Press.
Ober, Josiah (2008), *Democracy and Knowledge*, Princeton, NJ: Princeton University Press.
Ober, Josiah (2010), 'Wealthy Hellas', *Transactions of American Philological Association*, **140**(2), 241–86.
Olson, Mancur (1965), *The Logic of Collective Action, Public Goods and the Theory of Groups*, Cambridge, MA: Harvard University Press.
Rhodes, P.J. (2013), 'The organization of Athenian public finance', *Greece and Rome*, **60**(2), 203–31.
Roselli, David K. (2009), 'Theorika in fifth-century Athens', *Greek, Roman and Byzantine Studies*, **49**(1), 5–30.
Stiglitz, Joseph E. (2012), *The Price of Inequality: How Today's Divided Society Endangers our Future*, New York: W.W. Norton and Co.
Tridimas, G. (2011), 'A political economy perspective of direct democracy in ancient Athens', *Constitutional Political Economy*, **22**(1), 58–72.
Tridimas, George (2012a), 'Constitutional choice in ancient Athens: the rationality of selection to office by lot', *Constitutional Political Economy*, **23**(1), 1–21.
Tridimas, George (2012b), 'How democracy was achieved', *European Journal of Political Economy*, **28**(4), 651–8.
Tridimas, George (2013), 'Homo oeconomicus in ancient Athens: silver bonanza and the choice to build a navy', *Homo Oeconomicus*, **30**(4), 143–62.
Tullock, Gordon (1980), 'Rent seeking as a negative sum game', in James M. Buchanan, Robert D. Tollison and Gordon Tullock (eds), *Toward a Theory of the Rent-seeking Society*, College Station, TX: Texas A&M University Press, pp. 16–36.
Wallinga, Herman T. (1993), *Ships and Sea-power Before the Great Persian War: The Ancestry of the Ancient Trireme*, Leiden: E.J. Brill.

PART V

CONSTITUTIONS AND INSTITUTIONS

26. Rent seeking and constitutional political economy

Randall G. Holcombe

SUMMARY

Rent seeking and constitutional political economy are based on different foundations. Constitutional political economy models politics as exchange, and depicts government action as a cooperative endeavor in which people work together to collectively achieve goals that they would be unable to accomplish with bilateral exchange. In contrast, rent seeking depicts a political system in which some people are able to use the force of government to provide benefits for themselves at the expense of others. One is the calculus of consent; the other is the calculus of coercion.

26.1 INTRODUCTION

Rent seeking and constitutional political economy are two of the major areas of inquiry that public choice scholars have investigated since the public choice revolution began in the 1960s. One might argue that constitutional political economy lies at the very foundation of public choice, partly because Buchanan and Tullock (1962), who subtitled their book *Logical Foundations of Constitutional Democracy*, made a clear distinction between constitutional and post-constitutional decision-making, and partly because, following their logic, post-constitutional collective decision-making is heavily influenced by the constitutional framework within which it occurs. Rent seeking, as the literature has depicted it, is a feature of post-constitutional decision-making that may be more or less prevalent depending on the constitutional rules. This chapter explores three different aspects of the relationship between rent seeking and constitutional political economy. First, it examines differences in the assumed nature of the political processes that underlie these two areas of public choice. Second, it considers the degree to which constitutional rules can limit rent seeking. Third, it evaluates the constitutional versus post-constitutional distinction to consider whether that theoretical distinction can exist in practice.

26.2 THE POLITICAL PROCESS: CONSTITUTIONAL POLITICAL ECONOMY

Buchanan and Tullock (1962, p. 13) begin their study by depicting the political process as one of exchange, saying, 'Collective action is viewed as the action of individuals when they choose to accomplish purposes collectively rather than individually, and the government is seen as nothing more than the set of processes, the machine, which allows such collective actions to take place . . .' The constitutional contract is a set of rules that allows individuals to cooperate to achieve their individual goals through collective action. The market mechanism works well when people can accomplish their ends through bilateral exchange, but in other cases that require collective action, the political process serves to facilitate multilateral exchange in much the same way as the market mechanism facilitates bilateral exchange. As Buchanan and Tullock (1962, chapter 6) make clear, the constitutional framework as they depict it is based on agreement among members of a group to accomplish goals that are in everyone's interest; to use their words, the decision-making undertaken to accomplish those collective goals is the calculus of consent.

Buchanan and Tullock use unanimity as the benchmark for political agreement, because unanimous agreement demonstrates that everyone in the group believes that they are better off because of the collective action, but they note that because of decision-making costs everyone in a group could unanimously agree to make some decisions using a less-than-unanimity decision-making rule. Buchanan and Tullock (1962, chapter 6) incorporate this idea to make the distinction between constitutional and post-constitutional collective decisions. Constitutional decisions establish the rules under which collective action takes place, whereas post-constitutional decisions are made under those constitutional rules. The constitutional contract consists of those constitutional rules that are approved by unanimous agreement.

Even when post-constitutional decisions can be made with less-than-unanimous approval, the politics as exchange framework holds within the constitutional political economy framework, because the less-than-unanimous decision rule facilitates people being able to accomplish their collective goals. Buchanan (1990) argues the importance of this constitutional–post-constitutional distinction, even when – and especially when – it is sometimes difficult to discern in practice.

In practice, few people have actually agreed to the constitutional rules under which they are governed, which opens up the question of the real-world relevance of the idea of agreement with those rules. That issue is dealt with by Rawls (1971) and Buchanan (1975), who offer different but similar criteria for determining whether constitutional rules are based on agreement. Constitutional rules meet the agreement criterion if they would be agreed to behind a veil of ignorance, or in a renegotiation of the constitutional contract from anarchy. Holcombe (2011) offers a critical assessment of these criteria, and Yeager (1985, 2001) offers a strong critique of the constitutional paradigm, emphasizing in particular contractarian frameworks of Rawls and Buchanan that are based on implied agreement. These criteria of hypothetical agreement, Yeager argues, mean that there is no actual agreement. As the constitutional literature has developed, however, the concept of optimal constitutional rules that meet some criterion of implied agreement lies at the foundation of constitutional political economy. The constitutional rules are agreed to, which brings with it agreement with the post-constitutional procedures that govern collective action.

The foundation of constitutional political economy is the idea of politics as exchange, where people agree collectively to undertake activities that require collective action to accomplish. The political process is based on agreement, and constitutional political economy depicts political exchange as an extension of the idea of market exchange, undertaken for the benefit of those who engage in the process.

26.3 THE POLITICAL PROCESS: RENT SEEKING

The theoretical foundation of rent seeking differs substantially from that of constitutional political economy. Rent seekers use the force of government to generate income for themselves at the expense of others. Businesses lobby government to provide them with monopoly franchises, or erect barriers to entry in other ways, to give themselves profits at the expense of their customers and potential competitors. They lobby government to erect tariffs and quotas to insulate their businesses from foreign competition, at the expense of customers and potential competitors. They lobby for subsidies to make their businesses more profitable at the expense of taxpayers and potential competitors. They lobby for favorable regulations, for tax breaks, and to have costs imposed on rival firms. Rent seeking is based on coercion: the use of the force of government to allow some people to impose costs on others, not agreement and exchange, where people work together to achieve ends they all value.

Tullock (1967 [2008]) lays the foundation, noting that not only are there the welfare costs associated with monopolies, tariffs and other rent-seeking activities but also the costs of engaging in rent seeking that use up resources unproductively to try to gain those rents. Krueger (1974 [2008]) offered specific examples, noting that at the time she was writing, many of the best and brightest people in India were not engaged in productive activity, but rather were employed to try to work the legal system to get favorable treatment for their employers – for example, getting import licenses in a system where imports were restricted – that provided private benefits to some, but at the expense of others. Not incidentally, rent seeking also lowered the productivity of the economy. Bhagwati (1982) calls rent-seeking activities directly unproductive but privately profitable, but the inefficiencies the rent-seeking literature have emphasized point only indirectly to the different ways that rent seeking and constitutional political economy depict the political process.

The rent-seeking literature has focused on the welfare losses entailed by rent seeking, but because rent-seeking activity imposes costs on some for the benefit of others, it can only occur through the force of government. Some people use the power of government to coercively transfer resources from others to themselves. Constitutional political economy and rent seeking depict the political process as resting on completely different foundations. Constitutional political economy views government as an embodiment of politics as exchange, whereas rent seeking is founded on the idea of government being able to forcibly extract resources from some for the benefit of others. One is based on the idea of politics as agreement; the other is based on the idea of politics as coercion. One is based on the idea that government is a way for people to achieve their common ends through collective action; the other is based on some people being able to use the force of government to benefit themselves at the expense of others.

26.4 A CONSTITUTIONAL RECONCILIATION

The different foundations of the literatures on constitutional political economy and rent seeking might be reconciled within the constitutional political economy framework. Constitutional political economy divides political decision-making into two stages, and deals explicitly with the constitutional stage, whereas rent seeking is a post-constitutional activity. Thus, everyone might agree to a set of constitutional rules that enables some post-constitutional rent seeking, because even though individual activities of rent seeking benefit some at the expense of others, in the aggregate, political activity provides net benefits to everyone. Everyone is better off with the constitutional framework that allows some rent seeking, rather than one with higher decision-making costs that would prevent all rent seeking. This proposed reconciliation implies a constitutional trade-off that exchanges lower post-constitutional decision-making costs for more post-constitutional rent seeking.

The constitutional literature rests on a procedural foundation. Procedures are agreed to at the constitutional level, which implies agreement with post-constitutional political decisions. The Buchanan and Tullock (1962, chapter 6) framework recognizes that not every post-constitutional decision will be unanimously supported, but that the constitutional framework that constrains post-constitutional decisions implies that if the constitutional rules are agreed upon, then post-constitutional politics provides net benefits to everyone.

The implication that on net, everyone benefits from all the rent-seeking activity, only applies under situations in which the constitutional framework meets the criteria for agreement. If the constitutional framework was imposed on some by others rather than being the product of agreement, then the procedural argument pointing toward agreement with rent-seeking activities does not hold up. Only if the constitutional rules were generally agreed upon is the implication that rent-seeking activity in the aggregate provides benefits to everyone supported. Without such agreement at the constitutional level, rent seeking can create the welfare losses the literature emphasizes.

So, even recognizing that constitutional political economy analyzes constitutional decision-making whereas rent seeking is a feature of post-constitutional decision-making does not completely resolve the tension between the constitutional 'politics as agreement' framework and the rent-seeking 'politics as coercion' framework. Because constitutional agreement is hypothetical, there are no real-world indicators to reveal whether the rules meet the agreement criterion, and therefore whether rent seeking is a transaction cost that comes with political exchange or a transfer activity that relies on the force of government to benefit some at the expense of others. The dichotomy remains: consent versus coercion.

This points to another difference in the two literatures. Constitutional political economy, at least as it has been developed by Buchanan, rests on a normative foundation, whereas rent seeking is based on a purely positive foundation. The constitutional literature argues that optimal constitutional rules are those that would command unanimous agreement under some set of hypothetical circumstances, but this does not imply that real-world constitutional rules command unanimous agreement under any circumstances. Rent seeking and its attendant welfare losses can be the result of non-optimal constitutional rules that do not meet the test of hypothetical unanimous agreement. Rent seeking describes the positive facts of political activity, whereas constitutional political economy uses agreement as a normative benchmark for evaluating constitutional rules.

The foundation for rent seeking is explicitly positive. The conclusion that rent seeking results in welfare losses injects a normative element into the analysis, because welfare is a normative concept, but the judgment that rent seeking lowers welfare is a conclusion that emerges from the analytical framework, along with a specific and generally accepted normative criterion for welfare, which goes back at least to Pigou (1920). Despite conclusions with normative overtones, rent seeking does not rest on a normative foundation.

The normative foundation of constitutional political economy is somewhat tenuous because it is based on a hypothetical conjecture about agreement that is unobservable and unverifiable. Twentieth-century contractarians like Rawls (1971) and Buchanan (1975) rest their normative arguments on a hypothetical agreement from behind a veil of ignorance, or from a renegotiation of the social contract from anarchy, which can never occur. It is easy to imagine that with regard to specific real-world constitutional rules one person could argue (and believe) that people would unanimously agree from behind a veil of ignorance or with a renegotiation from anarchy, while another person could argue (and believe) that unanimous agreement could not be obtained even under those hypothetical conditions. There would be no way to reconcile such a disagreement. Ultimately, then, these hypothetical devices become more tools for persuasion than analytical tools that could actually determine whether specific constitutional provisions meet the test of agreement.

A constitutional analysis goes some distance toward reconciling the very different foundations underlying the two literatures. At the constitutional level hypothetical unanimous agreement is the benchmark for evaluating whether constitutional rules are optimal, but not all constitutional rules satisfy this benchmark. The benchmark provides a normative criterion for evaluating the desirability of constitutional rules, not a positive description of the characteristics of actual constitutional rules. Rent seeking and its attendant welfare losses may occur because actual constitutional rules do not meet the benchmark, so political institutions allow some to use the force of government for their benefit, at the expense of others, and without the agreement of those others. They may also occur because even if constitutional rules are optimal, the high decision-making costs that would be required to eliminate rent seeking are not worth the cost of preventing those costs. Some rent seeking is likely compatible with optimal constitutional rules.

26.5 BUT SOME TENSION STILL REMAINS

Constitutional political economy depicts politics as exchange, and depicts government as a way for individuals to accomplish ends collectively that they could not accomplish individually. At the same time it recognizes that actual constitutional frameworks are not optimal, which allows people to use the force of government to impose costs on some for the benefit of others, as depicted in the rent-seeking literature. Buchanan's own work makes this argument in specific cases (Buchanan and Devletoglou 1970; Buchanan and Wagner 1977). Thus, in reality this exchange model of government may not be descriptive, and contrary to the constitutional framework, coercion is a more descriptive term for the way individuals interact in the public sector than consent.

Yeager (1985, 2001) points out that no matter how much someone agrees with the activities of government, the ultimate basis of government is force, not agreement. For example, even someone who agrees that government should levy the taxes it does to provide government goods and services for the benefit of all is still forced to pay those taxes, and despite approving of government taxation still is threatened with punishment by government if those taxes are not paid. Government uses force against those who violate its mandates and regulations, or who try to pay less than it demands to finance its operations. Joseph Schumpeter (1950, p. 198) observed, 'The theory which construes taxes on the analogy of club dues or of the purchase of the services of, say, a doctor only proves how far removed this part of the social sciences is from scientific habits of mind.'

Can people 'agree to be coerced', as Hochman and Rodgers (1969) suggest? Their argument is that people have an incentive to free ride on the production of public goods, so everyone would be better off if they could agree with each other that everyone would pay, so everyone could get the optimal amount of the good. Government facilitates this exchange by forcing people to pay and then producing the Pareto optimal amount of a public good. The problem with this argument is its hypothetical nature. Are the people who say, 'No, I really do not want the public good' trying to free ride, or stating their true preferences about believing the cost of the good is greater than the benefit it will return to them? The hypothetical agreement argument can be used to justify government coercion in almost any circumstance, simply by saying that under some hypothetical circumstance people would agree to be coerced. The argument cannot be refuted because there is no way to observe whether it is true. As Yeager emphasizes, these devices suggesting that people would hypothetically agree under some circumstances mean that in reality, people have not agreed.

One might try to reconcile the different foundations of the literatures on constitutional political economy and rent seeking by noting that one addresses decision-making at the constitutional level and the other at the post-constitutional level, but that does not fully reconcile the differences, and there remains a tension between literatures that depict politics as based on consent versus on coercion. Using agreement at the constitutional level for less-than-unanimous agreement in post-constitutional decision-making, the constitutional political economy framework can be used to argue that in some cases rent seeking is hypothetically agreed upon and optimal. Yet we know that Buchanan (Buchanan and Devletoglou 1970; Buchanan and Wagner 1977), the biggest promoter of the 'politics as exchange' constitutional paradigm, does not believe that all post-constitutional activities meet this test of agreement. Thus, the inherent tension between the politics as agreement foundation of constitutional political economy and the politics as coercion framework of rent seeking remains.

26.6 CONSTITUTIONAL CONSTRAINTS ON RENT SEEKING

Recognizing that constitutional political economy deals with the choice of constraints, whereas rent seeking is the result of political activity within those constraints, one might evaluate the degree to which constitutional rules can constrain the ability of people to engage in post-constitutional rent-seeking activity. The constitutional political economy literature has done that, not so much with direct reference to rent seeking, but rather by analyzing constitutional rules as a more general constraint on government discretion.

Buchanan and Tullock (1962) specifically subtitle their book *Logical Foundations of Constitutional Democracy* and evaluate institutions such as voting rules and bicameralism as constraints on government. More generally, constitutional rules limit the scope of government activity, which was an intention of the American Founders. The American Constitution is specifically written as a doctrine of enumerated powers specifying that the federal government does not have any powers not granted explicitly to it in the Constitution. If the government has little in the way of discretionary powers, it cannot provide benefits to rent seekers.

Buchanan (1967, p. 219) discusses the selection of fiscal rules this way, saying 'if no prospective player can predict his own position in the various rounds of play anticipated, consensus on the rules moves within the realm of possibility . . . each prospective player will be motivated to select a set of rules that will seem "efficient" or "fair" . . .' Extending this line of reasoning, Brennan and Buchanan (1980) examine ways in which a fiscal constitution can be designed to constrain a Leviathan government. Brennan and Buchanan (1980, pp. 7–8) say, 'The logic of constitutional restrictions is embodied in the implicit prediction that any power assigned to government may be, over some ranges and on some occasions, exercised in ways that are at variance with the desired usage of such power, as defined by citizens behind the veil of ignorance.' They later note (1980, p. 9), 'One aspect of such rules is the application of restrictions on the possible misappropriation of public funds by legitimate public officials . . . Further, restrictions are typically placed on the legitimate activities of government, in terms of both the nature of the services that government provides and of the type of laws that governments may enact.' While not dealing directly with rent seeking, Brennan and Buchanan's volume on the power to tax does suggest that constitutional constraints can limit discretionary activity by those in government.

Ostrom (1987) examines the role of federalism as a constraint on government in an explicitly constitutional framework. He recognizes the constitutional versus post-constitutional levels of decision-making, and argues that a federal constitutional design can constrain those in government because it divides political power among many individuals, or groups of individuals. The literature on federalism suggests other ways in which constitutional design can limit rent seeking, by allowing citizens to 'vote with their feet', as described by Tiebout (1956), and move to jurisdictions that are more effectively governed, and by allowing 'benchmark competition' where, even if citizens are not mobile, they can compare the performance of their government with governments in other jurisdictions.

Brennan and Buchanan (1985) argue more generally for 'the reason of rules', noting that constitutional constraints serve the purpose of limiting the discretionary activities of government. The literature does not mention the ability to limit rent seeking specifically, but points toward constitutional constraints as one way in which the losses from rent seeking can be limited. However, the ability to limit rent seeking through constitutional constraints would appear to apply only in cases where constitutional rules eliminate the possibility of post-constitutional decision-making.

The easy case in which to illustrate this is with regard to constitutional constraints that prohibit government activity. Tullock (1967 [2008]), for example, uses tariffs to illustrate rent-seeking activity. The Constitution of the United States prohibits tariffs on exports, so there are no rent-seeking losses associated with tariffs on exports, because the Constitution places them outside the scope of post-constitutional decision-making. Here is an example of a constitutional rule that prevents rent seeking. But because tariffs are allowed on imports, they provide Tullock's prototypical example of rent seeking activity. Similarly, Stigler's (1971) capture theory of regulation argues that over time regulatory agencies tend to favor the firms they regulate, providing benefits to those regulated firms at the expense of the general public whom the regulations were initially designed to protect. Regulatory capture is an example of rents going to regulated industries as a result of the regulations the regulatory agency is supposed to enforce. Those rents could be eliminated by eliminating the regulation. Tullock (1975 [1980]) offers examples of rent-seeking losses due to regulations on taxicabs, airlines and trucking, all of which could be eliminated by eliminating the regulations. If constitutional rules prohibit government post-constitutional decision-making, they can eliminate any rent-seeking activity that would have accompanied those post-constitutional decisions.

One way to do this, the above paragraph illustrates, is through constitutional rules that limit the scope of government. This also might be done with a constitutional provision that eliminates discretion in post-constitutional activity. For example, the tax code generates a substantial amount of rent seeking as taxpayers attempt to have the tax code changed for their benefit. In the United States, the progressivity of the tax system, and income that might be excluded, deducted or credited in the tax system are the object of much rent seeking. One way to limit rent seeking would be to specify these characteristics of the tax system as constitutional rules. If the 16th Amendment to the United States Constitution, which generally allows income taxation, were instead written to specify that all income would be taxed at a single specific rate, rent seeking over that characteristic of the tax system would be constitutionally prohibited.

The rent seeking for tariffs on imports that Tullock used as a prime example would be eliminated if the Constitution specified that all imports would be subject to a tariff of 3 percent, for example. Constitutional rules can limit rent seeking by making decisions that might be deferred to the post-constitutional stage at the constitutional stage instead.

Making all decisions at the constitutional stage would require more foresight than would be humanly possible, which is why people do not choose – even from behind a veil of ignorance – to be constrained to that degree by constitutional rules. Constitutions are to a degree constraints on the discretion afforded governments at the post-constitutional stage, but also are largely a set of rules for making post-constitutional decisions. Buchanan and Tullock's (1962) initial distinction between constitutional and post-constitutional decision-making was illustrated with the way that people could, at the constitutional stage, unanimously agree to make post-constitutional decisions with a less-than-unanimous decision rule, such as the majority rule that is often used. The example recognizes that there is potential value in allowing government the discretion to make post-constitutional decisions rather than having all government decisions specified within the constitutional rules.

Once post-constitutional discretion is allowed, rent seeking is inevitable. Tullock's initial examples were on obvious cases where firms engaged in rent-seeking activity to protect themselves from competitors, by gaining government-granted monopolies or through tariff protection to make foreign firms less competitive. Consider, however, public goods that most people would like to see government produce, like national defense and roads. If government decides to produce a new military aircraft, to build a new road, some private firm will be contracted to build the aircraft, or the road, and there will be rent-seeking activity by firms that are attempting to win the contract. A potential way to avoid that rent seeking would be to have the government build its own aircraft and roads, but even here unless that work-around is a constitutional rule, private firms will lobby to privatize the government activity. Governments are contracting out to operate prisons, to replace government janitors with private custodian services, to contract out government cafeterias to private food services and so forth. Any government discretion on how its budget will be spent will lead to rent seeking by those who want to receive those revenues.

The same is too obviously true of taxes to discuss in detail. Any portions of the tax code that are not specified in the constitutional rules will be subject to rent seeking by those who want the tax code changed in their favor. Even in cases where the tax rate is flat, such as state sales taxes in the United States or value added taxes in Europe, rent seekers look to gain exemptions and exclusions from the tax. Rent seeking for regulatory benefits fits the same mold. If government has the discretion to make post-constitutional decisions, people will engage in rent seeking to have those decisions made in a way that favors them.

The reasoning goes back to the consent versus coercion framework that is the fundamental difference between the constitutional political economy and rent-seeking paradigms. Post-constitutional decisions are made in markets all the time, within the constitutional framework that defines property rights and the parameters within which exchange can take place. In markets, however, activities actually are based on consent, because a market exchange will not take place unless all parties to the exchange are in agreement. If the terms are not favorable to a participant – if the participant views that the costs of the potential exchange exceed the benefits – then the participant can walk away without engaging in the exchange. With government decisions, taxpayers have no choice but to pay their taxes and citizens are offered no alternative but to abide by government regulations. People have no choice but to pay the cost of the post-constitutional decisions government makes, even though they may not agree. Rent seeking uses the force of government to try to obtain benefits from the discretionary decisions those in government can make, imposing a cost on those who have no choice but to pay the cost.

This is true even for those who fully buy in to the social contract. An individual can agree that it is socially beneficial for everyone to pay taxes and to abide by government regulations, but that does not alter the fact that government forces everyone to do so. When the costs of government are forced on everyone, rent seekers then have the means by which they can impose costs on others for their own benefit.

Constitutional constraints can limit rent seeking by shifting decision-making from the post-constitutional stage to the constitutional stage. Whenever post-constitutional decisions are made, however, the benefits can be tilted toward some rather than others. Building a public good like a road, the selection of the exact route will favor some property owners over others, setting up the incentive for rent seeking to get the road favorably located, and the road must be built by someone, setting up the incentive for firms to engage in rent seeking to get the construction contract. Constitutional constraints cannot eliminate rent seeking, because they cannot eliminate post-constitutional decision-making.

26.7 IS CONSTITUTIONAL DECISION-MAKING POSSIBLE?

The idea behind constitutional political economy is that people can agree on the constitutional rules of the game from a position in which they will not have good information about the way that the specific configuration of rules will affect their post-constitutional position. Brennan and Buchanan (1985, p. 34) note with regard to the choice of constitutional rules,

> It is much more difficult for a person to determine which of the several choice options confronted will, indeed, maximize whatever set of values that person desired to maximize. There are two reasons for this loss of interest identity as we shift to the level of choice among rules or institutions. In the first place, rules are, almost by definition, applicable to a number of instances or cases . . . A related but somewhat different characteristic of rules is that they embody an extended time dimension . . . Rules tend to be quasi-permanent; they 'live' longer than the outcomes of decisions made under them.

Brennan and Buchanan go on to say (1985, p. 35), 'The "veil of uncertainty" may be approached, if never fully realized, if persons are modeled as though they were faced with choices among rules of social order that are generally applicable and guaranteed to be quasi-permanent.' These are persuasive arguments, but they do not quite get to the point of implying that constitutional rules are made behind the Rawlsian veil. In many cases people are well aware of their long-run interests when constitutional rules are being designed. They may not know the implications of specific rules with certainty, but they can make good conjectures about how specific rules will affect them in the future. Also, in many cases rules are subject to post-constitutional interpretation, so may not be as permanent as they appear. In reality people are never behind a veil of ignorance and always know their own personal interests. The question this section considers is the degree to which people can further their own interests in constitutional decision-making.

Buchanan has used the sports analogy that constitutional rules are the rules of the game and post-constitutional decision-making occurs within those rules. Using this analogy, depending upon their specific strengths, teams will know in advance whether they will benefit from certain rules. For example, in American football, whether pass interference is a spot foul or has a specific yardage penalty associated with it will differentially benefit teams that have a comparative advantage in passing rather than running the ball. For another example, when the three point line was added to basketball, that differentially benefited teams with better long shooters. Yes, it is possible that a decade in the future the teams with the good three point shooters today will not still have that advantage, but (1) people still anticipate their immediate benefits from the rule; (2) the people who benefit from those rules today will be different people who play under them in the future, even if they are the same teams; (3) a positive discount rate implies that people value immediate benefits over long-term outcomes; and (4) the rules can change again in the future. There are many reasons why people both know and favor rules that will provide them with immediate advantages over others. Decisions on rules of the game are made with full knowledge of one's post-constitutional position, which often implies that individuals know ahead of time whether rules will provide differential benefits to them.

Charles Beard's (1913) analysis of the Constitutional Convention that produced the Constitution of the United States argued that the economic interests of those who attended the Convention were a significant determinant of the provisions that ultimately appeared in the document. For example, many of those in attendance had purchased government bonds to help finance the Revolutionary War, and there was the prospect that those bonds might not be redeemed. This is the origin of the provision in Article

VI, 'All debts contracted and engagements entered into, before the adoption of this Constitution, shall be as valid against the United States under this Constitution, as under the Confederation.' McGuire and Ohsfeldt (1989) initiated a literature empirically testing Beard's hypothesis using voting records from the Constitutional Convention, and that literature strongly supports the conclusion that the authors of the Constitution of the United States wrote the document in such a way that their personal interests were furthered by the constitutional rules they designed.

When rules apply over a long sequence of decisions, people may not know exactly how those rules will affect them in the future, but those actually making the decisions are not behind a veil of uncertainty and must have a good idea of how they anticipate the rules will affect them. As a result, rent seeking occurs even over constitutional rules, and there may not even be a constitutional stage of decision-making. Because people anticipate how rule changes will affect their own personal interests, even decisions over constitutional rules may be post-constitutional decisions, to use the terminology of constitutional political economy.

Constitutional rules have the appearance of being semi-permanent, but it may be that they appear that way only as long as the rules favor those who have the power to keep them in place. A striking example is the series of bailouts of 'too big to fail' firms following the recession that began in 2008. Contrary to the bankruptcy rules that seemed to define the constitutional framework for firms that become insolvent, the US government bailed out General Motors, AIG and a number of banks. In the General Motors case, the United Auto workers that represented the firm's union labor received a substantial ownership share in the new General Motors, ahead of bondholders who should have been in line before the union under normal bankruptcy rules. The appearance here is that even though there were rules that would normally apply to most firms going through bankruptcy, those rules did not apply to these companies (and labor unions) that had the political power to alter the rules for their benefit.

This example is anecdotal, and arguing the case too strongly would pull the chapter away from its main subject, but note that around the same time Delta Airlines and American Airlines went through bankruptcy proceedings that followed the old and long-standing rules. The airline industry was not as politically connected as the financial industry or the auto industry. Using the bailouts as an illustration, it may be that what appear to be semi-permanent rules of the game remain in place only as long as they benefit those who have political power. When different rules would favor those who have the power to change them, the rules change. Thus, rent seeking occurs even in the design of the rules of the game, and it appears that constitutional rules are the product of post-constitutional decision-making.

Another factor is that constitutional rules are not made all at once, after which all post-constitutional decisions are made under those rules. Rather, constitutional rules are continually evolving as post-constitutional decisions are made. The result is that constitutional rules evolve in response to the demands of those who have the political power to change them. One way to look at this, from the standpoint of constitutional political economy, is that everyone agrees that a change in the rules would be beneficial – that is the calculus of consent. But when one looks at the way the political process actually works, people with political power are able to redefine the rules, often with considerable dissent and substantial opposition, for their own benefit – that is the calculus of coercion.

Decisions over constitutional rules in real-world politics do not meet the normative standards of constitutional political economy because, first, changes in the rules are often made without any substantial consensus behind them, and second, because those who are pushing for changes in the rules are well aware of their own interests in the changes they advocate. In contrast to the hypothetical worlds of decision-making from behind a veil of ignorance, or renegotiation of the rules from anarchy, people know their own interests, and some people have more political power than others due to their status within the existing institutional structure. All decisions are post-constitutional decisions, made after the veil has been lifted, because in reality the veil was never there.

Because constitutional rules have longer-lasting effects than the post-constitutional decisions made under those rules, there is a greater incentive to use political pressure for constitutional rule changes than for favorable political decisions made under those rules. And because people know their interests and are not behind a veil, this means that rent-seeking activity will tend to be at least as prevalent with regard to changing the constitution as with regard to post-constitutional politics. There really is no veil behind with people make constitutional decisions, and there really is no requirement for consensus when those decisions are made.

Consider real constitutions, like the Constitution of the United States. For it to be formally amended, two thirds of the members of the House of Representatives and the Senate must agree, along with three quarters of the states. This is a higher bar than simple majority rule, but falls way short of real consensus, especially when one recognizes that all of those making these decisions are politicians. No private sector citizens are even involved. However, the constitutional rules that are actually in effect depend on the Supreme Court's interpretation, and that is continually evolving, based on the judgment of nine individuals. They do come closer to meeting the veil of ignorance criterion than the politicians who can formally amend the document, however. Indeed, one significant issue in US presidential campaigns is that the president appoints justices to the Supreme Court. This would not matter if Court decisions were in some way analogous to decisions behind a veil of ignorance, but people realize the political interest group considerations behind Court decisions. Those Supreme Court decisions that actually define constitutional rules are widely recognized as political decisions that favor one interest over another, rather than decisions based on the consensus criterion that underlies constitutional political economy.

When one looks at state constitutions within the United States, many can be amended with majority approval of ballot initiatives that can be placed on ballots after collecting a certain number of signatures. What is required is the financial backing to get the signatures, along with ballot wording persuasive enough to attract the votes of rationally ignorant voters. Using the criteria of constitutional political economy, constitutional rules are not necessarily only those rules in a written constitution, and all of the rules in a written constitution may not meet the criteria of consent that constitutional political economy specifies. Still, it is instructive to consider how written constitutions line up with the normative criteria of constitutional political economy, especially since Buchanan and Tullock (1962) cite the Constitution of the United States as inspiration for their work.

Of course there is a counter-argument to this position that all decisions are post-constitutional decisions: the argument that Brennan and Buchanan gave, which was quoted earlier in this section. So, the section is more intended to raise the question of whether there really is a distinction between constitutional and post-constitutional decision-making, rather than to answer that question. If the distinction is not complete, so that people do have at least some idea of their interests with regard to constitutional rules, that opens up the opportunity for rent seeking at the constitutional stage.

26.8 CONSTITUTIONAL RULES AND CONSTITUTIONAL DECISION-MAKING

The perspective one takes on constitutional political economy depends in part on whether one is discussing the existence of generally agreed-upon constitutional rules or on whether one is discussing the process by which those rules are changed. There are certain rules that likely would command general agreement, mostly with regard to the protection of individual rights. Most people would agree that people have an obligation not to kill or injure each other, and not to violate other people's property rights, for example. However, what constitutes an injury, and what constitutes property, is subject to debate, and at this point constitutional decision-making comes into play. For example, certain types of speech might be deemed to injure someone, even though no physical injury occurs, and rights of property ownership have continually been modified. An owner of real estate may be prevented from building certain types of structures on that land or may be prevented from building anything at all. Intellectual property rights have been continually debated, without apparent consistency. Fashions and food recipes have no protection as intellectual property, whereas formulas for medicinal drugs and computer programs do. One way to explain this is that computer programmers have more political power than chefs, and have been able to design the rules to their favor. While there may be some constitutional rules that do command general agreement, constitutional decision-making occurs when those rules are subject to change through a collective decision-making process.

Constitutional political economy discusses the process by which constitutional rules are determined, not the rules that emerge from that process. Buchanan (1975, p. 175) criticizes Rawls for attempting to identify constitutional outcomes, saying that he 'attempted to identify those precepts that might be predicted to emerge'. Doing so, Buchanan argues, 'is drawing attention away from his more basic contribution, which is the relationship of justice to the outcome of the contractual *process* itself'. That emphasis is in the original, and illustrates that the focus of constitutional political economy is on the process of defining constitutional rules rather than the constitutional rules themselves.

Without denying that there are certain constitutional rules that are supported by consensus, the actual process by which those rules are changed involves decision-makers who are well aware of their own interests, and who are able to use their political power and the force of government to get the rules changed in ways that favor those with political power. Because the process does not take place behind a veil, the constitutional decision-making process is subject to rent seeking.

26.9 CONCLUSION

The literatures on constitutional political economy and rent seeking are based on different foundations. Constitutional political economy models politics as exchange, and depicts government action as a cooperative endeavor in which people can collectively achieve goals that they would be unable to accomplish with bilateral exchange. Rent seeking depicts a political system in which some people are able to use the force of government to provide benefits for themselves at the expense of others. One is the calculus of consent; the other is the calculus of coercion.

A partial, but only partial, reconciliation can be made within the constitutional political economy framework, by recognizing that constitutional political economy applies to determining the constitutional rules whereas rent seeking is post-constitutional activity that takes place within those constitutional rules. Different frameworks apply because the two literatures are considering two different levels of collective decision-making. The bigger difference between the two literatures, however, is the normative element in constitutional political economy, typified by Rawls (1971) and Buchanan (1975), in contrast to the positive foundation of the rent-seeking literature. Constitutional political economy specifies normative criteria for optimal constitutional rules, whereas rent seeking offers a positive description of one aspect of the political decision-making process.

A purely positive analysis of constitutional decision-making causes the distinction between constitutional and post-constitutional decisions to recede, and perhaps vanish altogether. In actuality, the normative criterion of consensus is rarely met, and in actuality people always have a good idea of their own interests and how changes in the rules will differentially affect them. This means that the real-world rules of the game will be determined in the same way as the post-constitutional decisions that are made within the constitutional rules. There is no constitutional stage, and changes in the rules are driven as much by private interest, and by one group imposing costs on others, as any political decisions. Therefore, the rent-seeking framework applies as much to decisions made on constitutional rules as it does to everyday post-constitutional decision-making.

One reason Leland Yeager (1985, 2001), a strong critic of the constitutional political economy project, objects to it is because it depicts government as if it is based on agreement. All government action is based on coercion. This fiction that government action is based on agreement is dangerous, he argues, because it offers justification for government's coercive activities – activities that may harm individuals and on net lower welfare. Using the arguments of constitutional political economy, one might argue that just as people might agree to bear the external cost associated with political decision rules of less-than-unanimity, people might also agree to rent-seeking costs to further their collective interests. This argument turns rent seeking from a welfare cost, to use Tullock's (1967 [2008]) term, into a transaction cost as a part of politics as exchange. The welfare cost Tullock attributes to rent seeking arises precisely because some people can use the force of government to impose costs on others. This is politics as force, not politics as agreement. Government exists only to force people to do things they would not voluntarily choose to do in the absence of government coercion, and Yeager argues that the constitutional political economy framework that is based on some hypothetical consent is dangerous propaganda because it conceals the coercion that actually lies at the foundation of all government's activities.

Rent seeking describes the actual process whereby people use the coercive power of government to gain at the expense of others. This chapter has looked at ways in which the foundations of the literatures on constitutional political economy and rent seeking might be reconciled, and despite some arguments along those lines, it appears that a complete reconciliation is not possible. One describes the calculus of consent; the other describes the calculus of coercion.

REFERENCES

Beard, Charles A. (1913), *An Economic Interpretation of the Constitution of the United States*, New York: Macmillan.

Bhagwati, J.N. (1982), 'Directly unproductive, profit-seeking (DUP) activities', *Journal of Political Economy*, **90**(5), 988–1002.

Brennan, Geoffrey and James M. Buchanan (1980), *The Power to Tax: Analytical Foundations of a Fiscal Constitution*, Cambridge: Cambridge University Press.

Brennan, Geoffrey and James M. Buchanan (1985), *The Reason of Rules: Constitutional Political Economy*, Cambridge: Cambridge University Press.

Buchanan, James M. (1967), *Public Finance in Democratic Process: Fiscal Institutions and Individual Choice*, Chapel Hill, NC: University of North Carolina Press.

Buchanan, James M. (1975), *The Limits of Liberty: Between Anarchy and Leviathan*, Chicago, IL: University of Chicago Press.

Buchanan, James M. (1990), 'The domain of constitutional economics', *Constitutional Political Economy*, **1**(1), 1–18.

Buchanan, James M. and Nicos E. Devletoglou (1970), *Academia in Anarchy: An Economic Diagnosis*, New York: Basic Books.

Buchanan, James M. and Gordon Tullock (1962), *The Calculus of Consent: Logical Foundations of Constitutional Democracy*, Ann Arbor, MI: University of Michigan Press.

Buchanan, James M. and Richard E. Wagner (1977), *Democracy in Deficit: The Political Legacy of Lord Keynes*, New York: Academic Press.

Hochman, Harold M. and James D. Rodgers (1969), 'Pareto optimal redistribution', *American Economic Review*, **59**(4), 542–57.

Holcombe, Randall G. (2011), 'Consent or coercion? A critical analysis of the constitutional contract', in Alain Marciano (ed.), *Constitutional Mythologies: New Perspectives on Controlling the State*, New York: Springer, pp. 9–23.

Krueger, Anne O. (1974), 'The political economy of the rent-seeking society', *American Economic Review*, **64**(3), 291–303, reprinted in Roger D. Congleton, Arye L. Hillman and Kai A. Konrad (eds) (2008), *40 Years of Research on Rent Seeking 2 – Applications: Rent Seeking in Practice*, Heidelberg: Springer, pp. 151–63.

McGuire, Robert A. and Robert L. Ohsfeldt (1989), 'Self-interest, agency theory, and political voting behavior: the ratification of the United States Constitution', *American Economic Review*, **79**(1), 219–34.

Ostrom, Vincent (1987), *The Political Theory of a Compound Republic*, 2nd edn, Lincoln, NB: University of Nebraska Press.

Pigou, Arthur Cecil (1920), *The Economics of Welfare*, London: Macmillan.

Rawls, John (1971), *A Theory of Justice*, Cambridge, MA: Belknap Press.

Schumpeter, Joseph A. (1950), *Capitalism, Socialism and Democracy*, 3rd edn, New York: Harper & Row.

Stigler, George J. (1971), 'The theory of economic regulation', *Bell Journal of Economics and Management Science*, **2**(1), 3–21.

Tiebout, Charles M. (1956), 'A pure theory of local expenditures', *Journal of Political Economy*, **64**(5), 416–24.

Tullock, Gordon (1967), 'The welfare costs of tariffs, monopolies and theft', *Western Economic Journal*, **5**(3), 224–32, reprinted in Roger D. Congleton, Arye L. Hillman and Kai A. Konrad (eds) (2008), *40 Years of Research on Rent Seeking 1 – The Theory of Rent Seeking*, Heidelberg: Springer, pp. 45–53.

Tullock, Gordon (1975), 'The transitional gains trap', *Bell Journal of Economics*, **6**(2), 671–8, reprinted in James M. Buchanan, Robert D. Tollison and Gordon Tullock (eds) (1980), *Toward a Theory of the Rent-seeking Society*, College Station, TX: Texas A&M University Press, pp. 211–21.

Yeager, Leland B. (1985), 'Rights, contract, and utility in policy espousal', *Cato Journal*, **5**(1), 259–94.

Yeager, Leland B. (2001), *Ethics as a Social Science*, Cheltenham, UK and Northampton, MA, USA: Edward Elgar Publishing.

27. Rent seeking and organizational governance: limiting losses from intra-organizational conflict

Roger D. Congleton

SUMMARY

This chapter demonstrates that efforts to curtail rent-seeking losses can explain much about the architecture and procedures of all formal organizations, including governments, firms and others. To be successful, every organization has to reduce internal rent-seeking losses to well below full-dissipation levels.

27.1 RENT SEEKING, RULES AND ORGANIZATIONS

Every organization confronts three general kinds of managerial problems, only two of which have attracted significant attention in the new institutional economics literature. First, there are problems associated with team production as noted by Alchian and Demsetz (1972), Williamson (1975, 1996) and a very large number of talented scholars inspired by their research. Second, there are a variety of problems associated with information gathering, processing and asymmetries, which also have implications for organizational design as noted by Jensen and Meckling (1976, 1979), among many others. In addition, there is another neglected class of problems that must be solved by all organizations, namely, the problems associated with intra-organizational conflict over organizational resources and surplus, that is to say, intra-organizational rent seeking.[1]

Although neglected by most of the literature on the theory of firms and non-profit organizations, potential losses from intra-organizational rent seeking are sufficiently important that they have had major effects on organizational design. Without rules to solve free riding and coordination problems, team production would be less productive and thus less likely to be used. Without rules and procedures that reduce internal conflict, any organizational surplus that might be created through team production would be consumed by intra-organizational rent seeking among the various persons staffing the organization, including employees, management and owners (Congleton 1989). The latter is sufficiently important that reward, recruiting and decision-making procedures within organizations all appear to reflect the insights of the rent-seeking literature, although most were adopted long before rent-seeking theory was worked out.

It bears noting that both the contract and theory of the firm literatures use the term 'rents', but they rarely mention potential rent-seeking losses. Instead, they focus on

[1] Throughout this chapter, I use the term rent seeking in the broad sense suggested by Tullock (1967 [2008]) and Congleton (1980 [2008]), as resources consumed by a process of competition or conflict.

how principals can extract rents from their agents through contract design – often of the take-or-leave variety. In doing so, these researchers indirectly point out that rents can be shifted from one party to another within firms, which implies that intra-firm rent seeking is possible. Shifting rents does not necessarily increase total organizational surplus, although it may insofar as it aligns the interests of team members with that of the organization.[2] Conflict over the distribution of rents, however, nearly always reduces organizational surplus by shifting resources from productive to unproductive uses.

The literature on rent seeking suggests that losses from conflict for organizational rents can be reduced by adjusting the 'rules of the game'. This chapter suggests that many such adjustments have taken place within robust organizations. Nonetheless, intra-organizational rent-seeking losses remain greater than zero, although standing rules and procedures make those losses much smaller than they would have been without them.[3] Rent seeking is not a single activity, but a broad class of activities in which innovation can and does take place, which makes it difficult to eliminate.

This chapter demonstrates that the rent-seeking approach can shed considerable light on the institutions of firms and non-profits. Anecdotes from classic works in organizational theory and history are used to illustrate both the existence of intra-organizational conflict and solutions adopted.

27.2 RENT SEEKING AS THE DUAL OF PRODUCTIVE EFFORT

To be 'organized' means that a rule-based system has been created for conducting the affairs of interest. Thus, every organization is substantially rule bound. Part of the explanation for this is the difficulty of team production. To realize advantages from team production, *formateurs* and their managers adopt a variety of rules to solve a variety of coordination, informational, free rider, and exit problems. In addition to encouraging productive activities, unproductive activities have to be discouraged. Thus other rules and procedures are adopted to reduce the extent of rent-seeking losses. Among the rules adopted are those specifying procedures for recruiting team members, and the conditional rewards and punishments associated with team membership, including wage rates, raises, promotions, demotions and dismissals.

As in any 'contest', an organization's rules determine the returns from alternative strategies at the margin, which in turn encourages some forms of behavior and discourages others within the organization. In this manner, the standing rules determine the equilibrium behavior within the organization – the stable pattern of life that exists within organizations during 'office hours'. These rules are not entirely rigid or written down, but tend to be relatively stable. Nonetheless, management can adjust the rules as circumstances or goals change.

---

2 See, for example, Khalil et al. (2013), who show among other things that 'more productive' employees need to receive (limited) rents in order to be induced to fully benefit from their productivity. Early discussion of intra-firm rents are included in Coase (1937), Williamson (1985) and Crémer and McLean (1988).

3 See Congleton et al. (2008a, 2008b) for compendiums of the rent-seeking literature.

Table 27.1 The team production dilemma and solutions

The shirking dilemma of the natural cooperative			Organizational solution to the rent-seeking dilemma		
	Team Member B			Team Member B	
Team Member A	Work	Shirk	Team Member A	Work	Shirk
Work (A)	3,3	1,4	Work (A)	**R,R**	R,4 − P
Shirk (A)	4,1	**2,2**	Shirk (A)	4 − P,R	2 − P,2 − P

Note: The cell entries are utilities, the rank order of subjective payoffs for the team members (A, B). The dilemma in the 'natural case' is that both team members shirk rather than work.

27.2.1 An Illustration: Using Rules to Promote Team Production

Team production is useful when the productivity of individual team members is increased by the efforts of others on the team. In such cases, a team's output is greater than the sum of the outputs that would be produced by the independent efforts of the same individuals. The essential problem of team production is illustrated in Table 27.1. In the game on the left, which I refer to as the natural cooperative, the group's output is shared equally by all team members. In the game on the right, a *formateur* has created an artificial reward structure for his or her team in which rewards are conditioned on effort levels. Shirking in either game by individual team members frees time for their own use but reduces the productivity of other team members.

In the game on the left, the reward structure of the natural cooperative fails to encourage sufficient productive work to realize all of the advantages of team production. Mutual shirking is the equilibrium outcome. The game on the right demonstrates that the shirking dilemma can be solved by creating a different reward structure. In the managed organization on the right, each team member receives a reward (R) for work and faces a penalty (P) for shirking that is independent of the efforts of other team members.

Team members in the organized enterprise avoid shirking if $R > 4 - P$ and $R > 2 - P$, thus any combination of rewards and penalties such that $R + P > 4$ is sufficient to solve this particular intra-organizational shirking problem. The reward for mutual cooperation has to be greater than 2 to attract team members from natural cooperative(s). In order to be self-sustaining, the promised rewards can be no greater than 3, since the maximal output is 6. An organization is viable only when conditional rewards reduce the shirking problem, attract team members and generate sufficient net revenue to sustain the organization.

The effectiveness of team production tends to increase as better rules for encouraging effort from team members are adopted and as specialized methods of production are refined. Without appropriate rules, most team members would be inclined to shirk or free ride rather than engage in team production.

Note that shirking in this context can be considered to be a form of rent seeking, because shirkers attempt to secure a total reward that is above their marginal revenue product. In the natural cooperative, the entire team rent seeks, yielding a less desirable combination of leisure and income than the (work, work) equilibrium. That time is wasted rather than put to its highest-valued use is indicated by the unrealized Pareto superior move from the lower right-hand cell to the upper left-hand one. Achieving such moves, however, requires incentives of the sort illustrated by the game on the right. Such artificial rewards and penalties simultaneously increase productive activities (working) and reduce rent-seeking activities (shirking).[4]

It is such possibilities that lead *formateurs*, managers, and team members to invest in organizational design. These efforts, together with survivorship, promote the development of rules for curtailing intra-organizational rent seeking and for encouraging team production at least cost.

In cases in which rent seeking is simply the dual of the usual maximization of productive effort problems addressed by the mainstream organizational literature, little is added to the theoretical analysis by focusing on conflict rather than production. Nonetheless, in practice the distinction may still be important because recognizing the form of rent seeking to be punished may be easier than specifying the productive activity to be encouraged. However, not all intra-organizational rent-seeking losses can be analyzed as the dual of the standard team effort problem.

27.2.2 Incomplete Contracts and Rent Seeking Within Organizations

Most optimal contract research assumes that potential team members are passive participants in a one-sided bargaining process in which principals attempt to prevent team members from obtaining rents (income above some hypothetical opportunity cost) through shirking. Team members are represented as second movers in a Stackelberg game in which the first move is made by *formateurs* or their agents, which is often a reasonable assumption at the point when a new member is recruited to a firm or other organization. This is also implicitly assumed in the above illustration, but it is less likely to be the case after contracts are signed.

As Williamson stresses, contracts are never complete. As a consequence, after team members are recruited, gaps in the rules allow both conventional shirking behavior to arise and also other forms of conflict over the organization's surplus (Congleton 1989 [2008]; Konrad 2000 [2008]; Wärneryd 2003 [2008]). Even hierarchical organizations with well-defined areas of responsibility may suffer from intra-organizational conflict over that surplus, although hierarchy itself can be a method for reducing rent-seeking losses, as developed above by Wärneryd and further elaborated below. For example, Hillman and Katz (1987 [2008]) demonstrate that the entire surplus of a hierarchical organization can be consumed by intra-organizational conflict within and between the levels of a hierarchical organization. In general, the rent-seeking literature suggests that ongoing conflict over organizational surplus can be very intense and significantly reduce the surplus realized by any organization.

---

4 The illustrations may strike the reader as overly simplistic, but it bears noting that a good deal of the theoretical literature on optimal contracts and mechanism design relies upon similar two-player two-strategy set contests. The underlying discreteness of strategy choices in sequential versions of such models makes the analytical mathematics more complex and often produces counterintuitive results, albeit ones similar to the tables here. See, for example, Crémer and McLean (1988).

27.3 ON THE PRODUCTIVITY OF ORGANIZATIONAL RULE OF LAW: REDUCING INTRA-ORGANIZATIONAL CONFLICT

In at least some cases, rent-seeking losses and productivity are not dual problems, because reducing rent-seeking activities does not always increase productive activities. Avoiding losses can be as important a determinant of organizational surplus as seeking profits.

To see this, suppose that an organization has accumulated a reserve, which is used for capital investments and as a buffer for fluctuations in external conditions, such as weather or market demand shocks. The reserve may be thought of as a cumulative organizational surplus, or as an insurance fund for use in future emergencies. In either case, the existence of such reserves can generate significant conflict. The following two-game matrices illustrate possible gains and losses associated with such conflict. In these games, the payoffs in one cell are negative sum, in two cells they are zero sum and in one they are positive sum. The latter represents the non-conflictual outcome under which the organizational reserve benefits each team member through increased income security, insurance-like payouts, or profit sharing. Ideally, each team member would try to maintain the reserve rather than capture it for themselves.

The off-diagonal cells represent the temptation to use time and other scarce resources to capture or increase one's share of those reserves. Rent seeking can take aggressive forms as with expropriation and sabotage that increase one party's share of the reserve but undermines the reputation of the organization or fellow employees, or otherwise unprofitably consumes the organization's capital. It may also take relatively unaggressive forms as with 'dressing for success,' which requires time, money and energy for shopping and grooming. Engaging in social activities to attract the attention and favor of superiors might also require investments in homes and restaurant meals after hours. Aggressive forms of rent seeking may also take place at social events with 'whispering campaigns' against fellow employees or executives.

The Nash equilibrium of the contest on the left is the Hobbesian one of 'fight, fight' and the result is the classic Hobbesian social dilemma of the all-consuming war of every 'team member' against every other. The organization on the right simply forbids particular actions by team members with the aim of reducing losses from intra-organizational conflict. Enforcing such rules (by imposing punishment P on those who violate the rules) increases total team member surplus, but does not necessarily increase 'output' in the usual sense of the word. Savings would be realized even if the original forms of conflict were simply replaced with less destructive ones of equal cost. For example, penalties for violence and sabotage may encourage less costly networking and apple polishing at social gatherings.

Increasing rewards for (productive) work can also be used in some cases to motivate reductions in conflict, as noted in Table 27.1. However, this is not always possible. Rewarding productive effort rather than punishing unproductive activities reduces reserves and thereby reduces prospects for organizational survival. Moreover, the use of rewards to reduce unproductive conflict can create other incentive problems, as team members may attempt to invent new arenas of conflict in order to secure new rewards for avoiding new counterproductive activities. As a consequence, solutions to intra-organizational conflict problems often involve the use of 'thou shall not' rules, supported by penalties that discourage unproductive activities, rather than conditional rewards that encourage productive activities.[5]

The use of penalties is constrained by participation constraints, insofar as team members have exit opportunities. The acceptance of possible penalties by team members implies that members prefer continued membership on productive teams to membership on other less managed teams without penalties.[6] This requires punishments to be systematically targeted at rent-seekers and shirkers, in an appropriate manner, rather than arbitrarily imposed. Participation constraints thus indirectly encourage the emergence of organizational rule of law, as noted in Congleton (2011).

That intra-organizational conflict of the sort discussed above can occur and be solved through rules is more than a hypothetical possibility, as indicated by the following anecdote from Frederick Taylor's classic book on scientific management (1914, pp. 50–51, emphases added).

> No one who has not had this experience can have an idea of the bitterness which is gradually developed in such a struggle [to motivate workers to increase output]. *In a war of this kind* the workmen have one expedient which is usually effective. They *use their ingenuity* to contrive various ways in which the machines which they are running are broken or damaged – apparently by accident . . . He [Taylor] was told that if he continued [attempting to increase team member effort] it would be at *the risk of his life*.

The intra-firm conflict described above was solved through Taylor's (1914, p. 51) adoption of the following rule:

> There will be no more accidents to the machines in this shop. If any part of a machine is broken the man in charge of it must pay at least a part of the cost of its repair, and the fines collected in this way will all be handed over to the mutual beneficial association to help care for sick workmen. This soon stopped the willful breaking of machines.

Indeed, it was the conflict that Taylor encountered as a young man over his modifications of a pre-existing piecework system (at the Midvale Steel Company) that led him to look for entirely new methods for motivating workman and organizing their work.[7]

---

[5] It is interesting to note that Taylor's solution included a device that reduces the firm's incentive to over-punish personnel for engaging in conflict or other uncooperative behavior by giving the fines to charity rather than using them to increase profits.

[6] The search costs and lost income associated with temporary unemployment may be sufficient to make punishments possible in firms. Montesquieu's organizational solution to the Hobbesian jungle was the creation of mutual defense societies. Exit costs in such cases could be substantial – a departure from a relatively safe society to the undefended world of the Hobbesian jungle. In such cases, the threat of expulsion from an organization can be a sufficient penalty to address a wide variety of problems.

[7] Taylor was a pioneer in the development of scientific management methods, and his book *The Principles of Scientific Management* is regarded as a classic in the field. The book has more than 9000 Google citations as of November 2013. (Midvale was a specialty steel company based in Philadelphia.)

Table 27.2 Intra-organizational conflict

Negative sum conflict in winner-take-all games (without rules)			Organizational rules and sanctions as solutions (rules)		
	Team Member B			Team Member B	
Team Member A	Maintain	Fight	Team Member A	Maintain	Fight
Maintain	1, 1	−2, 2	Maintain	**1, 1**	−2, 2 − P
Fight	2, −2	**−1, −1**	Fight	2 − P, −2	−1 − P, −1 − P

Note: The cell entries are utilities, the rank order of subjective payoffs for teams (A, B) or average payoffs for team members.

27.4 A DIGRESSION ON FRAGILE PARTNERSHIPS AS THE FIRST ORGANIZATIONS

The games analyzed above tend to make the solutions to team production problems appear more straightforward than they actually are. There are many forms of rent seeking, and each problem may require a unique solution, as in the anecdote above. It is likely that the penalties and conditional rewards necessary to solve team production and rent-seeking problems were initially difficult to imagine and implement. If so, the first organizations were likely to have been ones for which team production was extraordinarily effective yet the teams themselves were very fragile.

Let us define 'fragile teams' as teams that only produce a surplus (increase in desired output) if all members of the team contribute to its production. Fragility of this sort can discourage intra-organizational rent-seeking activities if the rewards of membership are sufficient. To see this, suppose that a single rent seeker eliminates the advantages of team production. If the team production of Table 27.2 continues only as long as all persons work, the payoffs of the (work, work) cell in each period remain (1, 1). In a repeated game the time period of rational calculation shifts from single period interactions toward perpetuity. The conflict payoff in such fragile organizations is realized only once, because the organization disappears after it is realized. Given this, the present value of the n-period strategy of always working or cooperating is 1/r, where r is the player's discount rate. In contrast, the conflict payoff for each player is at most (2, −2), because it can be realized just once. A commitment to work rather than attempt to capture the reserve is self-enforcing whenever $1/r > 2$; that is, in cases in which each team member's discount rate is less than 0.5.[8] The 'centipede-game structure' of fragile organizations yields long-term cooperation, rather than shirking or conflict.

To sustain long-term cooperation on such fragile teams, *formateurs* should only recruit team members with relatively low discount rates ($r < 0.5$) or high exit costs (which reduce the net benefits of expropriation). Persons who are likely to take the long

[8] Note that the fragile organization game has a structure that is similar to the counterintuitive centipede contest but has the opposite and more intuitive implication. The fact that the result is more intuitive may imply that such organizations are actually fairly commonplace.

view (as with family members) would always be preferred to those likely to leave, other things being equal.

Conflict in fragile teams can also be reduced through rules for sharing team output. For example, equal-sharing rules might be adopted, although they undermine team production as noted in Table 27.1. On fragile teams such distributional rules can serve an important function by further reducing temptations to engage in unproductive intra-organizational conflict. The realization that 'we are all in this together' tends to encourage loyalty (increase subjective exit costs) as well.

This may explain why payouts to the founders of new organizations often resemble the natural cooperatives of Table 27.1. New partnerships tend to be small, and when they are composed of persons who bring different skills to the organization, they are often fragile in that the loss of one team member greatly reduces the team's effectiveness and survival prospects. New partnerships often share the proceeds of their enterprises more or less equally and make decisions through consensus. That many businesses disappear with a founding member's retirement or death is evidence that fragility often remains even years after an organization is established.[9]

Success, paradoxically, tends to undermine the durability of such relatively simple organizations by reducing their fragility. As reserves are accumulated, the temptation to engage in conflict over the reserves increases. When reserves increase to the point where they exceed 1/r in the game above, the development of more robust organizational forms becomes necessary for an organization's survival.

27.5 ORGANIZATIONAL ARCHITECTURE: INSIGHTS FROM THE RENT-SEEKING LITERATURE

The rent-seeking literature indirectly suggests that a variety of rules, procedures and architectures can increase organizational robustness by reducing intra-organizational conflict. And, it turns out that large organizations often have such rules, procedures and architectures. Although relatively few papers from the rent-seeking literature directly apply their insights to issues of institutional design, most reach conclusions about how efforts in rivalrous contests can be increased or decreased by adjusting various parameters of the rent-seeking contests of interest. Many of these have institutional interpretations.

---

[9] The fragility of startup firms in the post-war period is evident in numerous studies. Several studies find failure rates on the order of 80 percent after three or four years. This is especially true of small firms and new firms, firms without significant management structure or experience. Nenadic (1993) notes that in Victorian England, very few firms survived their founder's death. Average survival rates of medium-sized firms with deeper management structure are somewhat larger. Audretsch (1991), for example, reports ten-year survival rates of firms large enough to be tabulated in the USELM data set of the US Small Business Data Base. They find ten-year survival rates of between 23 and 45 percent, varying with the particular industry entered. Survival rates tend to increase with years already survived.

27.5.1 Intra-organizational Rigidity – Bureaucratization – as a Method of Reducing Conflict

The simplest way to reduce the extent of counterproductive conflict within an organization is to adopt completely rigid rules that make it impossible for anyone to increase his, her or their share of organizational resources through their own initiative (Congleton 1980 [2008]). By reducing the returns from rent seeking to essentially zero, no rational individual within the organization of interest will engage in rent-seeking activities. Bureaucratization in this sense reduces team members to cogs in an organizational machine, which mechanically advance organizational goals.[10]

Bureaucratic rigidities may include the centralized assignment of organizational equipment and space (as with academic offices and class rooms); salaries that are determined by exogenous factors such as initial salary, age, experience or college degree; or in the case of task-specific rewards, through essentially permanent assignments of individual team members to specific tasks. Such customary assignments and fixed rewards may be taken for granted by team members after they join an organization. Insofar as similar structures are used by most other durable organizations, such assignments may be regarded as simply 'facts of life'. Long-term alignment of team member interests with those of their organization may be promoted by mechanically linking salaries with time spent in the organization (seniority), which tends to increase loyalty and exit costs.

That bureaucratization can increase organizational surplus by reducing wasteful conflict has been mentioned in passing by the microeconomic of the firm and contract literatures. For example, Williamson (1996, p. 98, emphases added) suggests that 'hierarchy uses *flat incentives* because these elicit greater cooperation and because *unwanted side effects* are checked by added internal controls . . . workers and managers [are] more willing to accommodate, because their compensation is the same whether they "do this" or "do that" . . . an unwillingness to accommodate is interpreted not as an excess of zeal but as a predilection to behave in a *noncooperative way* . . . Long-term promotion prospects [within the organization] are damaged as a consequence.'

It seems evident that 'unwanted side effects' and 'noncooperative way' should be interpreted as team member efforts to use time, energy and other resources to engage in unproductive conflict with other team members or with management, as in the Taylor anecdote above. The rent-seeking literature implies that 'flat incentive systems' indirectly increase organizational surplus by reducing the losses from intra-organizational conflict (Congleton 1980 [2008]; Tullock 1980 [2008]).

Note that such structures do not directly address the team production or asymmetric informational problems. No financial incentives are used to align individual interests with organizational interests. Instead, rigidity and flat incentives are used to reduce intra-organizational rivalry and individual initiative in order to reduce losses from unproductive intra-organizational conflict. Other methods are used to induce productive

---

[10] The Merriam-Webster online dictionary characterizes bureaucracy as follows: 'Bureaucracies are often known for their rigid rules and lack of flexibility. Government characterized by specialization of functions, adherence to fixed rules, and a hierarchy of authority. A system of administration marked by officialism, red tape, and proliferation.'

effort, such as recruiting persons with a strong work ethic, 'self starters' and 'team players'. That such rigid systems are commonplace in large organizations suggests that potential losses from conflict are often greater than the productivity gains that can be induced by more responsive compensation schemes.

27.5.2 Surprise, Flexibility and Delegation: How to Share Authority

Bureaucratization and centralized management, thus, have a variety of advantages in static, predictable circumstances. However, complete rigidity has disadvantages in a dynamic environment. Creatively responding to unexpected problems and opportunities can often increase organizational surplus. Consider, for example, the unexpected breakdown of a critical machine or absence of a critical team member. In the short run, such events can reduce team output to zero, until a repair is made or the critical team member returns, or is replaced. Rapid responses to such problems tend to reduce cumulative losses more than slower ones.

Knowledge about such problems and their solutions is often readily available only to persons in the organization who can directly observe the problem. Central management cannot adapt as quickly or effectively to changing circumstances, because they either completely lack the information necessary to make adjustments to such problems or receive the necessary information only after a considerable delay.

As a consequence, delegating some authority to persons on the spot – as opposed to reserving it all to the organization's central government – potentially allows more rapid responses to be made and losses to be diminished (Taylor 1914; Jensen and Meckling 1995). Such institutional refinements, however, also open avenues for intra-organizational rent seeking.

The literature on rent seeking implies that the potential rent seeking associated with decentralization and delegation have to be managed to realize the advantages associated with flexible, rapid responses to both pleasant and unpleasant surprises. Indeed, if avoiding intra-organizational conflict is as important as argued above, losses from missed opportunities and unaddressed problems will have to be relatively great to justify reductions in rigidity.

One method of reducing the conflict associated with delegated authority is to constrain discretion and limit the 'prizes' that can be handed out by individual managers or committees of managers. Once again, what Williamson calls 'flatness' in the reward and resource allocation systems can be used to reduce rent seeking by reducing returns from lower-level efforts to influence upper-level managers to secure greater personal rewards or resources (Congleton 1980 [2008]; Tullock 1980 [2008]).

27.5.3 Some Organizational Architectures Work Better than Others: Function-based versus Product Line-based Divisions of Authority

Wärneryd (1998) suggests that rent-seeking losses within somewhat flexible hierarchical organizations can be further reduced by dividing an organization into more or less self-sufficient independent units. The individual unit surpluses of such 'divisions' are smaller and the number of contestants for those surpluses are also smaller, which in contests with Tullock-like contest success functions reduces rent-seeking losses, other things being equal. This process of delegation and division of responsibilities creates an internal structure analogous to federalism, with 'upper' levels of organizational governance specifying areas of authority for 'lower' levels of management.

The delegation of limited policy making and allocative authority to departments and divisions in turn allows local knowledge to be used to increase productivity and to respond to (local) emergencies. Structural rigidities can further limit rent seeking at the department and divisional levels, by reducing scope for engaging in 'turf battles'. It bears noting that organizational structures do, as predicted by this analysis, tend to be somewhat rigid; insofar as the hierarchy and domain of authority are rarely adjusted whole cloth.

The rent-seeking literature also implies that some partitionings of a work force are more effective than others. Indeed, some divisional structures can increase losses from rent seeking by creating new, more destructive methods of competition over the organization's surplus and resources.

27.5.3.1 Functional divisions of authority

For example, functional divisions of authority in which individual stages of production are organized into independent subunits can address emergency response problems and pool expertise, but also place an organization's entire surplus at risk. When the divisions each control a particular stage of product development or production, each subunit can lobby for an increased share of the organizational surplus by blocking or slowing down production in a manner difficult for the organization's central government to monitor, as was the case for workers destroying equipment in the Taylor anecdote.[11] In effect, each division can stop or slow down the organization's 'assembly line', and may use that ability to negotiate for additional resources, higher salaries, shorter hours, longer vacations (downtimes) and so on. Emergencies will be 'invented' if they tend to increase discretion and thereby a manager's or division's potential share of the organization's surplus or control over resources.

For example, imagine that every product sold by a firm needs plastic packaging and that the packages are designed by a single subunit. Packaging designers make aesthetic as well as protective contributions to each product. Thus during the design phase, it is difficult to assess such a unit's effort level, because the creative process is not entirely predictable. Given this, the managers in charge of package design could insist on greater manpower and equipment than necessary to maximize the net revenues generated by well-designed packages. To lobby for additional resources, new or revised packaging may be delayed to the point where it affects the output of other divisions. Such effects would, of course, demonstrate the importance of their request for additional resources or need for higher salaries to retain their talented team members.

Similar bottleneck-based rent-seeking risks exist in all organizations in which policies

---

[11] This is one possible application of the anti-commons problem explored in Buchanan and Yoon (2000). Similar problems have also been addressed in the fiscal federalism literature regarding tax authority of higher and lower levels of government (Flowers and Danzon 1984). The rent-seeking interpretation of these situations within a single organization simply points out that the ability to veto or tax a firm's total output can be used strategically as a lobbying method, which induces deadweight losses among those competing for organizational resources.

or products are produced in a series of stages, and a divisional 'gate keeper' controls a stage of production.

27.5.3.2 Parallel divisions of authority

One method for reducing unproductive intra-division conflict is to reduce the extent to which a single unit can impact the entire organization's output or surplus. Rather than create divisions by function or phase of production, parallel systems of production can be created. Such organizational structures will be profitable whenever anticipated losses from rent-seeking activities exceed gains from economies of scale. The independence of parallel units reduces a single unit's ability to affect the organization's profits through effects on other units, while the average net output of similar units can be used to assess both productivity gains and discourage rent-seeking activities.

A regional or product line architecture also reduces the size of the potential prize that can be achieved through intra-divisional rent seeking and the number of persons actively engaged in rent seeking. All these effects tend to reduce the extent to which resources are diverted to unproductive conflict, as developed in Wärneryd (1998) and Inderst et al. (2005).

Chandler (1962) notes that the first large commercial organizations of the nineteenth century initially adopted functional divisions of authority, but began switching to decentralized parallel systems in the 1920s. Williamson (1975) calls this organizational structure the M-form, and notes the informational advantages of this system. Armour and Teece (1978) provide econometric evidence that the M-form yields higher profits than organizational divisions along functional lines. Indeed, during the period of their study (1955–73) the M-form essentially replaced the other organizational forms in the petrochemical industry. Similar arguments are found in a variety of managerial texts, including the popular text on the *Toyota Way* (Liker 2004).

Nonetheless, those authors fail to appreciate that many of the informational advantages realized by the M-structure are ones associated with reducing counterproductive conflict over organizational surplus. It is more difficult to hide 'soldiering' when independent rivals performing similar tasks exist. Moreover, reducing unproductive intra-organizational conflict differs from shirking or opportunism problems of the sort focused on by Williamson, because organizational resources may be consumed by the conflict without actually increasing average private rents. In many rent-seeking contests, the average individual participant gains no (net) rents, in spite of significant efforts to obtain them.[12]

[12] Williamson (1996, p. 378) defines opportunism as follows: 'Self-interest seeking with guile, to include calculated efforts to mislead, deceive, obfuscate, and otherwise confuse. Opportunism should be distinguished from simple self-interest seeking, accordance to which individuals play a game with fixed rules that they reliably obey.' Essentially, opportunism is behavior that violates the organization's rules and is difficult to detect.

27.6 RENT SEEKING BY CENTRAL MANAGEMENT AND ORGANIZATIONAL GOVERNANCE

Realizing the potential advantages of flexibility requires a systematic process for revising existing rules to address short-run surprises and long-term problems as they emerge. That is to say, it requires an organizational government. How such rule-making bodies should be structured is not much discussed in the economic literature on governance, which for the most part focuses on internal incentive mechanisms that align agent interests with those of the principals, who are usually assumed to be shareholder-owners. It is simply assumed that risk-adjusted returns to equity will be maximized. In an M-form organization, for example, 'central management' chooses overall goals and allocates organizational resources among divisions at the margin. Nonetheless, that a centralized rule-making body will adopt rules to advance an organization's overall surplus rather than simply to increase its own share of that surplus cannot be taken for granted.

A firm's top-level policy maker(s) rarely consist(s) of a single residual claimant or group with perfectly aligned interests as imagined in most economic analyses. Instead, ownership and policy-making authority are usually distributed among managers, owners and other stakeholders, each with somewhat different interests. Differences in underlying risk preferences or economic theories may lead to disagreements about policies, as may efforts to secure a large share of the organization's surplus for major or minor shareholders, or corporate leadership. Insofar as planning, resource allocation and rule making are active processes, the usual problems of team production exist within organizational governments, but without an outside authority to correct them through incentivization and organizational design.[13]

Fortunately, an organization's *formateurs* do not have to be constitutional or organizational geniuses to adopt rule-making procedures that produce good results on average, because survivorship pressures tend to produce templates for organizational governance that reduce rent-seeking losses, plan effectively and allocate resources in a manner consistent with maximizing organizational surplus or reserves. Only the systems that have successfully done so in the past will remain on the menu of organizational templates that attract the attention of *formateurs*.

Possible governing structures include formal club or corporate charters of the sort explored in Buchanan and Tullock's (1962) classic work on constitutional design, the various threat rent-sharing schemes outlined in North et al. (2009) and designs based on the king and council variety analyzed by Congleton (2011, part I). The divisions of authority and recruitment procedures used are likely to be reinforced by internal norms and pecuniary incentives that encourage an encompassing interest for members of an organization's leadership team (Congleton 2011, chapter 2). Reliance on rules and conditional rewards is likely to be supplemented by efforts to recruit senior office holders known for their honesty, hard work and organizational spirit, as well as their job-specific talent and experience. However, recruiting persons with the right internalized norms or

---

[13] By this I mean that the government of the organization is its top rule-making body. However, external rules may be devised by government to incentivize an organization's top office holders, as with accounting standards and fiduciary duties in civil law.

values is unlikely to completely eliminate rent-seeking losses, in part because internalized norms are difficult to observe.[14]

Institutional architecture is also likely to be useful. The above analysis suggests that fairly rigid divisions of authority and decision-making procedures tend to reduce conflict. This is also true at the highest levels of an organization's management. Nonetheless, the architecture of governance may occasionally have to be revised, because it fails to fully use the resources at hand or resolve problems associated with rent seeking.

When technological advances are taking place that alter the economics of production and distribution, new modes of conflict or other problems may arise that affect the optimal distribution of intra-organizational authority. For example, the rapid dissemination of information made possible by well-designed data storage and retrieval systems increases the efficiency of centralized emergency responses and inventory control. It also allows more informed decision making by lower levels of management; but it also creates new methods for using informational access as a method of rent seeking and programming techniques as methods of sabotage.

In dynamic settings, standing procedures for revising an organization's governing system can be an important feature of robust organizational governance, although it may also encourage rent seeking at the organization's constitutional level.

27.6.1 An Illustration: How Committees and Majority Rule can Reduce Rent-seeking Losses

One little-analyzed institutional device for reducing rent-seeking losses is the use of standing committees to make decisions at both the top levels of organizational governance and within organizational units. Congleton (1980 [2008], 1984 [2008]) demonstrates that competition among rent seekers tends to elicit larger total efforts (and losses) when favors are conferred by single decision makers than when decisions are made by committees. Thus more resources tend to be consumed in conflict for the favor of a single administrator than for that of a committee, such as a board of directors.

Consider the case in which two parties attempt to 'purchase' a special privilege from a manager with complete control over the policy of interest. Suppose that the privilege is worth R to the rent seekers and that the highest bidder wins the prize. Party 1 may bid amount $A_1 < R$, which can be beaten by Party 2's bid, $A_1 < A_2 < R$. In a single-round contest, the second mover would always win and the amount received by the manager would be larger than the smallest bid capable of attracting his attention. Bids tend to escalate in such contests. In a second round, Party 1 would be inclined to raise its bid to A_1', with $A_2 < A_1' < R$, as would Party 2 after the new bid by Party 1 is observed

[14] Note that the knowledge asymmetry problem associated with functional divisions of authority, which are nearly unavoidable in top management, can be reduced to some extent by promoting especially productive managers to higher levels. Such honest managers can use their experience to set output targets, effectively monitor quality and recognize and punish rent seeking when it occurs. Accurately targeting penalties and promotions is itself a significant form of quality control. However, the parallel divisional measure sketched out below provides a more effective solution, because it allows local knowledge to be used to increase productivity and discourage intra-unit rent seeking.

(or anticipated). In the limit, the amount paid would tend to escalate toward R and the manager would be able to extract the full 'rent' associated with his authority. (Note that pre-committing to a maximal bid, A*, would not be self-enforcing by the participants in a sequential contest, because each player would benefit in the next round by bidding a bit more than A* to secure the prize, as long as that bid was less than R.)

Now consider efforts to assemble a majority in a three-person committee of managers under the assumption that their votes are for sale or subject to influence through lobbying. Party 1 may initiate the bidding with a bid of (1, 1, 0), which would secure the votes of committee members 1 and 2 in the absence of efforts by Party 2. Party 2 may, however, bid (0, 1.5, 0.25), which would defeat Party 1's effort by obtaining the votes of members 2 and 3. Party 1 could respond with (0.25, 0, 0.5) and so on. Note that in contrast to the two-party contest for a single pragmatic manager's favor, there is no tendency for bids to escalate when seeking the favor of pragmatic committees. In the illustration, the total bids fall in each subsequent round (from 2 to 1.75, to 0.75). The bids tend to de-escalate toward the lowest levels sufficient to attract a member's attention.

Notice also that the nature and losses from the bidding process will vary with the rules that constrain (or are supposed to constrain) the behavior of organizational leadership and intra-organizational favor seekers. If votes are literally up for sale, then there is no Tullock-type loss from the rent-seeking game. Thus, purchasing votes from shareholders (proxies) tends to reduce losses from conflict for the votes of shareholders. Resources may be misallocated within the organization if, however, the 'auction' is not an open one or authority is misused, but rent-seeking losses would be smaller (Congleton 1980 [2008], 1988).

When votes are not literally sold, but are merely influenced through lobbying or favor trading, rent-seeking investments take a more roundabout form and losses are more likely. These lobbying efforts are likely to generate smaller benefits for the persons that need to be influenced than the amount spent by the rent seekers. This difference represents losses of the Tullock variety.

27.6.2 Another Illustration: The 'King and Council Template' and Rent-seeking Losses

Although committees are widely used within all organizations, committees are normally combined with a more or less independent chief executive of some kind, as with a firm's chief executive officer (CEO) and board of directors. This structure has various informational and succession advantages, but it creates an institutional venue for conflict, because the CEO and board of directors may disagree about the distribution of control over organizational surplus.

A board of directors and top level of management function as a team, and as true of other teams may be well or poorly motivated to increase organizational surplus according to the selection process and rewards associated with membership on the team. Losses from potential conflicts have historically been reduced through recruiting methods and relatively flat reward systems.

The manner in which a board of directors is constituted clearly affects the degree of conflict within the board, the upper reaches of an organization's management, and shareholders. The board members of publicly held corporations are selected through share weighted elections. This tends to align board member interests with those of major shareholders, the shareholders whose information about a given corporation tends to be best. CEOs are subsequently recruited by and serve at the pleasure of their boards of directors. This process tends to align CEO interests with those of the board and shareholders, which reduces unproductive conflict.

In the case of private firms without publicly held shares, the advisory boards are normally recruited by founders, senior management and other major stakeholders (financiers, labor and so on), rather than elected by shareholders. These selection processes also tend to produce boards and CEOs with relatively congruent interests, although in this case it is the board that is selected to be congruent rather than the CEO.

Such recruiting procedures are neglected or taken for granted by much of the economics literature, but the fact that they reduce unproductive conflict is doubtless important for organizational robustness and survival. Without procedures that align the interests of CEOs and boards of directors, intense disputes over the distribution of a firm's profits – between the CEO and shareholders, or senior management and the board of directors – would tend to be the norm rather than the exception.

The extent of such unproductive conflict can be further reduced through the standard methods, including selection of persons who are predisposed to cooperate ('team players'), flat reward systems and penalties for engaging in conflict. Decision processes may simultaneously aggregate information and avoid conflict, and also limit the number of persons that are eligible to participate (or lobby). Most of these are features of organizational governance structures, although reward structures have become somewhat less 'flat' in the past few decades in corporate America.

Losses associated with too much 'team playing' by insiders are countered to some extent through the selection of external directors, the number of which is often quasi-constitutional at the level of organizations, and by takeover threats in the case of publicly held companies. In publicly held corporations, capture of the board of directors by management, which is likely to affect the distribution of an organization's surplus, rather than its magnitude, tends to be reduced by frequent shareholder elections for boards of directors. Major shareholders often hold positions on the board and can directly monitor and attempt to reduce such problems by persuading other directors or shareholders.[15]

27.7 LOSSES FROM CONFLICT AND THE ORGANIZATION OF RELATIONS BETWEEN ORGANIZATIONS

Although the main focus of this chapter is the extent to which organizational structures have evolved to reduce losses from intra-organizational rent seeking, the analysis also

[15] Baysinger and Butler (1985) provide an excellent survey of the early literature on corporate policy making, and one of the earliest and most thorough analyses of the effects of board of director composition on (relative) corporate profits. They find considerable evidence that the composition of board members matter, although with a lag. Dalton et al. (1999) provide a meta-analysis of the empirical literature in this area, which also finds support for the claim that the number and composition of boards of directors matter – in spite of external market pressures (survivorship and takeovers) on firms.

has implications for conflict among organizations and the size of existing organizations. A short discussion of some common steps taken to reduce inter-organizational conflict is sufficient to demonstrate that the rent-seeking model sheds light on many aspects of market structure.

Organizations interact with one another in more or less rule-bound settings, rules that associate different rewards with different modes of interaction. Civil law encourages some sorts of interactions, as with trade, contracts and price competition; and discourages others, as with fraud, theft and murder. Within that context, organizations will adopt agreements that reduce unproductive conflict with each other. Contracts will be formal, explicit and incentive compatible; arbitration boards will be efficient and unbiased. In some cases, implementing the desired rules will require organizations of organizations, consortia, with rules for all members. Such organizations will also use a variety of rules and flat incentives to reduce temptations for conflict among members. In medieval Europe, such consortia were often themselves a form of government, as in the Hanseatic League of medieval northern Europe.

Organizations also have incentives to lobby governments to provide legal systems that reduce unproductive conflict among organizations, because the cost of enforcement can be shifted to other taxpayers and/or economies of scale may be realized. Thus, civil law itself may have emerged from organizational efforts to reduce losses from inter-organizational conflict. Such legal systems increase surplus for a wide range of organizations and persons by reducing the costs of extensive exchange networks, facilitating specialization and reducing counterproductive forms of conflict.

Consortia of organizations naturally attempt to reduce all forms of conflict that reduce organizational surplus, even if they produce losses for non-members (consumers). As stressed by the industrial organization literature since Adam Smith, economic organizations often attempt to coordinate price and output decisions. As stressed by the rent-seeking literature, they would also lobby governments for monopoly privileges and for rules that directly or indirectly facilitate cartelization and block entry.

When formal cartels or trade associations are difficult to form or illegal, firms will ask governments to adopt rules that achieve similar ends, that is to say, regulations that formally or informally limit competition among existing firms or restrict the formation of new organizations with similar goals, as argued by Stigler (1971). It is such activities that caused Tullock (1967 [2008]) to realize that there are potentially many counterproductive forms of competition in contemporary political-economic systems. The existence of such efforts and their consequences are well described and documented in several of the chapters of this volume.

Inter-organizational conflict also has implications for the optimal size of an organization. Rather than forming a consortium or lobbying government for conflict-reducing rules, an organization may simply expand to bring more of its overall input and output 'markets' within the organization's own rules. Vertical integration reduces conflict (and uncertainty) when input suppliers or output distributors have market power and can renegotiate contract terms at will. The problems are similar to those developed above concerning functional based divisions within large organizations. Such suppliers and distributors can use various holdup techniques to extract rents from those both above and below them in the production process. Consistent with this, Chandler (1962) notes that the first large industrial firms undertook vertical integration and expanded sales networks at the same time that they developed internal formal administrative structures that allowed the new larger enterprises to be managed.

Horizontal mergers can reduce conflict over market prices for outputs and allow economies of scale from capital-intensive modes of production to be realized (and safeguarded). Both mergers and formal trusts were common in the late nineteenth century, as new more capital-intensive methods of production were developed and declining transport and communication costs allowed broader distribution of a single firm or factory's outputs.

Of course, as emphasized by economic textbooks, some forms of inter-organizational conflict are productive for society, if not for the organizations themselves. When firms compete with one another for resources to attract and retain team members or to expand sales, the resultant conflict assures that resources shift to highest-valued uses, the total cost of production is minimized and that consumer surplus is maximized. Similarly, when politicians compete for elected office, information about policy issues is disseminated and the officials elected have incentives to take into account the interests of a broad cross section of voters if they want to remain in office. Such contests can produce more value than lost from the resources consumed by them.[16]

For this reason, societies must be careful to avoid adopting rules that reduce all forms of conflict. Some forms of conflict produce positive benefits (positive externalities) for persons and organizations not directly involved in the conflict at hand, as an audience benefits from competition in sporting events, and most consumers benefit from product innovation.

27.8 CONCLUSIONS: SOLUTIONS AND THE DILEMMAS THAT REMAIN

This chapter has argued that much about the nature of formal organizations can be understood as efforts to reduce losses from rent seeking. This is not to say that the informational and team production problems focused on by the mainstream literature are unimportant, but that many features of organizations cannot be easily explained by such problems. Many common features of organizations address losses from unproductive conflict, rather than attempt to increase productivity per se. For example, flat incentive systems and bureaucratization clearly reduce conflict, but do not otherwise encourage greater productivity or align employee interests with those of their organizations. Contests for promotion may encourage increased productivity (in a very coarse manner) but only if they promote productive forms of competition rather than intra-organizational rent seeking.

Of course, the organizational solutions in place did not require a complete game-theoretic theory of rent-seeking losses to be worked out. Many specific problems are

[16] Note that campaigns for votes may produce useful information, but may at some point cease to do so. In the latter case, campaign finance rules may increase the surplus obtained from electoral competition (Congleton 1986 [2008]). In others, it may serve to cartelize politics by making the entry of new candidates and parties more difficult.

'obvious', and their solutions critical for the survival of organizations. At the level of day-to-day problem solving, 'necessity is the mother of invention', as the saying goes. Nonetheless, placing a wide range of solutions in a general theoretical framework helps us to understand why some institutions are more productive than they appear (for example, bureaucratization) and may also point to new more effective ones, insofar as the problems addressed come to be better understood.

The problems of intra-organizational conflict are not static, nor always as tractable as illustrative models suggest. This is most evident when new technologies of production or types of organization emerge that inadvertently create new potential modes and venues for conflict that are not addressed by the existing rules. When more roundabout modes of production replaced simpler ones during the industrial revolution, sabotage and other forms of intra-organizational conflict often became individually less costly and more effective as bargaining strategies.

Nineteenth-century conflicts associated with the mechanization of production are legendary and provided many new words for the English language. The power loom riots of 1826 in Lancashire, England, gave rise to the term Luddites. 'Strikes' and other work slowdowns ('soldiering') became commonplace as specialization within and among firms and persons increased. Twenty-first century internet-based sales and distribution also create new possibilities for conflict. Such networks can be disrupted through denial of service and other attacks on rival websites. Misinformation campaigns can be conducted via social media though networks that are hard to trace. These were not and are not ordinary principal-agent problems, but instances of organized, aggressive conflict over organizational and social surplus.

Necessity often produced efforts to reduce the level of unproductive conflict, and various partial solutions were worked out as industrialization proceeded. Evidence that the new management and administrative methods associated with the industrial revolution reduced conflict is provided in Frederick Taylor's classic book on *The Principles of Scientific Management* (1914) and Chandler's history of the organizational designs of large firms (1962). What Taylor refers to as scientific management simultaneously increased productivity and reduced intra-organizational conflict:

> [D]uring the thirty years that we have been engaged in introducing scientific management there has *not been a single strike* from those who were working in accordance with its principles . . . Scientific management will mean, for the employers and the workmen who adopt it – and particularly for those who adopt it first – the *elimination of almost all causes for dispute and disagreement* between them. (Taylor 1914, p. 135, emphases added)

> What constitutes a fair day's work will be a question for scientific investigation, instead of a subject to be bargained and haggled over. Soldiering will cease because the object for soldiering will no longer exist. The great increase in wages which accompanies this type of management will largely eliminate the wage question as a *source of dispute*. But more than all other causes, the close, intimate cooperation, the constant personal contact between the two sides, will tend to *diminish friction and discontent*. (Taylor 1914, pp. 142–3, emphases added)

Similar efforts to reduce losses from unproductive forms of conflict have evidently long affected organizational design and management methods.[17]

[17] Note that Taylor's 'scientific bargain' is a method of introducing rigidity (an exogenous rule) into this potential area of conflict (deciding what a fair day's work entails).

That organizational designs and contracts among organizations have evolved to reduce rent-seeking losses does not imply that losses from rent seeking have disappeared. Even in the contemporary West, where the legal setting and organizational institutions are as well developed and binding as anywhere, there is evidence of both legal and illegal rent seeking by organizations and individuals. These activities are sufficiently commonplace to have stimulated a broad range of academic research, including the rent-seeking literature reviewed and extended in this volume.

The rent-seeking literature has not very often directly addressed problems associated with intra-organizational conflict, but doing so is an obvious direction for further research. This chapter demonstrates that the literature on rent seeking can shed very useful light on several important core features of organizational design.[18]

REFERENCES

Alchian, A. and Harold Demsetz (1972), 'Production, information costs, and economic organization', *American Economic Review*, **62**(5), 777–95.

Armour, Henry O. and David J. Teece (1978), 'Organizational structure and economic performance: a test of multidivisional hypothesis', *Bell Journal of Economics*, **9**(1), 106–22.

Audretsch, David B. (1991), 'New-firm survival and the technological regime', *Review of Economics and Statistics*, **73**(3), 441–50.

Baysinger, Barry D. and Henry N. Butler (1985), 'Corporate governance and the board of directors: performance effects of changes in board composition', *Journal of Law, Economics, and Organization*, **1**(1), 101–24.

Buchanan, James M. and Gordon Tullock (1962), *The Calculus of Consent: Logical Foundations of Constitutional Democracy*, Ann Arbor, MI: University of Michigan Press.

Buchanan, James M. and Yong J. Yoon (2000), 'Symmetric tragedies, commons and anticommons', *Journal of Law and Economics*, **43**(1), 1–14.

Chandler, Alfred D. (1962), *Strategy and Structure: Papers in the History of the Industrial Enterprise*, Cambridge, MA: MIT Press.

Coase, Ronald H. (1937), 'The nature of the firm', *Economica*, **16**(4), 386–405.

Congleton, Roger D. (1980), 'Competitive process, competitive waste, and institutions', in James M. Buchanan, Roger D. Tollison and G. Tullock (eds), *Toward a Theory of the Rent-seeking Society*, College Park, TX: Texas A&M University Press, pp. 153–79, reprinted in Roger D. Congleton, Arye L. Hillman and Kai A. Konrad (eds) (2008), *40 Years of Research on Rent Seeking 1 – The Theory of Rent Seeking*, Heidelberg: Springer, pp. 69–95.

Congleton, Roger D. (1984), 'Committees and rent-seeking effort', *Journal of Public Economics*, **25**(1–2), 197–209, reprinted in Roger D. Congleton, Arye L. Hillman and Kai A. Konrad (eds) (2008), *40 Years of Research on Rent Seeking 1 – The Theory of Rent Seeking*, Heidelberg: Springer, pp. 279–91.

Congleton, Roger D. (1986), 'Rent-seeking aspects of political advertising', *Public Choice*, **49**(3), 249–65, reprinted in Roger D. Congleton, Arye L. Hillman and Kai A. Konrad (eds) (2008), *40 Years of Research on Rent Seeking 2 – Applications: Rent Seeking in Practice*, Heidelberg: Springer, pp. 297–311.

Congleton, Roger D. (1988), 'Evaluating rent-seeking losses: do the welfare gains of lobbyists count', *Public Choice*, **56**(2), 181–4.

Congleton, Roger D. (1989), 'Monitoring rent-seeking managers: advantages of diffuse ownership', *Canadian Journal of Economics*, **22**(3), 662–72.

Congleton, Roger D. (2011), *Perfecting Parliament*, Cambridge: Cambridge University Press.

Congleton, Roger D., Arye L. Hillman and Kai A. Konrad (eds) (2008a), *40 Years of Research on Rent Seeking 1 – The Theory of Rent Seeking*, Heidelberg: Springer.

---

18 Indeed, this chapter suggests that reducing losses from rent seeking was necessary for contemporary market economies to have emerged. Institutional innovations occurred in both private and public sector organizations. National reforms reduced the extent of rent protection by local and national governments, and also allowed more extensive use of roundabout production and extended trading networks.

Congleton, Roger D., Arye L. Hillman and Kai A. Konrad (eds) (2008b), *40 Years of Research on Rent Seeking 2 – Applications: Rent Seeking in Practice*, Heidelberg: Springer.
Crémer, Jacques and Richard P. McLean (1988), 'Full extraction of the surplus in Bayesian and dominant strategy auctions', *Econometrica*, **56**(6), 1247–57.
Dalton, Dan R., Catherine M. Daily, Jonathan L. Johnson and Alan E. Ellstrand (1999), 'Number of directors and financial performance: a meta analysis', *Academy of Management Journal*, **42**(6), 674–86.
Flowers, Marilyn R. and Patricia M. Danzon (1984), 'Separation of the redistributive and allocative functions of government: a public choice perspective', *Journal of Public Economics*, **24**(3), 373–80.
Hillman, Arye L. and Eliakim Katz (1987), 'Hierarchical structure and the social costs of bribes and transfers', *Journal of Public Economics*, **34**(2), 129–42, reprinted in Roger D. Congleton, Arye L. Hillman and Kai A. Konrad (eds) (2008), *40 Years of Research on Rent Seeking 1 – The Theory of Rent Seeking*, Heidelberg: Springer, pp. 523–36.
Inderst, Roman, Holger M. Müller and Karl Wärneryd (2005), 'Distributional conflict in organizations', *European Economic Review*, **51**(2), 385–402.
Jensen, Michael C. and William H. Meckling (1976), 'Agency costs and the theory of the firm', *Journal of Financial Economics*, **3**(4), 305–60.
Jensen, Michael C. and William H. Meckling (1979), *Theory of the Firm: Managerial Behavior, Agency Costs, and Ownership Structure*, Heidelberg: Springer.
Jensen, Michael. C. and William H. Meckling (1995), 'Specific and general knowledge, and organizational structure', *Journal of Applied Corporate Finance*, **8**(2), 4–18.
Khalil, Fahad, Jacques Lawarree and Troy J. Scott (2013), 'Private monitoring, collusion and the timing of information', CESifo Working Paper No. 4497, Munich.
Konrad, Kai A. (2000), 'Sabotage in rent-seeking contests', *Journal of Law Economics and Organization*, **16**(1), 155–65, reprinted in Roger D. Congleton, Arye L. Hillman and Kai A. Konrad (eds) (2008), *40 Years of Research on Rent Seeking 1 – The Theory of Rent Seeking*, Heidelberg: Springer, pp. 409–19.
Liker, Jeffrey K. (2004), *The Toyota Way, 14 Management Principles from the World's Greatest Manufacturer*, New York: McGraw-Hill.
Nenadic, Stana (1993), 'The small family firm in Victorian Britain', *Business History*, **35**(4), 84–114.
North, Douglas C., John J. Wallis and Barry R. Weingast (2009), *Violence and Social Orders: A Conceptual Framework for Interpreting Recorded Human History*, Cambridge: Cambridge University Press.
Stigler, George J. (1971), 'The theory of economic regulation', *Bell Journal of Economics*, **2**(1), 3–21.
Taylor, Frederick W. (1914), *The Principles of Scientific Management*, New York: Harper.
Tullock, Gordon (1967), 'The welfare costs of monopolies, tariffs and theft', *Western Economic Journal*, **5**(3), 224–32, reprinted in Roger D. Congleton, Arye L. Hillman and Kai A. Konrad (eds) (2008), *40 Years of Research on Rent Seeking 1 – The Theory of Rent Seeking*, Heidelberg: Springer, pp. 45–53.
Tullock, Gordon (1980), 'Efficient rent seeking', in James M. Buchanan, Robert D. Tollison and Gordon Tullock (eds), *Toward a Theory of the Rent-seeking Society*, College Park, TX: Texas A&M University Press, pp. 97–112, reprinted in Roger D. Congleton, Arye L. Hillman and Kai A. Konrad (eds) (2008), *40 Years of Research on Rent Seeking 1 – The Theory of Rent Seeking*, Heidelberg: Springer, pp. 105–20.
Wärneryd, Karl (1998), 'Distributional conflict and jurisdictional organization', *Journal of Public Economics*, **69**(3), 435–50.
Wärneryd, Karl (2003), 'Information in conflicts', *Journal of Economic Theory*, **110**(1), 121–36, reprinted in Roger D. Congleton, Arye L. Hillman and Kai A. Konrad (eds) (2008), *40 Years of Research on Rent Seeking 1 – The Theory of Rent Seeking*, Heidelberg: Springer, pp. 487–502.
Williamson, Oliver E. (1975), *Markets and Hierarchies*, New York: Free Press.
Williamson, Oliver E. (1985), *The Economic Institutions of Capitalism*, New York: Free Press.
Williamson, Oliver E. (1996), *The Mechanisms of Governance*, Oxford: Oxford University Press.

Name index

Subject index

Cover description: Rents and Reynard

The cover is an accompaniment of a tale of Reynard the fox ('Renart' French, 'Reineke' German, 'Reinaert' Dutch), who is a central figure in European folklore. Reynard produces nothing and there is nothing to which he adds value. He lives for his own consumption and for his own pleasure. Reynard is, in this regard, similar to other animals. Reynard is, however, an anthropomorphic character who epitomizes particular human attributes. He benefits at the expense of others and usually emerges well from interactions with higher authority. Is Reynard the fox the quintessential rent seeker?

The origins of tales of Reynard (or Renart) the fox are attributed to Pierre de St Cloud (1174, sequel 1177). The cover illustration is from a manuscript copied in northern France, late thirteenth century (BnF, Manuscripts, France 1580 fol. 1). The description of the illustration is 'the Noble Lion King convenes the court animals'. The text (translation from French) informs us that: 'Word of tricks of Reynard reaches the king of beasts, the Noble Lion. The full Court convenes. Ysengrin (the wolf) complains of having been dishonored by Reynard and demands justice. But the king, liking Reynard, finds extenuating circumstances, and leaves it to the Court to decide Reynard's fate. The animals are divided on the sentence. It is decided that Reynard should swear to make amends but Hersent (the she-wolf) wants revenge. She hands Reynard a trap with the help of the dog Roonel, falsely dead and false saint. Reynard thwarts the ruse and narrowly escapes the pack launched in pursuit.'

Reynard is about to swear his innocence on a holy relic, which he discovers at the last moment to be the teeth of Roonel the dog, who is feigning death and feigning being a holy relic (clarification from Bouwnan and Besamusca 2009, pp. 46–7).

The anthropomorphic animals avoid attributions to actual people or social classes. Ysengrin the wolf accuses Reynard of dishonor through his consort Hersent, but Grimbeert the badger says that the fox Reynard and the she-wolf Hersent have long been secret lovers. Hersent the she-wolf prefers a story that blames Reynard and leaves her in good stead with the wolf Ysengrin, the father of her cubs. Ysengrin and Reynard are not on good terms. Referring to the accusations of Ysengrin, Grimbeert points out that 'as everyone knows and it is an old saying: Sweet words rarely fall from the enemy's mouth' (ibid., p. 53).

The Noble King sees extenuating circumstances and delegates judgment to the court of animals. Has Reynard with the complicity of Hersent benefited at the expense of the honor of Ysengrin? Or, given the claim of Hersent's consensual behavior, are rents through unwarranted retribution being sought from Reynard?

We do not usually describe the competition for food in nature as rent seeking but the anthropomorphic animal characters speak their minds and remind us of a Nietzschean world in which the strong dominate the weak. Reynard often behaves unethically. He tricks and eats other animals when they trust him. He is a chicken killer (not a chicken thief because the animals have no owners). He is imaginative. When he is accused of killing and eating the rooster's children, Reynard's defense is that he has of late been a vegetarian.

Reynard makes an appearance in Nietzsche's Twilight of the Idols (written in 1888 in Sils-Maria near Silvaplana). In the twentieth century, Reynard appears in a story (van Genechten 1937) that teaches children to be racist and prejudiced. Reynard is portrayed as prototypically European in contrast to a non-European anthropomorphic animal character who creates rents through control of capital markets and also encourages miscegenation so that the local animals will lose their distinct identities. The circle is complete. In the thirteenth-century tale accompanying the cover illustration, Reynard is involved in miscegenation (the fox and a wolf) and benefits at the expense of others. In the twentieth century, it is the now-declared pure Reynard who is placed in the role of making accusations about miscegenation and unearned benefit from rents.

REFERENCES

Bouwnan, André and Bart Besamusca (eds) (2009), *Of Reynaert the Fox*, Amsterdam: Amsterdam University Press. See http://books.google.co.il/books?id=vtEe8fONXgMC&pg=PA47&lpg=PA47&dq=dog+Roonel&source=bl&ots=ji0s6Ah46w&sig=mqWZfhNtLkY_I8d4icakkX8jRnA&hl=en&sa=X&ei=VtxVVMBl6dfsBtaZgfgM&redir_esc=y#v=onepage&q=dog%20Roonel&f=false (accessed December 10, 2014).

de St Cloud, Pierre (1174, sequel 1177), *Le Roman de Renart*. See http://www.etudier.com/sujets/pierre-de-saint-cloud-le-roman-de-renart-vers-1174-1177/0 (accessed December 10, 2014).

Nietzsche, Friedrich (1889), *Twilight of the Idols*. See http://www.lexido.com/EBOOK_TEXTS/TWILIGHT_OF_THE_IDOLS.aspx (accessed December 10, 2014).

van Genechten, Robert (1937), 'Van den vos Reynaerde, in Nieuw-Nederland'. See http://www.awn.com/mag/issue1.7/articles/barten1.7.html (accessed December 10, 2014).